THE RISE OF THE
MONOPHYSITE MOVEMENT

The Rise of the Monophysite Movement

*Chapters in the History of the Church
in the Fifth and Sixth Centuries*

By W. H. C. FREND

James Clarke & Co. Ltd

James Clarke & Co. Ltd
PO Box 60
Cambridge
CB1 2NT
UK

www.jamesclarke.co.uk
publishing@jamesclarke.co.uk

First published by Cambridge University Press, 1972
Corrected edition by James Clarke & Co. Ltd, 2008

ISBN: 978 0 227 17241 4

British Library Cataloguing in Publication Data
A catalogue record is available from the British Library

Copyright © W. H. C. Frend, 1972

All rights reserved. No part of this edition may be reproduced, stored in a retrieval system, or transmitted in any form or by any means, electronic, mechanical, photocopying, recording or otherwise, without the prior permission in writing from the Publisher.

CONTENTS

Preface	*page*	vii
Introduction		ix
Abbreviations		xvii
1 The road to Chalcedon, 428–451		1
2 The emperor and his church		50
3 The intellectuals and the monks		104
4 The *Henotikon* of Zeno, 451–484		143
5 Towards a Monophysite solution, 484–512		184
6 The orthodox reaction, 513–527		221
7 Justinian: the end of compromise		255
8 The Monophysite kingdoms		296
9 'To Syria, a long farewell' (the Emperor Heraclius)		316
Epilogue		354
Appendix		360
Bibliography		369
Index		393

FIGURES

Fig. 1 Monophysitism in the
    patriarchate of Antioch, 512-18.   250-51

Fig. 2 The Roman Empire *circa* 560.   258-59

PREFACE

This work is a revised edition of the Birkbeck lectures for 1968 on the *Rise of the Monophysite Empire*. It was inspired largely by a suggestion from Rev. Professor Henry Chadwick, now Dean of Christ Church, that not a great deal had been written in English on the period following Chalcedon, while my own interest in the Monophysites had been aroused during the excavations at Q'asr Ibrim in 1963-4, when I was associated with Rev. Professor J. M. Plumley in the direction of work on this important Nubian site on behalf of the Egypt Exploration Society. I had also been encouraged by reviewers of my *Martyrdom and Persecution in the Early Church* to push my research further down the time scale, so that this survey represents a third volume of what might be called a 'social history of the early church' taking the story down to the Arab invasions of the 630s.

To write about the Monophysites, as those who opposed the Council of Chalcedon have come to be known, demands a greater knowledge of philosophy and Christian doctrine than a historian can usually claim. Yet there must be an attempt to understand the doctrinal issues if any sense is to be made of the history of the fifth and sixth centuries. It is sometimes proposed in university courses that 'while theology will be avoided, Justinian's ecclesiastical policy will be assessed' (*Cambridge University Reporter*, 7 May 1969), but this is not an option open to the historian of the period. The present work therefore aims at presenting an integrated study, combining factors of secular and ecclesiastical history with the outlines of doctrinal development, spanning the two hundred years from the Council of Ephesus in 431 until the expulsion of the Byzantines from the mainly Monophysite provinces of Egypt and Syria by the Arabs.

The author is grateful to many who have helped and encouraged him, especially since departure from Cambridge in September 1969 entailed also loss of ready access to a copyright library. He would like to thank his former colleagues, Professors H. Chadwick and G. W. H. Lampe, for advice on Chapters 1 and 3 respectively, and Mr P. R. L. Brown, Fellow of All Souls, for suggestions on Chapter 2. To the Rev. Justin Taylor, Fellow of Downing College, Cambridge, he owes much help with references

Preface

which had to be checked in the University Library; he thanks also Miss M. Webb, Miss G. Barnes (now Mrs Henry Hart) and Mrs D. Brodie for their assistance in typing the original Birkbeck Lectures and the first draft of the book, and Mrs P. Larsen for retyping practically the whole of the revised draft and for help on the maps and index, and finally the Cambridge University Press, especially Mrs Christine Linehan and Miss Gillian Limbert (now Mrs Law) and the proof-reader, for patience, help and advice at all times freely given.

W. H. C. FREND

Glasgow University
15 October 1971

INTRODUCTION

The two centuries that separate the meeting of the Council of Ephesus in 431 from the Arab invasions have a vital place in the history of the Mediterranean peoples. On the one hand, they witness the magnificent achievement of Justinian in reuniting for a moment the whole Mediterranean world in a single religion and civilisation; on the other, they reflect the slow working out of the religious, political and social tensions that made Justinian's ideals incapable of fulfilment. In the end the northern and southern halves of the Mediterranean were to be divided between Christian and Arab-Moslem, while in the territories retained by the Christians, east and west were to go their separate ways.

In these developments the passionate religious controversy following the Council of Chalcedon in 451 played a primary role. The Byzantine Empire was a church state. Already by the reign of Theodosius II (408–50) the imperial monarchy and the church represented an integrated structure of society in which the secular and religious formed a single whole. The civilised world corresponded to Christendom and its sole ruler was the emperor at Constantinople. In the provinces, people felt that whether they were Egyptians, Syrians or Illyrians by birth they belonged to 'the race of Christians', distinct from Jews and barbarians, assured of their own destiny under Providence. This solidarity reflected in unswerving allegiance to the 'God-loving' or 'orthodox' emperor was a significant factor in the survival of the east Roman provinces from attacks by external enemies in the fifth century.

Within the framework of religious unity, however, the church was being subjected to increasingly severe strains. Christianity was in origin a religion preached in an Aramaic and non-Classical medium. How were its truths to be interpreted in the context of traditional Greek philosophy in which the great majority of the Christian leaders had been educated, but which the mass of the Christians particularly in Egypt and Syria were finding an increasingly alien medium? Moreover, the four eastern patriarchates, Constantinople, Alexandria, Antioch and (after 451) Jerusalem, coincided with territories that possessed their own distinctive histories, cultures and ecclesiastical traditions, and this facilitated the emergence of regional bias in what ostensibly were purely ecclesiastical problems. In

Introduction

the background, too, lay the perpetual clash between the collegial outlook of the eastern patriarchates based on their autocephalous relationship to each other and the authoritative and authoritarian claims of the Roman see grounded in the belief that the living voice of Peter spoke through his successors, the popes.

At the Council of Chalcedon these latent divisions came to a head. The council's decision representing an alliance between Rome and Constantinople, that Christ was to be acknowledged as existing in two natures inseparably united, was bitterly opposed in Egypt from the outset and increasingly so in most of Syria, on the grounds that there could only be one reality or nature, namely the divine nature, in the incarnate Christ. He could be 'out of two natures' but not 'in two natures'. This movement of opposition has become known to history, though not to contemporaries, as Monophysitism. Our problem here has been to study its development in the two centuries following Chalcedon. Despite the wearisome doctrinal hairsplitting that much of its history involves, it also seems to provide the main clue to the ultimate failure of the east Roman emperors to continue the work of the Hellenistic monarchies and their own pagan predecessors to weld the diverse peoples of their empire into an homogeneous whole. In a few years during the seventh century the Arabs succeeded in dismembering a large portion of the empire where the Huns and Persians had failed. Why?

In this survey, therefore, an attempt has been made to see beyond the exasperation of both contemporary and modern critics who would relegate the whole religious issue to a 'quarrel about words',[1] and at the same time to look carefully at the arguments of those who conclude perhaps too easily that 'Monophysitism became a symbol of the separatist movements in Syria, Egypt and Armenia'.[2] Regional identity does not necessarily imply separatism. The wise study by A. H. M. Jones, 'Were the ancient heresies national or social movements in disguise?',[3]

[1] Thus M. Jugie's summing up, 'Monophysitism' was 'moins une hérésie qu'un schisme, moins une controverse de doctrine, qu'une querelle de mots', in 'La Primauté romaine d'après les premiers théologiens monophysites', *Echos de l'Orient* 33, 1934, p. 181. Compare J. Maspero's view that 'Monophysitism was not a heresy, but merely a schismatic intention', in his *Histoire des patriarches d'Alexandrie* (Paris, 1923), p. 11. For a contemporary view to the same effect see Evagrius, *HE* II. 5, or John of Damascus (*c*. 750 A.D.), *De haeresibus* 83.

[2] A. N. Stratos, *Byzantium in the Seventh Century* (Amsterdam, 1968), p. 4.

[3] *JTS*, n.s. 10. 2, 1959, pp. 280–98.

Introduction

warns against too ready an acceptance of the 'nationalist' approach to the study of non-orthodox movements, especially in the east Roman provinces.

At the same time a study of the Monophysites cannot be confined to the history of Christian doctrine. The issues raised by the councils of Ephesus and Chalcedon touched on many, perhaps nearly all, aspects of the relations between government and governed in the east Roman provinces in the fifth and sixth centuries. Religion was the medium through which this relationship was expressed both in its harmony and its dissent. Indeed, it was the only medium that would have been understood at this period. Nearly all the art, much of the finest architecture and a great deal of the literature of the times were inspired by religion. It was the work of men, whether clerical or lay, working in the interest of Christianity to win victory for the people of God and its rulers over demonic forces represented by paganism, schism and civil disorder. Through the whole range of society the line between secular and lay was finely drawn. Justinian was not a mere amateur theologian but a ruler whose chief concern was his own and his subjects' right religion, and who immersed himself in the doctrinal questions of the day to become no mean performer in the intricate logic by which Chalcedon was defended in the interests of the patriarchate of the capital and the unity of *Romania*. The Emperor Anastasius (491–518) was personally a deeply religious man and had been actually short-listed as patriarch of Antioch three years before he became emperor.[1] His nephew John, Justin I's rival for the throne in 518, found himself metropolitan of Heraclea. Justin himself appointed his former military commander (*comes Orientis*) Ephraim to be patriarch of Antioch in 526, and a vigorous choice he was, during his eighteen years in that see. One of Justinian's more curious appointments was that of Photion, described as a 'monk of high rank', to command the levies used to put down the revolt of the Samaritans in 564.[2] The list of high officials who end their days as churchmen, and churchmen who conduct affairs of state, is a long one. They include many of the great men of the day, from Cyrus the prefect under Theodosius II, who became for a short time bishop of Cotiaeum in Phrygia,[3] to Constantine of

[1] Theophanes, *Chron.* A.M. 5982.
[2] John of Nikiou, *Chron.* (ed. Charles), ch. 95. 17.
[3] Cyrus had originally been a pagan but had been forced to convert to Christianity by the emperor (Theophanes, *Chron.* A.M. 5937). Other fallen ministers less lucky could find themselves ordained deacon (John Malalas, *Chron.* XVIII. 184).

Introduction

Laodicea, a one-time *magister militum* who for a decade or so (540–50) was a sort of Monophysite pro-patriarch of Antioch, and Dometianus, archbishop of Melitene, who achieved a role something like that of Chief Minister in the reign of Maurice. The tendency is perhaps summed up in the person of 'Cyrus the Caucasian' whom Heraclius appointed as the governor as well as orthodox patriarch of Alexandria in 631. He epitomises the interlocking of the concepts themselves of the Christian church and Byzantine state. When eleven years later he capitulated to the Arabs and sailed away from Alexandria, an era of Mediterranean history had come to an end.

These trends found their response among the people as a whole. From the middle of the fourth century public and private life was coloured by religion, indeed the more abstruse the doctrine in question the livelier the public interest. The well-known expostulation by Gregory of Nyssa about the level at which theology was discussed in the capital was typical of the situation, and was made in a sermon devoted to doctrinal issues.[1] 'If in this city [Constantinople] one asks anyone for change, he will discuss with you whether the Son is begotten or unbegotten. If you ask about the quality of the bread you will receive the answer, "the Father is greater, the Son is less". If you suggest a bath is desirable, you will be told "there was nothing before the Son was created".' This familiar text is confirmed, however, by other evidence from the capital. A decade later, about 390, we find the Arians there split over the issue of whether it was right to call God 'Father' when referring to the time when 'Christ was not'. The point was hotly disputed, and those who believed that there was a time when the term Father was inappropriate took their name Psathyrians from an ardent supporter who spent his spare time selling crumbly cakes (*psathyropoles*).[2] The concern for theological questions was indeed world-wide. In almost every village in Syria there would be monks to keep discussion going, waxing the more fanatical as the issues became less intelligible. In the west also, theological debates provided public spectacles; on 22 August 392 Augustine's controversy with his old friend, the Manichee Fortunatus, was brought to a halt by demonstrations in the crowded ranks of the spectators.[3] Even in the midst of the barbarians' invasions two decades later Pelagianism was being argued in many provinces in the west.

[1] *De filii deitate*, PG 46, col. 557.
[2] Philostorgius, *HE* II. 15; Socrates, *HE* V. 23.
[3] Augustine, *Contra Fortunatum* I. 19 (*PL* 42, col. 121).

Introduction

In this era of deep and avid theological inquiry Chalcedon assumes overwhelming importance. The two centuries of Byzantine history that follow may be regarded as a long aftermath, ended only when the success of the Arabs in conquering Egypt and Syria rendered efforts to find doctrinal compromises academic. The story unfolds slowly. There could be no greater mistake than to think that the opponents of Chalcedon formed a separate church from the outset; indeed, 'Monophysitism' is relatively a modern concept. No one used the term in the period with which we are dealing. To the emperors, opponents of Chalcedon were the 'Hesitants', the *diakrinomenoi*, those who 'had reservations' about accepting its definition. Orthodox clergy and laymen often found their position baffling. As the Patriarch John the Faster (582–95) complained in the reign of Maurice, their doctrines were irreproachable yet they would not communicate with Chalcedonians.[1] In moments of impatience, as after the ending of the Acacian schism in 518, the opposition became 'dissidents' (*aposchistae*) or more sinister, the 'headless ones' (*acephaloi*), referring to the apparent anonymity of their leadership. Though I use the term 'Monophysite' in this work I do so mainly to avoid circumlocutions; but it is only apt as a description of the anti-Chalcedonians after the establishment of a separate Monophysite hierarchy in the second half of Justinian's reign.

Even this move was undertaken with extreme reluctance. Severus and his colleagues were forced into it by the circumstances of the persecution in Justin's reign. Fifty years later, however, in *circa* 600, the Monophysite 'empire' stretched almost unbroken from the Black Sea, down Rome's eastern frontier with Persia, thence to Egypt and the Nile valley to Ethiopia, a vast expanse of territory, greater than that covered by Latin and orthodox Christianity combined. This Monophysite tradition became the tradition of the Armenian, Jacobite, Coptic, Nubian and Ethiopian churches, and insofar as these have survived they have continued to be loyal to it. At the outset, however, except in Egypt, it would be hazardous to see Monophysitism as an expression of regionalism on the part of the non-Hellenistic provincials. Ultimately it developed in that direction, but study of the evidence even in the relative detail attempted here reveals that Monophysitism owed little of its initial impulse as a reaction against Chalcedon to non-religious factors. It is not true, for instance, that 'at an early period in their history the Monophysites and Nestorians attracted to

[1] John of Ephesus, *HE* (Part iii) III. 12 (ed. Brooks, *CSCO* III. 3, p. 102).

themselves the Semitic population of the eastern provinces of the Roman empire who found in their adherence to a schismatic church an opportunity of expressing hatred of foreign rule'.[1] There was no 'Monophysite church' for nearly a century after Chalcedon, and in the early stages of the movement the Hellenistic element was just as prominent as the native. Neither Cyril nor his 'Monophysite' successors were Copts, nor was Severus of Antioch a Syrian. The issue at the back of their minds and those of their followers was whether the life-giving elements of the Eucharist had been dispensed by a cleric who had a truly orthodox attitude towards religion, and Chalcedon was not truly orthodox. Even in Egypt, the amalgamation of resentment against ecclesiastical rule from Constantinople and Alexandrian and Egyptian particularist feeling was slow to develop. Elsewhere it was centuries before Monophysites would express themselves in words attributed to the Armenian Catholicus, Gregorius VII (1293–1307), 'We are prepared rather to be in hell with our fathers than ascend to heaven with the Romans'.

In this respect the contrast with the history of the Donatist schism in the west is instructive. Whereas the Donatists questioned the right of the emperor to intervene in ecclesiastical affairs and their movement derived its strength largely from the single province of Numidia, the Monophysites invited it. The emperor's sovereignty embraced the government of both church and state in imitation of his Master, the divine Word. They abhorred the very idea of provincial separatism, schism and rebellion. Their object, down even to the eve of the Arab invasions, was to persuade the emperor to renounce Chalcedon and accept the Christology of Cyril as interpreted by them. Even the great Monophysite missionary, James Bar'adai (d. 578), who was responsible more than anyone else for the establishment of a permanent Monophysite church, would have been willing to return to communion with the emperor on the latter's rejection of Chalcedon, or even his acceptance of the *Henotikon* of Zeno understood in the sense of cancelling the synod.[2]

The final parting, therefore, between the adherents of Chalcedon and the Monophysites was only gradually brought about. The landmarks are the *Henotikon* of Zeno in 482, followed by the Acacian schism between Rome and Constantinople lasting from 484 to 519, the election of Severus

[1] T. W. Arnold, 'The pictorial art of the Jacobite and Nestorian Churches', *BZ* 30, 1929–30, p. 596.
[2] See below, p. 319.

Introduction

to the patriarchate of Antioch in 512, and the persecution of the anti-Chalcedonians in Syria in 519 and even more violently in 532 and 536. Each time hopes of reunification became more slender and the tone of polemic more abrasive as the doctrinal differences between the two sides became harder to define. The experts became the more rancorous because they were convinced that it was possible to achieve agreement on a shared body of doctrine. Only after the death of the Empress Theodora in June 548, however, was hope abandoned of an 'orthodox emperor' who would restore Second Ephesus ('the Robber Council') as symbol of orthodoxy and dethrone Chalcedon. After that, the establishment of an episcopate and clergy in direct opposition to the Chalcedonian grew apace, but even in the early years of Justin II's reign the two communities came within an ace of agreement. One cannot say that political rejection of Byzantium was inevitable before the failure of the Emperor Maurice's policy of coercion.

In this work I have followed the beaten track established by the past generation of Continental and British scholars. The essays contained in the first two volumes of A. Grillmeier and H. Bacht's work commemorating the 1,500th anniversary of Chalcedon must be the starting point of any research. I am indebted also to the encyclopaedic studies of Eduard Schwartz, especially for the chronology and elucidation of events in the complicated period from the accession of Leo I to the end of the Acacian schism. To R. V. Sellers, *The Council of Chalcedon*, I owe many insights, particularly those relating to the period leading up to Chalcedon. To the works of R. Draguet and A. de Halleux I owe guidance towards understanding the doctrinal intricacies of the Monophysite position, and to E. Honigmann's detailed surveys of the bishoprics and bishops in the patriarchate of Antioch, some grasp of the actual distribution of Chalcedonian and Monophysite opinion in the sixth century.

The present work claims to be no more than a survey. Tchalenko's classic study of the north Syrian villages shows what can be done in the field to demonstrate the connection between religious attitudes and livelihoods of the inhabitants in a specific area.[1] More of the same kind of work is needed before one will be in a position to say why one area of the Byzantine Empire preferred Monophysitism to Chalcedon and vice versa. For instance, why should the province of Pamphylia in southern Asia Minor be described by John of Ephesus as having been 'ex initio' 'orthodox'

[1] G. Tchalenko, *Villages antiques de la Syrie du Nord* (Paris, 1953–8).

(i.e. Monophysite)?¹ Was it the commanding personality of the powerful metropolitan, Amphilochius of Side, the only prelate who voted 'the wrong way' in Leo I's plebiscite concerning Chalcedon and Timothy the Cat, or did he represent merely the *genius loci* derived from the province being dominated by its monasteries and villages (*pagi*)? Why, moreover, should Pamphylia have been a hotbed of the Tritheist brand of Monophysitism and the whole province characterised by popular religious zeal? Similarly, the island of Chios: why should this island have been singled out as the seat of John, one of James Bar'adai's bishops? One would give much for more documents such as Athanasius of Nisibis' collection of Severus of Antioch's letters, which shed so much light on obscure local situations that often played a great part in influencing opinions for or against Chalcedon. At the moment one must accept one's authorities and wait for the archaeologist and student of prosopography to provide more evidence on the ground.

The historian is always dealing with incomplete evidence. His assessment of the facts as he finds them must reflect to a large extent the ideas of his own age. The questions he asks, however, may have a longer validity. How did the development of Monophysitism affect the relations between the Greek and Latin-speaking worlds? What light can be thrown on the breakdown of confidence that led to the Monophysites preferring Moslem to Byzantine rule? How did Monophysitism emerge by the end of the sixth century to become a third religious force in the Mediterranean world distinct from both Latin and orthodox Christianity? What factors, if any, lay behind this debate about seemingly unanswerable trivialities? These are questions of interest to the historian of Europe as well as to the specialist in Christian doctrine. Some attempt at answering them was made in the lectures on which this book is based.

¹ John of Ephesus, *HE* v. 6.

ABBREVIATIONS

AB	*Analecta Bollandiana* (publ. Société des Bollandistes), Bruxelles, 1882–
ACO	*Acta Conciliorum Oecumenicorum*, ed. E. Schwartz, Strassburg, Berlin and Leipzig, 1914–40
AHR	*American Historical Review*, New York, 1895–
AJP	*American Journal of Philology*, Baltimore, 1880–
AJT	*American Journal of Theology*, Chicago, 1897–1920
BZ	*Byzantinische Zeitschrift*, Leipzig, München, 1892–
CAH	*Cambridge Ancient History*
CHS	*Church Historical Society*
CIG	*Corpus Inscriptionum Graecarum*, Berlin, 1828–77
CIL	*Corpus Inscriptionum Latinarum*, Berlin, 1862–
CMH	*Cambridge Medieval History*
CSCO	*Corpus Scriptorum Christianorum Orientalium*, Paris, 1903–
CSEL	*Corpus Scriptorum Ecclesiasticorum Latinorum*, Vienna, 1866–
DTC	*Dictionnaire de Théologie Catholique*, ed. A. Vacant, E. Mangenot and E. Amann, Paris, 1909–50
EHR	*English Historical Review*, London, 1886–
GCS	*Die griechischen christlichen Schriftsteller der ersten drei Jahrhunderte*, Leipzig, Berlin, 1897–
HE	*Historia Ecclesiastica*
HTR	*Harvard Theological Review*, New York, 1908–
IGLS	*Inscriptions grecques et latines de la Syrie* (ed. L. Jalabert and R. Mouterde, Paris, 1929–)
ILCV	*Inscriptiones Latinae Christianae Veteres*, ed. E. Diehl, Berlin, 1961
JEH	*Journal of Ecclesiastical History*, London, 1950–
JHS	*Journal of Hellenic Studies*, London, 1880–
JRS	*Journal of Roman Studies*, London, 1910–
JTS	*Journal of Theological Studies*, London, 1899–
MGH AA	*Monumenta Germaniae Historica*, Auctores Antiquissimi
PG	*Patrologiae Cursus Completus*, Series Graeca, ed. J. P. Migne, Paris, 1857–1934
PL	*Patrologiae Cursus Completus*, Series Latina, ed. J. P. Migne, Paris, 1841–90
PO	*Patrologiae Orientalis*, ed. R. Graffin and F. Nau, Paris, 1907–
PS	E. Schwartz, 'Publizistische Sammlungen': see below, p. 145n 1, for full details
PW	*Paulys Realenzyklopädie der klassischen Altertumswissenschaft*, ed. G. Wissowa and W. Kroll, Stuttgart, 1894–
RHE	*Revue d'histoire ecclésiastique*, Louvain, 1900–
RHR	*Revue de l'histoire des religions*, Paris, 1880–
TU	*Texte und Untersuchungen*, Leipzig, Berlin, 1882– (ed. O. von Gebhardt and A. von Harnack and successors)
ZNTW	*Zeitschrift für neutestamentliche Wissenschaft*, Giessen, Berlin, 1900–

Chapter 1

THE ROAD TO CHALCEDON
428-451

Like 1066 and 1485 the date 451 has taken on a significance of its own. While in Gaul the Romans and their Visigothic allies under Aetius were winning their decisive victory over the Huns on the Catalaunian Plains near Troyes,[1] more than 500 bishops were assembled in the nave of the Church of St Euphemia at Chalcedon on the east side of the Bosporus opposite Constantinople.[2] There, between 8 October and 10 November 451, in sixteen long and often turbulent sessions, they laid down what has remained the orthodox definition of faith regarding the person of Christ to the present day, and in addition, attempted to regularise a series of problems concerning ecclesiastical discipline, including that of the position accorded to the see of Constantinople, better known to the bishops as New Rome.

The council affirmed at its sixth session on 25 October:

'Following then the Holy Fathers, we all unanimously teach that Our Lord Jesus Christ is to us one and the same Son, the self-same Perfect in Godhead, the self-same Perfect in manhood, truly God and truly Man, the self-same of a rational soul and body, consubstantial with the Father according to the Godhead, the self-same consubstantial with us according to the manhood, like us in all things, sin apart; before all the ages begotten of the Father as to the Godhead, but in the last days, the self-same for us and for our salvation [born] of the Virgin Theotokos as to the manhood, one and the same Christ, Son and Lord, Only-begotten, made known to us in two Natures, unconfusedly, unchangeably, indivisibly, inseparably; the difference of the Natures being in no way removed because of the Union, but rather the properties of each nature being preserved and concurring into one Prosopon and one Hypostasis, not as though he were parted or divided into two Prosopa, but One and the self-same

---

[1] The actual site of the battle fought on 20 June 451 is not known. See E. A. Thompson, *Attila and the Huns* (Oxford, 1948), p. 141.

[2] In its letter to Pope Leo after the conclusion of proceedings the council claimed that 520 bishops had participated: included in Leo's correspondence, Leo, *Ep.* 98 (*PL* 54, col. 959).

Son and only-begotten God, Word, Lord Jesus Christ, even as from the beginning the prophets have taught concerning him, and as the Lord Jesus Christ Himself hath taught us and as the symbol of the Fathers hath handed down to us.'[1]

This complicated statement, reminiscent of the intellectual pitfalls prepared for the unwary in the Athanasian Creed, conceals a wealth of controversy.[2] Almost every word had a technical and special meaning for the signatories. Thus the four adverbs 'unconfusedly, unchangeably, indivisibly, inseparably' (ἀσυγχύτως, ἀτρέπτως, ἀδιαιρέτως, ἀχωρίστως), Harnack's 'four bald, negative terms',[3] nonetheless represented a neat balance between rival theological opinions. The first two were designed to confute those who suggested that in Christ there had been a mingling and modification of the divine and human natures to form a composite being whose flesh was not 'human flesh',[4] while 'inseparably' and 'indivisibly' were designed to exclude the possibility of division between those same two natures so as to make 'two Christs'. There was the effort, too, to harmonise the terms *physis* (nature in the sense of a quality or property in which more than one individual may share), *hypostasis* (individuality), and *prosopon* (personality) that had bedevilled theologians for the previous seventy years, a hopeless effort as it proved, at squaring a circle that prompted the feeling that Chalcedon marked the bankruptcy rather than the triumph of Greek theology. The terms, almost synonymous though they had come to be, had nonetheless retained distinct meanings, the result of different philosophical approaches to the mystery of the incarnation. Attempts to redefine their relationship could be regarded as the victory of one approach over its opponents. The hasty efforts to arrive at compromises at the council raised more problems than they solved.

The most important statement of all, however, was the phrase 'but in

[1] Text in *ACO* 2. 1. 2, pp. 129–30; see also notes on the text in Bindley/Green, *Documents*, pp. 191–9, and the commentary by R. V. Sellers, *The Council of Chalcedon: a historical and doctrinal survey* (London, 1961), pp. 207–28.

[2] See the almost word-by-word analysis of the text by I. Ortiz de Urbina, 'Das Symbol von Chalkedon, sein Text, sein Werden, seine dogmatische Bedeutung', in A. Grillmeier and H. Bacht, *Das Konzil von Chalkedon; Geschichte und Gegenwart* (Würzburg, 1953–62), I, 389–418, and Sellers, *Council of Chalcedon, loc. cit.*

[3] A. von Harnack, *History of Dogma* (Eng. tr., London, 1898), IV, 222.

[4] This was also made clear in the passage καὶ τοὺς οὐρανίου ἢ ἑτέρας τινὸς ὑπάρχειν οὐσίας τὴν ἐξ ἡμῶν ληφθεῖσαν αὐτῷ τοῦ δούλου μορφὴν παραπαίοντας ἐξελαύνει. See *ACO* 2. 1. 2, p. 129, and Bindley/Green, *Documents*, p. 193, line 105 of the Definition.

the last times for us and for our salvation [born] of the Virgin Theotokos as to the manhood...made known to us in two natures...'[1] It had only been accepted after dramatic scenes which demonstrated the conflicting forces present and nearly brought the council to a premature end.[2] Four days before, a draft doctrinal formulary had been prepared under the direction of Anatolius, patriarch of Constantinople. This was read to the council at its fifth session on 22 October and received practically unanimous approbation.[3] Unfortunately the text has not survived, for immediate objection was encountered from the papal legates supported by some of the bishops from the patriarchate of Antioch: that it contained no direct mention of the 'two natures' of Christ, a phrase fundamental to western Christological thought. It is clear, however, that it affirmed Christ was 'of two natures' and the Blessed Virgin was *Theotokos* (God-bearing).[4] The legates threatened to return home and hold a new council in Italy. A considerable number of the bishops would not have been sorry to see them go. 'Let the formula stand, or we depart', they shouted, 'these men are Nestorians, let them be off to Rome.'[5] Such a contingency, however, could have split the empire in two just as the danger from the Huns seemed at its most serious. Amid growing uproar the imperial commissioners who presided over the proceedings intervened. The bishops were reminded that they had accepted as orthodox Pope Leo's *Tome* written two years before to Anatolius' ill-fated predecessor Flavian,

---

[1] ἐπ' ἐσχάτων δὲ τῶν ἡμερῶν τὸν αὐτὸν δι' ἡμᾶς καὶ διὰ τὴν ἡμετέραν σωτηρίαν ἐκ Μαρίας τῆς παρθένου τῆς Θεοτόκου κατὰ τὴν ἀνθρωπότητα, ἕνα καὶ τὸν αὐτὸν Χριστόν, Υἱόν, Κύριον, μονογενῆ, ἐν δύο φύσεσιν ἀσυγχύτως, ἀτρέπτως, ἀδιαιρέτως, ἀχωρίστως γνωριζόμενον.

[2] See *ACO* 2. I. 2, pp. 121–4 = Mansi, *Collectio* VII, cols. 100–5, and R. V. Sellers' account, *Council of Chalcedon*, pp. 116–21.

[3] *ACO* 2. I. 2, p. 123, paras. 7 and 8: Ἀνατόλιος ὁ θεοφιλέστατος ἐπίσκοπος Κωνσταντινουπόλεως εἶπεν· Ἤρεσε χθὲς πᾶσιν ὁ ὅρος τῆς πίστεως; Οἱ εὐλαβέστατοι ἐπίσκοποι εἶπον· Ὁ ὅρος πᾶσιν ἤρεσεν. ἄλλως οὐ πιστεύομεν.

[4] *ACO ibid.* p. 124: ὁ δὲ ὅρος ἐκ δύο φύσεων ἔχει (=Mansi, *Collectio* VII, col. 104B). I cannot agree with Sellers' view (*Council of Chalcedon*, p. 117) that the draft Definition omitted the title of 'Theotokos'. The interventions by members of the council in favour of the title were protests against objections from Antiochenes, especially John, bishop of Germanicia. The mass of bishops feared with good reason that the alliance between the papal legates and the Antiochenes would prevent the acceptance of Mary as Theotokos, and hence the repeated shouts that she was so and that those who objected were 'Nestorians'.

[5] *ACO ibid.* p. 125 = Mansi, *Collectio* VII, col. 105B.

and that this had contained the formulary 'two natures are united without change, without division and without confusion in Christ'.[1] The definition to be agreed by the council must take this into account – a neat example of a decisive intervention in ecclesiastical affairs in the east by laymen. On the Emperor Marcian's suggestion a fresh committee of bishops was set up to reconsider the matter.[2]

The result of their deliberations was the formulary known as the Chalcedonian Definition, already quoted. Eventually, 452 bishops among those present signed,[3] but despite its acceptance of the Virgin as *Theotokos* it was instinctively repellent to a large number of the signatories. Only two years before at a council held at Ephesus in August 449 many of these same bishops had howled down any suggestion that Christ existed 'in two natures' after the incarnation.[4] The formula, however, was known to correspond to the will of the emperor supported both by the papal legates and the lay presidents of the council. It therefore carried the day. In retrospect, these four days of consultations were to have a decisive effect on the history of Christianity in the Mediterranean. Though, as in the Arian controversy a century earlier, a single letter separated the rival positions (*en* as against *ek*), the difference was wider than met the eye.[5]

---

[1] *ACO* ibid. p. 125 = Mansi, *Collectio* VII, col. 105C. The *Tome* of Leo = *Ep*. 28; see also text and notes in Bindley/Green, *Documents*, pp. 168–80.

[2] This committee consisted of Anatolius, patriarch of Constantinople, the three papal legates, together with Julian of Cóos, Leo's personal representative, Maximus of Antioch, Juvenal of Jerusalem, Thalassius of Caesarea and Eusebius of Ancyra (the last three of these had taken a prominent part in the proceedings of Ephesus II in August 449), three Illyrian bishops, three from the diocese of Asia, Eusebius of Dorylaeum (who had been deposed and outrageously treated at Ephesus II), four bishops from the patriarchate of Antioch (who could be regarded as in favour of the two-nature definition), and three others from sees in Thrace (*ACO* 2. 1. 2, pp. 124–6 = Mansi, *Collectio* VII, col. 105A). It was as representative a group as was ever likely to meet, and went far to vindicate the presiding officials' claim that Chalcedon was to be a 'just synod'. *ACO* 2. 1. 1, p. 120, para. 337; see Sellers, *Council of Chalcedon*, p. 120 n3.

[3] *ACO* 2. 1. 2, pp. 141–55; only 324 bishops signed their names as being present at the sixth session (*ibid.* pp. 130–8), but others signed later, and on behalf of absent colleagues, bringing a final tally up to 452.

[4] At Ephesus the bishops had cried out, 'If anyone says "two" [natures] [let him be] anathema': *ACO* 2. 1. 1, p. 140, para. 495.

[5] At the end of the sixth century the Syrian Melchite (pro-Chalcedonian) writer Evagrius commented on the minuteness of the difference that separated the two sides and attributed the situation to 'the device of the envious and God-hating demon' (Evagrius, *HE* II. 5).

Christ compounded 'out of two natures', divine and human, followed logically from the current Word-flesh theology of the Greek east, derived ultimately from St Paul but refined and interpreted by generations of minds steeped in the tradition of Stoic and Platonic psychology. The formula did justice to those who accepted that the mystery of salvation was contained in the union of the divine and human in one being, Jesus Christ, and it corresponded to the way in which people might define an individual in ordinary speech as composed of two natures, a rational soul and a body.[1] In these circumstances, the formula was acceptable to the eastern bishops as a whole, as they had demonstrated when it had been put to them on 22 October. For them the only-begotten Son of God was indeed God. The 'in two natures' school, while equally concerned with human salvation in Christ, emphasised the reality of Christ's humanity and his permanent identity with man. This Word-man theology saw Christ as atoning for the sins of mankind by his sacrifice on the cross and, by the example of his life, death and resurrection, leading man on to communion with God. The emphasis lay more on the high priesthood of Christ than on Christ as incarnate Word. Thus, behind the two formulae lay two distinct interpretations of Christ's work and even the nature of his church, as well as of his essential being. These differences had already begun to harden along cultural and geographical lines. Alexandria, Antioch, Rome and Constantinople were confronting each other at the council as representatives of potentially exclusive traditions.

If Anatolius had been able to gain his point and include both 'Theotokos' and 'out of two natures' in the definition of faith he would probably have averted schism in the east.[2] The Egyptian bishops, divided over the personal worthiness of their patriarch Dioscorus, and chastened by the

---

[1] Thus Christ's manhood was described in the Definition of Chalcedon as ἐκ ψυχῆς λογικῆς καὶ σώματος as well as in Flavian's confession of faith.

[2] 'Out of two natures' had been accepted in the previous two years: (a) by Flavian in a confession of faith written to the Emperor Theodosius on 17 December 448 – 'Ex duabus utique naturis confitentes Christum post Incarnationem ex sancta virgine et inhumatum in una substantia et in una persona unum Christum, unum filium, unum Dominum confitemur' (*ACO* 2. III. 1, p. 5, lines 17–19). (b) Eutyches the archimandrite, condemned by Flavian on 22 November 448, had accepted the same formula under pressure (*ACO* 2. I. 1, p. 140, paras. 488–9). (c) Dioscorus also accepted it at Chalcedon itself: τὸ ἐκ δύο φύσεων δέχομαι· τὸ δὲ δύο οὐ δέχομαι (*ACO* 2. I. 1, p. 120, para. 332). The formula therefore had been accepted both by Alexandria and Constantinople, and by Eutyches representing the outlook of many of the monks.

revelations concerning his administration revealed by members of his own clergy, would almost certainly have rallied to it with relief, and, on Dioscorus' ejection, accepted a new patriarch at the hand of the council. This solution would have been, however, at the expense of a rupture with the papacy and considerable opposition from Antioch. Moreover, so great was the revulsion caused by Dioscorus' tyrannical conduct in the recent past, and in particular by what was believed to be his responsibility for the violent death of the Patriarch Flavian of Constantinople in 449,[1] that any Christological formula to which he could have agreed immediately became suspect. Instead, the bishops were prepared to accept the 'in two natures' formula that had been proposed by Pope Leo in his *Tome*, and were ready to argue somewhat disingenuously that it corresponded to traditional eastern theology.[2] When the choice was put squarely to the assembly by the lay commissioners 'Dioscorus or Leo', the cry went up, 'As Leo we believe. Leo has expounded [the faith] rightly. He who contradicts is a Eutychian.'[3] They were to repent their rash enthusiasm at leisure.

For the next century the great majority of Egyptian Christians and their Syrian allies strove by every means to wipe out the effects of this defeat and to secure the renunciation of the 'two natures' formula by the church as a whole. They failed, partly because the papacy was involved in upholding the definition, and successive popes refused to consider any modification, and partly because both Constantinople and Jerusalem had a common interest in maintaining the ecumenical status of the Council of Chalcedon as the best means of safeguarding the rights and privileges of their sees. In the background also lay the growing particularist self-consciousness of the Coptic- and Syriac-speaking Christians who were already beginning to throw up from among the monks of Egypt and Syria individuals who leant strongly towards the one-nature Christology and to whom any compromise proposed from the imperial capital was to

---

[1] E.g. *ACO* 2. 1. 1, p. 143, para. 530 – the outcry of the Oriental bishops (i.e. from the patriarchate of Antioch) against the 'out of two natures' formula: ἀνάθεμα τῷ εἰπόντι. ὁ φονεὺς ταῦτα εἶπεν. ταῦτα οἱ Αἰγύπτιοι εἶπον. ταῦτα τοῦ Φαραώ εἰσιν. ἀνάθεμα τοῖς εἰποῦσιν. The spontaneous shout against 'the Egyptians' and 'Pharaoh' is significant for the exasperation felt at the domination of eastern Christendom by the Alexandrians.

[2] Thus the archdeacon Aetius of Constantinople argued at the third session of the council that the formula corresponded to the great Cyril of Alexandria's views (*ACO* 2. 1. 2, p. 82, paras. 24–5). See also Liberatus, *Brev.* XIII. 86 (*ACO* 2. v, p. 120).

[3] *ACO* 2. 1. 2, p. 125, para. 27.

be anathema. At the same time, the theologians and people of Constantinople were developing their own imperial self-consciousness and loyalty to the person of their patriarch, not least the memory of the 'martyr' Flavian.[1] This came increasingly to express itself in an insistence on the full doctrinal orthodoxy of Chalcedon and respect for the privileges of the patriarchate. Their self-esteem clashed not only with the popular Christianity of Egypt and Syria but with the equally strongly held authoritarian views of the bishops of Rome.

The resulting divergence of views between Rome and Constantinople gave rise to even more far-reaching consequences. The quarrel between the old capital and the new, typified in this period by the Acacian schism (484–519), emerged almost by accident at the end of the proceedings of the council. After the doctrinal formula had been agreed, the council, like its predecessor at Nicaea in 325, moved on to consider sundry matters of discipline. There had been long-standing dispute between the churches of Constantinople and Ephesus over the right of the church of the imperial capital to intervene in the affairs of the churches of the province of Asia and of Ephesus itself.[2] Ephesus had claimed primatial status over the churches in the provinces of Asia Minor. This had contributed to the hostility of its bishop towards the patriarchs of Constantinople in the two previous councils held there in 431 and 449, but at the twelfth session of the Council of Chalcedon the bishops were confronted with the spectacle of rival bishops of Ephesus, each demanding recognition by the council. Having declared, however, both deposed, the judges put off stating an

---

[1] Note the cry of the clergy of Constantinople at the council, Φλαβιανὸς μετὰ θάνατον τὴν πίστιν ἐξέθετο (*ACO* 2. 1. 3, p. 51, para. 44).

[2] The status of Ephesus was not very clear. Traditionally, Ephesus 'led the bishops of Asia' (Eusebius, *HE* v. 24. 1) and Bishop Polycrates (*ibid.* v. 24. 4) claimed that John the beloved disciple was buried there. On the other hand, Ephesus was not accorded special primatial rights (πρεσβεῖα) in Asia beyond those of a metropolitan (see canon 2 of the Council of Constantinople), and with the growing authority of Constantinople, its claims to special prerogatives were increasingly challenged. In 400 John Chrysostom seems to have regarded Ephesus as having some rights over churches throughout Asia Minor, but he accepted an appeal by the church at Ephesus itself to settle a disputed episcopal election, and previously he had deposed six bishops from Asia for various offences, with the agreement of an incipient Home Synod assembled in the capital (Palladius, *Dial.* chs. 13 and 14). Nestorius' intervention in the affairs of Ephesus provoked great resentment, but a generation later the bishop had clearly no great claim to the restoration of what the council of 475 defined as τὸν πατριαρχικὸν δίκαιον lost at Chalcedon (Evagrius, *HE* III. 6, ed. Bidez and Parmentier, p. 106).

opinion on whether the right of consecrating a new bishop belonged to the see of Constantinople or not.¹ At the end of the council, to settle this issue and perhaps, too, with an eye to preventing the capital from suffering further attacks by the rival see of Alexandria, 185 bishops who remained behind assigned to the patriarch of Constantinople not only the right of consecrating the metropolitans of Asia (which included Ephesus), Pontus, Thrace and 'bishops in lands held by barbarians', but also 'primacy of honour after the bishop of Rome because that Constantinople is new Rome'.² The wording of the decision, known to history as the 28th canon, was exceedingly carefully chosen and designed to avoid any impression that something new was being conceded to the capital. The bishops recalled canon 3 of the Council of Constantinople in 381 which had declared that Constantinople as New Rome had honorary pre-eminence (πρεσβεῖα) after Old Rome.³ In justification of the prerogatives that were now granted it could be argued that the see of Constantinople had been assigned jurisdiction over Thrace (with its former metropolis of Heraclea) by the Council of Constantinople in 381.⁴ In addition, it had occasionally exercised appellate jurisdiction in areas as far afield as Bostra in Arabia. It had been represented at important trials of bishops,

---

¹ The whole of the twelfth and thirteenth sessions were devoted to this issue. The clergy of Constantinople asserted their rights vigorously. Leontius of Magnesia, however, pointed out that 'from the holy Timothy until now 27 bishops have been consecrated, all in Ephesus. Only Basil was made bishop here [in Constantinople] violently and much rioting was the result' (*ACO* 2. 1. 3, p. 52, para. 57). Anatolius had the wit to come forward with the generous suggestion that both rival bishops should be allowed to retain their titles of bishop and be compensated with 200 solidi each from the revenue of the church. The new bishop was to be chosen by bishops of the province but nothing was said about his consecration except that it was to be 'according to the canons of the church of Ephesus'.

² The official version was that the aim was 'to cut out all confusion and to confirm ecclesiastical discipline'. On this subject, see T. O. Martin, 'The twenty-eighth canon of Chalcedon: a background note', in Grillmeier/Bacht, *Das Konzil von Chalkedon*, II, 433–58, and E. Schwartz, 'Der sechste nicaenische Kanon auf der Synode von Chalkedon', Sitz. der preussischen Akad. der Wiss., Phil.-hist. Kl. 1930, pp. 611–40, especially p. 612. Also, W. Bright, *Notes on the Canons of the First Four General Councils* (Oxford, 1882), pp. 92 and 192ff., an old but still valuable work, and C. J. Hefele and H. Leclercq, *Histoire des conciles* (Paris, 1907), II. 1, 24.

³ On the term πρεσβεῖα see E. Herman, 'Chalkedon und die Ausgestaltung des konstantinopolitanischen Primats', in Grillmeier/Bacht, *Das Konzil von Chalkedon*, II, 459–89 at pp. 464ff.

⁴ Socrates, *HE* v. 8.

including that of Ibas of Edessa for heresy and peculation at Berytus in 448,[1] and it had become the normal place of recourse for aggrieved clergy. Finally, it had frequently consecrated metropolitans in provinces of Asia Minor.[2] In 421, during the dispute with Rome over the right of ecclesiastical jurisdiction in the Illyrian provinces,[3] Theodosius II had ruled that this belonged to Constantinople, as the latter 'enjoys the prerogative of Old Rome'. Any other solution was condemned as 'innovation'.[4] All this was now to be put to the test.

The immediate question of principle had been simmering in the background for over a year.[5] The papal legates had been briefed before departure from Rome that the claims of Constantinople might be urged and had been instructed how to resist them.[6] The way in which the question arose may have caught them unawares, though it should not have done so

[1] *ACO* 2. 1. 3, p. 19.

[2] Socrates, *HE* VII. 28, refers to a law which forbade the church of Cyzicus to consecrate a bishop without the sanction of the bishop of the capital, and several of the metropolitans in Asia Minor declared at Chalcedon they had been consecrated by him. See Herman, 'Chalkedon', in Grillmeier/Bacht, *Das Konzil von Chalkedon*, II, 459–89 at pp. 472–7, and A. H. M. Jones, *The Later Roman Empire* (Oxford, 1964), II, 892.

[3] These formed a vital bridge between east and west, since they consisted of Illyria and the Danube provinces of Dacia, Dardania and Moesia, which were Latin-speaking, and Macedonia and Epirus which were Greek-speaking. Papal efforts to control this vast area through a papal vicar at Thessalonica caused obvious difficulties with Constantinople.

[4] *Cod. Theod.* XVI. 2. 45, of 14 July 421. In a subsequent exchange of letters between Theodosius II and Honorius, between 421 and 423, Theodosius climbed down to the extent of recognising that Rome had a claim to jurisdiction in Illyricum based on 'old canons', and had ordered the *praefectus praetorio* in Illyricum to see that 'the bishops' plottings ceased' there, but the original mandate (*Cod. Theod.* XVI. 2. 45) was retained in the *Codex Theodosianus* when this was published in 438, and was repeated in the *Codex Justinianus* a century later as *Cod. Just.* I. 2. 6 and II. 21. 1. See P. R. Coleman-Norton's valuable note, *Roman State and Christian Church* (London, 1966), II, 617–21; also R. P. Venance Grumel, 'Le Vicariat de Thessalonique et le premier rattachement de l'Illyricum oriental au patriarcat de Constantinople', *Annuaire de l'école de législation religieuse*, 1950–1, pp. 49–63. The whole dossier of papal, imperial and other letters bearing on the rival claims between Rome and Constantinople over Illyricum is printed in Mansi, *Collectio* VIII, cols. 749–72.

[5] See below, p. 46.

[6] *ACO* 2. 1. 3, p. 95, para. 14. They were to stand firm on Nicaea. Papal prerogatives were to be protected at all costs, and any attempt to interfere with these on the basis of the authority reposing in any city was to be resisted on legal grounds (Mansi, *Collectio* VII, col. 443).

as they had already been warned of the patriarch's intention.¹ In their indignation they mismanaged their case. This in essence was a strong one, for Constantinople was not an apostolic see, and at the time of Nicaea when primatial jurisdiction had been granted to Rome, Antioch and Alexandria, it was merely a suffragan see of Heraclea.² Moreover, Rome had real grounds to fear that the claims of New Rome, if accepted by the council, would gain readier acceptance throughout the east than those of the see of Peter.

The legates, however, confused substantial and formal grounds of objection and they antagonised the council, some of whose members were already prepared to regard them as heretics. They claimed, first, that the new canon had been accepted in the absence of many of the bishops and that the signatures of some who did sign were forced.³ Then, after asking what Constantinople, having enjoyed its prerogatives 'for about eighty years', was now demanding, they referred to their own see's version of canon 6 of Nicaea which opened with the words 'Quod ecclesia Romana semper habuit primatum',⁴ and which had been shown thirty years before (in 419) by the African bishops to be a gloss. The bishops at Chalcedon were deferential enough to Leo not to point this out, but when Anatolius, patriarch of Constantinople, referred immediately afterwards to the

---

¹ Especially during the twelfth session on 29 October: *ACO* 2. 1. 3, pp. 52–3. At the opening session also, Paschasinus Bishop of Lilybaeum, the senior legate, had expressed surprise that at Ephesus II, Constantinople had been relegated to fifth in order of seniority. 'As for us', he said, 'we look upon Anatolius [of Constantinople] as the first.' The bishop of Cyzicus replied, 'Yes, for you know the canons', i.e. canon 3 of Constantinople, 381 (Mansi, *Collectio* VI, col. 608B). It looks as though there were divided counsels at Rome itself, for Paschasinus had declared that Anatolius' position was 'by the will of God'.

² This point had been made by implication by Boniface I during the dispute over Illyricum, in his letter to the bishops there, on 11 March 422 (*Ep.* 15. 5, *PL* 20, col. 782): 'Servant Ecclesiae magnae praedictae per canones dignitates, Alexandrina et Antiochena, habentes ecclesiastici juris notitiam...' (but Constantinople had not!).

³ *ACO* 2. 1. 3, pp. 94–5 = Mansi, *Collectio* VII, col. 442. This was a false move, recalling needlessly the violence used by Dioscorus to extort signatures from the bishops at the second Council of Ephesus for the deposition of the Patriarch Flavian.

⁴ *ACO ibid.* p. 95 = Mansi, *Collectio* VII, col. 443, and for the version of Rusticus (Latin *Acta*), *ACO* 2. III. 3, p. 109. See Schwartz, 'Der sechste nicaënische Kanon', p. 611; H. Chadwick, 'Faith and order at the Council of Nicaea: a note on the background of the sixth canon', *HTR* 53, 1960, pp. 171–95, especially 180–1 where the rival texts are set out, and T. G. Jalland, *The Church and the Papacy* (London, 1944), p. 308.

eastern version of the same canon, which contained no such phrase, and to canon 3 of the Council of Constantinople,[1] the lay judges asked the bishops of Asia and Pontus whether they had been coerced into agreement. With only one dissentient voice (that of the metropolitan of Ancyra) they received the answer 'No', and thereupon decided that the canon must stand since, they pointed out, New Rome was the seat of government and should have the same privileges as possessed by Old Rome. 'The Fathers', they said, 'formerly gave the primacy to the see of Old Rome, because she was the imperial city, and gave like privileges to New Rome, rightly judging that the city which enjoyed like imperial privileges should also be honoured in matters ecclesiastical being next in rank.' Behind this reasoning was the idea that *Rome* was one, whether 'old' or 'new', and that each should possess the privileges of the other.[2] This typically layman's view of ecclesiastical history, a sort of secular *communicatio idiomatum*, and of the relative importance of episcopal sees, had something to be said for it. Only a short time before, the council had laid down that civil and ecclesiastical boundaries should coincide,[3] and this was beginning to be accepted in the west as well.[4] Moreover, canon 9 of the council had already granted the 'throne' of Constantinople appellate jurisdiction in cases of dispute between a bishop and his metropolitan. The legates do not appear to have opposed this,[5] though it must have been clear to them that the way was being prepared for some such canon as the 28th. In the

[1] For doubts whether Anatolius did refer to canon 6 of Nicaea which made no reference to Constantinople, see Jalland, *The Church and the Papacy*, p. 309.

[2] Schwartz, 'Der sechste nicaënische Kanon', p. 612. The senators of Constantinople certainly regarded themselves as 'Romans' and senators of the imperial city. At Chalcedon Anatolius was usually referred to as 'archbishop of royal Constantinople, new Rome', and Leo as 'archbishop of the royal and elder Rome'. See Mansi, *Collectio* VI, cols. 960C and 1048D. 'New Rome' was not quite like 'New York'.

[3] Canon 17: 'If any city has been, or shall be, new-built by imperial authority, let the arrangement of the ecclesiastical dioceses conform to the civil and public standards.'

[4] Though the legates had absented themselves from this session, the principle was accepted in the west. Thus on 24 March and 3 October 417 Pope Zosimus had informed the Gallic churches of the need for dioceses to correspond with traditional city territories (*Ep.* 1. 3, *PL* 20, cols. 644–5) and the Council of Orange in 441 accepted this view of ecclesiastical and secular jurisdiction (canon 10). See K. Müller, 'Kleine Beiträge zur alten Kirchengeschichte', *ZNTW* 18, 1933, pp. 167, 171 and 178.

[5] See F. Dvornik, *Byzance et la primauté romaine* (Paris, 1964), pp. 45–6. Canon 28 did not deny the 'presbeia' of Old Rome but there was no question of its having the 'pronomia' that Constantinople was asserting over Ephesus.

event, the legates could only protest against 'the humiliation' of their see, and state that they would inform Leo. The metropolitan of Armenia I, speaking for the bishops, said they agreed with the judges and the decision must stand.[1] On this discordant note the council had come to an end. Both sides rested on positions already established in the previous half-century.

The history of the next century is the history of the working out of these twin disagreements. Failure to find acceptable solutions resulted in the division of Christendom in all but name between the Greek-speaking eastern churches and Rome, and within the Greek-speaking community between those who accepted the Council of Chalcedon and its definition, and those who did not. We must now consider in outline how this situation had arisen.[2]

The deep differences of doctrine must be held over until later. Suffice it to say that once the bishops at the Council of Nicaea had decided that for man's salvation to be guaranteed through Christ, Christ must be thought of as fully God, consubstantial with God, true God from true God, and to be worshipped as God, discussion about the relationship of the human and divine natures within him was bound sooner or later to arise. That this was delayed for half a century was due largely to the long-continued battle over the exact formulation of the Trinitarian doctrine. Instinctively, the mass of the eastern bishops had distrusted the term *homoousios* by which consubstantiality was defined. It was not to be found in Scripture, and it smacked of earlier heretical statements associated with the names of Sabellius the Libyan and Paul of Samosata. Above all, it seemed to place Christian belief too near to that of Judaism, for by diminishing the emphasis on the human ministry of Jesus it seemed to reduce Jesus' life to a prolonged 'appearance' of God on earth such as Jews could accept concerning Jahwe's appearance to Moses.[3] Nonetheless, *homoousios* triumphed, partly because the eastern bishops were unable to agree on an alternative, partly owing to the unifying effect of the short and sharp pagan reaction under Julian (361–3) which rallied opinion in

[1] *ACO* 2. III. 3, p. 114, para 46: 'Ioannes revs. eps. Sebastiae d.: "Omnes in sententia vestrae magnificentiae permanemus."'

[2] On this question, see N. H. Baynes' essay 'Alexandria and Constantinople: a study in ecclesiastical diplomacy', *Byzantine Studies, and Other Essays* (London, 1955), pp. 97–116.

[3] Basil of Caesarea, *Ep.* 210 on fears that in reality Judaism lurked behind Sabellian interpretations of Trinitarian theology. Compare *Ep.* 263. 5.

favour of Athanasius and the prestige that he lent to the term. In the 370s it was already being asserted that the symbol of Nicaea was the 'cliff against which heretical waves dispersed into foam', and that it was not subject to the slightest addition, even, said Basil, concerning the incarnation.[1] The decision of the '318 Fathers' remained from now on the rock of orthodoxy.

Yet even the staunchest defenders of the *homoousios*, including Athanasius himself, saw the implicit difficulty arising from this in defining the nature of Christ and especially his manhood. In a long and laboured letter to Bishop Epictetus of Corinth in *circa* 371, Athanasius insisted time and again on the reality of Jesus' humanity, without, however, being able to demonstrate exactly how this could be reconciled with his consubstantiality with God. Within a year or so, his loyal supporter Apollinarius, bishop of Laodicea in Syria, cut the Gordian knot by asserting that in Christ that part which is occupied in a man by the rational soul was occupied by the divine Word. There was no distinction, he argued, in Holy Scripture between the Word and his flesh (cf. Jn. 1. 14), but he was one nature, one *hypostasis*, one energy, one person, at once wholly God and wholly man.[2] 'One incarnate nature of the Logos' was to become the slogan first of the Alexandrian theologians and thence of the Monophysite movement.

Immediately, however, this teaching was challenged by the rising school of Antiochene theologians represented by Diodore, bishop of Tarsus (died *circa* 395), and Theodore, bishop of Mopsuestia in Cilicia (d. 428). They held that the problem of how the divine and human elements in Christ could be related could best be understood by accepting these natures as separate but united by will and grace so completely as to form one person (*prosopon*).[3] But unity of human and divine wills in one being

---

[1] Basil of Caesarea, *Ep.* 258. 2.

[2] Apollinarius, *De fide et incarnatione* 6. See below, p. 115.

[3] Theodore of Mopsuestia, *Comment. in Johann.* VIII. 16 (ed Vosté, p. 119) 'Dominus noster quando de humanitate sua et de divinitate loquebatur, pronomen "ego" retulit ad personam communem' (*prosopon=persona*), and *Comment. in Ep. ad Romanos* (cited by Facundus of Hermiana, *Pro defensione trium capitulorum Concilii Chalcedonensis* III. 6 = *PL* 67, col. 601C), 'Duae naturae unum autem quiddam connexione intellegunt. Altera quidem est assumpti hominis, altera vero Dei Verbi.' For the Antiochenes *prosopon* was more than outward appearance. It included the real element in the being of an individual, and as applied to Christ the point of unity between the human and divine elements. It still implied, however, an external and personal connection as opposed to a unity of essence. The Antiochenes always differentiated between *prosopon* and *physis*,

saving mankind by example, and the incarnate Word manifesting the totality of God to humanity were two different things, and whereas the Antiochene view had its supporters among critical theologians, and later, in the restored church in North Africa, the Monophysite tendencies inherent in its rival became predominant among the Christians in the east and particularly in the patriarchate of Alexandria. Moreover, the growth of intense popular piety not least in the great cities of the eastern empire demanded veneration of the Virgin Mary as God-bearer (*Theotokos*). This was not easy to reconcile with the Antiochene Christology, for without serious mental reservations and circumlocutions she could according to the latter only be *Christotokos*, or Mother of Christ.[1]

In the summer of 381 the Second Ecumenical Council under the influence

the one being the form or image of the other, but allowed identity between *hypostasis* and *prosopon*. (See L. Hodgson's discussion of 'The metaphysic of Nestorius', *JTS* 19, 1917, pp. 49–53, and for Theodoret of Cyrrhus' views see M. Richard, 'La Lettre de Théodoret à Jean d'Egées', *Les Sciences philosophiques et théologiques* 2, 1941–2, pp. 415–23.) The Alexandrians, on the other hand, conflated *physis* with *hypostasis* and, virtually, with *prosopon* also. Flavian of Constantinople had confessed Christ as 'out of two natures', 'in one *hypostasis* and one *prosopon*, one Christ, one Son, one Lord', i.e. he combined *hypostasis* with *prosopon* but distinguished *physis* from both. Hence his quarrel with the Alexandrians (*ACO* 2. 1. 1, p. 35).

[1] This was pointed out by Nestorius in his sermons in the capital. 'He who says that God is born of Mary makes the Christian teaching ridiculous to the heathen.' What Mary bore was the human nature, but the Godhead was united to it. This sermon has survived in Latin translation at the hands of Nestorius' enemy, Marius Mercator, but may be accepted with caution as being accurate: *PL* 48, cols. 775ff., and *ACO* 1. v. 1, p. 37. Also *ibid*. pp. 39–45 for the text of Nestorius' sermon devoted to the subject, preached shortly after 6 December 430.

For Nestorius' theology, see F. Loofs, *Nestorius and his place in the history of Christian doctrine* (Eng. tr., Cambridge, 1914) commenting on J. F. Bethune Baker's *Nestorius and his Teaching* (Cambridge, 1908), and A. Grillmeier's chapter on 'The reactions of the Antiochenes' in *Christ in Christian Tradition* (Eng. tr. by J. S. Bowden, London, 1965).

In a passage quoted by Severus of Antioch in reply to 'the impious grammarian' (*Liber contra impium grammaticum* 1. 134–5), Theodore of Mopsuestia is recorded as saying, 'When they ask whether Mary was *Anthropotokos* or *Theotokos* we shall answer that she was both: he who was in the womb of Mary was man, and he came forth from there. She is *Theotokos* because God was in the man that was born.' Theodoret of Cyrrhus in accepting the term (*Ep.* 83) interpreted it to mean that the Virgin was the instrument by which the divine form of the Logos was united to 'the form of a servant': *PG* 76, col. 392. See Hefele/Leclercq's valuable note, *Histoire des conciles*, II. 1, 269 n1.

of the emperor, Theodosius I, had condemned Arianism in all its forms and also Apollinarianism; then, almost as an afterthought – the clause starts with the word *mentoi*, 'however' – had conferred on the bishopric of Constantinople 'the primacy of honour after the bishop of Rome, because Constantinople is new Rome'. To clerics to whom the organisation of the church was becoming continuously more assimilated to that of the state, and who had seen only a few years before in 372 the vast but traditional ecclesiastical province of Cappadocia divided into two halves by imperial order, this would have seemed a natural step marking the importance of the bishop of the capital of the empire, but it appeared to contradict the emperor's decision of the previous year whereby Rome and Alexandria had been named by Theodosius I as 'guardians of orthodoxy',[1] and in doing so offended against the religious sense of those who believed that episcopal seniority rested on association of a see with an apostolic founder. Rome, Alexandria, Antioch, Jerusalem and even Ephesus had such claims, but Constantinople could make no claim on its own behalf. Status as imperial capital was no compensation.[2]

The period 381 to 431 is dominated by the efforts of the aggrieved bishoprics of Rome and Alexandria to undo so far as possible the work of the Council of Constantinople. The three sees were potential rivals in almost every conceivable way, including the mission field, where Alexandria and Constantinople both claimed jurisdiction over Christians beyond the southern frontier of the empire, Alexandria on the grounds of Athanasius' consecration of Frumentius of Axum *circa* 351 and the founding of the church in Ethiopia, Constantinople by virtue of a general authority to appoint bishops to churches founded among the barbarians and the emperor's activity in doing so.[3] At the same time, the growing doctrinal divisions between the representatives of the Antiochene and, from the beginning of the fifth century, the Alexandrian Christologies added to existing discords. Between 402 and 404, Theophilus the Alexandrian patriarch was instrumental in having John Chrysostom, patriarch of Constantinople and originally a presbyter at Antioch, sent into exile,

---

[1] *Cod. Theod.* XVI. 1. 2.

[2] Compare Leo to Anatolius, *Ep.* 106. 2 and 5, and *Ep.* 104. 3 (to the Emperor Marcian). See below, p. 146.

[3] For the clash between Athanasius and Constantius II over the church in Axum see Athanasius, *Apol. ad Constantium* 31 (*PG* 25, col. 636), and for Constantius' despatch of Theophilus the Indian to build churches for the Roman merchants in the Red Sea market centres and in Ethiopia, see Philostorgius, *HE* III. 4 (*GCS*, p. 34).

by taking advantage of some of John's more spirited but less tactful utterances against the Empress Eudoxia to discredit him at court. One notices in passing that the Emperor Arcadius signed the order banishing John, and John had no option but to obey. Matters had been different in the west in the struggle some twenty years before between Ambrose and the court of Valentinian II and Justina at Milan.

The real test, however, was postponed until the period 428–31. In April 428 largely as a result of conflict within the church at Constantinople, the Emperor Theodosius II had chosen Nestorius, an Antiochene monk and presbyter as well as a disciple of Theodore of Mopsuestia, as bishop of the capital.[1] Nestorius has been described by the contemporary Constantinopolitan historian, Socrates, as a man of extreme tactlessness, ignorance and garrulity, who first of all enraged the citizens of the capital by harsh treatment of long-standing (and respected) heretics, the Arians, and the Macedonians who maintained the subordination of the Holy Spirit to the Son and the Father, and then outraged popular piety by emphatically and repeatedly rejecting the term *Theotokos* 'as though it were some terrible phantom'.[2] 'It was obvious', says Socrates, 'that Nestorius had very little acquaintance with the old theologians, men such as Origen and Eusebius who had discussed the term.'[3] Unfortunately for him the see of Alexandria was occupied by Theophilus' nephew, Cyril (412–44). He was a master-theologian whose deep perception of the mystery of the incarnation has influenced Greek theology from that day to this, and he could formulate his ideas in such a way as to make them appear acceptable in the west also. Against this, he was utterly unscrupulous, overbearing, turbulent and greedy for power, ready to use the mob and the monks to do his bidding against his opponents such as the Alexandrian Jews and the pagans. He can hardly avoid responsibility for having approved the murder of the philosopher Hypatia in Alexandria in 415. Thirteen years later he was at the height of his powers and the combination of Nestorius' ill-judged utterances and the appeal of some of

---

[1] Socrates, *HE* VII. 29.

[2] *Ibid.* VII. 32. In view of Nestorius' own *Bazaar of Heraclides* (*Liber Heraclidis*) written during his exile and expressing his own view, this seems a harsh judgement. He seems to have been a man who found hidden reserves of character in adversity. In view of the antipathy felt by the Antiochenes for Eusebius and Origen it is not surprising, perhaps, that Nestorius knew little or nothing of their works.

[3] The term *Theotokos* had been in use in the capital for some time. Gregory of Nazianzus uses it in his Letter to Cledonius, *Ep.* 101 (*PL* 37, col. 177).

his clergy to Constantinople complaining against a sentence of deprivation gave him the opportunity to deal a deadly blow to the authority and prestige of the church of the capital.[1] With a mixture of sincere attachment to a doctrinal position, lack of scruple in action and subtle diplomacy, Cyril manoeuvred himself during 430 into the position of being papal plenipotentiary in what was designed as a trial of Nestorius for heresy. He wrote in flattering terms to Celestine of Rome at a moment when the latter was irked at the presence of Pelagians at Constantinople against whom he was waging unremitting war.[2] Celestine was also ill advised by his agent, Marius Mercator, who accused Nestorius unjustly of being a disciple of the heretic Photinus.[3] He was jealous of the claims of his own see, and perhaps remembering that the term 'Mother of God' had been used in a sermon by Ambrose,[4] at once supported Cyril. Nestorius, on the other hand, had written about the alleged Pelagians to Celestine courteously but as an equal ('brother to brother'), as he was bishop of 'New Rome', and he had also written in Greek, whereas Cyril had supplied the pope with a Latin translation.[5] Nestorius, backed by the court, was

---

[1] For the detail of this and the ensuing period see L. Duchesne, *Early History of the Christian Church*, III (Eng. tr. by C. Jenkins, London, 1924), chs. 10 and 11, and Hefele/Leclercq, *Histoire des conciles*, II. 1, 248ff.; and from the point of view of the papacy, E. Caspar, *Geschichte der Papsttums von den Anfängen bis zur Höhe der Weltherrschaft* (Tübingen, 1930–3), I, ch. 10.

[2] Especially in Britain. See Prosper Tiro, *Chron.* ad ann. 429 (*PL* 51, cols. 594–5 = ed. Mommsen, p. 472) and *Contra collatorem* XXI. 2 (*PL* 51, col. 271B–C).

[3] Marius Mercator, translation of Nestorius' *Sermo* 4, *PL* 48, col. 785 and note *b*. Photinus was bishop of Sirmium and was deposed in 351, *inter alia* for denying the pre-existence of Christ and saying that the Word was born of Mary. For further misinterpretation of Antiochene views by Marius, see A. Mingana, 'The Christian faith and the interpretation of the Nicene Creed by Theodore of Mopsuestia (c. 350–428)', Woodbrooke Studies, fasc. 10, *Bull. of John Rylands Library* 16, 1932, pp. 200–318 at p. 215.

[4] A fragment of a sermon by Celestine preached *circa* August 430 is preserved (*PL* 50, col. 457), in which he cites a Christmas Day sermon by Ambrose referring to the Virgin as one who 'bore God' ('talis decet partus Deum') as equivalent to Cyril's 'Theotokos'. This sermon is lost. Ambrose himself in *Hexaemeron* v. 65 (*PL* 14, col. 248A) refers to Mary as 'Dei Mater'. The only previous western text using these terms is Tertullian, *De patientia* 3. See W. Bright, *St Leo and the Incarnation* (London, 1886), pp. 126–7.

[5] See Celestine, *Epp.* 8 (from Cyril) and 13 (to Nestorius) (*PL* 50, cols. 447ff. and 469ff.). Nestorius' two letters ap. Celestine, *Epp.* 6 and 7, remained untranslated for several months.

able for the moment to avoid Cyril's direct aggression, and the emperor sternly rebuked the latter for stirring up trouble (November 430). A general council, however, was convoked by the emperor at Ephesus and this was entirely under his enemies' control. 'Cyril presided: Cyril was accuser: Cyril was judge. Cyril was bishop of Rome. Cyril was everything', or so it appeared to Nestorius.[1] On the evening of 22 June 431 Nestorius was condemned as 'the new Judas' and deposed 'on account of his impious sermons and disobedience to the canons'.[2] The sentence was greeted with demonstrations of popular fervour in favour of Cyril (Cyril, *Ep.* 20).[3] 'Mary has triumphed over Nestorius', the crowd seemed to shout in their joy.

Cyril's triumph, however, was not to be complete. In his controversy with Nestorius in the two years before the council he had defined his theological standpoint in three letters which he had sent to his opponent. The first two letters, written in the autumn of 429 and in February 430 respectively, despite the violence of tone which characterised especially the second, were acceptable as statements of faith. In his first he had confined himself to urging Nestorius to restore peace in the church by employing the term *Theotokos* (*Ep.* 1 *ad Nestorium*). In his second letter, he made what was to become the usual criticism of the Antiochene view, namely that the latter claimed that the incarnate Word became man in the sense of 'being united merely as a result of will or good pleasure'.[4] He pointed out instead, that as a logical result of the definition of Nicaea the nature of the Word must be united, though 'in an ineffable and inconceivable manner',[5] with flesh animated by a rational soul, and that though they were different and the Word retained its full divinity, the two natures of Christ were united and perfected in one Lord, the Christ and Son. The Virgin bearing the Word in his human nature was rightly called *Theotokos*. Moreover, Scripture did not state that the divine Word united itself with the *prosopon* of a man but that it 'became flesh' (Jn. 1. 14).

[1] Nestorius, *Liber Heraclidis* (ed. Nau), p. 117.
[2] *ACO* 1. 1. 2, p. 54.
[3] Theodoret of Cyrrhus, *Ep.* 152, also bears witness to popular support for Cyril and Memnon; and similarly Nestorius himself, *Liber Heraclidis*, p. 119, referring to 'idlers and peasants' led by Memnon.
[4] *Ep.* 4 in *PG* 77. A convenient text in Bindley/Green, *Documents*, pp. 95–7 at pp. 95–6, and line 43 of the letter: γέγονεν ἄνθρωπος καὶ κεχρημάτικεν υἱὸς ἀνθρώπου οὐ κατὰ θέλησιν μόνην καὶ εὐδοκίαν, ἀλλ' οὐδὲ ὡς ἐν προσλήψει προσώπου μόνου.
[5] *Ibid.* lines 48–9: διὰ τῆς ἀφράστου καὶ ἀπορρήτου πρὸς ἑνότητα συνδρομῆς.

This teaching, founded on a closely interwoven pattern of Scripture and philosophy, was to be Cyril's most lasting and constructive contribution to the study of the mystery of Christ's nature. In stressing its essential unity he represented the opinions of the eastern Christians as a whole.

In his third letter,[1] however, despite a disclaimer that the incarnation involved no change of the Godhead into flesh or vice versa, he went further towards accepting a complete Apollinarian thesis by alluding to the 'One Hypostasis of the Incarnate Word'. Here he used the term *hypostasis* which usually bore the theological definition of 'individuality' as a synonym of *physis* (or 'nature' as 'inner quality of existence'), and he attached to his statements twelve propositions which he called upon Nestorius to anathematise. These had been agreed by an Egyptian council before despatch and the church in Egypt was henceforth committed to them. It did not take John, bishop of Antioch (428–41), and others very long to see that some of these Twelve Anathemas, as they came to be called, notably the second insisting on the hypostatic union of Word and flesh[2] and the twelfth which spoke of the Word suffering in the flesh, contained statements not only unscriptural but culled from the writings of Apollinarius which had been condemned at the Second Ecumenical Council at Constantinople fifty years before.[3] Ibas, the metropolitan of Edessa (d. 458), claimed a few years later that Cyril's teaching was Apollinarian, in that it failed specifically to distinguish between the temple that Christ dwelt in (the body) and the dweller.

Therefore when John arrived at Ephesus with forty-three Syrian bishops, on 26 (or 27) June 431, he not only espoused the cause of Nestorius but excommunicated Cyril and Memnon, the bishop of Ephesus who had rallied public opinion in the city to the latter's side, and all bishops who

[1] *Ep.* 17, *PG* 77, cols. 105–21. See text and notes in Bindley/Green, *Documents*, pp. 108–15.

[2] σαρκὶ καθ' ὑπόστασιν ἡνῶσθαι... Compare lines 253–70 of the letter (Bindley/Green, p. 113).

[3] That he came to this conclusion before the Council of Ephesus, see Theodoret, *Ep.* 112 (to Domnus). For Theodoret's view that the Anathemas were 'full of Eunomian and Arian heresies', *Ep.* 152, and compare *Ep.* 171. Events had moved fast. Representatives of Cyril had reached Constantinople bearing the letter with the Anathemas on 6 December 430. Before the opening of the Council of Ephesus in June 431, Nestorius had circulated his Antiochene friends with the Anathemas and they had already taken up their position on them.

accepted the Twelve Anathemas.[1] At first, the emperor's representative Count Candidian supported John, but once again local public opinion proved decisive, and in the ensuing negotiations, laced with stupendous bribes from Cyril to the court at Constantinople,[2] the court, largely guided by the Augusta Pulcheria, agreed that Nestorius' deposition should stand and the term *Theotokos* should be accepted as orthodox, but no judgement was passed on Cyril's Twelve Anathemas. It was agreed also, rather as a tailpiece to the council, that no doctrine that sought to add to the definition of the Council of Nicaea should be regarded as orthodox.[3]

Looking back, it is clear that Ephesus really represented the mind of the east, 'the belief of the whole world', as the participants had claimed. From now on it was to be linked with 'the great and holy synod'[4] of Nicaea as representing an orthodoxy from which no deviation was permissible. It had also been Cyril's council, and this was never forgotten. Cyril's theology as set out in his letters to Nestorius formed an inseparable part of that concept of orthodoxy. The future debate among the eastern bishops concerned the standing of the Twelve Anathemas and letters in which he had pursued the logic of his argument towards Monophysitism, but the core of his position remained inviolate. At Chalcedon, time and again approval was given to views 'because they were in agreement with Cyril'. In contrast, the Christological views held by Nestorius which up to now had been influential in Syria and the neighbouring province of Cilicia and in southern Armenia suffered a decisive defeat. The strict Nestorian party began to hive off and form an exclusively Nestorian church. This, apart from a foothold in east Syria, was eventually to be

---

[1] Theodoret, *Ep.* 112 and see also Ibas' account in his letter to the presbyter Maris, read at the Second Council of Ephesus (see *Akten*, ed. Flemming, pp. 49–53).

[2] For details, see F. Loofs, *Nestorius* (Cambridge, 1914), p. 55, commenting on the surviving texts.

[3] Not so much a 'canon', but a 'decision' (ὅρος) as Dioscorus himself admitted at Chalcedon (Mansi, *Collectio* vi, col. 632 = *ACO* 2. 1. 1, p. 91, para. 159). It was agreed at the sixth session on 22 July 431. This was another point won by the Alexandrians as much of their case against Nestorius turned on the fact that Cyril's letters 'agreed with Nicaea'. As early as *circa* 369, Athanasius had written on behalf of ninety Egyptian and Libyan bishops to the Catholic bishop of Carthage stressing that one object of the Council of Nicaea had been to prevent local synods being summoned to solve problems regarding the Faith. Nicaea was the sole point of reference (Athanasius, *Ep. ad Afros* 2, *PG* 26, col. 1032).

[4] Cyril's phrase: see his Second Letter to Nestorius in Bindley/Green, *Documents*, p. 95, line 32.

driven across the Roman frontier, to be accepted by the Christians in Persia as a mark of distinction between them and their neighbours on Roman soil. It became the first in time of the national churches of the east. Finally, though pleasure was expressed that Celestine was 'one with the synod' and 'the guardian of orthodoxy',[1] the jurisdictional claims made by the legates on behalf of Rome were passed over in silence.[2] The council and its immediate sequel showed how the patriarchates of the east under pressure might be able to settle their affairs without accepting doctrinal formulae from the west. Rome, after all, had played no great part at Nicaea.[3]

Two years later, despite their deep mistrust of each other,[4] and after painstaking negotiations, harmony was formally restored between Alexandria and Antioch. The latter, in exchange for acquiescing in Nestorius' downfall, secured Cyril's assent to a dogmatic definition known as the Formula of Reunion[5] (April 433). In this, Christ was defined as 'of two natures', 'in a union without confusion', 'consubstantial with the Father as touching his divinity, and with us as touching his humanity; a union therefore of two natures, and hence we confess one Christ, one Son and

---

[1] *ACO* I. I. 3, p. 57; Caspar, *Papsttums*, I, 409.

[2] The legates had declared solemnly: 'ad hoc usque tempus et semper in suis successoribus [Petrus] vivit et iudicium exercet, huius itaque secundum ordinem successor et locum tenens beatissimusque papa' (Mansi, *Collectio* IV, col. 1296 = *ACO* I. I. 3, p. 60).

[3] Though perhaps more than is usually credited. Pope Liberius alludes to correspondence between Alexander of Alexandria and Pope Silvester on the eve of the council, in which Alexander reports the dismissal of eleven pro-Arian presbyters and deacons: Liberius' letter to Constantius, para. 5, published in Hilary of Poitiers, *Opera*, ed. H. Feder (*CSEL* 65, Vienna, 1916), p. 91. This contact is confirmed by papyri relating to correspondence between the two bishops, published by M. Richard, 'Quelques nouveaux fragments des Pères Anténicéens et Nicéens', *Symbolae Osloenses* 38, 1963, pp. 76–83 at p. 82. Even so, all this seems to have been forgotten by the fifth century.

[4] Ibas, Letter to Maris, insists that the emperor himself had compelled the opening of negotiations: *Akten*, ed. Flemming, p. 51, lines 32–8. Liberatus (*Brev.* VIII) indicates that Theodosius threatened to have both John and Cyril put under surveillance at Nicomedia 'unless they made peace with one another' (*PL* 68, col. 983A = *ACO* 2. v, p. 106). Following precedents going back to Constantine, Theodosius regarded episcopal dissension as 'intolerable' and himself took the initiative towards ending it.

[5] Included in Cyril's letter, *Laetantur coeli* (*Ep.* 39, in *PG*). See also Bindley/Green, *Documents*, pp. 141–4. On the events see Duchesne, *Early History of the Christian Church*, III, 263–5.

Lord'. It was agreed, too, that 'as regards the evangelical and apostolic utterances respecting Christ, we know that theologians apply them differently; the one class, referring to the one person, they relate to both natures in common; the other class separate them as referring to two natures (ὡς ἐπὶ δύο φύσεων)'. It was as far as Cyril could fairly be expected to go and much further than many of his supporters went, including the archimandrite Eutyches in the capital. It safeguarded confession of the Godhead and true humanity of Christ inseparably united at the incarnation without, however, Cyril's favourite terminology μία φύσις. For this there had been substituted the Antiochene ἐν πρόσωπον, and the formula spoke of δύο φύσεων ἕνωσις or ὡς ἐπὶ δύο φύσεων but not their '*hypostatic union*': i.e. the signatories accepted the concept of two natures rather than one. On the other hand, Antiochene though much of its phraseology was, the acceptance of Jesus being formed from 'the union of two natures' satisfied the Alexandrians.[1] Both sides had gained just enough for unity to be restored.

The Formula of Reunion was the first of a long succession of attempted compromises between radically opposed views of Jesus Christ and his mission, which were to continue down to the Arab invasions and beyond. The concessions which both sides had been obliged to make under the emperor's pressure were to have lasting results, since on the strength of Cyril's agreement to them it became possible to interpret his theology in a two-nature sense. On another issue of almost equal importance in the future, Cyril also failed to get his way. A study of the evidence suggests that all the time Cyril's main object had been the condemnation of the theology of the Antiochene teachers Diodore and Theodore, and that Nestorius' overthrow was merely an incident in this campaign. Within a year of Ephesus he was trying to pin down the Antiochenes further, while his supporters Rabbula of Edessa and Acacius of Melitene endeavoured to persuade the Armenian church to condemn these theologians and so renounce all Antiochene influences in their theology. The Armenians, however, played safe and decided to seek the advice of the patriarch of Constantinople before agreeing. All this took time, and when the delegation eventually arrived, the Formula of Reunion had been signed and the new Patriarch Proclus (434–46), though strongly favourable to Cyril's theology, was not prepared to condemn his opponents outright. The

---

[1] Compare Cyril's εἷς δὲ ἐξ ἀμφοῖν Χριστὸς καὶ Υἱός, line 45 of his Second Letter to Nestorius (Bindley/Green, *Documents*, p. 96).

celebrated letter which he sent back with the delegates in 435 spoke of 'the unique hypostasis of the incarnate Word' (μίαν ὁμολογῶ τὴν τοῦ σαρκωθέντος Θεοῦ λόγου ὑπόστασιν) and confessed that 'one of the Trinity was incarnate', but did not condemn Diodore and Theodore by name.[1] John of Antioch also stood firm, agreeing to sign the *Tome* but pointing out that both theologians had died in the peace of the church.[2] Cyril found himself checked. The issue, however, was never far from his mind. As late as 438 he was writing once more against the Antiochene doctors,[3] and Proclus' unwillingness to further his efforts in this direction placed an additional obstacle in the way of theological harmony between Alexandria and the capital. When at the Fifth General Council in 553 the works of Theodore were at last condemned, the initiative came from the emperor and Alexandria derived no benefit.

For the moment, however, Cyril was more successful in dealing with the disappointment of his powerful supporters than was John of Antioch. His letters to Succensus of Diocaesarea[4] and Acacius of Melitene[5] show him at his dialectical best, arguing that nothing of substance had been conceded to his opponents and that his whole position, including the Anathemas, stood as previously. It was too subtle, however, and the result was that at Chalcedon and for the century after each party was able to claim Cyril for their own and set one quotation from his works against another. This was to ensure theological stalemate, with the advantage lying with Constantinople as primatial see in the east. For the moment, the Antiochenes showed more signs of strain. Angry synods were held by the bishops of Cilicia and Euphratesia (bordering Syria), and the bitterness expressed among the leaders there, such as Alexander of Hierapolis, demonstrated how even under a leader of John's calibre the patriarchate of Antioch refused to be united.

The reaction of Xystus III of Rome (432–40) was instructive. Like his predecessor, Celestine, he had been more interested in the fate of Pelagianism than in Nestorius. He had, however, kept in touch with both

---

[1] See Liberatus, *Brev.* x. 44 (*ACO* 2. v, pp. 110ff.). For the text of the *Tome* of Proclus, see *ACO* 4. II, pp. 187–95 and below, p. 311.

[2] Ap. Cyril, *Ep.* 66. For Cyril's final effort to persuade John of Antioch and Proclus to accept the condemnation of Diodore and Theodore, see Cyril, *Epp.* 66–72.

[3] For this incident see G. M. de Durand, *Cyrille d'Alexandrie; deux dialogues christologiques*, Sources chrétiennes 97 (Paris, 1964), pp. 27–31.

[4] *Epp.* 45 and 46.

[5] *Ep.* 41.

Cyril and John though he appears to have exerted little influence on the actual negotiations leading to the Reunion Formula. Even so, he claimed what credit he could and wrote to John of Antioch, 'You have learnt by the outcome of this affair what it means to be like-minded with us'.[1] The papacy meant to impress its indispensability on the two sides, and Leo found a valuable precedent to follow.

For the next decade there was relative peace. Two straws in the wind, however, showed in which direction imperial policy was moving. In 435 Theodosius ordered the removal of Nestorius from the bounds of the patriarchate of Antioch (he had been at Petra in Arabia since 432) to the remoteness of the Western Oasis in Egypt, and forbade his followers to call themselves 'Christians'.[2] In 437 he accepted the cession of the eastern part of the diocese of Pannonia from the west in return for the marriage of his daughter, Licinia Eudoxia, to Valentinian III, the formal transfer of sovereignty taking place on Valentinian's visit to Constantinople.[3] This completed the acquisition of eastern Illyricum and coincided with further pressure on the Illyrian bishops to transfer their allegiance from the papal vicar of Thessalonica to the patriarch of Constantinople, against which Pope Xystus protested. These lands were to be Byzantine and not Roman despite another papal protest.[4] Old feuds, however, were gradually dying down, and when in 439 the historian Socrates concluded his *Ecclesiastical History*, he did so with a paean of praise for 'the flourishing nature of the church at this time', and the comment that 'so long as peace continues those who desire to become historians will not find materials for their purpose' (*HE* VII. 48). Even Nestorius had become forgotten.

Gradually, the scene changed. In August 440 Pope Xystus III ended a relatively uneventful eight years' pontificate, and his place was taken by one of the ablest and most thrustful of the mediaeval popes, Leo I. Leo was not only a capable theologian, who knew his own mind even if sometimes he did not understand that of his opponents; he was also supremely a man of business. He missed nothing, his grasp of affairs was formidable and his activity was incessant. On one occasion he told his agent in

[1] Xystus, *Ep.* 6. 5 (*PL* 50, col. 609A).
[2] *Cod. Theod.* XVI. 5. 66.
[3] Cassiodorus, *Variae* XI. 1. 9 (ed. Th. Mommsen, *MGH*, AA 12, Berlin, 1894, p. 329), and Jordanes, *Romana*, p. 42. See S. I. Oost, *Galla Placidia Augusta* (Chicago, 1968), p. 185 n56.
[4] Xystus, *Epp.* 9 and 10 (*PL* 50, cols. 612–18).

Constantinople, Julian, bishop of Cóos, that he had begun to answer his letters not only the self-same day but that very hour.[1] Budgets of letters were sent off on the same day, combining wisdom and probity with an eye for detail and above all for the advantage of the claims of the see of Peter.

In 441 John of Antioch was succeeded by his nephew, Domnus, a disciple of the great monastic leader in Palestine, Euthymius, and a monk in his monastery. The Antiochene church, however, was to pay dearly for this single mistake by an otherwise great bishop of attempting to imitate his rival at Alexandria by founding an episcopal dynasty, for Domnus was a man of clay. On 27 June 444 Cyril himself died, and his formidable archdeacon Dioscorus became bishop. Finally, in 446 Proclus was succeeded in the capital by the less gifted and less fortunate Flavian.[2]

Inevitably some of the new men would be seeking to revise in their own interests the compromise of 433, while there were still sufficient surviving victors and vanquished (including Nestorius himself) of the period of the Council of Ephesus to fan trouble if anyone were to provoke it. There was first the zealous prosecutor of Christian orthodoxy, Eusebius of Dorylaeum, who had arraigned Nestorius and nearly twenty years later was to be responsible for accusing Eutyches of heresy. There was Count Irenaeus, one of the friends of Nestorius whom Cyril feared, as he shows in a memorandum which he is said to have given to the monk Victor before leaving Alexandria for Ephesus,[3] and who now, after a spell of exile, was in Orders and had been bishop of Berytus since 444; there was a new metropolitan of Edessa, Ibas (435-58), a convinced adherent of Antiochene theology, as his predecessor, Rabbula, had been of Cyril, and he was supported by a considerable group of relatives in some of the chief sees of east Syria.[4] On the other side there was Eutyches himself, the *éminence grise* among the archimandrites of Constantinople, who in 431 had served Cyril by enlisting the support of Theodosius' sister Pulcheria for his doctrine, and was the godfather of the eunuch Chrys-

---

[1] Leo, *Ep.* 127. 1, written on 9 January 455 (*PL* 54, col. 1071B).

[2] Nestorius' view of him that he lacked eloquence (Nestorius did not!), *Liber Heraclidis* (ed. Nau), p. 294, must be treated with some reserve.

[3] W. Kraatz, *Koptische Akten zum ephesinischen Konzil vom Jahre 431, TU* 26 (n.s. 11), Leipzig, 1904, no. 2, pp. 6 and 136. The document is probably fictitious as it stands, but may include genuine material.

[4] Such as Sophronius of Tella and Daniel of Harran, both nephews, and arraigned at Second Ephesus.

aphius who since 441 had been Theodosius II's Grand Chamberlain. There was Juvenal of Jerusalem (422–58) whose determination to make himself patriarch had had to be abandoned after Ephesus, but whose ambition was merely increased with age.[1] Above all, on the Antiochene side stood the zealous missionary, historian, controversialist, and friend of monks including Simeon Stylites, Theodoret, bishop of Cyrrhus (northeast of Antioch). His correspondence shows that he was on good terms with the greatest of the time and he was bitterly opposed to Cyril's theology, denouncing the Twelve Anathemas as 'full of Eunomian and Arian heresies',[2] and 'Apollinarian'.[3] He was one of the few men Dioscorus feared. His alleged comment on the death of Cyril is revealing. 'At last, at last he is dead, that bad man ... His departure gives joy to those who survive, but it will bring grief to the dead ... We must cover his tomb with a heavy stone so that we may never see him again.'[4] He had not bargained on the character of his successor.

Dioscorus has gone down as one of the great villains of ecclesiastical history, but this is not how he appeared to contemporaries at the time of his consecration or even to later historians.[5] Theodoret himself wrote (*Ep.* 60) congratulating him and commenting on his universal reputation for modesty and reason, while at Antioch Domnus believed that at last

[1] Juvenal's inordinate ambition got on the nerves even of Cyril. He 'shuddered at his unlawful attempts', and in *Ep.* 56 counsels the Abbot Gennadius not to sever relations with Proclus of Constantinople merely because the latter remained in communion with Juvenal. See E. Honigmann, 'Juvenal of Jerusalem', *Dumbarton Oaks Papers* 5, 1950, pp. 211–79 at p. 217.

[2] Theodoret, *Ep.* 152. [3] *Ep.* 153.

[4] The letter (*Ep.* 180) circulated under Theodoret's name was, however, addressed to John of Antioch who had died in 441! It was quoted against Theodoret at the fifth session of the Fifth General Council (Mansi, *Collectio* IX, col. 295), and may have been written to Domnus.

[5] Zacharias Rhetor, *HE* III. 1, says that he was 'vir pacabilis et ἀγωνιστής quamquam Cyrilli facilitatem et παρρησίαν non habebat '(ed. Brooks, *CSCO* III. 5, p. 101) – a curious comment on his behaviour at Ephesus II. The account of the second session of the proceedings preserved in the Syriac MS published by Flemming (*Akten*) shows him following in the wake of the discussion, despite his indignation at the doctrines taught by Ibas and Theodoret. It must be admitted that if there was any truth in the detailed circumstantial accounts of the words and actions of the Syrian bishops produced at this session, it is difficult to see how they could have been acceptable to any theologian brought up in the Cyrillian tradition. For the later and more usual view of Dioscorus as a tyrant and an 'Origenist' in doctrine see Theophanes, *Chron.* A.M. 5940 (ed. Classen, I, 151).

Alexandria had elected a bishop with whom he could work.[1] From Rome, Leo wrote a kindly and patronising letter, as one might write to an amiable and inexperienced subordinate, and sent it via the presbyter Posidonius (*Ep.* 9). After reminding Dioscorus that Mark was Peter's disciple he laid down the proper procedure for ordaining clergy – before dawn on Sunday morning after fasting was the correct moment, and if the churches were too small in Alexandria for all to attend the great festivals at one time, then Dioscorus should not hesitate to celebrate the liturgy twice on the same day, and Leo admonishes the new patriarch to observe his injunctions strictly.

What Dioscorus thought of this advice history does not relate. He soon made it clear that he stood for two things: first, the complete destruction of all vestiges of the two-nature Christology, in particular the form in which it was continuing to be preached by the new leaders of the Antiochene school, Theodoret and Ibas; secondly, he was determined to vindicate the status of his see as an apostolic see, senior to Antioch and in particular to Constantinople. 'No one', he wrote in an encyclical to the bishops present at Ephesus II, 'who shared the outlook of Nestorius or thought similarly to him was worthy of the priesthood.'[2] He himself accepted Nicaea and Ephesus only, as ecumenical councils. He cared nothing for the decrees of Constantinople in 381 whose canon 2 forbade bishops to intervene in the affairs of sees other than their own,[3] and he allowed himself to be addressed as 'ecumenical patriarch' by his supporters.[4] Every rumour about the alleged beliefs of Antiochene clergy was grist to his mill. That he 'turned the see of St Mark upside down' was no exaggeration,[5] and had his zeal for Cyril's doctrine and Cyril's see been matched by a minimum of tact and a sense of justice towards Cyril's surviving

---

[1] Note Domnus' lament to Flavian (ap. Theodoret, *Ep.* 86), 'I thought I should find an ally and fellow-worker in the most godly bishop of Alexandria, the lord Dioscorus, and so sent him one of our pious presbyters...' Perhaps drafted by Theodoret (see Caspar, *Papsttums*, I, 466).

[2] *Akten*, ed. Flemming, p. 155.

[3] So wrote Domnus to Flavian (ap. Theodoret, *Ep.* 86); the letter was cited at Ephesus II against him. See Flemming, p. 121, lines 43ff.

[4] For instance, by Olympius, bishop of Evaza, at the Council of Ephesus II: Mansi, *Collectio* VI, col. 855.

[5] Domnus, ap. Theodoret, *Ep.* 86. Dioscorus, however, would fully have agreed with the presbyter Alypius, Cyril's correspondent, that 'through his valiant struggles, Athanasius had exalted to the highest degree the holy see of St Mark, the Evangelist, and Cyril was following in his footsteps' (*Ep.* 29, *PG* 77, col. 148B). This was precisely Dioscorus' ambition.

relatives, his position would have been unshakeable. Even when pressed on all sides at the Council of Chalcedon he could still give a brief and trenchant account of his own acts and critique of the views of his opponents.¹ Despite the legates, no one dared adjudge him a heretic.

His vindictive nature, overweening ambition and lack of scruple, however, involved him in a serious mistake. While accepting Cyril's theology he objected to Cyril's clan. The brutal treatment he meted out to Cyril's nephew, the presbyter Athanasius,² roused a party in the church in Egypt against him, and at this crucial moment their indignation outweighed their theological loyalties. Their leader was Nestorius, bishop of Phragon, one of Cyril's financial officers. He accused Dioscorus of conniving with Chrysaphius in using no less than 1,400 lbs. of gold, Cyril's legacy, for his own purposes. Nestorius' knowledge of affairs in the patriarch's see and his personal influence were strong enough to organise a local opposition to Dioscorus which at Chalcedon his enemies were only too glad to use.³

Meantime, however, all went well for him. He first turned on the Antiochenes. Malcontents from Domnus' vast patriarchate flocked to Alexandria to unburden themselves on the subject of the heresies and ecclesiastical abuses that were reigning there. Already in 446 Theodoret was complaining to Domnus of attacks on the former Count Irenaeus, now bishop of Tyre, that he was twice-married and did not subscribe to the Theotokos.⁴ Soon he too was under fire, for the same offences and that while at Antioch he had preached 'two sons'.⁵ He

---

¹ He was rigid and unbending even in adversity (*ACO* 2. 1. 2, p. 27=Mansi, *Collectio* VI, col. 1041) but his doctrine was not extreme for the time. He was no Docetist, and in a letter written from exile he emphasised the similarity of Christ to men (but not the consubstantiality). 'Christ was made like us so that we through his mercy might become similar to him.' He was certainly aware of the problem of how to explain that 'Jesus was our brother' if his body was different from ours, but he failed to solve it. (Cited from Zacharias, *HE* III. 1, p. 105.)

² The scandalous treatment of Athanasius was reported by him in a letter to the Council of Chalcedon: *ACO* 2. 1. 2, p. 20=Mansi, *Collectio* VI, col. 1021.

³ At the third session of the council at which Dioscorus was deposed: *ACO* 2. 1. 2, p. 27=Mansi, *Collectio* VI, col. 1044. A further accusation, contained in the *Libellus* of the deacon Ischyrion, charged Dioscorus with disobedience to the emperor's order to send corn to Cyrenaica during a drought, and selling it for his own benefit at an outrageous profit: *ACO* 2. 1. 2, p. 17.

⁴ *Ep.* 110. For Irenaeus see *ACO* 1. IV, pp. 10-15.

⁵ *Ep.* 83.

protested to the Alexandrian[1] and his letters to Flavian, the patricians Taurus and Florentius and other senior officials in the capital indicate his alarm at these events.[2] In September 447 Domnus himself complained to Flavian of Dioscorus' machinations against the see of Antioch and his obvious contempt for canonical prohibition of the interference of one bishop in the affairs of other dioceses.[3]

The scene now shifts to the capital. There since 441 the all-powerful influence had been the Grand Chamberlain, Chrysaphius.[4] He and other imperial eunuchs, the *cubicularii* who served the personal needs of the Emperor Theodosius II, were immensely important in forming the religious ideas and policy of the court. Theirs was a monkish outlook pushed to extremes and they tended to side with Alexandria. A near-contemporary describes them as 'living in the palace as though a monastery', devoting their time to fasts and prayers.[5] But they were also unscrupulously active in the politics of the court. Chrysaphius had gradually ousted from influence the emperor's sister the Augusta Pulcheria who narrowly escaped consecration as a deaconess, and then his wife Eudocia. His persistence, the medieval Byzantine writer Nikephorus Kallistus comments, was like that of drops of water wearing away a stone.[6] The two women also quarrelled and in 443 Eudocia retired to Palestine, there to establish the tradition of Byzantine empresses as patrons of the arts as well as of religion. Flavian, too, Chrysaphius hated, for Flavian had refused to send him a *eulogion* of gold on his consecration.[7] Behind the chamberlain stood his god-father Eutyches, aged, venerated, but no wiser for his grey hairs, ruling over a great monastery of 300 monks. He was bent on trouble. By 447 he was not only openly proclaiming the one nature of the Word incarnate but attributing to the Word itself the

---

[1] *Ibid.*   [2] *Epp.* 85–103.

[3] *Akten*, ed. Flemming, pp. 119–23. The same complaint against Alexandrian interference in the affairs of Antioch is made by Nestorius in his sermon preached just after 6 December 430.

[4] See Nikephorus Kallistus, *HE* XIV. 47 (*PG* 146, cols. 1221–4), and P. Goubert, 'Le Rôle de Sainte Pulchérie et de l'eunuche Chrysaphios' in Grillmeier/Bacht, *Das Konzil von Chalkedon*, I, 303–21, for the ideas and policies of the Grand Chamberlain.

[5] John Rufus, *Vita Petri Iberi* (ed. Raabe), p. 24.

[6] Nikephorus Kallistus, *HE* XIV. 47 (*PG* 146, col. 1224B).

[7] Evagrius, *HE* II. 2. More circumstantially in Theophanes, *Chron.* (ed. Classen, I, 151), the incident providing a good illustration of Chrysaphius' dominance over Theodosius II.

sufferings of the Passion. Evidently through misunderstanding Cyril he transformed the latter's formula μία φύσις τοῦ Θεοῦ Λόγου σεσαρκωμένη (one nature of God the Word, made flesh) into an assertion that the one nature of the Word incarnate had been made flesh, μία φύσις τοῦ Θεοῦ Λόγου σεσαρκωμένου, i.e. this could not be human flesh, but the flesh of the Word incarnate, however that might be defined. He challenged therefore the view that Christ's humanity was as our humanity, or in theological language, that Christ was 'consubstantial' with man.[1] In addition, he continued to foment demands for the condemnation of the Antiochene theologians Diodore and Theodore.[2]

The reaction of the Syrians had been immediate, and in the same year (447) Domnus complained to Theodosius. His friend was more effective, Theodoret writing a trenchant reply called *Eranistes* or 'The beggarman'. This was arranged as a dialogue between an orthodox and a Eutychian representative in which Theodoret exposed the main Eutychian errors of asserting the mutability and passibility of God and maintaining the confusion of the natures in Christ, and insisted in his turn that the example of Christ as the perfect man was essential for human salvation. Hence Christ's human nature must be regarded as a reality distinct from his divinity.

This time, however, the court backed Eutyches. Already Irenaeus of Tyre had been deposed by imperial order,[3] and an inquiry was set up under an imperial official to investigate the teaching of Ibas of Edessa. He was reported to have made blasphemous pronouncements in the

---

[1] See R. Draguet, 'La Christologie d'Eutychès, d'après les Actes du Synode de Flavien, 448', *Byzantion* 6, 1931, pp. 441–57, and T. Camelot, 'De Nestorius à Eutychès' in Grillmeier/Bacht, *Das Konzil von Chalkedon*, I, 213–42 at p. 237. To the imperial officials who were present at Eutyches' trial the monk appeared to teach 'that the body of our Saviour was not of our substance' (*ACO* 2. 1. 2, p. 120, para. 107 = Mansi, *Collectio* VII, col. 77). When pressed by Flavian, however, Eutyches had drawn a distinction between Christ having the body of a man (σῶμα ἀνθρώπου) which he refused to accept, and a 'human body', derived from the flesh of the Virgin, which he would (σῶμα ἀνθρώπινον) (*ACO* 2. 1. 2, p. 142, para. 522 = Mansi, *Collectio* VI, col. 741).

[2] Facundus of Hermiana, *Pro defensione trium capitulorum* XII. 5: 'Domnus Antiochenus, qui... Eutychi Apollinaris heresiarchae impietatem renovare tentanti et ob hoc Diodorum atque Theodorum anathematizare praesumenti primus restitit, ad imperatorem Theodosium scribens' (*PL* 67, col. 852).

[3] September 447: for dating see *Regesten*, ed. Seeck, p. 379. His successor Photius was consecrated on 9 September 447 without reference to Domnus, and was an ardent Cyrillist.

presence of his presbyters that 'I do not envy Christ that he had become God; for I have become that; for he is of my own nature',[1] and to have criticised the Twelve Anathemas. On 16 February 448 an edict was despatched to the praetorian perfect Hormisdas[2] ordering the burning of 'Nestorian works' and those of the anti-Christian philosopher of the late third century, Porphyry. It also reaffirmed the deposition of Irenaeus, 'so that no one should feign ignorance of these matters'. A copy was sent to be read in the Egyptian monasteries.

The monks, too, were beginning to move. Under the leadership of a certain Palestinian, Theodosius, they accused Domnus and Theodoret to Dioscorus at Alexandria. The charge of heresy was well received there. Meantime (spring of 448), in Constantinople, Eutyches wrote to Leo complaining that the Nestorians were raising their head once again (Leo, *Ep.* 20). The stage was being set for a final reckoning with Antioch and Constantinople. Leo, however, was not Celestine. He merely acknowledged Eutyches' letter (1 June). Perhaps he did not like the monk's references to Cyril being 'the leader and chief of the holy synod at Ephesus',[3] for the papal view of those events was different. Prosper Tiro had made it clear that while Cyril's pertinacity had aided the unmasking of Nestorius, the authority of Rome had really been responsible for his downfall.[4] This divergence of approach was to have far-reaching effects in the storm that was about to break.

In the capital Flavian felt strong enough to act against Eutyches. Theologically, the patriarch represented the ideas of the Formula of Reunion but was open on analysis to similar criticisms on the score of imprecision and contradictions.[5] However, he had the support of a considerable array of monastic leadership as well as the bishops at court who formed a sort of permanent council in the capital.[6] Before this 'Home

---

[1] *Akten*, ed. Flemming, p. 41.   [2] *Cod. Just.* I. 1. 3.

[3] Leo, *Ep.* 21, Appendix (*PL* 54, col. 718A).

[4] *Chron.* ad ann. 428: 'Cui impietati [Nestorius] praecipua Cyrilli Alexandrini episcopi industria, et papae Coelestini repugnat auctoritas' (*PL* 51, col. 594=ed. Mommsen, p. 472).

[5] As Dioscorus did not fail to make clear at Chalcedon, accusing him of contradicting himself: *ACO* 2. 1. 1, p. 115.

[6] By this time the Home Synod was a well-established institution. At the fourth session of Chalcedon, Anatolius explained (Mansi, *Collectio* VII, col. 92): 'A custom has long prevailed that bishops who are staying (ἐνδημοῦντας) in Constantinople should assemble when occasion requires for such ecclesiastical affairs as may by chance occur.'

Synod' (σύνοδος ἐνδημοῦσα) consisting of eighteen archimandrites and thirty-one bishops, Eutyches was summoned to defend his views. After two refusals he eventually appeared on 22 November accompanied by court officials and a crowd of monks at a session presided over by the patrician Florentius.[1] His accuser was Eusebius of Dorylaeum. His previous horrified rejection of a two-nature Christology was modified to the extent of confessing 'two natures before the Union, one after it'. His judges were more puzzled than hostile. What did he mean by this? Was this not to admit that the incarnation resulted in a confusion between God and man?[2] Perhaps Eutyches was simply muddled as well as being at times diabolically artful.[3] His answers nonetheless may have deserved more attention than the contemptuous judgement they received from Leo (*confabulationes eius*) when he heard of them.[4] Leo regarded him more as a fool than a heretic ('imperite atque imprudenter errare detectus sit'),[5]

---

[1] Florentius, described as 'trustworthy and orthodox' by Flavian, was appointed by Theodosius to watch over the proceedings (*ACO* 2. 1. 2, p. 14, para. 103 = Mansi, *Collectio* VI, col. 731–4). His role may have been equivocal. Ostensibly, it was he who challenged Eutyches with the direct question, 'Do you confess "two natures after the union"? Speak, or else you will be condemned', and finally, 'He who does not say "out of two natures" and "two natures" does not rightly believe'. At the examination of the *Acta* of the Synod in April 449 Florentius had to explain this outburst, and he stated that he was merely warning Eutyches of what was likely to happen if he persisted (*ACO* 2. II. 1, p. 69, paras. 328 and 332), and he denied that he added 'and two natures' (*ibid*. para. 334). This sounds like the truth, and is supported by the fact that there was nothing illogical or cynical in Florentius' reasoning throughout the proceedings. However, the fact that Eutyches brought to the session Theodosius' letter appointing him as his official observer and then spoke to him privately after his condemnation and told him of his proposed appeal, leave the suspicion that somehow Florentius may have been engaged in double-dealing at the expense of Flavian. On the other hand, he was also a correspondent of Theodoret (Theodoret, *Ep*. 89). I prefer to leave the question open.

[2] Basil of Seleucia's question (*ACO* 2. II. 1, p. 17, para. 137).

[3] For instance, in an exchange with Flavian that formed the climax of the session; he stated that 'until that day I have not said that the body of the Lord and God was consubstantial with us, but that I confess that the holy virgin is consubstantial with us and that our God was made flesh from her', but nevertheless he was now prepared to accept instruction from his superiors and confess that 'the Son was *homoousios* with us' (Mansi, *Collectio* VI, col. 741). Under the pretence of being a humble monk, Eutyches was claiming perhaps that Flavian was innovating, and hence violating the decisions of Ephesus, thus anticipating Dioscorus' accusation against him next year.

[4] Leo, *Epp*. 28, 29, 31 and 35; also *Ep*. 47, 'imperitissimus senex'. See H. M. Diepen's comments in *Les Trois Chapitres de Chalcédoine* (Oosterhout, 1953), p. 67.

[5] Leo, *Ep*. 29.

and even when he was vindicated by Dioscorus at Ephesus the next year there were those who pointed out that he had made the task of the judges difficult by not making clear that it was an *incarnate* nature that he was asserting.[1] It would seem that behind all his prevarication he was determined to hold to the view that there was only one nature in the God-made flesh of Christ. He feared the consequences of admitting that Christ 'was consubstantial with us'[2] and he believed that any overt acceptance of two natures could be interpreted as 'Nestorianism'.[3] Above all, he believed that his views were founded firmly on the opinions of the Fathers including Pope Julius, Athanasius, Gregory of Nazianzus and Cyril. In failing to realise that the 'papal letters' that he so confidently produced were really Apollinarian forgeries he was no worse advised than most of his contemporaries, including Cyril. His plea, however, that 'his Fathers of Rome and Alexandria' did not enjoin him to speak of two natures was not accepted, and after the failure of considerable efforts by Florentius and the assembled clerics to get him to accept a two-nature formula he was condemned to deposition and loss of priestly status. In a letter to Leo, Flavian characterised his teaching as that of an Apollinarian and of a Valentinian Gnostic.[4]

This was a blow to Dioscorus, and in the summer and early autumn of 448 his offensive against the Antiochenes also had encountered resistance. Following the proscription of the works of Porphyry and Nestorius in February and the deposition of Irenaeus of Tyre, Dioscorus had opened

[1] Basil of Seleucia, who had been one of Eutyches' judges, pointed out to Dioscorus that 'dicente autem monacho "ex duabus naturis dico dominum nostrum Iesum Christum, post autem unitionem unam esse naturam" et non addente incarnatam... intellegeris commixtionem dicere et confusionem; sin autem addideris incarnatam, haec dices quae et patres nostri...' (*Gesta Synodi Ephesinae=ACO* 2. II. 1, p. 55, para. 120). For Basil's utterance at the trial, as reported, see *ACO* 2. II. 1, p. 18, para. 157. His career might be compared to that of the Vicar of Bray. In 448 he was a correspondent of Theodoret. He condemned Eutyches in November. He was present at Ephesus II, rehabilitated Eutyches and condemned Theodoret, August 449. Attended Chalcedon, condemned Dioscorus and Eutyches, signed the Definition and rehabilitated Theodoret. Died in possession of his see *circa* 460 (see Theodoret, *Correspondance*, ed. Azéma, I, 32).

[2] For instance, 'Florentius vir inlustris dixit: Matre nobis consubstantiali, sine dubio et filius consubstantialis est nobis. Eutyches presbyter dixit: Hactenus non dixi...' (*ACO* 2. II. 1, p. 17, paras. 139–40).

[3] See Draguet, 'La Christologie d'Eutychès'.

[4] Flavian to Leo=*ACO* 2. II. 1, p. 22.

an exchange of correspondence with Domnus of Antioch which with its free use of threats interlarded with copious asseverations from Scripture recalled Cyril's letters to Nestorius nearly twenty years before. He accused Domnus of harbouring Nestorians, including Theodoret of Cyrrhus, and allowing them freedom of speech in the churches throughout his patriarchate. He brushed aside Domnus' protests and hinted that the monks might soon be stirring up trouble for those who stood in his way. It was clear that only abject surrender of the whole Antiochene position, including acceptance of the Twelve Anathemas, would satisfy Dioscorus, and this even Domnus was unprepared to concede.[1] From his point of view, however, the weak link was Ibas, metropolitan of Edessa. The latter had succeeded the Cyrillist Rabbula in 435 and showed himself a tactlessly outspoken adherent of the two-nature Christology and a disciple of Diodore and Theodore. He made no bones about his view that Cyril was a heretic. There is no doubt that Edessa, strategically placed near the frontier with Persia, was deeply divided on all these issues. Thither also the long arm of Eutyches had reached out to grasp that of Dioscorus, each bent on rousing Ibas' suffragans against their metropolitan.[2] They succeeded, for Ibas was accused of heresy to which were added other charges including nepotism, perversion of justice, toleration of magic and peculation. These were all referred to Domnus as patriarch. Ibas defended himself and carried conviction even before tribunals which included his enemies, first at Berytus and then at Tyre. In hearings that extended from September 448 to February 449 he was acquitted, probably after giving a satisfactory declaration to his clergy.[3] With Eutyches' condemnation it appeared as though Dioscorus had been decisively checked.[4]

Once again as at Ephesus the anti-Alexandrian bishops had failed to read the tide of public opinion. Cyril's posthumous reputation was even greater than it had been while he lived. His evil deeds were quietly forgotten.

[1] The text of these letters was read at the second session of Ephesus II on 22 August 449 to discredit Domnus (*Akten*, ed. Flemming, pp. 133-47).

[2] Ibas complained that Uranius of Himera had been bribed by Eutyches (pro gratia Eutychis) to incite certain of his clergy to accuse him: *ACO* 2. III. 3, p. 16.

[3] The final hearing at Tyre before the tribune and notary Damascius is dated in precise terms 25 February 449 (*ACO* 2. III. 3, p. 17). Ibas promised to preach against Nestorius in Edessa, affirmed his acceptance of the Formula of Reunion and swore an oath to forgive his accusers. This dating is quite compatible with Ibas' return to Edessa in time for Easter on 27 March. The riots would have started immediately after.

[4] See Duchesne, *Early Church*, III, 283.

His championship of orthodoxy at Ephesus remained. There can be little doubt that 'Nestorius' had become a bad name even in the patriarchate of Antioch and that 'two natures' in any form was suspect to the masses and perhaps to Theodosius himself.[1] Ibas' unwise comments about 'Hell being only a threat' and 'the Jews crucified a man' helped his enemies' case. These suspicions were also being fanned by the latent antipathies between the bishops and clergy established in the largely Greek-speaking cities and the monks, largely Syriac-speaking, who dominated the countryside.[2] Their leader Barsaumas was to play an important part in the approaching crisis.

The story of this great crisis that engulfed the church between 449 and 451 has often been told.[3] The main factors were the support of the court of Theodosius II for Eutyches, and the fanatical devotion bestowed on the old archimandrite by the Egyptian and Syrian monks, co-ordinated and pressed forward by the determined and ruthless patriarch of Alexandria. Against such a combination of forces upheld by the emperor himself, Flavian and Leo were helpless. Only the sudden death of Theodosius II on 28 July 450 as the result of a hunting accident brought about the changes of policy at the court that led to Chalcedon. It is impossible to acquit Theodosius II of treachery towards his patriarch, though it might be argued in mitigation that, confronted by the overwhelming tide in favour of Cyrilline Christology which corresponded to his own views, he swam with it. For him as for many others in the east, Alexandria represented orthodoxy. In addition, he was irked at Flavian's inability to patch up what he considered to be an unnecessary personal dispute with Eutyches.[4]

[1] At Chalcedon, Count Helpidius, who had been at Ephesus II as one of the two executive officers deputed to supervise proceedings, claimed that Theodosius' fear of Nestorianism was the main factor in the summons of Ephesus II (Mansi, *Collectio* VI, col. 619). Theodosius seems to have believed that Nestorius' teaching was the work of demons hostile to both church and empire.

[2] See below, p. 90. The simple influence of difference of language must not be overstressed. Ibas' own supporters among his clergy numbering sixty-six who petitioned on his behalf included fifteen Syriac-speakers (*ACO* 2. III. 3, pp. 43–6, para. 141).

[3] See Sellers, *Council of Chalcedon*, pp. 30ff.; T. G. Jalland, *The Life and Times of St Leo the Great* (London, 1941), pp. 260ff.; Duchesne, *Early Church*, III, ch. 11; Hefele/Leclercq, *Histoire des conciles*, II. 1, 499ff.; Caspar, *Papsttums*, I, ch. 12; and O. Seeck, *Geschichte des Untergangs der antiken Welt* (Stuttgart, 1920), VI, ch. 14.

[4] On the relative shrewdness of Theodosius II's foreign policy, particularly in regard to the Huns, see E. A. Thompson, 'The foreign policies of Theodosius II and Marcian', *Hermathena* 76, 1950, pp. 58–75.

The best that can be said for him is that in 449/50 in the crisis which touched the beliefs of most of his subjects, combined with a serious external threat from the Huns on the Danube,[1] and growing disorder in some of the key cities on the Euphrates frontier, he manoeuvred skilfully and successfully, and handed over his dominions intact to his successor. In this respect he did better than his more orthodox cousins in the west.

The spring of 449 had swung the pendulum once more in Dioscorus' favour. Eutyches had carried out his threat to appeal to 'the councils' of Rome, Jerusalem, Thessalonica and Alexandria. He had sent his *libellus appellationis* to the emperor and the bishops he had named. Significantly for the authority attributed to the bishop of an imperial capital, he had included Peter of Ravenna.[2] The latter was embarrassed; Leo was angry and confused as Flavian had failed to inform him immediately of the findings of the Home Synod, but Theodosius acted. He had seconded Eutyches' appeal to Leo, and now he accepted the archimandrite's plea that there had been faults of procedure in the synod and even that Flavian's sentence deposing him had been prepared in advance of the vital session of 22 November. After a painful scene between himself and the patriarch in church on Easter Sunday (27 March), Theodosius, on 30 March, summoned a general council to meet at Ephesus on 1 August. By now the matter had passed beyond any personal dispute between Flavian and Eutyches.

The task of convening the council was entrusted by Theodosius not to his patriarch but to the latter's enemy, Dioscorus. The emperor's rescript to the Alexandrian laid down that the council was to be strictly limited in numbers to ten metropolitan bishops and ten other learned bishops from their provinces. The 'controversies which had suddenly arisen' (i.e. the dispute between Flavian and Eutyches) were to be settled, and in more general terms, 'error was to be rooted out' and that 'with zeal'.[3] Where Theodosius believed error to lie was indicated by a special ban on Theodoret. He must remain in his diocese and not participate in the synod unless the synod itself so demanded. Elsewhere, too, events were playing into

---

[1] His concern is evident from his letter to the council in which he claims to have told Flavian several times to abandon the question of Eutyches, in order not to stir up trouble throughout the world, but that Flavian had refused (*ACO* 2. I. 1, p. 73, para. 51 = Mansi, *Collectio* VI, col. 597).

[2] *ACO* 2. III. 1, p. 6.

[3] Text in *Akten*, ed. Flemming, pp. 3–5, and *ACO* 2. II. 1, p. 42, para. 10. 1.

Dioscorus' hands. At Edessa Ibas' home-coming from Tyre had given rise to massive demonstrations. The authorities in the city sided with his opponents, and he was forced to withdraw again. By the end of March the situation had become so tense that the governor of Osrhoëne, Count Chareas, came to Edessa on 12 April to conduct a full inquiry. He reported his detailed findings in three long memoranda through the patricians Florentius, Romanus, Protogenes and through other notables at court to the emperor himself.[1]

If the latter had needed any reassurance of the rightness of his assessment of Dioscorus' authority throughout the whole of the east he received it now. An evil spirit, Chareas reported, had been responsible on two occasions for turning the city of Edessa into a state of uproar and confusion. He had no doubt of the cause of this unwelcome visitor.[2] Agitation against Ibas had reached unparalleled lengths. The outcries of clergy and citizens, faithfully tabulated by the governor's staff, would have convinced anyone of the inflamed state of opinion. Amid loyal shouts for 'the empire' and 'Theodosius' there were others more menacing: 'No one accepts the enemy of Christ', 'To the gallows with the Iscariot', 'Ibas has corrupted the true doctrine of Cyril', 'Long live archbishop Dioscorus', 'The Christ-hater to the arena', 'Down with the Judophile', 'The books of Nestorius were found with Ibas', 'The writings of Theodore were found with Ibas', 'Where has the church property gone?', 'Ibas has laid waste Osrhoëne', 'Let Ibas burn', 'No one accepts this Nestorian bishop' – and very much more.[3] The cries show a strongly pro-imperial and anti-Nestorian outlook and were supported by an abundance of individual sworn depositions by magistrates, clergy, monks and artisans. Even though he had denied at Berytus the more hair-raising of his alleged utterances and had been acquitted, his opponents were not persuaded. He was not to be forgiven.

Meantime, in the capital the procedure and sentence of the Home Synod against Eutyches was under review. Exhaustive sessions on 8, 13 and 27 April had indeed established that Flavian had given sentence 'abrupte',[4] without reading out the arguments (*prosecutiones*) against Eutyches, but apart from the inadequacies of the secretarial system and the natural wish of the patrician Florentius and the bishops present not to have everything

---

[1] Texts in Flemming, pp. 15–55.
[2] Chareas' Third Report, Flemming, p. 33.
[3] Flemming, p. 19 (First Report).
[4] *ACO* 2. II. 1, p. 71, paras. 344 and 345 (8 April).

they said recorded,¹ no serious irregularities had been established. Flavian, however, was not restored to favour. Previously, he had been forced to give a personal declaration of faith to the emperor (17 December).² He now had to await events.

His position was indeed desperate. Almost too late he had informed Leo of Eutyches' deposition. Not until mid-May did a letter from him arrive in Rome. The Pope had been irked by what he considered to have been negligence by Flavian in failing to write to him at once about his handling of the affair, and seems to have been wholly unaware of the peril the patriarch had been placed in by subsequent events. He took his time. He had received his summons to the council on 13 May, but it was not until 12 June that he despatched to Constantinople his reply (*Ep.* 28) to Flavian known to history as the *Tome* of Leo.³ In this he asserted in uncompromising language the mystery of the distinction between the two natures of Christ and their unity through the mutual sharing of properties, the *communicatio idiomatum*. Even now he berated his unfortunate colleague and his clergy for not being severe enough on Eutyches and allowing nonsensical statements about 'one nature after the union' to pass without censure. He had little idea of the real situation in the east and the approaching trial of strength was to demonstrate this fully.⁴

By the time Leo's *Tome* reached Constantinople the net had closed. In vain Flavian had appealed to Leo to stop the council, to condemn Eutyches and to influence Theodosius to accept this advice.⁵ On 20 June Leo had agreed. In his view 'there was no need for a synod to deal further with the matter'.⁶ Too late. On 15 May Theodosius had written personally to Dioscorus telling him how it had come to his ears that many of the monks and Christian people throughout the east (i.e. Syria) were combating

---

¹ *Ibid.* para. 348. See the account of the successive inquiries given in Hefele/Leclercq, *Histoire des conciles* II. 1, 545ff.

² Text in *ACO* 2. 1. 1, p. 35.

³ For text and commentary see Bindley/Green, *Documents*, p. 159.

⁴ This is abundantly clear from the fact that as late as 23 July he sent another letter to Flavian urging him to treat Eutyches mildly if the latter corrected his error (*Ep.* 38). Neither this nor *Epp.* 36 and 37 reached their destination before the council opened, and the legates had to sail direct to Ephesus without calling at the capital; see Caspar, *Papsttums* I, 483.

⁵ Leo, *Ep.* 26 (*PL* 54, col. 747B).

⁶ *Ep.* 36. His letter (*Ep.* 37) to Theodosius stated his inability to attend himself, but indicated an intention to be represented, as had his *Ep.* 29 sent on 13 June.

Nestorianism favoured by the bishops in some cities there and that he was to accept Barsaumas as representative of all the monks in the east and to sit with him in council at Ephesus.¹ On the same day an executive instruction to Count Helpidius referred to Eutyches as 'venerable archimandrite'.² The previous day he had invited Barsaumas to attend, praising his stand against Nestorianism.³ The reference to its persistence 'in some of the eastern cities' boded ill for the bishops in their struggle against the ever-encroaching influence of the monks.

The monk's acquittal of the charges brought by his adversaries at the Home Synod was assumed. On 27 June, having perused the reports from Edessa sent by Count Chareas, the emperor passed these on for consideration by the council, with instructions that it should act to free the city from the disgrace of blasphemy.⁴ By 21 July the case of Ibas had already been judged, for a new, pro-Cyrilline bishop had been consecrated in his place at Edessa.⁵ Finally, on 6 August, though Flavian was already in Ephesus, Dioscorus received an imperial mandate conferring on him the presidency of the council. He was to act as the emperor's deputy 'not only in the matter of Theodoret but in all else that concerns the holy synod' (e.g. the case of Eutyches). With Juvenal of Jerusalem and Thalassius of Cappadocia he was to vindicate the memory of Cyril against recent attacks by Theodoret and others, and re-establish the symbols of Nicaea and Ephesus 'without enlargement or diminishing'. No freedom of speech (παρρησία) was to be permitted to contrary views.⁶ Neither Flavian nor Domnus of Antioch, nor Leo, his legates or his *Tome* were mentioned. In the rescript addressed on 15 May to the Counts Helpidius and Eulogius who were to act as executive officers at the proceedings, Theodosius stated that the judges of Eutyches were to have their opinions reviewed again and his case was therefore open. They were to call on such military power as they needed.⁷

Thus the council of about 135 bishops together with Barsaumas which met at the Church of the Theotokos at Ephesus on 8 August was a foregone

---

¹ *ACO* 2. II. 1, pp. 44–5.

² Text in *ACO* 2. II. 1, p. 46, no. 14. Both Flavian and Eutyches were termed by Theodosius 'religiosissimus' in his letter to the Council, *ibid.* p. 47.

³ *ACO* 2. I. 1, p. 71.

⁴ *Akten*, ed. Flemming, pp. 55–7.

⁵ *Chron. Edessenum* (ed. Guidi), p. 7, para. 64; see *Regesten*, ed. Seeck, p. 383.

⁶ *Akten*, ed. Flemming, p. 5. Theodosius declared that 'he had turned his countenance away from Theodoret'.

⁷ Text in *ACO* 2. II. 1, pp. 45–6, para. 14.

affair.¹ True, the papal legates, Bishop Julius of Puteoli and Hilarus a deacon and Leo's successor, were there,² as were Domnus, Juvenal and Flavian, flanking Dioscorus as he sat on his throne high above the assembled bishops.³ Flavian, however, had been depressed into fifth in order of precedence, below Juvenal. The letters of the emperor strongly critical of the two-natures doctrine were read, but not the *Tome* of Leo, for though Dioscorus did not refuse to read the latter, he (or Juvenal) saw to it that it was propelled down the agenda until lost sight of in the crowded moments that ensued.⁴ The emperor's instructions had given him everything he needed to crush 'Nestorianism' and humiliate his fellow-patriarchs; nor did he need to face Theodoret, the only man living who could have worsted him in debate. It was a strong position, the greatest opportunity ever presented to the see of St Mark to assert for itself the leadership of the Christian Mediterranean world.⁵ It was one of those occasions in history when developments can be disproportionately influenced by personality, and on the day Dioscorus failed by overplaying his hand.

He had only to follow the imperial instructions without vindictiveness, avoiding needless offence to a distant Leo, keeping within the bounds of

[1] Note, however, the figure of 150 given by E. Honigmann in his article 'The original list of the members of the Council of Nicaea, the Robber Synod and the Council of Chalcedon', *Byzantion* 16, 1942–3, pp. 20–80 at p. 34. Michael the Syrian, *Chron.* VIII. 7, gives the number of bishops present as 128, plus Barsaumas (ed. Chabot, II, 29). At Chalcedon, Basil of Seleucia said that 'there were between 120 and 130' present (*ACO* 2. I. 1, p. 94, para. 178). In the Latin *Acta* of the first session of the council there are 140 signatures including seven of presbyters signing for bishops, and Barsaumas (*ACO* 2. III. 1, pp. 252–8, para. 1070).

[2] The third delegate, the presbyter Renatus, had died en route at Delos (cf. Mansi, *Collectio* VII, col. 1061).

[3] See Sellers, *Council of Chalcedon*, p. 78 for the events.

[4] At Chalcedon it was revealed that Dioscorus was willing 'to receive the letter of his distinguished brother and fellow-bishop, Leo', but that Juvenal had insisted that the emperor's missives were read first. When later in the session the legates again requested that the letter of Leo be read, Eutyches himself immediately interjected that the legates were not impartial and had dined with Flavian in Constantinople, and that Leo's letters should not be read before his own case had been disposed of. The Council thought this was fair, and of course from then on there was no further chance of reading them. Dioscorus merely let matters take their course. See *ACO* 2. II. 1, p. 51, para. 54.

[5] That this in fact may have been Dioscorus' aim is suggested by his later Monophysite biographers. See F. Haase, 'Patriarch Dioskur I nach monophysitischen Quellen', *Kirchengeschichtliche Abhandlungen* 6, 1908, p. 204; also Prosper Tiro, *Chron.* ad ann. 449, *PL* 51, col. 601c.

Cyrilline orthodoxy and ecclesiastical decorum. The first session of the council, however, was marked by scenes unparalleled in ecclesiastical history. The immediate task was to rehabilitate Eutyches. The monk was on his best behaviour. He produced copies of documents ostensibly written by Gregory the Wonderworker and Pope Julius to support his case. Since Julius' 'Letter to Prosdocius' condemning the Christology of Paul of Samosata had already been accepted at the first Council of Ephesus, this was a valid line of defence,[1] and Eutyches followed it up with a confession of faith in which he admitted that the incarnate Christ was made from the flesh of the Virgin and was made man for our salvation. He condemned Mani, Valentinus, Apollinarius, Nestorius 'and all those who say that the flesh of our Lord and God Jesus Christ came down from heaven'. The council was entranced. 'Two natures before the union, one afterwards. Is that not what we all believe?' asked Dioscorus.[2] Whatever the merits or demerits of Flavian's procedures the previous November, the issue was soon transported from the realms of theology to those of hysteria. 'Eusebius to the flames. Burn him alive. Cut in pieces this man who divides the Christ', cried the bishops.[3] 'Anathema to him who says two natures after the incarnation'. Eutyches was declared orthodox and rehabilitated. Then came a brilliant but unscrupulous manoeuvre by Dioscorus and Juvenal which caught the council unawares. Dioscorus had extracts from the sixth session of the previous Council of Ephesus read: in these it was forbidden on pain of deposition to teach any creed other than that of Nicaea. Everyone, including the legates, approved.[4] Dioscorus then showed his hand. Eusebius and Flavian with their formulas regarding the two natures had infringed this canon; moreover they had caused disturbance among the holy churches and orthodox laity and merited deposition. Even the assembly was dumbfounded. 'I appeal', protested Flavian.[5] 'Contradicitur', shouted the deacon Hilarus and disappeared to the comparative safety of the sanctuary. He could have saved himself the trouble, for in this purely

---

[1] Mansi, *Collectio* v, col. 545, and see *ACO* 2. II. 1, p. 75, para. 397.

[2] *ACO* 2. I. 1, p. 143, paras. 528–9 = Mansi, *Collectio* VI, col. 744.

[3] *ACO* ibid. p. 140, para. 491 = Mansi, *Collectio* VI, col. 737.

[4] *ACO* ibid. p. 190, para. 952 = Mansi, *Collectio* VI, col. 905.

[5] Φλαουιανὸς ἐπίσκοπος εἶπε · παραιτοῦμαί σε (Mansi, *Collectio* VI, col. 908 = 'Appello' of the *Coll. Novariensis*, *ACO* 2. II. 1, p. 76, para. 403). His surprise is indicated in his account of the proceedings he sent to Leo (*Coll. Novariensis* 11 = *ACO* 2. II. 1, p. 78, lines 34ff.). Dioscorus had even had the sentence written out in anticipation, the very thing which Flavian was accused of doing to Eutyches!

Greek-speaking assembly he was not understood.¹ Some bishops tried to protest. Dioscorus brought in the Counts. The proconsul of Asia himself led in the military who brandished manacles at the bishops. No one was allowed to leave the church. The bishops were presented with blank forms which, urged on by the tumult of the soldiers and the vociferations of Barsaumas' monks, they were forced to sign.² Flavian was disgracefully manhandled, to die not long after, perhaps even as the result of his injuries.³ He was declared deposed. Juvenal, who had acted as Dioscorus' faithful henchman, received patriarchal dignity and six provinces at the expense of Antioch, whose patriarch was completely overawed by the occasion.⁴

The second session on 22 August was almost equally riotous, though neither the papal legates nor Domnus of Antioch were present.⁵ The reading of Count Chareas' three long reports on his mission to Edessa the previous April occupied much of the time.⁶ Ibas' name was greeted with shouts of execration. In quick succession he, his nephews Daniel of Harran and Sophronius of Tella were deposed, and the same fate accounted for Theodoret (amid lurid shouts that he should be burnt as an example to others), Irenaeus of Tyre and Aquilinus of Byblos whom he had consecrated. These sentences were duly reported to Domnus and he agreed to them.⁷ His baseness availed him nothing. He had sinned too grievously against Dioscorus for forgiveness: he was accused of being 'worse than

---

¹ The word is transcribed into Greek as κοντραδικίτουρ with the explanation ὅ ἐστιν, ἀντιλέγεται: *ACO* 2. 1. 1, p. 191, para. 964 = Mansi, *Collectio* VI, col. 908. Hilary's own account written to Pulcheria = Leo, *Ep.* 46.

² Mansi, *Collectio* VI, cols. 602 and 626–30. Also, Flavian's appeal to Leo 'statim me circumvallat multitudo militaris et volentem me ad sanctum altare confugere non concessit...', for the ensuing scenes of violence (*ACO* 2. II. 1, p. 78, lines 34ff.).

³ It would appear that Flavian was still in good enough health to pen his desperate but dignified appeal to Leo. His *natalis* was kept on 17 or 18 February, and the possibility exists that he died in exile on that day in 450. Compare Prosper Tiro, *Chron.* ad ann. 449, which indicates death on the way to exile (*PL* 51, col. 602B = ed. Mommsen, p. 481). See H. Chadwick, 'The exile and death of Flavian of Constantinople: a prologue to the Council of Chalcedon', *JTS*, n.s. 6. 1, 1955, pp. 17–34.

⁴ Juvenal received Arabia, the three Palestinian provinces and the two provinces of Phoenicia. Domnus meantime tamely agreed to the deposition of both Flavian and Eusebius of Dorylaeum. Mansi, *Collectio* VI, col. 909.

⁵ Domnus was ill, and of the legates Bishop Julius was apparently hiding somewhere in the suburbs of Ephesus, and Hilary in the martyrium of St John: *Akten*, ed. Flemming, pp. 9–11.

⁶ Flemming, pp. 15–55.   ⁷ *Ibid.* p. 113.

Ibas', of having supported Theodoret actively, and of preaching Nestorianism to catechumens.[1] He was deposed. The Synod ended with the solemn acceptance of Cyril's Twelve Anathemas.[2] In November Dioscorus completed his triumph by securing the election of his deacon and representative (*apocrisarius*) in the capital, Anatolius, as patriarch in Flavian's stead.[3]

Despite the violence of the proceedings the decisions of Ephesus II also represented what a large proportion of the east believed, though in their anxiety to rehabilitate Eutyches the bishops had failed to emphasise the inadequacy of his previous theological statements. For without the words 'made flesh and made man', his one-nature Christology fully deserved later criticism of 'Manichaeism'. This failure seriously weakened the Alexandrian position in the future debate. Meantime, at the court no one except Pulcheria took the part of the papal legates. The second session of the council had proceeded without them, and none had raised objection to Dioscorus' description of the meetings as 'this great and holy synod'. The bishops had cried out that its decrees 'agreed with Nicaea',[4] and that sufficed. The patriarch's own orthodoxy went unquestioned. In the view of the west, he had asserted his primacy over Christendom[5] and his supporters regarded him as 'the supreme guardian of the faith'.[6] With a rare unanimity that included even the Latin-speaking bishops from Illyricum, Dioscorus had been able to secure the unequivocal condemnation of the champions of the Antiochene school and depose the patriarch, Domnus. At the end of the proceedings Theodosius sent him a rescript thanking him for his services and instructing him to inform all metropolitans of the results through an encyclical letter.[7]

Alexandria had proved its claim to be 'the city of the Orthodox', and as long as Theodosius lived it remained so. The ensuing months, however,

[1] *Ibid.* p. 119. That his rejection of the Twelve Anathemas was his cardinal sin, see Theodoret, *Ep.* 147 to John of Germanicia.

[2] *Akten*, ed. Flemming, p. 147.

[3] This seems the most probable dating (rather than June 450). See the arguments of Chadwick, 'The exile and death of Flavian'. For Anatolius as deacon and *apocrisarius* of Dioscorus, see Liberatus, *Brev.* XIII. 76.

[4] *Akten*, ed. Flemming, p. 145.

[5] Prosper Tiro, *Chron.* ad ann. 449: 'In quo concilio Dioscorus Alexandrinus episcopus primatum sibi vindicans...' (*PL* 51, col. 601c = ed. Mommsen, p. 480).

[6] For the acclamation of the synod in honour of Dioscorus see Michael the Syrian, *Chron.* VIII. 7 (ed. Chabot, II, 31).

[7] *Akten*, ed. Flemming, pp. 151–5.

were to demonstrate the innate strength of the see of the capital and the difficulties of finding general acceptance in the east of any theological and ecclesiastical system which was openly rejected by the papacy. The latter's authority is revealed as one of veto, rather than positive ability to impose its own views in the face of opposition. At first, however, Leo was impotent. Instinctively, the opponents of Dioscorus had turned to him as a last resort. Flavian's piteous appeal to him 'to save the Church from ruin' survives,[1] and so also does Theodoret's more indignant expostulation at what he describes graphically as the 'massacre of the bishops' at Ephesus.[2] Eusebius of Dorylaeum, restless and calculating as ever, wrote and then betook himself to Rome to canvass his own views about Dioscorus and Eutyches. Leo, however, could do nothing effective. So long as the judgement of Ephesus II stood his own position was in jeopardy. The *Tome* could be reconciled with the Formula of Reunion, but was blatantly at variance with Cyril's Anathemas. A false move, and Dioscorus' excommunication of him would not have been merely the defiant gesture that it was to be on the eve of Chalcedon.

The thirty letters (nos. 43–72) that he wrote between Ephesus II and Chalcedon betray Leo's embarrassment. In mid-October, fortified by the views of the council of his own Italian 'province', he wrote a budget of letters to the court, to the anti-Eutychian archimandrites in the capital, and to the clergy and people of Constantinople exhorting them to accept no bishop other than Flavian.[3] Horror was expressed at Dioscorus' proceedings, and the name of 'latrocinium'[4] with which he dubbed these has stuck for all time. In the winter and spring 449/50 his repeated attempts, however, to move Theodosius to convoke a new general council in Italy failed, and so did the personal appeals of the court of Valentinian III[5] and even the emperor's daughter Licinia Eudoxia[6] (February 450). Eutyches, whose heresy Leo had eventually found so damnable and nonsensical, remained in

[1] *ACO* 2. II. 1, p. 77. Hilary took it back to Rome with him.
[2] *Ep.* 113. Neither was an 'appeal to Rome' *qua* jurisdictional head, but an appeal in desperation to the one power which seemed to stand aside from the maelstrom of Ephesus II.
[3] *Epp.* 45–51.   [4] *Ep.* 95, to Pulcheria, 20 July 451.
[5] *Epp.* 55–7.
[6] Text in *ACO* 2. III. 1, p. 15, *Epist. ante Gesta Collectio* 21. Theodosius' reply was kindly but said that he had ordered Flavian's banishment ('ab humanis rebus ablatus'), and that there was no going back on the steps taken to remove the dissensions among the churches.

high honour. Theodosius was immovable. Probably in April he replied to his cousins at Ravenna in letters which summed up his opinions. At Ephesus, in full respect for the truth various disturbers of the peace had been removed from the office of the priesthood, and 'nothing contrary to the rule of faith or of justice had been done there'.[1] The synod had been concerned with matters of discipline, which had been settled, and the faith of Cyril had been vindicated.

Meantime other influences were beginning to make themselves felt at Theodosius' court. From Liberatus we gather that schism threatened to break out, the Egyptian, Palestinian and Thracian bishops supporting Dioscorus, while those of Pontus, Asia and Syria held to the memory of Flavian.[2] There were murmurs against the 'Manichaean' doctrines prevailing in the capital.[3] Sometime before 17 March 450 Pulcheria disclosed to Leo her own disapproval of the 'heretical error' of the council,[4] and at the same time, the new patriarch, Anatolius, began to assert his independence from Dioscorus. Whether he was working in concert with Pulcheria is quite uncertain, but he seems to have decided in the course of the early summer to seek recognition from Leo.[5] His first step in this direction succeeded, for on 15 July Leo let it be known to Pulcheria that Anatolius would be acceptable if he would concur with Cyril's Second Letter to Nestorius and his own *Tome*, and he wrote to Theodosius to that effect.[6] Legates were on their way east when Theodosius' sudden death on 28 July intervened.

In the capital the ensuing revolution was complete. Pulcheria's star had been visibly rising in the previous months[7] and now she took over the government, choosing as her consort the elderly Thracian officer Marcian (25 August). Short shrift was accorded to Theodosius' ministers. Chrysaphius, whose influence had begun to crumble despite his brilliant diplomatic success in negotiations with Attila that same spring, was charged with avarice and plotting, and executed even before the new reign opened![8]

---

[1] Leo, *Epp.* 62–4.

[2] An interesting description of the distribution of parties in 449–50. The schism continued until Theodosius' death. Liberatus, *Brev.* XIII. 76 (*ACO* 2. v, p. 119).

[3] Leo, *Ep.* 59.   [4] *Ep.* 60.

[5] Chadwick, 'The exile and death of Flavian', p. 26.   [6] *Epp.* 62–4.

[7] See Goubert, 'Le Rôle de Sainte Pulchérie'. Nikephorus Kallistus indicates that Chrysaphius had already fallen from favour and been exiled by the summer of 450 (*HE* XIV. 49).

[8] Theodore Lector, *HE* I. 1 (*PG* 86, col. 165), says that he was executed 'through Pulcheria'. Also Nikephorus Kallistus, *HE* XIV. 49, indicating that Theodosius was

The rise of the Monophysite movement

Eutyches was sent into exile. Flavian's body was brought back to Constantinople and his name restored to the diptychs (October 450). In this situation Anatolius and Leo were able to negotiate. The patriarch's position was relatively strong. He had taken part in the coronation ceremony, if not actually crowning Marcian as emperor.[1] Meantime the decisions of Ephesus II had been accepted in the east, and stood. The *Tome*, however, had not been condemned by name and was therefore negotiable. Anatolius himself, would have no difficulty in agreeing with any Cyrilline document proposed by Leo. What he wanted from Leo was explicit acceptance on the papacy's part of canon 3 of the Council of Constantinople with its reference to the privileges of 'New Rome'.[2] Then Leo could have his council. Eusebius of Dorylaeum states that Leo was prepared to agree to these terms in April 451 when Anatolius' own legates visited him; but between then and June when he issued instructions to his representatives for the Council of Chalcedon he had evidently changed his mind.[3] Perhaps the emperor in his anxiety to restore unity in the church had spoiled Anatolius' scheme. On 23 May 451 he summoned an ecumenical council – not merely an enlarged judicial tribunal – to meet in September at Nicaea to end the disputations and settle 'the true faith more clearly, and for all time'. He ignored Leo's plea for a postponement.[4]

In fact, the opening of the council was delayed until October and then it met at Chalcedon on the Asiatic side of the Bosporus. Once more events showed the pivotal position of the emperor, and the importance of the traditional policies of the great sees, independently of the views of indi-

already intent on punishing him for his misdeeds. The vital change was in foreign policy, however, where Marcian reversed Chrysaphius' policy of trying to treat with Attila and using payments and subsidies for this purpose. He was lucky that Aetius' victory in 451 did not put this strong line to the test. See Thompson, *Attila and the Huns*, pp. 133 and 189.

[1] Probably because Marcian had not received the assent of Valentinian III to his elevation. See P. Charanis, 'Coronation and its constitutional significance in the later Roman Empire', *Byzantion* 15, 1940–1, pp. 49–66 at p. 53. For the view, however, that Anatolius only witnessed the coronation, the act being performed perhaps by Pulcheria, see W. Ensslin, 'Zur Frage nach der ersten Kaiserkrönung durch den Patriarchen', *BZ* 42, 1943–50, pp. 101–15 and 369–72.

[2] Chadwick, 'The exile and death of Flavian', pp. 27–8.

[3] *ACO* 2. III. 3, p. 112, para. 31 (Versio a Rustico edita): 'Eusebius revs. eps. Dorylaei d.: "Sponte subscripsi, quoniam et hanc regulam sanctissimo papae in urbe Roma ego relegi praesentibus clericis Constantinopolitanis eamque suscepit."'

[4] Leo, *Ep.* 89 (written on 24 June 451).

viduals who happened to be their bishops. Dioscorus arrived early with sixteen or seventeen Egyptian bishops and promptly excommunicated Leo, but Anatolius did not support him, and neither did Juvenal. In the first session of the council on 8 October, the latter dramatically changed sides, having, it was reported, been assured of the status of Jerusalem as a patriarchate.[1] Confronted with a new, pro-western emperor, and their discussions supervised by watchful and studiously fair-minded high officials from the capital, the bishops, with the exception of thirteen Egyptians, found little difficulty in modifying their views enough to satisfy the new regime. They agreed that 'they had erred' in condemning Flavian and Eusebius, and besought pardon.[2] The *Tome* of Leo was accepted as 'orthodox' with a great show of enthusiasm.[3] Dioscorus was deposed and Flavian vindicated, while somewhat reluctantly Theodoret and Ibas were restored to their sees, and monkish power curbed to the advantage of the bishops. Eutyches himself was exiled. Doctrinally, the council built on the foundation laid by the Formula of Reunion eighteen years before. Once again, Cyril's concept of the hypostatic union of the Word and the incarnate Christ was sidetracked, and instead a formula substituted which taught two natures inseparably joined in one person and one *hypostasis*, each nature retaining its own properties yet sharing in the properties of the other. It was not an easy formula to grasp at the best of times, the product of an uneasy compromise. It invited dispute, especially among those whose theology was rooted in Athanasius and Cyril.

The extent, however, of the rejection of Alexandria must not be exaggerated. Dioscorus was not condemned as a heretic, but as contumacious and for having excommunicated Leo. At the first session of the council he was unflinching amid growing adversity. He conspicuously held his own in the heated exchanges on matters of doctrine, explaining trenchantly and briefly why he believed Flavian had been wrong and hence had been excommunicated.[4] 'I can prove from Athanasius, Gregory and Cyril that after the union we ought to speak of only one incarnate nature of the Logos. I will be rejected together with the Fathers, but I am defending the doctrine

---

[1] Zacharias Rhetor, *HE* III. 3 (ed. Brooks, *CSCO* III. 5, p. 80, line 7).

[2] *ACO* 2. 1. 1, p. 94, paras. 181–4 = Mansi, *Collectio* VI, col. 936. Most had been present at Ephesus II. Only twenty-six metropolitans and bishops attending that council did not attend Chalcedon. See Honigmann, 'The original list of members', p. 40.

[3] *ACO* 2. 1. 2, p. 81, para. 23 = Mansi, *Collectio* VI, col. 972.

[4] *ACO* 2. 1. 1, p. 117, para. 299 = Mansi, *Collectio* VI, col. 684.

of the Fathers and yield on no point.'[1] He was no mere follower of the monk. He was willing to condemn Eutyches 'even to the fire, if Eutyches had taught wrongly',[2] and his interpretation of Cyril was supported by the majority of his own bishops and a considerable faction of the monks. Had not his conduct at Ephesus and against Cyril's kin been so abominable he might yet have triumphed, for again and again the bishops made clear that they equated orthodoxy with Cyril. But this time the clergy of the capital were bent on revenge, their archdeacon Aetius and not Dioscorus' servant was chief secretary at the council and guided the argument. Vindication of 'the martyr Flavian' necessitated acceptance of Leo's Letter to Flavian, with its two-nature Christology. The remainder of the bishops were only too glad to find a scapegoat for their own shortcomings in Dioscorus. So all rejoiced in his downfall. It was 'Cyril and Leo taught alike',[3] 'Flavian's doctrine accorded with Cyril'.[4] The problem whether or not it did was to occupy theologians for the next century.[5] Even worse, if the *Tome* and its author were regarded as orthodox,[6] what was to be thought of Flavian's confession of faith which affirmed that Christ existed 'out of two natures'?[7] In their relief, however, at the removal of the tyrant Dioscorus and perhaps at their own reprieve from merited deposition, the assembled bishops were unprepared to delve into possible contradictions between the two formulae. Most of those present did not regard the Chalcedonian formula as a Symbol of Faith. One of the very few occasions when the lay commissioners put a foot wrong was at the beginning of the second session

[1] *ACO loc. cit.*
[2] *ACO* 2. 1. 1, p. 92, para. 168 = Mansi, *Collectio* VI, col. 633, and *ACO* 2. 1. 2, p. 111 = Mansi, *Collectio* VII, col. 53 for similar views by other Egyptian bishops.
[3] *ACO* 2. 1. 1, p. 81, para. 23 = Mansi, *Collectio* VI, col. 972, and *ACO* 2. 1. 2, p. 124, para. 20. Here the bishops cried out that Leo, Celestine and Xystus simply confirmed Cyril's teaching.
[4] *ACO* 2. 1. 1, p. 115, para. 277 = Mansi, *Collectio* VI, col. 681.
[5] Even at Chalcedon, Aetius had to read extracts from Cyril's works to show that he did accept the *communicatio idiomatum* just as Leo did (*ACO* 2. 1. 2, p. 82, paras. 25–6 = Mansi, *Collectio* VI, col. 973).
[6] The Illyrians and Palestinians objected to the *Tome* at the end of the second session and had to be convinced of Leo's orthodoxy (*ACO* 2. 1. 2, p. 82, para. 24 and p. 93, para. 6 = Mansi, *Collectio* VI, col. 972 and VII, col. 9).
[7] The point was made clearly to the bishops by the judges, Mansi, *Collectio* VII, col. 104. In the first session the Syrian bishops and others after hearing Flavian's doctrinal statement made at the Home Synod cried out 'the martyr Flavian rightly explained the Faith' (*ACO* 2. 1. 1, p. 115, para. 280 = Mansi, *Collectio* VI, col. 681).

when they proposed that the bishops should draw up an expression of the true faith. There was an immediate protest against the very idea that there should be 'another exposition' over and above 'that taught by the Fathers'.[1] Only Nicaea, confirmed by Constantinople and Ephesus I, could be regarded as a Symbol or Rule of Faith. As the archdeacon Aetius put it, 'The holy fathers Cyril and Celestine and now the most holy Pope (πάπας) Leo have compiled letters interpreting the Symbol [of Nicaea], not setting out faith or teaching'.[2] Some easterners would not even accept the definition of Chalcedon for purposes of baptismal catechism.[3] It was a 'buckler against those who denied the real character of the incarnation', a legal definition for the extirpation of the two heresies of Nestorius and Eutyches, and thus in their view it was to remain. For Leo, however, it was a binding document and a definition of faith which was not susceptible to negotiation.[4] The 'in two natures' formula became in the west the touchstone of all orthodoxy. In the east, however, it was not only the Eutychian minority at the council that rejected this interpretation. Out of the discordant views on the validity of the decisions taken at Chalcedon, relations between the eastern and western halves of Christendom were to strain and ultimately to founder.

[1] Mansi, *Collectio* VI, col. 953: οἱ εὐλαβέστατοι ἐπίσκοποι ἐπεβόησαν· ἔκθεσιν ἄλλην οὐδεὶς ποιεῖ.

[2] *ACO* 2. 1. 2, p. 119, para. 98 = Mansi, *Collectio* VII, col. 73.

[3] The views of Epiphanius of Perge in 457 cited from the *Codex Encyclius* (*ACO* 2. V, p. 59): 'veluti scutum eam [definitionem] contra haereticos opponentes et non mathema fidei existentem' – this view was to have a long life in the east. The acceptance of formulae for purposes of baptismal catechism was recognised as a 'second string'. Westerners had excused their own Serdican Creed of 342 on the grounds that since the Council of Nicaea heresies had arisen which required more detailed refutation for the purposes of instructing catechumens.

[4] Note, for instance, *Ep.* 145 of 11 July 457 to Leo I: 'quia in illo concilio per sanctum spiritum congregato tam plenis et perfectis definitionibus cuncta firmata sunt, ut nihil ei regulae quae ex divina inspiratione prolata est, aut addi possit aut minui'.

Chapter 2

THE EMPEROR AND HIS CHURCH

The real victors at Chalcedon had been Marcian and Pulcheria. They had initiated the vast change of religious policy that followed the sudden death of Theodosius II. Marcian himself had guided the crucial sixth session.[1] He and his consort, who had also attended this session, had convoked the council, and had seen their concept of orthodoxy accepted by the largest gathering of bishops ever assembled. This assembly had changed decisively the ecclesiastical balance in Christendom. It had humbled Alexandria, while the patriarch of the capital had emerged immensely strengthened. At the same time relations with Rome had been saved from disintegration. The emperor's success emphasised what had been true since the time of Constantine, namely that whoever sat as ruler on the throne at Constantinople held the initiative and nearly always the control of the ecclesiastical affairs of the empire. Where Constantine and Constantius II had led Theodosius II and Marcian followed.

The great struggle between the patriarchates that reached its climax at Chalcedon had tested the statecraft of the emperor to the uttermost. In the years to come Marcian's successors were to seek by every available means to maintain intact the essentials of the hard-won settlement. The story of the next two centuries is the story of their increasing failure to do so in face of the conflicting religious outlooks of Latin and Greek Christendom, the intransigence of the papacy, and the forces of popular religion in Egypt and Syria hostile to the council. In this chapter we consider some of the factors that influenced the course of events. First, there is the position of

[1] Marcian deliberately followed Constantine's precedent in addressing the synod. See Mansi, *Collectio* VII, cols. 129–30 and 169–78 (= *ACO* 2. III. 2, p. 150, line 27). For critical comments on the Latin and Greek versions of the speech, see Coleman-Norton, *Roman State and Christian Church*, II, 792–9.

In later years Marcian's part at this session was emphasised by Byzantine historians, Evagrius saying 'at the command of the emperor the formulary was read by the archdeacon of Constantinople, Aetius, and all subscribed to it' (Evagrius, *HE* II. 18), and this is indeed what happened (*ACO ibid.* p. 152). For Pulcheria's presence, see Theodore Lector, *HE* I. 6, and see E. Schwartz, 'Die Kaiserin Pulcheria auf der Synode von Chalkedon', *Festgabe Jülicher* (Tübingen, 1927), pp. 203–12.

the emperor at Constantinople as guardian of orthodoxy and the extent to which this role was accepted by the church and its leaders in the east. How far was it to be challenged by the growth of regional particularism in Egypt and Syria, and to what extent may the growth of opposition to Chalcedon be attributed to social and political forces implicit in this development as well as to contrary religious beliefs? Is it true that in the century after Chalcedon 'the Syriac and Coptic masses felt the power of the empire to be a hated yoke',[1] and rejected Chalcedon accordingly? To attempt an answer involves an assessment of the cultural as well as the religious forces at work within the eastern patriarchates and especially the part played by the monks as representatives of popular religion in influencing the course of events within them. Finally, from the situation in the east we turn to the different presuppositions that governed church–state relations in the west. Only thus can the attitude of Pope Leo and his successors towards the emperor and his religious policy be understood.

The emperors at Constantinople regarded their office as involving a 'common oversight' over their realm, in all matters and especially in the religion of their subjects.[2] They felt themselves to have been elected 'by divine providence',[3] and their interpretation of kingship was theological. Royal and priestly office were derived from the same divine source; their exercise was different but complementary, and involved the emperors in the duty of leading their people spiritually as well as materially to victory and salvation.[4] The peace and prosperity of the church, its ministers united in their doctrine and discipline, were essential to the prosperity of the em-

[1] The phrase is A. Schmemann's, *The Historical Road of Eastern Orthodoxy* (London, 1963), p. 139.

[2] Thus Marcian addressing the bishops at Chalcedon: 'Studium autem nostrum est ut omnis populus per veram et sanctam doctrinam unum sentiens in eamdem religionem redeat et veram fidem catholicam colat' (Mansi, *Collectio* VII, cols. 129–30 = *ACO* 2. III. 2, p. 151, line 2).

[3] Leo, *Ep.* 73 (Marcian to Leo).

[4] Thus Justinian's well-known pronouncement in *Novel* 7. 2. 1: 'The priestly power and the royal power are not widely separated, and sacred property is not far removed from that which all mankind hold in common or from that which is owned by the state, because the churches are endowed with all their material resources and their status by the munificence of the royal power...' Compare also *Novel* 6, Prologue: 'Maxima quidem in hominibus sunt dona dei a superna collata clementia sacerdotium et imperium, illud quidem divinis ministrans, hoc autem humanis praesidens ac diligentiam exhibens.' The contrast to the western view of the nature of the Imperium and Sacerdotium is striking.

pire.¹ The pagan *pax deorum*, to maintain which persecution had been unleashed on the Christians in the past, was taken over and given an even more drastic application against heretics and dissidents by the Christian emperors. Fear of the results of its loss explains much of the feverish initiative of successive emperors in attempting to settle even the details of religious controversies. Theodosius II had written to Cyril before Ephesus I that 'the stability of the state depends upon the religion by which we honour God',² and he repeated almost exactly similar views to Dioscorus seventeen years later when he instructed him to convoke Ephesus II.³ At Chalcedon itself the presence of the lay element in the form of eighteen senators and high officials who acted as the judges before whom the bishops pleaded their causes, demonstrated the indissolubility of the ties that bound church and state in the fifth-century eastern Roman Empire.

The practical results of this outlook were far-reaching. The emperor was responsible for the summons and conduct of church councils with the object of maintaining the unity and peace of the church, and even Leo accepted his right of doing so. He founded new episcopal sees and might determine the status and boundaries of the existing ones. Whether it was a disciplinary matter like the dispute that had 'suddenly arisen' between Flavian and Eutyches and which had provoked Ephesus II, or the wider question of 'the establishment of the true faith', as was the purpose of Chalcedon, the emperor was personally concerned. He drafted ecclesiastical canons, and gave his own judgement on matters of doctrine and liturgy. The site even of Chalcedon was chosen, Pope Gelasius claimed forty years later, 'because it was near the palace',⁴ and Marcian's officials had the

¹ Compare the claim by Justinian (*Novel* 133. 5. 1) that religious orthodoxy was necessary for procuring 'prosperous cities, peace, public order, flourishing crops and even seafood', with Maximin's similar claim to justify the enforced re-conversion of Christians to the service of the 'immortal gods' during the Great Persecution (Eusebius, *HE* IX. 7. 10–12).

² Mansi, *Collectio* IV, col. 1112 = *ACO* I. I. 1, pp. 114–15; dated 19 November 430.

³ 'Constat apud universos esse manifestum quod nostrae conversationis status et universa mortalia erga deum pietate probatur et continetur et propitia divinitate prospere (et) ex sententia procedunt et reguntur humana' (*ACO* 2. II. 1, pp. 42–3 = *Coll. Novarienses de re Eutychis*). Note the phrase, too, in Zeno's *Henotikon*, 'cum sic igitur immaculata fides et nos et Romanam servet rempublicam', from Liberatus' translation, *Brev.* XVII.

⁴ Gelasius, *Gesta de nomine Acacii* = *Coll. Avellana* 99. 1 (ed. Guenther, *CSEL* 35. 1, p. 444): 'propter palatii vicinitatem'. Note Athanasius' plea, 'if the emperor really cares about ecclesiastical peace ... the synod should meet far away from the palace,

The emperor and his church

council in their hands from start to finish. Though Pulcheria had assured Leo that the council would be held 'under your authority',[1] the precedence accorded to the Pope's legates was simply the right to speak and vote first. It has been pointed out how Paschasinus' role was analogous to that of *princeps senatus* functioning under the overall presidency of the emperor.[2] Administrative matters also, such as Eustathius of Berytus' claim of metropolitan status (accorded in 448) vis-à-vis the metropolitan of Tyre, came to Marcian's notice. The emperor told the bishops that this must be solved 'not by sacred [imperial] letters, nor by pragmatic sanctions, but according to what has been ordained by the Fathers'.[3] On more purely religious issues, Marcian regarded it as his duty to 'confirm the faith' by his presence at the council,[4] and subsequently approving its decisions by edict. It was only a short step for the Emperor Zeno, acting on the advice of his patriarch, to set out what he considered should be the faith of Christendom in the terms of the *Henotikon* of 482.

This degree of involvement with the 'right religion' of the empire required considerable control over episcopal appointments and dismissals. Here, too, Marcian and his successors followed the precedents established

where neither emperor nor *comes* can come, where no judge can threaten... In no other way can the church's faith be upheld as the Fathers defined it at the Nicaean Council': *Historia Arianorum* 36 (*PG* 25, col. 736). Compare *ibid.* 11, 15 and 76 (cols. 705, 709 and 785).

[1] Leo, *Ep.* 77 (*PL* 54, col. 907A): 'te auctore decernant [omnes episcopi]'.

[2] I have accepted F. Dvornik's view, *Early Christian and Byzantine Political Philosophy*, Dumbarton Oaks Studies 9 (Washington, 1966), II, 779. For Marcian's presidency 'lending splendour to the proceedings' see the letter of the bishops to Leo after the conclusion of the sessions: Leo, *Ep.* 98. 3 (*PL* 54, col. 961B).

[3] At the fourth session of the council on 20 October (see Mansi, *Collectio* VII, col. 89 and *ACO* 2. 1. 3, p. 105). Eustathius, a strong supporter of Dioscorus and, later, of Timothy the Cat, had been raised to metropolitan status in 448 (*Cod. Just.* II. 22. 1) and given six suffragan bishops. What were to be his rights vis-à-vis the metropolitan of Tyre whose suffragan he was, especially when Tyre ranked as second see (*protothronos*) to Antioch? (See H. G. Beck, *Kirche und theologische Literatur im byzantinischen Reich*, Handbuch der Altertumswissenschaft 12. 11. 2 (Munich, 1959), p. 191.) In fact, Eustathius was allowed to keep his title but not his suffragans. For this and a collection of other administrative decisions made by Marcian and the senators and officials at Chalcedon, see Coleman-Norton, *Roman State and Christian Church*, II, 778–90.

[4] Mansi, *Collectio* VII, col. 129: 'For to confirm the faith, not to wield any power, by the example of Constantine a religious emperor, we have wished to be present at this synod lest the people be divided any longer by wicked persuasions' (tr. Coleman-Norton, *Roman State and Christian Church*, II, 793).

by the emperors before them. Jovian had ordered the return of Athanasius to his bishopric of Alexandria in 363,[1] Gregory of Nazianzus resigned his see of Constantinople, accepting that the emperor could shift and choose his bishops as he would,[2] John Chrysostom, Nestorius and Flavian were all patriarchs of New Rome who had trod the weary road to lifelong exile and in Anastasius' reign Euphemius and Macedonius followed them. In Alexandria, Athanasius had been exiled no less than five times in his career before Dioscorus was dismissed to Gangra. In 511/12 Sabas, the most illustrious of the Palestinian monks, was warned by the Emperor Anastasius that if the Patriarch Elias of Jerusalem 'remained a protagonist of Chalcedon and the whole heresy of Nestorius',[3] he would have to resign. A few years later the threat was carried out. Only the incumbents of 'Peter's see', who lived beyond the immediate control of the emperor at Constantinople, were personally inviolate, but even this privilege was to be lost with Justinian's reconquest of Italy, when that emperor would treat Vigilius in precisely the same manner as Constantius II had treated Pope Liberius two centuries before.

In asserting these prerogatives the emperors in the fifth century were drawing on traditional beliefs regarding the nature of their office. Two sets of assumptions underlay their claims to religious as well as to secular supremacy. First, they were the heirs to the Roman imperial tradition reinforced in the east by ideas of divine rulership that had surrounded the Hellenistic kings. It is sufficient to remember how in the age of Augustus poets and writers had proclaimed that the Roman Empire was co-terminous with the inhabited world, and the emperor was its ruler. Jupiter's promise to the Romans, 'His ego nec metas rerum nec tempora pono; Imperium sine fine dedi' (*Aen.* 1. 278), is echoed in Livy bk. 1 as Romulus predicts '... caelestes ita velle, ut mea Roma caput orbis terrarum sit'. In the first three centuries A.D. the emperor had been to his subjects 'restitutor' and 'reparator orbis', the intermediary between the immortal gods of Rome and mankind.[4] In the east he had been *basileus* since Augustus' day, worshipped as the one who imitated the gods and provided peace and safety to all. Gradually the Hellenistic view of the monarchy, emphasising its semi-

[1] *Petitiones Arianorum ad Jovianum imperatorem* (*PG* 26, cols. 820–4).
[2] *Poemata de seipso*, lines 1871ff. (*PG* 37, cols. 1160–1).
[3] Cyril of Scythopolis, *Vita Sabae* (ed. Schwartz), p. 144.
[4] See J. Vogt, 'Orbis Romanus' in *Orbis, ausgewählte Schriften zur Geschichte des Altertums* (Freiburg, 1960), pp. 161ff.

divine character, was accepted by the emperors, until from Diocletian onwards their person, office and everything that touched it became 'sacred'. The same word 'sacer' was used to describe orthodox dogma or imperial legislation. On the other hand, the Christian emperor was also heir to the Alexandrian Jewish and Greek Christian traditions that elevated monarchy as the godly principle of government, and accepted the emperor as the reflection of the divine reason that controlled the universe.[1] Both principles led to the acknowledgement of the supreme powers of the emperor as just ruler and saviour of all men,[2] and it was in virtue of this acknowledgement that the emperors were to determine the course of ecclesiastical affairs.

The full development of the imperial position was largely the legacy of Constantine who successfully wove both strands of monarchical theory into an almost unchallengeable ideal of Christian absolutism. That emperor had the genius first to recognise the significance of the religious revolution brought about by the spread of Christianity especially in the east, and then to guide it to suit his ambitions. His claim to be 'bishop', and more specifically to be 'bishop of those outside the church', entailed use of authoritative powers both in his self-appointed role of universal proclaimer of God's word and also in curbing what he regarded as the unreasonable attitudes of individual clerics.[3] Even before he had made up his mind that the 'summus deus' was to be worshipped only through the Christian church, he had told the authorities in Roman Africa at grips with the intractable dispute between Caecilian and Donatus, that he himself would come to Africa and there 'demonstrate with unequivocal verdict as much to Caecilian as to those who seem to be against him just how the supreme deity ought to be worshipped', and this task he considered to be part and parcel of his duties

---

[1] See E. Peterson's essay, *Der Monotheismus als politisches Problem* (Leipzig, 1935), pp. 31ff., and Dvornik, *Early Christian and Byzantine Political Philosophy*, II, chs. 11–12.

[2] There is little to choose between the pagan philosopher Themistius' assertion that the emperor should be like God in all respects, a heavenly being dispensing *philanthropia* – *Oratio* VI (ed. W. Dindorf, Leipzig, 1832), addressed to Valentinian when he took Valens as co-ruler, March 364 – and the views expressed in Eusebius' *Tricennial Oration*; cf. C. H. Williams, 'Christology and church–state relations', *Church History* 20, 1951, pp. 17–23.

[3] Eusebius, *Vita Constantini* (ed. Heikel) IV. 24, and Socrates, *HE* I. 9. See W. Seston, 'Constantine as a "bishop"', *JRS* 37, 1947, pp. 127–31, and S. L. Greenslade, *Church and State from Constantine to Theodosius* (London, 1954), ch. 1.

as Roman emperor.¹ After Nicaea, when ecclesiastical affairs occupied an increasing proportion of his time, he intervened in the internal affairs of Alexandria by informing Athanasius in *circa* 331 that if he did not accept Arius and his supporters back into communion, 'I will immediately send someone to depose you at my command and remove you from your place'.² Four years later Athanasius was packed off into exile at Trier. In all this he was paving the way for the policies of Theodosius II and Marcian.

Christendom and the emperor's authority were regarded as coterminous.³ Even beyond the political frontiers of the empire Christians in Gothia and Persia were often looked upon as the emperor's men and were sometimes treated accordingly.⁴ The emperors themselves had no compunction in trying to enforce their views on independent Christian rulers. 'We order that the same doctrine be observed equally by Romans and yourselves' Constantius II had written to the princes of Axum (Ethiopia) ordering them to reject the offices of Frumentius, even though he had been largely responsible for their conversion, because he was a supporter of 'the most wicked Athanasius'.⁵ There was to be no argument, let alone disobedience. In their day Justin and Justinian both attempted to enforce Chalcedonian orthodoxy on Christian rulers outside their frontiers with the same sense of divine mission.⁶

In the eastern provinces this view of the emperor's office was accepted by bishops and laity alike. In theory a bishop, as prince of the church, might possess greater dignity than the emperor.⁷ In practice, Athanasius'

---

¹ Letter to Domitius Celsus, cited in Optatus of Milevis, *De schismate Donatistarum* (ed. Ziwsa), App. VII, p. 212. Compare Marcian's view of his responsibilities in his address to the sixth session of Chalcedon, Mansi, *Collectio* VII, col. 132 = *ACO* 2. III. 2, p. 150.

² Athanasius cites the letter in *Apol. contra Arianos* 59 (*PG* 25, col. 357).

³ Cf. Eusebius, *Tricennial Oration* (ed. Heikel), ch. I. 3, and *Demonstratio evangelica* III. 2. 22 and 37 (ed. Heikel, *GCS* 23, Eusebius Werke 6, Leipzig 1913). For Justinian's feeling that the welfare of Christians in Vandal North Africa was his responsibility, see Procopius, *Wars* III. 10. 19.

⁴ For Gothia see the account of the reason for the persecution of Christians given by Epiphanius, *Panarion* LXX. 15. 4 (ed. Holl, p. 248), καὶ πρὸς ζῆλον τῶν Ῥωμαίων, διὰ τὸ τοὺς βασιλεῖς τῶν Ῥωμαίων εἶναι Χριστιανούς. For Persia, note Constantine's alleged letter to Sapor recorded in Eusebius, *Vita Constantini* IV. 8 and 9.

⁵ Athanasius, *Apol. ad Constantium* 31 (*PG* 25, col. 636).

⁶ See below, ch. 8.

⁷ So, John Chrysostom, *In Oziam, vidi Dominum*, Homil. IV. 5, *PG* 56, col. 126: 'Bodies are committed to the care of the king, souls to the care of the priest.' Spiritual

The emperor and his church

challenge to the claims of Constantius II to arbitrate in the affairs of the church was not repeated.[1] At the time of Chalcedon, none of the opposition, not even Dioscorus, cited his defiance to that emperor as a precedent. The examples of Pope Liberius' opposition to Constantius II in the 350s or Ambrose's excommunication of Theodosius I after the massacre of Thessalonica were remembered by church historians and admired as acts of personal bravery,[2] but they were not regarded as providing examples to be followed. Almost to a man, the eastern episcopate accepted the implications of the Eusebian ideal of the godly monarchy. One king on earth corresponded to one king in heaven, one royal law and Word.[3] Just as the divine Word bound together the different parts of the world in concord and universal harmony,[4] so his servant the emperor governed the peoples of mankind in the same sublime interest. Constantine 'the friend of God'[5] represented the Word on earth, and 'in imitation of his superior directs the helms of all the affairs of this world'.[6] Two generations later Synesius (*circa* 400) spoke of the wish of the ideal king that everything here should

weapons had greater power than temporal and for that reason, 'the king bends his head to the hand of the priest and in the Old Testament kings were always anointed by priests'.

[1] It is to be remembered that Athanasius' opposition to Constantius was due to the latter's championing the Arian cause and not to any disparagement of the imperial majesty. In his *Apol. ad Constantium* 43 he had told Constantius that if Truth were the partner of his throne, she would be his defence as a Christian emperor and would make his rule secure.

[2] Theodoret, *HE* v. 18. It is interesting that the fullest and most dramatic account of Theodosius' humiliation comes from the pen of this Antiochene theologian. In historiography as well as in doctrine there is some evidence for sympathy between western and Antiochene views.

[3] Eusebius, *Tricennial Oration*, ch. III (ed. Heikel, p. 201, lines 19ff.).

[4] Basil, *Hexaemeron* II. 2 (*PG* 29, col. 33A).

[5] Eusebius, *HE* x. 9. 2, and *Tricennial Oration*, ch. II (ed. Heikel, p. 199).

[6] Eusebius, *Tricennial Oration*, ch. I. 6 (ed. Heikel, p. 199). For the Eusebian political theory, see Peterson, *Der Monotheismus als politisches Problem*, pp. 71ff., and H. Eger, 'Kaiser und Kirche in der Geschichtestheologie Eusebs von Käsarea', *ZNTW* 38, 1939, pp. 97–115; also E. Barker, *Alexander to Constantine* (Oxford, 1956), pp. 472–9, and N. H. Baynes, 'Eusebius and the Christian empire', *Byzantine Studies, and Other Essays*, pp. 168–72. For the symbolism of Constantine's burial in the Church of the Apostles surrounded by the twelve niches representing the twelve apostles (Eusebius, *Vita Constantini* IV. 60), see A. Kaniuth, *Die Beisetzung Konstantins des Grossen, Untersuchungen zur religiösen Haltung des Kaisers* (Breslau, 1941) and Dvornik, *Early Christian and Byzantine Political Philosophy*, II, 757ff.

be in imitation of the wish of the world above.¹ The same viewpoint was echoed by the Constantinopolitan lawyer Sozomen, *circa* 440,² and fifteen years later by the Patriarch Anatolius writing to Pope Leo regarding Marcian. The emperor was 'the most religious and Christian prince who governs the entire range of human affairs by the virtue of his most wise providence and whom the philosophy of divine virtues glorifies'.³ He was 'lord of the earth and sea and of the human race',⁴ Bishop Eunomius of Nicodemia had affirmed in a petition presented at Chalcedon. A less exalted bishop of the time, Agapetus of Rhodes, wrote in 457 to the Emperor Leo I on the occasion of the 'plebiscite' concerning Timothy the Cat that 'he existed truly priest and by nature emperor'.⁵ To the Syrian bishops of this period he was Peter, the rock on whom the church was founded. His empire 'came from God', the bishops in the metropolitan diocese of Myra added,⁶ and there was no difference of opinion whether the bishops came from Illyricum, Thrace, Galatia or Syria, or whether they were pro- or anti-Chalcedon, that this indeed was so. The eastern provinces of the empire were united in their views, and it was the papacy who was the odd man out. Nor did the situation change with time. Two centuries later, in the crisis of the Persian war during Heraclius' reign (610–41), the emperor's mystique remained just as powerful. 'How fair a thing is monarchy with God for guide', exclaimed the deacon George of Pisidia, and in so doing he reflected the spirit of the whole Byzantine world.⁷

---

¹ *De regno* 3 (ed. FitzGerald, pp. 113–14).

² Sozomen, *HE*, Prologue 9 (ed. Bidez and Hansen, p. 3). Theodosius II 'imitated his Protector the Heavenly Emperor', and hence his reign prospered.

³ Included in Pope Leo's Letters, as *Ep.* 132. 1: 'Quia tamen piissimus et Christianissimus princeps, qui consultissimae suae providentiae bono tam res universas regit humanas, quam philosophia divinarum pollet ubique virtutum...'

⁴ Mansi, *Collectio* VII, col. 301 = *ACO* 2. 1. 3, p. 58.

⁵ Agapetus of Rhodes cited in *Codex encyclius* (*ACO* 2. v, p. 64, no. 33): 'vere namque sacerdos et natura imperator existis'. Similarly, Socrates, *HE* VII. 22, where Theodosius is compared to Moses as 'a true priest of God'. Theodoret, *HE* v. 18, adds the detail that at Constantinople the emperor would stand within the altar enclosure with the priests during the liturgy. In the west this was evidently not the custom.

⁶ *ACO* II. 5, p. 61, 'qui imperium a deo sortitus es', and compare *ibid.* p. 70, where the Emperor Leo is represented as reflecting 'robur et fundamentum immobilem Christi petram' (not the Pope!).

⁷ Georgius Pisida, *De exped. Pers.* II, line 24 (ed. A. Pertusi). See P. J. Alexander, 'The strength of empire and capital as seen through Byzantine eyes', *Speculum* 37, 1962, pp. 339–57.

Significantly, perhaps, it was in Alexandria that this view was challenged, but then only privately by Athanasius in his anger and desperation against Constantius.[1] Even so, the church remained a divine society and 'not of this world'. If the emperor could not guarantee the 'accuracy of doctrine', to cite the phrase often used by Severus of Antioch and his colleagues, consonant with that position, then his interpretation of orthodoxy could be rejected. In that event a conflict between the sacramental community of true believers and the emperor was possible. Monophysitism was to preserve the spark of independence, and in the mid sixth century John Philoponos argued in the Monophysite interest that the king was not the image of God,[2] and that government rested on the free will of the governed. If there was to be a movement towards religious and political independence in the east, Alexandria was the most likely starting point.

The aura, however, that surrounded the divinely appointed emperor was all-pervading, and it accounts for much that appears pusillanimous in the conduct of the eastern clergy in the period following Chalcedon. The successive changes of imperial policy for or against Chalcedon illustrated by Leo I's 'plebiscite' in 457, the encyclical of Basiliscus in 475, the *Henotikon* of Zeno in 482, and the restoration of Chalcedon to full canonical status by Justin in 519, all appear to have won the overwhelming support of the bishops, often the same bishops approving both Chalcedonian and anti-Chalcedonian formulae within a few years. An opponent of Chalcedon such as John of Tella (in north-east Syria) had the greatest difficulty in convincing his clergy and people who were otherwise favourable to his views that it was right to resist Justin's edict. 'If the edict comes that we accept the council we shall first try to persuade our bishop to accept', they said, 'since this is nothing, for no one can resist the king's decree.'[3] For many Christians indeed, the difference between 'in two natures' and 'out of two natures' could be reduced, as the Syrian Chalcedonian Evagrius pointed out,[4] to microscopic proportions; so long as the emperors' dogmatic requirements remained within the presuppositions of Cyril's theology and their own unitive concept of the imperial office they could count on general support.

[1] *Historia Arianorum*, PG 25. In ch. 3 (col. 693) he tells his readers to read and return the copy immediately to himself without making another copy.
[2] *De opificio mundi* VI. 16 (ed. W. Reichhart, Leipzig, 1897). See Dvornik, *Early Christian and Byzantine Political Philosophy*, II, 711.
[3] Elias, *Vita Johannis episcopi Tellae* (ed. Brooks), p. 36.
[4] *HE* II. 5.

The rise of the Monophysite movement

If an openly 'Nestorian' definition of faith had ever been proposed, it is more doubtful whether the loyalty of the episcopate to the throne would have survived. Christ 'divided' could also have introduced schism into the concept of imperial monarchy.[1]

For the ordinary provincial the sacred and hieratic character of the imperial office and its holder was attested not only by the example of bishops and the definition of jurists, but more directly by the artistic conventions of the day. Since the time of Constantius II ruler followed ruler on the coinage he used in his daily life, with the same stark hieratic features reminiscent of the fixed and awesome stare of the Pantocrator looking down from the mosaics of the basilicas where he worshipped. In Byzantine pictures and mosaics the majesty and authority of the monarch were demonstrated to the people by his association with the kingly attributes of Christ from whom he received his divine power and indeed his insignia in the act of worship.[2] He was both 'priest and king' moved by paternal and priestly interest for his subjects, as the Egyptian patrician Strategius told the Syrian bishops who had come to the capital in 532 for a colloquy aimed at ending the religious disputes.[3] He spoke for the popular mind of the day.

There was thus no two-swords theory of church–state relations in the east, no episcopal alternative to royal power. Division of authority would have been regarded as 'anarchy'.[4] In the fifth and sixth centuries, no eastern bishop dared excommunicate an emperor even in the heat of controversy. The Monophysite leaders in exile gave thanks for Justinian's survival of the Nika revolt in 532.[5] Synods opened with prayers for the

---

[1] An interesting sidelight on this attitude comes from the anti-Chalcedonian Bishop James of Serug (d. 521) concerning Justin. James asks why, if Justin failed to believe that the crucified one was God, could he still wear a cross on top of his crown. If it were simply the cross of a man, as those pretend who wish to deceive the emperor and outrage God, the emperor would never have wished to wear the cross of a man on top of his crown. *Chronicle of Edessa* cited from A. A. Vasiliev, *Justin the First* (Harvard, 1950), p. 234. The symbol of crown and cross only made sense in the framework of Cyrilline theology. Earlier Athanasius himself (*De incarnatione* 24. 4) had argued that the Word-flesh Christology was in itself a guarantee against schism.

[2] See A. Grabar, 'L'Empereur dans l'art byzantin', *Publications de la Faculté des Lettres à l'Université de Strasbourg*, fasc. 75 (Paris, 1936), pp. 95–122 at pp. 95–7 and 98ff.

[3] Mansi, *Collectio* VIII, col. 818 (*ACO* 4. II, p. 170); 'paterna et sacerdotali confunctione'.

[4] See Georgius Pisida, *De exped. Pers.* II, lines 25–8, and compare with Eusebius, *Tricennial Oration*, ch. III. 6 (ed. Heikel, p. 201).

[5] See below, p. 264.

emperor and his realm. The patriarch of the capital blessed the troops as they departed to war.[1] In times of crisis, such as in 387 in the affair of the imperial statues at Antioch, a monk might remind the emperor that he himself was mortal and should forbear from slaying other mortals made like him in the image of God,[2] but all recognised that in the last resort the emperor had 'no peer in the world'[3] and must be obeyed by all, whether priests, monks or laymen. Theodosius I had every right to take vengeance on those who had insulted his majesty. This did not mean that the provincials possessed no scope for the expression of discontent, but it was always set in Biblical and theological rather than political contexts. Theologically unpopular rulers were bitterly abused – Marcian was 'the new Assyrian',[4] Pulcheria a 'false virgin'[5] to the anti-Chalcedonians; Anastasius was a 'Manichaean'[6] to his opponents; but there was no thought of rebellion or secession. Indeed, the Monophysites were to blame Marcian precisely because he broke the unity of the empire, by what amounted to a usurpation of the throne and by Chalcedon.[7] Hopes rested on the reprobate's removal by a more favourable ruler, and meantime 'persecution' was to be endured with that same mixture of resignation and expectancy as under Decius and Diocletian.[8] All disorder, especially political disorder, was regarded as the work of 'the devil, the enemy of truth who

---

[1] Procopius, *Wars* III. 12. 2 (Patriarch Epiphanius on the eve of the Vandal expedition of 533).   [2] Theodoret, *HE* v. 20.

[3] John Chrysostom, *De statuis*, Homil. II. 2. (*PG* 49, col. 36); compare *Homil.* XXIV. The tumult on 4 March 387 was no more than a riot lasting about three hours in protest against over-taxation, but everyone realised that the direst punishment could result (Zosimus, *Historia nova* IV. 41, Theodoret, *HE* v. 20, Sozomen, *HE* VII. 23 and Libanius, *Orat.* XIX, XX and XXII). Theodoret tells the story of the intervention of Macedonius. See also Homes Dudden, *The Life and Times of St. Ambrose* (Oxford, 1935), pp. 356–70, and R. Browning, 'The riot of A.D. 387 in Antioch', *JRS* 42, 1952, pp. 13–20. The attitude of Flavian, bishop of Antioch, described by Sozomen as having psalms of supplication and contrition sung to appease Theodosius, and Ambrose of Milan's forthright excommunication of the latter after the massacre of Thessalonica three years later, illustrates the difference of outlook among the eastern and western episcopates towards the emperor at this time. Easterners admired Ambrose's attitude but did not imitate it (Theodoret, *HE* v. 18).

[4] John Rufus in the *Plerophoria* cited by Michael the Syrian, *Chron.* VIII. 11 (ed. Chabot, II, 69–88) and VIII. 14 (II, 122).

[5] *Ibid.* VIII. 12 (II, 89).   [6] Evagrius, *HE* III. 32.

[7] Michael the Syrian, *Chron.* VIII. 14 (ed. Chabot, II, 122).

[8] For instance, under Basiliscus, *Vita Danielis*, ch. 73 (ed. Peeters, pp. 121–219; Eng. tr. by Dawes and Baynes, *Three Byzantine Saints*, pp. 1–84).

envied the prosperous state of Christianity'.[1] Bishops, as the Monophysite Severus of Antioch told the bishop of Tripolis, had the duty 'of cutting short and restraining unregulated movements of the mob, if these should indeed occur, and setting themselves to maintain all good order in the cities and watch over the peaceful manners and customs of those fed by them'.[2] For all the rancour of the controversy, the anti-Chalcedonians were far from being in intention political rebels. The Monophysite kingdoms developed in independence of the Byzantine monarchy largely despite themselves.

There could be no greater mistake than to try to see the Monophysites as Donatists in Egyptian or Syrian form.[3] Chalcedon was followed by schism of hearts and minds throughout the whole of the east, but no 'altar was set up against altar' as it had been in Africa in 312.[4] No formal break occurred until a very considerable number of Christians throughout the east came to feel that it was intolerable to receive sacraments at the hands of one who was not strictly orthodox, especially when in some areas in the east these were only received once a year.[5] It was not until the time of Severus of Antioch, and due largely to his 'strictness' (ἀκρίβεια) in relation to the reception of sacraments from Chalcedonians that permanent division between supporters and opponents of Chalcedon was rendered inevitable, and even then the organisation of a rival Monophysite hierarchy took a very long while. For the generation following the council this step was not even considered, a fact which must influence any assessment of the nationalist or particularist and indeed any non-theological element in Monophysitism. It must also influence discussion on why religious controversy, though

---

[1] Cf. Eusebius, *HE* IV. 7. 1 and Evagrius, *HE* II. 5. For riots in Edessa see above, p. 37. For demons causing the Nika riot, see John Malalas, *Chron.* XVIII. 213 (ed. Dindorf, p. 473), and Basiliscus' usurpation, *Vita Danielis*, ch. 68.

[2] Severus of Antioch, *Select Letters* I. 9 (ed. Brooks, p. 46). For bishops being responsible for building a fort in the reign of Anastasius, see R. Mouterde and A. Poidebard, *Le Limes de Chalcis* (Paris, 1945), pp. 69–70 (Bouz el Hanzir).

[3] For the 'nationalist' thesis applied to the east, see E. L. Woodward, *Christianity and Nationalism in the Later Roman Empire* (London, 1916). Against Woodward's thesis see A. H. M. Jones, 'Were ancient heresies national or social movements in disguise?', *JTS*, n.s. 11, 1959, pp. 280–98 – a brilliant but perhaps too negative survey.

[4] For the phrase see Augustine, *Contra Cresconium* II. 1. 2 (*PL* 43, col. 468), and Optatus of Milevis, *De schismate Donatistarum* I. 19 (ed. Ziwsa, p. 21).

[5] John Rufus, *Plerophoria* 38 (Eucharist, i.e. bread, sent yearly by Peter of Iberia to Anianus, the advocate, in Cilicia), ed. Nau, p. 89. See also, for laymen's concern that Communion should be received at orthodox hands, *ibid.* 78, pp. 134–5.

intensely bitter, did not play the same destructive role in the history of the eastern provinces of the empire as it did in the west. The historian is confronted with the fact that, despite the recurrent crises between the patriarchs of Alexandria and Constantinople, despite barbarian invasion and Persian threat, and despite social and economic pressures every whit as serious as those in Roman Africa and Gaul, the Byzantine Empire did not follow its western counterpart into disintegration and collapse. Until the Persian wars and Arab invasions of the first half of the seventh century, the Monophysite movement developed against a background of relative internal peace, with warfare mainly confined to the frontiers. Gaiseric far away in Africa was cast in the role of chief disturber of the emperor's and his subjects' sleep.[1]

Part of the explanation is purely military. Constantinople was massively protected by the Walls of Anthemius even in the first decade of the fifth century. Rome was less defensible; the Germanic barbarians on the Rhine and upper Danube were better organised and their movements more skilfully co-ordinated than those of the Huns who threatened the eastern provinces. For long periods in the fifth century the Roman and Persian empires were at peace, while the core of the eastern world, the provinces of Asia Minor, lay beyond the grasp of invaders. The confidence of John Chrysostom, bishop of the capital (398–404), in the peaceful future of the empire[2] and the serenity and security of the Greek ecclesiastical writers in the 430s may be compared with the pessimism of their western contemporaries. To some extent it reflects the military situation of the two parts of the empire. There was, too, a significant difference in the upper echelons of society in east and west. In the west, the Constantinian religious revolution had been balanced by the emperor's conservatism in social outlook. His successors found themselves checked by the power of a traditional aristocracy that progressively entrenched itself in high offices of state allied to vast landed properties. Constantinople also had its senate and senatorial

[1] For Leo I's fear that Gaiseric would move against Alexandria, see *Vita Danielis*, ch. 56, and for the impression he left on the minds of Syrian provincials, see *The Oracle of Baalbek* (ed. P. J. Alexander, Dumbarton Oaks Studies 10, Washington, 1967), line 129.

[2] For instance, in his *Homil. in Isaiam* II. 5 (*PG* 56, col. 33): 'Now those vast spaces which the sun shines upon from the Tigris to the isles of Britain, the whole of Africa, Egypt and Palestine, and whatever is subject to the Roman Empire live in peace. You know the whole world is untroubled and of wars we hear only rumours' – an astounding statement in view of the situation in Italy at that time. For the reactions in the east Roman world to the progressive collapse of the western empire in the fifth century, see W. E. Kaegi, *Byzantium and the Decline of Rome* (Princeton, 1968).

spokesmen such as the historian Zosimus, and the traditional local aristocracies retained their authority in their provinces of origin, but they made their influence less felt in public administration. The emperors' trusted officials were often men of comparatively humble birth.[1] The administration of the eastern provinces did not depend so much on the will of a small class to govern, a will that failed in the west in the crucial years of the first decade of the fifth century.

Determination to survive, however, was all-important, and when one looks at the western and eastern writers respectively one notes a significant contrast in their attitudes. In the west Augustine accepted the downfall of the empire as in the order of things. It was mere pride that aimed at the secular unification of the world, destined to pass and perish, under one dominion.[2] Lust of domination had brought the Romans their empire, and it had no special call on the consideration of God.[3] It was destined to perish as other terrestial empires had done before it. The fall of Rome in 410 was only a tragedy in terms of pagan thought. His contemporary, Synesius, later to be bishop of Ptolemaïs in Cyrenaica, had other ideas. Not only did he take an active part in the defence of his provinces against Berber invaders,[4] but when on embassy in Constantinople he addressed the emperor Arcadius reminding him of the splendid example of frugality and personal prowess shown by the pagan Roman emperors,[5] and upbraiding him for

[1] For instance, Philippus, praetorian prefect in the east, was son of a sausage-maker: Libanius, *Orat.* XLII. 24–5 (ed. Foerster). In the west one might quote the example of Vulcacius Rufus who was praetorian prefect under both Constantius and the rebel Magnentius as a member of a noble house who could hold his position regardless of war and revolution around him. See Peter Patricius, frag. 16. I owe these insights to a pupil, Mr M. Arnheim of St John's College, Cambridge. For the importance of Rome and its aristocracy in the fourth century, see A. Alföldi, *Constantine and Pagan Rome*, tr. H. Mattingly (2nd ed., Oxford, 1969).

[2] Thus *De vera religione* XLV. 84, representing Augustine, even in his 'liberal' phase, 387–96: 'Habet ergo et superbia quendam appetitum unitatis et omnipotentiae sed in rerum naturalium principatu, quae omnia transeunt sic ut umbra' (*PL* 34, col. 160). Prudentius, reflecting the optimism of the Theodosian age, was almost alone among western Christian writers in believing in the providential future of the empire.

[3] *De civitate Dei* III. 14, V. 12 and 19. See A. A. T. Ehrhardt, *Politische Metaphysik von Solon bis Augustin* (Tübingen, 1959–69), III, ch. 2.

[4] *De regno* 10–15 (*PG* 66, col. 1076).

[5] For his sense of civic responsibility, see *Epp.* 104, 108 and 125 (*PG* 66, cols. 1477–81, 1489–92 and 1504–5), and see C. H. Coster, 'Synesius, a *curialis* of the time of the Emperor Arcadius', *Byzantion* 15, 1940–1, pp. 17–37.

recruiting Goths rather than Romans in the army.¹ In the west, however, at this very moment Maximus of Turin mocked the belated efforts of the chief citizens (the *primores*) to put the city in a state of defence against the Goths. It would be better if they put their souls in readiness for the approaching Last Day.² Thirty years later, Salvian of Marseille (*circa* 439) demonstrated the extent to which provincials had lost confidence in themselves and the institutions of the empire. The rough justice of the barbarian was preferred to the extortion of the emperor's tax collectors, and many of those who did not join the barbarians went over to the even more destructive and revolutionary Bagaudae.³ In Africa, Possidius' *Life of Augustine* tells the same story of rapid collapse of the will to resist before the onset of the Vandals.⁴ For all their praise of Rome the western aristocracy organised no resistance movement against the barbarians.⁵

When one turns to the story of the eastern provinces, one is struck by the existence of an articulate and active popular opinion in favour of the Christian empire which often atoned for the lack of military competence among the emperor's generals.⁶ Acts of treachery there were, such as that which led to the capture of Castra Martis in Moesia by the Huns in 408,⁷ and more seriously to the loss of Horrea Margus, also to the Huns, in 442.⁸ Some percipient individuals like the Greek merchant from Viminacium whom Priscus encountered in the Hunnish camp in 449 had imitated the bishop of

---

¹ *Ibid.* 15, col. 1093.
² Maximus of Turin, *Sermo* 85. 2 (ed. A. Mutzenbacher, p. 348).
³ Salvian, *De gubernatione Dei* (ed. Sanford) v. 5 and following: 'Roman citizenship had been brought to nought through Roman extortion', and as a result 'men are passing over everywhere now to the Goths, now to the Bagaudae, or whatever other barbarians that have established their power anywhere and they do not repent of their expatriation, for they would rather live as free men...'
⁴ Possidius, *Vita Augustini* 28 (*PL* 32, col. 58). See H. J. Diesner, 'Die Lage der nordafrikanischen Bevölkerung im Zeitpunkt der Vandaleninvasion', *Historia* 11, 1962, pp. 97–111.
⁵ See the interesting study of eastern and western attitudes to barbarian invasion by F. Millar, 'P. Herennius Dexippus; the Greek world and the third century invasions', *JRS* 59, 1969, pp. 12–29.
⁶ For their wretched showing against the Huns in 447, see Theophanes, *Chron.* A.M. 5942 (ed. Classen, I, 158–9).
⁷ Sozomen, *HE* IX. 5. 2.
⁸ Priscus, frag. 1 (ed. I. Bekker and B. G. Niebuhr, Bonn, 1829, p. 140). He acted, however, not out of hostility to the empire but to save his own skin after being accused by the Huns of robbing their royal treasures.

The rise of the Monophysite movement

Margus, but these seem to have been exceptions worthy of remark,[1] and most accounts speak of a readiness of the people of the east Roman provinces to defend themselves against the barbarian invaders. In many parts of Illyricum the local inhabitants imitated the people of Constantinople after the disaster of Adrianople in 378[2] and took up arms against the Huns to harass the raiders in the campaigns of 447–9.[3] Thracian provincials had similarly harassed the retreating army of Gainas the Goth forty-five years before.[4] On Rome's eastern frontier the clergy were numbered among the most active defenders of the empire. Bishop James' encouragement of his people's defence of Nisibis against the Persians in 349 is well known, and the province of Mesopotamia where Monophysitism was to be strong provides examples of passionate loyalty to the empire in time of crisis in the fourth and fifth centuries. At Nisibis itself Ephraim Syrus and Ammianus Marcellinus both remark poignantly on the despair of the citizens at the prospect of their surrender to the Persians by the Emperor Jovian in 363. To the last they hoped that the city would be retained within the Roman frontiers, and they begged to be allowed to fight the Persians with their own resources.[5] Jovian was hissed in the hippodrome at Antioch on news of the surrender. One notes in contrast the existence of what may be termed movements of revolutionary separatism among the cities of Britain and in Armorica in Honorius' reign.[6] In the western empire the tendency was for separatism, heresy and schism to be associated.

One of the most interesting examples of loyalty to Byzantium comes

[1] Priscus, frag. 3 (pp. 190–5). See Thompson, *Attila and the Huns*, p. 184. Priscus' conversation with this renegade shows that the evils of lack of proper protection and extortion which had eroded the loyalty of the Gauls were rampant in the Danubian provinces also.

[2] Socrates, *HE* IV. 38.

[3] Priscus, frag. 3, on the valiant conduct of the people of Azemon in face of the Huns (pp. 143–4). In contrast to conditions in the west morale seems actually to have improved in the east during the fifth century. There had been times when the provincials there were also prepared to welcome the barbarians (Zosimus, *Historia nova* IV. 32) but this feeling did not come to prevail.

[4] Zosimus, *Historia nova* V. 19.

[5] Ammianus Marcellinus, *Res gestae* XXV. 8. 13–15 and 9. 2–4; cf. Ephraim Syrus, *Carmen* XXI (ed. E. Beck, Louvain, 1961). See R. Turcan, 'L'Abandon de Nisibe et l'opinion publique', *Mélanges André Piganiol*, II (Paris, 1966), pp. 875–90.

[6] Zosimus, *Historia nova* VI. 4–6 (Britain), Rutilius Namatianus, *De reditu suo*, lines 213–16 (Armorica), and *Chron. min.* I, 660. See Bury, *History of the Later Roman Empire*, I, 250.

from the strongly pro-Monophysite city of Edessa on the eve of Ephesus II in 449,[1] an area where two centuries before anti-Roman and pro-Parthian feeling had been strong. Count Flavius Chareas who arrived on 12 April to enquire into the riots against Bishop Ibas earlier in the year was overwhelmed with loyal shouts of jubilation, 'One God, victory to the Romans', 'Long live the Roman Empire', 'Multiply the victories of Theodosius', 'Long live the Patrician Anatolius. May he be preserved to Romania.' Persia and Persians were feared and hated. 'Banish the Persians, Babbai, Barsauma and Balas', the people cried, 'these men are the cause of evil.'[2] This was not an isolated demonstration. Sixty years before, the western pilgrim Etheria had been shown by the bishop of Edessa where the fountains in the city had appeared miraculously when the 'Persian enemy' had cut the city's water supplies during a siege.[3] The presence of imperial officials was to some extent a guarantee of peace among the mixed populations of the descendants of Macedonians, Syrians, Armenians, Jews and Persians that composed the populations of the eastern cities, and the counts did their job well of acting as channels of communication between the people and the emperor.[4] There is little doubt, however, that the latter inspired a loyalty among the populace that was reflected in the adulatory addresses of the episcopate to the emperor and his officials. Whatever forces lay behind Monophysitism must be assessed against the background of a loyalism in the east which was in no way matched in the west.

The remoter causes of the difference of morale in the two halves of the empire reflect not only material factors but the difference in the impact of the Christian religion on the provincials in east and west respectively. The pace of the church's progress had varied from province to province, being noticeably slower in the Celtic lands of western Illyricum, northern Gaul and Britain than elsewhere. It had resulted, however, from two main movements which, though finally universal, operated unevenly between the Greek- and Latin-speaking territories. First, beginning in the latter part of the third century there had been a cumulative rejection of the traditional territorial gods in favour of Christianity by the mass of the provincials. This had been most marked in its initial stages in North Africa, Egypt and parts of Asia Minor and Syria: but the Christianity that the rural

---

[1] *Akten*, ed. Flemming, pp. 15–21.   [2] *Ibid.* p. 27, lines 40–1.
[3] *Peregrinatio Sanctae Silvae* 19. 10 (*CSEL* 39, pp. 62–3).
[4] For the *comes* as the official channel between the emperor and the provincials, see *Cod. Theod.* I. 16. 6 and 7 (A.D. 331).

populations had welcomed with such enthusiasm was of a Biblical type dominated by apocalyptic and prophecy and in which the Lord's commands in favour of martyrdom and rejection of wordly values were accepted literally.[1] Meanwhile, the steady expansion of established Christian communities in the cities of the empire, especially in the east, had continued, until by the end of Constantine's reign the Christians were becoming, except in north-western Europe, an effective majority. The Christianity of these communities was hierarchical and episcopal and for the most part had long outgrown the apocalyptic yearnings of the new native Christians on the land.

The causes of the victory of Christianity as the religion of the mass of the peoples of the Mediterranean remain obscure. The historian would give much to know just why the cult of Saturn in rural North Africa fell out of favour in the last decades of the third century.[2] Certainly, one of the records of the Great Persecution shows that the Christianity of the up-country areas of North Africa had an appeal to the idealism of city-dwellers in Carthage.[3] During the first half of the fourth century in Asia Minor and Egypt the Christian church achieved the reputation of being a charitable organisation with a sense of justice and care for those in need that far outshone that of the traditional gods.[4] Too often temples had become associated with secular matters such as collection of taxes and other government business.[5] In this climate of opinion the message of the New Testament with its uncompromising commands, its promise of salvation to all regardless of social standing, and its dramatic descriptions of the fate of the ungodly, must have exercised a powerful appeal. Whatever the reasons, the Great Persecution of 303–12 failed signally in the countryside as well as in

---

[1] See my analysis of this movement in *Martyrdom and Persecution in the Early Church* (Oxford, 1965), ch. 14, especially pp. 464–7.

[2] For the cult of Saturn, M. Leglay's researches have confirmed my own, namely that the latest dated inscription to the god in Numidia and Mauretania is A.D. 272, and that the lack of dedications that can be dated later than the Tetrarchy is consistent with the worship suffering a decline in popularity *circa* 300. See M. Leglay, *Saturne africain: histoire* (Paris, 1966), final chapter, and my *The Donatist Church; a movement of protest in Roman North Africa* (Oxford, 1952), pp. 83–4.

[3] *Acta Saturnini* 14 (*PL* 8, col. 698): 'et illi [i.e. the Christians of Abitina in the upper valley of the Mejerda] sunt fratres mei qui Dei praecepta custodiunt' – statement by the confessor Victoria from Carthage.

[4] Julian, *Epp.* 22 and 89b (ed. J. Bidez, Paris, 1924, p. 157).

[5] See J. M. Fennelly, 'Roman involvement in the affairs of an Egyptian shrine', *Bull. of John Rylands Library* 50, 1968, pp. 317–35.

the towns, and the Emperor Julian's efforts to resuscitate paganism in the eastern provinces fifty years later were a fiasco. By the middle of the fourth century paganism and much of the society and way of life that went with it had fallen without hope of recovery.

All this had profound effects. In the west especially, one result of the bitter struggle that had characterised the era of persecution was to perpetuate among all classes the traditional suspicion Christians there had felt for the state. The church had never been disloyal in a political sense, but it had tended to regard itself in terms of the Remnant, a gathered community bidding defiance to the pagan world and its authorities, and inspiring its converts with the ideal of martyrdom to be sought at their hands. The victory achieved in 312 did not change its basic attitude. The Devil still worked through the state, only more cautiously than before.[1] In addition, the emphasis on the gathered nature and otherness of the church had resulted in the Christians being profoundly concerned about its institutional character. How were the church and its members to be defined? To break communion with the brethren in the visible church demonstrated a lack of charity which was the gravest of sins. Schism rather than heresy was the main preoccupation of leaders such as Cyprian of Carthage. When, however, the 'rivalry of bishops' did lead to schism it almost inevitably developed on a territorial basis, and this was recognised by contemporaries.[2] The Donatist schism in Africa in 312 was concerned with the theological issue of the nature of the church. It divided those who in the tense period of the Great Persecution were prepared to accept compromise with the world and its institutions and those who were not; and the intransigents held the upper hand down to the time of Augustine. But it was also a regional schism, the outcome of rivalry between the clergy of the province of Numidia and those in the capital, Carthage, and the Donatists of later years were not ashamed to assert that the shade in which it was stated that the Lord had made his flock lie down 'in the south' was Numidia.[3] The

---

[1] For this view see the Donatist pamphlet *Passio Donati* 2, written *circa* 320 (*PL* 8, col. 754A).

[2] For instance, the Donatist writer Tyconius defines schism in terms of localisation as well as being an internal quarrel between people belonging to the same religion: 'In aliquibus provinciis aut in una civitate' (cited from T. Hahn, *Tyconius-Studien*, Leipzig, 1900, pp. 68–9). Augustine's famous 'securus iudicat orbis terrarum' against the Donatists also presupposes a correlation between truth and geographical extent.

[3] Augustine, *Ep.* 93. 8. 24 and *Ad Catholicos epistola* 16. 40 (*PL* 43, cols. 421–2). The gospel had reached Africa last, and 'the last shall be first'! See *ibid.* 15. 37, col 419.

The rise of the Monophysite movement

evidence of Optatus of Milevis (*circa* 365) and Augustine leaves little doubt also as to the rapid association of the Donatist Christianity of the majority with the social and economic grievances of the countryside.[1] This often expressed itself in violence against the landowners and zeal for martyrdom at the hands of the authorities. In times of repression, such as under the Emperor Constans in 347–8, the emperor and his court were denounced in unbridled language as 'anti-Christ', and such terms were never far from the minds of western theologians if the emperor deviated from their concept of orthodoxy.[2] Though details may be open to discussion, the justice of the description of Donatism as a 'movement of protest' with a firm regional basis in rural Numidia can hardly be gainsaid.

In the eastern provinces, on the other hand, less concerned with the nature of the visible church than with the assertion of right belief concerning the Trinity, similar situations took much longer to mature even where the provincials had the strongest reasons to protest against the empire and its rulers. People, whether Armenians, Egyptians, Syrians or Anatolians, felt a certain unity in that they all belonged to 'the race of Christians'. Greek theology had been universalist from the outset and that legacy was not to be cast away except as the result of sheer force of circumstances after the ending of the Acacian schism in 519. The effect of the conversion of masses of the rural populations in Syria and Egypt was, however, to import an element of fanaticism into the consideration of metaphysical problems. Reactions were instinctive yet often shrewd, and in the hands of a demagogue like Dioscorus reflected secular hatreds as well as new-found pieties.

The example of Egypt where rural monasticism was to form the core of

---

[1] Both Optatus of Milevis, *De schismate Donatistarum* III. 4 and Augustine, *Ep.* 105. 2–3, 108. 5. 14, 185. 4. 15 and *Contra litteras Petiliani* II. 83. 184 *inter alia*, make the revolutionary role of the Circumcellions under Donatist leadership clear. The modern literature on the subject is vast. See H. J. Diesner, *Kirche und Staat im spätrömischen Reich* (Berlin, 1963), pp. 53–78 and 78–91, and E. Tengström, *Donatisten und Katholiken; soziale, wirtschaftliche und politische Aspekte einer nordafrikanischen Kirchenspaltung* (Gothenburg, 1964), especially Bibliography, pp. 194–200.

[2] See *Passio Marculi* 1 (*PL* 8, col. 761) and *Passio Maximiani et Isaaci* 1 (*PL* 8, cols. 767–74) for Africa, and Lucifer of Cagliari, *Liber contra Constantium imperatorem* 2 (*PL* 13, col. 962) for Italy in the period 347–61. In general, my article 'The Roman Empire in the eyes of the western schismatics', *Miscellanea Historiae Ecclesiasticae* 1 (Louvain, 1961), pp. 9–22.

the Monophysite movement is instructive. There, as in North Africa, the popular trend towards Christianity began to gather force in the latter part of the third century, and is symbolised by Antony and the beginnings of monasticism. By A.D. 300 Bibles in both Sahidic and Bohairic dialects seem to have been in existence,[1] and during the century Coptic became the usual language of the great majority of the monks.[2] It is significant for the importance of the language as a medium for ideas that it was also used by the Manichaean missionaries who began to proselytise among the Egyptians at this time.[3] Christianity was certainly a liberating force as it freed the Copt from the thraldom of age-old fears and superstitions, and established the self-governing community of the monastery alongside the traditional villages. Even so, identity of language and culture, we are reminded, did not of themselves imply 'any conscious desire to remove the yoke of Rome'.[4] They would contribute to this, however, once emotional antagonisms on religious and other grounds had been aroused.

Egypt had always been to some extent a special case. The Nile gave the country a unity unattained elsewhere in the empire, but such Egyptian national pride as existed in the third and fourth and even later centuries seems to have been expressed by Greek-speaking pagans, perhaps continuing the anti-imperial tradition of the *Acts of the Pagan Martyrs*.[5] Among the Christian converts it seems even as though there had been some upsurge of a latent residue of the Jewish-Christian and prophetic forms of Christianity which are known to have found support in parts of the Nile valley

[1] See G. Steindorff, 'Bemerkungen über die Anfänge der koptischen Sprache und Literatur', in *Coptic Studies in honour of W. E. Crum* (Boston, 1950), p. 211.

[2] See Rufinus, *Historia monachorum* 7 (*PL* 21, col. 420A) for non-Coptic speakers in monasteries being provided with interpreters. Greek was also spoken in the monasteries Rufinus visited.

[3] The Medinet Madi collection of fourth-century Manichaean psalms and other documents was in Coptic. For Manichees proselytising among the lower classes, and their connections with monastic extremism, see particularly *Cod. Theod.* XVI. 5. 9. (A.D. 382).

[4] P. R. L. Brown, 'Christianity and local culture in Late Roman Africa', *JRS* 58, 1968, p. 94.

[5] On this theme see R. Macmullen, 'Nationalism in Roman Egypt', *Aegyptus* 44, 1964–5, pp. 179–99; also by J. Maspero, for the Byzantine period, *Histoire des patriarches d'Alexandrie depuis la mort de l'empereur Anastase jusqu'à la réconciliation des églises jacobites* (Paris, 1923), pp. 24ff., and H. I. Bell, *Egypt from Alexander the Great to the Arab Conquests* (Oxford, 1948), p. 110.

The rise of the Monophysite movement

from the middle of the second century onwards.[1] The new Christians of the era of the Great Persecution were as disdainful of their Egyptian past as they were of the idolatry of the imperial authorities. At Caesarea some Egyptian confessors surprised the judge by renouncing their birth-names 'as being those belonging to idols', and giving themselves instead names of Hebrew prophets, such as Jeremiah, Elijah and Isaiah.[2] Indeed, Egypt, with its temples of Serapis and tombs infested with pictures of demonic idols, was a land of sin. All this the Christian had abandoned for the desert.

One factor which gradually led to a more conscious identity of Coptic Christian with Egyptian was the continuance of an association between paganism and the old Greek-speaking settlers and urban aristocracies.[3] Antony had despised paganism as being derived from Greek philosophy which inspired no martyrs and asked questions instead of answering them.[4] In the next century the great Aba Shenute of the Pachomian White Monastery, himself the son of a Coptic farmer, had a smattering enough of Greek to explain who Hephaistos was and to quote Aristophanes and Plato, but only in scorn.[5] Though he had strong views on the wickedness of the traditional Egyptian practice of embalming bodies and would not even honour the tombs of his ancestors as they had died pagans,[6] the real venom of his sermons was directed against the Greek-speaking pagans in the neighbouring towns.[7] With him one can detect the growth of a self-conscious Coptic

[1] See my 'The Gospel of Thomas: is rehabilitation possible?', *JTS*, n.s. 18, 1967, pp. 13–26 at p. 23, and for Millenarianism in the second half of the third century in the Nile valley, see Eusebius, *HE* VII. 24, concerning Nepos of Arsinoë.

[2] Eusebius, *Mart. Pal.* 11. 8 (ed. H. J. Lawlor and J. E. L. Oulton, London, 1952). Antony had no use for the old Egyptian gods, their oracles and incantations: see Athanasius, *Vita Antonii* 79 for 'Egyptian incantations' (*PG* 26, col. 952c). In contrast, Horapollon, a pagan philosopher of the late fifth century, was the author of a work on the antiquities of Alexandria and perhaps on hieroglyphs also. See Bell, *Egypt from Alexander the Great to the Arab Conquest*, p. 148.

[3] Theodoret, *HE* IV. 18, relates how in Valens' reign (364–78) the greater part of the inhabitants of Antinous near Thebes were still pagans.

[4] Athanasius, *Vita Antonii* 72–8.

[5] On Shenute, the authorities are still J. Leipoldt, *Schenute von Atripe*, TU 25 (n.s. 10), Leipzig, 1904, no. 1 and E. Amélineau, *Oeuvres de Schenoudi* (Paris, 1911), especially the Introduction. For Shenute's hostility to the Greek-speaking pagans, see Leipoldt, *Schenute*, p. 26, and his distaste for Plato and Aristophanes, *ibid*. p. 72. Some of his sermons have been translated and edited by H. Wiesman, *CSCO*, Scriptores Coptici II. 4 and 5 (Paris, 1931).

[6] See Leipoldt, *Schenute*, pp. 31–2.   [7] *Ibid.* pp. 24–6 and 177.

spirit growing away even linguistically from the previously dominant Greek, and which combined Monophysitism and prophecy as formidable weapons against outsiders. Shenute's work, too, of gathering in the traditional riff-raff of Egyptian society and giving its members the standing of monks and an assurance of personal salvation, as well as his passionate eloquence in their native tongue, provided the Monophysite movement in Egypt with a popular basis that it never lost.

Shenute died in 451. Some sixty years later, in 516, the monks and people of Alexandria rioted against the Emperor Anastasius' choice of patriarch even though he and the emperor favoured the Monophysites, on the ground that the 'rulers' (*archontes*) had invited him.[1] This incident, in which Theodosius the Augustal prefect was killed by the mob, may be perhaps the watershed in Egyptian church history. After this, Coptic loyalty to Monophysitism, combined with Alexandrian chauvinism and self-assertiveness[2] and suspicion of any form of imperial intervention in their ecclesiastical affairs, made an Egyptian 'national religion' based on the teaching of Cyril and Cyril alone a reality. If this cause was threatened, as it was in Justin's reign, it could be claimed by an eye-witness that 'the whole people of Egypt are ready to strip themselves for like contests'[3] and rise in its defence.

Even so, another century passed before indisputable evidence exists for the Coptic Monophysite monks regarding themselves consciously as both Egyptian and anti-imperial. Like Antony before them,[4] the Monophysite

[1] Theophanes, *Chron.* A.M. 6009 (ed. Classen, I, 251). The reason for the rage of the people against the prefect, διὰ τὸ ἐπαινεῖν τὸν βασιλέα 'Ἀναστάσιον, is interesting. The situation was aggravated by a shortage of olive oil in the city (see John Malalas, *Chron.* XVI. 119 (ed. Dindorf, p. 401).

[2] Note the interesting comment by Severus of Antioch in his letter to Hippocrates the lawyer (*Collection of Letters of Severus*, ed. Brooks, PO 12. 2, p. 318) criticising Dioscorus II's view of Cappadocia as a 'waste country', the opinion of whose clergy might be treated with contempt. 'For it is the habit of the Alexandrians to think that the sun rises for them only, and towards them only the lamp burns, so that they even jestingly term outside cities "lampless".

[3] Severus of Antioch, Letter to John and the presbyters, written 520–34 (*Select Letters* v. 2, ed. Brooks, p. 328). Severus describes indignation embracing every age and sex against the imposition by Justin of Chalcedon.

[4] See Palladius, *Hist. Lausiaca* XXI (ed. Butler, p. 66), where Antony is related to have asked his disciples to find out from visitors 'whether they were Egyptians or men of Jerusalem', i.e. grave and serious individuals. Only if the latter would he give his time to discussing spiritual matters with them. See G. Bardy, 'Le Patriotisme égyptien dans

ascetics still looked upon nationality as an Egyptian as very secondary compared with true Christian citizenship as 'a man of Jerusalem'.[1] The statement, however, preserved in the *Book of the Patriarchs* concerning the attitude of the monks of the episcopal monastery of Metras on the eve of the Arab invasions admits of no doubt. 'The inmates', we are told, 'were especially powerful. They were Egyptians [*Misrwani*] by race, all natives, and there was no stranger among them. Therefore, Heraclius could not make their hearts pliant, and therefore they received Aba Benjamin [the Monophysite patriarch] when he returned from Upper Egypt, because they kept the orthodox faith and did not deviate from it.'[2] Other monasteries might bow to 'Heraclius the heretic', but not these men. One wonders whether a Coptic writer would have expressed himself similarly on behalf of Athanasius. Even so, hostility to the empire was confined to religion.[3] Coptic historians attribute the Arab triumph of the 640s to divine punishment on the Byzantines for accepting the *Tome* of Leo and Chalcedon. Of an Egyptian national rising against Heraclius or a peasant rising against the Byzantine landowners there is little trace.[4]

These events lie far in the future. At the time of Chalcedon, the second major factor in the success of the Constantinian revolution still counteracted particularist tendencies among the native Christians of Egypt and elsewhere in the east. Attention to the upsurge of Christianity in the countryside must not be allowed to obscure the importance of the steady advance of the church in the Greek cities. These cities provided its leadership and its theology, and the urban congregations contributed greatly to its wealth and power. Of their loyalty to the institution of the empire and to the emperors there can be no doubt.

la tradition patristique', *RHE* 45, 1950, pp. 1–24. Bardy indicates rightly that neither Athanasius nor Cyril evince any conscious Egyptian patriotism.

[1] The monk Isaiah is described by Zacharias Scholasticus as 'cum corpore Aegyptius esset animae autem nobilitate Hierosolymitanus' (Brooks, p. 3).

[2] *History of the Patriarchs*, part I, ch. XIV (ed. Evetts, p. 498).

[3] John of Nikiou, *Chron.* circa 680, chs. 121. 1 and 123. 4: 'And everyone said, "This expulsion [of the Romans] and the victory of the Moslems is due to the wickedness of the Emperor Heraclius and the persecution of the orthodox through the patriarch Cyrus. This was the cause of the ruin of the Roman and the subjugation of Egypt by the Moslem."'

[4] For possible Coptic support of the Arab forces in Cyrenaica in 645, see R. G. Goodchild, 'Byzantines, Berbers and Arabs in seventh-century Libya', *Antiquity* 41, 1967, pp. 115–24.

The emperor and his church

Even in Origen's time (*circa* 230–40) the church in some of the eastern cities had been strong enough to act as a magnet to those who wanted to prosper in this world.[1] In the last half of the third century the bishops who presided over the wealthy sees of Antioch and Alexandria included powerful political figures such as Paul of Samosata and Dionysius 'the Great'. In the west also, where Christianity was relatively strong in towns, especially on the Mediterranean seaboard and in the provincial capitals, it was tending to come to terms with the state. The Council of Elvira's canons (perhaps May 309) show how Christians could find themselves holding nominal pagan priesthoods that formed part and parcel of municipal administration.[2] An influential African rhetorician, Lactantius, a convert to Christianity, became tutor to Constantine's son, Crispus. It has been pointed out that 'compared with the vast and menacing stretches of their own countryside and the new horizons of the barbarian world, a hair's breadth separated pagan and Christian members of the intelligentsia'.[3] Since Lucian of Samosata's time (*circa* 170) few members of the former had taken the 'old, ill-behaved gods of classical paganism'[4] seriously: Christian and pagan shared the conservative ethics of the Diocletian era – 'pious, religious, quiet and chaste'. *Beata tranquillitas* of the *folles* of the Tetrarchy could equally have been a Christian watchword. Whereas, however, the Tetrarchy had placed their hopes on the 'dii immortales' of Rome, and on the officials of the city and provincial councils as the executors of their will,[5] Constantine had seen the failure of both to crush the Christians. The 'Summus Deus' worshipped by them and served by their clergy had won, and in the crisis of his fortunes in the battle against Maxentius had saved him as well.

[1] Origen, *Homil. in Jeremiah* XII. 8 (ed. E. Klostermann, *GCS* 6, Leipzig, 1901), p. 94; *Contra Celsum* III. 9, and *Comment. in Matt.* XVI. 8, ed. Klostermann, *GCS* 40, Origenes Werke 10, Leipzig, 1935, pp. 493–4 (Christians in larger towns show arrogance towards the poor).

[2] Council of Elvira (ed. Hefele/Leclercq, *Histoire des conciles*, I. 1, 221ff.), canons 2 and 3. Dating: I have accepted H. Grégoire's suggestion from *Les Persécutions dans l'empire romain* (Brussels, 1951), pp. 128–30.

[3] P. R. L. Brown, 'Approaches to the religious crisis of the third century', *EHR* 328, July 1968, p. 555.   [4] The phrase is Brown's, *loc. cit.*

[5] Maximin (306–13) in particular used the city and provincial councils as vehicles of opinion against the Christians. His attempted restoration of paganism was based on the association of the councils with the temples and their priesthoods: see Eusebius, *HE* VIII. 14. 9 and IX. 4. 2–5. 2. Compare also *ibid.* IX. 7. 3 (Tyre) and the inscription from Aricanda (*ILCV* 1b) for requests by these bodies to the emperor for action against the Christians.

He gradually identified his aims with those of the next most powerful group within the cities, namely the Christian churches and their clergy. Their leaders such as the two Eusebii became his guides and counsellors. Bishops obtained a jurisdiction parallel in many respects to that of civil magistrates,[1] and by the reign of Justinian had acquired also many of their duties, such as those connected with allocating and accounting for funds to be spent on public works and provisions for the populace.[2] It is impossible to imagine civil administration continuing in the fifth and sixth centuries in the east Roman provinces without the church. Once again, Constantine turned the policies of his predecessors on their head. Like them he accepted that the consolidation of his empire depended on the revival of the cities, but as the people of Cotiaeum in Phrygia noted, imperial favour was bestowed on Christian cities.[3] Constantine's chosen instruments were the Catholic church and its bishops.

In the east the success of this policy was guaranteed by an uncovenanted piece of good fortune. The strongly anti-Hellene and anti-imperial trend of Christian apologetic represented by Tatian and perhaps Bardaisan did not prevail. Instead, the loyalist element among apologists reared in the Greek philosophic tradition was able to stamp its ideal of the harmony of church and empire on the beliefs of succeeding generations of Christians. What had been the wishful thinking of Justin and Melito of Sardes became with Origen part of the intelligent Christian's *credo*. Eastern Christians not only accepted the empire as the guarantor of earthly peace to whom obedience and general good conduct was due, as did their western brethren, but developed a far more positive approach towards it. The birth of Christ had taken place in the reign of Augustus. This represented a providential association between church and empire, foreshadowing the time when all men would be Christians under a Christian emperor and when the Prince of Peace would reign everywhere.[4] The charge made by Celsus *circa* 178 that Christianity produced revolution and was a danger to the state was by-

---

[1] *Cod. Theod.* I. 27. 1. See T. M. Parker, *Christianity and the State in the Light of History*, Bampton Lectures for 1954 (London, 1955), p. 51.

[2] *Cod. Just.* I. 4. 26 (A.D. 530).

[3] *Monumenta Asiae Minoris antiqua*, ed. W. M. Calder (Manchester University, 1960), VII. 305. For Constantine's policy favouring Christian cities, Eusebius, *Vita Constantini* III. 38 and 39.

[4] Melito of Sardes, cited by Eusebius, *HE* IV. 7. 26. Compare Origen, *Contra Celsum* II. 30 and Eusebius, *Demonstratio evangelica* I. 4 (ed. I. A. Heikel, *GCS* 23, Eusebius Werke 6, Leipzig, 1913).

The emperor and his church

passed and finally was rendered obsolete and irrelevant by Constantine's victory over his pagan rivals.

In addition to inbred loyalism, the predominance of Origenist theology throughout the east in the third and fourth centuries ensured that the values represented by the Christian leadership would be those of Plato. Despite polemic and the glorification of Jewish heroes, this interpretation of Christianity implied no great break with the pagan past whose values it proceeded to rationalise and absorb. Furthermore, it emphasised the providential character of the empire and its ruler as reflections of the harmony of the divine world, it accepted the *polis* and the duties connected with the city as divinely ordained and it interpreted both Christianity and the monastic vocation within it in terms of a philosophical ideal. Under the aegis of Clement, Origen, and Eusebius of Caesarea, the monks became less refugees from society than 'true philosophers' seeking communion with God through asceticism and contemplation.[1] Allegorical interpretation softened the outlines of the dominical imperatives, and apocalyptic, so powerful an influence in the west, was denounced as the mark of a 'weak intelligence'.[2]

The leaders of the eastern church, whether Chalcedonian or anti-Chalcedonian, identified themselves with this tradition. Severus of Antioch, for instance, is stated by his biographer Zacharias Scholasticus to have been an admirer of Libanius before he conceded that the Platonic Christianity of Basil of Caesarea attracted him even more.[3] Others before him, from Origen to Basil himself, had regarded pagan wisdom as desirable preparation for probing the divine mysteries.[4] This stage, therefore, of Severus' development towards the 'true philosophy' of monasticism is recalled not as the moment of his conversion from a reprobate past (which

---

[1] For monks 'practising philosophy' see Sozomen, *HE* II. 14, III. 14. 28 and VI. 28. 1. Severus of Antioch frequently uses the same terms, e.g. Philip the presbyter and monk is described as 'one of those who live an ascetic life of philosophic labour' (*Ep.* 52 = *PO* 12. 2, p. 326). For Christianity as a 'philosophy', see Melito of Sardes, cited by Eusebius, *HE* IV. 7. 26. See also F. Dölger, 'Zur Bedeutung von φιλόσοφος und φιλοσοφία in byzantinischen Zeit', *Byzanz und die europäische Staatenwelt* (Ettal, 1953), pp. 197–208.   [2] Eusebius, *HE* III. 39. 13.

[3] Zacharias Scholasticus, *Vita Severi* (ed. Kugener), pp. 12–13. Severus is described as being a zealous and honest student even when accepting Libanius as his master.

[4] 'Having accustomed ourselves to seeing the [reflection of the] sun in water, we shall [then] direct our gaze to the true light.' Basil, *Homil.* XXII *ad adolescentes*, a classic statement of Christian humanism (*PG* 31, col. 568).

The rise of the Monophysite movement

it might have been) but as the normal progress of an already brilliant man destined to become a spiritual leader. An eastern archimandrite or bishop presided over 'rational souls' rather than 'miserable sinners',[1] and he did not expect to find instruction in the art of reasoning on behalf of the faith in the Bible.[2] For that he must turn to philosophy. The contrast with the western outlook is striking. Caesarius of Arles, a contemporary of Severus, for instance, could not envisage studying the grammar and philosophy of the classical past while remaining a monk.[3] Like Jerome, he was warned in a terrible dream that the rule of salvation could not be associated with the wisdom of this world and he reacted accordingly. At the end of the sixth century, Pope Gregory informed the luckless Desiderius, bishop of Vienne, that his teaching of grammar was a cause for scandal.[4] The combination of the theology of the gathered church with profound fear of the approaching end of the world and the Judgement was responsible even to a greater extent than the barbarian conquests for the creation of attitudes of mind associated with the term 'The Dark Ages'.

In the east, on the other hand, Christianity was a religion which had been built upon and had absorbed previous pagan tradition. The emperor's monarchy had its due place of authority in the divine order together with the church and its clergy. If in the west the church's sense of opposition to the world and its wisdom and rulers was never lost, in the east Severus and his colleagues saw their task as that of convincing the emperor and hence the Christian world of the truth of their anti-Chalcedonian teaching by argument. Rebellion would be an act of unreason, surrender to the impious demons who hated the peace of the church and were the cause of every outbreak of chaotic violence in the cities of the empire.[5]

---

[1] For instance, as stated by Severus of Antioch, *Select Letters* VII. 3 to Simeon the archimandrite (ed. Brooks, p. 371).

[2] See Socrates, *HE* III. 16.

[3] *Vita Caesarii* 9 (*PL* 67, col. 1005). See A. D. Nicol, 'The Byzantine church and Hellenic learning', *Studies in Church History* V (Leiden, 1969), p. 25.

[4] Gregory, *Ep.* 11. 54: 'quia in uno se ore cum Iovis laudibus Christi laudes non capiunt'. Contrast the attitude of Zacharias Scholasticus, *Vita Isaiae Patris* (ed. E. W. Brooks, *CSCO*, Scriptores Syri III. 25, Paris, 1907), p. 8, in which a certain Aeneas is recommended as being 'sophista Gazae urbis, vir Christianissimus et doctissimus'.

[5] Note the role attributed to demons in the riot at Antioch in 387, Sozomen, *HE* VII. 23. 5, and for Severus' instructions to a colleague on his duty as a bishop, see above, p. 62. Also, Synesius' denunciation of 'the mob rule and democracy of the passions', which could also be applied to ideas of government: *De regno* (ed. FitzGerald), p. 119.

Thus the visible authority of the bishops was buttressed by a coherent religious philosophy that promoted loyalty to the empire and subservience to its ruler. In practice, the philosophical ideal of communion with God and contemplation was grafted on to monasticism and damped down the underlying apocalyptic and sense of protest against established society which had brought that movement into being. The result was that in the east, religious controversy, however bitter, did not extend consciously to political controversy and social upheaval as it did in the west. There, apocalyptic hopes dominated movements of protest such as the African Circumcellions, and these became revolutionary in the accepted sense of the term.[1] So long, however, as hope remained that the emperors would repudiate Chalcedon, the Monophysite leaders did not set up their own rival church and they kept their followers loyal to the institution of the empire.

Their followers were the monks, the heart and soul of popular Christianity in the east.[2] Their effect on the beliefs and attitudes of the people towards the controversies of the fourth, fifth and sixth centuries was incalculable. As Sozomen, writing *circa* 440, explains in his account of the rejection both of Eunomianism and Apollinarianism in Syria in the 370s, 'they [the Eunomians and Apollinarians] incurred the full weight of popular aversion when it was observed that their sentiments were regarded with suspicion by the monks, whose doctrines were invariably received and followed by the people on account of the virtue they exhibited in their actions'.[3] This virtue included not only exorcism of demons and miraculous cures from every type of ailment,[4] but also making grievances known to the emperors and their officials; and the latter, whatever they might think in moments of exacerbation,[5] took heed of what they said as individuals inspired by God.

[1] See my article, 'Circumcellions and monks', *JTS*, n.s. 20, 1969, pp. 543–9.
[2] For a comprehensive bibliography of eastern monasticism to 1958, see H. G. Beck, *Kirche und theologische Literatur*, p. 120 n3, and H. Lietzmann's account in *Geschichte der alten Kirche*, IV, ch. 6.
[3] Sozomen, *HE* VI. 27.
[4] A good example of what people expected of the monks is given in a letter quoted in Bell, *Egypt from Alexander the Great to the Arab Conquest*, p. 110: 'To Ammonius, I beg and entreat you, most valued father, to ask for me [help?] from Christ that I may obtain healing, for by ascetics and devotees revelations are manifested. For I am afflicted with a great disease in the shape of grievous shortness of breath.'
[5] Note the outburst of the *magister militum* Timasius at Milan in 388 against Ambrose, concerning the activities of the monks in east Syria: Ambrose, *Ep.* 41. 27.

The contrasting influences for or against the bishops which the monks exercised in the three great patriarchates at the time of Chalcedon was to demonstrate amply their strength.

Monasticism had probably originated independently in Egypt and Syria. Perhaps far back in the second century one can point to the common formative influence of the Jewish Christianity found in the *Gospel of Thomas* which was in use in both areas,[1] but thereafter for a century the development and direction of monasticism is obscure. By the time of the Great Persecution, however, it had become an explosive mass movement which drew its strength in both provinces from the non-Greek-speaking peasants. In Egypt the Pachomian monasteries were packed thickly around Alexandria, and in the Fayum, and the middle Nile round the original settlement of Tabennesi, and they counted their inmates in thousands. Jerome's figure, *circa* 400, of 'nearly fifty thousand monks' taking part in the annual chapter of the Pachomian order may not be far from the mark.[2] We hear of 10,000 monks in monasteries around Oxyrhynchus in the fifth century,[3] and of Shenute's White Monastery with a population of 2,200 monks and 1,800 nuns.[4] These great houses were self-sufficient economic and social units. At Panopolis, for instance, the Pachomian monastery is described as containing numerous trades, including fifteen tailors, seven smiths, four carpenters, twelve camel-drivers and fifteen fullers among three hundred monks, and there they 'work at every kind of craft and with their surplus output they provide for the needs of the women's convents and the prisons'.[5] Similarly, Shenute's White Monastery seems to have been self-sufficing, as Besa's *Life* tells of work at the mill and of monks digging drains (chs. 17 and 24). By the inevitable process of bequest, gift and the permanence of their own institutional lives, they became in their turn landlords from whom peasants would hire equipment and to whom they paid their rents.[6] Spiritually and economically they became the representative institutions of Coptic Egypt.

[1] See my 'Gospel of Thomas', *JTS*, n.s. 18, 1967, pp. 25–6. For early Syrian monasticism see especially A. Vööbus, *A History of Asceticism in the Syrian Orient*, vol. II, *CSCO*, Subsidia 17 (Louvain, 1960).

[2] Jerome, *Regulae Sancti Pachomii*, Praefatio, 7 (*PL* 23, col. 64).

[3] John Rufus, *Vita Petri Iberi* (ed. Raabe), pp. 61ff., and compare Rufinus, *Historia monachorum* 5 (*PL* 21, cols. 408–9). See Lietzmann, *Geschichte*, IV, 139.

[4] Leipoldt, *Schenute*, p. 93.

[5] Palladius, *Hist. Lausiaca* (ed. and tr. W. K. Lowther Clarke) XXXII. 9.

[6] See E. R. Hardy, *Christian Egypt: Church and People* (New York, 1952), p. 167.

Their importance in both respects can hardly be exaggerated. Spiritually, the mantle of the Coptic martyr had descended on to the shoulders of the Coptic monk. His abstinences and combats with demons simulated the pangs and combats of the martyrs, whom he imitated in will and intention and whose rewards were his also. Aba Shenute spoke as a matter of course with the Hebrew prophets, and on occasion would, like the confessors of the past era, speak direct with the Lord.[1] Seeing visions and uttering prophecies were his by right. Whatever the depth of his theological ignorance, his prestige was enormous. Time and again his biographer records how he brought needed and sometimes dramatic relief to the oppressed. Pagan landowners who owned vineyards on an island in the Nile and were extorting high rents from the husbandmen saw their possessions suddenly sink below the waters of the river at Shenute's command.[2] Such actions were not regarded as detracting from the status of an abbot as a holy man. The monks regarded the fight against the demons as an active one in which prayer, relief of distress and work for their own and other people's livelihoods were all essential parts of their lives as ascetics. 'I have spent all my life in sowing, reaping and making baskets', said the monk Serenus.[3] When a monk visited Silvanus' monastery on Mount Sinai and claimed that in not working for food that perished Mary was better than Martha, his hosts told him that if that was so, he did not need to have any lunch.[4] Shenute was characteristically to the point, quoting 'He who would not work, let him not eat' (2 Thess. 3. 10).[5]

These rough, individualistic but socially conscious monks provided the patriarchate of Alexandria with the force it needed to further its ambitions. That the alliance between the two was by no means inevitable is evident from the story of the rise and fall of the Meletian movement in the fourth century. The Meletians were based on the Coptic-speaking Thebaid, and they had developed a monastic movement by the 330s.[6] With Alexandria

[1] Besa, *Life of Shenute*, chs. 94 and 95 (conversation with Jeremiah and Ezekiel). Compare Leipoldt, *Schenute*, p. 57 (conversation with Jesus concerning a dispute with a bishop). For similar examples of monks' words having the force of oracles, see W. Bousset, *Apophthegmata Patrum* (Tübingen, 1923), p. 80, and visions, *ibid.* p. 85.
[2] Besa, *Life of Shenute*, chs. 85–6.
[3] *Apophthegmata Patrum*, De abbate Sereno 2 (*PG* 65, col. 417).
[4] *Ibid.* 409 (De abbate Silvano).
[5] See Leipoldt, *Schenute*, pp. 64 and 123–4.
[6] See H. I. Bell, *Jews and Christians in Alexandria* (Oxford, 1924), ch. 2, pp. 45 ff., and E. R. Hardy, *Christian Egypt*, p. 53.

unpopular in the eyes of many Egyptians as representing foreign domination, their success could have resulted in a permanent shift in the balance of Egyptian Christianity from Alexandria to the Thebaid. That this did not come about was largely due to Athanasius. In the first years of his episcopate, secure in the friendship of Antony, and ordaining Pachomius, he outbid the Meletians for the leadership of the monks. This was a stroke of genius, as far-reaching in its effects as his championship of Nicaea. It resulted in the alliance of monks and patriarch and also in the blending of the Logos theology of the intellectual Alexandrian clergy with the Hebraic Biblicism of the Coptic monks.

The alliance, however, could never quite be taken for granted. Under Athanasius and his immediate successors the monks gave devoted support to the patriarch. Athanasius owed his liberty to them in 356, and Theophilus his ability to destroy paganism in the heart of Alexandria. 'Once upon a time', wrote the author of the *Gesta Theophili* concerning the destruction of the Serapeum in 391, 'the fathers came to Alexandria, called by Archbishop Theophilus that he might make prayer and destroy the temples.'[1] Theophilus, Cyril and Dioscorus all courted the monks, and the rowdy swarm that accompanied them on their encounters with the patriarchs of the capital did much to ensure their victory. It was not, however, all plain sailing. An undercurrent of monastic suspicion persisted. Both the crises involving Theophilus with John Chrysostom in 404 and Cyril with Nestorius in 429 were set off by appeals by monks to the capital against their patriarch's tyranny. Similar misdeeds led to Dioscorus' downfall and the long-standing alienation of the great Pachomian monastery of Canopus in the suburbs of Alexandria from his successors.[2]

Where the patriarchs were tactful, and Cyril's handling of the monks was usually masterly, the power of Alexandria was irresistible. The story of Shenute's striking down Nestorius at Ephesus I typifies the legendary collaboration between monk and patriarch that Cyril achieved.[3] In addition to monastic support the patriarch had complete control over his suffragan bishops who feared for their lives if they expressed beliefs that were other

[1] *Apophthegmata Patrum*, Gesta Theophili 3 (*PG* 65, col. 200A).

[2] The story is told by the presbyter Athanasius in his appeal to the Council of Chalcedon and read at the third session. The only way of getting rid of Dioscorus was to condemn his contumacy for not answering this and other complaints. Canopus provided Athanasius with a refuge against Dioscorus: Mansi, *Collectio* VI, col. 1021 ff.

[3] Besa, *Life of Shenute*, ch. 128.

than his.¹ In material terms, too, the see was enormously wealthy. Cyril's bribes to potentially hostile court officials at the time of Ephesus I were legendary – 2,500 lbs. of gold in 'benedictions', carpets, tapestries, ivory-inlaid furniture and ostriches, and even then he left a private fortune of 1,400 lbs. of gold, for Dioscorus to seize.² In 505 John Nikaiotes promised 2,000 lbs. of gold to the Emperor Anastasius in return for complete rejection of Chalcedon.³ Strong in an alliance with the Roman see that went back to the days of Athanasius and even beyond, controlling a great territory extending from the borders of Libya to the Nubian frontier, with missions in Ethiopia and Yemen whose bishops depended on Alexandria for their consecration, the patriarch of the church of Alexandria could claim to be 'ecumenical patriarch' and 'judge,' and defy any opposition from Antioch or Constantinople.

At Antioch the monastic movement had exactly the opposite effect on the standing of the patriarch, monks being in the main out of sympathy with the specifically Antiochene theology of the first half of the fifth century.⁴ Ostensibly the see of Antioch was every whit as powerful as Alexandria at this period. It was the capital of the Oriental diocese, a vast area extending from the Taurus mountains to the Egyptian frontier, including wealthy Greek cities of the coast and western Syria, the client kingdom of Osrhoëne with Edessa, 'city of the believing people of Mesopotamia',⁵ the Euphrates fortress towns, and also at this period Jerusalem. Its influence extended northwards into Cappadocia and Galatia where its bishop, Vitalis, presided over a council at Ancyra in 314,⁶ and eastwards into Persia whose church continued to maintain close contact with Antioch until the last decades of the fifth century when Antioch broke decisively with Nestorian-type theology. At the beginning of the fifth century, the

---

¹ The pitiable plight of the Egyptian bishops if they accepted the *Tome* without the assent of their patriarch roused the sympathy even of the council: Mansi, *Collectio* VII, cols. 58–60.

² See J. B. Bury, *History of the Later Roman Empire* (London, 1923), I, 354, for the list. For Cyril's private fortune, see Letter of the Presbyter Athanasius, Mansi, *loc. cit.*

³ Theodore Lector, *HE* (fragments, ed. Miller), p. 396.

⁴ The important exception is Theodoret's influence on the monks in his own diocese at Cyrrhus. See for instance, *Epp.* 127, 128 and 151, all addressed to monastic leaders.

⁵ Rufinus, *HE* II. 5 (*PL* 21, col. 513).

⁶ In the sixth century Severus was not only well informed about the situation in Cappadocia but able to influence affairs there: *Select Letters* (ed. Brooks), pp. 55 and 258.

patriarch presided over 14 metropolitans and 127 bishops, some of whom, such as Edessa, had staffs numbering hundreds of clergy.[1] The patriarch, moreover, had a wealth of intellectual talent to call upon, clerics such as Theodoret of Cyrrhus, Ibas of Edessa or Theodore of Mopsuestia being outstanding in any company and representing far greater resources than were ever available to Cyril or Dioscorus. Moreover, to many eastern bishops Antioch was the mother-church of the east[2] and it could claim unimpeachable Petrine foundation, as well as being associated with Paul and the earliest Christian missions. This alone should have won for it the support of Rome and consequent freedom from Alexandrian assault.

Antioch, however, never achieved the same sense of disciplined purpose that was the strength of Alexandria and Rome, and after Chalcedon, of Constantinople. Granted that Jerusalem and the three small Palestinian provinces totalling about sixty bishoprics[3] were likely sooner or later to break away and become a fifth patriarchate, the vast area presided over by Antioch lacked the geographical and historical unity possessed by its main rival Alexandria. First, the territories under its sway were divided along linguistic lines, Greek being the *lingua franca* of the towns and Syriac of the countryside. Syriac was the language of the people on both sides of the Persian frontier from Ctesiphon northwards to Zeugma and Edessa and southwards to the Egyptian border. Men like Aphraat moved easily in the mid fourth century from southern Mesopotamia to Edessa and only found it necessary to launch into pidgin-Greek on reaching Antioch.[4] John

---

[1] For Edessa, see *ACO* 2. 1. 3, p. 27. Ibas speaks of 'our clergy' who knew his views personally, and hence would be those of his own cathedral rather than the diocese as a whole (compare, however, Jones, *The Later Roman Empire*, II, 912). At Apamea in 518 the petition of the church there against Severus of Antioch's friend Peter was signed by seventeen priests, more than forty-two deacons, three subdeacons and fifteen readers. In general, see Beck, *Kirche und theologische Literatur*, pp. 191–5, and R. Devreese, *Le Patriarcat d'Antioche* (Paris, 1945), pp. 133f.

[2] Theodoret, *Ep.* 86. Compare Basil, *Ep.* 66. 2. To Severus of Antioch, Antioch was always 'the apostolic see'.

[3] Canon 7 of the Council of Nicaea had treated the position of Jerusalem as exceptional, but not sufficiently so to upset the metropolitan rights of Caesarea. See S. Vailhé, 'L'Erection du patriarcat de Jérusalem, 451', *Revue de l'Orient chrétien* 4, 1899, pp. 44–57 at pp. 56–7. Vailhé points out, however, that as late as 415 the Council of Diospolis was presided over by Eulogius of Caesarea despite the presence of John of Jerusalem (p. 48).

[4] Theodoret, *Historia religiosa*, ch. 8 (*PG* 82, col. 1368B). See P. R. L. Brown, 'The diffusion of Manichaeism in the Roman Empire', *JRS* 59, 1969, pp. 92–103 at

Chrysostom speaks of farmers who spoke only Syriac flocking into the city to hear his sermons at the time of the crisis over the imperial statues in 387.[1] That this difference of medium had its effect on the development of Christianity in the territories dependent on Antioch is shown by the fact that in the 260s the Christians at the episcopal city of Yaransahr, swelled by captives brought thither by Shapur, divided themselves into Greek- and Syriac-language congregations.[2] It would be hazardous, however, to argue from this a difference in doctrinal interpretations along linguistic lines, though in the controversy caused by Paul of Samosata's Adoptionist Christology, 265–70, Malchion the presbyter and head of the Aristotelian school in Antioch clearly represented an opposition based on Origenistic teaching against Paul's ideas, while these were accepted in other parts of Syria.[3] Some tension, too, is perceptible between representatives of the two language-groups. For instance, the observant writer of the *Pilgrimage of Egeria*, circa 385, describes how the bishop of Jerusalem would insist on celebrating the liturgy in Greek though he knew Syriac and the congregation consisted of Syriac-speaking peasants.[4] The indignation, too, of even so pro-Cyrillist an ecclesiastic as Photius of Tyre against the 'arrogant blasphemies' of the masses of Mesopotamian monks who swarmed into his city in 449 to demonstrate against Ibas suggests some hostility between the two groups,[5] while the monks themselves reserved much of their gall for Greek-speaking bishops during the turbulent years 449–51. On the other hand, language alone would hardly have been decisive any more than it was in Egypt. At Edessa, for instance, Ibas himself was Syriac-speaking

p. 96. Also, R. Macmullen, 'Provincial languages in the Roman Empire', *AJP* 87, 1966, pp. 1–17, especially references in n9.

[1] John Chrysostom, *De statuis*, Homil. XIX. 1 (*PG* 49, col. 188).

[2] *Chronicle of Séert* (ed. Scher), *PO* 4, p. 222.

[3] The Christology of the bishop of Carrhae in the account of his 'debate' with Mani on the Syro-Persian frontier, recorded in *Acta Archelai*, is remarkably similar to that of Paul (see below, p. 108).

[4] *Peregrinatio Sanctae Silvae* 47. 3: 'licet siriste noverit, tamen semper graece loquitur'; a presbyter interpreted to the congregation (*CSEL* 39, p. 99; for dating, see *ibid.* p. xiii). On the other hand, the people of Tarsus seem to have accepted Mar-Benjamin, an east Syrian monk of Persian birth, as their bishop, according to the *Life of Mar-Benjamin* (died in 466), ed. V. Schiel, *Revue de l'Orient chrétien* 2, 1897, pp. 254–5. The incident is, of course, legendary but could not have been completely impossible in the period.

[5] Council of Chalcedon, eleventh session = *ACO* 2. 1. 3, p. 18, para. 22. He ordered them out of the city.

The rise of the Monophysite movement

and his clergy consisted of both Greek and Syriac speakers. Of the latter, eighteen were among the signatories of a petition in support of his orthodoxy by sixty-seven clerics addressed to the judicial inquiry at Tyre in 449.[1] In Cyrrhus the monks with whom Theodoret was corresponding so amiably were bilingual with Syriac as their native language.[2]

Just as important in preventing a sense of unity developing within the patriarchate was the relative isolation of Antioch as a Christian centre. If a strong pagan minority continued to exist in many of the Egyptian towns, an even stronger one was able to maintain itself in many of the towns in Syria. Gaza was largely pagan until the beginning of the fifth century, Carrhae and Heliopolis (Baalbek) until a century later.[3] For a long time Antioch itself was an isolated Christian enclave. Sozomen points out how for a long time the city was cut off from more Christianised areas to the south and east. 'Coele Syria', he says, 'with the exception of Antioch was only slowly converted to Christianity.'[4] As in Egypt the monks were the missionaries, as destructive of the old Graeco-Syrian culture as their counterparts in the Nile valley.[5] The upshot was, however, that Antioch could exert little real influence on the development of Christianity in the outlying areas of its great diocese, and in the eastern parts the main representatives of the faith were Marcionites and Gnostics. There were also the Manichees.[6] The religious debate was predominantly between these strongly ascetic and Christologically Docetic groups and representatives of the more rationalist two-nature Christology of the spiritual descendants of Paul of

---

[1] Ibas is said by John of Egea, *HE* v (fragmenta, ed. Miller, p. 402), to have translated the works of Theodore of Mopsuestia into Syriac. Concerning his clergy, see Council of Chalcedon, eleventh session = *ACO* 2. 1. 3, pp. 35–7 and Mansi, *Collectio* VII, cols. 252–5.

[2] Theodoret, *Historia religiosa*, ch. 5, monks of Zeugma singing hymns 'some in Greek' and some in their native language.

[3] For Gaza, see Mark the Deacon, *Life of Porphyry* (ed. and tr. G. F. Hill, Oxford, 1913), ch. 64; Carrhae, see Theodoret, *HE* IV. 18 (fifth century) and Elias, *Vita Johannis episcopi Tellae*, chs. 43 and 55 (showing the existence of a pagan priesthood in the 530s); Heliopolis, see Michael the Syrian, *Chron.* x. 12, ed. Chabot, II, 318 (situation in sixth century). A landowner could still be called 'Eusebius the Christian' in 369, *IGLS*, 598.

[4] Sozomen, *HE* VI. 34. 4.

[5] *Ibid.* VI. 34. 5–7, and Theodoret, *HE* V. 29, Bishop John using monks to destroy pagan temples in Phoenicia.

[6] See Brown, 'Diffusion of Manichaeism', pp. 96–7, Syria as a 'bridgehead' of Manichaeism.

Samosata. The Origenism so strong in Antioch itself throughout most of the fourth century was less important. In addition, Antioch lacked the material means of enforcing the views of its bishop on clergy who chose to be recalcitrant. It was a very much poorer see than its rival, Alexandria. John Chrysostom declared that its revenue was about comparable to that of one of the more wealthy residents of the city, but not the very richest,[1] and it had to do a great deal of charitable work with it. In the early years of the sixth century Severus was to wax eloquent about the impoverishment and debt he inherited from his predecessor.[2] There was no question of a bishop of Antioch undertaking any policy involving massive expense to influence his suffragans. The occasional gift of vestments and sundry ecclesiastical 'treasures' is all that even an ambitious and desperate patriarch like Flavian II could afford.[3]

There was a further complication. Traditionally, Antioch had always been the home of a flourishing Jewish community. Unlike Alexandria there had been no pogrom or massive expulsions such as had followed the end of the Jewish revolt of 115. The Jews had continued to prosper. In the fifth century they could be found supporting the 'Blue' or pro-Chalcedonian party in the city,[4] a fact which gave point to the smear of 'Judaism' attached to any Chalcedonian patriarch of the city. Their influence at least in the background of the theological controversies is not to be underestimated. At the time of Nicaea, the church in Antioch still celebrated Easter on the Sunday after the Jewish Passover whose date was accepted from the Jews. Sixty years later, Jewish influence was still strong. The amount of time and invective expended by John Chrysostom in his sermons against Christians, even his own clergy, who observed Jewish fasts,[5] attended the synagogues, swore fiduciary oaths in them in the course of a business transaction and kept Jewish usages and feasts,[6] demonstrates the influence of Judaism on a personal level on Antiochene Christianity. Was there really only a small difference between 'us and the Jews', he asks.[7]

---

[1] John Chrysostom, *Homil. in Matth.* LXVI. 3 (*PG* 58, col. 630). See Jones, *The Later Roman Empire*, II, 905.   [2] See below, p. 223.

[3] Severus of Antioch, *Select Letters* I. 4 and 22 (ed. Brooks, pp. 26 and 80).

[4] John Malalas, *Chron.* XV. 103 (ed. Dindorf, p. 389). See below, p. 158.

[5] John Chrysostom, *Adversus Iudaeos orationes* I. 1 (*PG* 48, col. 844) and 4 (*ibid.* cols. 871ff.).

[6] *Ibid.* I. 4. John made an exception regarding the feast of the Maccabees on 1 August: see *Homil.* XI *de Eleazaro et septem pueris* 2 (*PG* 63, col. 525).

[7] *Adversus Iudaeos orationes* IV. 3 (*PG* 48, col. 875).

The rise of the Monophysite movement

Perhaps the coincidence of strong Jewish colonies in the towns of Cilicia and the popularity of the Antiochene school of theology there may not be accidental, for the exact approach of Diodore and Theodore of Mopsuestia to the text of the Bible and their emphasis on the humanity of Christ in accordance with the New Testament account of him would not be wholly unsympathetic to Jews.

All these factors contributed to the lack of a consistent theological tradition in Antioch until the final decade of the fourth century. There was nothing comparable to the school of thought which had matured slowly through two centuries of Alexandrian church history to reach its climax with the genius of Cyril. From the moment that the Origenist bishops secured the deposition of Paul of Samosata in 268, Antioch was seldom free from schism. In broad terms, the Origenists kept the upper hand throughout the fourth century, their opponents in the first part of the fifth. From Nicaea the dominant trend was represented by Flacillus, Stephen, Leontius, Eudoexius, Meletius and Flavian I; all Origenists, with Antioch serving as the headquarters of the *Homoiousion* party against Athanasius in the 350s. These prelates deposed or reduced to impotence the rival line of Eustathius, Paulinus and Evagrius, who may perhaps be reckoned as forerunners of the Antiochene school of theology of the end of the century.[1] Only one worthy representative of this latter sat on the patriarchal throne, and that was John (428–41). He successfully frustrated Juvenal's attempts to build his own patriarchate after Ephesus I, but even he could not command the undivided loyalty of his bishops. None was more devoted to Cyril than Rabbula (d. 435), metropolitan of Edessa, and in the presbyter Maximus Cyril had a firm supporter among the clergy in Antioch itself.[2] Moreover, Alexandria had a precedent in interfering in Antiochene affairs. Athanasius had refused to accept Meletius as bishop and had consistently supported his rival, Paulinus. After the Formula of Reunion in 433 it would have taken a man of rare calibre to hold the patriarchate together. Domnus, John's nephew and successor, was not such a man.

Lacking either decisive leadership or theological inspiration from Antioch, Syrian monasticism developed anarchically. The predominant trend was towards extremes of individual austerity inspired by a perfec-

---

[1] Theodoret, *HE* v. 25, reckons that the Eustathian tradition in Antioch re-started with the monastic bishop Alexander, Cyril's contemporary.

[2] See Cyril, *Epp.* 56–7. For Apollinarians in Antioch in Cyril's time, see Theodoret, *HE* v. 38 (Theodotus' episcopate).

tionism that sought communion with God through suffering, asceticism and contemplation. One of the centres from which the *Gospel of Thomas* had circulated was in all probability Edessa and the strongly ascetic character of that gospel had found ready hearers. 'Blessed are the solitary and the elect' was accepted literally.[1] The first organised Christian community there seems to have been Marcionite,[2] and this contributed towards the Marcionite predominance in eastern Syria in the second and third centuries,[3] in its turn to be challenged by the Manichaeans, the Messalians ('men of prayer'), Audians and a host of other encratite sects. All these were ascetics 'fasting like serpents and clothed in sack-cloth' and envied by their detractors.[4] They, together with more orthodox monks, made Syria the land *par excellence* of fanatics and eccentrics such as Jerome describes in his stay in the desert of Chalcis between 375 and 379.[5] There were pillar saints, cavern saints, monks wearing iron collars and clanking chains, or engaged, like the Boscoi, in diets of formidable rigour. Their theologies were as diverse and argumentative as their ways of life, but all emphasised the supreme virtue of the practice of asceticism.[6]

By the first half of the fifth century parts of Syria had become as peopled with monks as parts of Egypt.[7] Disused forts, pagan mausolea, and even

---

[1] Gospel of Thomas, *Logion* 4. For the connection between the Gospel and Edessa see G. Quispel, *Makarius, das Thomasevangelium und das Lied von der Perle* (Leiden, 1967), pp. 18ff. For the continuation of this outlook in Syria compare *Liber graduum* (*Patrologia Syriaca* 3, Paris, 1926), p. 476: 'Men and women who do not marry are as angels.' Some Marcionites castrated themselves on baptism so as to seal their complete rejection of the works of the creator-god: see Tertullian, *Adv. Marcionem* IV. 11.

[2] See W. Bauer, *Rechtgläubigkeit und Ketzerei* (2nd ed. by G. Strecher, Tübingen, 1964), p. 27, and H. J. W. Drijvers, 'Edessa und das jüdische Christentum', *Vig. Christ.* 24, 1970, pp. 4–33.

[3] W. Bauer, *loc. cit.*; compare Eusebius, *HE* IV. 30 (Bardaisan's work directed against Syriac Marcionites).

[4] Such as Ephraim Syrus. See references in A. Vööbus, *A History of Asceticism in the Syrian Orient*, vol. I, *CSCO*, Subsidia 14 (Louvain, 1958), p. 48.

[5] Jerome, *Ep.* 17. 2. 'De cavernis cellularum damnamus orbem. In sacco et cinere volutati de episcopis sententiam ferimus.'

[6] See Vööbus, *History of Asceticism*, II, 319ff. for examples. That these physical rigours were not always appreciated by the Greek ecclesiastics is shown by even Meletius of Antioch expostulating against Simeon Stylites' chains. The only chains should be spiritual ones. Iron was superfluous! (Theodoret, *Historia religiosa* XXVI, *PG* 82, col. 1472B).

[7] Etheria commented *circa* 385 on the area between Carrhae and Nisibis 'being full of monks', who used to come into Carrhae to venerate the house of Abraham and martyrium of Helpidius: *Peregrinatio Sanctae Silvae* 20. 5.

bath-buildings were used, monasteries would be built almost overnight, set up especially where the bones of some martyr were believed to lie, or by apparent caprice in a village where a holy man decided he would settle.[1] Once there, however, the monk would soon make his presence felt. The Syrian countryside was as much a prey to economic and social scourges as Egypt and North Africa. As in the latter, fifth- and sixth-century Syria was a land of olive culture and villages.[2] Debt and endemic poverty, however, caused by extortionate taxation, corvées requisitioned by the state and landowners who lived in the cities, and even the uncertainties of the weather combined to force many a smallholder to leave his land or remain and accept conditions akin to slavery. Both John Chrysostom[3] and Theodoret[4] speak of the tyranny of debt, of peasants being used no better than beasts of burden and of oppression by officials, especially those in charge of requisitions and billeting. It is the same picture that one gets from the pages of Optatus of Milevis for North Africa,[5] but the Syrian monks were too individualist and ill-organised to imitate the Donatist Circumcellions and foment peasant uprisings against the landowners. Their personal acts of charity and relief were, however, not dissimilar in range and effectiveness. Simeon Stylites, prince of ascetics, spent part of his days giving judicial decisions and corresponded direct with the emperors and officials in favour of distressed persons who came to him for help.[6] The monk Alexander had debtors' bonds burned in his presence. Others championed villagers against extortion by landowners and tax-collectors,[7] or were instrumental in building hospices for strangers and caring for the sick.[8]

The attitude of these monks towards the clergy varied. By the end of the

[1] See Vööbus, *History of Asceticism*, II, 161ff.

[2] See G. Tchalenko, 'La Syrie du nord: étude économique', *Actes du VIe Congrès international des études byzantines* (Paris, 1950), pp. 389–97.

[3] *Homil. in Matt.* LVIII. 3. (*PG* 49, col. 591).

[4] *Ep.* 42, very valuable evidence, and *Historia religiosa* XVII (*PG* 82, col. 1420D). Compare also *Ep.* 43.

[5] For instance, Optatus of Milevis, *De schismate Donatistarum* III. 4.

[6] Theodoret, *Historia religiosa* XXVI (*PG* 82, col. 1484).

[7] Theodoret, *Historia religiosa* XIV, col. 1413 (Maisumas) and *ibid.* XVII (Abraames who had settled as trader in walnuts and then proceeded to champion the villagers against oppressive tax-collectors). Compare Vööbus, *History of Asceticism*, II, 376ff. regarding Alexander.

[8] Hospices: Theodoret, *Historia religosa* XIV, col. 1412; Maisumas is described as 'Syrian by speech and reared in the countryside' near Antioch as a shepherd. Hospital: *ibid.* XXIV, col. 1461D (Zebrinas).

fourth century some of their number had become the bishops of Carrhae and Edessa whom Etheria met on her pilgrimage tour.[1] Simeon Stylites was conspicuously loyal to the patriarchs of Antioch; but more typical was the reputation of Barsaumas (d. 459), the monastic leader summoned to Ephesus II by Theodosius II as representative of all the monks of Syria, and accused, though perhaps with exaggeration, of being personally responsible for the death of Flavian of Constantinople. He had a huge reputation built up on his fifty-four years as an ascetic; he was 'leader of the mourners'.[2] There was none like him, we are told. His monastery, perched high up on the Nimrod Dagh near the Armenian frontier, was preferred to Antioch as the seat of residence of the medieval Monophysite bishops.[3] This man, a countryman who spoke no Greek, had little use for Domnus and the Syrian episcopate, but his influence in northern and eastern Syria was enormous. 'This is the man who has perverted all Syria in favour of Dioscorus and against the bishops', asserted Diogenes of Cyzicus at Chalcedon.[4] With Shenute in Egypt, Barsaumas was probably the major individual influence in the conscious association of the one-nature Christology with a monastic Christianity that drew its strength from the adherence of the non-Greek populations of Egypt and Syria. Quite rightly the bishops at Chalcedon saw him as their enemy.

The monks in Constantinople were playing an intense but ambivalent part in the ecclesiastical affairs of the capital. Monasticism itself seems to have been a late development there. The year 383 may be taken perhaps for the foundation of the first monastery, that of Isaac and his son Faustus at Psamathia just outside the city.[5] During the next two decades their numbers increased and they were already a powerful 'democratic' force in the time of John Chrysostom (398–404). Their rioting and attempts to bar the churches to John's opponents set off the final crisis which resulted in John's exile. Not only their egalitarian outlook but their squalor and excesses combined with apparent contempt for public affairs were criticised.[6]

[1] *Peregrinatio Sanctae Silvae* 19. 2 and 20. 2.

[2] See Vööbus, *History of Asceticism*, II, 206–7.

[3] See E. Honigmann 'Le Couvent de Barṣaumā et le patriarcat jacobite d'Antioche et de Syrie', *CSCO*, Subsidia 7 (Louvain, 1954) – a defence of Barsaumas.

[4] Mansi, *Collectio* VII, col. 73; also *ibid.* col. 68: ἐπίσκοποι ἐβόησαν· πᾶσαν Συρίαν Βαρσουμᾶς ἠφάνισεν. 'He led thousands of monks against us.'

[5] For the comparative lateness of monasticism in the eastern capital, see J. Pargoire, 'Les Débuts du monachisme à Constantinople', *Revue des questions historiques*, n.s. 21, 1899, pp. 67–143.   [6] Zosimus, *Historia nova* V. 23.

Though these strictures came from pagans, they were pagans in the official classes, and therefore reflect a certain measure of dislike in these quarters.

They were far from being the patriarch's allies on every issue. In the Nestorian crisis the archimandrite Dalmatius and his fellow-monks dramatically threw their weight behind Cyril,[1] and the latter acknowledged their help in winning him the day. Eutyches, with his monastery of 300 monks, also had been on the same side. In the interval, however, between the two councils of Ephesus, monastic opinion had become divided. It was still Cyrillian in outlook, but so were both Proclus and Flavian, and when in 448 the latter at last decided to move against Eutyches, he could count on at least twenty-three archimandrites and other monastic leaders, despite Eutyches' great influence at court.[2]

The first half of the fifth century shows a gradual increase in the real power of the patriarch, a power not based purely on court patronage which could be easily withdrawn, but on a widening influence in the neighbouring provinces, their traditional rights over bishops consecrated for work in heathen areas beyond the frontiers,[3] and above all in an increase of religious identity with the patriarch among the citizens of the capital. Three times, indeed, Constantinople had been humbled by Alexandria. Theophilus, Cyril and Dioscorus had all emerged from their conflicts victorious over the patriarchs of the capital. Over the years, however, the latter had become progressively stronger. Theodosius II had been prepared to support his bishop's jurisdictional claims over the Illyrian bishoprics in 421 and despite protests from successive popes to leave his decision in the *Codex Theodosianus* whose compilation was completed in 438.[4] Proclus' *Tome* to the Armenian church in 435 answering a number of important doctrinal questions showed how the patriarch's influence was making itself felt beyond Rome's eastern frontiers. New Rome was regarded as an acceptable resort, if not of appeal, at least for receiving considered doctrinal advice. Moreover, despite persistent conflict with Ephesus over consecration rights

---

[1] Note the impassioned scene between Theodosius II and Dalmatius in which the latter rebuked Theodosius for his defence of Nestorius and persuaded him, invoking 'the tribunal of Christ', to abandon his cause: Nestorius, *Liber Heraclidis* (ed. Hodgson and Driver), pp. 272–7.

[2] See above, p. 31.

[3] A good example is Eudoxius' consecration of Ulfilas for work among the Goths; Philostorgius, *HE* II. 5. Was the Pope's consecration of Palladius as bishop for the Irish in 431 a riposte?

[4] *Cod. Theod.* XVI. 2. 45.

which the patriarch claimed on the mainland of Asia, these were clearly being accepted by the provincial metropolitans themselves by the time of Chalcedon.[1] All the time, the standing council of bishops in residence at the court – the Home Synod – gave the patriarch the power of comparatively rapid decision on important matters affecting the east in general, supported by clergy drawn from a wide distribution of provinces. This institution was probably the greatest single factor in the rise of the patriarchs of New Rome.

Flavian had been better placed with regard to his clergy than Nestorius had been, and his tragic death had influenced opinion at Chalcedon in favour of the claims of his see. These had also been constantly kept to the fore by the existence of a vocal and coherent public opinion in the capital, as chauvinist and 'orthodox' as its counterpart in Alexandria. Politically this opinion was represented by the factions of the Circus whose members had made themselves responsible for the actual building of the Long Walls and the defence of the city against the Goths.[2] In matters of religion, it expressed itself in a fanatical adherence to orthodoxy, ideally the religion of the court and the patriarch, but always Greek Christianity elevating the status of their city. Already by the year 400, orthodoxy was the only road to acceptance by the populace. Gothic leaders such as Gainas and Tribigild who had taken service with the empire were always feared and suspected. They were Germani and Arians. They dressed and worshipped differently. Even Catholic Goths were described to their faces in unflattering terms by John Chrysostom as 'the most barbarous of all men', who should regard it as a privilege to 'stand along with the sheep of the church in a common pasture and one fold and one table set before all alike'.[3] Others were reminded how they had crossed the Danube in skins![4] On the side of the patriarch, popular chauvinism was a force to be reckoned with. At the end of the fifth century the emperor Anastasius was to tell Pope Gelasius how it would be impossible to have Acacius removed from the diptychs without a tumult.[5]

In the last resort, however, the position of the patriarch of the capital depended on the policy and personality of the emperor. A great figure he

[1] See above, p. 11.
[2] See the article by G. Manojlovic translated and republished by H. Grégoire, 'Le Peuple de Constantinople', *Byzantion* 11, 1936, pp. 616–716, at pp. 632–4.
[3] John Chrysostom, *Homil. habita postquam presbyter Gothus* I (*PG* 63, col. 502).
[4] Theodoret, *HE* v. 32.
[5] Gelasius, *Ep.* 12. 10 (*Epist. Rom. pontif.*, ed. Thiel, p. 357).

The rise of the Monophysite movement

already was by the time of the Second Ecumenical Council in 381, the rival in splendour 'to consuls, governors and the most illustrious commanders', Gregory of Nazianzus ruefully remarked,[1] but he was also the personal chaplain of the ruler, whose confidence he had to retain. Arcadius who exiled John Chrysostom and Theodosius II who destroyed Flavian show where the ultimate power in ecclesiastical affairs lay. Both emperors have been harshly treated by western historians, who have misunderstood some of the values that counted most in the east Roman world of the fifth century. For Arcadius little perhaps can be said, and one can detect the note of exasperation in Synesius' *De regno* at his indolence and unwillingness to act as leader of his people,[2] but even he left a favourable memory with the peoples of the east, as one who cared for their welfare and protected his realm through his orthodoxy and piety.[3] He deserved his share of divine intervention to disrupt the rebellion of Gainas.[4] In Alexandria, the Serapeum converted into a Christian church was named after him.[5] On the other hand, the picture of Theodosius II as a weak and effeminate ruler overshadowed by his sister Pulcheria and surrounded by eunuchs who kept him in the seclusion of his palace has been overdone. There are elements of truth in this, but in addition to the quality of mercy that impressed contemporaries concerning him,[6] Theodosius was capable of rapid decision and action, as the unfortunate Ibas of Edessa found to his cost.[7] Senior officials whom he appointed, such as the prefect Cyrus or Chareas the

---

[1] Gregory, *Oratio* XLII. 24 (*PG* 36, col. 488).

[2] *De regno* 10–15 (ed. and tr. FitzGerald). Piety might be the foundation for success, but leadership including personal leadership in battle was also necessary. Arcadius was criticised as being 'amazingly inactive' (p. 125).

[3] To the Arab Jacobites he was a virtuous emperor (*Synaxarium* under 17 Tout = 14 September, *Synaxaire arabe jacobite*, ed. R. Basset, *PO* 1, Paris, 1907, p. 277). Also, Michael the Syrian, *Chron.* VIII. 1 and Socrates, *HE* VI. 23. While Honorius was regarded as weak and pitiable (Procopius, *De bello vandalico* 1. 2. 25 and 34, and Sozomen, *HE* IX. 16), Arcadius was credited with positive virtue that merited divine reward.

[4] Sozomen, *HE* VIII. 4. 12–14 and 18–20 (ed. Bidez and Hansen, pp. 355–7). Socrates, *HE* VI. 6: the defeat of Gainas 'an astounding act of divine providence'.

[5] Sozomen, *HE* VII. 15. 10.

[6] See Sozomen, *HE*, Prologue, 9 (ed. Bidez and Hansen, p. 3).

[7] The dating of developments relating to Ibas' removal before Ephesus II is interesting. Chareas and his staff visited Edessa to take evidence of popular feeling concerning Ibas on 12–14 April 449, the report was in Theodosius' hands by the fourth week of June. By the 27th the emperor had sent this to his council for judgement on Ibas, and on 21 July a new bishop was consecrated at Edessa (*Chron. Edessenum* LXIV).

governor of Osrhoëne in 449, were often men of great ability and character, prepared to make on-the-spot decisions even if contrary to a previously drafted brief.[1]

No man could survive for forty-two years as an imperial ruler in the fifth century without some gifts of statesmanship. Theodosius showed skill in diplomacy and after Ephesus I a sureness of touch in ecclesiastical affairs.[2] He recognised the monks, particularly the Syrian monks, for the important influences on public opinion that they were. In 434 his letters to Simeon Stylites, James and Baradotus contributed much towards securing the acceptance by all parties of the Formula of Reunion. In 449, feeling the tide of opinion in Syria in favour of Dioscorus, he invited James and Barsaumas as monastic representatives at Ephesus II, and both accepted. It was hard on Domnus, Flavian and Theodoret, but it put the emperor on the side of public opinion, and this was never to be forgotten among the Monophysites.[3] Theodosius was to remain their hero.

In fact, he had been following wise precedent. Ever since Constantine had demonstratively reconciled himself and his office with the Egyptian confessor Paphnutius at Nicaea, the eastern sovereigns had courted ascetics and monks.[4] Constantine and even Constantius had corresponded with Antony.[5] Theodosius I had accepted the illiterate Macedonius' rebuke during the crisis of 387, Arcadius had founded monasteries in Palestine. Only Valens had been against the monks[6] – and he had perished at Adrianople! When the emperor was at Constantinople there were no incidents like the massacre of Thessalonica. In moments of dire peril such as

[1] Chareas himself admits that he was persuaded to forward the petitions against Ibas by their very force, contrary to his instructions: *Akten*, ed. Flemming, p. 33, line 25.

[2] Note J. B. Bury's view (*History of the Later Roman Empire*, I, 215): 'The truth is, that this emperor, though weak like his father [Arcadius] was far more intelligent and profited more by his education.'

[3] In the anti-Chalcedonian 'visions' recorded by John Rufus *circa* 500, Palestinian monks heard angelic voices crying out that 'the heavens were falling' for 'the great emperor, Theodosius the orthodox, is dead' (*Plerophoria* 32, ed. Nau, p. 75). To Timothy the Cat, he was 'our venerable emperor' (*ibid*. p. 83).

[4] Theodoret, *HE* I. 7, emphasising the 'martyr' aspect of these clerics at the hand of Constantine's predecessors. Also, Socrates, *HE* I. 11.

[5] Athanasius, *Vita Antonii* 81.

[6] His law, *Cod. Theod.* XII. 1. 63 of January 370, ordered that no *curialis* could become a monk; and for retribution foretold by Isaac the monk, see Sozomen, *HE* VI. 40. 1 (ed. Bidez and Hansen, p. 301). Compare Theodoret, *HE* IV. 34. 1–2.

beset Anastasius in 511–12 over the *Trishagion* and Justinian in the Nika riot of 532, he would listen to his subjects, and survive. The identification of successive eastern emperors with the religious feelings of their subjects established a relationship which was proof against barbarians and Persians alike and took some of the edge off the theological and social rancour of the times. Loyalty founded on a common theology was one of the main factors in preserving the eastern provinces from the fate of their western counterparts in the first half of the fifth century.

The emperor's relations with the Pope and with the church in the tottering remains of the western empire were based on equally important but different assumptions. Just as their establishment at Constantinople seems to have affected the outlook of even the most western-oriented rulers such as Theodosius I, the same is true only in the opposite sense in the west. The religious policy of the western emperors, whether of a soldier such as Valentinian I or of a figurehead like Honorius, shows remarkable continuity. They appear to have accepted without question a theory of church–state relations based on parallel and autonomous jurisdictions which would have been rejected in the east.

Events had assisted these developments. The transfer of the centre of imperial authority from Rome to Constantinople by Constantine, the defection of North Africa to the Donatists and the unity of the western episcopate behind the formula of Nicaea, each contributed towards strengthening the hand of the western bishops, and in particular the Pope, against imperial authority. Already under Constans in 342, the western bishops at Serdica had conceded an appellate jurisdiction to the Pope, and restricted recourse by clergy to the civil power.[1] A decade later Constantius II's attempt to foist a non-Nicene *credo* on the west after creating great bitterness ended in failure, and his successors wisely accepted that on matters of doctrine the emperor had little or nothing to say. Thus, Valentinian I told the bishops assembled at Lampsacus in 364, 'I am a layman and should not interfere in such matters [i.e. matters of faith]. Let the priests whose concern these things are assemble where they like.'[2] Just as pertinently Honorius told Apollodorus, proconsul of Africa, that 'so far as matters of religion are concerned the bishops should act, but other matters which

---

[1] See Jalland, *The Church and the Papacy*, p. 220, for comment on canons 5 and 6 of the Council of Serdica.
[2] Sozomen, *HE* VI. 6. 2.

pertain to appointed magistrates or to the enforcement of the public law should be settled according to law'.[1] There was a dual control. Church and empire worked in harmony but on parallel lines. Magistrates and bishops kept to their own separate functions. Disputes between them concerned the frontiers of authority only. As the power of the emperor declined, so that of the bishops increased. Valentinian III's edict of 8 July 445[2] handing over the supreme authority of the churches in Gaul to Leo came just at the time when his cousin Theodosius II was asserting his own prerogatives over the churches in the east.

The principles that governed a balance of authority so favourable to the church were as long-standing as those in the east that led in the opposite direction. The world-view of the western and eastern churches contrasted at many points. If in the east theologians and historians believed that, despite everything that 'the envious demon' might do, all creation was moving towards a harmony between God and the universe under the providential rule of the emperor, in the west the tendency, except for a brief period under Theodosius I, was towards a dualistic concept of the created order. *Civitas Dei* stood over against *civitas terrena*, as did Jerusalem against Babylon, the church contrasted with the world, and priests with rulers. If the world belonged to God, what was worldly belonged to the devil,[3] and for those who remained attached to the world there awaited not gradual improvement and purification, but rapidly approaching divine judgement and hell fire.[4] Thus the separation of the religious and secular was a matter of vital moment for the Christian. Baptism for the religiously-minded involved not only illumination but renunciation of the learning and philosophy of the world, and monasticism a rejection of all forms of service to it.[5]

More at home with a Biblical typology ultimately derived from Jewish

[1] *Cod. Theod.* XVI. 11. 1 (A.D. 399).

[2] Valentinian, *Novel* 17, agreeing that the papal verdict against Hilary of Arles would have been valid throughout Gaul even without imperial enforcement. 'For what limits can there be to the authority of a bishop so great as he?'

[3] Tertullian, *De spectaculis* 15: 'Sed tamen in saecularibus separamus quia saeculum dei est, saecularia autem diaboli.'

[4] This is universal in the west. For instance, Maximus of Turin *circa* 400: 'Considera itaque iudicii inmittentem diem et inextinguibiles gehennae flammas stridorem horridum dentium tenebrarum ultimum cruciatum, et si potes relicta ecclesia saecularibus sollicitudinibus inplicare!' (*Sermo* 32. 2). No purging fire this, as envisaged by Origen, *Contra Celsum* II. 24.

[5] Thus, Paulinus of Nola, *Carmen* X, lines 166–8. Those contemplating God 'otia amant strepitumque fori rerumque tumultus cunctaque divinis inimica negotia donis

interpretations of Scripture than the free-ranging allegory of Greek Christianity, the westerners regarded the church as 'the people of God', the prolongation and fulfilment of Israel. The Christian was a member of the congregation of the faithful, accepting its law[1] and conditions of service, whose only interpreters were the clergy. The Christian emperor was a member of the church, and he too was subject to its laws. His office indeed was sacred and ordained by God. He was protector of the church. His laws vindicated its freedom[2] and the sanctity of its doctrines against its enemies. Like any other layman, however, he must accept the discipline of its clergy. He was 'within the Church' and not above it,[3] and his chief glory would be found in service to it.[4]

The practical results of these ideas in the fourth and fifth centuries are well known. The dualism implied in Donatus of Carthage's famous question to the representatives of the Emperor Constans in 346, 'What has the emperor to do with the Church?',[5] would have been accepted by practically every bishop in the west. Ten years later, Constantius was defied by the aged Hosius and reminded of the injunction, 'Render unto Caesar...'[6] For Ambrose, Caesar's sphere was confined strictly to the control of those secular matters where the church had no interest. Where religion or matters affecting morals were concerned, any question 'in causa

ab Christi imperiis et amore salutis abhorrent'. Note also Pope Damasus' praise for soldiers who threw away their weapons, thus courting martyrdom: *ILCV* 1981, (*Nereus et Achilles martyres*). See my article 'Paulinus of Nola and the last century of the western empire', *JRS* 59, 1969, pp. 1–11.

[1] The emphasis in North Africa on Christianity as a 'law' is shown by an inscription from Koudjiat Adjala in Mauretania Sitifensis dating to 361. Gaius Iulius Castus is described as 'sacerdotalis legis sacrae' and buried near a chapel dedicated to martyrs (see P. A. Février, 'Inscriptions funéraires de Maurétanie', *Mélanges* 76, 1964, p. 158).

[2] So Maximus of Turin, *Sermo* 106. 2 (ed A. Mutzenbacher, p. 418): 'Principes quidem tam boni christiani leges pro religione promulgant, sed eas exsecutores non exerunt conpetenter', a nice sidelight on the religious situation in north-west Italy *circa* 400.

[3] So Ambrose, *Sermo contra Auxentium* 36 (*PL* 16, col. 1018) and *Ep.* 10, 22 and 21. 10. Compare Lucifer of Cagliari's assertions that the emperor was 'unus ex conservis' of the church: *PL* 13, cols. 826, 883 and 1002.

[4] Thus Augustine, regarding Constantine and Theodosius I, *De civitate Dei* v. 24–6. Compare Ambrose, *Ep.* 17. 1, 'You are serving almighty God and our sacred faith', to Gratian.

[5] Optatus of Milevis, *De schismate Donatistarum* III. 3 (ed. Ziwsa, p. 73). See my 'The Roman Empire in the eyes of the western schismatics'.

[6] Cited by Athanasius, *Historia Arianorum* 44 (*PG* 25, cols. 743–8). See Greenslade, *Church and State from Constantine to Theodosius*, p. 45.

Dei', the church's views must prevail, even against the requirements of civil order. Excommunication awaited any ruler who refused to accept the authority of its representatives.[1] Schism between Pope and emperor was always a possibility.

In Milan in 385 and 386, Ambrose had had popular opinion on his side in his refusal to hand over a church to the emperor's court for Arian worship. Not surprisingly perhaps, for the outlook of the western Christians corresponded to that of their clergy. One notices how, for instance, the Biblical scenes expressed in the popular arts of the lamp-maker and sculptor depict Noah's ark or the Hebrew youths defying Nebuchadnezzar in the fiery furnace, representing the exclusive attitudes of the church towards external society and the emperor.[2] Even at the end of the fourth century Millenarianism, originally inspired by late-Jewish apocalyptic, was by no means extinct among western Christian writers. Far from identification of church and Roman empire being regarded as an acceptable ideal, the empire remained, in orthodox and schismatic circles alike, as merely the last of the great secular realms which had dominated humanity for a season before extinction at the hand of God. The emperor or barbarian king was the 'rex saeculi'[3] in an age where doom was expected and persecutions were in the natural order of events.

Just as important in forming the climate of opinion was the fact commented upon by Sozomen writing *circa* 440 that in his time, 'the Thracians, the Illyrians and the other European nations possessed no congregations of monks' though there were 'many men devoted to Christian philosophy among them'.[4] The lack of a popular monastic movement in the west had a significance that cannot be overestimated. At a crucial moment in the history of the western empire it left the provincial without the vision of a better life to achieve by his own efforts, an antidote to fatalistic predictions

---

[1] Ambrose, *Epp.* 40 and 41 (on the affair of Callinicum, 388). See also the collection of texts in C. Morino, *Church and State in the Teaching of St Ambrose*, Eng. tr. by M. J. Costelloe (Washington, 1969), ch. 6 and notes.

[2] See for examples from Numidia, A. Berthier *et al.*, *Les Vestiges du Christianisme antique dans la Numidie centrale* (Algiers, 1942), p. 188.

[3] Petilian of Constantine ap. Augustine, *Contra litteras Petiliani* II. 92. 202: 'Quid autem vobis est cum regibus saeculi quos numquam Christianitas nisi invidos sensit.' Compare *Liber genealogus* (ed. Mommsen, *MGH*, AA 9, Berlin, 1892), p. 195, referring to Gaiseric. For a study of Augustine's concept of human history and the state, see R. A. Markus, *Saeculum: history and society in the theology of St Augustine* (Cambridge, 1970).

[4] Sozomen, *HE* III. 14. 38.

The rise of the Monophysite movement

of approaching doom, and no channel through which he could make his grievances known to his rulers. Until too late, monks were unpopular and often regarded as Manichaeans in disguise.[1] Even the renunciation of their possessions by some members of the nobility brought little joy to the provincials who formed the mass of the tenants on the great estates. They might simply find themselves the prey to a horde of lesser men who seized on the estates when they were broken up and sold.[2] The result was a spirit of despair leading to separation and revolt. The long persistence of these attitudes in the west made it impossible for the emperors to make concessions to anti-Chalcedonian opinion with any hope of retaining western loyalty. In Pope Gelasius (492–6) the popular mood found a papal champion.

In all essentials the popes spoke for the west in their dealings with the emperor at Constantinople and the eastern episcopate. In an important letter to Marcian, Leo states unequivocally the difference of premiss that determined divine and human law.[3] To the long tradition of the separation of powers, the popes added prerogatives of their own. They were undisputed heads of the church in the west. We have seen, too, how Celestine and Xystus III considered that their views, however uninstructed, should be accepted as a matter of course by the easterners.[4] Similarly, appeals by eastern bishops should be directed to them rather than to the emperor. The long struggle of the popes to retain control over the diocese of Illyricum illustrates the importance they laid on the acknowledgement by the emperor of their jurisdictional authority. All this legacy was maintained, systematised and wherever possible extended by Leo.

Significantly perhaps, it is not easy to grasp at the real personality of Leo, despite his voluminous sermons and correspondence. He sees himself in a strictly depersonalised role, a mere office-holder. He is Peter's mouthpiece but as such the heir (*haeres*) to the apostle in a juristic sense (*Sermo* III. 4). Just as Peter held the *plenitudo potestatis* as Vicar of Christ, so the claims of the papacy to obedience were also untrammelled.[5] Long before he became

---

[1] Compare Jerome, *Ep.* 22. 13 and 38.

[2] For Ausonius' view of what would happen on Paulinus of Nola's estates in south-west Gaul if he were to retire from the world, Ausonius, *Ep.* 27 (ed. and tr. Evelyn White, lines 115–16).

[3] 'Alia tamen ratio est rerum saecularium alia divinarum'; *Ep.* 104. 3 (*PL* 54, col. 995A).   [4] See above, p. 23.

[5] For instance, *Sermo* III. 4, IV. 3 and V. 2. See Walter Ullmann, 'Leo I and the theme of papal primacy', *JTS*, n.s. 11, 1960, pp. 25–51 for the development of this outlook from the time of Damasus and its expression by Leo.

involved with Eutyches and Flavian, he had written to the bishops in Illyria, 'Moreover, because our care extends throughout all the Churches, since our Lord demands this of us, who entrusted to the most blessed apostle Peter the primacy of apostolic honour in reward for his faith, establishing the universal Church on his firmness as a foundation, we share the duty of responsibility which we possess with those who are joined to us in collegial love.'[1] Before Chalcedon he had written to the Gallic bishops, 'Through the most blessed Peter, chief of the Apostles, the holy Roman Church holds the principate over all the churches of the whole world'.[2] Christ had provided for the monarchic rule of the church, and it was hopeless for the other patriarchs, especially that of Constantinople who had no claim to apostolic authority, to try to build up their own jurisdictions against the will of the see of Peter.

Regarding the emperor, Leo was not quite so clear. Certainly he had the power and duty of safeguarding the liberty of the church and upholding Catholic truth. This could also be extended to the summons of councils whereby that truth could be established. Leo did not dispute Theodosius II's right to assemble Ephesus II. He complained it had been subverted by Dioscorus and that the best remedy was for the emperor to summon another council speedily, this time to meet in Italy. He went even further, and in a remarkable letter (*Ep.* 24)[3] written in February 449 he conceded that Theodosius did possess a priestly role. He was not only 'guardian of the faith', but Leo rejoiced in 'the even priestly soul' that resided in Theodosius (*sed etiam sacerdotalem inesse animum gaudeamus*) through which he exercised 'the most pious solicitude for the Christian religion apart from imperial and public affairs'.[4] To Leo, then, the 'two societies' of church and empire might coalesce to the extent of it being possible for the one to share the properties of the other. Yet though his words might be the same as those used by some eastern bishops, it is doubtful whether the meaning behind them was the same also. This was to prove the case regarding the doctrinal issue. Yet both pope and emperor still regarded the empire as an unbreakable whole, and, as we have seen, it was far from Theodosius' intention to

[1] Leo, *Ep.* 5. 2 (*PL* 54, col. 615), Jan. 444.
[2] *Ep.* 65. 2 (*PL* 54, col. 881).
[3] *Ep.* 24. 1 (*PL* 54, col. 735): 'ut vobis non solum regium, sed etiam sacerdotalem inesse animum gaudeamus'.
[4] Compare similarly Vigilius on Justinian's 'priestly soul', *Ep.* 4 (Mansi, *Collectio* IX, col. 35).

break with Rome after Ephesus II. The correspondence with Leo is markedly polite. The pope asks the emperor to help the church. He does not make demands. Theodosius and Marcian are always 'your clemency'[1] and not, as with Felix III and Gelasius, 'my son'.

Like the other patriarchates, the see of Rome had its internal difficulties that impeded its freedom of action. The schisms that tied the hands of Damasus and Symmachus through much of their reigns had social and political aspects that rendered them violent and intractable. The minority groups among the Roman Christians hated the papacy for its wealth.[2] In its external relations the long dispute with Constantinople over the Illyrian provinces has been alluded to.[3] The heated exchange with Hilary of Arles (*Epp.* 10 and 11) indicates that even in Gaul, Rome's supreme jurisdictional authority was not acknowledged unreservedly. Africa, however, the centre of the conciliar tradition under Augustine, was no longer an ecclesiastical power by the time Leo became pope. But meanwhile the see of Ravenna was beginning to loom on the horizon as the seat of the imperial court and Eutyches took his case thither after his condemnation.[4] Had the western empire survived, more might have been heard of the prerogatives of this imitation Rome. A more serious if more insidious danger perhaps was the situation in Sicily, where the predominance of Greek as the language of the majority of church and people gave Constantinople an unlooked-for foothold in its rival's camp.[5] Not for nothing did Leo and his successors attempt to Latinise the liturgy and calendar of the Sicilian church.[6] Their lack of success foreshadowed the ready acceptance of Byzantine ecclesiastical control by the Sicilians a century later.

[1] Leo, *Epp.* 31 and 117.

[2] Note the *Preces Luciferianorum* 121 (= *Coll. Avellana* 2, ed. Guenther, *CSEL* 35.1, p. 43): 'Habeant illi basilicas auro coruscantes, pretiosorumque marmorum ambitione vestitas vel erectas magnificentia columnarum; habeant in longum possessiones ob quas fides integra periclitata est.' The Donatist view of the African Catholics was similar; compare Possidius, *Vita Augustini* 23 (*PL* 32, col. 53): 'Dum forte [ut assolet] de possessionibus ipsis invidia clericis fieret.'

[3] See above, p. 9.

[4] Ap. Leo, *Ep.* 25.

[5] See M. I Finley, *Ancient Sicily to the Arab Conquest* (London, 1968), pp. 166 and 176–8 (gives references).

[6] Leo, *Ep.* 16. The issue was the Sicilian custom of celebrating baptism at the festival of the Epiphany instead of at Easter or Pentecost. Epiphany was mainly an eastern feast. See T. G. Jalland, *The Life and Times of St Leo the Great* (London, 1941), p. 88 on the incident.

The emperor and his church

There are few inevitabilities in history. Even making every allowance for the coincidence of interest between pope, emperor and patriarch of Constantinople and the extension of the *communicatio idiomatum* to cover the relations between church and state, it is difficult to see that east and west could have worked together for long. Sooner or later the emperor would have had to choose between the eastern and western view of his prerogatives and no Byzantine emperor would have accepted the role assigned to him by the Latins, that of an Israelite monarch, or even of a repentant Nebuchadnezzar.[1] As it was, the issue was forced by the most difficult of intellectual disputes, in which not only was the east divided within itself, but much of the east and the west took views which, however subtly enunciated, were at heart diametrically opposed.

[1] As Augustine, *Contra litteras Petiliani* 11. 92. 204 and *Ep.* 185. 2. 8.

Chapter 3

THE INTELLECTUALS AND THE MONKS

We now turn to the battle of the intellectuals.[1] Three general points may be made at the outset. We are dealing with long-standing issues, debated in in the east over the two previous centuries before Chalcedon. There was nothing sudden about the Christological controversy. Secondly, behind the seemingly unending wrangle over whether Christ existed 'in two natures' or 'out of two natures' lay deep questions of human salvation, not least those embodied in the doctrines of the Eucharist and the Atonement. Thirdly, in a world in which combat by the individual with evil spirits and destructive powers was accepted as in the nature of things, the masses of the faithful led by the monks could not accept what they believed to be prevarication and uncertainty over matters affecting their ultimate salvation. The victory of Christianity as the religion of the Mediterranean peoples made religious compromises impossible.

The germ of the future conflict is to be found far back at the turn of the third century with the outbreak of the Monarchian controversies in Rome. Orthodox theologians had opposed Valentinian gnosticism and Marcionism with the assertion of the reality of Jesus' mission and sufferings, and pointed to the Gospels as sufficient warrant for the true character of Jesus' humanity. In the fourth century there were many who saw the Christology of Apollinarius and his disciples as nothing better than a recurrence of these ancient heresies.[2] The problem, however, was just how to define the relationship between the divine and human elements in Christ.

By A.D. 200 some Christians in Rome, such as Noetus and Praxeas, immigrants from the province of Asia, were claiming that in order to exalt

---

[1] On this theme see the masterly work of A. Grillmeier, *Christ in Christian Tradition*, and J. N. D. Kelly, *Early Christian Doctrines* (London, 1958), chs. 11 and 12, to which I am much indebted in this chapter.

[2] Compare Basil, *Ep.* 261 (*PG* 32, col. 969C), and Didymus the Blind, *Comment. in Psalmos* x. 9, lines 12–14 (A. Gesché, 'La Christologie du Commentaire sur les Psaumes découvert à Toura', *Univ. Cath. Lovaniensis Dissertationes*, ser. III. 7, Gembloux, 1962, p. 108).

Christ's divinity so that he was worshipped truly 'as God',[1] it was necessary to conceive of the Father in some way being associated with his sufferings.[2] This Patripassian or Modalist-Monarchian view of Christ (as a 'mode' of the Father) persisted in the background of much of the thought of Christians in Asia and may be a factor in the popularity of the Monophysite cause there in the fifth and sixth centuries. As against this understanding of Christ, however, were the theories of individuals such as the two Theodoti, also immigrants to Rome, who could point to a text such as Jn. 8. 40 and claim that it proved that Christ was a man in origin in whom the divine power (δύναμις) of the Holy Spirit took up his abode, symbolised by the descent of the dove at Jesus' baptism.[3] This Dynamic Monarchianism represented Jesus in Trinitarian terms, but failed to do justice to the belief that he was truly God. External inspiration and resulting adoption into the Godhead were unconvincing of themselves as attributes of God and smacked too much of Jewish angel-worship or Ebionism. Both Theodotus and Praxeas were condemned. Even so, it was evident that Theodotus' views were shared not only by some intellectual Christians in Rome who used their ethical appeal to bridge Christianity and Aristotelianism,[4] but also among Syrian Christians, perhaps influenced by a Judaic environment, who tended to prefer a literal interpretation of the Gospel narratives. The teachings of Theodotus were carried on by his pupil Artemon in the 230s, and a generation later these were associated with Paul of Samosata at Antioch. Already at this period Christology was beginning to take on a regional colour.

Meantime, in Alexandria one of the impulses that drove Origen to elaborate his Logos-theology was an indignant mistrust of the two Monarchian Christologies. At the end of his lengthy and teasing examination of a Bishop Heraclides who seems to have been suspected as a Modalist-Monarchian,[5]

---

[1] The requirement occurs already in *II Clement*, ch. 1, the opening words of his sermon ('Brethren, we must think of Jesus Christ as of God, as of the Judge of the living and the dead'). For the emphatic assertion of his humanity against Docetism at this period, see Ignatius of Antioch, *Ep. ad Trall.* IX. Theodoret, *Ep.* 151, claims Ignatius in the succession of the same Christology as he.

[2] Note pseudo-Tertullian, *Adversus omnes haereses* 8 (ed. A. Kroymann, *Corpus Christianorum* 2, Turnhout, 1954, p. 1410): 'Hic [Praxeas] Deum patrem omnipotentem Iesum Christum esse dicit; hunc crucifixum passumque contendit mortuum.'

[3] Eusebius, *HE* v. 28. 6. Compare Hippolytus, *Refutatio* VII. 35. See M. F. Wiles, *The Spiritual Gospel* (Cambridge, 1960), p. 112.   [4] Eusebius, *HE* v. 28. 14.

[5] Origen, *Dialogue with Heraclides* (Eng. text in *Alexandrian Christianity*, ed. Chadwick and Oulton, pp. 437–55, especially p. 439).

Origen defends his assertion of the existence of a duality between Christ and God on the grounds that only thus could the obvious errors of the Monarchians be avoided. 'In this way', he says, 'we avoid falling into the opinion of those who are separated from the church and turned to the illusory notion of monarchy, who abolish the Son as distinct from the Father and virtually abolish the Father also. Nor do we fall into the other blasphemous doctrine which denies the deity of Christ.'[1] The anger roused in Origen at the idea of Dynamic Monarchianism, compared with his tone of admonition towards the Modalists, is significant in itself, and it foreshadows the attitude of the school of Alexandrian theologians towards both alternatives to their own Trinitarian doctrine and Christology. Paul of Samosata, rather than Heraclides, was the enemy. The one was to be deposed by a council, the other merely rebuked. Against Heraclides, Origen emphasised the separation of Father and Son and dwelt on their method of conjunction as 'God'. This leads him to discuss the nature of the Son and in doing so he anticipates the standard anti-Apollinarian reasoning of the Cappadocians at the end of the fourth century. In reply to a certain Maximus, in the same dialogue, Origen points out 'the whole man (body, soul, and spirit) would not have been saved unless Christ had taken upon him the whole man. They do away with salvation', he adds, 'when they say that the body of the Saviour is spiritual.' He has, however, to confess his ignorance of how the body, soul and spirit of Christ became separated at the time of the Passion and reunited after the ascension.[2] As in so much else, he saw the issue clearly and his inability to contribute more significantly to its solution boded ill for the efforts of his disciples.

Origen's main problem was the relationship between God and his Word within the Trinity. Christology was not the decisive issue. He realised, however, in his *Commentary on John* that the apparent conflict between texts such as Jn. 7. 28 and 8. 19, or Jesus' actions to satisfy material needs, like sending his disciples to buy bread, compared with the miracle of the loaves and the fishes, could only be accounted for if Jesus was sometimes speaking of himself as man and at other times as God.[3] Elsewhere, he shows that he had meditated on the significance of Christ's soul, putting forward the view that this alone had escaped blemish at the Fall 'as being the Wisdom and Word of God', and therefore served as the meeting-point of divine and

[1] *Ibid.* p. 439.
[2] *Ibid.* p. 442. See Chadwick's comment, *Alexandrian Christianity*, p. 435.
[3] See Wiles, *The Spiritual Gospel*, p. 112.

The intellectuals and the monks

human through the incarnation.[1] He thought of Christ's soul as the link between the Logos and the body in which the Logos was revealed to mankind. Through its unity with the Logos it provided a model for the association of the believer with God. These views were, however, peripheral both to his Logos theology and to the urgency of his concern for moral reform and virtuous conduct which he proclaimed as the hall-mark of a Christian.[2] For all his assertion of the real humanity of Christ, the Word-flesh Christology which developed from his teaching made no allowance for a human directing mind or soul in Christ animating the body.

One reason for this may be that in the Neo-Platonist system that formed the background to the theology of Origen and his successors, the body was regarded as alien from the soul in man, and the soul alone was capable of immortality; but the soul itself was looked upon as a 'mixed' substance aspiring towards the sphere of the intellect but also involved in the corporeal world.[3] Christ, however, was the divine Logos who had taken to himself a body like ours (the form of a servant) to manifest the fullness of God to man, for the purpose of man's instruction and salvation.[4] Since the Logos did not change in any way at the incarnation,[5] the human soul in Christ could only be considered as an adjunct, present because humanity would not be complete without it, but wholly passive. Little wonder then, that at the Council of Antioch in 268 Origen's disciple Malchion took the logical step and denied its existence in Christ. 'The God-Logos is in him what the inner man is in us.'[6] The bishops present approved.

[1] Origen, *De principiis* II. 6. 3, ed. P. Koetschau, GCS 22, Origenes Werke 5, Leipzig, 1913, pp. 141–3 (gives other references) and *Contra Celsum* IV. 15 and 18.

[2] This comes out clearly in the passage from the *Dialogue with Heraclides*. He reminds his hearers that 'the divine tribunal' was concerned with matters other than doctrine.

[3] See R. A. Norris, *Manhood and Christ* (Oxford, 1963), pp. 39–40: 'For the Neo-Platonist the soul is an ontological Janus, forever turned towards the world of sense, yet – no doubt more fundamentally – forever aspiring to the world of the intellect.'

[4] Origen, *Homil. XIX in Luc.* (ed. M. Rauer, GCS 49, Berlin, 1954, pp. 114–15). Christ 'appeared as weak because he had assumed a weak body and is strengthened again because of that body. He had emptied himself as Son of God and therefore was filled again with wisdom.' The use of Phil. 2. 7 as evidencing a kenotic theory of Christology was to be followed by Origen's Alexandrian successors.

[5] Origen, *Contra Celsum* IV. 15: 'The Word suffers nothing of the experience of the body or the soul.' It remained always 'one', *ibid.* II. 9.

[6] Cited from the bishops at the council in reply to Paul of Samosata: H. de Riedmatten, *Les Actes du procès de Paul de Samosate* (Fribourg, Switzerland, 1952), p. 154, frag. 30

Unfortunately for the establishment of a two-nature Christology in response to this view, emphasising the humanity of Christ and the New Testament account of his life, Malchion's opponent was Paul of Samosata, bishop of Antioch under Queen Zenobia of Palmyra from 261 to 272. His questionable personal life (Eusebius, *HE* VII. 30. 6–11) made it easy for him to be condemned as a heretic for denying the essential or hypostatic union of the Word with Jesus in Christ without credit being given to the positive aspects of his beliefs. Paul separated the Logos and man in Jesus. He asserted that Jesus was a man in whom the Holy Spirit had taken up his abode as in a temple at his baptism (compare Jn. 2. 21) and that the Word was therefore 'conjoined to him who came from David'.[1] That is, Christ could be regarded as inspired in the same way as the prophets, though in his case the spiritual inspiration was total and permanent whereas with the prophets it was partial and intermittent.[2] If this, however, sounded blasphemous to Alexandrian ears, it seems to have been what a large proportion of Syrian Christians believed. The *Acts of Archelaus* (fourth century), for instance, which record an alleged debate between the bishop of Carrhae (?) and the Persian heresiarch Manes (Mani), show the former asserting, like Paul, that Mary gave birth to a man (not the Word), that he was not perfected until the dove descended on him at baptism[3] and that the Christian was saved through redemption from sin at baptism and by following a Christ-like life thereafter.[4] The emphasis was on Christ as true man undergoing real temptations and on man's salvation being won by his triumph. It is worth noticing that Antiochene theology, if influenced by Judaism, was being

(reviewed by H. Chadwick, *JTS*, n.s. 4, 1953, pp. 91–4). Also M. F. Wiles, 'The nature of the early debate about Christ's human soul', *JEH* 16. 2, 1965, pp. 139–51 at pp. 143–4.

[1] De Riedmatten, *Les Actes*, p. 158, frag. 37. For a selection of Paul's utterances see J. Stevenson, *A New Eusebius* (London, S.P.C.K., 1957), pp. 277–9, and E. G. Bardy, *Paul de Samosate* (Louvain, 1929).

[2] Compare the extract of Paul's discussion with Malchion, cited by Severus of Antioch, *Philalethes* (ed. Hespel), p. 124: 'The unique Lord was in him fundamentally. For he was equally in the prophets, and above all in Moses. The Lord is also in many mortals, but above all in Jesus, as in the temple of God.' The temple simile of Jn. 2. 21, 'he spake of the Temple of his body', was to be a favourite one among Antiochene theologians.

[3] *Acta Archelai* (ed. Beeson) 58. 11: 'Dic mihi, O Manichaee, si ais Iesum non esse ex Maria natum, sed apparuisse quidem ut hominem, cum homo non esset... dic mihi super quem spiritus sanctus sicut columba descendit?'; and *ibid.* 60. 3: 'Dico autem de eo qui ex Maria factus est homo.' Beeson unfortunately throws little light on the problems of date and authorship. Jerome, *De vir. illustr.* 72, places the debate in the reign of Probus (276–82). [4] *Acta Archelai* 60. 10.

forged in conflict with Manichaean missionaries who asserted the unreal or Docetic character of Christ.[1] In Egypt the Jews were now less powerful, but the Manichaeans were a real threat to Christianity in parts of the Nile valley. In east and west alike during the fourth and early fifth centuries Judaism and Manichaeism were always in the background, never strong enough to prevail against Christianity but powerful enough to be feared, and to force on the Christians definitions of doctrine designed deliberately to avoid contamination with either.

The Arian controversy, stretching over the whole of the middle years of the fourth century, brought the latent problems of Christology into the open. Each of the great patriarchates was to emphasise a different aspect in their defence of orthodoxy. The legacy of Origen led through Arius himself to Athanasius, to Apollinarius and to Cyril, on the one hand, and to the Cappadocians and the fifth-century patriarchs of Constantinople (except Nestorius) on the other. All these represented the theology of the Word-flesh, the Alexandrians interpreting it in terms of a one-nature Christology, albeit with lesser or greater degrees of reservation, the theologians who followed the lead of the Cappadocians in terms of two natures. It was the attempt to find the middle ground of agreement between adversaries who were at heart exponents of the same tradition that frustrated theological intellects and exacerbated strife. Opposed to them on the basic issues of the character of Christ's humanity but often approaching them verbally were the Word-man theologians of the Antiochene school, Eustathius (d. after 330), Diodore of Tarsus (d. *circa* 395),[2] and Theodore of Mopsuestia (d. 428). Allied to them in their theology, but separate from them in every other way, including matters of discipline and sentiment, were the westerners, and especially Leo.

All authorities were agreed that the Arians taught that in Christ the Word had united himself to a human body lacking a rational soul, himself taking the place of one.[3] Their views were expressed in a creed attributed to

[1] It is significant that it is the Manichaean who quoted Phil. 2. 7 to prove the Docetic character of Christ: *ibid.* 59. 3. 'Manichaeism' was to be among the accusations against the exponents of the Alexandrian school.

[2] For a different assessment of Diodore, see A. Grillmeier, 'Vorbereitung der Formel von Chalkedon', Grillmeier/Bacht, *Das Konzil von Chalkedon*, I, 140ff.: 'Das sind ohne Zweifel Elemente, welche auf einen echten Zusammenhang Diodors mit der Logos-Sarx-Christologie hindeuten.'

[3] See A. Gesché, 'L'Ame humaine de Jésus dans la christologie du IVe siècle', *RHE* 54, 1959, pp. 385–425 at pp. 385–8 and 403–20.

Eudoxius (d. 370) who was successively bishop of Antioch and Constantinople. 'We believe in one the only true God... and in one Lord... firstborn of all Creation... who was made flesh but not man (σαρκωθέντα οὐκ ἐνανθρωπήσαντα). For he did not take a human soul, but became flesh so that God might have dealings with us through flesh as through a veil. [He was] not two natures, for he was not a complete man, but God in place of a soul in flesh. The whole is one nature resulting from synthesis (μία κατὰ σύνθεσιν φύσις).'[1] At Nicaea the creed contained the emphatic statement aimed against the Arians, that the Son 'was made flesh, becoming man (σαρκωθέντα καὶ ἐνανθρωπήσαντα)'.[2]

This clause was intended to express Christ's permanent union as God with human nature, but like many formulae it could mean different things to different people. How was the 'flesh' of the Godhead to be understood? How was God to be united to man? It is evident from the sharp conflict at Nicaea itself that many of the ingredients of the future Christological controversy were already present at the time of that council.[3] At this stage the Antiochenes realised the dangerous trend of the Arian argument and had the clearest answer to it.[4] The Council of Antioch in December 324, presided over by the westerner Hosius of Cordoba, which censured Eusebius of Caesarea and elected as bishop of Antioch Eustathius (324 to 326 or 330), may be regarded as a partial turning of the tables on the Origenists who had deposed Paul of Samosata in 268. This becomes clear as Eusebius' Christology as well as his Trinitarian teaching was totally opposed to that of Eustathius. He states roundly that Paul of Samosata was deposed 'because he asserted a human soul in Christ', a view which he characterised as 'Ebionite'.[5] The foundation of Eustathius' beliefs was none other than this,

---

[1] A. Hahn, *Bibliothek der Symbole* (Tübingen, 1902), para. 191, and also Epiphanius, *Panarion* 69. 19 (ed. Holl, p. 164), ἀλλὰ καὶ ἀρνοῦνται ('Αρειανοί) ψυχὴν αὐτὸν ἀνθρωπείαν εἰληφέναι.

[2] See F. W. Green's valuable note in Bindley/Green, *Documents*, pp. 37–9.

[3] See Theodoret's account of the proceedings featuring Eustathius' role as champion of orthodoxy, *HE* I. 7–9, and R. V. Sellers, *Eustathius of Antioch* (Cambridge, 1928), ch. 2; and M. Spanneut, *Recherches sur les écrits d'Eustathe d'Antioche* (Lille, 1948).

[4] Westerners, such as Jerome, recognised this, when Jerome speaks of Eustathius as 'Eustathium nostrum, qui primus Antiochenae ecclesiae episcopus contra Arium clarissima tuba bellicum cecinit' (*Ep.* 73. 2). Eustathius' alleged speech to Constantine (*PG* 18, cols. 673–6) is regarded as fictitious: see Spanneut, *Recherches*, p. 83.

[5] Eusebius, *De ecclesiastica theologia* 1. 20. 43–4 (ed. E. Klostermann, *GCS* 14, Eusebius Werke 4, Leipzig, 1906, p. 88).

and he had little time for Eusebius personally.¹ The crushing defeat of Arius masks the fact that Nicaea itself was also in some ways a western and Antiochene triumph.

Against the Arians, Eustathius argued that Jesus' weaknesses and limitations of knowledge, which the Arians attributed to the subordination of the Word, were to be ascribed instead to the human soul of Jesus. This was subject to change like any other human soul. The Word and its tabernacle were not the same. Stephen beheld the glory of God,² and not the man Jesus. Eustathius' separation of 'tabernacle' and 'glory' was to be taken up by Ambrose half a century later in the west, also against the Arians.³ Again, Eustathius asks: 'Why do the Arians lay such emphasis on showing that Christ was a body without having taken on a soul, and relate such earthbound deceptions? ... They attribute changes of the senses (τὰς τῶν παθῶν ἀλλοιώσεις) to the divine spirit and therefore can convince themselves easily that what is changeable can be created out of an unchangeable nature.'⁴ Instead, he argued that Jesus was truly man, 'the Word and God raising him up gloriously as their temple'.⁵ It was not the Word, but the man Jesus who was born in Bethlehem, increased in wisdom, suffered and was crucified.⁶ The Word was not born of Mary.⁷ Human and divine within Jesus, however, always willed in harmony with each other. There was complete reciprocity between the two *personae* (πρόσωπα) that composed the Saviour:⁸ man was saved through Christ's example.

Eustathius had no difficult in accepting the Creed of Nicaea. His theology was naturally Trinitarian, but at the same time his concept of the Word as a 'divine energy' acting on and dwelling in the man Jesus as a separate nature links him ultimately with Paul of Samosata, and foreshadows Nestorius. Theodoret's praise of him⁹ as 'great', 'holy' and 'most ortho-

¹ Sozomen, *HE* II. 18. Compare Socrates, *HE* I. 23.
² Eustathius, *De anima adversus Arianos* = Theodoret, *Eranistes*, *PG* 83, col. 89A, cited by Spanneut, *Recherches*, no. 12.
³ Ambrose, *De fide* II. 9. 77. See below, p. 132.
⁴ *De anima* (*PG* 18, col. 690B) = Spanneut, *Recherches*, no. 15.
⁵ Spanneut, no. 19 = *PG* 18, col. 685C.
⁶ Spanneut, nos. 11 and 13 = *PG* 18, cols. 680B and C and 684C.
⁷ Spanneut, no. 18 = *PG* 18, col. 677A.
⁸ Sellers, *Eustathius of Antioch*, pp. 109–11.
⁹ Theodoret, *HE* I. 8. Compare *Ep.* 151 (an important letter aimed at vindicating Theodoret's own orthodoxy in the eyes of the monks of the whole of the Oriental diocese).

dox' is understandable, but that of Athanasius is more surprising. Despite Eustathius' assertion that Christ was God and man 'without division' and 'without confusion', it is difficult to understand how so acute an intelligence as Athanasius' evidently failed to detect the radical innovation that was being introduced into the anti-Arian armoury. For him also, Eustathius was 'very zealous for the truth, and hated the Arian heresy',[1] and he fell, probably at the end of 326, falsely charged with having insulted the emperor's mother Helena.

The interlude of Eustathius of Antioch was short-lived. His successor Flacillus was a strong Origenist and a powerful personality,[2] who began the tradition which was to prevail for a generation of Antioch serving as the headquarters of the Origenist opposition to Athanasius. During most of the reign of Constantius II (337–61) the main theological issue was the subordination of Christ to the Father. How could Christ as a 'creature' of 'like substance' with the Father redeem creation? Until the 350s the question of his humanity redeeming the individual man through his possession of a human soul had tended to fall into the background.[3]

Athanasius' Christology conformed to the same Word-flesh scheme as Arius', only that he attributed Christ's sufferings and limitations to his state as Word incarnate. These, he emphasised, were the traits of 'the flesh' in which the Word 'disguised himself' to manifest his power to men.[4] Apparently he accepted a Stoic view of the Word as the animating force of the universe – 'no part of creation is left void of him', he writes – and that the mind and reason within each human being was a tiny portion of this force.[5] Christ's human nature was, as it were, a part of the vast body of the universe, and so there was no incongruity of the Word encompassing a human body and at the same time vivifying and directing the whole of creation. 'The Lord [i.e. the Word] became man on our behalf.' Man's

---

[1] Athanasius, *Historia Arianorum* 4 (*PG* 25, col. 697D).

[2] Theodoret, *HE* 1. 22, makes him the third in a line of short-lived successors to Eustathius. To him, he was 'a secret Arian'.

[3] Though not completely so: for instance, note the inclusion in the Origenist Macrostichos Creed of 345 of the denunciation of the view that 'after the incarnation he was only by advance made God though by nature a mere man' (*Creeds, Councils and Controversies*, ed. Stevenson, p. 23). See also *Ep. ad Maximum* 3 (*PG* 25 col. 1089) for Athanasius' hostility to any Christology that resembled that of Paul of Samosata.

[4] *De incarnatione* 16. 1 or 'submitted himself' (ὑπέβαλεν ἑαυτόν).

[5] *Ibid.* 8. 1 and 17, and see Kelly's reconstruction, *Early Christian Doctrines*, p. 285.

redemption consisted in a return of the soul to its heavenly origin, its natural destiny, which had been interrupted by the Fall. Sin and death were destroyed through the perfect life and sacrificial death of the Son of God, that is, through the power of God himself. 'The Word', says Athanasius, 'itself immortal, partook of a body capable of death, so that it, by partaking of the Word who is above all, might be worthy to die in the place of all, and might because of the Word that came to dwell in it, remain incorruptible; and thenceforth corruption might be stayed from all by the grace of the resurrection.' 'For he was made man that we might be made God.' The famous passages from the *De incarnatione*[1] emphasise, first, the inseparability of the Word from its flesh – there could never be two 'natures' or 'individualities' of Word and flesh; and secondly, the profound connection between this Christology and human salvation. Yet opponents might ask, if Word and flesh were one, where was the difference between creator and created? Where was the solidarity between the Saviour and the individual, whose body also might hope to rise at the Last Day? To Athanasius, the willing and energising part of Christ was the Word. It alone possessed the will (θέλημα) while the 'flesh' was characterised by weakness. It was always the Word that acted, taking on the limitations of the flesh in order to deliver man. No more than in Origen's theology was there room for an active 'human soul' in Christ.[2] In this Athanasius stands as the natural successor of Malchion and forerunner of Apollinarius and Cyril.

Apollinarius (*circa* 310 to *circa* 390) was a friend and devoted supporter of Athanasius.[3] He had been brought up in the Alexandrian schools whose authorities were Plato, Pythagoras and Aristotle, but had emigrated to Syria where in Julian's reign he had championed the cause of the Christian intellectuals against the emperor's policy of forbidding all but pagans to

---

[1] *De incarnatione* 9. 1 and 54. 3, and compare Pseudo(?)-Athanasius, *Oratio contra Arianos* IV. 26 (*PG* 26, col. 524): 'Christ was God man [θεὸς ἄνθρωπος] born of the Virgin Mary.'

[2] *Oratio contra Arianos* III. 57 (*PG* 26, col. 444B). See the discussion of the issue in J. Roldanus, *Le Christ et l'homme dans la théologie d'Alexandrie* (Leiden, 1968), pp. 252ff. and M. Richard, 'Saint Athanase et la psychologie du Christ selon les Ariens', *Mélanges de science religieuse* 4, 1947, pp. 5–54, especially pp. 35–8 and 50–4, for the view that Athanasius' Christology in the period pre-362 was to all intents and purposes Apollinarian.

[3] Sozomen, *HE* VI. 25, and note the warmth of his praise of the bishops in Diocaesaea for their continuous support of Athanasius (H. Lietzmann, *Apollinaris von Laodicea und seine Schule*, Tübingen, 1904, p. 255).

teach the classics.¹ He was perhaps also a friend of Basil of Caesarea,² and as bishop of Laodicea in Syria might have been the architect of the reconciliation between the 'old' and 'new' Nicenes in the years following Julian's death. Events, however, were to divert his ideas into a different channel. The decade 362-73, covering the failure of Julian's pagan reaction and the last years of Athanasius' life, was to be crucial to the Christological controversy that lay ahead. Already at the council convoked by Athanasius at Alexandria in 362 the victorious Nicenes were becoming aware of the problem involved in the assertion that Christ was 'very God of very God' and was consubstantial with the Father. In Athanasius' account of the proceedings one may discern how the old divisions in the church of Antioch on this issue were once more coming into the open. Athanasius describes how while all accepted Nicaea, one group was criticising the other for affirming that in times past the Word had been present in Christ in the same manner as it had in the prophets and holy men. The critics believed, on the contrary, that the Word himself became flesh by his birth by the Virgin Mary for the sake of man to deliver man from sin and death and bring him to heaven. To this end, they went on, Christ must have possessed a soul as well as a body because he could not be without feeling or spirit, nor could he save the souls of men without possessing one himself. Athanasius accepted their view since the soul, like the body of Christ, could be understood as part of the Word, and he rejected the notion that it had entered Christ in the same way as it had entered the prophets.³

Discussion, however, was not stilled. A few years later, in *circa* 371, Athanasius received a letter from Epictetus, bishop of Corinth, in which the latter in some confusion asked for Athanasius' view regarding Christ's consubstantiality with man. Some people apparently were asserting that Christ's body came 'from above', i.e. a heavenly body, thus anticipating Eutyches. It was purely 'notional', it was being said, and the body which was born of Mary was co-essential with the Word. To this Athanasius

---

¹ Socrates, *HE* III. 16.

² See G. L. Prestige, *St Basil the Great and Apollinaris of Laodicea*, ed. H. Chadwick (London, 1956), pp. 6ff.

³ Athanasius, *Tomus ad Antiochenos* 7 (*PG* 26, col. 804); compare also *Oratio contra Arianos* IV. 26. See J. Roldanus, *Le Christ et l'homme dans la théologie d'Athanase d'Alexandrie* (Leiden, 1968), pp. 259-60. I do not accept R. Weijenborg's view that this part of Athanasius' letter is an Apollinarian interpolation dating to 373-5 ('Apollinaristic interpolations in the *Tomos ad Antiochenos* of A.D. 362', *Studia Patristica* 3 (= *TU* 78), Berlin, 1961, pp. 324-30).

reacted with horror, stressing the soteriological need behind the 'assumption of the whole man' by Christ.[1] Yet by now 'confusion was growing on all sides',[2] parties were canvassing for support, and it was in this situation that Apollinarius, building perhaps on the ideas of the victorious party in Antioch, elaborated his own theory.

Apollinarius' solution was the product of a brilliant and radical mind, of a man who wrote concisely and left not the slightest doubt what he meant. His ideas, as Harnack points out, corresponded wholly with 'the assumptions and aims of Greek piety and theology',[3] combining Pauline *Pneuma-Sarx* terminology with current Platonist interpretations of the relationship between soul and body. Scripture emphasised that Christ was 'one'. 'There is no distinction in Holy Scripture between the Word and his flesh: he is one nature, one energy, one person, one *hypostasis*, at once wholly God and wholly man'[4] – not a particular man, but man as representing the human race. His flesh as man was consubstantial with his Godhead, inseparable from the Godhead by whom it was vivified. What took place at the incarnation was a 'mixture' (μίξις or σύγκρασις) out of which only the predominant element, i.e. the Godhead, survived.[5] He delighted to speak, as Kelly says, of Christ as 'God incarnate', 'flesh-bearing God' and 'God born of a woman'.[6] Mary was therefore 'Theotokos', playing a part in an incarnation which owed nothing to the whim of man but was foreshadowed from eternity. The Jews in crucifying the body crucified God the Word.[7] Like Athanasius, he was deeply concerned with Christianity as a message of salvation and human redemption, and he was convinced that separation of the divine from the human in Christ would imperil this. If Christ could in

---

[1] Athanasius, *Ep. ad Epictetum* 2 (*PG* 26, cols. 1052–3). See also Epiphanius, *Panarion* 77. 24–5, who quotes these opinions and Athanasius' reply. Athanasius, however, does not concede that Christ was 'consubstantial with us'.

[2] Apollinarius, *Letter to the bishops of Diocaesarea* (Lietzmann, *Apollinaris*, p. 256).

[3] Harnack, *History of Dogma*, IV, 155.

[4] *De fide et incarnatione* 6: texts in Lietzmann, *Apollinaris*, pp. 198–9. See C. E. Raven, *Apollinarianism* (Cambridge, 1923), ch. 5; H. de Riedmatten, 'La Christologie d'Apollinaire de Laodicée', *Studia Patristica* 2 (= *TU* 64), Berlin, 1957, pp. 208–34; Norris, *Manhood and Christ*, pp. 80ff.; H. A. Wolfson, *The Philosophy of the Church Fathers*, I (Cambridge, Mass., 1956), 433ff.; and M. Richard, 'L'Introduction du mot *hypostase* dans la théologie de l'incarnation', *Mélanges de science religieuse* 2, 1945, pp. 5–32 at pp. 6–8.

[5] See Wolfson, *Philosophy*, p. 443.

[6] Kelly, *Early Christian Doctrines*, p. 291.

[7] Apollinarius, *De fide et incarnatione* 6 (Lietzmann, p. 198, lines 23–5).

any conceivable manner be thought of merely as man he would have no redemption to bestow, and the Arians could be right after all.

This trend of thought led Apollinarius to provide a reasoned argument for the rejection of a human mind (νοῦς) in Christ. If one granted that possibility one had also to concede the possibility of free will and ability to sin.[1] The *nous* in Christ must be ἄτρεπτος (changeless), not 'a prey to filthy thoughts, but existing as a divine mind immutable and heavenly'.[2] If not, all became uncertain. God could not assure *a priori* the sinlessness of a human mind without depriving it of its characteristic of humanity, namely its liberty. For Christ's mind, however, to possess even the tendency toward corrupt imaginings was out of the question, and hence there could be only one mind, a divine mind in Christ. There could not be two principles of thought and will dwelling in a single being at the same time.[3] Only if the entire essence of God were present in the Saviour could sinful man raise himself through Christ toward God and ultimately become divine. Christ could not give life and at the same time be of our nature.[4] No mortal could create life; he was 'in the form' of a servant only, but by his own voluntary self-emptying became incarnate. Perhaps Apollinarius, wedded to Aristotelian biological analyses, could only see the formative or psychic element which was believed to be implanted in humans by the semen, implanted by divine operation by God in the Virgin, and hence the Word displaced the human soul. If Christ were merely 'the temple of God', then his birth by a virgin would not be necessary.[5] The incarnate Christ was, in effect, 'a compound unity in human form', fused into a single life and single *hypostasis*,[6] and as the body of Christ could not exist of itself, it possessed no independent 'nature'. Thus 'the Lord existed not in two

---

[1] Apollinarius, *Apodeixis*, frag. 76 (Lietzmann, p. 222): ἐδεῖτο δὲ ἀτρέπτου νοῦ μὴ ὑποπίπτοντος αὐτῇ διὰ ἐπιστημοσύνης ἀσθένειαν, ἀλλὰ συναρμόζοντος αὐτὴν ἀβιάστως ἑαυτῷ. ('It was necessary therefore for the Nous to be unchangeable, not yielding to the flesh by any defect of knowledge, but by harmonising it to itself without violence.') In this way Word and flesh maintained their own characteristics in the one nature that was the incarnate Christ. Apollinarius attempted thereby to avoid the pitfalls of gnosticism.

[2] *Letter to the bishops of Diocaesarea* 2 (Lietzmann, p. 256).

[3] Frag. 2 (Lietzmann, p. 204): compare p. 179, οὐ δύο πρόσωπα, οὐ δύο φύσεις τέλειαι καθ' ἑαυτάς.

[4] Lietzmann, pp. 244–5. On the psychology of Apollinarius see Raven, *Apollinarianism*, pp. 189ff., and de Riedmatten, 'La Christologie d'Apollinaire', pp. 209 ff.

[5] See de Riedmatten, 'La Christologie d'Apollinaire', pp. 215–16.

[6] Lietzmann, p. 260.

substances but in one.'[1] Orthodoxy could be summed up in the formula 'one incarnate nature of the Logos', to be worshipped with his flesh in one worship.[2]

Nominally, Apollinarius was writing against the Arians; in reality it is not difficult to detect his strong bias against what was to become the Antiochene approach to the nature of Christ. After thirty years of storm and stress Athanasius had gone as far as he could to make the Alexandrian viewpoints acceptable in Antioch, his effort in 362 anticipating the Formula of Reunion seventy years later. Apollinarius was less willing to make subtle compromises for the sake of winning over possible enemies. 'I am astonished', he writes, 'to find people confessing the Lord as God incarnate, and yet falling into the separation wickedly introduced by those who imitate Paul [of Samosata]. For they slavishly imitate Paul of Samosata, differentiating between him from Heaven Whom they declare to be God, and the man derived from the earth.'[3] He rejected categorically the idea that God could be conjoined with man – perfect God with perfect man – for that would be two Sons, one by nature and the other by adoption;[4] and into which was the Christian baptised, he asked.[5] The sacramental issue was to be the vital one for the ordinary Christian. 'Rather', Apollinarius urged, 'the flesh [of Christ] united itself with the heavenly governing principle [i.e. the Word] and was fused with it... So, out of the moved and the mover was composed a single living entity – not two, but one composed of two, complete self-moving principles.'[6] 'Our salvation is the incarnation (σάρκωσις) of the Word.'[7] The challenge to the emerging Antiochene theology could not have been clearer.

Brilliant and logical though Apollinarius' position was, it was also open to serious objection without necessarily adopting the Antiochene standpoint. In particular, the suggestion that Christ lacked the most characteristic element in man's make-up, namely his rational mind and will, seemed monstrous, as did the obvious clash between Apollinarius' interpretation of Christ and the Christ of the Gospels. The ideas seemed too like traditional

---

[1] Apollinarius, *Ep. ad Jovianum* 1 (Lietzmann, p. 250); compare Ἡ κατὰ μέρος πίστις 31 (*ibid.* p. 178) and *De unione* 12 (*ibid.* p. 191) where Apollinarius points out that 'the body [of Christ] lived by the sanctification of the divinity and not by providing it with a human soul'.

[2] *Ep. ad Jovianum* 1 (Lietzmann, pp. 250–1).

[3] *Ep. ad Dionysium* 1. 1 (Lietzmann, pp. 256–7), Kelly, p. 290.

[4] Frag. 81 (Lietzmann, p. 224). [5] *Ep. ad Dionysium* (Lietzmann, p. 258)

[6] Frag. 107 (Lietzmann, p. 232). [7] Frag. 81.

Docetic and gnostic heresy, but it was difficult within the framework of the Word-flesh theology to do much more than assert the twofold character of the natures in Christ and to point to the unsatisfactory character of the Apollinarian solution. This the Cappadocian Fathers attempted to do in the decade leading up to the Council of Constantinople in 381, when in canon 1 of the council Apollinarianism was condemned. Their arguments laid the foundation of what was to become the theology of the patriarchs of the imperial city.[1]

For both parties the issue was how God could manifest himself in his fullness through Christ in order to redeem fallen man. Apollinarius had asserted that it was impossible to conceive of Christ assuming man's corrupted flesh for this purpose. His Cappadocian opponents took their cue from Origen and Athanasius and argued exactly the opposite. 'What has not been assumed cannot be restored. What is saved is what has been united with God.'[2] There was 'no need of the Holy Virgin', said Basil, 'if the God-bearing flesh was not to be assumed from the material from which Adam was moulded'.[3] Christ's flesh could not come 'from above' and save humanity.[4] It was 'by becoming exactly what we are that he united the human race through himself to God'.[5] Christ, the second Adam, must possess the fullness of the human nature of the first Adam in order to redeem it.[6]

This was now becoming easier to state in a fine series of paradoxes than to demonstrate, and there were plenty of people in Asia Minor who were prepared to dispute the official dogma. The presbyter Cledonius stated his doubts to Gregory in 382. If Christ came forth as God with what he assumed, that is one person but in two distinct natures composed of Godhead and manhood, was he not being preached as a 'flesh-bearing God rather than a God-bearing man'?[7] Gregory's answer, accepting the com-

---

[1] Note, for instance, that the Patriarch Atticus (406–27) is claimed by the Chalcedonians, at their conference with the Severan Monophysites in 531, together with the two Gregories and Amphilochius of Iconium as an upholder of the two-nature Christology: Mansi, *Collectio* VIII, col. 828.

[2] Gregory of Nazianzus, *Ep.* 101. 7 (*PG* 37, cols. 183–4); cf. *Ep.* 102.

[3] Basil, *Ep.* 261, written in 377. The Virgin birth thus plays an essential role in the Christology both of Apollinarius and of his Cappadocian opponents.

[4] Gregory of Nazianzus, *Ep.* 202 to Nectarius (*PG* 37, col. 332B).

[5] Gregory of Nyssa, *Contra Eunomium* XII (*PG* 45, col. 889).

[6] Gregory of Nazianzus, *Oratio* XXX. 21 (*PG* 36, col. 132); compare Gregory of Nyssa, *Contra Eunomium* IV.

[7] *Ep.* 102 to Cledonius (*PG* 37, col. 200). See also C. E. Raven's comments on the inadequacy of the orthodox rejoinder to Apollinarius, *Apollinarianism*, pp. 253ff.

plete domination of the divine over the human mind in Christ, was hardly reassuring. Nor was Gregory of Nyssa's classic definition of the littleness of humanity in contact with the majesty of the divine as 'though a drop of vinegar mingled in the deep was transferred to the substance of the sea'[1] more convincing than Demophilus' (semi-Arian, bishop of Constantinople 370–80) parallel of a measure of milk trickling into the ocean and being thereby lost.[2] The mingling of the two natures thus presumed must produce a hybrid of God and man. Was it not simpler to confess with Apollinarius that the 'humanity' of Christ was completely absorbed by the divine?[3] Only when Gregory raised the issue of Christ's will in relation to his sinlessness was he really grappling with the Apollinarian position. For the question whether possession of changeless and automatic goodness did not render Christ's temptations so much mockery and empty his sinlessness of any worth was a cardinal one. Human nature that was not limited by human conditions was not human. Without free will how could Christ be 'perfect man'?[4] So the debate went on. Though between 377 and 388 Apollinarius had been condemned alike in the west and east and by Emperor Theodosius I, his views had not been refuted. It became clear also that they coincided with those of a large proportion of the eastern episcopate and the people at large.

The two-nature Christology continued to be represented at the end of the century by Didymus the Blind at Alexandria (313?–98). The latter was characterised by Jerome as teaching the exact opposite to Apollinarius.[5] Didymus' *Commentary on the Psalms*, discovered in 1941 at Toura, was written probably between 370 and 385. In it he asserted not only the two natures, but that Christ possessed as part of his attributes as complete man

---

[1] Gregory of Nyssa, *Contra Eunomium* v. 5 (*PG* 45, col. 708).

[2] Philostorgius, *HE* IX. 14, thought this doctrine was confused.

[3] As the Eutychist speaker in Theodoret's *Eranistes* stated, ἐγὼ τὴν θεότητα λέγω μεμενηκέναι καταποθῆναι δὲ ὑπὸ ταύτης τὴν ἀνθρωπότητα (*PG* 83, col. 153C), and he goes on to use practically the same simile as Gregory of Nyssa, only with honey instead of vinegar. For him, however, the honey is quite washed away in the sea (*ibid.* col. 153D).

[4] Gregory of Nyssa, *Antirrheticus* 41 (*PG* 45, cols. 1217C and 1220A): 'Everyone knows that virtue is the right exercise of free will.' 'That which is without sin, if this is not the result of free will, is not at all to be praised; else we should be praising those who are restrained from their evil-doing by imprisonment.' See Raven, *Apollinarianism*, p. 270, and for a selection of Gregory of Nyssa's anti-Apollinarian arguments, see H. Bettenson, *The Later Christian Fathers* (Oxford, 1970), pp. 134–41.

[5] Jerome, *De vir. illustr.* 126, concerning Didymus' pupil Ambrose.

(τέλειος ἄνθρωπος) 'born of woman' the possibility of temptation (*propatheia*), which could be associated, however, with actual sinlessness.[1] The assumption of the manhood was therefore true assumption, and the manhood was of the same nature (*homoousios*) as our own.[2] Didymus opposed both Arians and Apollinarians. His assertion of the reality of Christ's humanity vis-à-vis mankind combined with his equally strong assertion of divine free will were permanently valuable in providing a two-nature alternative within the framework of the Word-flesh theology. The weakness of his position was, as Grillmeier has shown,[3] his inability to move from the Origenistic explanation of the unique purity of Christ's soul, namely that it alone did not descend into the land of death at the Fall and remained, albeit by its own free will, always bound up with the Logos. Christ always remained the Word made flesh. In this static concept there was no scope for Christ's development, his growth 'in wisdom and stature'.

Perhaps it is not altogether surprising that the clear-cut simplicity of the Apollinarian position continued to carry conviction. Though as a delegate to the anti-Apollinarian synod at Rome in 377 Peter II of Alexandria confessed that Christ was in 'two persons' (*prosopa*),[4] the popular debate moved steadily in favour of the one-nature Christology. From the later development of the controversy it is easy to see how the equation 'two natures = two sons' of Apollinarius' (pseudo-Athanasian) *Letter to the Emperor Jovian*, his assertion that 'manhood cannot save man', and that the Word himself suffered on the cross for man's salvation, sank into the religious consciousness of leaders and people alike. These ideas were to become the agenda for the debate between Chalcedonian and anti-Chalcedonian. When at the turn of the fifth century works of Apollinarius and his disciples began to circulate freely in the east under the names of accepted orthodox leaders such as Julius of Rome, who had vindicated Athanasius against his enemies, and of Athanasius himself, no one suspected their forgery.[5] These works provided Cyril with many of his fundamental ideas.

[1] Gesché, 'La Christologie du Commentaire sur les Psaumes', pp. 148ff., and dating, p. 409.

[2] See M. F. Wiles, 'ΟΜΟΟΥΣΙΟΣ ΗΜΙΝ', *JTS*, n.s. 16, 1965, pp. 454–61.

[3] Grillmeier, *Christ in Christian Tradition*, p. 275.

[4] Peter II, *Ep. ad episcopos Aegyptios* (*PG* 33, cols. 1291D–1293A). See Grillmeier, *Christ in Christian Tradition*, pp. 276–7: 'Alexandria therefore has a formula of the "two persons" in Christ as early as Antioch or even earlier.'

[5] For an example of subtle but telling alterations to Athanasius, *Ep. ad Epictetum*, which confused Cyril, even to the extent of his thinking that they were Nestorian

Cyril was brought up in the same school as Athanasius and Didymus, and within the limitations of the Word-flesh theology believed firmly in the full humanity of Christ. The 'flesh' (σάρξ) assumed by the Word was man with a soul and mind. At the same time, he was profoundly influenced by Apollinarian writings that were circulating under orthodox names. It may even be that his ambivalent Christology, demonstrated when one compares his Twelve Anathemas with the Formula of Reunion, was due partly to an inability to reconcile these two contradictory influences both of which he imagined to be orthodox. An ardent disciple of Athanasius,[1] he failed to distinguish between the genuine and the false in the works ascribed to his master. He anathematised Apollinarius without perhaps realising that some of his most important ideas were derived from that same source.[2]

To Cyril then, the Word always remained constant.[3] The 'nature' of Christ was always God. What happened at the incarnation was that while continuing to exist eternally as God, he 'took on the form of a servant' by assuming a body 'making the flesh his own by way of dispensation'. The single nature therefore which was the Word now became 'the Word made flesh' (as in Jn. 1. 14).[4] By the time of his controversy with Nestorius, Cyril had accepted the formula which he believed to be Athanasian of 'one nature, and that incarnate of the divine Word', and he was using *physis* and

(*Ep.* 46. 2 *ad Succensum*), see J. Lebon, 'Altération doctrinale de la lettre à Epictète de Saint Athanase', *RHE* 31, 1935, pp. 713–61.

[1] Grillmeier's view (*Christ in Christian Tradition*, p. 330): 'If we examine the characteristics of the Christology of the earlier works of Cyril, we find nothing but Athanasius', and Cyril's own avowal (*Ep.* 39), 'we follow in all respects the opinions of the holy fathers, but especially those of our blessed and all-renowned father Athanasius...' (*PG* 77, col. 180).

[2] He classes Apollinarius, Eunomius and Arius together as heretics (*Ep.* 31 to Maximian of Constantinople, *PG* 77, col. 151C), yet his favourite phrase 'one incarnate nature of the Word' was derived from the pseudo-Athanasian *Ad Jovianum*. Compare also his rejection of the idea of the 'flesh' borrowing its own 'nature' with that of Apollinarius.

[3] For an account of Cyril's theology, see Grillmeier, *Christ in Christian Tradition*, pp. 400ff., and Harnack, *History of Dogma*, IV, 174–8.

[4] See for a typical passage, *Oratio de recta fide ad Theodosium imp.* 16 (*PG* 76, col. 1157): εἷς κύριος Ἰησοῦς Χριστός, δι' οὗ τὰ πάντα· Θεὸν γὰρ ὄντα κατὰ φύσιν ἐπιγινώσκομεν τὸν δι' οὗ τὰ πάντα Λόγον, καὶ εἰ γέγονε σάρξ τουτέστιν ἄνθρωπος. For the Neo-Platonist influence on Cyril's views of 'the hypostatic union' of Word and flesh on the analogy of the union between the human soul and body, see E. L. Fortin, 'The *Definitio Fidei* of Chalcedon and its philosophical sources', *Studia Patristica* 5 (= *TU* 80), Berlin, 1962, pp. 489–98.

hypostasis as synonyms. Christ was in every way 'one and unique'. In reconciling this standpoint with the Biblical narrative of his ministry, suffering and death, the theory of *kenosis* played an indispensable part in his thought. Christ 'voluntarily' came 'under the Law' according to the condition of the human nature, suffered and submitted to death.[1] This voluntary 'self-emptying' of the incarnate Word enabled Cyril and his successors to assert the fullness of Christ's humanity without the corollary of accepting human nature as distinct from the divine. Cyril could preach Christ as man suffering for us men, buttressing his argument with a wealth of Scriptural texts, without yielding his cardinal point that the Word incarnate was 'one'.

The Word therefore assumed full humanity and united to himself ineffably 'flesh and a rational soul', as 'seed of Abraham' foretold in Scripture 'without mingling or confusion' for the purpose of overcoming on behalf of man the effect of sin which was death.[2] Human nature was thereby purified and offered to the Father as a 'sweet-smelling offering, to be present henceforth with Him always'.[3] This victory was, however, accomplished not by the Word becoming or dwelling in any individual man, but as second Adam Christ began by his sacrifice a new redeemed and regenerated humanity. This aspect of Cyril's theology is clearly illustrated from his Second Letter to Nestorius: 'We do not say that the Nature of the Word was changed and became flesh, nor that He was transformed into a complete human being, I mean one of soul and body; but this rather, that the Word had united to Himself in His own hypostasis in an ineffable and inconceivable manner flesh animated with a rational soul, became Man, and was called Son of Man' (tr. Bindley/Green, *Documents*, p. 210).[4] Thus every act which Christ was recorded in the Gospels as performing, whether the ordinary day-to-day tasks such as eating and sleeping or feeling weariness, or in his miracles and resurrection were the acts of a single being, God-in-Christ.

[1] *Ep.* 31 (*PG* 77, col. 151D). Compare *Ep.* 40 (*ibid.* col. 193C) etc.

[2] Inter alia, *Ad Theodosium imp.* 19 and 20 (*PG* 76, cols. 1160–4) and *Ep.* 31 to Maximian (*PG* 77, col. 151C).

[3] *In Ep. ad Hebraeos* IV. 14 (*PG* 74, col. 972D). See F. M. Young, 'Christological ideas in the Greek commentaries on Hebrews', *JTS*, n.s. 20. 1, 1969, pp. 150–63, especially pp. 152–3 and 159.

[4] *Ep.* 4 (*PG* 77, col. 45B); compare *Ep.* 45 (*ibid.* col. 232A), and *Liber thesaurorum* 34, where Cyril points out that the Saviour was born of the Holy Spirit, therefore not of the blood or will of a man, but from God (*PG* 75, col. 592).

The negotiations with the Antiochenes during 432–3 leading to the Formula of Reunion in 433 witnessed rather more than verbal concessions on Cyril's part to a two-nature Christology. 'Word' and 'flesh' were indeed opposites, as Cyril had always admitted. Even though the Word and his flesh were essentially and inseparably united in the incarnate Word, in the act of contemplation (θεωρία or ἐπίνοια) they could be distinguished as separate entities.[1] In the Second Letter to Nestorius, cited above, Cyril explained how 'the one Son and Christ' might be regarded as formed 'out of two natures'.[2] He could not, however, subsist 'in two natures'. Difference he would allow, division not. In the Formula of Reunion, however, he had been obliged to accept a definition whose emphasis lay on the two natures, united certainly, but not 'organically united', as he had insisted in his Third Letter to Nestorius. Perhaps even more important, he had to agree also that some theologians 'distinguish as relating to two natures, applying those God-befitting to the Godhead of Christ and those lowly in reference to his manhood'.[3] It was not his view, but it formed part of his agreement with the Antiochenes, and he inserted it in his famous letter *Laetentur coeli*. The reaction of its recipients is instructive. 'Why did the bishop of Alexandria tolerate and even praise those who speak of two natures?' asked the presbyter Eulogius.[4] In Isauria the congregation of the metropolitan Succensus flung themselves into debate. If Christ suffered in his rational soul he must by definition have suffered voluntarily, and how then can one avoid granting that the two natures existed without separation after the union?[5] Cyril's replies insisted that nothing had changed in his theo-

[1] *Homil. Paschalis* VIII (*PG* 77, col. 596D). Compare Letter to Acacius (= *Ep.* 40, *PG* 77, cols. 193D–196A). The long-standing importance of the idea of contemplative perception in Greek-Christian piety can be demonstrated by Gregory Thaumaturgus' assertion to the pagan Aelian that Father and Son, though 'one', could 'in theoria' be seen as two: Ὑἱὸν ἐπινοίᾳ μὲν εἶναι δύο, ὑποστάσει δὲ ἕν ('The Son is two in contemplation, but one in individuality'). This fragment is quoted by Basil, *Ep.* 210, but Basil has considerable doubts whether this point made by Gregory in the course of a debate with a pagan could be accepted as Gregory's real teaching. It did not come from his ἔκθεσις πίστεως (confession of faith). Compare, however, Gregory of Nazianzus, Letter to Cledonius (*PG* 37, col. 180). [2] *Ep.* 4 (*PG* 77, col. 45C).
[3] *Ep.* 39 (*PG* 77, col. 177A). See R. V. Sellers' translation, *Council of Chalcedon*, pp. 17–18, and Grillmeier, *Christ in Christian Tradition*, pp. 400–9 and 430–2.
[4] *Ep.* 44 (to Eulogius, *PG* 77, cols. 224D–225A). Cyril found himself conceding that Nestorius had been right to demonstrate the difference between Word and flesh, though he had failed to acknowledge their unity (*ibid.* col. 255A).
[5] *Ep.* 46 (the Second Letter to Succensus, *PG* 77, col. 245A).

logy. There was still one incarnate nature of God.¹ Christ was indivisible, even though he now concedes that the suffering was 'in the nature of the manhood'.² Yet, it was not 'another Son' who was born of Mary, but the Word whose flesh was just as much part of him as our flesh is part of us. In particular, the Anathemas stood, and Cyril assured Acacius of Melitene that he had no intention of going back on the Fourth Anathema which condemned those who attributed passages of Scripture now to the Godhead and now to the manhood of Christ.³ It was a piece of ecclesiastical tightrope walking, successful at the time only by making the utmost of 'the obscure phraseology' of the Antiochenes⁴ and exaggerating Nestorius' views to draw a distinction between them and those of the Antiochenes.⁵ It justified the subsequent Chalcedonian claim on Cyril's theology, and provided its apologists with a basis for their case.⁶

Cyril illustrates the strength and weakness of the Alexandrian position. He felt in the whole of his being the majestic concept of God suffering through Christ to redeem man and that the incarnation was not merely a fact in time but the eternal condition of the nature of God. 'One of the Trinity suffered for us', 'in the flesh', Cyril would add, and for the Greek-speaking Christian of the fifth and sixth centuries this was the unshakeable guarantee of salvation. And, just as Christ was from all eternity Word united by nature to God, so through the Eucharist of the body and blood, man had the means of participating in the life-giving Word. Christ's own flesh was given to the communicant, and hence only the most fundamental and indissoluble union, the ἕνωσις καθ' ὑπόστασιν, could endow the human flesh with the divine power to guarantee its invincibility against the powers of death.⁷ The Eucharist lay emotionally at the heart of Cyril's Christology. His criticism of his Antiochene opponents was that by insisting on the unbridgeable separation of God and creation and hence on the division of

---

¹ *Ep.* 44: μίαν τὴν τοῦ Θεοῦ φύσιν σεσαρκωμένην.

² *Ep.* 46 (the Second Letter to Successus).

³ *Ep.* 40 (*PG* 77, col. 193A and B) as, for instance, the westerners would be doing through Leo. See below, p. 134.

⁴ *Ep.* 44 (*PG* 77, col. 227A). ⁵ *Ep.* 40.

⁶ See below, p. 208, especially the use made by Severus of Antioch's opponent, the 'impious grammarian' of Cyril's letters to Acacius and Successus.

⁷ *In Evang. Ioann.* XII. 26 (*PG* 74, col. 725C). See H. Chadwick, 'Eucharist and Christology in the Nestorian controversy', *JTS*, n.s. 2. 2, 1951, pp. 145–64. Cyril's views are summed up in his Third Letter to Nestorius = *Ep.* 17 (*PG* 77, col. 112) and Bindley/Green, *Documents*, p. 110.

the human and divine natures, they made Christ a 'mere instrument' of the Godhead,[1] and denied to Christians the full benefit of the Eucharist. As he wrote poignantly in his Third Letter to Nestorius, if Nestorius was right, how could Christians be 'partakers both of the holy flesh and the precious blood of Christ the Saviour of us all? Not receiving it as common flesh – surely not – nor as the flesh of a man sanctified and associated with the Word in a unity of dignity, or at least having a divine indwelling, but truly as life-giving and of the Word's very own.'[2] The Eucharist, he writes elsewhere against Nestorius, 'raises us above corruption and destroys the law of sin which prevails over us in the flesh';[3] God 'transformed the elements into the activity of his own flesh'.[4] This was the driving force of Cyril's defence of the Alexandrian position against the Antiochenes. The body of life received in the Eucharist united the Christian with the Word to make him immortal and incorruptible. Either Mary was 'Bearer of God', or of a being that was not God, and that would be blasphemy.

Yet for all this, Cyril's Christ remains an abstraction, his humanity so much part of the divine world as to be unrecognisable in human terms, and the salvation offered to man only intelligible in a pantheistic setting in which the destiny of the soul was reabsorption into the source of life whence it had come. There was no Biblical ring in his thought for all his commentaries on the books of the Bible. Christ could not learn by obedience, and suffer temptation, for he could not become more perfect than he was already. He had no need to become man in order to know man, for he was man's creator.[5] In the *kenosis* his glory remained always with him.[6] Man's salvation lay in his knowledge of this mystery.

It was not easy to find a half-way house between Apollinarius and Nestorius. Cyril devoted a lifetime to the task but it would be a bold man who asserted his success. If Christ was really consubstantial with us, pos-

[1] *Ep.* 1 (*ad monachos*), *PG* 77, col. 37C: ἄνθρωπος δὲ ψιλὸς καθ' ἡμᾶς καὶ θεότητος ὄργανον.

[2] *Ep.* 17 (*PG* 77, col. 113) and Bindley/Green, *Documents*, p. 111 and 215–16.

[3] *Adv. Nestorium* IV. 4 (*PG* 76, col. 197C).

[4] *Comment. in Lucam* V. 19 (*PG* 72, col. 912A). See J. Mahé, 'L'Eucharistie après Saint Cyrille d'Alexandrie', *RHE* 8, 1907, pp. 677–96.

[5] This point is excellently made by F. M. Young, 'Christological ideas', p. 155.

[6] *In Isaiam orat.* III (*PG* 70, col. 129B): πλὴν οὐ δίχα δόξης, καὶ εἰ γέγονε σάρξ. See A. Dupré la Tour, 'La *Doxa* du Christ dans Saint Cyrille', *Revue des sciences religieuses* 49. 1, 1961, pp. 68–94.

sessed a rational human soul and suffered in it, then there were two natures, and they must subsist after the incarnation.[1] On the other hand, if there was only one nature, then only one nature – the divine nature – suffered, and how could that be?[2] Others were to ask the same question, and none more pertinently than the Antiochene theologians, who realised the profound weakness of the whole of the Alexandrian tradition of Christology which Cyril represented.

The Antiochenes accepted the current Platonic view of man, but with two important modifications which affected their Christology. First, they linked the rationality of the human soul with its mutability, and secondly, as a corollary, they thought of man not only in terms of philosophical categories, but also in an ethical way. Man's mutability implied freedom of choice and freedom of will. It was the means implanted by God by which man served God. 'The Lord made us rational, and wished to help that rationality to be effective in us, because in no other way could it be made manifest except by the choice of contraries. From among these, the choice of the better can be reached – for this is the highest attainment of every rational being.'[3] But for all this man remained man, and though 'made in the image of God' was part of the created order. God was by definition creator; therefore the gulf between the two could not logically be overcome. 'There is a great difference', said Theodore, 'between us and God; and we ought not to overlook this difference when we are thinking of the divine nature [of Christ] and the works done by it.'[4] The aim of man was not absorption into the divine by divinisation but communion with God by harmonising his will with God's. Christ as perfect man redeemed man by his example, restoring what had been thrown away in Adam's fall,[5] and

---

[1] Cyril, *Ep.* 46 *ad Succensum* 2. 5 (*PG* 77, col. 244D). See Grillmeier, *Christ in Christian Tradition*, p. 402.   [2] *Ep.* 46. 2. 1 (*PG* 77, col. 240A).

[3] Theodore of Mopsuestia, *Comment. in Ep. ad Galatas* (ed. Swete, I, 27). See R. A. Greer, *Theodore of Mopsuestia, Exegete and Theologian* (London, 1961), p. 17.

[4] Theodore, *On the Nicene Creed*, ch. 2 (Eng. tr. by A. Mingana, 'The Christian faith and the interpretation of the Nicene Creed, by Theodore of Mopsuestia (c. 350–428)', Woodbrooke Studies, fasc. 10, *Bull. of John Rylands Library* 16, 1932, pp. 200–318 at p. 232). The fact of their being created in the image of God enabled men to picture to themselves the higher things that belonged to God, but also emphasised the difference between man and God (*loc. cit.*).

[5] Compare J. F. Bethune Baker, *Nestorius and his Teaching* (Cambridge, 1908), pp. 109ff. for the argument used by Nestorius derived from Christ as high priest after the order of Melchizedek, and 'learning obedience' to God (Heb. 5. 7–9). Also, G. Koch, *Die Heilsverwirklichung bei Theodor von Mopsuestia* (Munich, 1965), pp. 65–6.

man was now destined to be saved in his complete human integrity. The Letter to the Hebrews, naming Christ *soter* and *archegos*, the great pioneer who had attained to life by victory over death and Satan, was the guiding light of Antiochene thought.

Theodore's doctrine of man did not require the essential or organic unity of the Word with manhood, indeed the contrary, for the Word was God and it could not therefore develop in excellence as was said of Jesus. Hence, however, he had to think in terms of two, Jesus and the Word as different subjects, attributing to each respectively divine and human characteristics of the New Testament Christ. Moreover, if the Word was confessed at Nicaea as of one substance with the Father, and was one *hypostasis* of the Trinity, his humanity must equally be another *hypostasis*. To redeem man, the Word assumed a man (not 'humanity' as in Cyril's theology), 'perfect man of the seed of Abraham and David'. 'The name [Jesus Christ] is that of the man whom God put on', Theodore stated.[1] Jesus then, though agent of redemption and to be worshipped as one with the Word, was still *homoousios* with man, and by his life and example showed the way whereby man might hate the evil and choose the good. Christ's human soul and will-power were not passive as in the Alexandrine teaching, but active in resisting temptations, accomplishing works of mercy, love and healing, and finally triumphant on the cross. The ethical example based on the New Testament account of Jesus was all-important. In addition, the approach to Scripture was historical and literal, with an absolute minimum of typology and allegory.[2] For instance, when he comments on Gal. 4. 24, Theodore states firmly that the apostle did not do away with the history, but presented these matters (Abraham's two wives) just as they happened at the time.[3] The Gospel narratives were treated in the same way. The 'third day' referred to in Jn. 2. 1 really meant the third day, i.e. two days after Andrew and his companions had spent the night with Jesus.

Applied to Christology the results were important, especially for the interpretation of the New Testament account of Jesus. If one wishes to

---

[1] *Expositio symboli* (ed. Swete, II, 328) and *On the Nicene Creed* 5 (Eng. tr. by Mingana, Woodbrooke Studies, fasc. 10, p. 260).

[2] Compare Theodoret of Cyrrhus, *Ep.* 132, to Ibas of Edessa: 'Let us cleave only to the doctrines of the Gospel, and with them, if need be, endure any extremity of pain, and choose honourable penury rather than wealth with its many cares.' Also *Ep.* 135 to Romulus of Berrhea, defending 'the plain truth of the Gospels against new-fangled impiety'.

[3] *Comment. in Ep. ad Galatas* (ed. Swete, I, 73–4).

contrast Antioch and Alexandria one has only to look at their respective approaches to the incident in Jesus' childhood told in Luke 2. 40–52. Athanasius (*Oratio contra Arianos* III. 52) maintains that the progress of which Luke speaks was 'the progress of the body; and as it progresses, there progresses in it the manifestation of the Godhead to those who saw it'. The Godhead was always present at full power but revealed itself more fully as the human envelope expanded. In this he follows Origen, who does violence to the Scriptural account by maintaining that Joseph and Mary were aware of the divine nature of Jesus and could not have been angry with him! Theodore's interpretation is more what one would expect of a modern exegete. 'Jesus progresses', he says, 'in age, as time passes; in wisdom, by acquiring understanding in accord with the passage of time; in virtue, by following the virtue that accompanies understanding and knowledge; from this virtue, favour with God takes its increase for him.'[1] Theodore considered that Jesus had a normal childhood but that all the time he was completely correlated with God until the climax of his baptism. Like the writer of the *Acts of Archelaus* he places great emphasis on this, for while before baptism he had fulfilled the law, only after baptism did 'he fulfil by the Spirit's co-operation with as great care [as he had previously observed the law] the life of grace' – hence through the grace of the Holy Spirit his miracles, his ministry and destruction of Satan and his work.[2] From now on, there was conscious union with the Word, union so complete as to form a single personality – one *prosopon*. 'We do not assert that the Sons are two, or Lords are two, but one Son is rightly confessed since there is one Son according to essence (εἷς υἱὸς κατ' οὐσίαν), God the Word, the only begotten Son of the Father to whom is conjoined he who participates in the Godhead, and shares the common name and honour of the son.'[3] As second Adam, Christ overcame genuine temptations, demonstrating thus the way of forgiveness and salvation for man. Finally, his resurrection was the resurrection of man, for how else, asks Theodore's

---

[1] Swete, II, 297–8. Compare also Diodore, frag. 36: '"Jesus grew in age and in wisdom." This cannot be said of the Word of God because he is born perfect God of the perfect Father.' Jesus grew in wisdom and the Godhead only gradually bestowed all wisdom on him. See R. Abramowski, 'Der theologische Nachlass des Diodor von Tarsus', *ZNTW* 42, 1949, pp. 19–69 at p. 51.

[2] *De incarnatione* XIII, frag. I (ed. Swete, II, 306–7). See Koch, *Die Heilsverwirklichung*, pp. 34–7.

[3] *Expositio symboli* (ed. Swete, II, 329). Compare *Ad baptizatos*, Lecture VIII (*ibid.* p. 323).

disciple Theodoret of Cyrrhus, could mankind's redemption be achieved?[1]

Thus Christ raised human nature to the level of the divine, and showed to individuals the way of salvation through his own works. The basis of his unity with God was through the will – the term Theodore used (εὐδοκία) is (not too happily) translated as 'good pleasure'.[2] Man drew near or rejected Christ also according to the exercise of his will. 'He cannot force his love on those who say "Evil be thou my good".'[3] There is no need to emphasise the relevance of this concept to westerners struggling with the Pelagian and Augustinian theories of grace. It was unfortunate that in 423 Theodore met and welcomed Pelagian exiles, thus damning his cause and that of Nestorius in the eyes of the popes.[4]

Even so, it must be conceded that however closely the union of the humanity and divinity was defined in terms of will, both were regarded by the Antiochenes as separate 'natures' which retained their identity as Godhead and manhood after the incarnation.[5] In exile, Nestorius sometimes writes of Christ existing in 'one *prosopon* in two *ousiai*' or 'in two natures', so anticipating the Chalcedonian formula, but he rejected the 'hypostatic union'. Though he implies the compenetration of the human and divine elements in Christ,[6] it is arguable whether at the time of his controversy

[1] *Eranistes* 3 (*PG* 83, col. 260c): 'If Christ did not receive a soul and if it was not his Godhead that conquered sin, there was no advantage to us in his achievements.' (Also Theodore, *De incarnatione* xv. 3.) Compare the interesting passage in *Acta Archelai* 58 (ed. Beeson): 'Quod si Jesus non resurrexit, nec alius aliquis resurget. Quod si nullus resurget, nec iudicium erit.' This is very near western Christology as stated by Tertullian, *De res. carnis* and *De carne Christi*. Both emphasised the judgement to come.

[2] Letter to Domnus (ed. Swete, II, 338–9). See J. Tixeront, *Histoire des dogmes*, vol. III, *La Fin de l'âge patristique* (Paris, 1928), p. 17: '*Eudokia* is in all probability a rendering of the Hebrew *raṣon* indicating an act of grace by God towards an individual.'

[3] *De incarnatione* VII (ed. Swete, II, 295).

[4] His contemporary Marius Mercator, Pope Celestine's agent in Constantinople, went so far as to infer that Theodore was one of the originators of Pelagian teaching: *Commonitorium* written in 439, text in *ACO* I. v, p. 5. See R. A. Norris, *Manhood and Christ* (Oxford, 1963), p. 240 and discussion of Theodore's 'Pelagianism' *ibid*. ch. 14.

[5] *Expositio symboli* (ed. Swete, II, 329).

[6] See Grillmeier, *Christ in Christian Tradition*, p. 448. More typical perhaps is Theodoret's outright rejection of the idea of hypostatic union, as wholly incompatible with Scripture and the interpretations of the Fathers: *PG* 76, col. 400A (Cyril, *Apol. contra Theodoretum pro XII capitibus*).

with Cyril he would have opposed Theodore's rejection of the *communicatio idiomatum*. There was no true sharing of properties, which Theodore suggested in any event was a doubtful piece of theological construction.[1] The emphasis which both theologians placed on the alternative teaching of 'association' (κοινωνία) or 'inseparable conjunction' (ἀχωριστή συνάφεια) of the natures seems decisive in this regard.[2] There was nothing 'interchanged' or 'mingled'. Christ's flesh was 'acquired': it did not pre-exist to be 'recognised' in contemplation, nor was it essentially united with the Word in one incarnate being. The sacrifice was that of the body, not of the Godhead.[3] Mary must be defined as 'Anthropotokos' as well as *Theotokos*, for 'he who was in the womb of Mary was man and he came forth thence. She is *Theotokos* because God was in the man who was born.'[4] The worship of the Christ was one but the two natures remained separate. The one *prosopon* was brought about by a personal union of opposites and not an essential union of the human with the divine. In the course of the long dispute between the two sides the differences narrowed but were not obliterated. Alexandria could not be satisfied; more decisively, nor could the majority of the monks.[5]

In this long-standing controversy the representatives of the western church appeared as innocents abroad. Their leaders tended to seize on some formula such as 'Apollinarius believed that Christ had no human soul', without enquiring further whether this was true, and even if so, how or why he had reached such a conclusion. When confronted by detailed theological argument they were at a hopeless disadvantage. Even Leo admitted naively

---

[1] *Contra Apollinarium* IV, frag. 2 (ed. Swete, II, 319); Raven, *Apollinarianism*, pp. 291–3.

[2] A good example of Theodore's exposition of the relations between the two natures is to be found in his Sermon on the Faith of Nicaea, Eng. tr. by Mingana, Woodbrooke Studies, fasc. 10, p. 236. Theodore cites Rom. 9. 5 in order to show that Paul used the words 'God' and 'in the flesh' concerning Christ 'in order to teach the close union of the two natures'.

[3] Cf. Theodoret, *HE* v. 3, criticising opponents who 'attributed suffering to the Godhead of the only begotten'. Hence, too, the emphasis on the message of Hebrews in Nestorius' works.

[4] Theodore, *De incarnatione* XV, frag. 2 (ed. Swete, II, 310). For an apparent outright rejection of the term *Theotokos* see *Contra Apollinarium* III, frag. 1 (Swete, II, 313–14). See Raven, *Apollinarianism*, pp. 294–5 and Koch, *Die Heilsverwirklichung bei Theodor von Mopsuestia*, p. 51. See above, p. 14.

[5] For Theodoret of Cyrrhus' attempts to woo monastic support for Antiochene doctrine at the time of Ephesus II, see *Ep.* 151, and 145 to the monks of Constantinople.

that for a long time he had little idea why Eutyches should be regarded as a heretic,[1] and he exaggerated Nestorius' teaching almost out of recognition.[2] Tactically and emotionally Rome was the ally of Alexandria, the fiction of Mark's discipleship to Peter being reinforced by the reality of joint grievances against Constantinople and memories of Athanasius' sojourn in Rome in 341 during his second exile. Theologically, however, the Roman and indeed the whole western view coincided more with that of Antioch, and hence the reversal of alliances that took place in 449 becomes easier to understand.[3] Indeed, had Celestine been an abler theologian and less ready to listen to the biased reports of his agents in the capital, the reversal must have taken place at the time of Ephesus I.[4]

Western Christology rested on three bases, all of which would have been understood better in Antioch than elsewhere in the east. First, there was a general soteriological position that Christ could not save what he did not himself possess that one finds as early as Tertullian's *De carne Christi*, in which he emphasises that Christ's soul had felt the full measure of human mental experiences.[5] Obviously, Tertullian states against Praxeas that the references in Matt. 26. 28 to Christ 'being sorrowful even unto death' must apply to Christ's soul. The 'two substances' (in Christ) acted distinctively, Christ hungering and thirsting and dying as man, but rising immortal as

[1] *Ep.* 34. 1: 'Diu apud nos incertum fuit, quid in ipso [Eutyche] catholicis displiceret.'

[2] For instance, *Ep.* 59 in which Nestorius is accused of preaching 'two Christs'. In contrast, Nestorius himself rejects the very idea of 'two sons'. Using the analogy of the burning bush (Exod. 3. 1–5) he points out how 'as the fire was in the bush and the bush was fire and the fire bush, each of them was bush and fire', but there 'were not two bushes nor two fires', nor were there two Christs, though Christ was in two natures. Cf. Grillmeier, *Christ in Christian Tradition*, pp. 449–50. Western apprehension of a 'two Christs' Christology goes back as far as Tertullian, *De carne Christi* 24, but Nestorius was not guilty of preaching it. The charge is neatly disposed of by Theodoret, *Ep.* 145 to the monks of Constantinople: 'It were the wildest folly to believe that there were two sons and to give the doxology to one alone!'

[3] Note Harnack's study of the west's doctrinal kinship with Antioch and Alexandria respectively, *History of Dogma*, IV, 183 n3, and Sellers, *Council of Chalcedon*, pp. 201–3, who stresses the correspondence with the Alexandrian position.

[4] For examples of bias and even misquotation of the Antiochenes by Marius Mercator, see Mingana, Woodbrooke Studies, fasc. 10, p. 215. See above, p. 17.

[5] Tertullian, *De carne Christi* 5: 'Christ's flesh will be mortal precisely because Christ is man, and Son of Man.' More generally, in Paulinus of Nola, *Ep.* 37. 6 (ed. Hartel, p. 322): 'That humanity which the Son of God assumed he must have assumed wholly, with that truth which he personifies and with which he created man, so that he might renew this work by saving it wholly.'

God.¹ Secondly, there was the doctrine of the Atonement, that as man's representative Christ paid in full the debt incurred to the devil by man at the Fall, and this involved 'the descent of the Son of God upon this lower world' (the *Tome* of Leo, *Ep.* 28. 4), sharing human nature to the full except for its sin. Thirdly, a developing theology of grace involved a concept of Christ in which the human and divine wills could be harmonised, and this would not be possible unless Christ offered an example of true and perfect humanity. The dominical injunction 'Be ye perfect as your Father in heaven is perfect' (Matt. 5. 48) would have been otherwise impossible to fulfil.

As it had done in the east, the Arian controversy consolidated the western Christological standpoint. In his victorious onslaught against the western Arians, Ambrose laid great stress on the reality of the distinction between Christ's human and divine natures. The Arians had, in his view, confounded these two natures and ascribed Scriptural passages referring to the 'weakness' and 'ignorance' of Jesus to a composite being of one nature inferior to and unlike God. 'Like Jewish vintners', Ambrose indignantly declared, 'they mix the water with the wine ascribing to the Divine Nature what could only be ascribed to the flesh.'² 'One must distinguish', he says elsewhere, 'the nature of the divinity and that of the body.'³ The Crucifixion was suffered by the body according to its nature so that man might benefit by the resurrection.⁴ There was an emotional undertone to these statements. A one-nature Christology, such as was the Arian, smacked of Manichaeism. Those who spoke of 'the one nature of the flesh and divinity of Christ' were 'uttering sacrilege'.⁵ From Rome too, Damasus' letter to the bishops of Illyricum, *Ea gratia*, written probably in 377, was asserting that 'the Son of God assumed perfect man, for at the Fall man had lost his

---

¹ Tertullian, *Adv. Praxean* 27 and 29.

² Ambrose, *De incarnatione* 23 (*PL* 16, col. 825). See Homes Dudden, *The Life and Times of St Ambrose* (Oxford, 1935), pp. 597–8.

³ *De fide* II. 9. 77 (*PL* 16, col. 576): 'Servemus distinctionem divinitatis et carnis. Unus in utraque loquitur Dei Filius, quia in eodem utraque natura est et si idem loquitur, non uno semper loquitur modo. Intende in eo nunc gloriam Dei, nunc hominis passiones. Quasi Deus loquitur quae sunt divina, quia Verbum est, quasi homo dicit quae sunt humana, quia in mea substantia loquebatur.' On this important passage, see G. Bardy, 'Sur une citation de saint Ambroise dans les controverses christologiques', *RHE* 40, 1944–5, pp. 171–6.

⁴ *De incarnatione* 45 (*PL* 16, col. 830), and compare *De fide* II. 58.

⁵ *De incarnatione* 23.

ability to choose between good and evil, and his entire nature therefore needed salvation'. The condemnation of Apollinarius and his doctrines was correspondingly unsparing.[1]

The general tendency of western theology in the first half of the fifth century continued to lean towards Antioch. It would be difficult to find a much more open avowal of the separation of the two natures than in Augustine's description of man's redemption in *De civitate Dei*, bk. IX: 'Man then, mortal and miserable and far removed from the immortal and blessed' needed 'uniting to immortality and blessedness'. But how? 'Through the Word of God', answers Augustine, 'but I do not say that He is Mediator because He is the Word, for as the Word He is supremely blessed and supremely immortal; and therefore far from us miserable mortals; but He is Mediator as He is man, for by His humanity He shows us that in order to obtain that blessed and beatific good, we need not seek other mediators to lead us through the successive steps towards this, but that the blessed and beatific God having Himself become a partaker of our humanity, has afforded us ready access to the participation of His divinity' (*De civitate Dei* IX. 15, tr. by Marcus Dods, altered slightly).

In this passage redemption is linked with Jesus' full humanity, the human mediator being decisive for the salvation of mankind.[2] In Augustine's Trinitarian thought also the mystery of the Trinity is expressed by Augustine in terms analogous to the human psychology. As the human mind knows itself and loves itself, so the Trinity is united through the quality of love.[3] This, too, could be harmonised with the Antiochene divine 'good pleasure' that united Word and man within Christ. More directly even than this, one can perceive how Ambrose's insistence on

---

[1] Damasus, *Ep.* II, frag. 2, text in *PL* 13, cols. 352–3: 'If human nature is taken incomplete then the gift of God is incomplete and our salvation is incomplete, because human nature has not been saved in its entirety.'

[2] Also, *Sermo* 174: 'Non liberaretur humanum genus nisi sermo Dei dignaretur esse humanus.' See H. E. W. Turner, *The Patristic Doctrine of Redemption* (London, 1952), p. 108.

[3] *De Trinitate* XV. 6. 10. Compare Theodore's assertion (*Ep. ad Domnum*, ed. Swete, II, 338) that 'the union of the natures [in Christ] is effected by the principle of grace [κατ' εὐδοκίαν]'. Also, compare Paulinus of Nola, *Ep.* 23. 14 where 'grace' united the two natures of God and man in Christ and brought them into harmony. Both assumed the activity of the Holy Spirit in bringing together two otherwise incompatible natures. Paulinus, a strong opponent of Apollinarianism, insisted also that the Son of God assumed 'a man' ('eum hominem quem suscepit dei filius'): *Ep.* 37. 6 (ed. Hartel, p. 322).

'preserving the distinction' of the divinity and flesh (of Christ), and on separating the 'glory' from 'the passion', for instance, contradicts Cyril's Fourth Anathema which condemned those who attributed 'some apostolic sayings as appropriate to the Divine Word and others as beseeming the human nature only', for this is precisely what both Ambrose and Leo in his *Tome* were doing. In contrast, neither could have disagreed with Nestorius' (or rather, Theodoret's) counter-anathema which while safeguarding the unity of Christ condemned those who attributed Christ's sufferings to the Word.[1] Dioscorus could not have read Leo's *Tome* at Ephesus II and upheld his own position. His excommunication of Leo just before Chalcedon as a new Nestorius followed logically. Christ's perfection *in* two natures was essential to the western position.[2] The interchange of human and divine qualities assured by the *communicatio idiomatum* in the *Tome* might paper over the cracks but could not satisfy the acute and recalcitrant minds of the Alexandrian theologians.

From the depths of his exile, Nestorius could appreciate that there were no essential differences between his theology and that contained in Leo's *Tome*. Leo's utterances, though sometimes penetrating, as in his *Sermo* XXVII. 1, often contained unclear ideas about the 'mixture' or 'mingling' of the natures which would have been condemned by both Alexandria and Antioch.[3] The *Tome*, for all its splendid rhetoric and resonant phrases, merely repeated without further definition traditional western concepts, concepts that had developed independently of Greek theological thought. The west, too, had little interest in *Theotokos*, or, beyond the Atonement, in the mystery of human redemption in the way that it agitated the monks and theologians of the east. Even today these preoccupations have been described as 'anarchy' by western Catholic theologians.[4] What, however, stood in the way of an understanding between Antioch and the west led by Rome which might have lessened the crises of 430–1 and 449–51, was not only Celestine's obsession with Pelagianism and the papacy's belief that Nestorius preached 'two Christs' (i.e. one pre-incarnation and one post-

---

[1] Counter-anathema 12 = *PG* 76, col. 449.

[2] For instance, Ambrose's affirmation of Christ 'in utroque unus, et utroque perfectus': *De excessu fratris sui Satyri* I. 12 (ed. O. Faller, *CSEL* 73, Vienna, 1955).

[3] Leo, *Sermo* XXXIV. 4: 'dei filius naturae carnis inmixtus'. Compare XXIII. 1, 'naturae alteri altera miscebatur', and Tertullian, *Apol.* 21. 14, '[Christus] nascitur homo Deo mixtus'.

[4] See, for instance, Dom René Dolle, 'Léon le Grande, Sermons III' (*Sources chrétiennes* 74, Paris, 1961), p. 9: 'anarchie doctrinale de l'Orient'.

incarnation), but the persistent rancour of the disciplinary issues that had bedevilled relations between Rome and the eastern bishops from the time of Athanasius. In handling these issues Rome showed intense preoccupation with the claims of the see of Peter that sometimes conflicted with considerations of doctrine. Indeed, in the case of Celestine these latter seem to have been secondary in his decision to support Cyril. Even in 449 Leo was concerned above all to furnish Flavian with dogmatic instructions of a somewhat hectoring character and to draw the Council of Ephesus' attention to what the see of Peter had already decided. The other great sees observed how the see of Peter calculated its priorities, and in this aspect of church life they took their lead from Rome.

Whether the doctrinal issues that separated the four great sees of Christendom could have continued to be held in tension is an open question. Even on the intellectual plane, the conflict was increasing in the last decades of the fourth century. Apollinarius attacked Diodore of Tarsus and was counter-attacked without compromise by Theodore of Mopsuestia.

With Cyril the dispute becomes more bitter. Cyril was incapable of writing an uncontroversial work; even the letter to John of Antioch accepting the Formula of Reunion lapses into menace before its end. His abiding passion was the destruction of Antiochene teaching whose true source, he reckoned, was Theodore, and which was represented only incidentally by Nestorius. In a significant letter to Rabbula, bishop of Edessa (dated perhaps to the end of 432), he indicated his belief that he was fighting a danger on a world front, and that the importance of Nestorius' role in the capital had been as representative of this. However, 'all the holy bishops that lived in the regions of the Romans were of one heart and mind with the decisions of Ephesus', but behind Nestorius had stood Theodore, the true author and origin of Nestorius' blasphemy.[1] Elsewhere, he shows that no language could be too violent in denunciation of Theodore.[2] Well before Nestorius arrived on the scene at Constantinople, Cyril had been denouncing those who 'divided Christ after the economy of the incarnation', or who spoke

---

[1] *Brief des hl. Cyrillus an Rabulas*, ed. G. Bickell (Kempten, 1874), pp. 246–9. In this letter Cyril hotly disclaimed Apollinarianism.

[2] *Ep.* 72 to Proclus (*PG* 77, col. 345). Severus of Antioch also cites Cyril as saying of Theodore, 'Sodom has been more justified than you. You have surpassed the babblings of the heathen which they uttered against Christ, "reckoning the Cross foolishness". You have shown that the charges against Jewish arrogance are nothing' (*Select Letters* v. 6, ed. Brooks, p. 317). Compare Mansi, *Collectio* IX, col. 235.

The rise of the Monophysite movement

of two Sons or two *prosopa*,[1] and had been urging instead that 'it is only in contemplation (*theoria*) that we may divide the natures, for it is written that the Word was made flesh, not that he was transformed into flesh'.[2] The impression is left that his real enemy was Theodore[3] dead or alive, and that personally Nestorius was simply a nuisance.[4]

Behind the intensity of feeling that led bishops to anathematise and manhandle each other and even to try to starve out each other's flocks, was the swelling tide of public opinion represented above all by the monks. In the crisis years around Ephesus in 430-1 and leading up to Chalcedon, monastic opinion, though tending towards division in the capital and in Palestine, was strongly behind Cyril and Dioscorus in the rural areas of Syria and Egypt. When one analyses who brought the charges against the Antiochene bishops and against Flavian at Ephesus II, we find almost without exception monks as accusers. Flavian, of course, was accused by Eutyches, Domnus by the presbyter-monks Marcellus of Emesa and Simeon of Antioch and charged with speaking against the Twelve Anathemas.[5] The charge of heresy and peculation against Ibas was mounted by twelve monks of his own diocese.[6] Theodoret of Cyrrhus was accused by the presbyter-monk Pelagius.[7] In all these cases the monks prevailed against the bishops. Ephesus II was their synod.

Why was the one-nature Christology so attractive to the Syrian and practically all the Egyptian monks? Mysticism of itself is not a complete answer, for we have seen how the monks in Syria rejected Apollinarianism

---

[1] *Comment. in Ioann.* v. 8. 12 (written 425-9), *PG* 73, col. 776B and c; compare 249C and 629C. See Chadwick, *Eucharist and Christology*, pp. 152-3.

[2] *Homil. Paschalis* VIII (A.D. 421). 5-6 (*PG* 77, cols. 568-72).

[3] See L. Abramowski, 'Der Streit um Diodor und Theodor zwischen den beiden ephesinischen Konzilien', *Zeitschr. f. Kirchengeschichte* 57, 1955-6, pp. 252-87. Abramowski, however, clearly believes that it was only as a consequence of his correspondence with Rabbula that Cyril opened his attack on Theodore, now four years dead. In view of the fury which Cyril developed against Theodore's theology in the next few years, I find it difficult to accept that up to then he had not concerned himself with Antiochene Christology as exemplified by its master.

[4] An utterer of δυσσεβεῖς περιττολογίας and κενοφωνίας (Cyril, *Ep.* 72), which the lay historians of the time found not unusual ecclesiastical faults.

[5] *Akten*, ed. Flemming, pp. 123-9.

[6] *Ibid.* p. 13, lines 12-14.

[7] *Ibid.* p. 87. See H. Bacht, 'Die Rolle des orientalischen Mönchtums in den kirchenpolitischen Auseinandersetzungen um Chalkedon (432-519)' in Grillmeier/Bacht, *Das Konzil von Chalkedon*, II, 193-314 at pp. 229-31.

when it seemed likely to gain popular acceptance, and moreover their fifth-century counterparts in the west and beyond the Roman frontier in Persia, the predecessors of Benedict and the Nestorian missionaries, were far from being Monophysites. A number of motives may have contributed. In Egypt loyalty to the patriarch was probably the strongest. There was also the appeal of Cyril's doctrine to the simple minds of the Coptic and perhaps the Syriac-speaking monks that real assurance of salvation could only come from the worship of one who was wholly God, and whose Eucharist guaranteed the partaker against the power of death, and the terrors of the underworld still thought of in terms of pagan legend.[1] The spontaneous cry of the Egyptian bishops at Chalcedon, 'Throw out the Nestorians. Christ is God',[2] lay at the heart of their religion. In the next century the simple, unhesitating belief in 'Christ, God' could inspire the deepest trust in the saving power of the cross and sustain humble Christians in the hour of martyrdom. The Himyarite heroine Habsa spoke for many.[3]

In Egypt monastic religion was based on two main principles, the Bible and the Council of Nicaea. It had been acceptance of the literal text of the New Testament command 'Sell all that thou hast ...' that had precipitated Antony towards solitary existence,[4] and according to Athanasius, Antony himself regarded reading outside the Bible as superfluous for salvation.[5] Accurate knowledge of the Testament in Coptic also played a great part in the training of the Pachomian communities, and for their leaders in the fifth century, men like Shenute and his successor Besa, a deep reverence for the

[1] For instance, see the Coptic-Monophysite 'Assumption of the Virgin' (*Apocryphal New Testament*, ed. James, pp. 194ff.) with its reference in ch. 11 to 'the accusers of Amenti and the dragon of the abyss, the river of fire that proves the righteous from the wicked'. See E. Amélineau, 'Le Christianisme chez les anciens Coptes', RHR 15, 1887, pp. 52–87 at pp. 87–8. Also below, p. 222.

[2] At the fifth session: see *ACO* 2. 1. 2, para. 124. Compare also their assertions at the first session: 'As he was begotten, so he suffered. Let no one divide the king of glory. Let no one divide the indivisible. Let no one call the one Lord two. Thus Nestorius believed.' *ACO* 2. 1. 1, paras. 171–5 = Mansi, *Collectio* VI, col. 636.

[3] Confronted by the victorious Jewish forces after the fall of Najran in 523 she said to her executioners, 'You must know that not only will I not say that Christ was a man, but I worship him and praise him because of all the benefits he has shown me. And I believe that he is God, Maker of all creatures, and I take refuge in his Cross' (*The Book of the Himyarites*, ed. A. Moberg, Lund, 1924, p. cxxiv). The *Book* was found in a corpus of Monophysite works (Moberg, p. xi). Others, 'Christians in name' (i.e. Nestorians?), were supporting the Jews. Cf. Michael the Syrian, *Chron.* IX. 29 (al-hareth).

[4] Athanasius, *Vita Antonii* 2.   [5] *Ibid.* 16.

The rise of the Monophysite movement

text much of which they knew by heart. Their surviving sermons suggest that the Biblical idiom was the one they used naturally.[1] Their approach to the text was literal, with little, if any, trace of the allegorism which was accepted as a matter of course by the Alexandrian theologians or of Greek piety in general.[2] Their preaching, too, was didactic with much emphasis on God's wrath and punishments, on Christ's judgement and retribution on the wicked, on the blood of martyrs, and the literal terrors of the beyond. All this might be expected to move Shenute and his contemporaries in the direction of the Antiochene and western interpretations of Scripture and of Jesus' earthly life, and indeed one can find traces of the *Acts of Archelaus*[3] with its Word-man Christology in Shenute's work. There is not a trace, Leipoldt points out, of Mariolatry in his writings.[4] But he seems never to have realised where this should be leading him regarding Christology. So far as he was concerned, Nestorius preached that Christ was 'a man like Moses' – therefore, anathema to Nestorius.[5]

At this point the other aspect of monastic religion, namely the monk's (and above all, the Coptic monk's) veneration of Nicaea, becomes important. It was demonstrated in many incongruous ways. For instance, at el Wizz, one mile north of Faras on the Egyptian–Sudanese frontier, excavators were surprised to find the walls of the seventh–eighth century hermit's cavern covered in rough characters with the complete Creed of Nicaea associated with versions of the Letter of James to King Abgar, the names of the Seven Dormants and the Forty Martyrs of Sebaste, and a Coptic version of the SATOR AREPO palindrome, now named the 'nails of Christ', and a large selection of pious stories of the desert Fathers.[6] But for this monk and his fellows, all roads led back to the creed and its great hero, Athanasius. This resulted in theological assumptions which could be at variance with the literal word of the Bible, and the Alexandrian patriarchs needed all their prestige and their skill to win the acceptance of these by the

---

[1] See J. Leipoldt, *Schenute von Atripe*, TU 25 (n.s. 10), Leipzig, 1904, no. 1, pp. 74ff.

[2] *Ibid.* p. 74: 'Nirgends habe ich auch nur eine Anspielung gefunden an den Grundgedanken griechischer Frömmigkeit, der Mensch werde durch den Logos vergottet.' Similarly, W. Bousset, *Apophthegmata Patrum* (Tübingen, 1923), p. 83 discussing the *Vita Arsenii*: 'In den Logien und Erzählungen dieser Mönche spielt das Dogma gar keine Rolle.'

[3] Leipoldt, *Schenute*, p. 86. Origen, on the other hand, was regarded as a heretic (*ibid.*). [4] *Ibid.* p. 83. [5] *Ibid.* p. 88.

[6] Excavations reported in 'Oxford excavations in Nubia VII' by F. Ll. Griffith, *Annals of Archaeology and Anthropology* 15 (Liverpool, 1927), pp. 81ff. The date was A.D. 739.

monks. Both Athanasius and Cyril took great pains to convince the latter of the rightness of their stand, Athanasius taking the monks into his confidence and spelling out in three considerable works his reasons for refusing to accept communion with the Meletians and Arians. His gift for repartee to monkish questions passed into legend. 'How was the Son equal to the Father? Like sight in the two eyes', replied Athanasius.[1]

It says much also for Cyril's shrewdness of judgement that fairly early in his controversy with Nestorius he sought out and brought to the surface the latent differences between his interpretation of the Word-flesh theology and the Biblicism of the monks, and convinced the latter of his orthodoxy. The monks had objected that the term *Theotokos* was not found in the Bible, and Cyril in a masterly reply (*Ep.* 1) with only the minimal Scriptural support (Eph. 5. 5 with its reference to the 'kingdom of Christ and God' is the only text Cyril quotes in direct support of the term[2]), reduced the argument in favour of *Theotokos* to the simplest terms. If Christ was not by nature God but equal to us and nothing more than an instrument of God, how could he overthrow death, and how could we be exhorted to worship a mere man? Nicaea had implied that what was born of the Virgin was 'homoousios tou Theou', hence the justification of the title *Theotokos* – and had not Athanasius been present at Nicaea? He always used the term. Could he err?[3] The argument worked, and Cyril, like Theophilus before him, could call on the devotion of the monks to his cause. At Ephesus I and II they were ready to dare all to destroy 'the divider of Christ', Nestorius and his followers. From then on, apart from the group of Pachomian monks alienated by Dioscorus, Egyptian monasticism was the heart and soul of Monophysitism.

The outlook of the Syrian monks was more complex. We have already described something of the extreme individualism of these and the influences of Marcionism and Manichaeism among them.[4] That a link existed also between these two forms of religious asceticism is clear from the statement of Ephraim of Nisibis regarding the middle of the fourth century that 'Marcion divided the sheep of Christ and Mani merely robbed the robber'.[5]

[1] *Apophthegmata Patrum*, reproduced by F. Nau, 'Histoire des solitaires égyptiens', *Revue de l'Orient chrétien* 12, 1907, p. 48, no. 1.
[2] He uses the reference to the 'kingdom of Christ and God' to show that what the Virgin made incarnate was 'God the Son': *PG* 77, cols. 20–1.
[3] Cyril, *Ep.* 1 (*PG* 77, col. 13C).   [4] See above, p. 89.
[5] Ephraim Syrus, *Contra haereses* XX. 1 (ed. E. Beck, *CSCO*, Scriptores Syri 174, Louvain, 1957).

The rise of the Monophysite movement

Among such Marcionite or Manichaean communities a Docetic Christology combined with an ascetic interpretation of Christianity would be accepted as a matter of course, and as the attractive power of these sects waned, Monophysitism would offer an alternative. An example is provided by Barsaumas, who asked like the Coptic monks, 'If the blood of the Crucified Only Son had been of the same nature as the blood of the sons of Adam, how could it have expiated the sins of the sons of Adam?'[1] A strong minority, however, were equally attached to the opposite Christology, continuing the Syrian tradition represented in the *Acts of Archelaus* and by Aphraates. In the sixth century the Persian frontier became the battle-ground not only of opposing armies but of Christologies. Further west the situation was more fluid. On the whole, in this area more deeply influenced by centuries of Greek culture, the theology of Cyril triumphed over that of the Antiochene school, but with contrasting shades of loyalty. If Antioch generally tended towards Monophysitism, the monks in the province of Syria II moved in the opposite direction and in favour of Chalcedon. It was some of these who seem to have been the first to expose the Apollinarian forgeries[2] and tear apart the most effective line of defence of the Monophysites, namely that one-nature Christology could claim unimpeachable patristic tradition in both the east and west. In the reign of Anastasius some of the great monastic houses in the province, such as that of Maro, south of Damascus, were pro-Chalcedonian to the extent of accepting Roman jurisdiction in preference to that of the Constantinople of the Emperor Anastasius.[3]

It is interesting to find how in these parts an apocalyptic tradition with social undertones, which one might otherwise have associated with non-orthodox religion, was in fact strongly anti-Monophysite. The *Oracle of Baalbek*, discussed by P. J. Alexander, dates probably to the period of the Persian war of 502–5.[4] It is modelled on Jewish-Christian Sibylline prophecies of three centuries earlier though written in prose and it also shows deep concern for economic relief. The prophesied messianic ruler 'would

---

[1] From the 81st Miracle told in the *Life* of Barsaumas written 550–650 and cited from E. Honigmann, 'Le Couvent de Barṣaumā et le patriarcat jacobite d'Antioche et de Syrie', *CSCO*, Subsidia 7 (Louvain, 1954), p. 18.

[2] Evagrius, *HE* III. 31. See below, p. 230.   [3] See below, p. 229.

[4] P. J. Alexander, 'Mediaeval Apocalypses as historical sources', *AHR* 73. 4, 1968, pp. 997–1018, especially pp. 1002–6, and *The Oracle of Baalbek*, Dumbarton Oaks Studies 10, Washington, 1967. The editor believes the *Oracle* was written circa 502–6 near Baalbek in Phoenicia Libanensis: *ibid* p. 65.

grant exemption from paying public tax and would restore all the people of the entire east [Syria] and Palestine'.[1] The *Oracle*, however, despite Docetism and even semi-Arian traits, is strongly biased in favour of Chalcedon. It castigates the anti-Chalcedonianism of the usurper Basiliscus (475–6) as 'blasphemy',[2] and criticises Anastasius himself for 'ruining the people either lawfully or unlawfully' and for 'hating all the poor'.[3] Neither were fair criticisms but indicated even among the pro-Chalcedonians of Syria II the beginnings of an underlying estrangement from the central authority of the capital. It was this sentiment that Monophysitism was eventually to represent.

The Chalcedonian crisis was not only a crisis of the intellectuals. It was a crisis involving the totality of Christians in the eastern Mediterranean. This marks it off from the Arian controversy a century before for the latter was primarily a crisis of bishops. Throughout the Monophysite dispute, the key role was always to belong to the monks. In perpetual warfare against the demons on the edge of the desert and haunted by subconscious fears of vengeance from the old, dispossessed national gods, the monks demanded as their protection the full armour of Christ. Nicaea, with its affirmation that Christ was indeed God and of one substance with the Father, assured them of the reality of his saving power for creation; the formula of the 'one nature' of the incarnate Word assured them also that through the Word made flesh the whole Godhead was manifested to humanity. Through contemplation of this mystery and participation in it through the Eucharist the Christian himself might become divine. Those who would 'divide Christ' or degrade him to the level of 'an instrument of God' were as much to be reprobated as those who had proclaimed 'there was when he was not'. The 'valiant Dioscorus', proclaiming to all hearers the oneness of the incarnate nature of Christ with the homely and obvious example drawn from Christ at the Cana marriage-feast, became the type of the embattled ascetic leader proof against the intellectual pitfalls laid by his adversaries.[4]

---

[1] *Oracle of Baalbek*, p. 20, lines 188–90.   [2] *Ibid.* lines 153–4.

[3] *Ibid.* line 168: μισῶν πάντας τοὺς πτωχούς, a somewhat surprising statement even if πτωχούς = 'beggars'. See Alexander, *Oracle of Baalbek*, pp. 95–6. I prefer Stein's appraisal of Anastasius' reign, *Bas-Empire*, II, 192.

[4] Makarius of Tkou relates how at Chalcedon Dioscorus put the argument to his accusers. 'When our Saviour Jesus Christ was invited to the marriage feast at Cana, was it in his quality as God or in his quality as man?' 'In his quality as man', they replied. 'Very well', said Dioscorus, 'And when he changed the water into wine, did

At Chalcedon the assembled bishops might shout in their relief: 'Peter has spoken through Leo', 'As Leo thinks, so do we', 'Leo and Cyril taught alike.' The monks were not so sure. Some were bold enough to voice their disagreement. They were prepared to condemn 'Mani and Nestorius and those who say that Christ's flesh came down from heaven',[1] i.e. the popular version of Eutychianism, but further they would not go. In their eyes the *Tome* of Leo seemed to consecrate the doctrine of Nestorius while condemning Nestorius by name. The majority of the Egyptian bishops had an even deeper premonition of the weight of public opinion against the two-nature formula. 'We shall all be killed if we subscribe to Leo's epistle', they cried in despair. 'Every district in Egypt will rise against us.' 'We would rather be put to death by you here than there [in Alexandria]. Have pity on us. We would rather die at the hands of the emperor and at your hands than at home.'[2] They spoke truly. The tragedy of Proterius, lynched in Alexandria by the anti-Chalcedonian mob in March 457, was to confirm these fears to the hilt.

he do that as God or as man?' 'Obviously as God', replied the assembly again. 'Well you see', concluded Dioscorus, 'that his divinity was never separated from his humanity and thus the separation proclaimed in the *Tome* of Leo was anathema'! See E. Amélineau, 'Le Christianisme chez les anciens Coptes', *RHR* 14, 1886, pp. 308–45 at p. 324.

[1] Mansi, *Collectio* VII, col. 51. [2] *Ibid.* cols. 58–60.

Chapter 4

THE 'HENOTIKON' OF ZENO
451–484

'All therefore shall be bound to hold to the decision of the sacred council of Chalcedon and indulge no further doubts. Take heed therefore to this edict of our Serenity: abstain from profane words and cease all further discussion of religion.'[1] The imperial edict of 7 February 452 addressed to the people of Constantinople expressed the finality of the emperor's decision. The Egyptians and their monkish allies apart, all had submitted. A few bold spirits such as Eustathius of Berytus, a supporter of Dioscorus, who had taken an active part at Ephesus II, wrote, 'I have signed under duress and without agreement.'[2] For most of the bishops, however, having heard the emperor's will, there was nothing more to be done than to accept Leo's *Tome* and hail Marcian as 'the new Constantine, the new Paul, new David' and 'the torch of orthodoxy',[3] and after the 'three or four days' the emperor had asked them to stay to deal with administrative problems,[4] to go back to their sees.

Ostensibly, the unity of Christendom, rudely disrupted by Dioscorus two years before, had been restored. In its later sessions, the council had been to all intents and purposes united, Palestinians, Illyrians, Syrians and the bishops from the provinces of Asia Minor, deeply divided only the previous year, voting their agreement to the canons. These had vindicated the position of the episcopate vis-à-vis the monks and were particularly pleasing to the bishops. No new monastery was to be built without the diocesan bishop's consent. Monks in city and village were to be subject to the bishops and were to keep to their calling. They were not to harbour fugitive slaves and enlist them as monks, under pain of excommunica-

[1] Text in *ACO* 2. II. 3, pp. 21–2. Compare also Marcian's edicts of 13 March and 6 July 452 (Mansi, *Collectio* VII, cols. 477–80 and 497–500 = *ACO ibid.* pp. 23–4 and *Cod. Just.* I. 3. 23)

[2] Zacharias Rhetor (= Zacharias of Mitylene), *HE* III. 1 (ed. Brooks, *CSCO* III. 5, p. 105). Zacharias also claims (*ibid.*) that another opponent of the Definition, Amphilochius of Side, was assaulted by the archdeacon Aetius and forced to sign.

[3] Mansi, *Collectio* VII, cols. 132 and 169 = *ACO* 2.1.2, pp. 140 and 155. Pulcheria was 'the new Helena'.   [4] Mansi, *ibid.* col. 177 = *ACO ibid.* p. 158.

tion.¹ Much of this was to remain a dead letter,² but the stand of the bishops against the encroachment of the monks had reaffirmed the authority of episcopal government and its vehicle the council.

If, however, the bishops showed a united front against their monastic tormentors, their own unity rested on a more fragile basis. The main axis was now Rome–Constantinople–Antioch instead of Rome–Alexandria, but however one looked at matters there was no real community of aim between the major sees. The thirty years that separated Chalcedon from the Emperor Zeno's letter of Unity to the Egyptian church in July 482 (the *Henotikon*) saw only a gradual hardening of traditional attitudes with little willingness to compromise even on matters of detail. Rome and Alexandria agreed in refusing to Constantinople the prerogatives assigned to it by the Second Ecumenical Council and canon 28 of Chalcedon, but were hopelessly at odds over the *Tome* of Leo and Chalcedon itself. Constantinople accepted Chalcedon with some reservations, but was intent on maintaining its prerogatives at the ultimate expense of Rome and Alexandria.³ Jerusalem tended to follow the capital on matters of doctrine and accepted its senior position in the east, but was also strongly influenced by the proximity of Alexandria. Antioch gradually lost cohesion and reverted to its fourth-century role as the prize of the victorious party. Rome insisted on the uniqueness of its apostolic authority against all comers.⁴ Among the people, opinion in the capital tended to consolidate into three groupings; those who continued to accept Eutyches as orthodox; a much stronger body who rejected Nestorius, Eutyches and the *Tome*, who later came to be known as the 'Hesitants' (*Diakrinomenoi*)⁵ and are the true forerunners of the Monophysites; and finally, the Chalcedonians. In the different provinces, Egypt found itself divided between the great majority who were anti-

---

¹ Canon 4. That Marcian himself proposed a draft of the canon is clear; see Mansi, *Collectio* VII, col. 173 = *ACO* 2. 1. 2, pp. 156–7. The bishops added the words 'It is the duty of the bishop of the city to make due provision for the monasteries' (see W. Bright, *Notes on the Canons of the First Four General Councils*, Oxford, 1882).

² Leo complains, for instance, of Thalassius of Caesarea permitting unlicensed monks to preach and write at will in his diocese (*Ep.* 118. 2).

³ For Zacharias Rhetor's interesting analysis of Anatolius' reasons for suggesting the questionnaire to the bishops in 457 (*HE* IV. 5), see below, p. 161.

⁴ See for instance, F. Dvornik, *The Idea of Apostolicity in Byzantium and the Legend of the Apostle Andrew*, Dumbarton Oaks Studies 4 (Cambridge, Mass., 1958), pp. 93ff.

⁵ John of Ephesus, *HE* II. 37 and 47 referring to the period after Chalcedon. See also G. Bareille, 'Diacrinomènes', *DTC* 7, cols. 732–3.

The 'Henotikon' of Zeno

Chalcedonian, a small group composed mainly of monastic enthusiasts who remained Eutychists, and another small but momentarily more powerful group of pro-Chalcedonians. In Syria, too, party lines were beginning to establish themselves, the east of Syria veering towards Monophysitism while the west and coastal areas remained loyal to Chalcedon. Throughout the other eastern provinces Chalcedon tended to win reluctant acceptance, more willingly in Illyricum than in Asia Minor, as being preferable to domination by Alexandria. The medieval Byzantine historian Nikephorus Kallistus' description of his chapter relating to the *Henotikon* as 'Concerning the emperor's so-called *Henotikon*, neither rejecting nor receiving the Holy Synod of Chalcedon', sums up the complexity of the times.[1]

From the outset it was clear that Rome did not regard the decisions of Chalcedon in the same light as the emperor and the eastern patriarchates. Though ostensibly Nestorius and Eutyches had both been condemned, eastern sentiment throughout had leaned heavily against the upholders of Nestorius' views. Ibas and Theodoret, though supported by Leo, had only been restored under protest, but no one contested similar concessions to those bishops who had so stridently supported Eutyches a mere two years before. Yet by March 453 Leo was branding any who questioned the binding character of the Chalcedonian Definition as 'Eutychians',[2] thus adding another heresy to the western catalogue and implicating a large proportion of the eastern episcopate in its toils.

More immediately menacing, however, was Leo's refusal to accept the 28th canon.[3] The council, the emperor, and Anatolius himself, all wrote to

---

[1] *HE* XVI. 12 (*PG* 147, col. 136). The best account, which I have followed here, is that of E. Schwartz, 'Publizistische Sammlungen zum acacianischen Schisma', *Abh. der bayer. Akad. der Wiss.*, Phil.-hist. Abt., n.s. 10. 4 (1934) (= *PS*). For Leo's policy down to his death in 461, see Jalland, *St Leo the Great*, chs. 13–15, and Caspar, *Papsttums*, I, 531ff.

[2] Leo, *Epp.* 111. 1 and 2: 'Nestorianis atque Eutychianis haereticis', and his denunciation of Anatolius' new archdeacon as a 'Eutychian'. In *Ep.* 109. 3 he equates Eutyches' supporters in Jerusalem with 'Manichees'. Western chroniclers also made no distinction between those who merely rejected Chalcedon and those who were Eutyches' supporters; cf. Paul the Deacon, *Historiae romanae* XVI. 2 (ed. Droysen, p. 216) on Anastasius, and similarly, *Vita Hormisdae* 82 for whom also Anastasius was a 'Eutychian'. Justinian himself was allegedly branded as a 'Eutychian' by Pope Agapetus in 536 (Paul, *Historiae romanae* XVI. 13).

[3] For this episode, see in particular A. Michel, 'Der Kampf um das politische oder Petrinische Prinzip der Kirchenführing' in Grillmeier/Bacht, *Das Konzil von Chalkedon*, II, 491–562.

Leo attempting to obtain his adhesion to it. In a most flattering letter signed by the patriarchs, the metropolitans and their bishops, members of the council, while defending their decision, suggested that the reason why the papal legates had rejected the canon was so that the Pope himself might have the pleasure of 'establishing good order as well as faith' in the church.[1] Leo, however, was not to be placated. In letters despatched on 22 May 452 to Marcian, Pulcheria and Anatolius, he rejected the canon in the strongest terms as being 'contrary to the canons of the Fathers, against the statutes of the Holy Ghost, against the examples of antiquity'. More explicitly, he alleged that it deviated from Nicaea, and he implied also his rejection of the relevant canon of the Council of Constantinople in 381.[2] 'For it is boasted that this [i.e. the prerogatives of the capital]', he wrote to Pulcheria, 'has been winked at for almost sixty years now, and the said bishop [Anatolius] thinks he is assisted by this boast; but it is vain for him to look for assistance from that which, even if a man dared to wish for it, yet he could never obtain.'[3] He was scathing on the subject of the patriarch: 'Let him remember what a man he has succeeded, and expelling all spirit of pride let him imitate Flavian's humility that raised him even to the glory of a confessor.'[4] To Marcian himself[5] he was even more direct, attacking his patriarch's obnoxious cupidity and reminding him of his ecclesiastical past. To Anatolius he stated that his see had no metropolitan rights at all and could not acquire any, however many bishops met in council and agreed them. Constantinople might be a royal city but nothing could make it an apostolic see.[6] Anatolius' consecration of Maximus as patriarch of Antioch was uncanonical, being contrary to the canons of Nicaea, and this particular misdemeanour was to be remembered for centuries.[7] The decrees

[1] Leo, *Ep.* 98. 4. Anatolius (ap. Leonem, *Ep.* 101. 5, *PL* 54, col. 981c) made out that the legates 'lacked instructions' on Leo's attitude towards his church ('ignorantes intentionem vestrae sanctitatis, quam habetis erga Constantinopolis sanctissimam ecclesiam').

[2] *Epp.* 104, 105 and 106; especially *Ep.* 104. 2 (*PL* 54, col. 993c, to Marcian).
[3] *Ep.* 105. 2.   [4] *Ep.* 105. 3.   [5] *Ep.* 104. 4.
[6] *Ep.* 106. 5. Compare *Ep.* 104. 3.
[7] *Ep.* 106. 2. Leo regarded Alexandria as being the second senior see and Antioch the third; nothing could extinguish this (cf. *Ep.* 106. 5). How seriously Constantinople's apparent control of Antioch was taken by the papacy is demonstrated by the fact that in 1053 Cardinal Humbert quoted Leo, *Ep.* 119. 3, to support his objection to Cerularius' consecration of the patriarch of Antioch, as offending 'the privileges of Antioch'. Cerularius was blamed for the sins of Anatolius which descended on him 'by contagion' (*PL* 143, col. 774). See A. Michel, 'Die römische Angriffe auf Michael

of the Council of Constantinople, on the other hand, Leo argued, 'had never been brought to the knowledge of the Apostolic see by Anatolius' predecessors'.[1]

Few, if any, in the east accepted Leo's view. Even his confidential agent, Julian of Cóos (or Kios in Bithynia),[2] seems to have had his doubts to judge by the tone of Leo's remonstrance to him at his apparent indifference to Anatolius' intrigues.[3] From New Rome matters looked differently. It is quite clear from the correspondence between Leo and Marcian that apart from the Definition, the prerogatives of the patriarch of New Rome were regarded by the emperor as the most important single decision that had been taken by the council. Anatolius too wrote reasonably in terms that foreshadowed his successors' attitude to the papacy in the reigns of Justin and Justinian.[4] The see of Constantinople, he said, regarded 'your apostolic see as a father, uniting itself in a most excellent way to you'.[5] It was in vain. Even this acceptance of Rome's *presbeia* failed to mollify Leo. Finally, on 15 February 453 Marcian lost patience and ordered Leo 'archbishop of Rome' to ratify 'quam celerrime' the decrees of the council.[6] On 21 June Leo again stated his reservations in letters addressed to all the bishops present at Chalcedon, to Marcian and Pulcheria, and his legate Julian.[7] His personal opinion of Anatolius he expressed forthrightly to Julian. 'There was in him no enthusiasm for the Catholic faith, and not much for the sacrament of salvation.'[8] Such statements even if true did not augur well for future co-operation between Old and New Rome.

In his letter to Leo, Marcian had urged that the continuing uncertainty regarding the Pope's attitude to the council was encouraging the supporters

Cerullarios wegen Antiocheia 1053/1054', *BZ* 44, 1951, pp. 419–27. Nearer home, note the objection raised by Pope Hormisdas' emissary, the deacon Dioscorus, in 520 to Patriarch John's intention of consecrating in Constantinople his presbyter Paul as patriarch of Antioch (*Coll. Avellana* 216, ed. Guenther, *CSEL* 35. 2, p. 675).

[1] *Ep.* 106. 5.

[2] For Julian's see as Kios in Bithynia rather than the island of Kos, see A. Wille, 'Bischof Julian von Kios der Nunzius Leos des Grossen in Konstantinopel' (diss., Würzburg, 1904). E. Caspar, *Papsttums*, I, 481, accepts this.

[3] *Ep.* 107 sent on 22 May 452 with the same post as letters to Marcian, Pulcheria and Anatolius.   [4] See below, p. 268.   [5] Anatolius to Leo = Leo, *Ep.* 101.

[6] *Ep.* 110.   [7] *Epp.* 114–17.

[8] *Ep.* 113. 2: 'quia in episcopo Constantinopolitano catholicus vigor non est, nec multum aut pro sacramento salutis humanae, aut pro sua est aestimatione sollicitus'. Theodore Lector, frag. 5, says that Anatolius had actually been in communion with Eutyches (*PG* 86. 1, col. 217D).

of Eutyches.¹ This was correct, for the unity represented by the bishops at Chalcedon was not reflected in the provinces to which they returned. Bishops like Thalassius of Caesarea or Juvenal of Jerusalem might trim their sails to meet the emperor's wishes, but not so the monks and the people.

The long-term popular verdict was expressed by Zacharias of Mitylene in the next century, namely 'that under the pretext of suppressing the heresy of Eutyches, Chalcedon had established and increased that of Nestorius, and that by substituting one heresy for another it had divided and confused the whole Christian world'.² The immediate popular reaction was one of scandalised shock. Chalcedon had vindicated Nestorius' 'two natures' and was not scriptural:³ it taught that he who was crucified was not God but man. The Jews were delighted with the news, it was said.⁴ The upshot was a series of outbursts of indignation in Egypt, Syria and Asia Minor. Only a few, but nonetheless influential, religious leaders, such as Simeon Stylites in Syria⁵ and Euthymius in his monastery not far from Jerusalem,⁶ were prepared to accept that Chalcedon could be reconciled with Nicaea.

Popular anger was concentrated at its fiercest in Alexandria and Jerusa-

---

¹ *Ep.* 110: 'Quod nonnullorum animis qui Eutychetis etiam nunc pravam opinionem et perversitatem sectantur, ambiguitatem multam injecit utrum tua beatitudo quae in sancto synodo decreta sunt confirmaveris.'

² Zacharias Rhetor, *HE* III. 1 (ed. Brooks, *CSCO* III. 5, p. 101).

³ See Cyril of Scythopolis, *Vita Euthymii* (ed. Schwartz, pp. 41–2). Compare also Timothy the Cat's verdict, expressed in his work 'Against Chalcedon' (fragments, ed. Nau, pp. 226–36), and in popular terms, John Rufus, *Plerophoria* 59.

⁴ Note the letter allegedly drawn up by Jews and sent to Marcian, reproduced in Michael, *Chron.* VIII. 12 (ed. Chabot, II, 91): 'To the merciful Emperor Marcian: the people of the Hebrews – for a long time we have been regarded as though our fathers had crucified a God and not a man. Since the synod of Chalcedon has assembled and demonstrated that he who was crucified was a man and not a God we request that we should be pardoned this fault and that our synagogues should be returned to us.'

⁵ The position of Simeon may have been somewhat ambiguous. Evagrius (Chalcedonian), *HE* II. 10, quotes the letters which he sent to Leo I in answer to the latter's encyclical in 457, which accept Chalcedon, and he encouraged the Empress Eudocia in the same direction (see below, p. 153); but John of Ephesus, cited by Dionysius of Tell Mahre, makes him, at least at the outset, opposed to the council (ed. F. Nau, *Revue de l'Orient chrétien* 2, 1897, p. 458). That the Monophysites would dearly like to have had him on their side is clear from Michael, *Chron.* VIII. 12 (p. 92) attempting to father on to him a forged anti-Chalcedonian letter. On the pillar-saints in general, see H. Delehaye, *Les Saints Stylites*, *Subsidia Hagiographica* 14 (Brussels, 1923).

⁶ Cyril of Scythopolis, *Vita Euthymii*, ch. 27 (ed. Schwartz, pp. 41 and 43).

lem. In Alexandria the four returning pro-Chalcedonian bishops had consecrated Proterius, Dioscorus' trusted arch-priest, as bishop. Proterius had had the reputation of being a staunch opponent of the council, but this now availed him nothing.[1] The people rose in fury against the magistrates and soldiers; many of the latter lost their lives when the Serapeum to which they had retreated was set on fire over their heads. Order was only restored after the despatch of 2,000 fresh troops from Constantinople.[2] In Jerusalem the situation was momentarily even worse. Juvenal could be regarded as a traitor, for he had not only been an ardent aide of Dioscorus at Ephesus but allegedly had told a concourse of clergy before he left for the council, 'The *Tome* is Jewish, and the ideas it contains are those of Simon Magus. Anyone who accepts it deserves to be made a Jew.'[3] Now, he had actually helped to draw up the obnoxious Definition. His conduct was motivated by ambition, and he has been treated by chroniclers with the contempt he deserved.[4] He was driven out of Jerusalem and forced to seek refuge at Constantinople. Elsewhere there were expulsions under threat of murder of pro-Chalcedonians, and the monks and their supporters seized control.[5] Theodosius, perhaps the same monk who had made trouble for Domnus before Ephesus II and had been present at Chalcedon, was consecrated bishop. He lost no time in consecrating others who were of the same opinion as he. Among the most famous of his disciples was Peter the Iberian (*circa* 409–88), a one-time royal hostage from the Black Sea kingdom of Iberia and now a devoted ascetic,[6] who on 7 August 452 became bishop of Maiuma, the port of Gaza, where Egyptian influence was traditionally strong.[7]

[1] Zacharias Rhetor, *HE* III. 2 and Liberatus, *Brev.* XIV. 99.

[2] Evagrius, *HE* II. 5, quoting Priscus of Paniou as an eyewitness account. The principal rioters were members of the Alexandrian guilds who since Athanasius' time had thrown their influence behind the patriarch.

[3] John Rufus, *Vita Petri Iberi*, written *circa* 500 (ed. Raabe, p. 53). Compare Zacharias Rhetor, *HE* III. 3, and John Rufus, *Plerophoria* 25. Raabe's text reads 'excommunicated'. I owe the truer reading of the Syriac, namely 'cut' or 'circumcised', to Rev. J. Sturdy (Dean of Gonville and Caius College, Cambridge).

[4] Zacharias Rhetor, *HE* III. 3 and *Plerophoria* 17–19.

[5] As at Ascalon: *Plerophoria* 52, and in general, Cyril of Scythopolis, *Vita Euthymii*, ch. 27 (ed. Schwartz, p. 42).

[6] For a sketch of Peter of Iberia and discussion of the two versions of his life, one written by John Rufus and the other by Zacharias Scholasticus, see D. M. Lang, 'Peter the Iberian and his biographers', *JEH* 2, 1951, pp. 158–68.

[7] Zacharias Rhetor, *HE* II. 4. For Egyptian contact with Maiuma and its influence on the Christianisation of the area, see Mark the Deacon, *Life of Porphyry* (ed. and tr.

The rise of the Monophysite movement

Elsewhere, the reminiscences of the popular reception put on record by John Rufus half a century later were impressive in unanimity. When John wrote during Severus' tenure of the patriarchate of Antioch, 512–18, there was extreme tension between the Chalcedonians and their opponents. John was an anti-Chalcedonian, but even so, the series of ninety-three prophecies after the event and narrative accounts known as the *Plerophoria* (Witnesses) may convey something of the spirit of the moment[1] as they appear to have done at the time of Ephesus I.[2] There were visions of Marcian roasting in hell,[3] along with Juvenal and other traitors. Disillusion was matched by anger. Congregations in Isauria, where the Encratite and monastic traditions were both strong, found it incredible that their monastic bishops such as Basil of Seleucia could restore Ibas and Theodoret and condemn Dioscorus a bare two years after having condemned to the flames the doctrine of the two natures and its adherents.[4] Monks saw visions of Christ cursing Chalcedon as Chalcedon had denied him, or of Satan taunting them by saying that as the bishops now worshipped him why should not they?[5] Some bolder spirits wrote to the emperor telling him that 'the world has perished, demons are dancing in the churches and people are dying without baptism'.[6] All over the east churches, friends and families were divided.[7] No greetings were exchanged in the streets between the two sides[8] and often no words were exchanged.[9] We hear of Anastasius and Theodore, young law students at Berytus, taking different sides in the dispute, each eventually destined to become ascetics in the Monophysite cause.[10] Those who opted for one side or the other often did so only after

G. F. Hill, Oxford, 1913), ch. 58. For Theodosius's consecrations, see Cyril of Scythopolis, *Vita Euthymii*, ch. 27 (p. 42), and John Rufus, *Vita Petri Iberi* (ed. Raabe), p. 54.

[1] Reproduced in full in *PO* 8. 1 (ed. F. Nau) and in an abridged form in Michael the Syrian, *Chron.* VIII. 11–12. On the career of John who succeeded Peter of Iberia as bishop of Maiuma in 488, see E. Schwartz, 'Johannes Rufus, ein monophysitischer Schriftsteller', *Sitz. der heidelberger Akad. der Wiss.*, Phil.-hist. Kl. 3. 16, 1912.

[2] Nestorius complains of his opponents claiming to have had dreams and revelations concerning him and his doctrines, and claiming for themselves the authority of 'angels of light': cited from *Plerophoria* (ed. Nau), p. 7.

[3] *Plerophoria* 27.   [4] *Plerophoria* 21 and 22 (Vision of Pamprepius).
[5] *Ibid.* 9.
[6] Michael the Syrian, *Chron.* VIII. 12 (ed. Chabot, II, 91).
[7] *Plerophoria* 38 and 39.
[8] *Ibid.* 61 (cited from Michael, *Chron.* VIII. 11, Chabot, II, 85).
[9] *Plerophoria* 40 (Boniface a 'Roman priest' and a Monophysite).
[10] *Ibid.* 71 (Anastasius); *Vita Petri Iberi* (ed. Raabe), pp. 78–9, concerning Theodore.

profound heartsearchings.¹ 'We have communion with our fathers' became the watchword of those who refused the ministry of apostate Chalcedonian clerics.² Schism was breaking out spontaneously all over the east.

That public order was restored within two years says much for the emperor's prestige and astuteness. He might be regarded as 'the new Assyrian' by many of the monks, but even the most hostile wished him 'long life' and requested only 'the restoration of the canon of the Fathers'.³ They might fight the soldiers sent to support Juvenal whom they knew as 'Romani' and equated with demons,⁴ but in the last resort the 'will of the emperor' was sovereign. Even in Alexandria 'the threats of King Marcian were feared'.⁵ In Jerusalem despite the violence of the opposition Juvenal was eventually restored by force in 453 to live out his life in the silent contempt of the monks. Marcian and Pulcheria wrote directly to the rebels explaining why in their view Chalcedon should be accepted.⁶ Once again, a fifth-century Byzantine emperor had taken the trouble to reason with the opposition, and the rebellion collapsed. Theodosius accepted a sentence of exile and advised his opponents to submit.⁷

Palestine was to be something of a special case throughout the whole of the Monophysite controversy. Lying between Egypt and Syria, the one almost wholly Monophysite and the other becoming increasingly so, Palestine after the first outburst of anger against Juvenal tended to move progressively into the Chalcedonian camp.⁸ There were three main reasons for this. First, the status of the patriarchate depended on acknowledgement

---

¹ As Peter of Iberia himself. He needed a vision before he was completely convinced that Chalcedon was wrong (p. 55). His profound hesitations may be symbolised also in his self-criticism as a 'heretic', before accepting consecration by Theodosius: see Zacharias Rhetor, *HE* III. 4.

² *Plerophoria* 62 (cited from Michael the Syrian, *Chron.* VIII. 11, ed. Chabot, II, 85). For Chalcedon as 'times of apostasy', see *Vita Petri Iberi* (ed. Raabe), p. 52.

³ Michael the Syrian, *Chron.* VIII. 12 (ed. Chabot, II, 91).

⁴ *Plerophoria* 4. For 'soldiers' being equated with 'Romans', see also Zacharias Rhetor, *HE* III. 2.   ⁵ Zacharias Rhetor, *HE* III. 11.

⁶ Text in *ACO* 2. v, nos. 2 and 3 of *Coll. Sangermanensis* (pp. 5–8).

⁷ *Vita Petri Iberi:* 'the king [Marcian] issued against him that which is called a *forma*. At that time all of them submitted and went away, this being what Patriarch Theodosius counselled...' (ed. Raabe, p. 58).

⁸ Its patriarchs tend to be harshly treated by anti-Chalcedonian writers. Peter of Jerusalem is described in the early years of Justinian's reign as 'having no courage and changing with each season' (Michael the Syrian, *Chron.* IX. 23, ed. Chabot, II, 199), and Severus had little use for Elias on the same grounds (*Select Letters* I. 42, ed. Brooks, p. 119).

of Chalcedon at least as a canonical synod, and therefore the constant demand by the Egyptians for its anathema could not be accepted. Secondly, the existence of the Holy Places involved Jerusalem in a much more thorough-going communication with the west and the court atConstantinople through the continuous stream of wealthy and pious pilgrims. This in turn attracted a vast concourse of monks from all parts of the east. The international character of Palestinian monasticism provided the uncertain factor in the situation. In the fifth and sixth centuries monastic leaders there were often strangers to the province. Euthymius himself came originally from Melitene near the Armenian frontier. His first twelve disciples in the *lavra* he founded in 428 included Domnus, future patriarch of Antioch, three brothers who were Cappadocians educated in Syria, four Melitenians, three desert-dwellers from Sinai, but only one Palestinian, a priest from Scythopolis.[1] In the sixth century one of the most famous Palestinian monks was Leontius 'from Byzantium'.[2] These men might accept the Egyptian example of piety, but they tended to judge the intellectual issues on their merits, Euthymius opting for Chalcedon, and Peter the Iberian, another 'foreigner', for its opponents. Thirdly, much of the rural population remained Samaritan and Jewish, both strongly anti-Christian and ready to assert themselves forcefully whenever opportunity arose. The Samaritans set upon the monks opposing Juvenal in 453, and they again rebelled under Zeno and again under Justinian.[3] In the sixth century the historian Procopius, speaking at first hand of his experience in his native Caesarea, describes how the great majority of inhabitants adopted Christianity to avoid trouble from the law, but when the chance offered 'instantly inclined to the Manichaeans and to the Polytheists, as they are called'. In Palestine therefore religious labels sometimes marked anti-imperial sentiment for one reason or another.[4] In this case the 'Manichaeans' may be

[1] See Cyril of Scythopolis, *Vita Euthymii*, ch. 2, p. 8. For Euthymius' companions in his *lavra*, *ibid*. ch. 16. See D. J. Chitty, *The Desert a City* (Oxford, 1966), p. 85.

[2] The Origenist: see E. Schwartz, *Kyrillos von Skythopolis*, TU 49 (ser. IV. 4), Leipzig, 1939, no. 2, p. 388.

[3] Michael the Syrian, *Chron.* IX. 6 (ed. Chabot, II, 148) says that the Samaritans even set up their own king, Justus, and suggests that 'the Romans of Palestine' simply formed one community among others. For the Samaritan revolt in Justinian's reign when the bishop of Neapolis was numbered among their victims, see Cyril of Scythopolis, *Vita Sabae*, ch. 70 (ed. Schwartz, p. 172).

[4] Procopius, *Anecdota* XI. 26 with reference to the Samaritan revolt under Sabarus. That Samaritans were expected to be hostile to Christians, *ibid.* XXVII. 27.

'Monophysites'.[1] Despite their number, the *lavrae* tended to remain somewhat isolated Greek-speaking enclaves, more tied to the international and pro-Chalcedonian world represented by the Holy Places than to any form of rural or provincial piety. Their security and even their existence depended on Constantinople.[2]

The situation which followed the restoration of Juvenal in 452 abundantly illustrates the cross-currents at work in Palestine. The key personality, apart from the patriarch himself, was the dowager Empress Eudocia who had settled near Jerusalem since 443 and had distinguished herself as a poetess and an ardent patron of the arts and buildings as well as a keen advocate of the doctrines of Cyril.[3] There was also Peter of Iberia. For a generation Peter's monastery inland from Maiuma was to be the main centre of anti-Chalcedonian resistance in Palestine. Among those who became inspired by the monastery 'full of holy men bearing the Cross' was to be a young nobleman from Pisidia named Severus, the future patriarch of Antioch.

Peter's cause, however, was destined to be that of the minority. At first Eudocia supported him warmly and upheld other monastic leaders such as the venerable Romanus who were opposed to Juvenal, but in 455 distant political events transformed the situation. The Vandal king Gaiseric captured Rome and with it Eudocia's daughter Licinia Eudoxia and her two daughters. At once Eudocia appealed to her relatives in Constantinople. They responded, but on terms.[4] She must be reconciled to Juvenal.[5] She had previously received letters from Simeon Stylites, Euthymius and the indefatigable Leo.[6] Now she submitted. Communion with Juvenal was

---

[1] See below, p. 254.

[2] The precarious position of Christians in Palestine in the sixth century is admitted by Cyril of Scythopolis in *Vita Sabae*, ch. 72 (ed. Schwartz, p. 175). He speaks of τῶν ἐν Παλαιστίνῃ ὀλιγωθέντων καὶ πραιδευθέντων Χριστιανῶν (i.e. 'few in numbers and preyed upon'), and their gratitude to Justinian.

[3] She was the first of the Byzantine empress-authoresses. A speech at Antioch was so well applauded that the citizens put up a statue in her honour. She wrote lives of saints in Homeric verse. See H. G. Beck, 'Eudocia', *Reallexikon für Antike und Christentum* 6, cols. 844–7.

[4] And not very successfully, for Licinia Eudoxia and one daughter, Placidia, were not restored to Constantinople until 462, while the other daughter, Eudocia, was married to Gaiseric's heir, Huneric.

[5] The main points of the story are given by Cyril of Scythopolis, *Vita Euthymii*, ch. 30, p. 47. Also, Nicephorus Callistus, *HE* xv. 13.

[6] *Ep.* 123, 15 June 453; and also from her relatives in Italy.

The rise of the Monophysite movement

restored. Though she continued to protect the abbot Romanus and others of his monastic opponents until her death in 460, the die was cast. In the last resort Palestine would accept the emperor's religion. Peter of Iberia withdrew to Egypt.[1]

In Egypt, however, the Chalcedonian cause was lost. Originally no less than ten bishops, including powerful individuals like the bishop of Oxyrhynchus, had opted against Dioscorus,[2] but they found it impossible to convince the population and the monks of the justice of Dioscorus' deposition.[3] Proterius himself might have won over the inhabitants of Oxyrhynchus, but for the intervention of Peter the Iberian who had gone into exile there.[4] He stood up for the rights of his see so far as he could, for instance in the protracted debate with Leo on the date of Easter for 455, which he won much to the anger of some westerners.[5] He had also been able to depose and have removed from Alexandria two prominent opponents, the presbyter Timothy, known as 'the Cat', and the deacon Peter, the Hoarse One or Mongus. Already by 453, however, shouts inspired allegedly by divine powers were heard in the theatre, 'Dioscorus to the city! The orthodox to the city! The confessor to his throne. Let the bones of Proterius be burnt! Drive Judas into exile. Cast Judas out!'[6] Dioscorus was being presented in the role of a great confessor who had defied the emperor and excommunicated the impious Leo and was paying the penalty for his righteousness. His death on 4 September 454 caused a momentary loss of confidence in the anti-Chalcedonian cause, but Proterius was unable to take advantage of this. On 1 August 455 Marcian himself wrote to the praetorian prefect Palladius, admitting that the inhabitants of the city of Alexandria and the whole diocese of Egypt were a prey to the heresies of Eutyches and Apollinarius, and ordered the infliction of the same penalties imposed on Manichees against those who followed these doctrines and the burning of heretical books.[7] Proterius was not master of his own house.

---

[1] *Vita Petri Iberi* (ed. Raabe), p. 59. He realised that in doing so he was cutting his links with the court. See Michael, *Chron.* VIII. 12 (ed. Chabot, II, 90).

[2] In 458 Leo addressed his *Ep.* 160 to fifteen bishops who had gone to Constantinople to represent the Proterian interest.

[3] Clear from the comment in *Chron. ad ann. 846*: 'Postquam eiectus est Dioscorus in exilium, multi tamen clam eum proclamabant in monasteriis' (ed. Brooks and Chabot, p. 163).

[4] *Vita Petri Iberi* (ed. Raabe), pp. 61–2.

[5] Leo, *Epp.* 121, 129, 133 and 137, Jalland, *St Leo the Great*, pp. 350–8.

[6] *Vita Petri Iberi* (ed. Raabe), p. 59.   [7] Text in *ACO* 2. II. 2, pp. 24–6.

His following was largely made up of 'nobles' and officials.[1] The great majority of the Egyptian church and people had separated themselves from him in disgust.

In vain he had urged on Leo the need for a more flexible presentation of Chalcedon[2] – and had he had his way, the example of the wavering of the congregation at Oxyrhynchus might have been followed elsewhere. Leo refused. Chalcedon must be accepted *in toto*. Alexandria was treated like a satellite of Rome, and Proterius' death-warrant was signed. The exclamations (*ekboeseis*) of the crowd in the Alexandria Theatre reflected accurately popular hopes of vengeance and these had not long to wait. On 26 January 457 Marcian died. By mid-February this was known in Alexandria. A small committee of monks and dissident clerics led by Longinus, abbot of the monastery at the Ninth Milestone (Enaton) from Alexandria, came into being and Timothy the Cat was smuggled into the city. Peter of Iberia was also hastening back from Oxyrhynchus, and on 16 March with two other bishops he consecrated Timothy as patriarch of Alexandria.[3] Opinion rallied to him. Though he had been at Ephesus II he was no Eutychist and Eutychist movements in Alexandria were suppressed by him;[4] he was a monk, a presbyter of Cyril's and regarded as fully in line of succession to Cyril and Dioscorus. There is slight evidence that the new emperor Leo I was also disposed to favour him, but before anything could happen Proterius had been lynched, his body dragged through the streets and burnt in the Hippodrome on Maunday Thursday, 28 March. Timothy had been rid of his rival.[5]

---

[1] Liberatus, *Brev.* XIV. 98 ('collecti sunt igitur nobiles civitatis'), and Michael, *Chron.* VIII. 12 (ed. Chabot, II, 91); cf. Zacharias Rhetor, *HE* III. 2.

[2] Indicated by Leo's reply to Proterius' letter presented by Nestorius of Phragon early in 454. Leo insisted that there was no new teaching in the *Tome* (*Ep.* 129. 1–2).

[3] The best account of Timothy is still J. Lebon, 'La Christologie de Timothée Aelure', *RHE* 9, 1908, pp. 677–702. His surviving works show him to be representative of the Monophysite element in Cyril emphasising the complete divinity of Jesus, that his 'nature' resided only in his divinity even after the incarnation, and that his humanity was assumed only by way of dispensation for the purpose of saving man. That humanity was, however, real. His opposition to Eutychism is illustrated in the collection of letters published by R. Y. Ebied and L. R. Wickham, *JTS*, n.s. 21. 2, 1970, pp. 321–69.

[4] Such as that led by John the Sophist, recorded in Zacharias Rhetor, *HE* III. 10.

[5] The sequence of events is given in *Vita Petri Iberi* (ed. Raabe), pp. 64–8, and Zacharias Rhetor, *HE* IV. 1, Evagrius, *HE* II. 8 and Theodore Lector, *HE* I. 8–9. The Emperor Leo, while despatching an official to investigate the murder, was also thought 'to feel compassion at the sorrows that had befallen Alexandria', and favoured Timothy against Proterius before the latter was murdered. See *Vita Petri Iberi*, p. 68.

The rise of the Monophysite movement

The sequel illustrates the realities of papal and imperial authority. The impotence of the one is contrasted with the power of the other wielded with superb skill with the aim of securing maximum unanimity among the bishops for any action decided by the emperor. Already Pope Leo's relations with the east and with Anatolius had suffered from distance, mistranslation of his opinions, perhaps malicious so as to make him appear as an out-and-out Nestorian,[1] and polite but determined obstruction. In the capital it was clear that while accepting the letter of Chalcedon, Anatolius had no qualms about staffing his cathedral with anti-Chalcedonian clergy. For years Leo had been complaining about the treatment accorded to the archdeacon Aetius, who had been chief of the secretariat at Chalcedon and was an outspoken supporter of the *Tome*. He found himself 'promoted' to the presbyterate and appointed to the exalted rank of cemetery-chaplain, while a suspected Eutychist, named Andrew, became archdeacon.[2] Aetius' lot was palliated, but he never regained the authority he had possessed at the time of Chalcedon. Equally vain had been Leo's protests against Anatolius' consecration of Maximus to the patriarchate of Antioch and his continued assertion of rights over the clergy in Illyricum.[3] The death of Pulcheria in July 453 was a blow to his influence in the east. This was now followed by the collapse of the Chalcedonian position in Alexandria.

Marcian's policy had been based on close understanding with Leo and with the western empire which he managed to combine with support for the ecclesiastical ambitions of his patriarch. To carry out these hardly reconcilable aims he had relied on the support of the bishops and of the senatorial aristocracy. 'He safeguarded', as Evagrius says, 'the riches of the wealthy.'[4] Taxes on their property such as the *follis* or tax on estates were abolished and arrears of taxation remitted. Their leading members had been

---

[1] E.g. *Ep.* 130. 3, 'ut commutatis quibusdam verbis vel syllabis receptorem me Nestoriani erroris assereret'; and compare *Ep.* 131 similarly.

[2] *Epp.* 111, 112 and 117; his judgement on the affair was that it was an 'injury to Catholicism' (*Ep.* 117. 4). Leo was also annoyed that the ordination had taken place on a date not in accordance with the canons. Anatolius made bland explanations, and in a letter to Leo (*Ep.* 132 ap. Leonem) pointed out that the status of his see was not his making but corresponded to the desires of his clergy and the bishops throughout the east. He himself 'had ever loved ease and repose in modest humility'. Leo continued to protest about the composition and Eutychian outlook of his cathedral staff, in vain: *Epp.* 143, 157. 4, 161 and 163.

[3] *Ep.* 117. 5.

[4] Evagrius, *HE* II. 1 (ed. Bidez and Parmentier, p. 38). See also E. A. Thompson, *Attila and the Huns* (Oxford, 1948), ch. 8.

The 'Henotikon' of Zeno

brought into a commanding role in ecclesiastical affairs through their nomination as judges at Chalcedon. The popular forces represented by the Green circus-faction in the capital and the monks in the eastern provinces had been rigorously curbed. Internally, ecclesiastically and externally, Marcian and Pulcheria's rule had contrasted with that of Theodosius II and yet in its way it had also been successful. The eastern provinces were at peace, a substantial amount of gold filled the treasury and the immediate crisis of Chalcedon had been overcome. What was to be expected of Marcian's successor?

The Emperor Leo (457-74), like his predecessor, was a Thracian staff-officer (*tribunus*), but to a far greater extent than Marcian had been, the nominee of the all-powerful minister Aspar.[1] He was a Chalcedonian of a puritanical cast of mind,[2] but less interested in placating the papacy than his predecessor had been, and more concerned with winning the active goodwill of the eastern provincials. Symbolical perhaps of the new course was that Anatolius performed the coronation rites[3] (thus validating Leo's succession, since Marcian had not formally nominated him). Another significant pointer was that despite the emperor's personal orthodoxy the Greens began to return to favour in the capital.[4] The Circus parties at Constantinople and in other eastern cities represented political and religious factions often associated with social distinctions. At Antioch the Greens

[1] See W. Ensslin, 'Leo', *PW* 12. 2, cols. 1947-62. He had been the equivalent of Aspar's quartermaster (Theophanes, *Chron.* A.M. 5961 and Zonaras, *Epitomae historiarum* XIII. 36, ed. Büthner Wobst).

[2] For his edicts enforcing Sunday rest and banning the playing of musical instruments, see Theodore Lector, *HE* I. 14 and John Malalas, *Chron.* XIV. 78 (ed. Dindorf, p. 371). His religion was regarded as 'orthodox' by George Cedrenus (*Historiarum compendium*, ed. Bekker, I, 607) and 'fide simplex' by Zacharias Rhetor, *HE* IV. 5.

[3] Theodore Lector, *HE* II. 65; George Cedrenus, *Historiarum compendium* (ed. Bekker), I, 607.

[4] See George Codinus, *De aedificiis* (ed. I. Bekker, Bonn, 1843), pp. 71-2. The Greens congratulated Leo for restoring the sea defences of the capital. The Empress Verina also favoured them and was compared to Constantine's mother Helena by them! (*Breves Enarrationes Chron.* I, *PG* 157, col. 675). On the importance of the Circus parties in the cities of the empire in the controversy for and against Chalcedon, see H. Grégoire, 'Le Peuple de Constantinople', *Byzantion* 11, 1936, pp. 616-716 at p. 657 (translating an article by G. Manojlovic published in Serbo-Croat in 1904). Also Y. Janssens, 'Les Bleus et les Verts sous Maurice, Phocas et Heraclius', *Byzantion* 11, 1936, pp. 499-536.

were the lower classes who were anti-Chalcedonian and anti-Jewish.[1] At Cyzicus also, in the reign of Justinian, members of the Green faction were said to be of those who had risen against the bishop, i.e. in all probability were also anti-Chalcedonians.[2] Theodosius II and Chrysaphius had been ardent patrons of the Greens,[3] Marcian of the Blues,[4] but in the capital the Blues and Greens lived in different quarters of the city and represented different orders of society. The Blues were the official and possessing classes, the Greens the artisans, port-workers and countryfolk.[5] Later on in the Nika riots of January 532, a leader of the Greens told Justinian, perhaps sarcastically, that they did not know where the palace and government offices were since he had only visited the city once, and then 'sitting on a donkey'.[6] Under Leo the balance was redressed in the Greens' favour, and the first great crisis of the reign indicated a slight but significant shift of policy in favour of purely east-Roman interests.

The issues confronting the new emperor involved a careful balance of the religious and political forces active in the capital and the provinces. The punishment of Proterius' murderers and the appointment of a successor was only one problem. Among those whose views he must consider were the Germanic military leaders and their mainly Arian and Gothic followers. In some ways the situations in the two halves of the empire were now parallel. In the west, the murder of Valentinian III in 455 opened the way to power for the *magister militum* Ricimer the Sueve, who was to make and unmake emperors according to his will until the institution of the western emperor became so discredited as to warrant its disappearance in 476. Leo seems to have realised the danger almost immediately. His promotion of Majorian first to Caesar and then in December 457 to Augustus was perhaps aimed

---

[1] See John Malalas, *Chron.* XV. 103 (ed. Dindorf, p. 389), concerning the rioters against the Jews.

[2] Procopius, *Anecdota* XVII. 42. For another indication of the religious divisions in Cyzicus on social lines, see Sozomen, *HE* V. 15. 6 (reign of Julian).

[3] John Malalas, *Chron.* XIV. 50 (ed. Dindorf, p. 352); a fact remembered over a century later when Maurice bowed to the Greens and christened his eldest son 'Theodosius' rather than the Blues' choice of 'Justinian' (Theophylact, ed. C. de Boor, Bibl. Teubner, Leipzig, 1887, p. 52).

[4] Marcian's favour to the Blues extended to banning any member of the Greens from taking civil or military office for three years, following a Green-inspired riot: John Malalas, *Chron.* XIV. 74–5 (ed. Dindorf, p. 368). Under Leo this seems to have been dropped.

[5] Grégoire/Manojlovic, 'Le Peuple de Constantinople', pp. 644–55.

[6] Theophanes, *Chron.* A.M. 6024 (ed. Classen, I, 280–1).

at checking Ricimer's authority by confining this to military matters.¹ The situation had, however, deteriorated too far and any hopes that the emperor, senate or the provincial leaders may have had of asserting their independence were compromised by the steady erosion of Roman authority in the west.

In the east the barbarians never attained quite the same power. The Alan warrior Aspar, who since the 440s had been *magister militum praesentalis*, was not a commander of the skill of Stilicho. He had been worsted by Gaiseric in 432 and was to show no stomach for renewing that encounter. Both Marcian² and Leo had been his officers and this, coupled with long experience at court, rendered his position a strong one. It was not, however, impregnable for he had remained an Arian in the midst of a court and populace fanatically pro-Nicene, if divided on the niceties of Chalcedonian interpretations.

The last thing Aspar wanted was an all-powerful patriarch in the capital supported by a strongly orthodox population. This combination had spelt death to Gainas and his Goths in the time of John Chrysostom nearly sixty years before, and even now these events, to judge from the prominence given to them by the historian Zosimus, were not forgotten.³ Aspar may have felt his position threatened,⁴ and the emergence of Timothy the Cat suited him well. As the chronicler Theophanes remarks, he opposed the punishment of the rioters in Alexandria and of Timothy

---

¹ See H. Meyer, 'Der Regierungsantritt Kaiser Majorians', *BZ* 62. 1, 1969, pp. 5-13. I find it difficult, however, to believe that Majorian's appointment as *magister militum* in February 457 could possibly have been dictated by such policies. Leo, owing his own position to Aspar, would hardly embark on an anti-Germanic policy in the first fortnight of his reign! Ricimer was also appointed *patricius* at the same time (*Chron. min.* I, 305). For a different interpretation of these events which would make Leo consider at one time taking over the government of the west, and in turn not being recognised by Majorian until May 458, see W. E. Kaegi, *Byzantium and the Decline of Rome* (Princeton, 1968), p. 31.

² Marcian was a *domesticus* of Aspar (Procopius, *De bello Vandalico* 1. 4). This clearly eased his choice by Pulcheria as consort. Jordanes, *Romana* 335 (ed. Mommsen, p. 43), says that 'Aspar made him emperor'.

³ Zosimus was writing *circa* 460 and devotes chs. 13-22 of book V of the *Historia nova* to the downfall of Gainas and Tribigild.

⁴ This is stated by Procopius, *Wars* III. 6. 4, in connection with Aspar's unwillingness to support Leo's Vandal war, for fear that if Leo won, he would be able to dispense with his services. An additional reason may have been that in any urban riot the Gothic troops tended to bear the brunt of popular wrath.

himself.¹ Anatolius also was jealous of his prerogatives, and, irked by Pope Leo's continuous attempts to interfere in the ecclesiastical affairs of the capital, was prepared to talk with Timothy; but his freedom for manoeuvre was restricted by the latter's refusal, conveyed through his embassy that reached the capital in the summer of 457, to accept the canons of the Second Ecumenical Council, i.e. to accept the ecclesiastical position of Constantinople as New Rome.² The emperor, however, may have had doubts about the wisdom of his predecessor's policy towards Alexandria. Timothy was not without friends at court.

At Rome, meantime, the full extent of the disaster at Alexandria had only gradually unfolded. Anatolius had informed Leo of Marcian's death and his successor's orthodoxy but neither he nor Julian of Cóos who wrote to Leo on 1 April mentioned the situation in Alexandria. The latter had merely referred to efforts by 'the enemies of Chalcedon' to take advantage of Marcian's death.³ By 1 June Leo had heard 'quidam rumores' of trouble, but had not associated Timothy with them.⁴ Only about a month later did the horror of Proterius' death become fully known to him⁵ and by that time Timothy's embassy was battling with a delegation of his opponents in the capital for the emperor's ear. The emperor himself was considering whether or not to accept Timothy's request and imitate his predecessor by summoning a new general council.⁶ Pope Leo's frantic activity, which included the despatch of six important and well-argued letters (*Epp.* 148–53)⁷ on a single day, 1 September 457, probably contributed towards preventing this plan from being put into effect. Instead, a new and original initiative was under-

---

¹ Theophanes, *Chron.* A.M. 5952 (ed. Classen, I, 173), and Theodore Lector (excerpta Vatoped. 42); and ed. Hansen, p. 106, para. 378.

² This is clear from Theodore Lector (excerpta Vatoped. 18) who adds the detail that an additional grudge which the Alexandrians felt against the council was its condemnation of Apollinarius; cf. Schwartz, *PS*, p. 173 n2 and 'Das Nicaenum und das Constantinopolitanum auf der Synode von Chalkedon', *ZNTW* 25, 1926, pp. 38–88 at pp. 84–5, where he points out, however, that Timothy himself did not go so far as his monkish delegates, and would have been prepared to rejoin the church of the empire if Chalcedon only were denounced.

³ *Ep.* 144, Leo's reply merely refers to Eutychist disturbances after Marcian's death. The 'rumours' about Alexandria had not come from Julian.

⁴ *Ep.* 144.

⁵ *Epp.* 145–7. Zacharias Rhetor, *HE* IV. 4, suggests that refugees from Alexandria first informed Leo of the details, followed by Anatolius' account (*Ep.* 145).

⁶ Leo, *Ep.* 150. 2.

⁷ With copies for less important recipients.

taken by the emperor and patriarch that also took little account of the Pope's susceptibilities.

In the autumn the emperor decided to confirm his predecessor's edicts in favour of Chalcedon, but there was to be no immediate action to restore the situation in Alexandria. Instead, an imperial letter was circulated to the Pope, to sixty-five metropolitans in the east and also to the three famous and venerable Syrian monks, Baradotus, Simeon Stylites and James, all of whom had been consulted by Theodosius II and Marcian. The recipients were informed that there had been 'much tumult and confusion in Alexandria' (not that Proterius had been foully murdered), and that the emperor had received rival petitions for and against Timothy. It asked them to consult provincial synods which were to be convoked at once and arrive at a clear opinion as to what they thought of Chalcedon and of Timothy's candidature.[1] As in Maximin's reign at the end of the Great Persecution, the populations of the eastern provinces were given the chance of expressing their will on a matter which touched them vitally, but now the vehicle for taking public feeling was not the provincial council, but the provincial assembly of bishops under the presidency of the metropolitan. The replies represented the views of about 1,600 bishops.

Zacharias of Mitylene attributes the idea of the 'plebiscite' to Anatolius.[2] Faced with the obduracy of Timothy's legates and the increasingly peremptory demands from Rome, and fearing that a new council might end by betraying the prerogatives of his see, this may have seemed the most obvious solution, and one which vindicated the authority of Constantinople against Rome and Alexandria alike. In addition, it was popular with the bishops themselves. One of these, Seleucus of Amasea in eastern Pontus, expressed his opposition to another general council on the grounds that bishops had already had to sell church vessels to pay their travel expenses to the last.[3] In the new year of 458 the results of the synodical consultation

---

[1] Text in Evagrius, *HE* II. 9. Anatolius had to consult his Home Synod.

[2] Zacharias Rhetor, *HE* IV. 5 (ed. Brooks, *CSCO* III. 5, p. 121). The Latin translation gives the significant account: 'Voluit ergo rex Leo qui a Timotheo Alexandriae litteras accepit synodum congregare: eumque impedivit Anatolius urbis regiae episcopus, non quod ea quae a Timotheo scripta sunt reprehendere potuit, sed commotus est, ne, si synodus congregaretur, omnia quae Chalcedone acta sunt abolerentur, non propter fidem: sed propter iura et honores quae sedi urbis regiae contra νόμον data sunt. Suasit ergo Anatolius regi ne synodum congregaret sed per epistulas litterarum quae vocantur encyclia de synodo et de Timothei χειροτονίας episcoporum sententiam exquireret.'

[3] *Codex Encyclius* 41 (*ACO* 2. v, p. 85).

began to arrive. They justified the emperor's and his patriarch's tactics. With the single exception of the Council of Pamphylia presided over by the metropolitan Amphilochius of Side, the bishops decided overwhelmingly in favour of Chalcedon and against Timothy.[1] The results recorded in the great *Codex Encyclius* testify to the depths of the reverence felt for the person of the emperor and respect paid to his decisions. They vindicated the utility of Chalcedon at least as a disciplinary synod, and demonstrated the honour in which the doctrines of Cyril were held throughout the east.[2] The appellate jurisdiction reserved to Constantinople in disputes concerning metropolitans by canons 9 and 28 of Chalcedon was shown moreover to be fully in force. Even so, the emperor, while ordering the pursuit of Proterius' actual murderers, still held his hand regarding Timothy.

In the west the *Codex Encyclius* came to be regarded as the most important piece of evidence for the eastern acceptance of Chalcedon, as indeed it was. One may detect the effort made by some bishops to equate the Council's 'two natures inseparably united' with Cyril's 'one incarnate nature', and to stress the disciplinary element of the definition. This was to become increasingly important in the eyes of those who in the next generation saw orthodoxy in terms of the council *plus* Cyril.[3] As an immediate result the 'plebiscite' induced Pope Leo to write two lengthy and important documents (*Epp.* 156 and 165)[4] setting out anew the western defence of Chalcedon. The second of these letters was one of the finest expositions of western theology in the patristic age. The positive aspects of the Atonement and man's redemption through the resurrection were plainly stated,

---

[1] Amphilochius was a strong opponent of Chalcedon (Zacharias Rhetor, *HE* III. 1, ed. Brooks, *CSCO* III. 5, p. 105) but even he condemned Timothy's conduct: see the text of his reply in Michael the Syrian, *Chron.* IX. 5 (ed. Chabot, II, 145–8).

[2] For instance, the letter of Basil of Seleucia on behalf of the Isaurians, *ACO* 2. V, p. 48. Most of the surviving replies also emphasise the compatibility of Chalcedon with Nicaea, Constantinople and Ephesus I, and pay tribute to Leo whose honorary precedence was acknowledged.

[3] This is particularly evident from the reply of Epiphanius of Perge (*Codex Encyclius*, *ACO* 2. V, pp. 58–9), arguing that 'two natures or substances in Christ' had firm patristic support. See Ch. Moeller's excellent account of the development of neo-Chalcedonian thought at this period, in 'Nephalius d'Alexandrie', *RHE* 40, 1944–5, pp. 110–28.

[4] 1 December 457 and 17 August 458 respectively. Much of what Leo says is repeated from the *Tome* and *Ep.* 124 to the monks of Palestine, but it represents the maturity of his thought.

and the need, therefore, for accepting the reality of the two natures of Christ. This was welded together into a pattern of Scriptural texts and concluded by an impressive array of proof-texts drawn from Athanasius, John Chrysostom, Theophilus, Cyril and western authorities. At least recipients could be made to understand that the west had produced a theologian of a calibre they could respect. One slight concession was allowed, perhaps as much by accident as by design, to the eastern view, in that the term 'in two natures' was not to be found in the exposition. Moreover, Eutyches' 'heresy' was more closely defined than previously, in that he was said to have 'dared pronounce Word and flesh as one nature'.[1] The legates who bore these missives also took a friendly letter to the emperor, and if they were forbidden to negotiate on (*certandum*) Chalcedon they were at least permitted to expound.[2]

The emperor forwarded the Pope's memorial to Timothy who rejected it. Eutychism he was ready to condemn but in company also with the *Tome* and Chalcedon ('The Fathers had never spoken of persons, properties or natures in the Incarnate Christ'), and he expressed the hope that the emperor would agree.[3] Leo, sure in the support of the eastern bishops, at last acted. At the end of 459 Timothy was arrested and taken by slow progress which sometimes resembled a triumph through Syria and Asia to Dioscorus' place of exile at Gangra on the Black Sea. Even then negotiations with him were not dropped.[4] But he proved obdurate and four years later was removed further off, to Cherson in the Crimea. In Alexandria his relegation gave the opposition their chance. It was evident that Proterius had some following, particularly among the wealthier classes and the Pachomian monks at Canopus where memories of Dioscorus' tyranny died hard. One of these monks, Timothy surnamed Salofaciolus or White Turban, or more probably 'Wobble-cap', was consecrated patriarch (spring of 460). He was a conciliatory character. Dioscorus' name was

[1] Leo, *Ep.* 165. 2. Timothy had already employed precisely the same method of debate to prove the council Nestorian (Lebon, 'Timothée', p. 683).

[2] *Ep.* 156. Compare *Ep.* 162 of 21 March 458. A study of this phase of ecclesiastical debate by textual accumulation would be interesting.

[3] Zacharias Rhetor, *HE* IV. 6. See Lebon, 'Timothée', p. 688.

[4] Rumours of Timothy's arrival in the capital for more negotiations early in 460 alarmed Leo: *Ep.* 170. E. Schwartz ('Codex Vaticanus graecus 1431, eine antichalkedonische Sammlung aus der Zeit Kaiser Zenos', *Abh. der bayer. Akad. der Wiss.*, Phil.-hist. Abt. 32. 6, 1927, p. 128) believes that the Emperor did grant him a final interview before committing him to exile at Gangra.

restored to the diptychs despite Pope Leo's protest,[1] but for all his efforts the mass of the Egyptian Christians regarded the other Timothy as their bishop. 'We like you very much', they might have said, 'but not as our bishop.'

Pope Leo died on 10 November 461, his objectives unfulfilled. The lesson of the period following Chalcedon and in particular after the death of Marcian was that no Roman bishop, however vigorous and dedicated, could hope to govern the church in the east. Leo, moreover, had made the mistake of continually interfering in purely local concerns or matters of internal administration in the eastern patriarchates, whose bishops he never seems to have accepted as more than simple metropolitans. There is a streak of arrogance too in his letters, that goes beyond the needs of his office, which must have encouraged the recipients to thwart him. Despite all his efforts, canon 28 had been accepted in the east, while his interpretations of Nicaea and Chalcedon were repudiated. From now on the emperor and his patriarch were to govern the church there, restricted only by the distant power of veto in the hands of the Pope. Even this only becomes effective when imperial policy looked back to the west haunted by the vanished glory of the united empire of Constantine and Theodosius I.

Anatolius had passed from the scene three years earlier, on 3 July 458. His successor was the presbyter Gennadius (458–71), a Biblical scholar and a far more convinced Chalcedonian than he had been. Once he had made up his mind that compromise with Timothy the Cat was impossible, he was prepared to isolate him and his followers, and consolidate his hold over the rest of the eastern church without the let or hindrance of the Alexandrian dissidents. He had opinion in the capital on his side despite the revival of the Greens in the Circus. While there was always to be a ground-swell of Monophysite piety among the populace, which Severus of Antioch and Theodora were to mobilise, this was counterbalanced by fears for the standing of the patriarchate if Chalcedon were denounced, and also the common-sense view that decrees banning Nestorius and Eutyches by a vast assembly of bishops could not be wholly bad. After all, had there not been 636 bishops at Chalcedon, just double the number of those at Nicaea?[2] The usurpation of Basiliscus in 475 and his attempt to enforce an anti-Chalcedonian policy were resented. There were demands for 'an orthodox emperor' (even Zeno), the burning of 'the enemies of orthodoxy' and the

[1] Zacharias Rhetor, *HE* IV. 10 and V. 5.
[2] Timothy the Cat (fragments, ed. Nau, p. 205) inveighs against this line of propaganda. For its application by Simeon Stylites, see Evagrius, *HE* II. 10.

return of the exiled pro-Chalcedonian bishops.[1] Monks and clergy of the capital fostered these sentiments. We hear of the emergence of poet-priests who used their talents to hymn the council in verse.[2] Representative of this whole movement of monastic–imperial piety was the Pillar-Saint Daniel, a Syrian by origin and favoured disciple of Simeon Stylites whose cowl he had received as a bequest on his master's death. He had emigrated to the capital soon after and had established his column some four miles north of the city. A Chalcedonian by conviction, he became Leo's leading spiritual adviser.[3] Another influence in the same direction was the arrival of the aristocratic ascetic Studius from Rome, who in 463 established a monastery dedicated to John the Baptist and filled it with recruits from the Sleepless Monks.[4] Its tendency from the outset was strongly pro-Chalcedonian and in addition the Studites retained important links with the Roman see. In Rome, however, Hilary, Leo's successor, seems to have dropped the latter's interventionist policies and no correspondence with Constantinople has survived for the whole of his reign (461–8). Our sources are almost silent about events, and it might appear that with Timothy the Cat in distant exile, the conflicting forces achieved some form of unstable equilibrium.

Two events only in Gennadius' rule require attention both of which, however, pointed to the growing challenge to the predominant Germanic influences at court. First, in 466 or 467 Aspar's son, Ardaburius, who was *magister militum per Orientem*, was implicated in an espionage affair with Persia, and though the charge was eventually found 'not proven', Ardaburius was recalled in disgrace and given no further command. Leo appointed his accuser, an Isaurian landowner who took the name of Zeno as his own could not be transliterated into Greek,[5] as his *comes domesticorum*

---

[1] *Vita Danielis*, ch. 83 (ed. Peeters, p. 198). Compare Theodore Lector, *HE* I. 32–3. See below, pp. 172–3.

[2] Theodore Lector, *HE* I. 19. On the influence of Chalcedonian poet-priests such as Romanos the Syrian in the century after the council, see E. C. Topping, 'The poet priest in Byzantium', *Greek Orthodox Theological Review* 14. 1, 1969, pp. 31–41.

[3] For Daniel's life see H. Delehaye, *Les Saints Stylites*, Subsidia Hagiographica (Brussels, 1923), pp. xxv–lviii, and E. Dawes and N. H. Baynes, *Three Byzantine Saints* (Oxford, 1948), pp. 1–84; and for the historical value of the *Vita* see N. H. Baynes, 'The Vita S. Danielis Stylitae', *EHR* 40, 1925, pp. 397–402.

[4] Theodore Lector, *HE* I. 17. These were also mainly Syrians, Antiochene in their Christological leanings.

[5] Tarasikodissa, son of Ronsoumblada. See E. W. Brooks, 'The Emperor Zeno and the Isaurians', *EHR* 8, 1893, pp. 209–38 at p. 212.

and sent him to Syria as Ardaburius' replacement.¹ Secondly, a year or so later, in 468, the Germanic cause in the capital received a further blow in the defeat of the vast expedition aimed at destroying the Vandal kingdom in Africa. Treachery inspired by Aspar was suspected, not without cause. The suggestion, however, that Aspar was promoting a sort of pan-Arian alliance with Gaiseric seems far-fetched,² but both he and the Emperor Marcian held the Vandals in healthy respect after their earlier defeat in Africa, and did not want to provoke them. It is interesting that Aspar's successor as *magister militum*, the Goth Theodoric Strabo, also stipulated that the Vandals would not be included among the enemies of the emperor he would be called upon to fight. Basiliscus, the commander of the expedition, was brother of the Empress Verina and, if we are to believe the biographer of Daniel Stylites,³ a barbarian in sympathy if not by descent, and his abject conduct both during and after the expedition seems to have further undermined Germanic influence at Constantinople. The hitherto all-important Germanic warlords were not forgiven by the nobility and people of the capital for the disaster.⁴

Meantime Zeno's promotion had brought him into contact with the religious situation in the great diocese of Antioch. His own province, Isauria, was largely anti-Chalcedonian, and so far as may be ascertained his views leant in the same direction. At Antioch itself, his headquarters, articulate opinion was veering away from Chalcedon, and the sober tradition of Simeon Stylites was being superseded on his death in 459 by more radical opinions.⁵ In Cilicia and Syria II (western Syria), episcopal and

---

[1] *Vita Danielis*, ch. 55; see Schwartz, *PS*, pp. 179–80, and Baynes, 'The Vita S. Danielis Stylitae', pp. 398–9.

[2] Nikephorus Kallistus, *HE* xv. 27. Aspar's attitude towards Gaiseric has been compared with that of Stilicho to Alaric: see B. Rubin, *Das Zeitalter Justinians* (Berlin, 1960), p. 37. On the expedition itself, see E. F. Gautier, *Genséric, Roi des Vandales* (Paris, 1932), pp. 255 ff.

[3] *Vita Danielis*, ch. 84. Compare Schwartz, *PS*, p. 189; see below, p. 172.

[4] In Justinian's reign the official account was of a combination of Aspar's treason and Basiliscus' negligence and incompetence. See Procopius, *Wars* III. 6. 4ff.

[5] The monastery associated with Simeon at Tell Neshim between Antioch and Aleppo became anti-Chalcedonian after his death. See Beck, *Kirche und theologische Literatur*, pp. 206–7, and for a possible indication that in these parts Syriac speaking was beginning to entail anti-Chalcedonianism, note the comment by Derwas Chitty that Simeon's monastery 'stands on the moorland which forms the watershed between the Orontes basin and the eastward-looking plains about Aleppo. It is Syriac, and the Syrian opponents of Chalcedon took possession of the monastery not long after the

monastic opinion remained loyal to the ideas of the Formula of Reunion and were to continue to do so.[1] On the other hand, in east Syria, the school of anti-Cyrillian theology represented by Ibas (d. 458) was losing ground fast, and the migration of the school of Edessa beyond the Persian frontier to Nisibis could be foreseen. The real hub of the Nestorianising movement was henceforth to be among the Christians in Persia, independent of developments further west, while eastern Syria tended increasingly toward Monophysitism.

Antioch itself was steadily becoming as much an anti-Chalcedonian centre as Alexandria. There had always been a vigorous Apollinarian party in the city, and they now found a leader in a presbyter from Chalcedon, named Peter the Fuller.[2] Peter had once been a monk in the monastery of the Sleepless Monks. He had quarrelled with the brethren, and for some reason accompanied Zeno to Syria where he showed strong anti-Chalcedonian leanings. While the Patriarch Martyrius was absent in Constantinople he was consecrated in his place, according to John Diakrinomenos at the instance of Zeno himself.[3] Martyrius returned and ousted the intruder, but wearying of intrigues renounced the see with the words, 'I renounce a rebellious clergy, an unruly people and a church defiled'.[4] This was in 469.

Peter enjoyed about a year as patriarch and used the opportunity to introduce an important innovation in the liturgy. At Antioch the doxology of the Kyrie Eleison had long served as a test of orthodoxy.[5] In *circa* 350 the Nicene opponents of Leontius of Antioch had composed a doxology, 'Glory be to the Father and to the Son and to the Holy Spirit', implying

saint's death.' The monastery of Simeon the Younger (521–92), however, 'lay between Antioch and the Mediterranean, an essentially hellenistic world', and remained Chalcedonian (*JTS*, n.s. 15, 1964, p. 180, reviewing Paul van den Ven's *La Vie ancienne de S. Syméon Stylite le Jeune (521–592)* = *Subsidia Hagiographica* 32, Brussels, 1962).

[1] Theodoret of Cyrrhus, for instance, restored to his see by Chalcedon, defended the Definition vigorously against pro-Nestorian colleagues in Cilicia, such as John of Egea. See M. Richard, 'La Lettre de Théodoret à Jean d'Egées', *Les Sciences philosophiques et théologiques* 2, 1941–2, pp. 415–23.

[2] Theodore Lector, *HE* I. 20. For Apollinarists in Syria in the fifth century, see Sozomen, *HE* VI. 27. 9. Martyrius was characterised by his enemies as a 'Nestorian'.

[3] John Diakrinomenos, *HE* v (fragmenta, ed. Miller, pp. 401–2). Compare John Malalas, *Chron.* xv. 88 (ed. Dindorf, p. 379): Peter 'received his consecration as bishop from Zeno'. See Schwartz, *PS*, p. 182.

[4] Theodore Lector, *HE* I. 21.

[5] For a similar, polemical (anti-Arian) purpose of Ambrose's hymns, see Ambrose, *Sermo contra Auxentium* 34 (*PL* 16, col. 1060).

The rise of the Monophysite movement

that both Son and Spirit were consubstantial with the Father, in contrast to the traditional Antiochene version, 'Glory to the Father through the Son and in the Holy Spirit',[1] which, however, seemed to imply a subordination of the latter two persons to the Father. In 431 the Antiochenes complained of people tampering with the doxology in Cyril's interest,[2] and at Chalcedon they shouted their approval of Dioscorus' condemnation with the cry, 'Holy God, holy and mighty, holy and immortal, have mercy upon us'.[3] It was into this doxology that Peter introduced the words 'thou who wast crucified for us' before 'have mercy upon us'.[4] This could still be orthodox if one referred it to the person of Christ and added the words 'in the flesh', and Severus of Antioch was to plead that it was merely an additional safeguard against Nestorius,[5] but it could also be interpreted in the sense that Christ as God and one of the Trinity had suffered on the cross. This was Patripassian and was the usual sense given to the phrase by its supporters. Soon it became the touchstone of Monophysite orthodoxy.

Peter's reign was not to be long. Once more the emperor and patriarch acted[6] and in 471 he found himself within the unwelcoming walls of the monastery of the Sleepless Ones in the capital.

Meantime, the advance of Zeno had been rapid. The Germanic element at court was discredited and the Isaurians provided a counterweight to them, barbaric enough, yet within the frontiers of the empire and orthodox in their faith. Time and Leo worked in favour of Zeno and the Isaurians. In 468 he married Ariadne, Leo's elder daughter, who had previously been promised to Aspar's son Patricius, an act which may have fired the relations between the Isaurians and Germans with an element of personal feud.[7] As

[1] Philostorgius, *HE* III. 13; also Theodoret, *HE* II. 24.
[2] *ACO* I. I. 7, p. 72, line 37.
[3] *ACO* 2. I. 1, p. 195, line 30. See Schwartz, *PS*, pp. 241–4.
[4] Evagrius, *HE* III. 44.
[5] *Homil.* 125 (*PO* 29, p. 249). Others attempted to safeguard an orthodox intent in the doxology by inserting 'Christ the king' before 'who was crucified for us'.
[6] Theodore Lector, *HE* I. 22, states that Leo ordered him to be sent into exile.
[7] For this period see Brooks, 'The Emperor Zeno and the Isaurians', pp. 212–14, and Baynes, 'The Vita S. Danielis Stylitae', p. 400. In 470 Aspar's son Patricius married Leo's second daughter, Leontia, on his acceptance of Chalcedon, the only condition under which the Sleepless Monks and their allies would accept him as Caesar and husband of Leontia, but the marriage-bond was broken after the revolution next year. Patricius was badly wounded and disappears from history. Zeno, himself the object of a mutinous outbreak in 470, was on the sidelines at Chalcedon when his rival, Aspar, fell (Schwartz, *PS*, pp. 183–4).

The 'Henotikon' of Zeno

Leo had no son, Zeno was now in line for the succession. In 469 he was consul and in 471 he benefited from the palace revolution that removed Aspar and his family from the scene. The Germans, however, defended themselves strongly. Leo was forced in 473 to appoint a relative of Aspar, Theodoric Strabo, as *magister militum* and continue to hold a balance between the Isaurian and German factions.[1] Zeno too showed serious weaknesses of character; he was indolent, and no warrior for all his ferocity.[2] Ecclesiastically, he was suspect to Gennadius and at first to his successor Acacius, who became patriarch in 471. In consequence of all this Zeno failed to become regent in 473, but had his infant son Leo (born in 469) made co-emperor in October of that year. When on 18 January 474 the elder Leo died, he had little difficulty in persuading the senate to request him to become co-emperor (9 February). The tragedy that removed Leo II on 17 November left him in sole control.[3] He had not, however, calculated on the unpopularity of the Isaurians in the capital,[4] and his own follies quickly roused up a party against him under the leadership of the Empress-Dowager Verina.

THE REVOLUTION OF BASILISCUS, JANUARY 475–AUGUST 476

The new palace revolution which put Basiliscus on the throne on 9 January 475 had profound repercussions on the religious life of the empire. Alexandrian monks had already acted on the news of Zeno's accession and a delegation full of denunciation for Chalcedon arrived in Constantinople to find Zeno had fled and Basiliscus emperor. At this point one can appreciate how much otherwise inexplicable decisions may have depended on some personal accident. Aspar had certainly protected the enemies of Proterius, but he was not a Monophysite. Why should Basiliscus also have offered such wholehearted support to them? Later Monophysite historians suggest 'desire to please the Alexandrians' as a motive.[5] The influence of Zenonis,

---

[1] On the end of Aspar, see John Malalas, *Chron.* XIV. 79 (ed. Dindorf, p. 371). Compare E. Stein, *Histoire du Bas-Empire*, vol. I (ed. J.-R. Palanque, Desclée de Brouwer, 1959), pp. 360–1.

[2] Evagrius, *HE* III. 1. Compare Zonaras, *Epitomae historiarum* XIV. 2. 2 (ed. Büthner Wobst). In contrast, however, *Vita Danielis*, ch. 85, whose writer had a high opinion of him and praised his orthodoxy.

[3] For dating, *Regesten*, ed. Seeck, pp. 425–6.

[4] 'The officers of the palace hated Zeno the emperor because he was an Isaurian by race': so Joshua Stylites, *Chron.* (ed. Wright), ch. 12. Similarly, Zonaras XIV. 2. 1.

[5] Michael the Syrian, *Chron.* IX. 5 (ed. Chabot, II, 144).

his wife, was a powerful factor,[1] and another was that by coincidence a member of the Alexandrian delegation was the brother of one of his senior ministers, the *magister officiorum*. Between them, Basiliscus was persuaded to pin his hopes on the out-and-out anti-Chalcedonians. After seventeen years in exile Timothy the Cat was recalled from Cherson and Peter the Fuller was allowed out of his monastery to proceed to Antioch once more.[2] Alexandrian seamen paraded their leader through the streets of Constantinople riding in triumph towards the 'Great church' (later Sancta Sophia) on an ass, as though he was the Lord himself. Basiliscus went out to greet him, and so did the populace of the capital.[3]

Basiliscus was now committed to supporting both Timothy the Cat and Peter the Fuller. His patriarch, Acacius, was in two minds. On the one hand, as a presbyter of Anatolius he disliked the teaching of the *Tome* and Chalcedon and sympathised with the outlook of Timothy the Cat. On the other hand, he was as determined as his predecessors had been to uphold the rights of his see against all comers. In the last resort both Timothy and Acacius regarded victory for their respective sees as the main objective.

In this uncertain situation Basiliscus was prevailed upon to acquiesce in the despatch on 9 April 475 of an important encyclical addressed 'to all cities and people throughout the empire', though in the first instance to Timothy, in which he outlined his religious policy.[4] As Theodosius II and Marcian had before him, he affirmed his trust that 'unity among the people of Christ was the preservation of ourselves and our subjects and the stout foundation and strong bulwark of our empire'; and he defined this bulwark as Nicaea, confirmed in regard to its doctrinal definition by Constantinople and *both* Councils of Ephesus. In contrast, 'the so-called *Tome* of Leo, and all things said and done at Chalcedon in innovation of the holy symbol of Nicaea', were declared anathema. The 'laws of Constantine' and of Theodosius II against heresy were reinvigorated. Bishops were called upon to sign and dissident clergy were threatened with banishment.

The encyclical based itself on the theology of Cyril and Dioscorus while

[1] Theodore Lector, *HE* I. 29.
[2] Peter's support of Basiliscus is indicated by John Malalas, *Chron.* xv. 89 (ed. Dindorf, p. 379).
[3] Zacharias Rhetor, *HE* v. 1; Theophanes, *Chron.* A.M. 5967 (ed. Classen, I, 187); Theodore Lector, *HE* I. 30, who cannot resist saying that he fell off the donkey and injured his foot badly!
[4] For the text see Schwartz, 'Antichalkedonische Sammlung', no. 73, p. 49, Evagrius, *HE* III. 4 and Zacharias Rhetor, *HE* v. 2.

castigating Nestorianism and Eutychianism impartially.¹ In the text preserved by Zacharias the teaching of 'the chief priests Celestine, Cyril and Dioscorus' was praised, and thus it was not directed against the see of Peter as such. On the other hand, the encyclical was ambiguous about the rights of the capital. The doctrinal canons of Constantinople were indeed confirmed, and explicitly that relating to the doctrine of the Holy Spirit, but the disciplinary canon (canon 3) regulating the position of New Rome as a see was passed over in silence.² Basiliscus had gone further than any other emperor in not only promulgating doctrine but deciding as between two rival synods which was to be regarded as orthodox. He prepared the way for the still more radical intervention in ecclesiastical affairs by Zeno in the *Henotikon*.

Acacius refused to sign the encyclical, and after accepting Timothy as a guest in his city closed the churches to him, while pro-Chalcedonian monks barred his entry to the 'Great Church'. On the other hand, Timothy disappointed the Eutychian element among the monks, stating his view that 'the humanity of Christ was in all respects similar to our own'.³ Zenonis also disapproved his sentiments and amid growing disenchantment Timothy left for Ephesus, where further triumph awaited him. He was determined to put the clock back a quarter of a century. The synod, allegedly of 600 bishops, which he held there repudiated Chalcedon 'as having turned the world upside down', and restored Ephesus to patriarchal dignity.⁴ He was dreaming of avenging Dioscorus. In Acacius, however, he met his match.

---

¹ The texts given in Zacharias Rhetor, *HE* v. 2 and Evagrius, *HE* III. 4 do not entirely agree. Zacharias adds after the phrase condemning Nestorius, 'et ea etiam quae Ephesi gesta sunt a duobus conciliis quae cum summis sacerdotibus Caelestino et Cyrillo et Dioscoro Romae et Alexandriae congregata sunt', which is omitted by Evagrius, but from Schwartz's text quite clearly belonged to the original decree.

² This was almost certainly intended. Timothy the Cat believed that Flavian had been quite properly condemned as a heretic at Ephesus II and that the Holy Spirit had spoken through the mouth of Dioscorus and the church of Alexandria (fragments, ed. Nau, pp. 208–9).

³ Zacharias Rhetor, *HE* v. 4. Clearly the Eutychians had been moving to the position of holding that the divine nature of Christ had wholly absorbed the human and that Christ's flesh was entirely 'heavenly'. Timothy reproached them for failing to accept that 'Emmanuel is, by the flesh, consubstantial with the Blessed Virgin, *Theotokus*, who has born Emmanuel' (Lebon, 'Timothée', p. 686). For the Eutychians Timothy and even Peter the Fuller were Chalcedonians.

⁴ Evagrius, *HE* III. 5; Zacharias Rhetor, *HE* v. 3 (text of petition to Basiliscus by the bishops assembled at Ephesus). Regarding the status of Ephesus, see above, p. 7 n2.

The rise of the Monophysite movement

In the previous thirty years, however, a great deal had happened to consolidate the position of the bishop of the capital. While his predecessors were content with the title of 'bishop' or 'archbishop', Acacius was 'patriarch'. Much had been due to the skill and clear-sightedness of Anatolius, with the result that Acacius was in a strong position both vis-à-vis the court and population of the capital and in the east generally. Events were to show that the standing of his see was all-important; for this he would be prepared to sacrifice the faith of the Chalcedonian Definition, and even communion with Old Rome. Now he played his trump card – Daniel the Stylite. Daniel had won the complete confidence of Leo and Gennadius. Demons had been chased out of a temple, cures performed, disasters accurately foretold, and Leo assured at an opportune moment that Gaiseric would not attack Alexandria.[1] He had never left his pillar, even his ordination as presbyter being carried out by Gennadius standing at the foot and in the presence of the emperor.[2] Now, however, he heeded Acacius' appeal to 'save the church from persecution', and descended his pillar. The effect was dramatic. A Gothic guard at the emperor's palace who ridiculed 'the new consul' fell dead;[3] Basiliscus was threatened with judgement and asked pointedly why he was acting like a 'new Diocletian'.[4] The battle was over. In an abject and significantly worded apology, the usurper affirmed emphatically that he accepted the Homoousion – he was not an Arian – but pleaded that 'as barbarians and educated to arms, we were not such as those who were instructed in the deep things (βάθη) of the holy faith'[5] – an interesting admission which illustrates the true weakness of the Gothic and pro-Gothic influence at court.[6] In Constantinople orthodoxy had become synonymous with the acceptance of Chalcedon. An emperor was expected also to guarantee the position of the patriarch as inviolable against external enemies.

Acacius had also called the papacy to his aid (autumn 475) using the monastic leaders of the capital for this purpose. The papacy could still be a powerful *deus ex machina* in an evenly balanced situation, and in particular

---

[1] The rumour was one of the reasons for Leo's determination to attack the Vandals. See *Vita Danielis*, ch. 56. Another example of his political influence was his mediation between Leo and King Gubazes of Lazica (*ibid.* ch. 51).

[2] *Ibid.* ch. 44.   [3] *Ibid.* ch. 75.

[4] *Ibid.* ch. 73.   [5] *Ibid.* ch. 73.

[6] *Ibid.* ch. 84. Basiliscus had also stressed his baptism into the Nicene faith in the text of the encyclical. For the possibility of his and therefore Verina's barbarian origin, see Schwartz, *PS*, p. 189 n1.

could deny an ecumenical character to any council simply by refusing to be represented. Rome thus re-enters the eastern scene after an apparent lapse of more than fifteen years, and was not to leave it again in a hurry. On 10 January 476 Simplicius replied, praising Acacius' firmness in the crisis, condemned Timothy as Leo had before him as a parricide, and urged Acacius not to allow a new general council to be summoned, thus frustrating Timothy's aim at convoking a council at Jerusalem and putting the patriarch in the dock. At the same time he wrote separately to Basiliscus, Acacius and the presbyter-archimandrites of the capital demanding the removal of Timothy.[1] Basiliscus capitulated: a new counter-encyclical, described in childishly emphatic terms as 'a sacred edict', reaffirmed the rights of the patriarch, denounced Nestorius and Eutyches 'and every other heresy', repudiated the idea of a new council but made no reference to Chalcedon.[2]

He dared not, for no less than 500 bishops of the east had subscribed to the encyclical,[3] and the patriarchates of Alexandria, Jerusalem and Antioch were in anti-Chalcedonian hands. The encyclical also commanded wide popular support.[4] Though the biographer of Peter the Iberian is prejudiced there can be little doubt that what he describes as 'a feast of gladness and spiritual joy possessed the souls of the God-fearing', and that in Palestine and Egypt there was a feeling of relief.[5] Timothy the Cat had entered Alexandria to tumultuous scenes of triumph. 'Blessed is he that cometh in the name of the Lord' (Matt. 21. 9), the crowds had chanted. His rival, Timothy Wobble-Cap, had been sent back to his monastery with a pension of one denarius a day – enough for a monk, it was thought.[6] Whatever else might happen, Timothy the Cat was immovable in the hearts of the people of Alexandria. Basiliscus' recantation did him no good.

---

[1] *Epp.* 2–5, *Epist. rom. pontif.*, ed. Thiel; *Coll. Avellana* 56–9 (ed. Guenther, *CSEL* 35. 1). Simplicius had been pope since 468, but appears to have taken little interest in eastern affairs up to then. Was it really the case, however, that no questions of interest were discussed between pope and patriarch between 468 and 475?

[2] Text published by Schwartz, 'Antichalkedonische Sammlung', no. 74, p. 52. Also Evagrius, *HE* III. 7.

[3] Evagrius, *HE* III. 5. Also Michael the Syrian, *Chron.* IX. 5 (ed. Chabot, II, 146).

[4] In a 'trial by ordeal' held in Pamphylia between rival groups of monks, John Rufus reports how the *Tome* of Leo and the Chalcedonian Definition were burnt up while the encyclical emerged from the fire undamaged. It was regarded as 'divine'. John Rufus, *Plerophoria* 46 (ed. Nau, p. 98).

[5] John Rufus, *Vita Petri Iberi* (ed. Raabe), pp. 76–7.

[6] Zacharias Rhetor, *HE* V. 4 (ed. Brooks, *CSCO* III. 5, p. 150).

By the end of August 476 Zeno was back in his capital. On 17 December an edict abrogated the usurper's acts and restored the ecclesiastical status quo. More important, the rights of Acacius over the churches in Asia were restated, and in the most solemn form the prerogatives of the capital see, 'mother of our Piety and of all Christians of the orthodox religion', affirmed.[1] The bond between emperor and patriarch was sealed as never before. The Asian sees submitted. Rome, for the moment, said nothing. Peter the Fuller and Paul of Ephesus were exiled, and an order was being sent to Timothy the Cat when he died, 31 July 477.[2] The problem, however, remained, whether Nicaea or Nicaea plus Chalcedon was to be the faith of Christendom, and Zeno was determined not to go on his travels again.

THE HENOTIKON

After the confusion caused by the usurper's encyclical and anti-encyclical it was inevitable that an attempt would be made to find a compromise. In Alexandria, in particular, schism continued, the death of Timothy the Cat being immediately followed by the consecration of Peter Mongus as bishop.[3] Though in hiding, with a severe impediment of speech, and a far from reliable character, his was the power in the city. In view of the schism which was to break out with Rome as the result of the ensuing compromise, it should be emphasised that the *Henotikon* of Zeno was not directed against the Roman see, and that the circumstances which provoked the latter's abiding anger were largely accidental. The original impulse towards compromise with the anti-Chalcedonians may have come from Acacius' colleagues in Palestine. Here, the unstable balance between the majority of the monks who were still anti-Chalcedonian, and successive patriarchs whose position was bound up with avoiding the outright renunciation of the council, continued. The Patriarch Anastasius[4] had signed Basiliscus' encyclical and while he had avoided signing the sequel had kept in communion with the Chalcedonian as well as the anti-Chalcedonian monks. When he died in July 478 it did not take Martyrius, his successor, long to attempt to unite the bickering factions. In an encyclical he proclaimed that

---

[1] *Cod. Just.* I. 2. 16.
[2] Evagrius, *HE* III. 11 and John Rufus, *Vita Petri Iberi* (ed. Raabe), p. 78.
[3] He was Peter's archdeacon: see Liberatus, *Brev.* XVI. 106.
[4] He was regarded later as pro-Monophysite: see Michael the Syrian, *Chron.* IX. 5 (ed. Chabot, II, 147).

The 'Henotikon' of Zeno

the true faith was to be found in the first three councils (i.e. Nicaea, Constantinople and Ephesus I) and that anyone who accepted any different doctrine, whether pronounced at Serdica, Ariminum or at Chalcedon, was anathema. In other words, the doctrines of Cyril were canonical, the position of Constantinople was safeguarded and Chalcedon was reduced to the status of a conciliar aberration.[1]

This took place probably in 479; the next year was to show that if harmony was to be restored in Antioch and Alexandria it could only be on the basis of a recognition of Peter Mongus and Peter the Fuller. In Alexandria, the restored Timothy Wobble-Cap had done his best to conciliate public opinion. Despite renewed protests from Rome, Dioscorus had been restored to the diptychs and the faith of the church proclaimed, as by Martyrius, as subsisting in the first three councils without a mention of Chalcedon.[2] In vain. However irregular Peter Mongus' consecration had been, he was regarded as true bishop in Alexandria. In Antioch, meantime, there was something like anarchy. Peter the Fuller was in exile, but the anti-Chalcedonians remained in control. Both there and in Alexandria the populace was firmly anti-Chalcedonian. The people supported Peter the Fuller, and Pope Gelasius included in his requisitory against Acacius in 494 the charge that Martyrius of Antioch had been expelled in favour of Peter in 469 by the mob and by heretics.[3] The situation was complicated because the Jews supported the more aristocratic Blue faction against the popular anti-Chalcedonian Green, and were massacred by them.[4] The new patriarch, Stephen, a Chalcedonian, was murdered in a tumult, pierced through and through by reed pens early in 479.[5] His successor, Calendio, also a firm Chalcedonian, was consecrated by Acacius himself in Constantinople in 481, but could not take possession of his see. In letters to Simplicius Acacius had promised that his election should be confirmed by a provincial synod at Antioch itself.[6] He had also condemned Peter Mongus in scathing

---

[1] Text in Zacharias Rhetor, *HE* v. 6. See Chitty, *The Desert a City*, p. 102.

[2] Zacharias Rhetor, *HE* v. 5.

[3] 'Ibi pulso Martyrio catholico episcopo per vilissimum populum et haereticos sedem ipsius occupasse [Petrus].' Gelasius, *Gesta de nomine Acacii* = *Coll. Avellana* 99. 25 (ed. Guenther, *CSEL* 35. 1, p. 450).

[4] John Malalas, *Chron.* XV. 103 (ed. Dindorf, p. 389). See also Grégoire/Manojlovic, 'Le Peuple de Constantinople', p. 646.

[5] Michael the Syrian, *Chron.* IX. 6 (ed. Chabot, II, 149).

[6] Referred to in Simplicius' letters to Zeno and Acacius, *Coll. Avellana* 66 and 67, June 479. For dating see Stein, *Bas-Empire*, II, 21.

The rise of the Monophysite movement

terms (autumn 477). He was a 'friend of darkness' who had 'subverted the canons of the fathers' by accepting consecration at dead of night while the body of Timothy the Cat still lay unburied.[1] This was, of course, a gross misrepresentation of the Alexandrian rite, whereby on the death of the patriarch his successor must make a vigil by the corpse, place his right hand on his head and with his own hands take the pallium of St Mark from off the dead man's neck and place it on his own.[2] That Acacius should write in such terms about Peter and ask that Rome should not recognise him,[3] and then come to an accord with him was to convince the popes of his perfidy. At this stage he was supporting the Chalcedonian Timothy at Alexandria, and the equally staunch Chalcedonian, Calendio, at Antioch.

Acacius, however, was not blind to events. The usurpation of Basiliscus had demonstrated the strength of anti-Chalcedonian feeling in the east. Rome was distant and the position of its bishop had deteriorated. Since 476 an emperor no longer ruled in the west; Simplicius was now, like himself, a subject of Zeno. There was also the perpetual instability in the capital and the European provinces caused by the rivalries between Germans and Isaurians for power. In addition, Peter Mongus had his troubles. In Egypt and Palestine serious rifts were beginning to appear in the ranks of the anti-Chalcedonians. Zacharias[4] refers to a certain Theodotus, bishop of Joppa, who had been consecrated originally by Theodosius of Jerusalem. This man was stirring up trouble, demanding unconditional condemnation of the *Tome* and Chalcedon, and he was being supported allegedly by no less than 30,000 monks in Egypt. These dissenters even now deserved the title of *aposchistae* (separatists). On the other hand, the former Proterian cause was visibly breaking up, and its members were seeking how to make their peace with Peter. There were strong reasons both in the capital and in Alexandria why an attempt should be made to heal past breaches. Perhaps, too, the lure of the title 'ecumenical patriarch' uniting all the eastern churches under his leadership influenced Acacius to accept the opportunity offered by Martyrius' declaration to the church in Palestine.

---

[1] *Acacii epistula ad Simplicium* (ed. Schwartz, *Coll. Veronensis* 4, in *PS*, pp. 4–5 = *Epist. rom. pontif.*, ed. Thiel, *Ep.* 8).

[2] Compare Liberatus, *Brev.* xx. 142.   [3] *Ibid.* xvii. 110.

[4] Zacharias Rhetor, *HE* v. 4 (ed. Brooks, *CSCO* iii. 5, pp. 150–1) and compare also vi. 1.

The 'Henotikon' of Zeno

Events in the winter 481/2 played into Acacius' hands. At the end of 481 Timothy Wobble-Cap sent his fellow Pachomian monk and *oeconomos*, John Talaia, to the capital with a request that his successor should be chosen from among the Egyptian clergy (i.e. not like Calendio). This was granted, but John apparently sought to contact the all-powerful Isaurian general Illus, to whom Zeno owed his return to his throne; but Zeno was already suspecting his benefactor of plotting a revolt against him in concert with the prefect of Egypt. John also gave Illus presents, which he failed to do for Acacius. Before he left an oath was allegedly extracted from him, that though he might accept any other post, he would deny himself the patriarchate. Timothy died in February 482,[1] and his supporters prevented John from keeping his word and he was consecrated Chalcedonian patriarch. He gave further colour that he might be disloyal by informing Illus at Antioch of his consecration and failing to do the same to Zeno and Acacius.[2] Meantime, a rival delegation headed by Peter Mongus himself had reached the capital, and Acacius took his chance to state his terms for recognising him.[3]

The *Henotikon*, or instrument of unity, was drafted on Acacius' advice, and on 28 July 482 was addressed to the bishops, monks and laymen of Alexandria, Egypt and Cyrenaica.[4] Its immediate aim was the complete

[1] For dating, Schwartz, *PS*, p. 196 n3.

[2] Liberatus, *Brev.* XVII. 111. See Brooks, 'The Emperor Zeno', p. 222 for dating of Illus' move to Antioch during 482. Zeno himself is recorded by Evagrius (*HE* III. 15) to have told Pope Simplicius that his objection to John Talaia was based on the latter's perjury 'and that for this reason and no other he had been ejected from his bishopric'. However, ten years later Gelasius claimed he could not have sworn as alleged (*Coll. Avellana* 99, ed. Guenther, *CSEL* 35. 1, p. 449). Compare P. Peeters, 'Sur une contribution récente à l'histoire du Monophysisme', *AB* 45, 1936, pp. 143–59 at pp. 152–6 regarding this aspect of the affair.

[3] Liberatus, *Brev.* XVII. 112. For the probable existence of correspondence between Acacius and Peter during the period leading up to the *Henotikon*, see G. Krüger, 'Monophysiten', Herzog-Hauck, *Realencyclopädie für protestantische Theologie und Kirche*, vol. XIII (Leipzig, 1905), 372–401 at 381.

[4] Zacharias Rhetor, *HE* v. 8. Zacharias does not, however, give the full text, but it is completed by the version preserved in Schwartz, 'Antichalkedonische Sammlung', no. 75, pp. 52–4. See also Nicephorus Callistus, *HE* XVI. 12 and Evagrius, *HE* III. 14; and in Latin Liberatus, *Brev.* XVII. 113–17 and Facundus of Hermiana, *Pro defensione trium capitulorum* XII. 4. There is an anonymous and partial version in Armenian translated by F. C. Conybeare in *AJT* 9, 1905, pp. 735–7. See also Coleman-Norton, *Roman State and Christian Church*, III, 924–33 for English translation and notes.

The rise of the Monophysite movement

reconciliation of Constantinople and Alexandria,[1] including the reintegration of former supporters of Proterius. It is one of the basic pronouncements of the church policy of the eastern emperors and the patriarch of the capital. The letter opens with the statement reminiscent of statements by Theodosius II and Marcian: 'Considering the source and constitution of our power and the invincible shield of our empire as the only right and true faith pronounced through divine intervention only by the 318 holy fathers assembled in Nicaea...'; then follows a reaffirmation of the symbol of Nicaea and Constantinople. Faithful observance of this and praise of God, the Saviour Jesus Christ and the Virgin *Theotokos* would enable the enemies of the empire to be crushed and the earth to bring forth her fruits abundantly for the prosperity of all. The emperor then stated that he had received petitions from 'archimandrites and hermits and other venerable men' beseeching him to act towards the restoration of unity. He asserted that because of continued disagreement in the church, baptisms had not been conferred, and the Eucharist not received, and in consequence there had been riots and violence that had resulted in countless murders and bloodshed. Hence, the emperor assured the Egyptians 'that both we and the churches everywhere neither have held nor hold nor shall hold nor know persons who hold' a creed other than Nicaea, confirmed by Constantinople and Ephesus where the 'impious Nestorius and those who were later of that one's mind' were deposed. Nestorius and Eutyches were anathematised, but the Twelve Chapters (Anathemas) of Cyril were received. In a confession of faith, the emperor affirmed that Jesus Christ was consubstantial with both God and man, and, 'incarnate from the Holy Spirit and Mary the Virgin and *Theotokos*, is one and not two, for we say that both his miracles and his sufferings which he willingly underwent in the flesh are of one person'. There was no Docetism on the one hand, nor on the other, did assumption of flesh imply any addition to the Son. The emperor concluded 'that every person who has thought or thinks anything else either now or any time either in Chalcedon or in any other synod whatever, we anathematise'. On these foundations all were enjoined to unite themselves to the church and hasten to reunite in agreement.

The *Henotikon* was to remain the official policy of Zeno for the remainder

---

[1] For the Egyptian inspiration of the text, see Evagrius, *HE* III. 12. For the emperor's hopes in this direction and his anger when the *Henotikon* only produced more schism in Egypt, see Zacharias Rhetor, *HE* VI. 2 (referring to the mission of Cosmas), and Evagrius, *HE* III. 22.

of his reign and also of his successor Anastasius. It was a masterstroke of Acacian diplomacy. It gave substance to the claim which Pope Gelasius subsequently put into his mouth of being 'praecipue pontificem regiae civitatis'.[1] It came as near as any other attempt before or afterwards to uniting the theologies of the great churches in the east. Under the explicit leadership of the capital the faith of the church was that laid down at Nicaea and subsequently confirmed at Constantinople and Ephesus I (but not Ephesus II). The standing of the monk and holy man was restored, for it was due to their initiative that the emperor had written. It gave full respect to the depth of religious feeling throughout the east, particularly among the monks, that somehow the created world could be made divine through the redemptive splendour of the incarnate Saviour. It had nothing, however, to say to the west, for though neither the *Tome* nor Chalcedon had been condemned explicitly, not the slightest concession had been made to Roman prerogatives and Roman views. Instead, Cyril's Anathemas were now declared canon, and Chalcedon was reduced, as it had been in Martyrius' pronouncement, to the status of the disciplinary body responsible for condemning the heretics Nestorius and Eutyches. Otherwise it was set in a pejorative light, but it was not condemned. This Zeno refused to do.[2]

In form the emperor had merely written a letter to the patriarchate of Alexandria; in fact, he had laid down detailed canons of belief on which church unity was to be restored throughout the empire. His lawyers could perhaps claim that even in this he had done no more than Theodosius I in his famous edict addressed to Thessalonica on 28 February 380 in which the Trinitarian teaching of Rome and Alexandria was declared canonical.[3] Zeno, however, had made no reference to the views of any see; nor was he like Marcian expressing simply the voice of the church as affirmed in a recent council. His was a consecration of the religious sentiment of what he believed to be the majority in the east. In this he was following the policies of Constantius II in the Arian controversy and of Theodosius II, and foreshadowing the Fifth General Council of 553, the *Ecthesis* of Heraclius and

[1] Gelasius, *Ep. ad episcopos Dardaniae* = *Coll. Avellana* 95. 2 (ed. Guenther, *CSEL* 35. 1, p. 370).
[2] See Evagrius, *HE* III. 22 (ed. Bidez and Parmentier, p. 120), Zeno's reply to the embassy of the Egyptian monks led by Nephalius who demanded the denunciation of *Tome* and council as well (οὐ συνθεμένου Ζήνωνος τὴν ἐν Χαλκηδόνι σύνοδον ἀναθεματίζειν).
[3] *Cod. Theod.* XVI. 1. 2.

the *Typos* of Constans II. 'Caesaro-Papism' was simply the application of the ideas of Constantine, and was accepted in the east as the normal role of the emperor as divinely appointed protector of Christians. There, and not among the barbarian kingdoms in Italy and the west, the heart of the empire was henceforth to lie.

Zeno's success was limited. Nominally Peter Mongus and Acacius were now in communion and the schism between Constantinople and Alexandria was thereby healed. In Alexandria most people seem to have been satisfied, and these included Peter the Iberian.[1] Pressures, however, were moving inexorably toward the rejection of any statement of belief that did not denounce Chalcedon outright. Peter Mongus lacked the personal authority and the prestige of long and arduous confessorship that had surrounded Timothy, and he was soon confronted by irreconcilable monks. He was forced by these extremists to condemn the *Tome* and Chalcedon in the same breath as he accepted the *Henotikon*.[2] This prevented a lasting schism between the patriarch and a large group of monks, but at the expense of hindering the reintegration of the former supporters of Proterius. It perpetuated the existence of a pro-Chalcedonian community in Alexandria, which formed the origin of the 'Melkite' or 'Imperial' church in Egypt.[3] The dissident monks became known among themselves as the 'Headless ones' (*Acephaloi*), denoting community of purpose without personal leader.[4] They wished for no accommodation with the capital nor with any other patriarchate that did not expressly condemn the *Tome* and council.

In Antioch, too, Calendio refused to accept the *Henotikon* as being too biased against Chalcedon. Since his entry into the city he had regarded himself as the heir to the theological tradition of Eustathius whose remains

---

[1] Zacharias Rhetor, *HE* v. 7; cf. Evagrius, *HE* III. 14 (end).

[2] Zacharias Rhetor, *HE* VI. 2 – thus setting the precedent for the attitude of Severus of Antioch.

[3] The exact moment when the Chalcedonians in Alexandria became consciously 'Melkites' is hard to determine; probably not until the period of Justinian.

[4] Zacharias Rhetor, *HE* VI. 2: 'Et monachi accipere noluerunt [*Henotikon*] dicentes: "Petrus cum summis sacerdotibus communicat qui non ut is synodum et Tomum expresse anathematizaverunt."' The name Acephaloi was perhaps an intentional revival of the name of those who after the Formula of Reunion rejected both Cyril and John of Antioch. See Liberatus, *Brev.* IX (*PL* 68, col. 988). According to Michael the Syrian, *Chron.* IX. 6, the opponents of Peter included Theodorus, bishop of Antinoë, two priests of Alexandria, two deacons and two 'great archimandrites'.

he had solemnly conveyed to Antioch[1] and he had added the phrase 'Christ our God' between the orthodox doxology and Peter's addition 'who was crucified for us', thus relating the specifically Monophysite invocation to Christ in his manhood. Now he joined John Talaia in complaining to Pope Simplicius. His days of authority were, however, numbered. Early in 484 the long-smouldering discord between Zeno and Illus broke out into civil war. Illus established himself at Antioch and, supported by the Empress-Dowager Verina, set up another Isaurian of consular rank, Leontius, as emperor. He may even have had wider visions involving some massive alliance of the Persians and Odoacer against his enemy. Ostensibly the rebellion (to judge from Verina's proclamation) was aimed against the *Henotikon*,[2] and as such it attracted Calendio's support. But, in addition, advised by the last of the Neoplatonist philosopher-statesmen, Pamprepius, the rebels permitted some restoration of paganism. At Aphrodisias, the capital of Caria, people remembered how the altars smoked again with incense and how the oracles foretold the destruction of Christianity.[3] The great effort failed (August 484), though it was not until 488 that Illus was finally cornered in his Isaurian stronghold and executed. The population had remained constant to Zeno and this time the anti-Chalcedonians paraded their loyalty to the emperor. Calendio was deposed in September 484 and Peter the Fuller returned to Antioch for the third time. He accepted the *Henotikon*.

Rome meantime had been caught off balance. As we have noted, in the autumn of 477 Acacius had informed Pope Simplicius of the evil ways of Peter Mongus and confirmed his support for the Chalcedonian Timothy in fulsome terms.[4] He had prevailed on Rome to excommunicate Peter and also John Codonatus, whom Peter had established as anti-Chalcedonian leader in Apamea.[5] A year later, however, Simplicius may have been beginning to suspect that Acacius was coming round to accepting Peter, for he demanded the latter's removal 'far off'. He was not prepared to

[1] Theodore Lector, *HE* II. 1.
[2] See Brooks, *The Emperor Zeno*, p. 226.
[3] Zacharias Scholasticus, *Vita Severi* (ed. Kugener, p. 40). At Alexandria the failure of the revolt was used as an argument against the remains of paganism there a decade later.
[4] Acacius to Simplicius, *Coll. Veronensis* 4 = *PS*, pp. 4–5.
[5] *Coll. Avellana* 70. 5 (ed. Guenther, *CSEL* 35. 1, p. 157). Simplicius was particularly angry that John had been later consecrated as bishop of Tyre at Acacius' own instance. Few incidents demonstrate more clearly the gradual change of policy at the capital in the years 480–2.

tolerate him even in his original office as a deacon.[1] The murder of Stephen at Antioch also filled him with grief,[2] and now Acacius' seemingly complete volte-face with his recognition of Peter Mongus appeared like an act of gross treachery. 'Even if he [Peter] were now orthodox, he should be admitted to lay communion only.' This was written on 15 July 482, a fortnight before the *Henotikon*.[3] The papacy, however, was out of touch with the situation and it is not known even how the emperor's decree was received in Rome. Towards the end of 482 Simplicius fell ill and did not recover. He died in March 483. Again, the time-lag consolidated the situation in the east to the patriarch of the capital's advantage. Acacius had been careful not to keep Simplicius informed[4] and Felix III took time to assess the situation. Then it was the Sleepless Monks, whose strongly Chalcedonian beliefs had been outraged by Acacius' actions, who alerted him. He summoned Acacius to answer for having restored Peter Mongus without permission and he upbraided him for asserting that 'he was head of the whole church'.[5] For six years the wound administered by Zeno's edict of 17 December 476 had festered. Now the challenge was take up, but in sorrow more than in anger. Acacius did not reply. A papal legation sent to the capital under the leadership of Misenus, bishop of Cuma, and Vitalis fell into a neatly laid trap and took communion with Acacius at a service at which the names of Dioscorus and Peter Mongus were read from the diptychs. This was too much. On their return, the wretched legates were disgraced, and on 28 July 484 a synod of twenty-seven bishops assembled at Rome and solemnly excommunicated Acacius on the grounds that he was a double-dealer ('hypocrita Acacius'), that he had promoted known heretics and insulted the Pope's legates.[6] A faithful monk from the Sleepless Ones pinned the sentence to the patriarch's pallium while he was celebrating

---

[1] *Coll. Avellana* 62, 'Olim divinorum', between 3 and 15 October 478. Compare *ibid.* 64, 'cui nec in diaconatu suus potuit ordo constare', and 65, Peter to be removed 'procul extra terminos patriae'.

[2] *Ibid.* 66–7 of 22 June 479 or 482.

[3] *Ibid.* 68, 'Miramur pariter' (*Epist. rom. pontif.*, ed. Thiel, *Ep.* 18).

[4] *Coll. Avellana* 69. The complaint of this letter is the silence of Acacius in face of the situation developing to the disadvantage of Chalcedon in Alexandria. Similarly, on 6 November 482 he makes the same complaint (*Epist. rom. pontif.*, ed. Thiel, *Ep.* 20 = *Coll. Veronensis* 3, *PS*, p. 4).

[5] Felix to Acacius (*Coll. Berolinensis* 21 = Schwartz, *PS*, p. 73 and Thiel, p. 238): 'Mihi crede nescio quemadmodum te ecclesiae totius asseras esse principem.'

[6] Felix to Acacius, 'Multarum transgressionum' = *Coll. Veronensis* 5, *PS*, pp. 6–7.

the Eucharist.¹ Acacius replied in kind, perhaps reluctantly. No question of belief had been raised, but the clash of aims and jurisdictions between Rome and Constantinople had now become open. On 1 August, Zeno himself was told to choose between the Apostle Peter and Peter Mongus.² The Acacian schism was to last thirty-five years – as long as the emperors regarded the eastern provinces as the area where their true interests lay.

¹ Liberatus, *Brev.* XVII. 125. Theophanes, *Chron.* A.M. 5980, says that the monks in question came from the monastery of Dius. Also Theodore Lector, *HE* (ed. Hansen, p. 120).
² Felix, *Ep.* 8 (*Epist. rom. pontif.*, ed. Thiel, p. 248 = *PS*, p. 81, lines 24ff.).

Chapter 5

TOWARDS A MONOPHYSITE SOLUTION
484-512

The unlikely partnership between Zeno and Acacius proved extraordinarily successful. As Ephesus I fifty years before, the *Henotikon* corresponded to what might loosely be called the mind of eastern Christendom. The theology of Cyril remained the yardstick against which all other teaching was measured, and with Nicaea formed the foundation on which the communion between the four eastern patriarchates rested. The schism with the Roman see was deeply regretted, but until a western-inclined emperor once more sat on the throne at Constantinople its continuance was regarded as preferable to the restoration of the *Tome* of Leo to canonical status. This point had been firmly grasped by Acacius. 'He was more partial to the emperor than to the faith' complained Pope Simplicius.[1] There were occasions on which communion even with Peter Mongus might be temporarily accepted in preference to accepting impossible conditions for communion with the see of Peter.

Yet under the umbrella of the *Henotikon*, popular feeling, represented by the monks and monkish writers, continued to boil, exacerbating latent differences between the Chalcedonian and anti-Chalcedonian leaders. Though the point had not yet been reached when rival organisations would be confronting each other, the schism of minds was complete. The *Tome* had been the 'divider' and Chalcedon 'the time of the Apostasy'. It is impossible not to perceive in the writings of the period the depth of anger that separated the two sides beneath appearances of outward calm. The biography of Peter of Iberia written *circa* 500 by John Rufus, bishop of Maiuma, describes the supporters of Chalcedon in terms akin to modern revolutionary propaganda. Proterius was depicted as 'a new Caiaphas', a man without a shadow of virtue, a 'hard-faced wolf' who relied on 'fierce barbarian soldiers' to keep his position, who rejoiced in Dioscorus' death and richly deserved his own fate.[2] Similar abuse was heaped on Calendio,

[1] Quoted by Evagrius, *HE* III. 21.

[2] *Vita Petri Iberi* (ed. Raabe), pp. 63–8. For John Rufus' authorship, see E. Schwartz, 'Johannes Rufus, ein monophysitischer Schriftsteller', *Sitz. der heidelberger Akad. der Wiss.*, Phil.-hist. Kl., 3. 16, 1912.

Towards a Monophysite solution, 484–512

patriarch of Antioch 481–4.[1] The innate savagery of the mob was affecting the outlook of the leaders. Digging up the bones of one's ecclesiastical opponents was a way to popularity.

There is perhaps one small indication that in north-east Syria words were passing to deeds. During the Persian war of 502–5, Marcellinus Comes implies that the Persians captured Amida, described as a most wealthy monastic city, through the treachery of the monks.[2] These were almost certainly anti-Chalcedonian. At the same time (i.e. 502), Philoxenus of Maboug (Hierapolis) was accused of some obscure actions that 'compromised him with the generals'.[3] Was it treachery, perhaps the first sign that anti-Chalcedonians would be prepared to stand aside in the event of the empire becoming involved in war in the east? We do not know, but these were straws in the wind which no ruler could ignore. Maboug was the major assembly point for all offensives against Persia down the Euphrates,[4] while on the Mesopotamian frontier Mardin, the great anti-Chalcedonian monastery and future Monophysite centre, lay within a stone's throw of the key fortress of Dara built by Anastasius in 505.[5]

The new situation was characterised by the emergence of leaders to whom rejection of Chalcedon was a matter of creed. The harsh, puritanical views of Xenaias (Hellenised into Philoxenus), bishop of Maboug 485–519, expressed in Syriac exclusively, represented the outlook of what was becoming a distinctly Syriac-speaking Monophysitism,[6] but alongside him

[1] *Vita Petri Iberi* (ed. Raabe), p. 79.

[2] Marcellinus Comes, *Chron.* ad ann. 502 (ed. Mommsen, p. 96): 'proditoresque eius monachos'. On the other hand, the Syrian tradition relates that the monks were simply drunk and asleep after celebrating the feast of John the Baptist (*Chronica minora*, ed. E. W. Brooks and J. B. Chabot, *CSCO*, Scriptores Syri III. 4, Paris, 1903, p. 261).

[3] Philoxenus, *Letter to the monks of Senoun* (ed. Halleux), pp. 7–9: 'And I pass over what was plotted against me with the generals at the time of the Persian war thanks to the heretic Flavian...' For Anastasius' reliance on the enterprise of the bishops of the frontier towns to defend them against Persian attack, see Joshua Stylites, *Chron.* XCI (ed. Wright, p. 71). For Philoxenus as anti-Byzantine, see Theophanes, *Chron.* p. 207.

[4] See V. Chapot, 'La frontière de l'Euphrate de Pompée à la conquête arabe', *Bibl. des écoles françaises d'Athènes et de Rome* 19, 1907, pp. 256–7 and 338–9 for its continued importance in Justinian's reign.

[5] For the reasons for Anastasius' decision, see Joshua Stylites, *Chron.* XC (ed. Wright, p. 70).

[6] Michael the Syrian, *Chron.* IX. 9 (ed. Chabot, II, 166) says that he was 'versed in everything that is contained in our writings and in our language'. See also Zacharias Rhetor, *HE* VII. 12. Theophanes, *Chron.* A.M. 5982, describes him as a Persian by race

there was still room for a leader of a more traditional stamp. Severus, patriarch of Antioch 512–18, was the embodiment of Hellenism in Asia Minor, the son of an aristocratic family in Pisidia, a law-student turned ascetic, whose early career resembles that of Gregory the Wonderworker or Basil of Caesarea. These two men illustrate the different aspects of the Monophysite movement in the first quarter of the sixth century. On the other side, this period sees the early stages of what was to develop into the neo-Chalcedonian defence of the council. Collections of patristic texts were being compiled, aimed at justifying the 'two-nature' formula as compatible with Cyril. In Heracleon of Chalcedon, the Patriarch Macedonius, and the stormy petrel Nephalius the Nubian, the Chalcedonian party were acquiring able and thoughtful spokesmen whose legacy was destined to survive.

All the time, the eastern patriarchates and Rome remained out of communion with each other. So long as Acacius lived nothing could be done to heal this schism. Pro-Chalcedonian appeals from Syria II in the course of 484–5 prompted Pope Felix to condemn again Acacius and the two Peters through a Roman synod in October 485.[1] But once more barbarian influence, this time Odoacer's, concerned to promote its own safety by maintaining unresolved ecclesiastical tensions, prevented these differences from interfering with advantageous political relationships between Italy and the eastern provinces of the empire. John Talaia, Chalcedonian patriarch of Alexandria, had to be consoled with the see of Nola.[2]

Against the deepening schism between Rome and the east, the eastern patriarchates and Ephesus with their suffragans continued on reasonable terms.[3] For the next thirty years the capital and Alexandria exchanged

and a slave who had no claim to the priesthood before Peter consecrated him (ed. Classen, I, 207). He was born in the middle of the fifth century at Tahal in the province of Beth-Garamai and studied at the school of Antiochene theology at Edessa but reacted strongly against this, to become its most convinced opponent. See also *Chron. ad ann. 846* (ed. Brooks and Chabot), p. 168, on Philoxenus' Nestorian background.

[1] *Coll. Avellana* 70: 'Olim nobis...' (ed. Guenther, *CSEL* 35. 1, pp. 155–61) = *Epist. rom. pontif.*, ed. Thiel, *Ep.* 11. It protested against Calendio's and other bishops' dismissal. These Catholics were compared with 'pearls cast before swine' (p. 160)! Acacius was likened to Satan whom Christ crushed, and the orthodox of the capital and Bithynia were enjoined to reject communion with him.

[2] See Stein, *Bas-Empire*, II, 33–4.

[3] Zacharias Rhetor, *HE* VI. 1. The outlook of Peter Mongus is probably represented by the anti-Chalcedonian collection of documents leading up to the *Henotikon* whose origin Schwartz places in Alexandria at this period: E. Schwartz, 'Codex Vaticanus

synodical letters and received each other's representatives, each aware of the anarchy that could result otherwise. Indeed nothing illustrates the absence of separatist intention on the part of the anti-Chalcedonian leaders at this period more than the continuance of communion between Alexandria and the capital throughout the reigns of Zeno and Anastasius, despite their differences over the interpretation of the *Henotikon*. The immediate effect of resumption of communion had been rejoicing in the capital and a fulsome letter from Acacius to Peter Mongus.[1] In Alexandria, however, Peter Mongus was forced to balance on the tautest of tight-ropes. On the one hand, the monks reproached him for being too pliant towards Acacius, and on the other hand, he tried to conciliate Acacius by referring to Chalcedon as 'a holy and ecumenical Council'[2] when in fact he had just anathematised it. Even so, the task of preserving unity in his see taxed him to the uttermost. As we have seen, immediately he accepted the *Henotikon*, dissident monks broke away to form their own anonymous or 'headless' body of irreconcilables, the ἀκέφαλοι, or ἀποσχισταί (separatists). Support for them in the monasteries gradually increased.[3] Peter lacked Cyril's ability to weld his doctrinal and political aims into a coherent whole. Despite a tradition of dissent going back for more than thirty years he was not trusted by anyone. To the Syrian Chalcedonian Evagrius he was a double-dealer, while Severus was to censure him for having anathematised the *Tome* yet remaining in communion with bishops who had not done so.[4] Pope Simplicius' assessment of him as 'unfit for the diaconate' was probably not far wide of the mark.[5]

In Antioch, opposition to the *Henotikon* came from the Chalcedonian and crypto-Nestorian bishops,[6] but fortunately for Zeno and Acacius their position had been compromised by the support of the patriarch, Calendio,

graecus 1431, eine antichalkedonische Sammlung aus der Zeit Kaiser Zenos', *Abh. der bayer. Akad. der Wiss.*, Phil.-hist. Abt. 32. 6, 1927, p. 136.

[1] Zacharias Rhetor, *HE* v. 11 (ed. Brooks, *CSCO* III. 5, p. 163).
[2] Evagrius, *HE* III. 17.
[3] Zacharias Rhetor, *HE* VI. 1–2; see above, p. 180.
[4] Evagrius, *HE* III. 17. Severus told the Alexandrine presbyter Ammonius that Peter was not a distinguished or reliable man in his view: see *Select Letters* IV. 2 (ed. Brooks, p. 254).
[5] *Coll. Avellana* 64: 'Proxime quidem...' (ed. Guenther, *CSEL* 35. 1, p. 145).
[6] Calendio wrote deploring the *Henotikon* to Zeno and to both Acacius and Simplicius, and is alleged to have regarded Nestorius favourably since he had called Cyril 'a fool': Zacharias Rhetor, *HE* v. 9 (ed. Brooks, *CSCO* III. 5, pp. 160–1). See above, p. 181.

The rise of the Monophysite movement

for the rebel movement of Illus and Leontius in 484. On its collapse, not only was Calendio deposed (September 484) but nine other senior bishops, including Nestor of Tarsus and Eusebius of Samosata, fell with him; and Peter the Fuller was reinstated for the third time as patriarch.[1] This was a revolution involving a clean sweep of the Nestorianising party among the Syrians, and the effect on the Christians further east across the Euphrates in Persia was immediate and profound. Up to now, despite the formal declaration of independence from the 'western' patriarchs in 424, the church in Persia had continued to lean on its Antiochene neighbour. Now, with the two-nature doctrine repudiated, ecclesiastical sentiment fell into line with political prudence. At synods held at Baylhapat in Susiana and at the capital, Seleucia, in April 484 and February 486 respectively, the creed of the church in Persia was defined as confession of the incarnation 'of two natures of Godhead and manhood, and let no one of us venture to introduce mixture, confusion or blending into the diversities of these two natures'. Both remained unchanged in their own characteristics, joined only in one majesty and adoration. This was pure Theodore. There was no reference to a *communicatio idiomatum*. Both the *Henotikon* and the *Tome* were thus repudiated, and repudiated partly because the Persian Christians wished expressly that their religion should not be the same as that of the Roman Empire. The Nestorian church had come into being, and after 489 its school at Nisibis provided it with a stronghold on the frontier with the empire.[2]

Meantime, in Antioch, Peter the Fuller consecrated a young Syrian agitator against Calendio, named Xenaias,[3] as *Chorepiscopos* and then in 485 metropolitan of Hierapolis (Maboug), the capital of the province of Euphratesia which had been hitherto largely pro-Nestorian. Nestorian

---

[1] Theophanes, *Chron.* A.M. 5982 (ed. Classen, I, 207); also, Evagrius, *HE* III. 16.

[2] See J. Labourt, *Le Christianisme dans l'empire perse* (Paris, 1904), pp. 131–41. Documents cited from B. J. Kidd, *Documents illustrative of the History of the Church*, vol. II (London, S.P.C.K., 1936), nos. 155 and 236. For the political motive for Persian preference for Nestorianism, see Michael the Syrian, *Chron.* VIII. 14, and John of Ephesus, *Life of Simeon the Bishop* (ed. Brooks), PO 17, p. 142. Nestorian bishops accused the Persian Monophysites of being 'traitors' to the king of Persia since their faith agreed with that of the Romans.

[3] See the monograph of A. de Halleux, *Philoxène de Mabbog, sa vie, ses écrits et sa théologie* (Louvain, 1963), part I on Philoxenus' career, reviewed by L. Abramowski, *RHE* 60, 1965, pp. 859–66. Xenaias had already been in the capital in 482 to protest against Calendio's election.

stalwarts a generation or so back, such as Andrew of Samosata, Theodoret of Cyrrhus and John of Germanicia, all came from this province. At Maboug itself the citizens had rejected Basiliscus' encyclical[1] with scorn. Now, however, a change set in and a generation later Euphratesia appears to have been won over for the opposite party. A large synod held by Peter in the same year consisting of the bishops from nearly every province of his patriarchate indicates that the *Henotikon*, albeit variously interpreted, was accepted.

Variety of interpretation was to be the order of the day. In Palestine where the terms of the compromise had originally owed some of their inspiration to the Patriarch Martyrius, opinion even among the monks was beginning to move decisively in favour of Chalcedon. Though Alexandria and Jerusalem remained in communion[2] and Monophysite bastions like Peter of Iberia's monastery at Maiuma retained their influence in the capital,[3] the *lavrae* springing up near Jerusalem and in eastern Palestine were tending increasingly to accept the council. One of the men behind this change was Sabas. In 483 this disciple of the Chalcedonian leader Euthymius founded a great *lavra* of 400 monks centred on a cave in a gorge on the River Kedron, and in the next decade he worked tirelessly to found others. His appointment in 494 by the Patriarch Sallust (486–94) as archimandrite of all the Palestinian *lavrae* was a portent. The episcopate was also moving in the same direction. From the *Life of Peter of Iberia* one gains the impression that by this time the opponents of Chalcedon were in the minority, islands of the steadfast in the sea of Chalcedonian conformity.[4] Despite

---

[1] Theodore Lector, *HE* (fragments, ed. Miller), p. 402. For the province's religious allegiance *circa* 500, see E. Honigmann, 'Evêques et Evêchés monophysites d'Asie antérieur au VIe siècle', *CSCO*, Subsidia 2 (Louvain, 1951), p. 66.

[2] Zacharias Rhetor, *HE* VII. 1 (ed. Brooks, *CSCO* III. 6, p. 13) – the joint démarche by Sallustius and Athanasius II to the emperor against Euphemius accusing the latter of heresy, *circa* 494. For the tendency towards Chalcedon by the monks and Sabas' influence, see Chitty, *The Desert a City*, ch. 6.

[3] See John Rufus, *Vita Petri Iberi* (ed. Raabe), p. 98. The ascetic Isaiah had 'many friends in Constantinople'.

[4] John Rufus singles out the bishop of Arca as 'a man of woe, overbold and all foul', but he was able to force Peter to leave his city despite the attitude of some of the chief men there: *Vita Petri Iberi*, p. 99. The neighbouring city of Orthosias was also in Chalcedonian control. Severus later claimed (*Ep.* 38, ed. Brooks, *PO* 12. 2, p. 294) that 'we, the few in number and small, by God's help completely checked the synod of Chalcedon that was already acting as absolute shepherd of the churches', and mentions Peter of Iberia, Bishop Theodosius of Antinoë and the monk Isaiah as among the very few anti-Chalcedonian stalwarts of the time.

The rise of the Monophysite movement

emergent tensions, however, for the remainder of the reign of Zeno the Roman east was outwardly united on the basis of the *Henotikon*. So far as the records go, there was no bishop in office who rejected it.[1] To that extent Zeno deserved his subsequent reputation among the Monophysites as an emperor 'who died religiously'.[2]

The years 488–91 ushered in a new phase. In turn, Peter the Fuller (488), Acacius (489) and his successor Fravitta (March 490),[3] Peter Mongus (490) and the Emperor Zeno (April 491) passed from the scene, and in February of the following year Felix III of Rome followed them. In Constantinople the *ekboeseis* that greeted Zeno's widow, Ariadne, on the death of her husband showed clearly what the people expected of the new Augustus. 'Long live the Augusta. Give the world an orthodox emperor.' Ariadne's speech was read for her by the *magister a libellis*. 'Anticipating your request we have commanded the illustrious ministers, the sacred Senate, with the approval of the brave armies to select a Christian and Roman emperor, endowed with every royal virtue, not a slave to money, and who is, as far as man may be, free from every human vice.' *People*: 'Ariadne Augusta, thou conquerest [shouted in Latin]. O heavenly king, give the world a *basileus* who is not avaricious.' Ariadne went on to ask for a short delay until after Zeno's funeral and the crowd dispersed after their demand that 'the thieving prefect of the city' be sacked and 'no foreigner be imposed on the Romans' was heard.[4] There was now real 'Roman' and 'Chalcedonian' patriotism in the capital and a ruler who failed to heed either might well lose his diadem.

In the event, Ariadne's choice was a curious one. The decurion silentiary

---

[1] Honigmann, 'Evêques et Evêchés monophysites', p. 6.

[2] For Zeno's anti-Chalcedonian outlook towards the end of his reign, see Evagrius, *HE* III. 22, and for his patronage of Peter of Iberia and Isaiah the Egyptian, see John Rufus, *Vita Petri Iberi* (ed. Raabe), p. 98, and Zacharias Rhetor, *HE* VI. 3. For 'dying religiously', Zacharias Scholasticus, *Vita Severi* (ed. Kugener), p. 35 and Kugener's note thereto.

[3] Fravitta lasted four months only. He informed both Pope Felix and Peter Mongus officially of his election: Felix, *Ep.* 14 (*Epist. rom. pontif.*, ed. Thiel), and Zacharias Rhetor, *HE* VI. 5. For the events of this period see G. Bardy's study, 'Sous le régime de l'Hénotique; la politique religieuse d'Anastase', ch. 2 of part 2 of *De la mort de Théodose à l'élection de Grégoire le Grand*, ed. A. Fliche and V. Martin, *Histoire de l'église*, vol. IV (valuable bibliography, pp. 299–300).

[4] From a contemporary document preserved in Constantine Porphyrogenitus, *De cerimoniis* (ed. Reiscke) I. 92; translation cited from Bury, *History of the Later Roman Empire*, II, 430.

Anastasius was a civil servant aged about 60.[1] He was well known in the capital but for a mixture of reasons. On the one hand, he was exceedingly generous in his almsgiving and care of orphans, but his doctrinal views were suspect. According to Theodore, his mother had been Manichaean and his uncle an Arian.[1a] He himself was a religious enthusiast, 'having generally the reputation of holding the Manichaean doctrine'.[2] To westerners he was a 'Eutychian', a heretic who must be restored to the church.[3] He gave unashamedly heterodox teaching in church to anyone who cared to listen to him.[4] Only a short time previously the new patriarch, Euphemius (490–6), a strong Chalcedonian and a former monk from Apamea where conflict between the two sides was bitter, had forbidden him to do this and expelled him from the church. Now, after stigmatising the new emperor as unworthy to rule over Christians, he insisted that before he took part in any coronation ceremony Anastasius should be required to sign a written declaration of orthodoxy.[5] This he did, and married Ariadne on 20 May.

This elderly couple were to govern the empire between them for 27 years. They were remarkably successful. The overweening power of the Isaurians in the capital was broken. In 498 Anastasius seized on the occasion of a riot in the Hippodrome to expel them from the capital. Their armed resistance was then crushed and they were resettled in Anatolia. The Isaurians had served their purpose, for from now on, except for the interlude of Vitalian's ascendancy (514–18), the capital was never again to be threatened by Germanic troops. On the eastern frontier the indecisive war with Persia (502–5) resulted in the construction of the great base at Dara over against the Persian strongpoint of Nisibis as a permanent guard to the Roman domains. In Thrace the Long Walls were built across the peninsula to give the capital a fortified perimeter come what may (Evagrius, *HE* III. 38). In the west, a *modus vivendi* was struck with Theodoric in 498, in which Anastasius recognised the latter as *rex* and returned to him the *ornamenta palatii*. Despite the outbreak of war in 505, this retained Italy

---

[1] Zacharias Rhetor calls him 'decurio silentiarius' (*HE* VII. 1). This seems preferable to imagining him as having eyes with a double pupil (δίκορος) as per Theophanes, *Chron.* A.M. 5983 (ed. Classen, I, 211). [1a] In Theodore Lector, *HE* (ed. Hansen, p. 126).

[2] Evagrius, *HE* III. 32; compare Theophanes, *Chron.* A.M. 5982 and 5983, for whom Anastasius was a Eutychian and a favourer of Manichaeans.

[3] Paul the Deacon, *Historiae Romanae* XVI. 2: 'Hic [Anastasius] Romani decus imperii Eutychianae haereseos inluvie maculavit' (ed. Droysen, p. 216).

[4] Theophanes, *Chron.* A.M. 5982 (ed. Classen, I, 208).

[5] Evagrius, *HE* III. 32.

The rise of the Monophysite movement

nominally within the empire but gave the reality of power to the Gothic king. A similar policy was applied to the now much more pliant Vandal kingdom in Africa. Financial and economic reforms gave the empire a fairer system of taxation by the abolition of the *chrysargyron* or trade tax, and some relief to the urban councils from the burden of assessing and collecting the taxes. There was an improvement in the status of the peasant, and more important, the institution in 498 of a new large bronze coin which after an interval of nearly a century provided the ordinary provincial with a reliable system of small change. Parsimonious though he was, Anastasius was one of the few Byzantine rulers to leave his successor with a well-stocked treasury.[1]

Until 510, whatever his own predilections, his religious policy was based on the letter of the *Henotikon*.[2] He was, Evagrius states, a man of peace who disliked religious change and, in particular, strife for or against Chalcedon.[3] This is certainly true of the first two decades of his rule. His episcopal choices such as Macedonius, patriarch of Constantinople from 496 to 511, and Flavian II of Antioch, 498–512, were ecclesiastics who were loyal to the decree and averse to trouble-makers.[4] There were however disadvantages, apart from the break with Rome. The period was remembered as one of confusion. Evagrius (III. 30) says that 'during these times the Council of Chalcedon was neither openly proclaimed, nor yet repudiated by all; but the bishops acted each according to his own opinion'. Most dioceses were therefore divided into three parties, the Chalcedonians, the Monophysites and a middle party that supported the *Henotikon*, and already *de facto* three rival churches no longer in communion with each other were coming into being. This was true especially in the years 512–518.

Only in Egypt does there seem to have been almost complete unanimity,

---

[1] In 518 there was a stock of 320,000 lbs. of gold in the treasury: see D. M. Metcalf, *The Origins of the Anastasian Currency Reform* (Amsterdam, 1969), p. 12.

[2] For the non-existence of the so-called Council of Constantinople of either 499 or 507, recorded by Victor of Tunnuna, *Chron.* ad ann. 499 (ed. Mommsen, p. 193, lines 14–30) and designed to condemn all the Antiochene enemies of the Twelve Anathemas, see L. Abramowski, 'La Prétendue Condemnation de Diodore de Tarse en 499', *Mélanges, RHE* 60, 1965, pp. 64–5.

[3] Evagrius, *HE* III. 30.

[4] Note, for instance, Flavian's alleged remark to Anastasius regarding Philoxenus' efforts to have the *Tome* and Chalcedon anathematised: 'We anathematise each in its place. We don't want to stir up the dragon against us' (*Chron. ad ann. 846*, ed. Brooks and Chabot, p. 168).

and this directed against Chalcedon and the *Tome*. Peter Mongus finally insisted on cursing both and only death saved him from another open conflict with the capital.¹ Despite protests from Constantinople, his successor, Athanasius II, 'openly and freely' copied him,² and so did the later patriarchs John Hemula and John of Nikiou when invited by the Patriarch of Constantinople to accept Chalcedon. The great landowners found ecclesiastical independence the best means of favouring the maintenance of a feudal society.³ Monophysitism was being accepted for quite different reasons by the local aristocracy, wealthy families such as Apion's, and by the Copts. Communion, however, with Constantinople was not broken and the Proterian succession was not continued. At the other extreme, the *Acephaloi* who had broken away from Peter Mongus at the time of the *Henotikon* did not go to the length of establishing a rival patriarchate. They remained in being, harassing successive patriarchs of Alexandria and demonstrating a growing tendency against any accommodation with the imperial capital.

For nearly twenty years, however, Anastasius' official policy was to attempt to restore religious unity in the empire, including the ending of the schism between Old and New Rome. His patriarch, Euphemius, was of the same mind. He accepted Chalcedon, had notified Pope Felix of his succession on the death of the short-lived Fravitta (March 490), and had even bid for his support against the defiance of Chalcedon demonstrated by the new patriarch of Alexandria, Athanasius II.⁴ That anything less than an open disavowal of Acacius and the withdrawal of the *Henotikon* would have healed the breach is doubtful,⁵ but Felix's successor, his archdeacon Gelasius, rendered hopes in this direction vain. Gelasius (March 492–

---

¹ Zacharias Rhetor, *HE* VII. 1.

² Zacharias Rhetor, *HE* VII. 1 (ed. Brooks, *CSCO* III. 6, p. 13): 'qui apertius ac liberius synodum et Tomum anathematizabat'.

³ Hardy, *Christian Egypt*, pp. 119–20, and Stein, *Bas-Empire*, II, 162. Apion himself fell into disgrace in 510 and found himself ordained presbyter.

⁴ Zacharias Rhetor, *HE* VII. 1: 'et [Euphemius] et Felicem Romae in auxilium vocabat'. Compare Theophanes, *Chron.* A.M. 5983 (ed. Classen, I, 209) and Evagrius, *HE* III. 23. Felix regarded Euphemius' synodical letter as orthodox, but refused to accept him as bishop, as he would not remove Acacius *and* Fravitta from the diptychs (*Ep.* 12). The insistence on Fravitta's condemnation was ominous.

⁵ Felix, *Ep.* 15 (*Epist. rom. pontif.*, ed. Thiel = *Coll. Berolinensis* 34, Schwartz, *PS*, p. 83), to Zeno: 'Quia dum per synodum Chalcedonensem... Eutychen atque Dioscorum constet esse damnatos et eorum sectatores plurimis illarum partium documentis Timotheus et Petrus extitisse monstrentur, atque eorum communionem etiam esse perhibeatur secutus Acacius.'

November 496), perhaps an African by birth, was a man of abounding energy cast in an utterly uncompromising mould and obsessed by fears of his own fate at the Day of Judgement. He was a Tertullianist in the papal saddle. His style of writing, compact, terse and trenchant, would have pleased his master. To those who did not agree he was unsparing. His irony was biting. 'One will discover before the sovereign Judge', he wrote to Euphemius, 'whether I am as you think harsh, severe, too unbending and difficult towards you.'[1] He failed even to announce his own election in Constantinople and treated Euphemius' protest as a mere piece of arrogance.[2] In the four and a half years he occupied the papal throne relations between the eastern and western churches grew perceptibly worse.

The detail of the negotiations between Gelasius and the east cannot be entered upon here.[3] Three points, however, may be stressed as relevant to the development of permanent anti-western sentiment in the east. First, though the Byzantines were anxious to heal the breach, as Gelasius admitted, the Pope offered no compromise. Acacius was a Eutychist 'by association'. He had entered into communion with Peter Mongus who was the direct heir of Timothy the Cat, Eutyches and Dioscorus, and he therefore shared their damnation. The 'root of his doctrine was tainted'. *In consortium damnatorum est damnatus Acacius*.[4] One may detect in these and other similar oft-reiterated statements an underlying 'African' influence, for both Cyprian and Donatus had stressed the contagious effect of association with heretics or apostates.[5] In face of this obduracy, arguments that Acacius could not oppose the emperor's will, that he had initiated no heresy, that though he was bishop of the imperial city he had not been

---

[1] Gelasius, *Ep.* 3. 16 (Thiel, p. 320 = *Coll. Veronensis* 12, Schwartz, *PS*, pp. 49–55 at p. 55).

[2] Gelasius, *Epp.* 2 and 3. Euphemius was told he belonged to 'an alien body', and Acacius was characterised as a worse sinner than Eutyches himself, as he 'had known the truth and yet allied himself with the enemies of the truth' (*ibid.* 8). See also F. Hofmann, 'Der Kampf der Päpste um Chalkedon', in Grillmeier/Bacht, *Das Konzil von Chalkedon*, II, 52–66.

[3] See Hofmann, *ibid.* and Caspar, *Papsttums*, II, 65ff.

[4] *Commonitorium Fausto magistro* (*Coll. Veronensis* 7 = Schwartz, *PS*, p. 17): Gelasius' brief for Faustus as his envoy in the capital, published by Thiel as *Ep.* 10.

[5] See for instance Cyprian, *Ep.* 67. 4, ed. W. Hartel, *CSEL* 3. 1 (Spanish bishops), while much of the Donatist justification for their break with Caecilian rested on their claim that he had been consecrated bishop of Carthage by a 'traditor' bishop. For contagion through corrupt root, compare Petilian cited by Augustine, *Contra litteras Petiliani* II. 5. 10.

Towards a Monophysite solution, 484–512

properly condemned by a council and that the population would not abide his permanent condemnation were brushed aside.[1] Christ had raised the dead from the grave, but did not absolve them from error, he affirmed.[2] Gelasius, while stressing his own Petrine tradition, shows extreme animosity against the claims of New Rome which he blandly reduces to its pre-Nicene level as a suffragan of the bishopric of Heraclea – thus rejecting the Council of Constantinople in 381 as well as the 28th canon of Chalcedon.[3]

Secondly, whereas Leo had emphasised to Marcian the positive role of the Christian emperor in the divine plan of salvation,[4] Gelasius emphasised to Anastasius in 494 in the so-called Tome of Gelasius the utter inferiority of the imperial as compared to the papal power. The well-known sentence reads, 'There are in fact two [powers], emperor Augustus, by which this world is sovereignly (*principaliter*) governed; the consecrated authority of the bishops (*auctoritas sacrata pontificum*) and the royal power (*regalis potestas*). Of these, the responsibility of the bishops is the more weighty, since even for the rulers of men they will have to give an account at the judgement seat of God.'[5] Anastasius was addressed as 'most gracious son' and reminded that he bowed his head in humility before those who dispensed the sacraments.[6]

---

[1] Gelasius *ad episcopos Dardaniae, Coll. Avellana* 95. 2 and 43, and *Ep.* 12 *ad Anastasium, Epist. rom. pontif.*, ed. Thiel, pp. 349ff.

[2] Gelasius, *Ep.* 10. 3: 'mortuos suscitasse legimus Christum, in errore mortuos absolvisse non legimus' (Thiel, p. 342; Schwartz, *PS*, p. 16).

[3] *Coll. Avellana* 95. 21 (ed. Guenther, *CSEL* 35. 1, p. 376) = *Ep.* 26. 4, Thiel, p. 398, Gelasius *ad episcopos Dardaniae*: 'an sedem apostolicam congruebat paroeciae Heraclensis ecclesiae, id est Constantinopolitani pontificis vel quorumlibet aliorum . . .' Constantinople had no more claim to special prerogatives than Milan, Ravenna, Trier or Sirmium (*ibid.* para. 53, ed. Guenther, *CSEL* 35. 1, p. 387). See also Dvornik, *Apostolicity in Byzantium*, pp. 111ff.

[4] *Ep.* 142. 2: '. . . fidei Christianae, ob quam iustus et misericors Deus tribuit ut vobis sicut divina sunt cara, ita sint mundana subjecta'. See W. Ullmann, *The Growth of Papal Government in the Middle Ages* (London, 1955), p. 14, especially n4.

[5] Gelasius, *Ep.* 12. 2–3. Analysed by Ullman, *Growth of Papal Government*, pp. 18–20.

[6] Simplicius had called Zeno 'filius', but had hedged this about with deferential epithets, such as in *Ep.* 3 (*Epist. rom. pontif.*, ed. Thiel, p. 180), 'gloriosissime ac clementissime fili, imperator Auguste'. Felix is still deferential ('dominum filium nostrum religiosum') while Gelasius says plainly concerning Anastasius, 'filius est non praesul ecclesiae' (*Ep.* 1. 10, Thiel, pp. 287ff. = Schwartz, *PS*, p. 35; *Coll. Veronensis* 11), not the most tactful utterance to the bishops of the eastern dioceses! It is noticeable too that while Simplicius, *Ep.* 6. 2, indicates a 'teaching' role for the emperor

The rise of the Monophysite movement

Much of this had been said before in the west: the Two Swords theory had been enunciated by Hosius to Constantius II in 355.[1] Ambrose had reminded Valentinian II and Theodosius I of their status within the church,[2] and Augustine had written that the emperor could only be accounted truly happy when he was serving the church and acting as its executive arm.[3] The choice also of words 'auctoritas' and 'potestas' to define the priestly and imperial powers respectively was common form and pointed in the same direction, the one being concerned with mystical and moral authority, the other with physical power.[4] But never before had these ideas been summed up in so cogent and unbending a form. 'We judge…', 'we decide…' 'we provide…', are, as Ullmann says,[5] the expressions characteristic of a legislator. While it is true that Gelasius did not attribute powers of the *imperium* to the *sacerdotium* and also used terms of respect and even affection towards Anastasius, the significance of his words should not be lost. What had been implicit in western Christian thought since the time of Irenaeus,[6] that Christ's kingdom stood over against the empire as its political rival, was now applied to an actual political situation. Coming from the Pope to an emperor for whom the concept of imperial power was as defined in the *Henotikon*, it was an explicit recognition of the incompatibility of the Byzantine and Latin theories of the church and state.

A third factor adds to the significance of these theoretical pronouncements. Gelasius made no secret of his contempt for the Byzantines. In a letter to the bishops of Dalmatia and Dardania (i.e. Illyricum) explaining why the *Tome* of Leo must be insisted upon, the easterners are referred to as 'Greeks among whom there is no doubt that heresies abound'.[7] Greeks

('in omnibus doceas causam tibi cum deo esse communem'), Gelasius concedes one of learning only.   [1] Athanasius, *Historia Arianorum* 44.

[2] Ambrose, *Epp.* 20–1 and *Sermo contra Auxentium* 36 (*PL* 16, col. 1061). See above, pp. 98–9.

[3] *De civitate Dei* v. 24 and 26. Compare Leo, *Ep.* 104, where the emperor's efforts to quell heresy are to be regarded as assisting the Pope in the same task.

[4] E.g. Leo, *Ep.* 156. 3 (to Leo I): 'Debes incunctanter advertere regiam potestatem tibi non solum mundi regimen sed maxime ad praesidium esse collatam.' See F. Dvornik, 'Pope Gelasius and the emperor Anastasius I', *BZ* 44, 1951, pp. 111–16.

[5] Ullmann, *Growth of Papal Government*, p. 12 n5.

[6] See Ehrhardt, *Politische Metaphysik*, II, 104ff.

[7] Gelasius (*Ep.* 7. 2), *episcopis per Dardaniam constitutis*, *Epist. rom. pontif.*, ed. Thiel, p. 335 = *Coll. Avellana* 79 (ed. Guenther, *CSEL* 35. 1, p. 220): 'Apud Graecos, quibus multas haereses abundare non dubium est…' By the mid-sixth century the Goths were also regarding the Byzantines simply as 'Greeks'.

and heretical teachings in his own and previous periods were associated in his mind. In his apparently intentional belittlement of 'the Greeks' he is the forerunner of those papal writers in the early European Middle Ages who insisted on addressing the Byzantine emperor as 'imperator Graecorum'.[1] Also, in his not unsuccessful effort to build up a strong pro-papal feeling in the two mainly Latin-speaking provinces of the empire Moesia and Dardania (Upper Macedonia) he was forging a counterweight to the hitherto predominant Syrian and Egyptian influence in the ecclesiastical affairs of the empire. As always, control of Illyricum remained a papal objective. The revolt of Vitalian and the Catholic reaction under Justin each indicated that the residual Latin-speaking areas of the empire could not be left out of account so long as a settlement with Rome appeared desirable and possible. Gelasius was the true architect of the papal victory in 519.

Italian ecclesiastical sentiment at the time[2] and medieval Italian patriotism were to take the side of Gelasius, for the reward of his short-lived successor, Anastasius II, November 496–November 498, was consignment by Dante to the sixth circle of the Inferno.[3] Anastasius, supported by the Roman senate, immediately attempted to reverse the policies of Gelasius.[4] In a letter written at the beginning of his pontificate, remarkably friendly in tone, he stated his unequivocal aim of restoring peace,[5] on the specific condition that the name of Acacius was dropped from the diptychs,[6] and that the emperor used his influence to persuade the Alexandrians to return to 'Catholic peace'. No reference was made to Fravitta, nor to Gelasius' various demands and admonitions. An explicit assurance was given that sacraments, including baptisms by Acacius and clergy ordained by him,

---

[1] See D. M. Nicol, 'The Byzantine view of Western Europe', *Greek, Roman and Byzantine Studies* 8, no. 4, 1967, pp. 315–39 at p. 318.

[2] Note the repeated salutations as to an emperor by the bishops and clergy at the council summoned by Gelasius on 13 May 495 to absolve Misenus: 'Vicarium Christi te videmus', 'apostolum Petri te videmus', 'exaudi Christe: Gelasio vita' = *Coll. Avellana* 103 (ed. Guenther, *CSEL* 35. 1, p. 487).

[3] *Inferno* XI. 8–9.

[4] See Schwartz, *PS*, pp. 226–30, and W. Ensslin, *Theodorich der Grosse* (Munich, 1947), pp. 107–9.

[5] *Ep.* 1. 1 (*Epist. rom. pontif.*, ed. Thiel, p. 615).

[6] *Ibid.* 3: 'Precamur igitur clementiam vestram, ut specialiter nomen taceatur Acacii.' This could be taken to mean (as Justin and Justinian assumed) that only Acacius need be dropped and not his successor – especially if sacraments at Acacius' hands were regarded as valid. See below, p. 244.

would be regarded as valid.¹ Acacius himself was not condemned as heretical but because of his 'excesses and presumptions'.² The Pope sent legates to explain his views more fully to the emperor personally, and like Leo at the time of the emperor Leo's 'plebiscite' was ready to discuss 'ambiguities' in the Greek version of his *Tome*. An embassy was also despatched by the senate under the *princeps senatus*, the patrician Festus, early in 497 to secure the emperor's recognition of Theodoric's position in Italy. This was successfully accomplished after a second mission at the end of the year, but Festus also intimated that the Pope could be persuaded to sign the *Henotikon* (if the reference hostile to Chalcedon were omitted).³ That there was the shadow of a possibility of this is evident from the latter's readiness to open negotiations with representatives of the Alexandrian Patriarch Athanasius II, in the capital. Here, too, the legates found a surprising degree of conciliation. The dogmatic statement which the Alexandrians gave them was flattering to the susceptibilities of the Roman see, emphasising the links that united the sees of Peter and Mark 'his imitator', and their joint immaculate guardianship of the true faith.⁴ It had been 'the enemy of the human race' (the Devil) that had caused division, through Leo's letters to the Council of Chalcedon being susceptible to an interpretation by the 'Nestorian heretics' Theodoret of Cyrrhus and his supporters, in a sense contrary to the creed of Nicaea. The Greek translation of these letters had made them appear to vindicate Nestorian blasphemy. Hence, 'our Godloving people divided itself from the unity of the Roman Church'. Mutual charges of heresy were unjustified, and the Alexandrians proceeded to put forward their confession of faith on the basis of the *Henotikon*, 'the onlybegotten Son of God was one whether in his miracles or indeed his sufferings (*passiones*)', and including acceptance of the Twelve Anathemas of Cyril. The guardians of this faith had been Dioscorus, Timothy (the Cat)

¹ *Ibid.*, and 9. Here, of course, Anastasius was following Augustinian teaching in the Donatist controversy on the validity of sacraments given by those outside the church (see Augustine, *De baptismo contra Donatistas* IV. 115 and *Contra epist. Parmeniani* II. 11). Gelasius, *Ep.* 12. 10, had pointed to the western acceptance of ordinations by Macedonius and Nestorius, but such was his hatred of the name of Acacius that he would not bring himself explicitly to accept the latter's sacraments.
² *Ep.* 3: 'Quantos vero excessus atque praesumptiones habuerit Acacius.'
³ Theodore Lector, *HE* II. 17.
⁴ Anastasius, *Ep.* 5 (*Epist. rom. pontif.*, ed. Thiel, pp. 628–33 = *Coll. Avellana* 102): 'Petrum memoramus beatum apostolum, cujus per omnia sanctus evangelista Marcus exstitit imitator.'

and Peter (Mongus), and if the Pope had aught against them he should either prove his case or restore them to the diptychs. Thus unity between the two churches could be restored.

Looking at the tone of the correspondence, it seems evident that this was one of the few occasions in the tangled history of the relations between east and west in the century following Chalcedon when the protagonists were willing to state their differences without heat and to seek solutions. Peace between the two Romes could be made on the basis of the *Henotikon* without the final offensive reference to Chalcedon,[1] the acknowledgement of the precedence of Old Rome, and the silent dropping of Acacius from the diptychs. With Alexandria restoration of unity with Rome would have been more difficult, but the tendency of the Alexandrian *Libellus* was to stress common ground with the translators as the scapegoats, and no mention was made on either side of the claims of John Talaia. It was an astonishing change from the menace and aggression of Gelasius.

The policy of Anastasius II has been dismissed as an aberration. This, however, was far from the way it was regarded by Justin and Justinian in negotiations with Hormisdas designed to induce the latter to agree to a flexible execution of the agreement that ended the Acacian schism in 519.[2] A party within the church in Rome was anxious for close co-operation with Constantinople. Its existence helps to explain later the relationship between Justinian and Vigilius. As it was, there were strong reasons why the Pope should seek the re-establishment of unity with Constantinople at this time. Ultimately, the emperor was the only person who could help the Catholic populations under Arian rule in Africa and Italy itself. If Theodoric was friendly, the successive Vandal kings Huneric (477–84) and Gunthamund (484–96) were hostile towards the Catholics and many of these were glad to find asylum at Constantinople. It was useless for Gelasius to tell exiled African bishops that Antichrist was striking there as much as in their homeland.[3] They were well aware that only the Byzantine emperor could restore them.

---

[1] The clause was, 'but everything different that has been believed or shall be believed both now or in any time, either at Chalcedon or at any synod whatsoever, we anathematise'.

[2] See Justin's emphatic reminder to Hormisdas, *Ep.* 132 (Thiel, p. 954 = *Coll. Avellana* 232, ed. Guenther, *CSEL* 35. 2, p. 702) of 9 September 520: 'Anastasius... palam aperteque constituerit, cum ob hoc idem scriberet negotium decessori nostro, satis esse pacem affectantibus, si nomen tantum reticeatur Acacii.' See below, p. 244.

[3] Gelasius to Bishop Succonius, *Ep.* 9 (Thiel, p. 339 = *Coll. Veronensis* 13, Schwartz, *PS*, pp. 56–7): 'Itane non senseras, quod duobus cornibus praeludendo uno eodemque

The rise of the Monophysite movement

Pope Anastasius died too soon for his far-reaching plans to come into effect. The sequel showed how the popular forces in Rome were moving away from ideals of a universal Roman world to more local loyalties represented by an 'Italian' ruler in Ravenna and a pope in the Gelasian tradition. Schism in Rome between the 'Anastasian' and 'Gelasian' factions represented by the arch-presbyter Laurentius[1] and Pope Symmachus (498–514) prevented further significant developments between east and west for a decade. The attempt, however, to place a pro-Byzantine pope on the papal throne failed. Like Damasus before him, Symmachus found that civil charges of inciting disorder and adultery provided a more realistic measure of the power of his see than lofty claims put forward in his predecessor's encyclicals and letters to the distant emperor. Theodoric found himself in the position of Constantine and Valentinian I, the judge of a bishop in a matter of civil law. It was 506 before Symmachus was able to clear himself completely but then his attitude towards the emperor was anything but conciliatory. Rome was not prepared to accept the leadership of Constantinople. Only surrender by the latter would end the schism.

Meantime at Constantinople Anastasius quarrelled with Euphemius because the latter was determined that the emperor's written assent to Chalcedon should be preserved and if necessary asserted. In 496 the patriarch found himself accused of intrigues with the Isaurians, having previously been indicted as a heretic by his colleagues of Alexandria and Jerusalem acting in unwonted concord.[2] He was deposed by a synod with Anastasius' agreement and he ended his days in the monastery of the Euchites in Pontus. The new patriarch, Macedonius (496–511), was the nephew of the former patriarch Gennadius. Though Chalcedonian in sympathy and anxious to heal the schism with Rome,[3] he signed the

tempore non minus in Oriente quam in Africa Iesum solvere niteretur Antichristus?' Gelasius was angry that Succonius had put himself in communion with the clergy of the capital and the east generally. For African Catholics' wistful hopes centred on Byzantium during Huneric's persecution in 484, see Victor of Vita, *Historia persecutionis africanae provinciae* (ed. Petschenig), III. 68. Also III. 30, concerning the subdeacon Reparatus at the court of Zeno.

[1] Laurentius, it was alleged, was also ready to accept the *Henotikon*: see Landolphus, *Additamenta ad Pauli historiam romanam* LVII. 216 (ed. Droysen, p. 364).

[2] Zacharias Rhetor, *HE* VII. 1, associates this démarche with Euphemius' downfall. It can hardly have been the direct cause as Sallustius died in 494 and Euphemius was not deposed until 496. It no doubt had its effect on the emperor's confidence in him.

[3] Theodore Lector says that the emperor prevented him from sending his synodical letter to Pope Anastasius (*HE* II. 17).

Henotikon. That this remained the touchstone of orthodoxy was confirmed by the emperor's choice of Flavian as patriarch of Antioch in 498. Flavian had previously represented his see in the capital, and he too signed assent to the *Henotikon.*

So matters continued for a decade largely occupied with fighting on the Persian frontier, 502–5, and against Theodoric in Pannonia in 508 – the latter conflict significant for the underlying ill will between the empire and the Latin west. In contrast, the war against Persia emphasised the ultimate dependence of the anti-Chalcedonians in the east on the emperor, for, as noted, since 484 the only recognised Christianity in Persia was Nestorian; and a number of Persian Monophysites found shelter within the empire's frontier. Their presence, however, increased local unrest, for they engaged in agitation against Flavian and in this they were abetted by the metropolitan of Euphratesia, Philoxenus.[1] In 508 the capital received a new and forceful visitor in the person of the monk Severus, accompanied by 300 Palestinian monks. He had been sent by his monastery at Maiuma to defend its interests against the pro-Chalcedonian enterprises of a turbulent monk from Egypt named Nephalius,[2] supported by the patriarch of Jerusalem, Elias.

SEVERUS OF ANTIOCH

Severus is one of the great figures of the religious history of the eastern Mediterranean.[3] He came from the type of wealthy landowning family which for generations had acted as the religious and political leaders of their communities. Like them he saw Christianity as a rational creed and a higher philosophy based on the Bible and the teachings of the fathers, but which

[1] For 'frequent embassies' from the Persian anti-Nestorian Christians to Anastasius, see Zacharius Scholasticus, *Vita Severi* (ed. Kugener), p. 112.

[2] Nephalius had been a fervent Monophysite twenty years before, but had changed his views (Zacharias Scholasticus, *Vita Severi*, ed. Kugener, pp. 100ff.). He had been in the capital in 499, and was at this stage an agitator, 'turbator populi' (Zacharias Rhetor, *HE* VI. 1). For his theology, see Ch. Moeller, 'Nephalius d'Alexandrie; un représentant de la Christologie néochalcédonienne au début du VIe siècle', *RHE* 40, 1944–5, pp. 73–140.

[3] For a sketch of Severus' life and the dating of his *Cathedral Homilies*, see M. Brière, *PO* 29. 1, pp. 9–72, and for an interesting appreciation which emphasises the influence of Severus' long flirtation with philosophic paganism and aptitude for a legal career on his life and work, see W. Bauer, 'Die Severus-Vita des Zacharias Rhetor', in *Aufsätze und kleine Schriften*, ed. G. Strecker (Tübingen, 1967), pp. 210–28.

one reached through the hard preparatory training of the philosophic schools. As Basil had before him, he combined personal asceticism with intense administrative activity and dedication in the service of a cause. He was born in Sozopolis in Pisidia in about 465.[1] His grandfather had been bishop of the town at the time of Ephesus I and had been among the 200 bishops who had deposed Nestorius. The Christianity of the family was, however, tinged strongly with philosophy, and Severus was a lover of Libanius before he was introduced by a friend to Basil of Caesarea's refutations of the philosopher.[2] Like Origen's famous pupil Gregory the Wonderworker he was destined for a legal career, and as a young man he went down with his elder brother to Alexandria to study Greek and Latin grammar. Then in about 486 he moved on to Berytus, to the school of Leontius, to learn jurisprudence. It was while he was at Berytus that he came into contact with keen propagandists for the monastic way of life, perhaps even with Peter of Iberia, who visited the city in 488. Years later, when in exile in Alexandria, he acknowledges how he came to reject 'the evil Chalcedonian impiety' and drew near to orthodoxy through Peter. 'This communion I so hold, I so draw near, as I drew near in it with the highest assurance and a fixed mind, when our holy father Peter of Iberia was offering and was performing the rational sacrifice.'[3] He accepted baptism, gave up the law, decided on the monastic ideal and visited Jerusalem. Then he stayed in the monastery of Romanus[4] in the wilderness near Eleutheropolis. Thoroughly imbued with Romanus' ideas he betook himself to Peter's monastery at Maiuma. He was ordained presbyter and founded his own house nearby, largely at his own expense. By 500 he had turned all his philosophical training to the service of the anti-Chalcedonian cause.

There are two Syriac *Lives* of Severus, one by his friend Zacharias Scholasticus (the lawyer), later allegedly bishop of Mitylene (?),[5] written

[1] It may be interesting that Sozopolis had been one of the centres of the Synousiasts in the 370s, who believed like Apollinarius that Christ's body was 'from heaven'. See Basil, *Ep.* 161 (*PG* 32, cols. 968–72).

[2] Zacharias Scholasticus, *Vita Severi* (ed. Kugener), p. 13.

[3] *Select Letters* v. 11 (ed. Brooks, p. 328).

[4] Athanasius Scriptor, author of the Ethiopian *Life* (or *Conflict*) of Severus, places great emphasis on Romanus' influence on Severus' ideas. His monastery was one of the remaining anti-Chalcedonian centres in Palestine (ed. Goodspeed and Crum, pp. 600–7).

[5] We have distinguished this Zacharias, friend and contemporary of Severus, from the writer of the documents covering the period 451–91 that form books IV, V

while Severus was patriarch of Antioch, and the other by John, abbot (*hegoumenos*) of the monastery of Beith-Aphthonia in Syria (died 536).[1] Both are valuable contemporary records. They were originally written in Greek, but have survived only in Syriac translation. That of Zacharias is extremely interesting concerning Severus' early life. It seems that for a long time he was accused of being a pagan at heart, and nearly two-thirds of the *Life* is devoted to clearing the patriarch of the charges that neither at Alexandria nor Berytus had he shown any real enthusiasm for the faith. The result is an extraordinarily interesting picture of ordinary student life in both centres of learning, including insights into the relations between professors and students and among the latter, the arrogance of the senior years towards the junior. Superficially, practically everyone was a Christian; but in fact, believing and practising Christians formed a small minority, a sort of 'ginger group', the so-called 'Philoponoi', rather officious and pious intellectuals, bent on sniffing out the remains of paganism. There were plenty. In Alexandria there were pagan cells organised by prominent teachers of grammar,[2] stories of a buried temple of Isis on the site of which the power of the goddess was still strong and sacrifices in her honour and that of other Egyptian and Roman deities took place.[3] One hears, too, of a

and VI of the *Ecclesiastical History* of Zacharias, and are inclined also to separate both from the bishop of Mitylene who signed the document condemning Severus in 536. The case is difficult, and comes down to a fine balance whether one believes that one man could be so enthusiastic a defender of Severus' reputation, yet as bishop of Mitylene condemn him without reserve, and could combine the distinctive Syrian-Palestinian flavour and zeal for Monophysitism of the *Lives* of Severus and the monk Isaiah with the balanced Henoticism and more ecumenical approach to the problems of the day shown by the historian Zacharias. The long list of works attributed by G. Bardy in his study of Zacharias in 'Zacharie le Rhéteur', *DTC* 30, cols. 3676–80, are so varied in outlook as to be hardly possible for even a Vicar of Bray to write. See however, E. Honigmann, 'Patristic studies', in *Studi e Testi* 173 (Vatican City, 1952), pp. 194–204, for a reasoned defence of the identification of Zacharias Rhetor with Zacharias Scholasticus.

[1] Both published by M. A. Kugener in *PO* 2. In addition there is an Ethiopian *Life* by Athanasius Scriptor who claimed to be a contemporary of Severus, published in *PO* 4, ed. E. J. Goodspeed (Ethiopian) and W. E. Crum (Coptic fragments).

[2] Zacharias Scholasticus, *Vita Severi* (ed. Kugener), p. 15. Severus was rumoured to have sacrificed to the gods while a student: *ibid.* pp. 9 and 75. For the ramifications of paganism in Alexandria among the grammarians there, see J. Maspero, 'Horapollon et la fin du paganisme égyptien', *Bull. de l'institut français d'archéologie orientale* 11, 1914, pp. 163–94.

[3] Zacharias Scholasticus, *Vita Severi* (ed. Kugener), p. 19.

great cache of heathen trophies hidden in a room covered with hieroglyphs in a village outside Alexandria after their evacuation from Memphis by pagan zealots. Secret sacrifices took place and blood-stained altars betrayed their character.[1] All this took place under the nose of the monks and the authorities.

At Berytus, paganism was, if anything, more active. Once more we hear of students dabbling in magic – an international group, including George of Thessalonica, Chrysaorius of Tralles, Asclepiodotus of Heliopolis and 'an Armenian and others of like brand', inspired by John the Fuller from Thebes in Egypt.[2] Their attempt to sacrifice John's Ethiopian slave in the circus of Berytus at dead of night in order to use his brain to win the charms of a beautiful woman with the help of demons, failed owing to the opportune arrival of passers-by. Another attempt, this time treasure hunting, using Persian and Egyptian magic and abetted even by clergy, coincided with an earthquake.[3] The misguided students were apparently confronted with their misdeeds by their fellows, among whom was Severus. They were forced to hand over their books of magic and promised to reform, not, however, before they had tried to raise a riot against their tormentors. An interesting sidelight on the affair was the fact that the priest who was custodian of a chapel called the Second Martyrion[4] was quite ready to assist in pillaging his own treasury in order to provide valuable objects which could be used for magical purposes, to locate a supposed buried treasure of King Darius.[5] Severus' own master, Leontius, also was a pagan and a spare-time magician, specialising in horoscopes and predictions.[6] On the other hand, the importance of the ultra-Christians is hard to exaggerate. Men like Evagrius of Samosata, their leader at Berytus in Severus' time, were in contact with the great monastic chiefs of the day. The resulting steady trickle of highly educated men into the 'philosophic', i.e. monastic, life prevented monasticism degenerating into ignorant fanaticism and provided the Monophysites with their political leaders and trained theologians.[7]

---

[1] *Ibid.* pp. 27–31.
[2] Zacharias Scholasticus, *Vita Severi* (ed. Kugener), pp. 57ff.   [3] *Ibid.* p. 72.
[4] *Ibid.* pp. 71–3.   [5] *Ibid.* p. 70.   [6] *Ibid.* p. 66.
[7] See E. Schwartz's study, 'Johannes Rufus, ein monophysitischer Schriftsteller', p. 4. Evagrius himself is described by Zacharias Scholasticus (p. 56) as 'president of this holy association, a practical philosopher in the way of Jesus Christ'. We hear of another monastic sympathiser, Plusianus, who was formerly on the staff of the prefect of Egypt (p. 88).

Towards a Monophysite solution, 484–512

Severus was certainly on the Christian side in all these affairs of magic, but by no means as prominently as his biographer would like to suggest. He confined himself to discreet, even 'secret advice' to the militant Christians.[1] He wanted, he said, to get on with his law studies. 'You will not make a monk of me, for I am a student of law, and I love law',[2] he told Evagrius, and for a considerable time resisted the advice of his friend Zacharias to be baptised.[3] Gradually, however, he was won over, and 'practical monasticism' on the anti-Chalcedonian side became the guiding motive of his life.

In the last decade of the fifth century not only was the episcopate of Phoenicia Chalcedonian, with Severus refusing to communicate with its members, but under the leadership of the Patriarch Elias (494–516) and Sabas the majority of the Palestinian monks had also come round to the same view. Sabas had increased his own prestige by converting Saracen tribes on the eastern borders of Palestine. His theology may best be described as 'Cyrillian but not Monophysite'. He was always a follower of Euthymius, that is to say, loyal to Chalcedon. At the same time, he seems to have admitted the Alexandrian Monophysite formula '*unus de Trinitate passus est*' (without the addition '*carne*'),[4] and may therefore be regarded as one of the influences that led to the Theopaschite solution as an alternative to the theology of Severus in the reign of Justin. His view of orthodoxy including the acceptance of Chalcedon was enforced on all the *lavrae* under his control.[5] At the same time the Patriarch Elias acted against the remaining anti-Chalcedonian monasteries on the Phoenician plain. In this offensive he was seconded by the Egyptian Nephalius, who after an interval of 25 years returns to history, this time as a Chalcedonian agitator. His activities menaced the very existence of the monasteries around Maiuma, and took Severus to Constantinople in 508.

Severus opened his literary account in the capital by writing against the Eutychians and Apollinarians, and there would be no greater mistake than to believe that he had any sympathy with either. While in the capital he opposed an elderly bishop who taught in Eutychist tradition that Christ did

---

[1] Zacharias Scholasticus, *Vita Severi* (ed. Kugener), p. 91.
[2] *Ibid.* p. 52.
[3] *Ibid.* p. 77.
[4] Cyril of Scythopolis, *Vita Sabae* (ed. Schwartz), pp. 127–8. Compare J. Lebon, *Le Monophysisme sévérien* (Louvain, 1909), pp. 70 and 479 n4. For the Palestinian part-inspiration for this formula, see below, p. 245.
[5] *Vita Sabae*, p. 125.

not suffer hunger and thirst like mortal men.¹ He was critical of a similar approach by the grammarian Sergius during his rule as Patriarch.² In his years of exile from 518 onwards he was to be involved in a long dispute with Julian of Halicarnassos, who believed like Eutyches that Christ was possessed of divine flesh which somehow was capable of suffering.³ For its part, the anti-Chalcedonian theology which Severus expressed and defined in his *Philalethes* (written 509–11) and *Against the Impious Grammarian* (*circa* 520) was remarkably consistent. It represented simply what eastern theologians believed Cyril had held. Indeed, Severus proclaimed in a moment of enthusiasm that every utterance of Cyril should be a law of the church.⁴ One of the strengths of the anti-Chalcedonians in the half-century after the Council was that they did not swing over to the opposite extreme. Cyril was not Eutyches. It was to maintain intact Cyril's deeply-pondered theology of salvation that men like Peter of Iberia, Philoxenus and Severus were prepared to battle all their lives and, if need be, end their days in exile.

One effect of Chalcedon had been to convince the eastern episcopate, including most of the Egyptians, that both Apollinarius and Eutyches had failed to give an adequate account of the mystery of salvation. No attempt was made to rehabilitate them. Even Dioscorus himself was not immune from criticism, as being 'contentious' and 'fighting unnecessarily about words'.⁵ Ephesus II was accepted not because Eutyches was vindicated but because the Twelve Anathemas of Cyril were declared canonical. Similarly, the anti-Chalcedonian writers did not criticise Flavian for his condemnation of Eutyches but because his theology was at heart two-nature. The struggle of those who opposed Chalcedon was always on two fronts, as much opposed to Apollinarius as to Theodore and Nestorius. Within about a decade of the council Timothy the Cat wrote a long letter to the church at Alexandria ordering the withdrawal of communion from Bishop Isaiah of Hermopolis and the presbyter Theophilus for having lapsed into Eutychianism in that they denied the reality of Christ's flesh. With a wealth of

---

¹ John of Beith-Aphthonia, *Vita Severi* (ed. Kugener), p. 251.

² Sergius was strongly anti-Chalcedonian but seems to have been an Apollinarian in outlook. He argued that as in Christ there was one person, so there must also be one quality, one property, one activity and one essence (*ousia*). His incarnation resulted in a 'mingling' rather than a 'composition' of Word and flesh. See Sellers, *Council of Chalcedon*, p. 272 n3.

³ See below, p. 262.   ⁴ *Select Letters* I. 9 (ed. Brooks, p. 45).

⁵ Severus, *Ad Nephalium* (ed. Lebon), p. 9 of translation.

proof-texts reminiscent of the form of Leo's defence of Chalcedon in Letter 156, Timothy shows with reference to Athanasius' letter to Epictetus, to (pseudo-)Gregory Thaumaturgus,[1] Basil, Ambrose, Cyril and the Apollinarian writing fathered on Julius of Rome, that the Word consubstantial with God was also co-natural in every way with man (except for sin), 'assuming the seed of Abraham'. The Word was not co-natural simply with himself even though the deity that assumed flesh was not thereby modified.[2] At the same time, Timothy was unsparing against Leo and the *Tome*. In his comments on the latter, addressed to the Emperor Leo in 459, he had pointed out that Chalcedon by dividing the Son into *hypostaseis*, natures, and *prosopa* was doing injustice to Scripture, to the Fathers, and to the definition of Nicaea. Hence it was not acceptable. To him, Leo was a Nestorian.

This was the foundation on which Severus built.[3] He left no great single work like Augustine's *De Trinitate* that summed up his whole theology, but he hammered out and refined his ideas in the course of long-drawn-out literary controversies with pro-Chalcedonians on the one hand and Eutychists on the other, in his sermons preached at Antioch and in a vast correspondence extending over thirty years. For their part, his opponents in the capital, Nephalius and Macedonius, begin the long line of Chalcedonian writers that extended through Leontius of Byzantium (485–543) and his colleagues in the reign of Justinian. The argument was conducted wholly in the language of Greek theology, with little reference to what the Latins may have had in mind. The question was whether the definition of Chalcedon could, so to speak, be naturalised into the Byzantine church in such a way that Greek piety could truly be reconciled with it. It was a similar problem which the Cappadocians had faced regarding the Creed of Nicaea, but the final success of the Chalcedonians was due less to superiority in argument than to the loss of Syria and Egypt to the Arabs in the seventh century.

[1] He quotes Apollinarius' κατὰ μέρος πίστις which was attributed to Gregory Thaumaturgus. See J. Lebon, 'La Christologie du monophysisme syrien', in Grillmeier/Bacht, *Das Konzil von Chalkedon*, I, 425–580 at p. 479 n67.

[2] Text in Zacharias Rhetor, *HE* IV. 12. Compare also Timothy's condemnation of the sophist John of Alexandria for introducing Apollinarian and Eutychian ideas for discussion, *ibid.* IV. 5. See J. Lebon, 'La Christologie de Timothée Aelure', *RHE* 9, 1908, pp. 679–708, and above, pp. 155 and 163.

[3] For Severus' theology, see J. Lebon, 'La Christologie du monophysisme syrien', and his earlier *Le Monophysisme sévérien*, both fundamental works.

The strength of Severus' position was that his thought was based on the acknowledged tradition of the great theologians of the past, the Cappadocian Fathers and Cyril. To the one he owed his Trinitarian concepts, to the other his Christology, and together these formed a single whole in his mind. The Trinity, he declares, was not indeed subject to definition, nor could it be investigated by human reason, but through Christ it could be apprehended, and it was evident that each person (*hypostasis*) of the Trinity possessed all the qualities of the Godhead, qualities such as goodness, creativity and all that belonged to the uncreated nature. 'Thus, we affirm that the Trinity shares one essence (*ousia*).' But just as three men (and both Severus and his opponent, John the 'impious grammarian', follow the Cappadocians in using the Apostles Peter, Paul and John as examples) share the same essence of 'humanity' while differing as individuals, so each one of the Trinity has what they share in common made distinctly and separately individual. As 'unbegotten', the Father differed from the Son 'who was begotten of the Father', and both in turn differed from the Spirit who 'proceeded', but each shared the Light and Life and Goodness of God.[1] This definition not only laid the foundation on which Severus could construct his Christology but the debt to the Cappadocians guaranteed its wide acceptance as orthodox. Severus' followers were to be thankful for the rigour of their master after events had forced them to establish their own hierarchy, and when they were confronted with Trinitarian heresy within their ranks in the 550s.

For some time collections of quotations from Cyril had been assembled, designed to show that Cyril could be properly interpreted in a Chalcedonian sense. One unnamed controversialist in the capital had put together no less than 244 proof-texts taken from Cyril's writings aimed at demonstrating this.[2] There was no essential difference, he argued, between the Chalcedonian 'two natures inseparably united' after the incarnation and the anti-Chalcedonian 'one incarnate nature of the word'.[3] Severus disagreed. In his *Philalethes*, written while he was in the capital, he set out to show that however defined, Christ was One. Cyril never separated, for instance, the body that suffered from the Word. 'The Fathers have

---

[1] *Liber contra impium grammaticum* (ed. Lebon), *CSCO* IV. 4 and 5; *Oratio* I. 18 (ed. Lebon, pp. 132–3), quoting Gregory of Nazianzus, *Oratio* VI. 22 (*PG* 35, col. 749) and *Oratio* XXXI. 14–15 (*PG* 36, col. 149). Compare a similar exposition by Severus in *Homil.* 125 (ed. Brière, *PO* 29. 1, pp. 237–41).

[2] Listed by Severus in *Philalethes* (ed. Hespel), pp. 6–105. [3] *Ibid.* p. 106.

taught us', Severus wrote, 'that God the Word, the Unique One begotten by his Father without beginning, eternally, impassibly and incorporeally, did in the last times for our salvation take flesh of the Holy Spirit and of the Holy *Theotokos* and ever-Virgin Mary, flesh consubstantial with us, animated by an intelligent and reasoning soul.'[1] This statement could be taken as Severus' creed, for it is repeated time and again in his writings and sermons. In this description of the divine nature the words *physis*, *hypostasis* and *prosopon*, when referred to Christ, coalesced into a single meaning, i.e. 'nature' in its Aristotelian sense, such as man being 'by nature' a political animal, so Christ was 'by nature' God, for no terminology could be permitted that detracted from the essential (or hypostatic) unity of the being who was the Word-made-flesh. 'All things', as Cyril had said, 'God-befitting and man-befitting were those of one Christ.' Christ's acts, whatever they were, were the acts of one being and not of two. Thus Severus argues against Sergius that 'when the hypostatic union, which is the perfect union of the two natures, is confessed, there is only one Christ, without mixture, one person, one hypostasis, and one nature, that of the Incarnate Word'.[2] There was no change or transformation of the Word, only its participation in the 'attributes of humanity', namely flesh and blood.[3] This point was made with equal clarity and persistence whether the opponent was an Apollinarian or a Chalcedonian. Against the latter, Severus argued in addition, that the intention of Chalcedon had been to vindicate the teaching of Nestorius. Had the council, argued Severus, confessed the hypostatic union, it would have confessed one incarnate nature of God the Word, and would not have defined that the one Christ existed in two natures, thereby dissolving the union.[4] In so doing, Chalcedon was heretical.

[1] *Ibid.* p. 107. Compare p. 113: 'It is obvious that the same being is at once God and man, consubstantial with the Father according to his divinity and consubstantial with us men according to his humanity.' This latter phrase excluded Eutychianism. Compare Severus' similar credal statements in his work against Julian of Halicarnassos (*Specilegium romanorum* X, *Anti-julianist Writings*, ed. Hespel, pp. 18–19) and *Ad Nephalium* (ed. Lebon), pp. 8–9.

[2] Letter to Sergius (ed. Lebon), p. 58.

[3] *Ibid.* p. 58. See Lebon, 'La Christologie du monophysisme syrien', pp. 440–1. Sergius was writing evidently in protest against the accord arrived at at the Synod of Tyre in 514, which temporarily brought Antioch, Alexandria, Jerusalem and Constantinople into agreement based on accepting the *Henotikon* as an anti-Chalcedonian document. See *Chron. ad ann. 846* (ed. Brooks and Chabot), p. 168.

[4] *Ad Nephalium* (ed. Lebon), p. 15.

All this was worked out in great detail, in laboured responses given to carping questions on the exact meaning of Cyril's words. Severus had to avoid on the one hand interpretations that suggested 'division' and on the other, 'mixture' or 'conflation' between the Word and his flesh. In the Alexandrian tradition both he and Philoxenus emphasised the divine *kenosis*, whereby the Word voluntarily divested himself of power in submitting to incarnation for the purpose of conquering death and saving man.[1] Thus it could be claimed that for the period of Christ's ministry, the Word was really man, not merely a being inhabiting a human envelope.[2] The union of Word and flesh was as soul and body in man – an inexpressible but essential unity. And similarly man also 'made in the image of God' was one *prosopon* 'without confusion'.[3]

Severus and his Chalcedonian opponents agreed that Christ was one *hypostasis* and one *prosopon*, but disputed the meaning of the crucial term *physis* (nature). Taking their brief from the Cappadocian Fathers, the Chalcedonians argued in favour of the double consubstantiality of Christ (i.e. with God and with man) but they deduced from this that Christ was 'in two natures without separation, that is to say in two substances (*in duabus* οὐσίαις)'. Both 'nature' and 'substance' meant the generic factor of a species, whether 'God' or 'man' as opposed to the particular and individual characteristics which would be translated 'hypostasis'.[4] Thus when the incarnate Word united to himself manhood it included the substance or nature of mankind, including a reasonable and intelligent soul, so making two substances or natures inseparably united. Man's salvation was guaranteed by this union.[5] Severus, however, refused to accept the identification of 'substance' and 'nature' on semantic grounds. He regarded 'substance' (οὐσία) as an unsatisfactory and 'unscientific term' in Christology, 'because

---

[1] Severus' emphasis on the soteriological aspect of his Christology is emphasised in his first sermon at Antioch, November 512 (ed. and tr. E. Porcher, *Revue de l'Orient chrétien* 19, 1914, pp. 69–78).

[2] Lebon, 'La Christologie du monophysisme syrien', p. 440.

[3] *Homil.* 81 (*PO* 20. 2, p. 356).

[4] *Liber contra impium grammaticum* I. 17, especially Lebon, pp. 113 and 126–7; also III. 1. 1 (Lebon, pp. 5–6). Note the conflation of *ousia* and *physis* by Epiphanius of Perge (*Codex Encyclius, ACO* 2. v, p. 58): 'duarum naturarum sive substantiarum in uno Christo declaratum invenimus a plurimis Patribus...' Similarly, the Orthodox speaker at the Colloquy of 532 equated *ousia* with *physis*: 'Sicut una substantia et una natura in Trinitate suscipitur' (Mansi, *Collectio* VIII, col. 822).

[5] *Liber contra impium grammaticum* I. 17 (ed. Lebon, pp. 113ff.).

of the varying use that is found in the holy fathers',[1] and preferred to confine it to a Trinitarian context. In justification he cited the Creed of Nicaea where the term was applied to the Word within the Godhead. Instead, 'physis' and 'hypostasis' were appropriate to the circumstances or 'economy' of the Word itself.[2] Hence the Word could not be in 'two substances' or 'in two natures', and Athanasius and Cyril insisted that after the incarnation there was only the one nature of Christ. As it stood, therefore, the Chalcedonian definition of two natures inseparably united with each maintaining its own properties[3] was simply nonsense. If the Godhead existed from all eternity its becoming flesh in no way altered it. In assuming humanity and so becoming consubstantial with man as he was with God, Christ remained the one *physis* as he had been before.

The question remained how the confluence of soul and body in Christ was achieved. How did the Word acquire 'a reasonable soul'? How could the Saviour truly suffer as man? Severus replied that while there was no confusion of properties between Word and flesh a synthesis of the two took place. At the incarnation the Word became composite or σύνθετος, not διπλός or double, which would imply distinction and separation.[4] Precisely

---

[1] *Ep.* 5, to Eusebius the Scholastic, *Collection of Letters* (ed. Brooks), *PO* 12. 2, pp. 195–6.

[2] Severus *ad Sergium Grammaticum*: 'Quis nescit quod οὐσία quidem ἀπὸ τοῦ εἶναι nomen sortitur, φύσις vero ἀπὸ τοῦ πεφυκέναι' (Lebon, p. 126), and also his Letter 6 to Maron, *PO* 12. 2, pp. 196–9, for the same point.

[3] Severus, *Philalethes* (ed. Hespel), p. 139: 'When those who assembled at Chalcedon spoke of the unique Christ as possessing two natures but one *hypostasis* and one *prosopon*, they fell stupidly into a first-class contradiction. We will demonstrate this from Saint Cyril's own words...' In his *Cathedral Homilies* he was less restrained: 'two natures' was 'Jewish turpitude' (*Homil.* 56).

[4] Note the passage in *Ep.* 25 to the clergy and magistrates of Emesa written while Severus was patriarch of Antioch (*PO* 12. 2, pp. 229–30) in which he tries to explain how the union took place: 'The divinity of the Word did not take anything into its essence [*ousia*] that was not its by nature', but 'from the unmixed union of the incarnation, and the composition out of two elements, the Godhead and the manhood, Emmanuel should be made up, who in one *hypostasis* is ineffably composite; not simple but composite; as the soul of a man like us, which by nature is bodiless and rational, which is naturally intertwined with the body, remains in its suprasensual and bodiless nature, but by reason of its composition with the body makes up one composite animal, man.' The assumption of the body made no addition to the essence (*ousia*) of the soul, nor did the assumption of flesh make any difference to the nature of the Word. For Severus' use of the term σύνθετος and its history in Alexandrian Christological terminology as far back as Origen (*Contra Celsum* 1. 60) see *A Patristic Greek Lexicon* (ed. Lampe), pp. 1329–30.

how Christ became endowed as Word with a 'reasonable soul', however, remained a divine mystery. Yet only thus could Christ save mankind from the results of the Fall. In this act 'one of the Trinity indeed suffered for us'.

Even so, the difficulty of this position, however clear-cut its presentation in the hands of a master theologian, was evident enough. Two realities, however they might be defined, did exist in Christ. Severus accepted this – Word and flesh did retain their 'properties', but this fact did not make the flesh a 'nature' apart from the Word.[1] As Cyril before him, Severus believed that these realities could be distinguished by intuition or contemplation (τῇ θεωρίᾳ),[2] and Christ confessed as being formed 'out of two' *hypostaseis* or existences (πράγματα), but there was, Severus insisted, only one nature after the incarnation, and one activity (ἐνέργεια), that of the God-man.[3] In all this one sees that Severus' objection to Chalcedon was not that it was the work of Leo and the Roman see. Indeed, he often quoted 'Pope Julius', whom he calls the 'spiritual and unshakeable tower of the church of the Romans', along with Athanasius, the Cappadocians, and Proclus of Constantinople.[4] He was not concerned with the ecclesiastical politics or origins, but with the issue of doctrinal emphasis and omission or innovation in the Chalcedonian decree.[5] Nowhere, he says, does one find in the decree either 'the one incarnate nature of the Divine logos' or 'the hypostatic union', or the confession of 'one nature out of two'.

---

[1] Sergius the Grammarian and his friends asked how, if there were 'two properties' in Christ, 'two natures' could be avoided; see Sergius, Letter to Severus sent via Antoninus, bishop of Haleba (Aleppo), ed. Lebon, pp. 51–3.

[2] *Liber contra impium grammaticum* III. 1. 17 (ed. Lebon, p. 196).

[3] For instance, *Ep.* 1 *ad Sergium* (ed. Lebon, pp. 60–1): see Sellers, *Council of Chalcedon*, p. 272, 'nam unus quidem est operans, id est Verbum incarnatum, et una operatio [ἐνέργεια], diversa sunt opera, id est res operatione perfectae.'

[4] See also Athanasius Scriptor, *Life* (or *Conflict*) of Severus, where 'the great Liberius', Athanasius, the Cappadocians, Cyril and Dioscorus are associated as champions of orthodoxy (ed. Goodspeed and Crum, p. 605). Severus clearly failed to realise that the works of Julius he was using were Apollinarian forgeries.

[5] For Chalcedon as 'innovating', see *Ep.* 34 (*PO* 12. 2, p. 272). The most trenchant criticism of the council comes in *Ep.* 36, written before 512. He tells Isaac the lawyer, who claimed that Chalcedon 'also placed the faith of the 318 before its definition', 'But in that case the innovation is obvious. First, it says in plain words, and that twice and three times, that it is making a definition. Secondly, because it said that our one Lord Jesus Christ is made known in two natures. Thirdly, to omit other points, because it called Leo's letter, which is full of the blasphemies of Nestorius, a "pillar of orthodoxy"' (*PO* 12. 2, p. 292).

Instead, Christ 'in two natures, perfect, undivided and unconfused' was taken straight from Nestorius.[1] How can Christ incarnate die 'in two natures', he asks. Which nature did Leo think had been nailed to the cross? It was these faults, as well as the acceptance of Theodoret and Ibas and the assertion of two natures 'after the incarnation', that made Leo appear in the eyes of Severus a 'blasphemer' and 'the common pillar of the heterodox'. He who 'numbered the persons' therefore 'divided them'. How else could one think in terms of 'two'? Indeed, Leo made each nature actually quote Scripture at the other, one declaring 'I and my Father are one' and the other 'the Father is greater than I'. His doctrine was simply a 'relative communion of forms', and therefore fallacious and heretical.[2]

Severus endowed the Monophysite movement with its philosophy and characteristic terminology. Whatever the subject on which he may be speaking he never strays far from the Fathers. He lived in the writings of the Cappadocians, Cyril and the canons of councils. It is interesting that this essentially Greek theologian who became patriarch of Antioch, rather an Alexandrian in Dioscorus' succession, should have become the spiritual leader of Monophysitism. Severus was in no sense a representative even of regional self-consciousness. His letters betray a profound deference to the emperor and loyalty to the empire[3] and he was not a man for martyrdom. It was typical of him that when after his flight from Antioch in 518 he was reproached for lack of courage, he replied in the words of Matt. 10. 23.[4] He was a cosmopolitan, as much at home in the capital or in Alexandria as at Antioch. He was not hostile to Old Rome or its primacy, but only to Leo as purveyor of false doctrine, based on what he considered to be traditional Roman misunderstanding of Trinitarian teaching.[5] He was a Biblical scholar in the mould of Origen and Basil, and like them he was both ascetic

---

[1] Severus, *Liber contra impium grammaticum* III. 1. 3 (ed. Lebon, pp. 20 and 22).

[2] *Ibid.* III. 1. 5 (Lebon, pp. 49–50). For Severus' criticism of Leo, see also his Letter to Count Oecumenius (*Collection of Letters*, ed. Brooks, PO 12. 2, pp. 180ff.) and compare the first sermon preached at Antioch (Porcher, *Revue de l'Orient chrétien* 19, 1914, p. 76). The *Tome* was 'Jewish' (*Ep.* 46, PO 12. 2, p. 321). Leo's acceptance of Ibas and Theodoret as blameless branded him as a Nestorian (*Ep.* 31, *ibid.* p. 265).

[3] See below, p. 265.

[4] *Ep.* 56 to Caesarea, PO 12. 2, p. 338.

[5] For instance, in *Ep.* 22, written *circa* 520, Severus quotes the Roman objection to the formula 'one of the Trinity suffered for us in the flesh', 'lest we subject the Holy Trinity to numeration'. He rejects its 'impiety' as being due to the Roman church confusing, as always, *ousia* which was indivisible with the *hypostasies* that were divisible (PO 12. 2, pp. 215–16).

The rise of the Monophysite movement

and reformer. His theological teaching was simply a vehicle by which he could lead his people towards God by example of ascetic contemplation.

Typical, perhaps, is Severus' first sermon to his congregation at Antioch, preached on 24 November 512. It was on the subject of Jacob's ladder and its symbolism demonstrated for the Christian how he might move upwards towards the glory of God manifest through Christ. As with Origen, conduct and creed went together. There is a ring of idealism in many of his *Cathedral Homilies*, as when preaching in Antioch on the Epiphany in 516 he says: 'Let us not accept the miracles so as to destroy and suppress the flesh, nor the human actions and voluntary poverty to deny and diminish the divinity. Let us return this semi-heritage to those who are man-worshippers or Docetists [Phantasiasts] and who in their malevolence and impiety cause division. As for us, we move along the middle of the royal road, turning our face away from the tortuous sins on one side or the other, and knowing that he who lives on the heights and dwells by nature in grandeur is worthy of the God who "emptied himself" (Phil. 2. 7)... to become the author of our salvation.'[1] In its fervour it could be Origen preaching. Like Origen too, he had a force of character that could influence any audience from the emperor to the least educated members of his flock. To the latter he represented the ruling civilisation, but in a way that had some relevance to their aspirations. This ability to communicate with the native as well as the Byzantine gave him eventually an historical significance similar to that of Athanasius and Donatus of Carthage. He deserved the title of 'Ecumenical teacher' with which later generations of Monophysites endowed him.[2]

For the moment, however, the popular forces that were to bring Severus to Antioch were controlled by Philoxenus of Maboug.[3] He more than anyone else was responsible for wrecking Anastasius' policy of uniting the east Roman provinces on the basis of the *Henotikon*. Anastasius' appointment of Flavian as patriarch of Antioch in 498 had ostensibly been wise. Flavian was a monk of the important pro-Chalcedonian monastery of

---

[1] *Homil.* 83 (ed. Brière), *PO* 20. 2, pp. 405–6.

[2] See the Letter of James Bar'adai and others to Patriarch Theodosius circa 564, in *Documenta* (ed. Chabot), p. 63, and compare p. 88, Patriarch Theodosius writing to the orthodox bishops of the east.

[3] Philoxenus was well supported by his suffragans, six of whom participated in Severus' consecration or were present at his inaugural address; cf. M. A. Kugener (ed.), 'Notices relatives à Sévère' (*PO* 2, Paris, 1907), pp. 317–25.

Tilmognon in Syria II[1] but he accepted the *Henotikon* and was prepared to go a long way to meet further Monophysite demands. Even to the Alexandrians his views did not seem unreasonable, but after a few years Philoxenus became determined to overthrow him. Looking back from the vantage points of old age and exile he speaks of 'a ten year duel' with his opponent, which ended in Flavian's fall in 512. Philoxenus' theology differed little from that of Severus. Christ was 'invisible God who appeared as man, and he who appeared as man was God invisible'. There was one *hypostasis* and one nature in the incarnate Christ. The Word of God was made man without change, confusion or amalgamation. The formula 'out of two natures' might be accepted so long as all idea of a pre-existent humanity in the union of the Word and his flesh was excluded. Humanity being 'enhypostasised' or 'en-natured', to borrow the terminology of Basil, it could thus be said that God himself suffered and died for man's salvation. The incarnation renewed and regenerated man.[2] These views were buttressed with a greater use of Scriptural text than Severus was wont to make, and were combined with a rabidly puritanical outlook demonstrated in his moral and ethical treatises, intense hatred of Leo and Chalcedon and a consciousness of Syriac culture that inspired him to initiate a new translation of the Bible into Syriac.[3] All this contributed to make him a man whom the monks would support, a rigorist who interpreted anti-Chalcedonism with 'accuracy', and he exploited the strength of his position as metropolitan of Euphratesia unmercifully against his colleague at Antioch.[4]

The outbreak of the feud between Philoxenus and Flavian may have been connected obscurely with the Persian war of 502–5,[5] and this was followed by incidents in Edessa, Apamea and Antioch.[6] Even to contem-

---

[1] For the pro-Chalcedonian allegiance of Tilmognon, see Evagrius, *HE* III. 32.

[2] 'He who is God by nature really became man and in himself created the nature of man anew' (*Three Letters of Philoxenus*, ed. Vaschalde, p. 38). Man was no longer 'in the image of God' and 'outside God' – arguments used, surely, to contradict the Nestorians with whom Philoxenus would have been in contact in his diocese. (For the Antiochene anthropology derived from the 'image of God' metaphor, see above, p. 126.)   [3] See Halleux, *Philoxène*, pp. 117–25.

[4] On Philoxenus' career in the decade 502–12, see *ibid.* pp. 57ff.

[5] See above, p. 185.

[6] Philoxenus' account of events is given in his *Letter to the monks of Senoun*, circa 521, written while in exile (ed. Halleux, pp. 94–5): 'Omitto quae adversus me tempore belli persici apud optimates molitus est praedictus Flavianus haereticus et quae mihi

The rise of the Monophysite movement

poraries, however, the cause of the trouble was uncertain. The evidence suggests that whereas Flavian intended that the *Henotikon* should remain the basis of doctrinal teaching, Philoxenus envisaged it as merely a stepping-stone for a total rejection of Chalcedon. His was an 'aposchist' (separatist) movement based on the monasticism of a strongly Syriac-speaking province similar to the 'aposchist' movement among the Egyptian monks. The differing fate of Peter Mongus and his successors compared with that of the Patriarch Flavian was the measure of the authority exercised by the patriarchs of Alexandria and Antioch respectively.

Philoxenus had visited the capital in 484 and again in 507.[1] This means that probably he did not meet Severus until the latter's return to his monastery in 511. Both were convinced, however, that the anti-Chalcedonian cause could triumph only with the removal of the patriarchs Elias and Flavian.[2] When in 507 Macedonius refused to receive Philoxenus and resisted a demand inspired by him to anathematise Diodore, Theodore, Nestorius and the 'eastern fathers', he was also marked down for destruction.[3]

Between 508/9 and 512 Severus and Philoxenus between them brought about a religious revolution in the east, Severus working in the capital and Philoxenus in Syria. Both succeeded through exercising continuous pressure on the opposition. Beginning with his discomfiture of Nephalius, Severus gradually took over the Patriarch Macedonius' role of spiritual adviser to the emperor. He became active in exposing various types of unorthodoxy which were being preached round about.[4] There was the Origenism of the ex-monk Isidore, and obscure beliefs of the followers of Lampetios and the Adelphians to be combated, as well as the more serious opponents against whom he wrote *Philalethes*.

Events in Syria gave him his opportunity to influence Anastasius. In 505/6 Flavian had broken communion with the new patriarch of Alexandria (John of Nikiou, 505–16) when the latter denounced Chalcedon. On his return from the capital in 508 (?) Philoxenus at once started agitation among the monks of Syria I, especially those in and around Antioch. He accused

acciderunt Edessae et in regione Apameesium et Antiochenorum, cum essem in monasterio beati Mar Bassi et in ipsa Antiochia...' In view of the suspected treachery of the monks of Amida at this period, the troubles of Philoxenus may not have been wholly the fault of others.   [1] For dating, see Halleux, *Philoxène*, pp. 59ff.

[2] For Severus' intrigues against Flavian at this time, see *Select Letters* I. 2 to Bishop Solon (ed. Brooks, p. 13).

[3] On the unravelling of this incident, see Halleux, *Philoxène*, p. 62.

[4] Zacharias Scholasticus, *Vita Severi* (ed. Kugener), p. 106.

Towards a Monophysite solution, 484–512

Flavian of insincerity, for no one who espoused the cause of Chalcedon could be other than a Nestorian.[1] For the time being Flavian held his own. At a council summoned at Antioch at the emperor's request, he not only reasserted his loyalty to the *Henotikon*, passing over Chalcedon in silence, but took the wind out of Philoxenus' sails by condemning by name Diodore and Theodore, Ibas, and Theodoret, and other lesser opponents of the Twelve Anathemas. In an accompanying letter to Anastasius, the Chalcedonian formula 'in two natures' was condemned as well.[2] Flavian's council thus followed the Home Synod of Constantinople and accepted the principle, hitherto denied, that the dead and their works might be condemned even though they had died in the peace of the Church and had been vindicated by a council. They anticipated by thirty-five years Justinian's decree of 544 denouncing the 'Three Chapters'.[3]

Philoxenus was not to be appeased. Both Flavian and he approached the emperor, and the latter turned to Severus to act as arbitrator. Severus' 'Formula of Satisfaction' (τύπος τῆς πληροφορίας), 510/11, while explicitly accepting the *Henotikon*, equally explicitly denounced the *Tome*, the formula 'in two natures', and the works of Diodore and his followers, and retained Chalcedon simply as the instrument through which Nestorius and Eutyches had been condemned.[4] Anastasius had himself confessed the formula 'out of two natures' in a letter written to the Palestinian monks in

[1] See the letter written by the pro-Chalcedonian monks of Palestine to Alcison, bishop of Nicopolis in Epirus, *circa* 515, for Philoxenus' tactics: Evagrius, *HE* III. 31. Like other agitators he continually raised his stakes to beyond what he knew his opponent could concede.

[2] Theophanes, *Chron.* A.M. 6000 (ed. Classen, I, 232). See Schwartz, *PS*, p. 240, and L. Abramowski, *RHE* 60, 1965, p. 65, who dates this event to *circa* 510 after Philoxenus had failed to force his hand the previous year. Philoxenus himself admits the general truth of this. See J. Lebon, 'Textes inédits de Philoxène de Mabbough', *Le Muséon* 43, 1930, pp. 24ff.

[3] See below, p. 280.

[4] Zacharias Scholasticus, *Vita Severi* (ed. Kugener), pp. 107–8. Part of the text of the *Typos* preserved in an Armenian translation is published by Ch. Moeller, 'Le Type de l'empereur Anastase I', *Studia Patristica* 3 (= *TU* 78), Berlin, 1961, pp. 240–7. This shows the emperor accepting the first three ecumenical councils, Cyril's Anathemas, 'the *Henotikon* of Zeno the orthodox emperor' and 'the letter of John, archbishop of Alexandria'. Moeller believes this was a letter written in 505 to Macedonius in which the denunciation of the *Tome* and Chalcedon was demanded (and no doubt the same as Flavian had refused to accept). If this text is genuine, it shows Anastasius actually prepared to denounce Chalcedon and to accept the position of Severus and his Alexandrian allies as orthodox.

The rise of the Monophysite movement

Severus' favour in 510,[1] but this further erosion of Chalcedon went just too far. Not only did Flavian refuse to accept, but he was supported by Elias of Jerusalem, and more significantly by Macedonius. The first half of 511 brought matters to a head. In the capital the monks who had accompanied Severus were openly using the Monophysite addition to the doxology 'who was crucified for us'. Anastasius at first favoured them, but very soon orthodox monks, reinforced by 'zealous and good men from Palestine', reacted.[2] There were riots, the orthodox calling on Macedonius, their opponents on the emperor himself.[3] On 20 July a confrontation took place between Severus and Macedonius, as a result of which the patriarch refused to allow the use of the new doxology. On 7 August he was deposed by a council for 'falsifying Scripture'.[4] He was told, 'the master of the world has decreed your banishment', and sent off, like his predecessor, to the monastery of the Euchites. Though he sent his synodical letter to John of Alexandria,[5] his successor Timothy was only slightly more favourable to Severus.

The narrowness of the theological issue between Severus and the patriarch is shown by Severus' own account of one of the questions debated between them. How was the writer of the Fourth Gospel to be interpreted when he spoke of Christ being dead before the soldier pierced him with a lance (Jn. 19. 34)? Did not then the water and blood flow out miraculously? What was one to make of Matthew's account which it was alleged stated that the incident took place before Christ's death? Archaeologists were set to work. A codex of Matthew was produced, said to have been dug up in Cyprus in Zeno's reign buried with the Apostle Barnabas. It was examined. The disputed passage was not there. Macedonius was in error through calling Jesus' body 'dead'.[6] This was Nestorianism, and Macedonius must go!

---

[1] Zacharias Scholasticus, *Vita Severi*, p. 105.

[2] Theodore Lector, *HE* (fragments, ed. Miller), p. 397.

[3] For the events, see Bardy, 'La Politique religieuse d'Anastase', pp. 311–12.

[4] Liberatus, *Brev*. XIX; Macedonius was accused of falsifying the text of 1 Tim. 3. 16 by altering ὃς ἐφανερώθη ἐν σαρκί into θς ἐφανερώθη ἐν σαρκί, i.e. that '*as* God' he appeared in flesh, not 'that he *was* God'. This could be interpreted as Nestorianism! Schwartz's view (*PS*, p. 243 n3) that verbal interpretations of Scripture hardly played a significant role in the dispute between Severus and Macedonius seems in this case to be mistaken.

[5] Severus, *Select Letters* IV. 2 (ed. Brooks, p. 255).

[6] Severus, Letter 108 to Thomas of Germanicea (*Collection of Letters*, PO 14, pp. 266–7). Compare Letter 1 to Oecumenius, 508–11, where Severus emphasises the life-giving character of the water that flowed from Christ's side (*PO* 12. 2, p. 183).

His work accomplished, Severus returned to Maiuma for a short time (September 511). Flavian and Elias still held firm. In Egypt, too, the Patriarch John was not impressed by a presbyter-monk arrogating to himself the leadership of the anti-Chalcedonian cause. A new synod at Sidon summoned at Anastasius' order to try to bring the eastern provinces into unity based on Severus' *Typos* resulted in a serious reverse for the Monophysites. Elias was supported by the majority of the Palestinian monks,[1] and though Isauria and east Syria opposed Flavian, west Syria as was to be expected rallied to him. The line of division between pro- and anti-Chalcedonian by provinces was hardening. Surprisingly, however, the Egyptians informed the Council that communion was not broken with those who accepted Chalcedon, so long as the *Henotikon* was accepted.[2] In the end only ten bishops, including Philoxenus, withdrew from communion with Flavian.

This success was short-lived. Though Sabas himself went to the capital to plead the Chalcedonian cause in 511/12, and won a respite for Elias at Jerusalem, Anastasius was won for Severus and Philoxenus. A new profession of faith (his signature to the *Typos*) was demanded of Flavian. Philoxenus appeared in Antioch with an imperial mandate. Rival groups of monks fought in the streets. The pro-Chalcedonians from Syria II battled successfully against the Monophysites from in and near Antioch.[3] Flavian, however, declared deposed by a council at Laodicea in Isauria, accepted the advice of imperial officials and withdrew from the city. He was eventually exiled at Petra with his supporters. Philoxenus had won at last. His letter to the lector Maro of Anazarba reveals him as a plotter and a revolutionary. But now, what he himself describes as 'ten years of resistance to Flavian' had ended triumphantly,[4] and on 6 November 512 Severus was elected and two days later consecrated patriarch of Antioch by twelve

---

[1] Theophanes, *Chron.* A.M. 6003. Marcellinus Comes, *Chron.* ad ann. 512, says eighty bishops were present. See E. Honigmann, 'Le Monophysisme jusqu'à l'accession de Sévère au patriarcat', *CSCO*, Subsidia 2 (Louvain, 1951), p. 13, who thinks the figure too high and refers to the Synod of Laodicea which deposed Flavian in 512.

[2] Severus, *Select Letters* IV. 2 (ed. Brooks, pp. 255–6). Severus regarded Sidon as a defeat. The actions of Egyptians 'cast great shame upon us who were combating on behalf of orthodoxy'. On the other hand, Chalcedonian commentators regarded it as a 'sacrilegious meeting'.

[3] Evagrius, *HE* III. 32.

[4] Philoxenus, *Letter to the Lector Maro of Anazarba*, chs. 27–32 (ed. Lebon, pp. 76–80), written probably *circa* 515.

bishops of Syria. These included six from Philoxenus' diocese.¹ Except for Palestine, the east was under Monophysite leadership. For the Chalcedonians, 'winter had descended upon the empire', as the imperial governor of Antioch wrote.²

Almost simultaneously, however, the first rumbles of the counter-revolution were to be heard. In the capital, the Sleepless Monks stirred up further riots against the use of the Monophysite doxology 'who was crucified for us'. So threatening did the situation become that Anastasius appeared in the Circus without his diadem and offered to abdicate (7 November 512). His tactic succeeded, but the orthodox doxology was resumed.³ A Syrian monk caught in the house of the emperor's powerful minister Marinus of Apamea was lynched and the house burnt to the ground.

The effect of these events was to be far-reaching. The exile of Macedonius and deposition of Flavian II virtually killed the Henoticist cause. Now there was a clear issue. It was not only for or against Chalcedon, but for or against Severus and his Egyptian friends. The papacy took its cue. In his anxiety to retain the goodwill of Syria and Egypt Anastasius appears to have forgotten that the Byzantine empire still included western and Latin-speaking provinces.⁴ These had been rallying steadily to the papal cause and among the barbarian officers quartered in Thrace was the commander of the federate troops (*comes foederatorum*) who happened to be the deposed Flavian's godson, Vitalian the Goth.

¹ Dating from 'Notices relatives à Sévère', ed. Kugener, *PO* 2, pp. 317–25, no. 2 p. 317. For Philoxenus' influence, *ibid.* no. 7, p. 321.

² Quoted by Severus in a letter to Hippocrates the Scholastic, *Ep.* 46, *Collection of Letters* (ed. Brooks), *PO* 12. 2, p. 321.

³ Evagrius, *HE* III. 44, suggests that the riot took place when Macedonius was still patriarch. The actual date seems, however, to have been 6 November 512 following a service on the previous Sunday at St Theodore's Church when the Monophysite *trishagion* was chanted in the presence of the emperor. Marcellinus Comes, *Chron.* ad ann. 512 (ed. Mommsen, p. 97), refers to the incident with a reference to Marinus' prominence to 512, the removal of Macedonius having taken place the previous year. Zacharias Rhetor, *HE* VII. 9, also indicates that Marinus' influence dated to after Macedonius' fall. See Schwartz, *PS*, pp. 247–8.

⁴ Anastasius attempted, however, to maintain control of the situation there through the archbishop of Thessalonica, whom he prevailed upon with bishops in Illyricum and Greece to remain in communion with the capital. See Theodore Lector, *HE* (fragments, ed. Miller), p. 399, and Theophanes, *Chron.* A.M. 6008 (ed. Classen, I, 250).

Chapter 6

THE ORTHODOX REACTION, 513-527

Severus had been consecrated as patriarch of Antioch for only a few months when Vitalian's revolt broke out.[1] It was still a distant phenomenon and in Syria the anti-Chalcedonian tide was in flood. He was the choice of the monks, and some who had been expelled from their monastery near Apamea by Flavian 'for their zeal against the doctrines of Nestorius' had appeared at his monastery at Maiuma each carrying a cross on his shoulder[2] to hail him as patriarch. According to Severus' other biographer, John of Beith-Aphthonia, the population of Antioch received him with enthusiasm. 'Anathematise the Council of Chalcedon. Anathematise the council that has turned the universe upside down. Anathematise the apostate council. Anathematise the council of renegades. Cursed be the council. Cursed be the *Tome* of Leo. Deliver the city from heresy. We want to participate in the holy mysteries. We want to baptise our children.'[3] The last two demands provide a clue to much that was to take place in the next few years. On 16 July 518, a mere week after the death of Anastasius, pro-Chalcedonian crowds in Sancta Sophia were to shout at the Patriarch John, 'For many years we have wanted to take communion. Why do we remain without communion? You are orthodox: who are you afraid of, [you who are worthy] of the Trinity? Long live the emperor. Long live the Augusta. Throw out Severus the Manichaean.'[4] With the arrival of Severus on the scene one may detect a heightening of the explicit doctrinal differences between the two sides. In Severus' correspondence the Chalcedonians are 'Diphysites', heretics to be converted to 'orthodoxy', while in the capital and among the hostile Palestinian monks Severus' followers were branded as 'Manichees' or 'Aposchists' ('Separatists'), dissenters to be punished

---

[1] The dating as between 513 and 514 is not certain: Marcellinus Comes, *Chron.* ad ann. 514. G. Bardy, 'La Politique religieuse d'Anastase', suggests 513, following Theophanes, *Chron.* A.M. 6005, who puts Vitalian's rebellion in the first year of Severus' pontificate.

[2] Zacharias Scholasticus, *Vita Severi* (ed. Kugener), p. 111.

[3] John of Beith-Aphthonia, *Vita Severi* (ed. Kugener), p. 241.

[4] Cited from A. A. Vasiliev, *Justin the First*, Dumbarton Oaks Studies 1 (Cambridge, Mass., 1950), p. 138.

and expelled.¹ The urgency, however, of popular demand for baptism and communion at the hands of an 'orthodox' cleric expressed deep anxieties whose appeasement contributed to the formation of two separate hierarchies. At Chalcedon the dispute between the rival bishops Bassian and Stephen led to fears that the city would be left without pastor and without sacraments. 'Our children will perish and our city will be ruined', the clergy cried.² Fear of the terrors beyond the grave that awaited those who died without the sacrament was universal. Severus himself defined these when he told one aged correspondent how in that event 'the soul was liable to be seized by the demons and prevented from moving to the abode of light'.³ Sometimes the demons could be more closely defined. In a time of plague at Antioch, Phoebus Apollo, usually the god of healing, was dreaded in his ancient role as the destroyer.⁴ Deep in the recesses of the minds of Syrians and Egyptians was a fear that perhaps the old gods might emerge and take their vengeance on those who had deserted them. To prevent such a catastrophe required the holy sacrament, taken perhaps as rarely as a single time each year, to be administered by a truly orthodox priest.

Severus' insistence on strict orthodoxy ('accuracy' was his favourite term) and uncompromising rejection of Chalcedon doomed the ideal of religious unity in the east for which successive emperors since Constantine had striven. Ascetic, upright, burning with zeal and intensely active, the new patriarch of Antioch had never made any secret of his rejection of the least concession to pro-Chalcedonian sentiment. In a letter written before his consecration, he told Bishop Constantine of Seleucia (Isauria) how he had warned Anastasius' emissary, John of Claudiopolis, why it was impossible for him to accept Chalcedon even as the formal means of condemning Nestorius and Eutyches. 'This argument is silly', he had said, 'for if one were to accept Chalcedon and the *Tome* of Leo 'which are the lifeblood of the abomination of Nestorius, how can we honestly say that we accept this synod against Nestorius?' The half-truth represented by Chalcedon's condemnation of Eutyches was no worthier than similar half-truths uttered by Arian councils directed against Sabellius.⁵ As for the

---

¹ 'Diphysites' – *Select Letters* I. 60 (ed. Brooks, p. 182); 'Aposchistae' – Cyril of Scythopolis, *Vita Sabae* (ed. Schwartz), p. 115 and pp. 140–1, and Theophanes, *Chron.* A.M. 6004 (ed. Classen, I, 241).
² *ACO* 2. 1. 3, p. 52, para. 53.   ³ *Select Letters* III. 4 (ed. Brooks, pp. 246–7).
⁴ John of Beith-Aphthonia, *Vita Severi* (ed. Kugener), p. 246.
⁵ *Select Letters* I. 1 (ed. Brooks, pp. 5–6).

Henotikon itself, Severus was ready to accept this, in the sense however that it cancelled Chalcedon. Thus there could be no question of agreeing to both. Elsewhere he had said that he regarded the *Henotikon* as 'superfluous' for 'it does not touch on the stumbling-block that sprang up at Chalcedon and separated the Churches'.[1] Only as a concession to the weak would he agree to it as a proof of orthodoxy, so long, however, as the *Tome* and Chalcedon were denounced at the same time.[2]

He forebore, however, from open breach with the aged emperor. In his allocution at the moment of his consecration on 8 November 512, he told his hearers that he accepted Nicaea, Constantinople and Ephesus I, with the *Henotikon* characterised as 'inspired by God', but Chalcedon and the *Tome* were condemned and with them 'the masters of Nestorius', Diodore and Theodore, and 'all their friends and disciples', including for the first time Bishop Barsaumas of Nisibis (435–84), the great Persian Christian leader.[3] Antioch had now parted company finally with its daughter church across the Euphrates. Not long after, on 24 November, Severus preached again in Antioch and delivered a more specific attack on Chalcedon. The heresy of Eutyches had been condemned there only to uphold the worse impieties of Nestorius. Only by complete acceptance of Christ as in nature one, his flesh, however, sharing the same substance (*ousia*) as ours, could death be overcome and man rise to immortality and sonship of God.[4] Early in 513 Severus held a general synod of his patriarchate at Antioch and offered the same terms to all clergy as a basis for unity, namely acceptance of the *Henotikon* coupled with denunciation of the *Tome* and Chalcedon.[5] The monks of Syria II refused, and they were supported by the Palestinian monks and the patriarch of Jerusalem, Elias. The unity of the churches in the east was not to be accomplished by a zealot.

Severus was not a man for half measures. In the next six years the flail of his reforming energy made itself felt from one end of his vast domain to the other. The church of Antioch was in a pitiable state: 'strangled by its creditors' and 'laden with a burden of interest' was how Severus

---

[1] *Ibid.* I. 3 (Brooks, p. 16).

[2] See *Ep.* 49 (ed. Brooks, *PO* 12. 2, pp. 323–4).

[3] Text of allocution with comment published by Kugener, *PO* 2, pp. 322ff. Theodore Lector states that the denunciation of the *Tome* and Chalcedon constituted a breach of faith by Severus, but in view of Severus' conversation with John of Claudiopolis this does not seem justified.

[4] Ed. and tr. E. Porcher, *Revue de l'Orient chrétien* 19, 1914, pp. 69–78.

[5] See Honigmann, 'Evêques et Evêchés monophysites', p. 15.

described it.¹ The patriarch's revenues were expected to finance costly gifts to provincial churches, and supplement the incomes of his more needy suffragans. To do this it would appear from Severus' letters that income was derived to a considerable extent from offerings supplemented by simoniacal payments from would-be priests.² At a time when the prestige of clerical office stood so high that people were prepared to pay even for the right to wear clerical dress without any intention of taking Orders,³ the temptation to accept such payments was great, and though Severus recognised the system for the abuse it was, his letters do not indicate that he was able to prevent it.

Poverty and the continuous pressure of theological controversy had made his subordinates edgy and quarrelsome and ready to accept bribes as payment for changing their views.⁴ Isauria gave him particular trouble, not always resolute in its orthodoxy and riddled with personal feuds. Severus did not spare the laggard from the lash of his tongue. Thus Musonius of Meloe was described as 'one known to us for his impudence and rustic denseness, and for love of money which is greater than all evil things'.⁵ He earned a princely stipend of 12 solidi a year.⁶ No wonder he was 'burdensome and hostile to the orthodox' and 'always bribing his neighbours'⁷, and that in reply to a charge by one of Severus' presbyters that he was acting as a moneylender he exclaimed, 'By God, what do you care, you who receive the stipend of the clergy of Antioch, while I possess nothing in my city, not so much as six denarii'.⁸ How could he be zealous on one solidus a month! Before long he gave up his see as a bad job.

There were others like him, bishops, such as Paul of Olba (Isauria) who first charged the bishop of Diocaesarea with performing ordinations in a monastery outside his diocese, then accused his archdeacon of simony and finally quit his own diocese without permission for the capital.⁹ He was ultimately deprived. Some were simply laggards, like the bishop of Arca

---

¹ *Select Letters* I. 9 (ed. Brooks, p. 44); compare I. 17 (Brooks, p. 64).

² Severus complains to Philoxenus that Flavian had abetted simony (*ibid.* I. 48, p. 131).

³ *Ibid.* I. 8, p. 43. Such people often claimed the pay of their 'rank'!

⁴ *Ibid.* I. 22, p. 80. Flavian gave 'both robes and treasures to the unholy Bisula and he drew the inhabitants of his country to him'. Compare I. 4, p. 26.

⁵ *Ibid.* I. 4, p. 23. See also Honigmann, 'Evêques et Evêchés monophysites', pp. 84ff., regarding Isauria.

⁶ *Select Letters* I. 22, p. 78. ⁷ *Ibid.* I. 4, p. 24.

⁸ *Ibid.* I. 4, p. 25. ⁹ *Ibid.* I. 26, p. 86; cf. I. 4, p. 29 and I. 23, p. 82.

near Tripolis, described by Severus as having no more initiative than an old pack-horse.¹ Another did nothing 'except for money or under the influence of passion'.² Among the lower clergy and even the monks the situation was not much better. Readers and choristers spent their time in the church of Perga in quarrels over matters of precedence;³ at Anazarba one of the presbyters was employing himself writing poetry,⁴ elsewhere another was embezzling church property,⁵ a third was guilty of forgeries for the same purpose so clumsy 'that they looked no more like the originals than an elephant resembled a sheep'.⁶ Others supplemented stipends by moneylending.⁷ The impression gained from Severus' voluminous correspondence is of an immensely busy administrator attempting to right in a few years disorders resulting from generations of neglect.

Severus was stern but scrupulously fair in matters of discipline, with an eye for the pretentious excuse and shady deal. 'The devout Julian [a presbyter of Tarsus] tried by the use of deception to make the illustrious Heliodorus an accomplice in his plot by giving him false information', Severus writes.⁸ The case, however, was tried on the spot to save expense, and Severus sent down two of his presbyters to conduct the inquiry. These roving commissions dealt with a wide variety of cases, as every type of problem, ranging from matrimonial rows to disputed episcopal elections, poured in for decision. And always it was by precedents established in church councils, based on Scripture and the Fathers, that Severus founded his verdicts. A case had to be established 'by the good and invincible arguments that we have, adducing the ordinances of the church and dispensations of the Fathers'.⁹

Dominating the whole scene, however, were the doctrinal issues, and the fissures in the vast patriarchate were plain to see. In the east, at the monastic town of Q'ennesrim (Chalcis), Severus received a tumultuous reception in the autumn of 514. He was obliged to preach an impromptu sermon to the townsfolk, only for this to be interrupted for him to settle some dispute in the city. He was heart and soul with its 'God-loving people'¹⁰ in an area

---

[1] *Ibid.* IV. 6, p. 265.   [2] *Ibid.* I. 14, p. 58.   [3] *Ibid.* I. 7, p. 40.
[4] *Ibid.* I. 27, p. 88; cf. I. 63, p. 196, where Severus condemned a deacon who was not only married twice but taught his children to dance and play the harp.
[5] *Ibid.* I. 40, p. 113.   [6] *Ibid.* I. 19, p. 69.
[7] *Ibid.* I. 4, p. 25 and I. 36, p. 103.
[8] *Ibid.* I. 40, p. 113.   [9] *Ibid.* v. 6, p. 316.
[10] *Homil.* 56 (*PO* 4. 1, pp. 78–82). The sermon breaks off and it is not known what the trouble was about. Compare *Homil.* 57, also preached at Q'ennesrim.

The rise of the Monophysite movement

where there were no less than sixty monasteries within twenty miles of the town. In Asia Minor, Pamphylia also was his, the metropolitan, Castor of Perga, communicating with the Alexandrian Patriarch Dioscorus II when the latter visited him in 516 on his way to the capital. Severus was glad at this news.[1] In Cilicia, however, and parts of northern Syria (Euphratesia), loyalty to Nestorius was still a force. In Tarsus particularly, though the bishop gave the appearance of agreeing with Severus, the name of Nestorius was left on the diptychs and he was commemorated among the martyrs.[2] At Cyrrhus, Theodoret's old see, Severus preached in vain against Antiochene doctrine, and once he had been removed to exile there were demonstrations in honour of Theodoret's memory.[3] In some villages we hear of Nestorians. Two aspiring clerics from coastal hamlets in Cilicia were reported to Severus as having 'sailed west' to be ordained at the 'hands of Nestorians'.[4] At the other end of the spectrum there were what Severus describes as 'abominable congregations of Adelphians' in eastern Cappadocia, heretics apparently of advanced Eutychist sympathies.[5]

But the real problem was always Chalcedon. Severus tried to combine extreme strictness of principle with a certain amount of flexibility towards individuals. When he became patriarch he laid down that 'each bishop should remove from the sacred tablets the names of those who had signed the impious deeds of Chalcedon'.[6] To those who were prepared to accept Severus' arguments yet found some difficulties in carrying out his instructions he was fair and even charitable. In particular he was opposed to humiliating those who wished to accept anti-Chalcedonian orthodoxy by re-ordination or rebaptism. He insisted on penance only, following the practice of Timothy the Cat towards repentant Proterians. 'In every matter whatever', he wrote, 'that is not contrary to the canons we ought to give help and to act in unison with one another.'[7] He kept his own precept. He knew of the Rebaptism controversy in Africa and of Cyprian's decisions, but in long letters to John the Tribune and to an unnamed bishop he points out how, granting the base character of the heretical administration of baptism and other sacraments, such severities could be modified by later examples.[8] He quotes at length those of Dionysius of Alexandria and of

---

[1] Another instance of Pamphylia being pro-Monophysite: Severus, *Select Letters* VI. 3, p. 259.
[2] *Ibid.* I. 24, p. 84.
[3] *Ibid.* V. 12, p. 341.
[4] *Ibid.* I. 6, p. 38.
[5] *Ibid.* I. 13, p. 55.
[6] *Ibid.* I. 19, p. 68.
[7] *Ibid.* I. 5, pp. 37–8.
[8] *Ibid.* V. 1 and V. 6.

Pope Xystus or Ambrose in regard to the followers of Auxentius, and later of Timothy the Cat to the Proterians. The sacrament was always the same, like a seal whether encased in gold or iron as Gregory of Nazianzus had argued.[1] Thus, those who had not been canonically ordained and now repented of their faults should be restored to their ministry.[2] 'Diphysites' did not need to be rebaptised or re-ordained.[3] The object in all cases, Severus added, was the salvation of those who had perished. Excessive zeal would tend to perpetuate heresy.[4]

To those, however, who remained unconvinced Severus was inflexible. 'Separation for piety's sake', he says more than once, 'is better than vicious concord.' There were no half-tones between heresy and orthodoxy. He wrestled with his conscience whether or not he should visit on his deathbed the former Bishop Cosmas of Apamea who had once been in communion with him but had lapsed. 'Woe is me', he lamented, 'that I should give a bodily greeting to any man when my soul does not agree to the greeting.' Eventually he went, remarking perhaps with unconscious cynicism after the event, 'I considered it a sin for us to enter upon a contentious and profitless conversation while the man was on the point of giving up the ghost'.[5] Heresy to Severus was always heresy. His duty was to maintain the church blameless, and compared with this comprehensiveness was secondary.

At one time he thought that 'the present condition of the holy churches in the east [i.e. Syria] and in Egypt was purer than the conditions in former times'.[6] For the first four years of his episcopate he had some justification. In 514 a great synod met at Tyre summoned at the emperor's order, but largely due to the energy of Philoxenus.[7] Alexandria and Jerusalem were represented, as well as the provinces of Severus' patriarchate. There the memory of the reverse at Sidon three years before was wiped out. The synod accepted the *Henotikon* as annulling Chalcedon.[8] 'All the bishops

---

[1] *Ibid.* III. 3, p. 240.   [2] As a certain Silvanus: *ibid.* v. 11, p. 326.

[3] *Ibid.* v. 6, p. 304. Another solution adopted at this period by anti-Chalcedonians was to accept sacraments given by a priest acting in ignorance of error but not those 'the moment his error has been revealed' – Letter attributed to Philoxenus, published by J. Tixeront, *Revue de l'Orient chrétien* 8, 1903, p. 629.

[4] *Select Letters* V. 1, p. 280.   [5] *Ibid.* I. 11, p. 50.

[6] *Ibid.* I. 11, p. 51.   [7] *Chron. ad ann. 846* (ed. Brooks and Chabot), p. 168.

[8] Zacharias Rhetor, *HE* VII. 12: 'Et [Severus] dum fidei veritatem oriri facit scriptum ipsius Henotici Zenonis in abolitionem eorum quae Chalcedone gesta sunt factum esse interpretatus est.' Compare *ibid.* 10.

assembled with Severus and Philoxenus and proclaimed the truth.'[1] As a final stroke Elias of Jerusalem, who had reluctantly accepted all the changes from 511 to 514 but remained at heart a firm supporter of Chalcedon, was deposed by the governor and exiled on 1 September 516. These years were the highwater-mark of the success of Severus and Philoxenus. Dioscorus and Timothy the Cat were once more restored to the diptychs. The east was now to all appearances Monophysite.[2]

Opposition, however, to Severus and Philoxenus gathered strength. Except for a few isolated though important centres, like Apamea, Syria II was united against him. The bishops refused to accompany their new metropolitan, Peter of Apamea, to another council summoned by Severus at the emperor's behest to meet at Antioch (spring 515).[3] Letters of Palestinian monks to their ally, Alcison of Nicopolis, though full of prejudice, give the impression of mounting confusion in that province and in neighbouring Arabia, with some of the leading bishops, such as Peter of Damascus and Julian of Bostra, abandoning their sees in protest.[4] In 516 the bishops of Epiphania, Rhaphania and Arethusa solemnly sent Severus a sentence of deposition and excommunication, and the military commander refused to restore Severus' authority against the will of the population of these towns.[5] In this he was supported by Anastasius himself.[6] The emperor, concerned above all for the loyalty of the eastern provinces, was not prepared to up-

[1] *Ibid.* 12. Severus himself shows his satisfaction when arguing against the rebaptism of 'Diphysites' by pointing to 'the sudden conversion to virtue' that had recently taken place throughout the Oriental diocese, 'where all by divine counsel under behest from above have cast forth and banned the heresy of the duality of the natures with definite anathemas' (*Select Letters* v. 6. p. 308).

[2] So the view of Zacharias Rhetor, *HE* VII. 12 (ed. Brooks, p. 38): 'Et sic praeter sedem Romanorum hoc consensu rursus fidei concordes erant sacerdotes.' For the restoration of Dioscorus and Timothy, see the petition against Bishop Peter by some of the clergy of Apamea, Mansi, *Collectio* VIII, cols. 1123–6.

[3] Severus, *Select Letters* I. 20, p. 71. Apamea was divided in allegiance, the city being Greek and pro-Chalcedonian at this stage, but overshadowed by the presence of the anti-Chalcedonian monastery of Kaphra-Birtha in the immediate neighbourhood, which took care to copy in 535 and preserve the *Acta* of Second Ephesus in Syriac (Hefele/Leclercq, *Histoire des conciles*, II. 1, 556n).

[4] Evagrius, *HE* III. 33. For the events of this period, see P. Charanis, *Church and State in the Later Roman Empire: the Religious Policy of Anastasius I, 491–518* (Madison, Wisconsin, 1939), pp. 69–74.

[5] Evagrius, *HE* III. 34. For Severus' summons of a council to deal with the disobedience of the two bishops, *Select Letters* I. 21, p. 73.

[6] Severus' letter to the archiatros Theotecnus (*Select Letters* I. 24, pp. 83–4).

hold Severus in the face of hostile public opinion. More menacing even, was the letter which 207 leading monks of the province, led by Alexander, presbyter and archimandrite of the great monastery of Maro south of Damascus, sent to Pope Hormisdas near the end of 517.[1] This attacked Severus, accused him of daily denouncing 'the holy synod of Chalcedon' and 'our blessed father Leo', and using violence, including responsibility for a shocking massacre of 350 monks while on a pilgrimage to extort assent to his views, and they claimed that their own appeal to the capital had fallen on deaf ears. They declared their will that Nestorius, Eutyches, Dioscorus, the two Peters and Acacius 'and those who communicated with them and all those who defended so much as one of those heretics' should be excommunicated. This was serious for the whole of the east. Not only had the authority of both the patriarch of Antioch and the capital been bypassed by a direct appeal to Rome, but the Pope was given a firm assurance that Acacius *and* those who had communicated with him or defended his memory could be struck from the diptychs with the agreement of a considerable body of opinion in the east. For the first time the system of patriarchal jurisdiction in the east through which Constantinople was the ruling see was challenged.

Other events showed that Severus' position was not as strong as it appeared. In Cilicia the neo-Chalcedonian movement represented by John the Grammarian was always a menace, drawing its strength from a traditionally Chalcedonian opinion in the province. In the south Severus' emissaries failed miserably to convince some important Arab tribes on the Syrian frontier that Monophysitism was a satisfactory belief.[2] His senior suffragan, Epiphanius of Tyre, who was the deposed Flavian's brother, refused to accept his synodical letters.[3] In 517 a rift appears to have opened between him and Dioscorus II of Alexandria.[4] The latter was less anxious than Severus for specific denunciation of the *Tome* and council to be coupled with acceptance of the *Henotikon*. In April 518, Severus complained

---

[1] *Coll. Avellana* 139. For Hormisdas' answer in February 518, see *ibid.* 140. A similar letter may have been sent by the monks of Transjordan in the autumn of 516 to Anastasius. See Victor of Tunnuna, *Chron.* ad ann. 516 (ed. Mommsen, p. 195, line 33).

[2] Theodore Lector, *HE* II. 35 (*PG* 86. 1). Also, Victor of Tunnuna, *Chron.* ad ann. 512 and Theophanes, *Chron.* A.M. 6005.

[3] *Ep.* 51 (ed. Brooks, *PO* 12. 2, pp. 325–6): 'Epiphanius exalted himself against my great weakness and became an example to others to secede.'

[4] *Epp.* 49–50 (*PO* 12. 2, pp. 323–5).

that the Monophysite addition to the *Trishagion* was not being accepted in Egypt even though it was in parts of the province of Asia.[1] As events later in the century showed, even common belief did not always suffice to hold Antioch and Alexandria together.

Ultimately, however, it was Severus' failure to bring Palestine and Jerusalem into his orbit, coupled with the loyalty of the European provinces to Chalcedon, that wrecked the emperor's and his ambition for Monophysitism to be the religion of the Byzantine world. Severus had a poor opinion of the Patriarch Elias,[2] probably without real justification, for he merely continued what had become the traditional policy of his see. He was loyal to the policies of the capital so long as these did not involve outright denunciation of Chalcedon, and in this he was supported by the great majority of the monks led by the archimandrite Sabas. The monks considered in particular the actions of Philoxenus damaging to the faith and resting on spurious documents. Though many leant towards Apollinarist views they hated Severus and they believed that Flavian and Macedonius had been unjustly deposed.[3] By 514 they were beginning to look for allies in the west by writing their grievances in detail to Alcison, the pro-Chalcedonian bishop of Nicopolis and metropolitan of Epirus.[4]

It is interesting that Severus is not mentioned in the letter, and that it had apparently taken all this time before the pro-Chalcedonians in the east had realised that many of the more striking anti-Chalcedonian proof-texts attributed to Athanasius, Gregory the Wonderworker and Pope Julius were not genuine. Now that they did, there was no possibility of Palestine accepting Severus' doctrine. One of the best weapons in Severus' armoury as a debater had been struck from his hand, for he himself did not hesitate to denounce Apollinarius as 'mad'[5] and yet he was using his works! The deposition of Elias only made the monks more determined. In Sabas they had found a leader of Severus' own mettle. When the new patriarch John (516–24) vacillated between anathematising Chalcedon or not, Sabas forbade him. With another monk, the holy man Theodosius, he mounted the *ambon* in the Church of St Stephen outside the walls of Jerusalem on

---

[1] *Homil.* 125 (*PO* 29. 1, p. 249).

[2] *Select Letters* I. 42 (ed. Brooks, p. 119): 'the man is utterly unstable and weak'.

[3] For instance, the Apollinarist grammarian Sergius who criticised Severus found support among the Palestinians. See *Chron. ad ann. 846* (ed. Brooks and Chabot), p. 168.

[4] Evagrius, *HE* III. 31.

[5] As in *Homil.* 80, *PO* 20. 2, p. 329, or *Select Letters* II. 3 (ed. Brooks, p. 215).

either side of the new patriarch and together, amid deafening shouts from the crowd, they anathematised all who did not accept Chalcedon, including Severus himself. Theodosius added the phrase which was to become the pro-Chalcedonian battle-cry, 'the Four Councils even as the Four Gospels'. Monks and bishops were in accord again, in favour of Chalcedon.[1] Severus' reminders of what happened to traitors in Jerusalem in the time of Juvenal fell on deaf ears.[2] Before the end of his reign Anastasius was being cursed in the churches there.[3]

Meantime, opinion in the European provinces had been veering strongly in favour of Chalcedon. One suspects that here also the fall of Macedonius had been the decisive event. Already in 512 the Illyrian bishops under Alcison of Nicopolis had written to Pope Symmachus stating their support for the council, and the Pope had replied with a letter of encouragement (6 October).[4] In 515 forty bishops withdrew communion from Dorotheus, metropolitan of Thessalonica, and petitioned the Pope to admit them to his communion.[5] Support for the Pope was emphatically renewed by the synod of Epirus under Alcison's successor in 516.[6] Hormisdas, who succeeded Symmachus in July 514, saw this meetings as a great step forward towards ending the schism with victory for his see.[7]

Meantime, the revolt of Vitalian had turned out to be more than the usual barbarian rumpus over pay and conditions; and Hormisdas knew well how to take advantage of it. Vitalian's demands at first had a purely eastern application, namely the restoration of the *Trishagion* in its old form and the recall of the patriarchs Macedonius and Flavian. These demands were supported almost to a man in the European provinces in the empire. With his army heavily defeated at Acra on the Black Sea (summer 514) and Scythia, Moesia and Thrace in Vitalian's hands, Anastasius agreed to restore the *Trishagion*, and in the late autumn of 514 indicated his willingness to make a further effort to end the schism with Rome. In two letters sent on 28 December 514 and 12 January 515, he formally invited the Pope to a coun-

---

[1] Cyril of Scythopolis, *Vita Sabae*, ch. 56 (ed. Schwartz, pp. 150–2); Theophanes, *Chron.* A.M. 6005.
[2] Severus, *Homil.* 125 (April 518) = *PO* 29. 1, p. 253.
[3] Evagrius, *HE* III. 34.
[4] *Coll. Avellana* 104 = *Epist. rom. pontif.*, ed. Thiel, *Ep.* 12. 2. See L. Duchesne, *L'Eglise au VIe siècle* (Paris, 1924), pp. 40–1.
[5] Theodore Lector, *HE* (ed. Hansen, p. 150, para. 521).
[6] Marcellinus Comes, *Chron.* ad ann. 516, and *Coll. Avellana* 119.
[7] *Ibid.* 120 (November 516).

cil to be held at Heraclea in Thrace on 1 July of that year.[1] The object, however, was to deal with the local matter of 'contentions about the faith that had arisen in Scythia', i.e. not necessarily the general religious situation and the validity of Chalcedon. But the Pope's mediation was asked. Hormisdas took his time before answering. He was able to tell the Gallic synod of the submission of the church in Dardania, Scythia and Illyricum to him,[2] and when legates led by Ennodius, the aristocratic bishop of Ticinum, were sent to Constantinople in the summer of 515 they were instructed to negotiate the end of the schism only on the terms of the complete acceptance of Chalcedon and the denunciation of Dioscorus, Timothy the Cat and Peter Mongus and of their abettor Acacius.[3] At this stage Hormisdas was prepared to attend a council himself, and he seems to have regarded Alexandrian recalcitrance as his principal enemy, with Acacius as an accessory. His *Libellus* mentioned neither Euphemius nor Macedonius, nor even Severus and his colleagues at Antioch.[4] The furthest Anastasius would go, however, in his answer to the Pope was to agree to accept Chalcedon as a disciplinary synod not conflicting with Nicaea, to restore exiled bishops to their sees, and berate the exuberance of the Egyptians for their continuous anathematising of the *Tome* and Chalcedon. Nestorius and Eutyches, already anathematised, would remain so.[5] Acacius, however, he would not sacrifice, claiming quite rightly that the effect on popular feeling might be disastrous. In all this Anastasius showed that, whatever his hopes for Monophysitism, his aim was religious peace and security for all his subjects. The living were not to be made to suffer for the errors of the dead. Unity achieved by force would be displeasing to God. His closing words citing the text 'My peace I give unto you, my peace I leave with you' (Jn. 14. 27) summarised his position.[6] He would hold to it even if it meant the continuance of schism with Old Rome.

For another eighteen months negotiations dragged on but without hope of success. There was now no Henoticist party in Rome, even in the Senate.

---

[1] *Coll. Avellana* 107 and 109. Anastasius addressed Hormisdas as 'archbishop and patriarch'.

[2] *Ep.* 9. 2 (*Epist. rom. pontif.*, ed. Thiel, p. 759). Compare *Coll. Avellana* 136, Avitus and the Gallic bishops to Hormisdas (dating end of 516).

[3] *Coll. Avellana* 115.

[4] *Ibid.* 116a. See Charanis, *The Religious Policy of Anastasius I*, pp. 60–1.

[5] Hormisdas, *Ep.* 10 (Thiel, pp. 761–4) = *Coll. Avellana* 125 (especially *CSEL* 35. 2, p. 539), winter 515–16.

[6] *Coll. Avellana* 125.

Emperor and Pope realised compromise was impossible. Anastasius refused to impose what he believed to be the creed of the Latin minority only on the empire as a whole. The defeat of Vitalian's attempt to take Constantinople in 516 gave him a respite, and to Severus far away in Antioch a cause for rejoicing.[1] After another embassy from Rome had intrigued to consolidate pro-Chalcedonian opinion against the emperor, Anastasius lost patience. On 11 July 517 he wrote to Hormisdas, 'From henceforth we shall suppress in silence our requests, thinking it absurd to show the courtesy of prayers to those who with arrogance in their mouth refuse even to be entreated'. 'Injuriari et adnullari sustinere possumus, juberi non possumus':[2] 'You may insult and thwart me, but you may not command me.'

The sands were running out for him. He was now ageing fast. His wife Ariadne had died in 515, in April 518 the Patriarch Timothy followed. His successor John felt the 'winds of change' sweeping in from the west, and was a temporiser. From Antioch Severus wrote, 'As to the man who has just been instituted and holds the prelacy of the royal city, we have learned that he is John... who is thought to be inclined to the right opinions and holds out some pleasing hopes to the orthodox, but is more desirous of adopting a deceitful middle course'.[3] Unfortunately there was no room for such. Five years of Severus' puritanical rule in Antioch, and the growing support for the papal policies in Illyricum and the west had destroyed the vision of the promoters of the *Henotikon* of a united church based on communion between the four eastern patriarchates. In the capital, Severus' star was waning. In April his excommunication by the new patriarch was rumoured.[4] All awaited the ending of the Anastasian era. Later critics such as a continuator of Joshua Stylites compared the last years of Anastasius with those of King Solomon in his decline.[5] With his death at the age of 88 on 8/9 July 518, the winter of the Roman Empire might be over, but what was the spring to portend?

The story of the revolution that shook the Byzantine world in the few weeks following the death of Anastasius has been told in detail by Vasiliev.[6]

---

[1] Severus wrote a hymn 'On Vitalian the Tyrant and on the Victory of the Christ-loving Anastasius the king' (Paul of Edessa, *The Hymns of Severus and Others*, ed. E. W. Brooks, *PO* 7, Paris, 1911, p. 710).

[2] *Coll. Avellana* 138 (ed. Guenther, *CSEL* 35. 2, p. 565).

[3] *Select Letters* VI. 1 (ed. Brooks, pp. 360–1). Severus himself wondered how long it would be before John was forced off his 'middle position'.

[4] *Ibid.* p. 362.   [5] Joshua Stylites, *Chron.* CI (ed. Wright, p. 76).

[6] *Justin the First*, pp. 136–60.

The rise of the Monophysite movement

Only a few points need be noted here. First, it would seem that the turning point in the capital had been the deposition of Macedonius. Like John Chrysostom and Flavian he was beloved by the people and when he died in exile was regarded as a martyr. The *ekboeseis* of the crowd in the tumultuous Sunday and Monday of 15 and 16 July in altercation with the Patriarch John during a solemn Eucharist in Sancta Sophia are extraordinarily interesting. 'Long live the new Constantine, long live the new Helena, long live the patriarch worthy of the Trinity', they cried. Warming to their theme they shouted, 'Either leave or proclaim the Synod [Chalcedon]. Now proclaim the Synod of Chalcedon. Whoever does not anathematise Severus is a Manichaean himself. Anathema to Severus the Manichaean. Throw out Severus, throw out the new Judas... The Holy Mary is the *Theotokos*. The Synod said so.' Next day, on the occasion of the commemoration of the 'Holy Fathers of Nicaea' there were further disturbances. 'Restore the relics of Macedonius to the church. Return to the church those who are in exile for the faith. Dig up the bones of the Nestorians, dig up the bones of the Eutychians. Who Nestorius is, I do not know, anathema to him from the Trinity... Send the decrees of the council to Rome at once.' The last sentence was pregnant with menace.

From these shouts one can deduce that Justin, the elderly comrade in arms of Vitalian and captain of the Imperial Guard (the *excubitores*) who had been proclaimed emperor, was expected to remove Severus, restore Macedonius to the diptychs, assert the Council of Chalcedon and take steps to end the schism between Old and New Rome. These demands were put in due form by monks in the capital to a Home Synod on 20 July and were accepted by the 43 or 44 bishops there present. Severus was declared deposed. On 6 August a synod of thirty-three bishops at Jerusalem also put the Four Synods on the diptychs, and on 16 September Severus' enemy Epiphanius of Tyre did likewise. Popular shouts were directed against Severus and 'the Manichaeans' and other symbols of unpopularity. Anti-Egyptian feeling was rife. 'The city does not want Egyptian wood merchants. Expel the Acephaloi [i.e. Severus' party]. If they prevail, we die. Restore Flavian to the diptychs.' More formally, Severus was accused of communicating with Jews, of sorcery and embezzlement. He had indeed had the doves representing the descent of the Holy Ghost removed from the baptismal fonts in Antioch[1] – a neat piece of liturgical symbolism, for

---

[1] Recorded among the accusations against Severus brought by Antiochene monks to the great Home Synod of 536: Mansi, *Collectio* VIII, col. 1039 and *PO* 2, p. 342.

whereas to the Antiochene theologian the descent of the dove of Jesus was the all-important act showing the achievement of unity with God, to the Monophysite such symbolism was blasphemous. 'One should not venerate the Holy Spirit in the form of a dove', Severus said.[1] He had offended, and the extent of the demands of the revolution in the east was roughly the restoration of the *status quo* of a decade back. There was no demand for the abrogation of the *Henotikon*. With the flight of Severus to Alexandria, where he arrived on 29 September, its purpose appeared to have been satisfied.

Justin and his advisers underestimated the price the papacy would exact in return for the restoration of unity. The new ruler was a Latin-speaker from Dardania. He made no bones about his acceptance of the *Tome* of Leo and Chalcedon,[2] and was a strong believer in the Roman or western interests of the empire. In the first vital two years of his reign he was forced to rely not only on his nephew, the Count Justinian, but on another Chalcedonian westerner and successful rebel, Vitalian. The pro-Monophysite element at court with whom Severus had had close contact was in eclipse. At Rome, Pope Hormisdas was a diplomat of the first rank. He had been kept informed of the steady swing of opinion towards Chalcedon through the empire by his faithful Sleepless Monks, and of the change of sentiment in the capital. The Latin-speaking provinces of the empire, and so also Syria II and, with reservations, Palestine, were entirely loyal to him. At his side was the Egyptian deacon Dioscorus, an exile who hated his fellow-countrymen and their heresies. His hour had come as well as the Pope's. The terms for a settlement would be stiff indeed.

It was not simply that Rome demanded the striking of Acacius 'and his associates' from the diptychs. Theologically also the papacy had moved further from eastern Christology than was apparent at Chalcedon. Duchesne has pointed out that while Leo had quoted the First and Second Letters of Cyril to Nestorius, Gelasius in his treatise ' On the Two Natures, against Eutyches and Nestorius' had not mentioned Cyril at all among sixty citations from the Fathers.[3] Nor did Hormisdas. Yet what concerned the east far more than the west was the paradox of divine suffering pondered

---

[1] *Loc. cit.*

[2] See the anecdote told of him in the *Chron. ad ann. 846* (ed. Brooks and Chabot), p. 169: also Theodore Lector's view, 'a blazing zealot' (Hansen, p. 151).

[3] See Tractatus III (*Epist. rom. pontif.*, ed. Thiel, pp. 530–57); Duchesne, *L'Eglise au VIe siècle*, p. 59. The interesting point is that Gelasius should have found himself in complete agreement with an Antiochene document which he used as his source.

and expounded by Cyril. To the east this was the way to salvation and on this issue Chalcedonian and anti-Chalcedonian were united. Rome appeared indifferent to this outlook and obsessed, as in the time of Leo, with matters of discipline. Great emphasis was laid by Hormisdas on the Petrine claims of the Roman see and need for obedience to it. There had been no change in the basic position of the parties since Chalcedon. It became clear within a year of the formal ending of the schism that not even the pro-western monks in the capital were prepared to accept an orthodoxy not grounded in Cyril, nor an ecclesiastical order that took no account of the status of the patriarch of Constantinople.

Meantime, the papacy had won what appears at first sight to have been a shattering victory over the pretensions of New Rome. On 7 September 518, Justin had informed Hormisdas of the steps he was taking to end the schism.[1] Negotiations between Rome and Constantinople went on through the winter and resulted in the despatch of legates to the imperial capital in January 519. The *Libellus Hormisdae*, which was presented to bishops in Illyricum for signature en route, contained the names of those who must be formally denounced ere communication could be restored. These were Acacius, Timothy the Cat, the two Peters 'and their followers' (*sequaces*). The mission was feted all the way across Illyricum. It was solemnly met by Counts Vitalian and Justinian with the Senate at the tenth milestone from Constantinople and received a rapturous reception when it reached the capital on 25 March.[2] What exactly happened in the next three days is still somewhat obscure, but the upshot was that the *Libellus*, which after some argument the Patriarch John signed on 28 March in the presence of the legates, the senate and the emperor, condemned not only Acacius but his four successors including Macedonius, together with the Emperors Zeno and Anastasius.[3] No wonder the original document was sent to Rome to be kept thereafter in the archives of the Roman church.[4]

---

[1] Three letters were drawn up on that day, from Justin, his nephew Justinian and the Patriarch John. Gratus, a 'comes sacri consistorii', was commissioned to take them to the Pope: *Coll. Avellana* 143, 147 and 146. See Vasiliev, *Justin the First*, p. 162.

[2] Dioscorus' report (*Suggestio*) to Hormisdas, *Coll. Avellana* 167 (ed. Guenther, *CSEL* 35. 2, p. 618) – a vivid account. Compare the less detailed summary by the legation, *ibid*. 223, also written on 22 April.

[3] *Ibid*. pp. 618 and 684: 'Anastasii quoque ac Zenonis nomina similiter ab altaris recitatione summota.'

[4] For the sequence of events September 518 to March 519, see Vasiliev, *Justin the First*, pp. 161ff. Most important for the final negotiations is Dioscorus' *Suggestio* = *Coll.*

The orthodox reaction, 513–527

The almost total collapse of the Byzantine position is not easy to explain. Reading the report which the deacon Dioscorus sent in his clipped but expressive Latin to Hormisdas about the final negotiations, the momentary personal failure of the relatively weak Patriarch John involving all his clergy cannot be ruled out.[1] Slavonic historians have seen with some justification the final act of the Acacian schism as a great disaster for the east, and much of the religious policy of Justinian towards the papacy as a sustained effort to repair what in retrospect was realised to have been a colossal blunder. Tactically, Hormisdas had gained more than even he had imagined possible when he despatched his embassy to the capital in January 519. Only a few years before, he had envisaged the likelihood of having to persuade Anastasius to restore Macedonius to his see.[2] Macedonius had been solemnly replaced on the diptychs on Anastasius' death: now he was equally solemnly proclaimed anathema. Even more incredible were the anathemas on the emperors Zeno and Anastasius. Admittedly both were dead, but such proceedings even against the imperial departed were unheard of, and were never to be repeated so long as the Byzantine Empire lasted. Not even Gelasius had demanded the denunciation either of Zeno or the *Henotikon*.[3] In the instructions to the legates, Hormisdas had been prepared to leave the term 'Acacii sequaces' vague. No one beyond the original Gelasian list of reprobates need be banned by name. Others (no doubt this included Macedonius and his immediate predecessors) would be

Avellana 167. One reads, however, 'certamina' as 'discussion' or 'debates' rather than 'struggles' (Vasiliev, p. 177). The sentence, for instance (p. 620), 'apud quos archimandritas et certamina nos habuisse suggerimus dicentibus illis: "sufficit quia archiepiscopus noster fecit; nos factum eius sequimur"', suggests absence of real resistance. The following phrase, 'post multa certamina', therefore, 'After much discussion'. For the use of 'certare' = 'negotiate', see Leo, *Ep.* 156.

[1] *Coll. Avellana* 167 (ed. Guenther, *CSEL* 35. 2, p. 620). The archimandrites told the legates, 'sufficit quia archiepiscopus noster fecit [signed the *libellus*]; nos factum eius sequimur'.

[2] *Coll. Avellana* 106. 19 (ed. Guenther, *CSEL* 35. 2, p. 517): 'Si dixerit imperator [Anastasius] "de Macedonio dicitis, intellego subtilitatem vestram: haereticus est: nulla ratione revocari potest", respondes, "nos, domine imperator, nullum personaliter vindicamus ... si haereticus est, iudicio cognoscatur et non sub opinione orthodoxi injuste dicatur oppressus"'; i.e. Macedonius should have a fair hearing and a chance to prove his orthodoxy. Four years later, his memory was to have neither.

[3] In his letter to Hormisdas reporting the agreement, Justin makes no mention of the inclusion of his predecessors in the anathemas: *Coll. Avellana* 160.

quietly left off the diptychs.[1] This, together with the confession that Rome had always been apostolic and orthodox, was regarded as a just settlement. Now all this had been gained and much more, for every enemy of Old Rome in the previous forty years lay prostrate under anathemas.

The completeness of the triumph, however, could not disguise one fact, namely that it had been largely due to the emperor himself. Justin and his consort Euphemia played analogous parts in the ending of the schism to Marcian's and Pulcheria's at Chalcedon. They too regarded the empire as incomplete without the unity of Old and New Rome. As the patriarch wrote to Hormisdas on 21 April 519, it had been the emperor 'who most wisely prepared the union of the churches'.[2] He had told the Pope that what had been accomplished had been sought for a long time by him with all his energy.[3] He had practically ordered the clergy of the capital to sign the *Libellus* brought by the legates.[4] Without this initiative the Pope would have been as helpless as Leo had been after Ephesus II. While the inclusion of Justin's predecessors in the anathemas may have been aimed at branding the strong 'Anastasian' party in the capital as heretics, Justin did not intend to humiliate his patriarch. John was the first prelate of the capital actually to use the title 'Ecumenical Patriarch',[5] and his correspondence with Hormisdas betrays no sign of defeat.

The clue towards understanding John's views may be found in the *Libellus* which he wrote on 28 March, the day he signed the Pope's *Libellus*, and sent off a month later with other correspondence. In this letter he writes, 'I accept that the two most holy churches, that is to say, your Old Rome and our New Rome, are one, and I admit that that see of St Peter and this see of the imperial city are one', i.e. as always, there was one Rome whether 'Old' or 'New'. Then John confessed acceptance of the four councils

---

[1] *Ibid.* 158 (p. 606): 'Saltem hoc acquiescite, ut anathemizato specialiter per libellum, quem vobis dedimus, Acacio de successorum eius nominibus taceatur abrasis eorum de diptychorum inscriptione vocabulis.'

[2] *Ibid.* 161 (p. 612): 'adunationem sanctissimis ecclesiis sapientissime comparavit [Justinus]'. Compare *ibid.* 147 (pp. 592–3), Justinian, 7 September 518, to Hormisdas.

[3] *Ibid.* 160 (pp. 610–11): 'Scias effectum nobis, pater religiosissime, quod diu summis studiis quaerebatur.' Compare *ibid.* 161 and 233, the views of the Patriarchs John and Epiphanius.

[4] *Ibid.* 167 (p. 620): his question to the clergy concerning the *Libellus*, 'et si vera sunt, quare non facitis?' Even so, how Macedonius was added to the list of excommunicated remains mysterious.

[5] Mansi, *Collectio* VIII, col. 1038.

by name, including Constantinople which first defined the rights of his see, as being valid 'regarding the confirmation of the faith and the ordering of the Church', *before* referring to the 'Tu es Petrus' text and relating it to 'the apostolic see'. There is no mention of the condemnation of any emperor. John therefore accepted, as his predecessors had done, the 'presbeia' of Old Rome, and swallowed the condemnation of his four predecessors in his see, though only Acacius by name.[1] Nothing else had been surrendered. Subsequently he writes to Hormisdas as an equal and rejoices simply in the new-found unity between Old and New Rome.[2] The all-important 28th canon of Chalcedon had not been renounced. Indeed it was never mentioned. Confirmation too had been implied for Constantinople as an ecumenical council. This meant that appeals to Rome, such as that from the monks and bishops of Syria Secunda a few years before, would not be tolerated. For all his deference to the person of the Pope, Justin intended little more than the *status quo ante Acacium* and the consequent return of Rome to the unity of Christendom. What that meant at the very outset to the thrusting Count Justinian who stood at his uncle's side was that the Pope could be ordered to hasten to the capital when required:[3] as Vigilius was to be. Hormisdas might appear to have gained a great victory. Neither he nor his successors were to find the situation so comfortable. His efforts meantime to play the part of a second Leo by maintaining a busy correspondence with all and sundry was to have little influence on the ecclesiastical policy of Justin and his nephew.[4]

The emperor had judged the situation well. The Byzantine world was ripe for a reconsideration of Chalcedon on its merits. For all their energy Severus and Philoxenus were at heart sectaries in a society that wanted religious unity round the person of the emperor. Christological heresy was abominated, but the continuous stress on the need of 'accuracy' of belief palled on the large number of eastern Christians outside Egypt who were beginning to see Severus' arguments against Chalcedon as so many quibbles. People were not prepared for venerated and long-dead bishops

---

[1] *Coll. Avellana* 159. See Dvornik, *Byzance et la primauté romaine*, pp. 53–9.

[2] *Coll. Avellana* 161 (p. 613); again Justin's personal role in the negotiations is stressed.

[3] *Ibid.* 147. On 7 September 518 Hormisdas was told 'sed absque quadam dilatione vestrum expectamus adventum'.

[4] One example is Justin's refusal to restore Helias of Caesarea and two other bishops to their sees on Hormisdas' demand: *Coll. Avellana* 193 (7 June 520). Helias must wait until his successor had died!

The rise of the Monophysite movement

to be anathematised simply because sixty years before they had been present at Chalcedon. So much is clear from Severus' and Philoxenus' own correspondence of the time. Many of their clergy had their doubts. Severus shows, for instance, how a certain presbyter-monk Mark first accepted Chalcedon, then rejected it and then revised his opinion again. He was 'repeatedly changing', wrote Severus.[1] His senior colleague Soterichus of Cappadocia had similar hesitations. He was not always, Severus implied, 'entirely on our side'.[2] He had been consecrated by Macedonius, but was an enemy of Flavian and one of Severus' few allies at Sidon in 511; at the same time, he had continued to regard the *Henotikon* as sufficient guarantee of orthodoxy, and threw his weight on the side of maintaining unity. He spoke for many. One can discern this from a letter to Severus, in which an archimandrite in Cilicia admitted that he had taken into his monastery his brother who was described as 'an avowed Nestorian'. In the course of an argument he had said, 'It's the same thing for us to speak of two natures as of one incarnate nature of God the Word.'[3] Ordinary educated citizens of Palestine and the Syrian seaboard for whom Procopius of Caesarea could speak, would have agreed heartily. The dogmas for which people were called upon to suffer were 'senseless'.[4] Not everyone even in sixth-century Byzantium was a religious fanatic.

Philoxenus had similar experiences. The lector Maro of Anazarba in Cilicia to whom he wrote *circa* 515 provides an interesting insight into pro-Chalcedonian arguments in the provinces. The 'two natures' confessed at Chalcedon were 'not separated', and if the Christian confessed that Christ was consubstantial with the Father in his divinity and with man in his humanity, there must be 'two natures'. This was the sort of argument that

---

[1] *Select Letters* v. 5 (ed. Brooks, pp. 291–2). Severus adds tartly that 'repentance was not the same sort of thing as superintendence or headship of a monastery', for which 'the devout Mark' was unsuitable (*ibid.* p. 292).

[2] *Ibid.* VI. 1 (pp. 361–2). For his outlook, see Severus, *Ep.* 46 (*PO* 12. 2, p. 319). He was typical of the Byzantine episcopate who would follow the religion of the emperor so long as it did not lead to outright Nestorianism. It illustrates also the influence exercised by the patriarch of the capital through his right of consecrating bishops in the provinces of Asia Minor.

[3] *Select Letters* VII. 4 (pp. 374–5), addressed to Naunus, bishop of Seleucia. In a letter to Dionysius of Tarsus (v. 7, p. 318), Severus blames him for receiving Indacus, bishop of Cotycus, 'when he has not agreed in confessing the same faith as we'.

[4] *Anecdota* XI. 25: τινα ὑπὲρ ἀνόητον φέρεσθαι δόγματος. See also A. Cameron's assessment of religious feeling in the capital in Justinian's reign, *Agathias* (Oxford, 1970), p. 123.

The orthodox reaction, 513–527

Cyril had encountered after the Formula of Reunion,[1] and it was now used in favour of the council. On these lines the *Tome* and council could be accepted at least because of the anathemas against Nestorius and Eutyches. Moreover, it was wrong to anathematise the dead, men such as Diodore and Theodore who had died in the peace of the church, and wrong also to curse bones and cinders which could do no harm to anyone.[2] The views of the great majority of clerics seem to be those described by Severus relating to preparations for the abortive synod called at Heraclea. 'Some said that the object of their endeavours was not to accept the impious synod that assembled at Chalcedon in respect of the definition of faith but in respect of the rejection of Eutyches and his doctrines.'[3] This was to be one of the big arguments by the neo-Chalcedonians of Justinian's reign. Underlying opinions had not altered much since the time of the *Henotikon*, and it is not surprising that more than 2,000 bishops eventually signed a *libellus* authorised by Justin accepting Chalcedon. The eastern episcopacy was prepared to accept two natures if explicable on Cyrillian terms, as 150 years before they had acquiesced in *homoousios* as expounded by the Cappadocian Fathers.

The Pope's legates asked for stern measures to be taken against those who opposed reunion.[4] Before their arrival the government under Vitalian's influence had acted vigorously against the anti-Chalcedonian leaders and replaced many of these with convinced supporters of the council. The Edessene Chronicle speaks of a veritable purge taking place in 518–19. Paul the presbyter of Constantinople, known as 'the Jew', Severus' supplanter, was typical of these new men, and his cruelty to the Monophysites in Edessa made him notorious. Perhaps, related to the rise of Justin's nephew, the Count Justinian, to power in the course of 519–20, one can detect a slowing down of tempo, if not a change of aim. In particular throughout Justin's reign Egypt remained largely unaffected by the events in the capital.[5] Alexandria was able to provide a refuge to the Monophysite

---

[1] See above, p. 123.
[2] See J. Lebon, 'Textes inédits de Philoxène de Maboug', *Le Muséon* 43, 1930, pp. 39–56, and Halleux, *Philoxène*, pp. 211–14.
[3] *Select Letters* 1. 24 (ed. Brooks, p. 84), to the archiatros Theotechnus. This was Anastasius' view also. See above, p. 217.
[4] Indicated in *Coll. Avellana* 192, 9 July 520.
[5] For Egypt's continued immunity from interference in Justin's reign, see Zacharias Rhetor, *HE* VIII. 5: 'Sedes vero Alexandriae haud commota est, et Timotheus Dioscoro successor factus est, nec recessit nec synodum accepit Iustini diebus.' Compare also Liberatus, *Brev.* XIX (*PL* 68, col. 1033D).

leaders. Severus describes the country as united against the *Tome* and council,[1] and possibly memories of Anastasius' failure to impose a patriarch in 516 counselled prudence. Nothing came of Hormisdas' offer in December 519 of Alexandria to his faithful deacon Dioscorus.[2]

For the rest, the government proceeded on its own cautious way. Over the remainder of the Oriental diocese it seems as though the authorities were prepared to watch events now that Severus and his friends were in exile. At Edessa, for instance, Justin refused to countenance the forcible removal of Bishop Paul from his see, and acquiesced in another Monophysite succeeding him (October 522).[3] Elsewhere in Syria pro-Chalcedonians took the law into their own hands. Theophanes notes that in city after city the Blue faction, i.e. the pro-Chalcedonians, took over power and 'cowed their opponents with violence and murders', and that this continued until the sixth year of Justin's reign.[4] Obviously in such situations there was no need for the government to act. Even so, the writer of the *Life* of John of Tella says that persecution 'did not cross the Euphrates' for two years after the death of Anastasius.[5] The consecration of John himself and of James of Serug, later known among the Monophysites as 'the flute of the Holy Ghost and harp of the Orthodox Church', took place in these years.[6] The severities too of Paul 'the Jew' in the patriarchate of Antioch involving wholesale expulsion of clerics and monks and the use of military force against monasteries were disavowed by

[1] *Select Letters* V. 11 (ed. Brooks, p. 328).
[2] *Coll. Avellana* 175, 3 December 519.
[3] *Chron. Edessenum* LXXXVII (ed. Guidi, p. 9), and also *Chron. ad ann. 846* (ed. Brooks and Chabot), pp. 173–4. See Vasiliev, *Justin the First*, p. 233.
[4] Theophanes, *Chron.* A.M. 6012 = A.D. 520 (ed. Classen, I, 256). Theophanes makes Antioch the starting place of the Blue reaction. The main reason seems however to have been economic. The Syrians had had enough of the parsimony of Anastasius. Momentarily his religious policy was involved in the revulsion against other aspects of his reign.
[5] Elias, *Vita Johannis episcopi Tellae* (ed. Brooks), p. 37.
[6] On James of Serug, see Michael the Syrian, *Chron.* IX. 15, and E. Tisserant, 'Jacques de Saro', *DTC* 15, cols. 300–3, and P. Peeters, 'Jacques de Saro appartient-il à la secte monophysite?', *AB* 66, 1948, pp. 134–98, especially pp. 194–8. Logically James may perhaps be claimed as Chalcedonian, but emotionally it seems clear that his sympathies were on the other side. According to the Nestorian Chronicle of Séert (History of Severus of Antioch), James was formerly a Chalcedonian, but converted to the opposite standpoint, was consecrated bishop of Batnai by Severus and Philoxenus and finally ended as a Julianist (ed. Scher, *PO* 7, p. 121).

Justin, and by the end of 520 Paul had in turn been removed.[1] James of Serug, who died in 521, praised the emperor's doctrine and his clemency towards Paul of Edessa.[2]

The correspondence between Constantinople and Rome in the years 519–21, especially the letters written by Justinian, gives some clue as to the mind of those who had brought about the reunion. On the one hand, Severus was repudiated.[3] On the other, no effort was spared to make the reunion palatable both on ecclesiastical and doctrinal grounds to the churches in the east, apart from Alexandria. This involved delicate and ultimately unsuccessful negotiations with Hormisdas. The aim of the authorities seems to have been to get the Pope to agree to the restriction of the anathemas to be pronounced in the churches as the price of unity to the names contained in the papal *Libellus* of January 519. Acacius could be sacrificed, so too the two Peters, Timothy the Cat and Dioscorus, but the correspondence makes no mention whatsoever of the inclusion of Zeno and Anastasius, while great pressure was exerted to persuade the Pope not to insist on the formal anathematisation of any other bishop by name. 'There was need', wrote Justin on 9 July 520, 'for a certain milder regulation in respect of the names of the bishops who were not specifically enumerated in the original letter which your Sanctity is known to have sent to us, but also of others whose memory those cities, in which while living they flourished, love especially.'[4] The somewhat ambiguous wording probably hid a plea for silence on Acacius' successors at the capital, but point was given to the plea by a report which Epiphanius, who succeeded John's successor as patriarch in February 520, sent to Hormisdas on 9 September. He stated openly that in Pontus, Asia and particularly in Syria the Pope's *Libellus* would not be accepted unless some concession was made concerning the names of bishops to be erased from the diptychs.[5] In

---

[1] Zacharias Rhetor, *HE* VIII. 1, accuses Paul of 'Nestorianism' and gives this as the reason for his expulsion. Justin, however, indicates to Hormisdas various secular crimes as the grounds: see *Coll. Avellana* 241, 1 May 521.

[2] See Vasiliev, *Justin the First*, p. 234, who translates a letter from James to the monks of Mar Bassus and Paul himself.

[3] In Syria II and Palestine he and his followers were already being denounced as 'Acephali' – true schismatics. See *Coll. Avellana* 232a (ed. Guenther, *CSEL* 35. 2, p. 704), from the clergy, abbots and landowners of Jerusalem and Syria Secunda to Justin (undated, but probably summer 520), a strongly pro-Chalcedonian document.

[4] *Coll. Avellana* 192 (ed. Guenther, *CSEL* 35. 2, p. 650); cf. *ibid*. 232, p. 702.

[5] *Ibid*. 232, pp. 707–8.

Thessalonica, the key to the papacy's hold on the western provinces of Byzantium, there were riots directed against the Pope's legates.[1] Weight was lent to these arguments by Justin himself on the same day, who pointed out, rather belatedly, that of Hormisdas' predecessors Anastasius II had required only the passing over in silence of Acacius. No one else had been named for anathema.[2]

Equally pressing was the doctrinal issue. For the previous thirty-five years the *Henotikon* had been the norm of orthodoxy. This had now been abrogated. What was to be put in its place? Since Gennadius' time Constantinople had been the stronghold of Chalcedonian orthodoxy, a position only temporarily overlaid by the events of the last years of Anastasius' rule. There had never been, however, the slightest prospect that as a reaction to this a 'Nestorianising' doctrinal solution would be accepted. Chalcedon was not sufficient guarantee, it was mooted, against Nestorius.[3] Even before the arrival of the papal legates for the reunion discussions there had been fears lest the Sleepless Monks in their zeal for Roman orthodoxy would force an openly two-nature Christology on the east.[4] When the legates did arrive there were many who said openly that those who communicated with representatives of the apostolic see were 'Nestorians'.[5] The lead in resisting any such doctrinal tendencies was taken by the Scythian monks (i.e. monks from the frontier province at the mouth of the Danube) who had arrived in the capital recently in the wake of Vitalian. They were anti-Nestorian, and took their stance on the letters of Cyril to Successus,[6] but they combined their acceptance of Chalcedon with the assertion 'one of the Trinity suffered in the flesh' (*unus de Trinitate passus carne*), that is, that Christ who was born, suffered and died was one of the Trinity.[7] They found allies in

---

[1] *Ibid.* 208, pp. 667–8, and 225, pp. 689–90.

[2] Justin to Hormisdas, 9 September 520 (*Coll. Avellana* 232, ed. Guenther, *CSEL* 35. 2, p. 702). See above, p. 199, and compare Justinian to Hormisdas, *ibid.* 147.

[3] *Ibid.* 216 (Dioscorus to Hormisdas, p. 676), and cf. *ibid.* 224, p. 686, 'non sufficit synodus contra Nestorium'.

[4] The emergence of Theopaschism in the first months of Justin's reign is indicated by Dioscorus in his statement that it was being discussed before the legates' arrival in the capital ('antequam nos Constantinopolim ingrederemur'): *Coll. Avellana* 224 (ed. Guenther, *CSEL* 35. 2, p. 685).

[5] *Ibid.* 217, p. 677 (the legates to Hormisdas).

[6] Thus, Dionysius Exiguus' letter to John and Leontius, *ACO* 4. II, pp. xi–xii.

[7] The documentation is collected in *ACO* 4. II, pp. 3ff. See also E. Amann, 'Scythes (moines)', *DTC* 14, cols. 1746–53, and Duchesne, *L'Eglise au VIe siècle*, pp. 59–69. Ch. Moeller, 'Le Chalcédonisme et le néo-chalcédonisme' (Grillmeier/Bacht, *Das*

the capital in representatives of the patriarchate of Jerusalem, who as in Zeno's reign attempted to act as honest brokers between the more moderate elements for and against Chalcedon.[1] The Theopaschite formula seemed to provide just such a possibility. It emphasised the role of Mary as *Theotokos*, it implied Cyril's assertion in his Twelfth Anathema that 'God the Word suffered in the flesh', and it could boast a respectable pedigree extending to the *Tome* of Proclus to the Armenians, which from now on was to assume an ever greater importance in the development of a distinctive Byzantine orthodoxy. Yet it lacked the Monophysite sectarian overtones of 'who was crucified for us'. The monks, too, shared something of the emergent neo-Chalcedonian vocabulary with their concept of the 'enhypostasisation' of the Word. This conceded the reality of Christ's human nature, without, however, accepting that it possessed an individuality (*hypostasis*) of its own. Theopaschism was to become the orthodoxy of the capital. With his sure feel for public opinion the powerful Count Justinian after some wavering made this teaching his own.

On both the doctrinal and disciplinary issues Hormisdas proved unco-operative. From June 519 onwards he had been receiving unfavourable reports from the deacon Dioscorus about the Scythian monks. Dioscorus suspected them rightly of being anti-Roman, and he described them as having been 'stirred up by the devil' and 'adversaries of the prayers of all Christians', and their leader, Maxentius, as a 'false abbot'. He reported his own stand as 'Chalcedon and nothing else', and urged Hormisdas to do the same.[2] Maxentius, finding himself baulked by the legates, set off with

---

Konzil von Chalkedon, I, 637–720 at pp. 676–9), is over-critical through judging the monks purely by Latin Catholic standards.

[1] See Philoxenus, *Letter to the monks of Senoun* (ed. Halleux), pp. 62 and 66. Philoxenus was contemptuous of their activities. 'Unus de Trinitate passus est' had often been on the lips of Palestinian monks as a guard against Antiochene theology, and they also admitted the hypostatic union though they were bitterly opposed to Severus. See Moeller, 'Le Chalcédonisme et le néo-chalcédonisme', p. 657.

[2] *Coll. Avellana* 224. 11. Compare *ibid*. 216. 5ff. He also pointed out that the eastern affirmation that the Son was 'consubstantial with the Father' lay at the root of the tendency to deviate from Chalcedon. 'Quia quotienscumque patres de dei filio domino nostro Iesu Christo disputaverunt, filium dei verbum consubstantialem patri, homousion patri dixerunt. Iste autem sermo ideo numquam est in synodis a patribus introductus, quia procul dubio Catholicae fidei minime poterat convenire' (216. 7).

some of the Scythian monks to Rome in the summer of 519. The brief they took with them after it had been refused by the legates contained an outline of current theological opinion in the capital. Prominent in it was the emphasis placed on the episcopal replies to the encyclical of the Emperor Leo I, the *Tome* of Proclus, Cyril's Letters to Nestorius, and the condemnation of the works of Theodore of Mopsuestia and his followers along with the usual reprobates Nestorius, Eutyches, Dioscorus, Timothy the Cat, Peter Mongus and Acacius.[1] Thus Theodore took his place formally among the villains of the Byzantine scene, while no patriarch of the capital apart from Acacius was to be sacrificed. In both these particulars, the démarche of Maxentius foreshadowed the future policy of the emperor and patriarchate of the capital. Already in July 519 the Count Justinian was warning Hormisdas that peace was unlikely to be restored in the churches without a rapid favourable response to the monks.[2] Meantime, the monks had reached Rome (August 519). Hormisdas at first received them well as protégés of Vitalian and approved Maxentius' *Libellus* 'in the presence of the bishops, people and Senate of Rome',[3] but afterwards he had second thoughts, delayed his judgement, and finally seems to have rejected the Theopaschite formula, not because he thought it actually heretical but because it was novel (Oct. 520). The assassination of Vitalian in July 520 at the instance of Justinian, however, made little difference to the popularity of the monks in Constantinople. They merely gained a more powerful patron. In this same month Justinian was attempting to assert his will over the papacy and pressing not only for acceptance of the Theopaschite formula as orthodox, but also that the Pope abate his demands regarding the names of the bishops to be removed from the diptychs.[4] Hormisdas was told, too, that three bishops whom he wished to see restored must wait until their supplanters had died. He was given no help in his efforts to oust his enemy Dorotheus of Thessalonica. Meantime the monks, disappointed in Rome, were befriended rather surprisingly by influential African bishops in exile in Sardinia, a further embarrassment for the Papacy.

Stalemate ensued. Hormisdas' aim, like that of Leo before him, was to

[1] Text in *ACO* 4. II, pp. 3–10.
[2] *Coll. Avellana* 191: 'celerrimo dato responso'. This letter contains no address and was sent through the brother of a certain Proemptor. It is clear, however, that it is addressed to Hormisdas and it is included in his correspondence.
[3] *ACO* 4. II, p. 3.
[4] *Coll. Avellana* 196 (ed. Guenther, *CSEL* 35. 2, pp. 655–6).

use the emperor as the executive arm of the church, giving nothing away himself. His emissaries were tactless. They left the impression of even refusing Mary the title of 'Theotokos', denying that the crucified Christ was one of the Trinity, and failing to anathematise Nestorius. They became increasingly unpopular, and regarded as representatives of an alien theology. Even so, the unity between the two Romes remained Justin's ideal, and he was prepared to listen to papal promptings at least to enforce a semblance of conformity in the provinces. Could Justin disagree with what Hormisdas wrote on 26 March 521 in one of the last documents of the *Collectio Avellana*: 'For the following saying sounds incessantly in my ears: No man having put his hand to the plough and looking back is fit for the kingdom of God'?[1] The Pope was a determined man as well as a shrewd one.

Sometime in 521 the fateful decision was taken to press home the persecution through the whole east apart from Egypt. By the end of Justin's reign at least fifty-five bishops had been expelled from their sees,[2] though often the authorities were prepared to wait for the Monophysite to die before replacing him with a Chalcedonian. Laymen were not molested, but the sternest action was taken against the anti-Chalcedonian monks. For them, Michael the Syrian's assessment that the whole of Justin's reign was marked by persecution was true enough.[3] They were treated by the Chalcedonian bishops with the utmost harshness. In Euphratesia (north-east Syria), Osrhoëne, Mesopotamia and around Antioch, where Syriac was the language of Christianity and Philoxenus' influence was strong, monks were given the alternative of signing a *libellus* of conformity with Chalcedon or being turned into the desert. Some, even the monks of the great monastery of Senoun, wavered. Others, little houses containing a bare half dozen inmates, collapsed.[4] In the *Life* of John of Tella, it is interesting to read how the majority opinion among John's congregation was that the emperor must be obeyed. Chalcedon, at least for the time being, must be accepted as the emperor's will, and John's act of defiance in remov-

[1] *Ibid.* 238. 14, p. 737.
[2] The *Chron. ad ann. 846* gives the names of fifty who were expelled at this time, including eighteen from Caria and Asia, and three from Cappadocia (ed. Brooks and Chabot, pp. 171–3). See Honigmann, 'Evêques et Evêchés monophysites', pp. 25ff.
[3] Michael the Syrian, *Chron.* IX. 13.
[4] Philoxenus, *Letter to the monks of Senoun* (ed. Halleux), p. 77. The lack of zeal in Maboug itself is interesting, but perhaps not surprising in view of the reception of the *Henotikon* there a generation before. Philoxenus was not popular personally there.

The rise of the Monophysite movement

ing the name of a Chalcedonian predecessor from the diptychs was not popular.[1] On the other hand, large numbers chose exile. John himself quitted his see with some twelve others from the same district.[2] Among the archimandrites expelled were those of Q'ennesrim and 'the monastery of the Syrians' in Antioch, both to be famous in Monophysite history. The desert areas were swamped with homeless bands.[3] Some among the more intrepid set up new communities in the desert described by Zacharias as 'quasi πολιτεία sacerdotum, insignium ac fidelium',[4] under the leadership of John of Tella and Thomas of Dara (both fortress towns of the Roman–Persian frontier).

From his place of exile at Philippopolis under the relentless care of a pro-Chalcedonian bishop, Philoxenus realised that the moment for final separation with Chalcedon and those who upheld it had come. Bishops like Flavian or Macedonius or John of Jerusalem, who was even now striving to interpret the *Henotikon* in Chalcedonian terms, had simply aimed at restoring the 'unclean doctrine of Nestorius': the successors of Leo were 'all Nestorians' and had worked unceasingly for the rehabilitation of that heretic. There was no question of accepting communion with such individuals.[5] Before he died in 523 he wrote in his Confession of Faith 'how the Hesitants [*Diakrinomenoi*] could be likened to the tribe of Judah when confronted with the idolatrous practices followed by the Ten Tribes'. They parted company with those who set up their 'two natures'; for how, he asks, could they who alone were worthy of the title of 'orthodox offer obedience to a council which had caused Israel to sin'? 'Nay, a curse lay on that council and all who agreed with it for ever.'[6] He anticipated his colleagues by fifteen years.

A study of the distribution of the areas mainly affected by the repression shows that, excluding the metropolitans who would naturally become the target for change, in Euphratesia 5 out of 7 known incumbents of sees at this time were exiled, in Cilicia II (immediately north of Antioch) the same proportion, in Isauria 9 out of 12,[7] Phoenicia Libanesia all 7 known

[1] Elias, *Vita Johannis episcopi Tellae* (ed. Brooks), pp. 37–9.
[2] John of Ephesus, *Life of John of Tella* (ed. Brooks), *PO* 18, p. 515.
[3] Zacharias Rhetor, *HE* VIII. 5.   [4] *Ibid.* VIII. 5, p. 56.
[5] Philoxenus, *Letter to the monks of Senoun* (ed. Halleux), p. 63.
[6] *Confession of Faith*, Anathema 10, ed. Budge, *Discourses of Philoxenus*, vol. II, p. xxxvi.
[7] That repression was severe in the province in 520–1 is confirmed by Severus himself, *Select Letters* I. 52 (ed. Brooks, p. 149).

bishops, Mesopotamia 3 out of 4, Oshroëne all 6, and Syria I 4 out of 7, but in Syria II none (out of 7) and none in Cilicia I, Maritime Phoenicia, and Arabia. While the evidence is far from complete, it suggests that south of the Taurus there was a tendency towards division along provincial lines. In Syria I also, the nucleus of important anti-Chalcedonian monasteries situated in the limestone massif east of Antioch was coming into being,[1] whereas in Syria II the most influential and articulate monks were pro-Chalcedonian. The contrast, too, between the strongly Greek Syria II and Maritime Phoenicia with the rest of the Oriental diocese is marked,[2] while Cilicia I, the old home of Antiochene theology, is also firmly Chalcedonian. In Asia Minor the pattern is less coherent, though often the site of a great monastery, such as Alabanda in Caria or Tagai near Seleucia in Isauria, seems to have betokened an anti-Chalcedonian bishop.[3] Both provinces seem to have been moved in the direction of Monophysitism at this period by these celebrated monasteries.[4] In Justin's reign Severus writes also to 'the presbyters and archimandrites of the holy cloisters of Caria', and praises his recipients as 'blazing with zeal'.[5]

As with other religious repressions in the fifth and sixth centuries the results of Justin's measures are not easy to determine. In Antioch during his short rule, Paul 'the Jew' was fiercely resisted and people clamoured for martyrdom.[6] Outside the city, monks were put to death when they refused to conform, but force certainly had some effect, as it had among the Donatists in Africa a century before. The bishops who did not go into exile conformed, and in Ephraim, a former military commander of the east (*magister militum Orientis*) whom Justin appointed as patriarch of Antioch in 526,[7] the Chalcedonians at last found a leader who combined drive,

[1] Michael the Syrian, *Chron.* IX. 14. See A. Caquot in G. Tchalenko's *Villages antiques de la Syrie du Nord* (Paris, 1953–8), III, 84.

[2] See Honigmann, 'Evêques et Evêchés monophysites', pp. 19ff. for discussion of the situation province by province, and map 1, pp. 250–1 below.

[3] Zeuxis, bishop of Alabanda, is listed among the exiles in Justin's reign: *Chron. ad ann. 846* (ed. Brooks and Chabot), p. 175.

[4] So the view of John Rufus to whom Tagai was 'the fountainhead of that splendour that illumined Isauria and thence the whole Orient': *Plerophoria* (ed. Nau), p. 55.

[5] *Select Letters* I. 60 (ed. Brooks, p. 179).

[6] Philoxenus, *Letter to the monks of Senoun* (ed. Halleux), CSCO, p. 67. In contrast, some of the citizens of Maboug joined the Chalcedonians (*loc. cit.*).

[7] He succeeded Euphrasius – also a strong Chalcedonian though at first he had denounced the council – after his death in the great earthquake of 526.

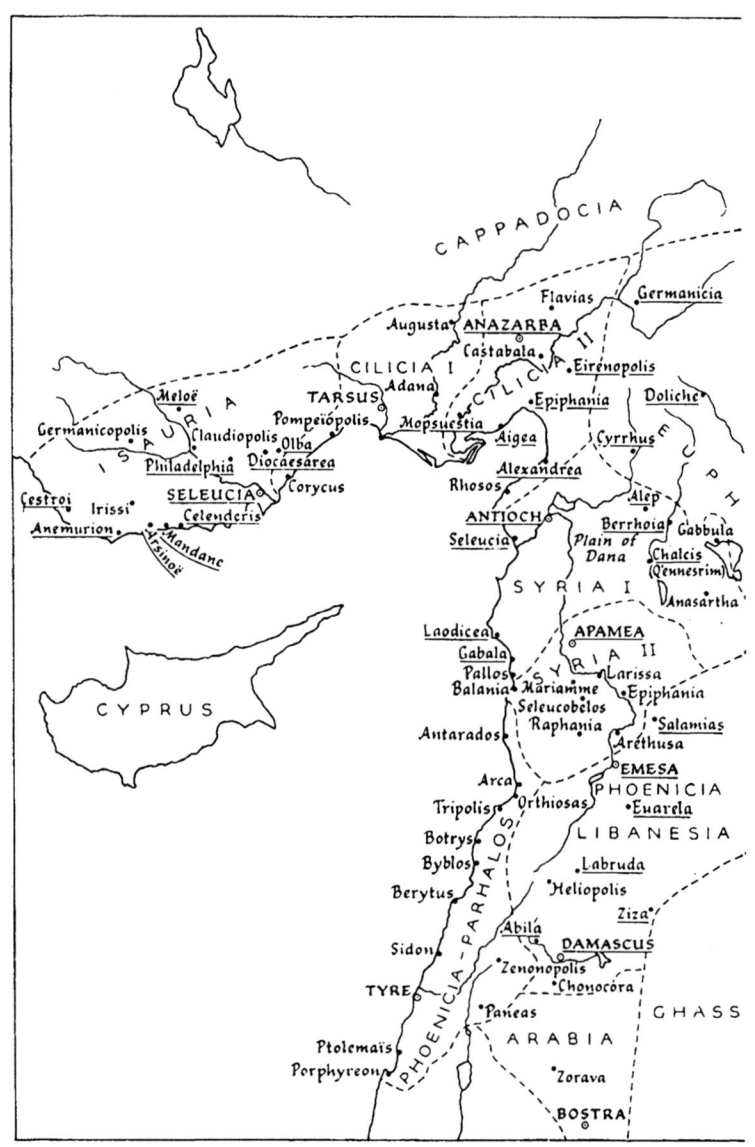

Fig. 1. Monophysitism in the patriarchate of Antioch, 512–18

(with acknowledgement to the work of E. Honigmann).

The rise of the Monophysite movement

probity and conviction in the rightness of his cause. In the eighteen years of his rule he gave his opponents little peace.

On the other hand, Severus in exile was almost as active as he had been as patriarch. At first all seemed black. 'The enemies of truth are laughing', he wrote. 'Cyrus has lapsed, Soterichus has fallen, Proclus and Eusebuna after many circuitous courses and useless movements have been cast down, and a whole trap has been spread about. Great champions of the faith Cappadocia displays to us!'[1] But the mood passed. Something like a standing Monophysite episcopal council was established in Alexandria and after a brief pause the flow of letters and directives to supporters both clerical and lay never ceased. All, especially the monks, were exhorted to stand firm.[2] Despite the persecution, Severus continued to administer the details of his diocese from Alexandria with the aid of his agents. 'As to the sub-deacon under a decree of separation from the miserable wicked Cyriac, if he repent of the sins he has committed the merciful sentence of God will absolve him through your holiness', he tells Bishop Sergius of Cyrrhus, where there had been strong Nestorian demonstrations at the time of Justin's accession.[3] For the healing of Cyriac himself, Severus says, he has mixed 'with severity a mild drug of penitence'. Archimandrites, Severus emphasised in the same letter, must take their responsibilities for appointing to the diaconate and priesthood seriously.[4] He apologises for the difficulty of communications from Alexandria that prevented an earlier answer to Sergius. In another letter Bishop Didymus was told how to deal with a deacon who had lapsed into old habits of theft.[5] He was to be put under surveillance but given another chance. Elsewhere, he gives to 'John and John the presbyters' detailed instructions about the reception of the lapsed penitent, and in particular regarding 'Silvanus who is of heretical ordination'.[6] Such were not to be re-ordained, but the precedents established by Timothy (the Cat) relating to Proterians in regard to the penances should be followed. To the same correspondents he is 'contemptuous of the Roman reason that had been reported to him of refusing to accept the Theopaschite formula, namely that the Trinity could not be numbered'. Rome never would understand the difference between the divine *ousia* which was incapable of division, and *hypostasis* of the persons

---
[1] *Select Letters* v. 13 (ed. Brooks, p. 344).
[2] *Collection of Letters, Ep.* 57 (ed. Brooks, PO 12. 2, p. 338).
[3] *Select Letters* v. 15, pp. 350–1. [4] *Ibid.* p. 357.
[5] *Ibid.* I. 58, p. 176. [6] *Ibid.* v. 11, p. 326.

of the Trinity that could be divided.[1] The Christians of Emesa, the metropolitan see of Phoenicia Libanesia, are warned against the arrival of wandering bishops like Isaiah the Armenian without credentials.[2] Clearly he had his finger on the pulse of his great diocese, and had imperial policy changed he would have been able to gather up the threads without difficulty.

Two serious threats, however, were beginning to emerge. First, the Chalcedonians controlled episcopal elections, and Justin's policy after the initial purges was to await the death of an incumbent and replace him with one who could be relied upon to accept Chalcedon. At the end of the reign there were only three places where 'believing bishops could be ordained', namely Alexandria, Mardin in north-east Syria, and beyond the Persian frontier.[3] Thither clergy from all over the east, including Armenia, came for ordination. Though the 'grass-roots' of Monophysitism in Syria remained intact and Armenia was in the process of coming into its orbit, the succession of clergy who would give a pure sacrifice was a growing difficulty for the anti-Chalcedonian leadership. Only in the next reign was the logical but radical solution of ordaining a rival hierarchy accepted.

The other problem was doctrinal. Among the exiles at Alexandria was Severus' friend and Monophysite leader in Asia, Julian, bishop of Halicarnassos.[4] With time on their hands, the exiles began to speculate into the deeper mysteries of their faith. Was the flesh of the Word really 'human flesh'? How was Christ 'consubstantial with man'? It was an old argument in Monophysite circles and had been canvassed in the capital during Severus' stay, 508–11. Julian maintained that the flesh of Christ was incorruptible from the moment of his conception, Severus that incorruption began with the resurrection. The controversy thus led back to the first principles of the movement, to interpretations of the words of Cyril and to the debate between Eutyches and his detractors. Julian was wary of the charge of Eutychism, but like Apollinarius he saw the problem in terms of Christ's liability to human sin. He maintained however (against Eutyches) that Christ could be 'consubstantial with man' through

---

[1] *Collection of Letters*, Ep. 22 (ed. Brooks, PO 12. 2, p. 218). See above, p. 213.
[2] *Select Letters* II. 3, p. 208.
[3] *Ibid.* v. 14, p. 346 (Mardin); cf. Vasiliev, *Justin the First*, p. 231.
[4] On Julian's theology and the development of the controversy, see R. Draguet, 'Julien d'Halicarnasse et sa controverse avec Sévère d'Antioche sur l'incorruptibilité du corps du Christ' (diss., Louvain, 1924). For its spread to Mardin, Severus, *Select Letters* V. 14, p. 349.

assuming the human nature of Adam *before* the fall.[1] According to one report, a monk questioned Severus and Julian on the composition of Christ's flesh and received contradictory answers, Severus asserting, but Julian denying, its mortal character. From these small beginnings the argument was to spread and grow bitter. Severus was angry in particular that the Julianists were giving his enemies in Palestine more ammunition that they gleefully used. 'See, those who pride themselves on being orthodox have been manifestly seen to be zealous for the semblances of Eutyches which is the error of the followers of Mani',[2] they were saying. Discord of an embarrassing and fundamental kind had been sown in the Monophysite ranks.

As the duel between Severus and Ephraim for the allegiance of Syria continued, the real aim of imperial policy in Constantinople was unfolding. Increasingly under the direction of Justinian this could be seen as the re-integration of Old Rome and thence western Catholicism into the orbit of the Byzantine church-state. It was aided by events in Italy where in 526 Theodoric, fearing for the future of the Gothic dynasty, sent Hormisdas' successor John I (523–6) on an embassy to Constantinople to try to persuade the emperor to lenience towards the Arians under his direct rule. The visit was a great occasion. The aged Justin allowed himself to be crowned again by his guest. Flattering statements were exchanged and doubt left as to whether pope or patriarch enjoyed the greater degree of eminence.[3] A period which lasted just over two centuries involving close relations and sometimes the dominance of the papacy by the empire had begun. As Vasiliev has so clearly seen, the short reign of Justin witnessed events which were to influence permanently the religious history of the eastern Mediterranean world.

[1] See R. P. Casey, 'Julian of Halicarnassos', *HTR* 19, 1926, pp. 206–13.
[2] Severus to the Eastern Monks, *Ep.* 35 (ed. Brooks, *PO* 12. 2, p. 290).
[3] See Vasiliev, *Justin the First*, pp. 212–21.

Chapter 7

JUSTINIAN: THE END OF COMPROMISE

The zigzag policy of Justinian towards the Monophysites in the first half of his reign is well known.[1] In this survey we confine ourselves mainly to the efforts made by the sinister and all-powerful monarch[2] to find a formula which would satisfy both Severus and the Chalcedonians, and how this failure led to the establishment of a separate Monophysite hierarchy. Justinian himself never deviated from support of Chalcedon, but his personal religion as well as the profound if imponderable influence of Theodora may have inclined him theologically towards the Monophysite position. The Aphthartodocetism that he adopted at the end of his life differed little from the views of Julian of Halicarnassos.[3] The determination with which he pursued the Theopaschite idea also suggests that this was something which corresponded to his own deeply held convictions and which he believed Severus and his colleagues would under pressure of personal argument come to accept within the framework of Chalcedon. Even so, the unity of the empire was to be Roman unity based on acceptance of the Four Councils by the five autocephalous patriarchates, while he himself acted as supreme arbitrator of religion down to details of administration.[4] To the hopelessness of attempting to gain Monophysite assent to these views Justinian added the folly of applying in political and military terms the western orientation of his uncle's and his own outlook. For contemporaries it seemed that by the last decade of his reign he had sacrificed the Roman east, and allowed the Balkans to be overrun by Hunnish and Slav barbarians far less tractable to romanisation than the

---

[1] The best account is that of E. Schwartz, 'Zur Kirchenpolitik Justinians', *Sitz. der bayer. Akad. der Wiss. zu München*, Phil.-hist. Abt. 1940, no. 2, pp. 32–81. Also, Ch. Diehl, *Justinien et la civilisation byzantine du VIe siècle* (Paris, 1901), ch. 7, and Stein, *Bas-Empire*, II, 376ff. On Procopius see B. Rubin, 'Prokopios von Kaisareia', in *PW* 23. 1, cols. 273–599.

[2] The awful picture presented by Procopius of Justinian as Lord of the Demons (*Anecdota* XII. 26 and XVIII. 1) is confirmed to some extent by Evagrius, *HE* IV. 32.

[3] See Michael the Syrian, *Chron.* IX. 34 (ed. Chabot, II, 272ff.).

[4] *Cod. Just.* I. 3. 41 and 47 for Justinian's concern for administrative detail relating to regulation of the choice and conduct of clergy.

Goths for the sake of empty conquests in the west.¹ Thus, claimed Procopius, he 'brought the empire to its knees'.² There was too a streak of unbalance in his character that made him a fanatical opponent of individuals who were not of his own way of thinking, such as the unfortunate Green party at Constantinople.³ With Justinian agreement by negotiation on any subject was always problematical.

To be fair, it is difficult to see how a western-oriented ruler with Justinian's power and ecumenical concept of the Roman Empire would have reacted differently when confronted by the almost simultaneous decline of the Vandal and Ostrogothic kingdoms and the appeals of the powerful Catholic interest in each for intervention.⁴ Regarding the Vandals, too, there was the nagging disgrace of the great disaster suffered under Leo I to be wiped out, as well as the Christian duty of overthrowing an Arian ruler. The immense initial success of the campaigns in Africa, Sicily, Dalmatia and Italy also show that the ending of Vandal quasi-independence and Gothic viceroyalty might be justified on political grounds. No sixth-century ruler could have been expected to foresee how the swift overthrow of the Vandals would merely open the way for a series of exhausting campaigns against the Berbers and few questioned Justinian's duty of protecting Christians against 'tyrants'. Indeed Cyril of Scythopolis, writing *circa* 554, claims that Saint Sabas had predicted to Justinian that God would restore the Roman Empire to its limits in the time of Honorius, including Africa and Rome, if the emperor adhered to an orthodox religious policy by destroying Arianism along with other heresies.⁵ Moreover, the reconquest of Africa itself had no immediately adverse effect on the emperor's aim of conciliating the Monophysites, and between 533 and 536 an observer might have conceded the possibility of all Justinian's plans succeeding. Within a decade, however, of their restoration in 535 the African Catholics were in the forefront of a movement aimed both at defying imperial authority in ecclesiastical affairs and, even more intolerably, at campaigning in favour of the theology of the Antiochenes, Theodore, Ibas and Theodoret. At a

---

[1] Procopius, *Anecdota* XVIII. 22–4, and XXIII. 6–8, written *circa* 550.

[2] *Ibid.* VII. 1.

[3] *Ibid.* XI. 36, and Evagrius, *HE* IV. 32.

[4] The importance of the Catholic 'lobby' in Constantinople in persuading Justinian into war is noted by Zacharias Rhetor, *HE* IX. 17 and Procopius, *Wars* III. 10. 19.

[5] *Vita Sabae*, ch. 72 (ed. Schwartz, pp. 175–6). See for this and other positive evaluations of Justinian's policies by John Lydus and Procopius, elsewhere than in *Anecdota*, W. E. Kaegi, *Byzantium and the Decline of Rome* (Princeton, 1968), pp. 212–14.

Justinian: the end of compromise

moment when the papacy seemed disposed to accept the will of the emperor so long as Chalcedon remained inviolate, the Africans produced in Facundus of Hermiana and the archdeacon of Carthage, Liberatus, active, able and well-informed defenders of the Three Chapters.[1] This development by itself sufficed to bring to nought Justinian's hopes of religious unity throughout the restored empire based on Chalcedon plus Cyril.

Justinian began his reign with a comprehensive edict against heretics.[2] In the few months (April–August 527) during which he reigned jointly with his uncle he subjected to severe legal disabilities 'heretics, Manichees and Samaritans', exempting only Gothic *foederati* from its penalties. In another edict issued in the first months of his reign he denounced the heresies of Nestorius, Eutyches and Apollinarius.[3] Adherents were denied the rights of worship and access to all state and municipal offices. A third edict[4] included Montanists, Manichaeans, Samaritans and various types of gnostics under the ban: there were executions of those suspected of being Manichees, while some notable pagans were driven to suicide.[5] In 529 the Academy at Athens, the main surviving centre of pagan thought and teaching, was closed.[6] Nothing but acceptance of the 'holy Catholic and Apostolic church of God' as defined at Nicaea was to be acceptable in the new reign. The emperor was zealous in enforcing this.[7]

In these early years the lot of the Monophysites was little altered. Bishops and monks alike remained scattered in exile. Four of the five patriarchs were now Chalcedonians, but Timothy IV (517–35) at Alexandria was as strongly opposed to *Tome* and council as his predecessors had been. Though divided among themselves between the supporters of Severus and those of Julian of Halicarnassos, the Monophysite leaders

---

[1] See R. A. Markus, 'Reflections on religious dissent in North Africa in the Byzantine period', *Studies in Church History*, vol. III (Leiden, 1966), pp. 140–50.

[2] *Cod. Just.* I. 1. 5.   [3] *Ibid.* I. 5. 12.

[4] *Ibid.* I. 5. 18.

[5] John Malalas, *Chron.* XVIII. 184 (ed. Dindorf, p. 449); Theophanes, *Chron.* A.M. 6022 (ed. Classen, I, 276).

[6] For a full discussion of this event, see A. Cameron, 'The last days of the Academy at Athens', *Proc. of the Cambridge Philol. Soc.* 195, 1969, pp. 7–30.

[7] Note Procopius' comment on Justinian's policy: 'For in his eagerness to gather all men into one belief as to Christ, he kept destroying the rest of mankind in senseless fashion, and that too, while acting with a pretence of piety' – *Anecdota* XIII. 8; and compare *ibid.* XI. 31 (persecution of pagans). For Justinian's own concern for the interests of the church, 'no less valuable than life itself', see *Novel* 57, Epilogue (to Menas, A.D. 537).

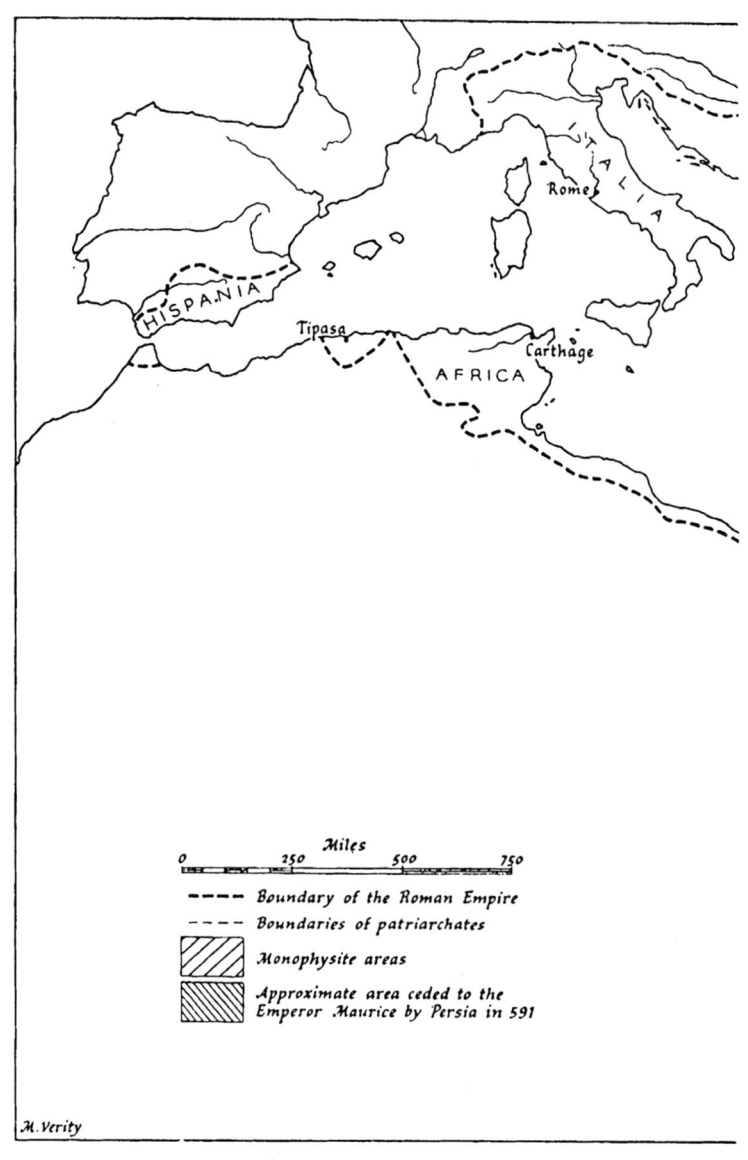

Fig. 2. The Roman

Empire *circa* 560.

remained a force to be reckoned with. Two factors prevented the disintegration of their cause. The first was the loyalty of considerable masses of the population, not only in Syria but throughout the Asiatic provinces of the empire and including many in and around Constantinople itself. Second, in a curious way representing this mood, was the personality of the Empress Theodora. The Monophysites had always had some influence at court, and in Caesaria, niece of Anastasius, Severus had retained a faithful disciple. Theodora, however, was altogether a different matter. Procopius has left a grim account of her character and misdeeds.[1] Whether she was the daughter of a *bestiarius* in the capital or an immigrant weaver from Paphlagonia, she was a woman of the people. She combined a powerful personality with the basic Monophysitism of the popular faith, and she interpreted this accurately in her career as empress. Already in 523 she had interceded on behalf of Mara, the deposed bishop of Amida, to enable him to be moved to a healthier place of exile than Petra, and until she died in 548 she was to throw all her considerable influence into the scale in favour of Severus and his friends.

Around 530 popular loyalty, particularly in east Syria, brought a fundamental change in Monophysite strategy which was to lead directly to permanent separation from the church of the empire. The story of the events resulting in this fateful decision is told by John of Ephesus in his *Life* of John of Tella who ordained him deacon at this time with fifty-nine others: 'At the end of ten years of persecution [i.e. 529/30], the faithful who remained in diverse places began to be concerned about ordinations and consulted the faithful bishops: but these latter feared to bring down on themselves even fiercer flames of persecution, and they refused to make ordinations openly, although they had made some in secret. Then complaints from the faithful persecuted arose from all sides against the blessed bishops because of the great deficiency of clerics; and they wrote and besought the bishops to make ordinations for the faithful, for the matter was urgent.'[2] The problem had gradually become more acute as the years went by with the Chalcedonians always in control. Severus had first resorted

---

[1] For instance, *Anecdota* XV. 1–4, XVII. 38–44, XXII. 27; 'a very ruthless person, filled with inhuman cruelty' (XXII. 23). On the other hand, she is praised by Malalas particularly for her redemption of the public prostitutes of Constantinople (*Chron.* XVIII. 173, ed. Dindorf, pp. 440–1).

[2] John of Ephesus, *Lives of the Eastern Saints* (ed. Brooks), *PO* 18, pp. 515–16. These were written not much later than 566, the first year of Justin II being the last recorded event in many of them.

Justinian: the end of compromise

to the idea of itinerant bishops with roving commissions to maintain the continuity of worship and sacrament. He had written to Julian, presbyter and archimandrite of the Mar Bassus monastery, in Justin's reign, 'Know therefore in times of persecution anyonesoever of the God-loving bishops who is of the same confession and the same communion with us in everything may properly supply the need [of ordaining priests and deacons] of any among the orthodox who is in need'.[1] The principle of an independent anti-Chalcedonian hierarchy had therefore been accepted by Severus if only as a purely temporary expedient for certain monasteries. Faced with John of Tella's demand for general ordinations, however, he hesitated. He may have realised that the effect on his relations with the capital would be grave. The bishops with him also feared to take the plunge. At first they refused to allow ordinations, but finally bowed to John's persuasion. The response was sensational. Hundreds of people came to him 'like a flooded river that has burst its banks'.[2] 'Every day fifty, a hundred and sometimes as many as two or three hundred men, came to him for ordination.' Supporters in areas where John was intending to come were secretly warned of his arrival and asked to bring to him suitable candidates in their neighbourhoods. All those produced were examined in reading the Scriptures and reciting the psalms and obliged before acceptance to show some evidence of literacy. Candidates, we are told, came from as far afield as Armenia, Phoenicia, Cappadocia and Arzanene on the Persian frontier.[3] Even if the number of ordinations, 170,000, is greatly exaggerated, the foundations of a Severan church extending throughout the whole of the Roman east had been laid. John of Tella himself claimed to have admitted no less than 840 members of his monastery to the diaconate in a single year (529/30).[4]

Elias' *Life* of John of Tella, written sometime after 542, claims that the success of John's mission persuaded Justinian to summon him together with eight other bishops to the capital for discussions concerning their differences over Chalcedon.[5] This would seem to be one of the main factors in Justinian's sudden relaxation of persecution in 530 or 531 and the restoration of the scattered communities of monks to their monasteries, but not the

---

[1] *Select Letters* I. 59 (ed. Brooks, pp. 178–9). Severus had written to his supporters Sergius of Cyrrhus and Marion of Sura to act together to carry out the ordinations at Mar Bassus.
[2] *Lives of the Eastern Saints*, p. 518.
[3] *Ibid.* p. 519.   [4] *Ibid.* p. 521.
[5] Elias, *Vita Johannis episcopi Tellae* (ed. Brooks), p. 39.

bishops to their sees.[1] The war with Persia also required urgent concessions to popular feeling in the frontier area, even though the return of the monks immediately caused a decline in the number of Chalcedonians.[2] Behind his move, however, was in all probability Theodora, even at this stage regarded with suspicion and loathing by Chalcedonians who visited the capital.[3]

Another factor which may have contributed to the change of policy was more to the emperor's advantage. In Alexandria, Severus and his friends were now engaged in a bitter warfare with Julian of Halicarnassos, and they were not winning. From its small beginnings the quarrel threatened to rend the Monophysite movement in Egypt asunder, and put even Severus among the minority. As already mentioned, the problem was as nice a metaphysical conundrum as had ever been propounded to philosophically-minded theologians. Was Christ's flesh inseparably united to the Word corruptible or not? Had the divine nature so absorbed the human into itself as to change its very nature and render the body itself incorruptible? Cyril had seen the problem, but failed to elucidate it. In his treatise addressed to the Emperor Theodosius II, he had written, 'It is by no means right (θέμις) for us to say that the flesh that was united to the Word could ever be corrupt',[4] but in another passage in the same letter (ch. 22), and in his first letter to Succensus, Cyril implied that the incorruptibility of the flesh freed from human weakness was only attained after the resurrection.[5] Severus, too, could be shown both to have been aware of the problem and to have

[1] The presence of Monophysite monks working on the populace in the capital may also have had its effect. That Justinian did not restore Severus and his followers to their sees is stated by Michael, *Chron.* IX. 21 (Chabot, II, 192).

[2] John of Ephesus, 'History of the convents of Amida' (ed. Brooks), *PO* 18, pp. 619–20. Later on, in Justin II's reign, the local leaders at Dara were only doubtfully loyal, 'hiding the keys of the town' so as to prevent the Roman garrison making good their retreat thither: see Michael, *Chron.* X. 9 (ed. Chabot, II, 311).

[3] See Cyril of Scythopolis' description of an encounter between Sabas and the empress while Sabas was on a delegation from Palestine. Sabas greeted the empress coldly and explained to his fellow Palestinians that they should not pray that Theodora had a child so that the teaching of Severus should receive no nourishment nor the hand of Anastasius bring confusion to the church (ed. Schwartz, p. 174).

[4] *Oratio de recta fide ad Theodosium imp.* 21 (*PG* 76, col. 1164C). Julian argued that the corruption of the flesh was only seeming, the result of Christ's voluntarily taking upon himself our infirmities (Isa. 53. 4). It was not due to the necessity of the nature of the flesh (Zacharias Rhetor, *HE* IX. 12).

[5] Cyril, *Ep.* 45 (*PG* 77, col. 236); cited by Julian for reputation in a letter to Severus recorded by Zacharias, *HE* IX. 10.

Justinian: the end of compromise

spoken publicly in favour of incorruptibility as the necessary corollary to conquest of death.[1] The debate, however, between him and Julian had now passed beyond the exchange of polite letters to the writing of angry treatises and mutual anathema. At heart the issue was whether the Monophysite movement would turn finally to Apollinarianism or not. Many of Julian's proof-texts were derived from Apollinarian forgeries of the Fathers, while Severus in his replies kept close to the genuine works of Athanasius and Cyril. But for the moment, while he could denounce Julian as a Manichee, the monks and the Eutychists in Alexandria supported him vehemently, and Severus' position was correspondingly weakened.[2]

Whatever the reasons, the wisdom of Justinian's change of policy towards the Monophysites[3] was confirmed by the events of 14–19 January 532 in the capital. The strength of the anti-Chalcedonian spirit among a large section of the poor was alarmingly demonstrated in the Nika riots, and next year after an earthquake had struck the city when the people assembled in the forum to intone the Monophysite doxology.[4] As long, also, as the nephews of Anastasius lived, Justinian's position remained fragile as they were the favourites of the Monophysites.[5] There had been ominous cries from the Greens that there should be baptism in the name of the One[6] (i.e. one nature, not two). That Justinian was saved by the resolve of Theodora also strengthened the hand of those who wanted a settlement with the Monophysites.

---

[1] Severus, *Homil.* 67 (*PO* 8. 2, p. 358).

[2] The account of the increasing intensity of the quarrel is given by Zacharias Rhetor, *HE* IX. 9–15. Michael the Syrian, *Chron.* IX. 21, emphasises that Julian's disciple Gaianus had the support of 'the rich' in his bid to become patriarch in 535 (ed. Chabot, II, 193). For Severus' anti-Julianist writings, see R. Hespel, 'La Polémique antijulianiste de Sévère d'Antioche', *CSCO*, Scriptores Syri 244 (Louvain, 1964).

[3] The exact dating is not certain. John of Ephesus (*Convents of Amida*, p. 620) implies 530 since he calculates $7\frac{1}{2}$ years' interval before Ephraim's persecution which can be placed in the second half of 536 and early 537. E. Schwartz, however (*Kyrillos von Skythopolis*, *TU* 49, ser. IV. 4, Leipzig, 1939, no. 2, p. 389 n1), prefers the summer of 531.

[4] *Chron. Paschale* A.M. 6041 = ad ann. 533 (ed. Niebuhr), I, 629, line 10. See also the article by G. Manojlovic translated and republished by H. Grégoire, 'Le Peuple de Constantinople', *Byzantion* 11, 1936, pp. 616–716 at pp. 659–62.

[5] Theophanes, *Chron.* A.M. 6024 (ed. Classen, I, 278).

[6] *Ibid.* pp. 280–1. See Bury, *History of the Later Roman Empire*, II, 39–48; for similar exclamations by the populace in June 539 (?) at the instance of Theodora, see Michael the Syrian, *Chron.* IX. 23 (ed. Chabot, II, 204).

The rise of the Monophysite movement

Meantime, the monks restored to their often ruined monasteries agreed on common action. Their episcopal leaders drew up a memorial of their case, which was sent to the emperor.[1] This took the form of a moving demonstration of loyalty to his person, unimpaired by their sufferings at his hands. They proclaimed that even in the depths of exile they had prayed daily for the emperor's majesty and for their own sins; and now, they cried blessings of every sort on his name and that of the empress and for the destruction of all rebellion[2] (they were not supporting the Nika revolution!). Their statement of belief was introduced with a long-winded deference that had come to characterise the attitude of Byzantine clergy towards the imperial court. Then, 'We confess that the Trinity should be worshipped, that is recognised in one holy co-natural power and one honour. For we adore the Father, and his only Son, God the Word who above all times was begotten of him eternally, and is with him always without change, and the Holy Spirit who proceeds from the Father and is co-natural with the Father and the Son. We say that one of the *hypostaseis* from this Holy Trinity, that is God the Word, by the will of the Father, was in these last days on behalf of man's salvation made incarnate from the Holy Spirit and the Virgin, God-bearing Mary, in a body with a rational and thinking soul, passible and co-natural with us, with a soul, and was made man without changing from what he was [before]. And so, while he is co-natural with the Father, we confess that in his humanity he is co-natural with ourselves.' In turn 'the fool Apollinarius', 'the impious Mani', and the 'deceiver' Eutyches were denounced, and the objection urged against Nestorius that he diminished both the divinity and humanity of Christ by dividing them into two natures and *hypostaseis*, and that this error had been repeated in the *Tome* and council. Moreover, at Chalcedon, the views of Nestorius, Theodore, Diodore and Theodoret of Cyrrhus had been vindicated, and a new definition of faith beyond that agreed at Nicaea had been sanctioned. Hence Chalcedon was not acceptable.[3] The demonstration was supported by

---

[1] The bishops only agreed to go when the emperor replied to their letter and guaranteed their safety (Schwartz, *Kyrillos von Skythopolis*, p. 389 n1).

[2] Zacharias Rhetor, *HE* IX. 15 (ed. Brooks, *CSCO* III. 6, p. 80); reproduced in the Appendix, p. 362 below. The reference to the rebellion, 'omnem populum rebellem', suggests that the memorial was drawn up in the spring of 532, and hence the conferences took place probably March 532 to March 533, and concluded with Justinian's letter to Pope John II; see below, p. 268.

[3] Zacharias Rhetor, *HE* IX. 15 (ed. Brooks, *CSCO* III. 6, pp. 81–4); see Appendix for full translation. The bishops met probably at Mardin.

quotations from Athanasius and Cyril, and for the first time in the history of the controversy from Dionysius the Areopagite. This devoted follower of Paul, it was claimed, had added his testimony that Christ while uniting to himself our humanity remained 'simplex'.[1]

Severus did not accompany the bishops to the capital. He too had received a summons but excused himself on the ground of age. In the long letter he wrote to the emperor[2] he denied strenuously accusations that he had been receiving money to stir up sedition. He lived in the poverty that suited a bishop and he wished to die in obscurity. Significantly for the heat of the internal dispute in Alexandria between Julian and himself, he devoted the latter part of the letter to a violent denunciation of Julian and his teaching – perhaps to anticipate a similar charge being made against himself.[3]

An account exists of only one of the conferences that took place in the capital and according to Zacharias lasted well over a year.[4] This meeting lasted three days, between the six Syrian bishops and five Chalcedonian opponents (one had dropped out through illness) and their supporters who included Leontius of Byzantium, representing the Palestinian monks,[5] and the results were inconclusive. An account was written by one of the Chalcedonian representatives, Innocentius of Maronia, to Thomas, one of the presbyters of the church of Thessalonica; but discounting the bias it is possible to get from it a fairly accurate idea of what took place.[6] The emperor's object was to persuade the Severans into union with the rest of the church by convincing them that once 'some contentions' (*quibus ambigitis*) were resolved there was no doctrinal point at issue, and Chalcedon suitably interpreted could be accepted.[7] This aim was stated by the presiding officer, the *comes largitionum*, the patrician Strategius, who explained pointedly to the Severan bishops how as an Egyptian his father, Apion, had come to the capital as an anti-Chalcedonian with strong reservations about accepting communion at Sancta Sophia, but that his doubts had been overcome by the emperors. By the end of the first day his hopes could have been justified. As the African Catholics in their controversies with the Donatists, the Chalcedonians had all the advantages in the discussion of the origins

---

[1] *Ibid.* p. 82. [2] *Ibid.* IX. 16. [3] *Ibid.* p. 88.
[4] *Ibid.* IX. 15, p. 84: 'et tempore haud parvo unius anni et amplius...'
[5] Schwartz, *Kyrillos von Skythopolis*, pp. 389–90.
[6] Text in *ACO* 4. II, pp. 169–84 = Mansi, *Collectio* VIII, cols. 817–33.
[7] That is, not as a definition of faith but as a means of condemning Eutyches and Nestorius, the position to which Justinian had reverted (see Zacharias Rhetor, *HE* IX. 20, p. 96).

The rise of the Monophysite movement

of the divisions. The Severans after accepting that Eutyches was a heretic were obliged to acknowledge that Dioscorus agreed with him and that he had condemned Flavian. How then was Dioscorus orthodox? To the plea that Eutyches probably had repented, the Chalcedonians asked, 'Why then do you regard him as a heretic?' By the end of the day the Severans were forced to admit that Dioscorus had been 'blind', that his condemnation of Flavian had been unfair, and hence the summons of a new council at Chalcedon had been justified.[1] On the following day, however, the orthodox were unable to press home their advantage. The Severans had said that their main objection to Chalcedon was that the two-nature doctrine was a novelty, and they were not impressed by the argument that not all novelties were bad.[2] Even when the orthodox were able to point to the Apollinarian and perhaps even Arian character of some of the works of the 'Fathers' that they produced, they were unable to shake the core of their opponents' position. This rested on two simple issues: first, that the council had not accepted Cyril's Twelve Anathemas but that it had restored Ibas and Theodoret, sworn enemies of Cyril and his allies, to their dignities; and second, that even if Cyril had spoken of Christ 'out of two natures', he had never uttered 'two natures after the union'.[3] The formula 'out of two natures' safeguarded the oneness of the incarnate Lord. If the Severan cause concerning the origins of the controversy was compromised, the Chalcedonians had been unable to convince them that Cyril would have agreed with Chalcedon.

On the third day there was a brief but important discussion in the presence of Justinian.[4] This enabled the emperor to put forward his Theopaschite solution as a possible compromise, and express the hope that

---

[1] Mansi, *Collectio* VIII, col. 819 = *ACO* 4. II, pp. 170–1. This admission was the precise opposite of Severus' defence of the apparent inconsistency of condemning Eutyches and glorifying Dioscorus. Eutyches, Severus told 'the orthodox brothers' of Tyre, had presented a proper confession of faith to Dioscorus that condemned Mani, Valentinus, Apollinarius and 'those who say that the flesh of our Lord God Jesus Christ came down from heaven', but afterwards 'seems again to have returned to his vomit': *Ep.* 32 (*Collection of Letters*, ed. Brooks, PO 12. 2, pp. 266–7). Further, Dioscorus had conditionally condemned Eutyches at Chalcedon: *Ep.* 33 (*ibid.* p. 268). Another admission at the conference made by the Severans was that Ibas and Theodoret were rightly re-admitted to office after condemning Nestorius.

[2] Mansi, *Collectio* VIII, col. 820 = *ACO* 4. II, pp. 171–2.

[3] Mansi, *Collectio* VIII, col. 821 = *ACO* 4. II, p. 173.

[4] Mansi, *Collectio* VIII, cols. 832–3 = *ACO* 4. II, p. 183.

it would be accepted in Rome also. Was it not true, he asked Patriarch Epiphanius, that the passion and miracles of Christ were to be attributed to the same being? In that case, was not he 'who suffered in the flesh one of the Trinity' (*deum esse, qui carne passus est atque unum esse de trinitate*)? The leader of the Chalcedonian delegation agreed, but there is nothing in the record to show that the Severan representatives followed suit, though this is what they had been asserting from the outset.[1] Nonetheless they had gained an important point; Christ was 'one', and in this respect the official position was nearer the *Henotikon* than to Leo. The discussions, however, had little practical effect. One of the Severan bishops, Philoxenus of Doliche, a friend and correspondent of Severus, accepted Chalcedon and so, according to Innocentius, did a number of priests and Syriac-speaking monks,[2] but the other leaders remained firm, and their attitude was soon to be rewarded by an outstanding defection from the Chalcedonian ranks.

On 15 March 533 Justinian published an edict addressed to the people of the capital and a dozen other large cities[3] setting out his confession of faith, which aimed at uniting the warring religious factions in the empire. The edict condemned Eutyches, Apollinarius and Nestorius, and its author explicitly disclaimed that the holy Catholic and Apostolic church 'innovated the faith'. The confession of faith proclaimed belief in familiar terms of a consubstantial Trinity of one substance in three *hypostaseis*, and Jesus Christ co-eternal with the Father who in the last days 'having descended from the Skies became incarnate from the Holy Spirit and Mary, the holy glorious Ever-Virgin and Theotokos, and assumed man's nature, and endured the Cross for us in the time of Pontius Pilate, and was buried and arose on the third day, recognising one and the same person's sufferings which he voluntarily endured in the flesh. For we know not God the Word to be one and Christ to be another, but one and the same person consubstan-

---

[1] Compare the Alexandrian confession of faith presented to Pope Anastasius II, above, p. 198. Western and Nestorian chroniclers always regarded the Severans as Theopaschites. See Victor of Tunnuna, *Chron.* ad ann. 512.

[2] Mansi, *Collectio* VIII, col. 833 = *ACO* 4. II, p. 184. Philoxenus had been one of Severus' consecrators. He ended his days as a Chalcedonian bishop in Cyprus (Michael the Syrian, *Chron.* IX. 29, ed. Chabot, II, 244).

[3] *Cod. Just.* I. 1. 6. The cities were Ephesus, Amida, Caesarea, Cyzicus, Trebizond, Jerusalem, Apamea, Justinianopolis, Sebastea, Tarsus, Theopolitus, Ancyra, Antioch. Jerusalem is not given precedence over Caesarea. Some but not all of these towns had been represented at the colloquies.

Justinian: the end of compromise

tial with the Father according to his divinity and the same one consubstantial with us according to his humanity. For as he is perfect in divinity, so the same is perfect in his humanity also. For the Trinity has remained the Trinity even after one of the Trinity was made incarnate as God the Word: for the Holy Trinity admits not the addition of a fourth person.' No mention was made of any council or of the *Tome* of Leo, and the final anathemas were confined to Eutyches, Nestorius and Apollinarius.

The emperor had given his views. It was up to those who had hitherto refused to communicate with his bishops to make up their minds. On 26 March, in a personal letter to the Patriarch Epiphanius addressed as 'ecumenical patriarch', Justinian repeated his ideas, but this time specified the Four Councils as proclaiming orthodoxy, Chalcedon both on the grounds that it condemned Eutyches and Nestorius and for the novel reason that its doctrine 'confirmed the letter of the great Proclus written to the Armenians about the necessity of saying that our Lord Jesus Christ, God's Son and our God, is one of the Holy Trinity'. The *Tome* of Leo was not mentioned but the Pope's status as 'head of all God's most holy priests' was recognised.[1] The emperor's letter to John II dated 6 June 533 shows how much store he set on unity between Rome and the eastern bishops and throws an interesting light on how he himself interpreted the papal primacy. It was a right to be kept informed (*innotescat*) of all that was being set in motion in the church, but not necessarily that the Pope should have any initiative. This belonged to the emperor. Once again, Justinian emphasised the Theopaschite formula, the unity of the two natures 'καθ' ὑπόστασιν' (spelt out in Greek) and he affirmed the Four Councils, reserving a special condemnation for Nestorius' 'evil and Jewish doctrine'. The *Tome* was again passed over in silence.[2]

These imperial decisions constituted the new *Henotikon*, the ultimate effort at compromise before the Monophysites established their own hierarchy. It was undertaken perhaps with an eye to the impending westward extensions of imperial jurisdiction and even with a side-glance towards Armenia, now anti-Chalcedonian. The Four Councils were to be accepted, Chalcedon because, Justinian told Epiphanius, it accorded with recognised eastern tradition represented by the Patriarch Proclus (i.e. not

[1] *Cod. Just.* 1. 1. 7.

[2] *Cod. Just.* 1. 1. 8, which preserves the text of both Justinian's letter and John's reply accepting its statements. The fact that both documents were included in the Code indicates that they were each to have the force of law.

268

by Leo) and because it condemned both Eutyches and Nestorius. The reference however to 'no addition of a fourth person' to the Trinity may reflect opposition to the Monophysite doxology which was criticised on these very grounds.[1] Also, though Cyril's Twelve Anathemas were not mentioned, Christ was to be regarded as 'one' and having suffered as 'one'. Instead, however, of the emphatic 'one and not two' of the *Henotikon* of Zeno, the perfection of his humanity was stated in unmistakable terms. As in the *Tome* of Leo, he was 'perfect God and perfect man' but must also be confessed as hypostatically united. Moreover, the Christological confession was firmly wedded to the Trinitarian confession. The theological pedigree combined Cyril with the Cappadocian Fathers, but rejected the interpretations of Severus.

For a moment it looked as though the grand design might succeed. The years 531–6 are the years of the great truce between adherents and opponents of Chalcedon throughout the east, when persecution ceased and each side rested on its position. In Alexandria both Severus and the Patriarch Timothy were ageing and were embarrassed by the activities of the supporters of Julian. In the capital the parties were in equilibrium. The colloquies had shaken the self-confidence of some Monophysites but had awoken pro-Monophysite feelings among some Chalcedonians. There is no evidence for violent reactions in the east such as greeted the *Henotikon* or the ending of the schism with Rome. At Rome, too, Hormisdas had been succeeded by the conciliatory John I and John II, and on 25 March 534 the latter accepted the edict as being 'in accordance with Apostolic teaching', and condemned the 'Nestorianising' activities of the chief agents of the papacy in the capital, the Sleepless Monks.[2] More extraordinary even was the arrival in the capital in the winter of 534/5 of Severus, again invited thither by the emperor and received by him with honour.[3] Religious unity (or, at least, acquiescence in the emperor's will) once more prevailed throughout the Christian world.

Zacharias credits Theodora for the invitation of Severus to Constanti-

[1] The view of Marcellinus Comes, *Chron.* ad ann. 512: 'in hymnum trinitatis Deipassianorum quaternitas additur'.

[2] *Cod. Just.* I. I. 7 = *Coll. Avellana* 84. Regarding the Sleepless Monks, see *ibid.* para. 26.

[3] Zacharias Rhetor, *HE* IX. 15 and 19. The dating of Severus' journey as taking place in the winter of 534/5 is accepted as against E. Stein's suggestion that he did not arrive in the capital before September 535. See Stein, 'Cyrille de Scythopolis, à propos de la nouvelle édition de ses œuvres', *AB* 62, 1944, pp. 169–86 at pp. 181–4.

nople.¹ His arrival with Peter of Apamea, the Stylite monk Zooras² and a monastic throng greatly increased the Monophysite presence in the city. The years 535–6 were to test the reality of the empress' powers to dominate the religious situation in the empire. On 7 February 535 Timothy of Alexandria died and four months later in June he was followed by the Patriarch Epiphanius. Few new elections could be more important. In Alexandria, after breath-taking hesitation, matters went Theodora's way. One of her *cubicularii* happened to be in Alexandria as Timothy died and he influenced the military commander to instal the deacon Theodosius in his place before Justinian could intervene (10 February). Once again, as twenty years before, the independence of the people showed itself. Theodosius represented the Severan party, but he was immediately challenged by a Julianist monk, Gaianus, who was supported by a formidable combination of the old Aposchist party and a large proportion of the Alexandrian monks and citizens. He held his position as rival patriarch for 104 days until his expulsion on 24 May.³ Theodosius could have found himself reduced to the situation of Proterius. His anti-Chalcedonianism was impeccable, however, and in June 535 he held a synod at which Nicaea, Ephesus and the Twelve Anathemas were declared to be of divine inspiration and the *Henotikon* restored to a place of honour as the weapon annulling the *Tome* and Chalcedon.⁴ Interestingly, neither Ephesus II nor Dioscorus was mentioned. The result was communicated to Severus who replied with a long letter on 25 July, reassuring him on the canonicity of his consecration and of his own unreserved support against the Julianists.⁵ Theodosius managed to hold on: the seventeen months he survived in Alexandria were just enough for him to lay claim to the leadership of the Monophysite cause, to ordain a succession of bishops loyal to him and reduce his rival to the position of a schismatic.⁶

In the capital, too, Theodora's star was in the ascendant. Anthimus of

---

[1] Zacharias Rhetor, *HE* IX. 19.

[2] Syriac = small. He was of humble origin. For his influence, Michael the Syrian, *Chron.* IX. 23.

[3] Liberatus, *Brev.* XX. See J. Maspero's account, *Histoire des patriarches d'Alexandrie*, pp. 110–17. For dating, *Documenta* (ed. Chabot), Praefatio.

[4] *Epistola synodica venerabilis et sancti archiepiscopi Alexandriae Theodosii ad beatum Mar Severum patriarcham Antiochae, Mense iunio*: *Documenta* (ed. Chabot), Document I.

[5] *Ibid.* Document II, pp. 6–22.

[6] See Michael the Syrian, *Chron.* IX. 21 (ed. Chabot, II, 194).

Justinian: the end of compromise

Trebizond had been one of the orthodox representatives at the colloquies of 532, but he was an ascetic, one who was said to have eaten no bread, oil or wine for years,[1] and the arguments of the Monophysite leaders must have impressed him. Soon after he had been consecrated patriarch, Theodora brought him into contact with Severus who convinced him completely both of his own orthodoxy and of the iniquity of Chalcedon. The letter which he wrote to him and whose text is preserved by Zacharias[2] probably dates to after his expulsion from office and Severus' return to Alexandria, but it could hardly have been very long before he aroused well-founded suspicion that he was at heart an anti-Chalcedonian.[3] To Severus, he proclaimed his acceptance of the Twelve Anathemas, of the *Henotikon* in the Severan sense, of the Theopaschite doctrines of Justinian and the condemnation of the Antiochenes, Ibas, Theodore and Theodoret. He urged – as though in defiance of orthodox apologetic – that the two-nature doctrine transformed Trinity into Quarternity. At the very moment when Justinian was engaged in the campaign for the capture of Rome this was an astonishing state of affairs in the capital. Zacharias states that the three patriarchs, meaning Severus, Anthimus and Theodosius, were now in communion,[4] and this is confirmed by Severus himself.[5] Every pro-Chalcedonian in the east took fright. Severus' old enemies, the 'monks of the Jerusalem desert' (i.e. Sabas' successors) and the monks from Syria II, both sent representatives to Constantinople. Ephraim of Antioch, feeling his position threatened, sent a special envoy to Rome.[6]

No document tells us exactly how this transformation took place. Common sense suggests that Theodora was behind the coup, and that it marks the highwater-mark of her influence. Her own devotion to the

---

[1] Michael the Syrian, *Chron.* IX. 21, describes him as a 'nazarean and ascetic'.

[2] Zacharias Rhetor, *HE* IX. 21. Schwartz, 'Zur Kirchenpolitik Justinians', p. 45 and *Kyrillos von Skythopolis*, p. 399 n4, argues that Anthimus' letters to Severus and Theodosius were written while he was in hiding under Theodora's protection but before Theodosius left Alexandria, i.e. between March and December 536.

[3] Apparently Ephraim of Antioch complained that his synodical letter despatched after his consecration did not condemn Eutyches strongly enough. See Schwartz, 'Zur Kirchenpolitik Justinians', p. 40 n3. Severus' letter to Theodosius replying to the latter's synodical epistle makes no mention of Anthimus.

[4] Zacharias Rhetor, *HE* IX. 19: 'Cum hi tres summi sacerdotes dilectione concordes essent nec fide inter se separarentur, Ephraim Antiochiae agitatus est...'

[5] *Ibid.* IX. 20.

[6] A celebrated physician, Sergius of Resaina, one of the more prominent pro-Chalcedonians in east Syria (see Michael the Syrian, *Chron.* IX. 23, ed. Chabot, II, 199).

Monophysite cause had, if anything, been sharpened by her baptism by Zooras in 535.[1] Justinian himself never wavered from support of Chalcedon, however he might interpret it, and from the subsequent events one must assume his rapid withdrawal of support from Anthimus once he grasped the truth about his views. As in the situation in the last years of Anastasius' reign, pressure first developed in those areas where Severus was least popular. The Palestinian and Syrian monks first tried to get Anthimus to accept explicitly Chalcedon and the *Tome* and for good measure anathematise Dioscorus. On his refusal they sent their delegation to Rome to join that of Ephraim. By a stroke of good fortune at that very moment (winter 535/6), King Theodahad the Ostrogoth had prevailed upon Pope Agapetus (535–6) to go to Constantinople with an appeal to Justinian to suspend operations in Sicily and Dalmatia. The Goth was prepared to offer almost any terms to save his throne. Agapetus hastened on his way. Early in March 536 he reached the capital. Once again, the mystique of Old Rome combined with the more solid assessment of the necessities of his western policies vis-à-vis the Pope carried the day with Justinian.[2] Anthimus was removed, not for heresy but for uncanonical election – once again Rome used the weapon of Nicaea canon 15 against a bishop whose presence was embarrassing – and Anthimus submitted. Liberatus says he returned his pallium to the emperor and departed to a place where Theodora protected him.[3]

On 13 March Agapetus himself consecrated his successor, the Alexandrian-born Menas (d. 552), and the letter which Justinian himself signed re-emphasised the orthodoxy of the two-nature Christology. Supported by the presence of the Pope he re-assumed command, and not even Agapetus' sudden death on 22 April could restore the Severan position. A lengthy and impressive Home Synod extending into five sessions condemned Anthimus as a heretic (May–June 536) and renewed the ban on Severus by acclamation. This decision caused some difficulty, for Menas pointed out that 'without the emperor's will and command nothing could

---

[1] Next year the Jerusalem monks at the synod that deposed Anthimus were loud in their demands that Zooras' 'cave' where allegedly he performed his 'false baptisms' should be destroyed! (*ACO* 3, p. 181, para. 129).

[2] Zacharias Rhetor, *HE* IX. 19 (ed. Brooks, p. 94), also indicates that the two men found much in common including the Latin language.

[3] Liberatus, *Brev.* XXI. 147; cf. John of Ephesus, *Lives of Five Patriarchs*, PO 18, p. 686. Anthimus seems to have survived another seven years, if not until after Theodora's death in 548 (Michael the Syrian, *Chron.* IX. 29).

happen in a matter touching ecclesiastical affairs'[1] – perhaps the most significant admission of the power of the emperor in church matters as seen through the eyes of the patriarch of Constantinople.

The emperor assented readily enough. On 6 August 536 an imperial edict banned Anthimus, Severus and their supporters from the capital and from all the great cities of the empire, and ordered the burning of all copies of Severus' writings. Severus himself was accused of waging 'undeclared war' in setting the churches against each other,[2] and charged with uttering blasphemies as damnable as those of Arius and Apollinarius. Harsh penalties were decreed against any who sheltered those who had been banned. 'We forbid to all men', Justinian declared, 'that any should possess the books of Severus. And just as it was not permitted to transcribe and possess the books of Nestorius because the emperors which have preceded us have decided in their edicts to assimilate those works with the writings of Porphyry against the Christians, so in the same way no Christian shall possess either the speeches of Severus, but these from now on shall be considered as profane and contrary to the Catholic church...'[3] Thus Severus was condemned; he left the capital and died in Egypt, an exile from his see, eighteen months later (8 February 538). His friend Anthimus had already disappeared into obscurity.

The reaction in favour of Rome and Chalcedon was extreme. All hope of compromise with the Monophysites disappeared. In the capital, Severus' influence was replaced by that of the Roman deacon Pelagius who begins a line of permanent papal representatives in the capital. He got on well with both Justinian and the empress, and it was not long before his influence began to be felt. High on the list of his priorities was the restoration of Chalcedonian obedience in Egypt. In Syria, meantime, Ephraim took on a new lease of life. To arguments and even miraculous signs sometimes unsuccessfully deployed against individual monastic leaders[4] was added force

---

[1] *ACO* 3, p. 181, para. 130 (fourth session): καὶ προσήκει μηδὲν τῶν ἐν τῇ ἁγιωτάτῃ ἐκκλησίᾳ κινουμένων παρὰ γνώμην αὐτοῦ καὶ κέλευσιν γενέσθαι. The *Acta* of the council are incorporated in those of the Council of Jerusalem that met to confirm its decisions. For a guide through the somewhat confused arrangement in *ACO*, see D. B. Evans, *Leontius of Byzantium; an Origenist Christology*, Dumbarton Oaks Studies 13 (Washington, 1970), p. 162 n44.

[2] Justinian, *Novel* 42 (= No. 56, ed. Z. Lingenthal, p. 369).   [3] *Ibid.* pp. 370–1.

[4] Ephraim's greatest success was the conversion of a Pillar Saint near Maboug related by John Moschos, *Pratum spirituale*, ch. 36 (*PG* 87, col. 2884). Even in this case he relied more on his position as patriarch than on pro-Chalcedonian arguments.

of arms. By the end of the year or early in 537 supporters of Severus were being hunted by police and soldiers in their strongholds in Mesopotamia on the Persian frontier.[1] Both John of Ephesus and Zacharias report that some of those caught were burnt alive,[2] and once again the Monophysite monks suffered the rigours of a harsh winter deprived of the shelter of their monasteries. John of Tella himself was arrested in the mountains near Singara while continuing to preach the anti-Chalcedonian cause, and died in prison.[3] With him the roll of Monophysite martyr victims of Chalcedon opens.

In Egypt for the first time the government took measures to root out the anti-Chalcedonians. In Alexandria the celebration of the anniversary of the death of Dioscorus was forbidden.[4] The Patriarch Theodosius, who owed his personal safety to the presence of imperial troops in 535–6, was convoked with other bishops and clergy to Constantinople (December 536),[5] Justinian hoping no doubt to bring him over to Catholicism. When this failed he was deposed (probably end of 537), and confined to the fortress of Derkos in Thrace,[6] but soon was brought back to the capital by Theodora and housed in the palace of Hormisdas with his supporters. Rid of Theodosius, the emperor turned to the Pachomian monks for a Chalcedonian patriarch, thus taking up the Melkite succession once more, which had been dormant since the fall of John Talaia in 482. The first choice prompted by Pelagius[7] was Paul the Tabennesiot and was unfortunate, for

[1] Elias, *Vita Johannis episcopi Tellae* (ed. Brooks), pp. 43ff. Elias claimed that Persian officials even co-operated with Ephraim.

[2] For Monophysite supporters in Amida being burnt by the Chalcedonian bishop, Abraham bar Kaili, see Zacharias Rhetor, *HE* x. 2 (*CSCO* III. 6, p. 120), and John of Ephesus, *History of the convents of Amida* (ed. Brooks), *PO* 17, p. 620. Also Michael the Syrian, *Chron.* IX. 18 (ed. Chabot, II, 187).

[3] Zacharias Rhetor, *HE* x. 1, Elias, *Vita*, pp. 52ff., and John of Ephesus, *Life of John of Tella* (ed. Brooks), *PO* 18, pp. 524–5.

[4] Severus, *Select Letters* IV. 9 (ed. Brooks, pp. 270–1).

[5] See E. W. Brooks, 'The dates of the Alexandrine patriarchs Dioskorus II, Timothy IV and Theodosius', *BZ* 12, 1903, pp. 494–7 at p. 494. John of Ephesus, *Life of John of Hephaestopolis* (ed. Brooks), *PO* 18, p. 528, suggests that the invitation to the capital followed removal from their sees. *Chron. ad ann. 846* affirms that Theodosius was with Anthimus and Severus in the capital (ed. Brooks and Chabot, p. 170), but this can hardly be true. Severus left after his condemnation in August 536. Theodosius did not arrive until the end of the year.

[6] Not far from the Black Sea and within striking distance of the capital.

[7] On Pelagius' activities at this time, see Diehl, *Justinien*, pp. 340–3.

soon after the new patriarch had been consecrated in the capital by Menas in Pelagius' presence he was implicated in a charge of murder. His successor (*circa* 540) was a Palestinian monk named Zoilus, the choice of Ephraim of Antioch.[1] The wheel had come full circle. Chalcedonian Antioch now dominated Alexandria. The Egyptian church had a foreign patriarch supported by a foreign government, but for the time being, bereft of its patriarch and most of its bishops, it submitted.

The events of 536–8 form the watershed in the history of the Monophysite movement. The condemnation of Severus and the equation of his works with those of Porphyry involved a complete break between his followers and the orthodoxy of the emperor and the capital. There was never again to be any real hope of the Monophysites ruling the church of the empire. Justinian's deep involvement in the west and the capture of Rome by Belisarius sealed the issue, for now both capitals were once more under the same political control. Pelagius' employment by Justinian in purely eastern matters emphasised this. Efforts continued to be made, sometimes strenuously as at the great monastic concourses which Justinian held in 558 and 563, to placate the Monophysites and meet them on any issue other than Chalcedon itself. Monophysite leaders such as John of Amida (John of Ephesus) or Constantine of Laodicea[2] might be welcome at court and given important assignments, but the Four Councils were now the religion of the empire. However fine might be the difference between neo-Chalcedonianism and Severan Monophysitism, the latter was not in communion with the church. In addition, among the Severans the hatreds and fears aroused by the *Tome* and Chalcedon and the persecutions in their name could not be washed away. Monophysitism had become despite itself a schismatic movement. 'I do not communicate with the synod' had become the stock answer to challengers.[3] The story of the Monophysites in the generation following the condemnation of Severus and the re-establishment of the Melkite succession in Alexandria is to be followed on two different planes. First, there was the continuing but progressively more

[1] Zacharias Rhetor, *HE* x. 1 (ed. Brooks, *CSCO* III. 6, p. 120).

[2] Michael the Syrian, *Chron.* IX. 30 (ed. Chabot, II, 249). Courtiers hastened to receive communion from him as a holy man.

[3] A good example of this attitude is the scene that took place in Amida when Abraham bar Kaili tried to proclaim Chalcedon on the emperor's orders. 'We will never accept the synod and the *Tome*', the people cried, and rioted against the bishop and magistrates (Michael the Syrian, *Chron.* IX. 26, ed. Chabot, II, 222). Compare John Moschos, *Pratum spirituale*, ch. 36 (*PG* 87. 3, col. 2885A) for another instance.

futile effort to win the Monophysite leaders to acceptance of the emperor's interpretation of orthodoxy by means of discussion and conference in the capital. Secondly, and far more important, was the establishment of a Monophysite hierarchy within the boundaries of the empire, and the missionary movement under its inspiration that carried the creed into Persia, down the Nile valley into Nubia and Ethiopia and consolidated its hold on Armenia.

We may review first the efforts to conciliate the Monophysites which led up to the Fifth General Council in 553. Thanks to Theodora, the Patriarch Theodosius continued to reside with his followers in the palace of Hormisdas where, until his death in 566, he presided over what had by then become world-Monophysitism. In the years 536–8 a last effort was also made by the empress to have the anathemas against Severus, Anthimus and Theodosius reversed. In Agapetus' deacon and representative in the capital, Vigilius, she found a sympathiser. Vigilius was an ambitious scion of a senatorial family who shared some of the emperor's aims of re-uniting the eastern and western Roman worlds. Allowing for Liberatus' prejudices,[1] it seems that he was flattered by the prospect of the Roman bishopric, and for a very substantial bribe he agreed to the restoration of Severus and his associates to communion. The plan miscarried temporarily through the election of Silverius as Agapetus' successor (536–7) but thanks to Theodora's relations with Antonia, the equally unscrupulous wife of Belisarius, Silverius was removed from Rome and exiled on a trumped-up charge of intrigue with the Goths. Before his death in December 537 Vigilius had succeeded him (29 March) and through Antonia sent a remarkable letter to the empress.[2] In this he condemned the wording of the *Tome* of Leo. 'We do not confess two natures in Christ but that Christ composed out of (*ex*)

[1] *Brev.* XXII, a severe critique.
[2] The text of two separate letters has survived: (*a*) that quoted by Victor of Tunnuna (*Chron.* ad ann. 542) addressed to Severus, Anthimus and Theodosius stating the writer's general agreement with their views and enjoining secrecy regarding the existence of the letter; (*b*) a more detailed letter preserved in long extracts by Liberatus (*Brev.* XXII), in which the *Tome* is criticised and the formula 'ex duabus naturis' preferred to 'in duabus naturis'. I find it difficult to agree that there is no foundation in fact for these letters (Schwartz, 'Zur Kirchenpolitik Justinians', p. 58 n3) and prefer the reconstruction of events by Krüger, 'Monophysiten', p. 395. The condemnation of the Three Chapters had traditionally been a touchstone of anti-Chalcedonian orthodoxy and the sequel was to show that it was very much on the theological *tapis* at the time.

two natures was one Son, one Christ, and one Lord.' He who spoke of 'two forms', or who attributed the miracles to one and the sufferings to another, was anathema. Anathemas were flung at the whole Antiochene tradition, naming in the same breath Paul of Samosata, Diodore, Theodore and Theodoret.

This secret letter, whether or not it existed, had no immediate practical effect. The interests of the Roman see made it impossible for Vigilius to denounce the *Tome*, while equally those of the capital were wedded to Chalcedon. On 17 September 540 Vigilius accepted in a somewhat abject letter Justinian's demand that he should ratify the anti-Monophysite edict of four years before.[1] With a permanent representative at the Byzantine court, the papacy had more reliable and less mercurial sources of information concerning opinion in the capital than had been provided once by the Sleepless Monks and a greater opportunity of avoiding the misunderstanding and ill will that had precipitated the Acacian schism.

Moreover, the defence of Chalcedon through the writings of the two Leontii[2] and Cyril of Scythopolis (d. 557), not to speak of the emperor himself, was developing a momentum of its own and was carrying conviction among large numbers of eastern Christians who accepted Chalcedon so long as it could be reconciled with Cyril.[3] This was Justinian's own

[1] *Coll. Avellana* 92. A further edict (*Novel* 109) dated to August 541 reiterated the proscription of those who followed the 'bad religion' (*prava religio*) of 'Dioscorus and Severus'.

[2] For the respective identifications of Leontius of Byzantium and Leontius of Jerusalem, see M. Richard, 'Léonce de Jérusalem, et Léonce de Byzance', *Mélanges de science religieuse* 1, 1944, pp. 54ff., and Evans, *Leontius of Byzantium*. Evans believes that Leontius of Byzantium was the Leontius referred to by Cyril of Scythopolis (*Vita Sabae*, ed. Schwartz, p. 188) as an Origenist, who attended the colloquies with the Severans in 532/3 as *apocrisiarius* of the delegation of Palestinian monks, and was also present at the Home Synod that condemned Severus and his colleagues in 536 (Evans, *ibid*. pp. 156–9). One of his orthodox opponents was his namesake, Leontius of Jerusalem.

[3] This is clear from the theology attributed to Ephraim of Antioch and his advisers who proclaimed 'Unus est Deus', believed that they were as good Cyrillists as John of Tella, and appear to have been genuinely hurt and surprised to find that John still demanded denunciation of Chalcedon as gauge of orthodoxy. See Elias, *Vita Johannis episcopi Tellae* (ed. Brooks), p. 52. Against this sort of argument, the Monophysite monks replied, 'Well, why if Chalcedon called Mary "Theotokos" and condemned Nestorius and Eutyches did it uphold Ibas who declared that Christ "was only a man

clearly expressed view. 'The holy church of God', he wrote *circa* 540 to the monks of the Enaton monastery near Alexandria, 'rightly accepts all the writings of the blessed Cyril, and in these writings it accepts also the unique incarnate nature of God the Word, as signifying that the nature of the divinity is one thing and that of the flesh is another, out of which the one and unique Christ was formed.' The very fact of incarnation pointed to a nature other than that of the Word.[1] The term that proved to be the philosopher's stone in this argument was 'enhypostasis', which we have already met with in connection with the Scythian monks. Though, Leontius of Byzantium (d. 543) argued, there could be no 'nature' without its individuality (*hypostasis*),[2] it did not necessarily follow that the two natures of Christ required two separate *hypostaseis*, since both were united in the same *hypostasis* which was the divine Word. At the incarnation the human nature became 'enhypostasised', so as to permit its unity with the Word which thus subsisted 'in two natures'.[3] One plus one therefore did equal two as the Council of Chalcedon had declared, and the 'ineffable and inexpressible' character of the union of the natures contemplated in Cyril's writings was given a closer definition. Could not unity be founded on this thesis?

The Monophysites thought not, and indeed on analysis the elaborate defence which Leontius of Byzantium made on behalf of Chalcedon seemed to lead to Origen rather than Cyril. It could be argued that Leontius' Jesus Christ was in reality not Word incarnate but an incorporated *nous* united to God through all eternity in the vision of God, taking a body while united

like me"?' The monks evidently knew their *Acta* of Ephesus II! (See Michael the Syrian, *Chron.* IX. 18, ed. Chabot, II, 188.)

[1] Justinian, *Tract. contra Monophysitas*: see E. Schwartz, 'Drei dogmatische Schriften Justinians', *Abh. der bayer. Akad. der Wiss.*, Phil.-hist. Abt., n.s. 18. 1, 1939). The Tract is a closely argued work drawing on a range of neo-Chalcedonian theses, and showing knowledge of the work of Severus and Timothy the Cat. It is another illustration of the willingness of the Byzantine emperors to argue out their ideas with their subjects. The *Tome* of Leo is only incidentally mentioned; that of Proclus, however, is emphasised. The Severans are termed 'Acephali' (not 'Monophysitae') and their ideas assimilated to Arianism or Manichaeism. The emperor was no 'amateur theologian' but as well-equipped in argument as his own patriarchs.

[2] *Libri tres contra Nestorianos et Eutychianos* I. 1 (*PG* 86. 1, col. 1277).

[3] So F. Loofs, *Leontius von Byzanz und die gleichnamigen Schriftsteller der griechischen Kirche*, *TU* 3 (Leipzig, 1887), p. 87. Compare, however, Evans, *Leontius of Byzantium*, pp. 132–46 (review of the relevant literature and conclusion that Leontius was an Origenist and not a Cyrillian).

Justinian: the end of compromise

to God to reveal His purpose to man and redeem him.[1] In rejecting Severus and his teaching eastern Christendom had still to agree on an acceptable alternative. What exacerbated the conflict was that, at heart, nearly all the Byzantine theologians were trying to express the same truth, that of the salvation of man through the suffering of the Christ-God. The problem was whether or not this could be done within the framework of Chalcedon, for how else could the unity of *Romania* be maintained? The Origenist monks in Palestine who became increasingly influential after the death of Sabas in 532 accepted Chalcedon on their own interpretation of 'two natures', but were just as hostile to the teaching of the Antiochene theologians as Origen and his immediate disciples had been. The argument was merely moved back a stage. The Origenist agitation of the period 532–42 illustrates how no sooner had Severus and his followers been relegated to the sidelines than the issues that had brought them into being began to emerge in a new form. The demand made by the Origenists to the Patriarch Peter of Jerusalem (524–44) to anathematise his colleague of Antioch, Ephraim, showed also that their acceptance of Chalcedon implied no acceptance of the Antiochene interpretation of its doctrinal definition, and in particular that anything not explicitly upheld at Chalcedon could be jettisoned. Their defeat, largely through papal influence at court, in Justinian's edict published in Jerusalem in February 543 condemning Origenism and Origen,[2] was not the end of the matter and opened the way to even more serious controversies within the Chalcedonian camp.

It is perhaps typical of the twists of Justinian's religious policy that one of the leaders of the defeated Origenists, Theodore Askidas, a Palestinian monk promoted to be bishop of Caesarea in Cappadocia, became his confidant, 'constantly about the person of Justinian',[3] Evagrius states, and that he gradually ousted Pelagius from favour at court. His opposition, however, to the Antiochene theologians was not, outwardly at least, inspired by love for Severus and his teaching. He was and remained a Chalcedonian. He believed, however, he could kill two birds with one stone if he could persuade the emperor to condemn the writings of Theo-

---

[1] Evans, *Leontius of Byzantium*, p. 144. Compare *ibid.*: 'It is indeed the tradition of Cyril and the decrees of the Council of Chalcedon that Leontius pretends to expound; but in fact he casts both tradition and decrees into the shape of the spirituality of Evagrius of Pontus.'

[2] Text in *ACO* 3, pp. 189ff.   [3] Evagrius, *HE* IV. 38.

dore of Mopsuestia, the works of Theodoret directed against Cyril's Twelve Anathemas and the letter of Ibas to the presbyter Maris which gave a strongly critical account of Cyril's actions and theology in the period after Ephesus I. It had commented bitterly on the efforts of 'the tyrant of Edessa' (Rabbula) to have Theodore condemned posthumously. By means of an anathema on these 'Three Chapters' he aimed at securing the condemnation of a theologian, Theodore, who was strongly opposed to Origen's views, and incidentally going some way towards meeting the Monophysite case without rejecting Chalcedon outright.[1]

It was an ingenious project. Condemnation of Theodore was now common ground between Chalcedonian and anti-Chalcedonian in the capital. A one-sided approach to Chalcedon might permit the argument that though the council had vindicated Theodoret and Ibas it had not necessarily vindicated all their writings, and the difficulty that both the papal legates and Maximus of Antioch had defended Ibas' letter could be dealt with by arguments as perverse as any employed in an ecclesiastical cause, including the assertion that Ibas had denied ever writing to Maris. Theodore, moreover, had not been mentioned at the council (he had died in 428!) and therefore his condemnation would not be an affront to its decisions. For their part, the Monophysites had been insisting on the condemnation of the Three Chapters for the previous half-century, and had informed the emperor during the conference of 532–3 that one of the stumbling-blocks in the way of their acceptance of Chalcedon had been its approval of the anti-Cyrillian works of Ibas and Theodoret.[2] Now they could be satisfied. The suspicion in the west that Justinian's condemnation of the Three Chapters in 544 owed much to collusion between Askidas and Theodora and her circle is probably justified.[3]

Whatever may have been suspected in the west, however, the Three Chapters had been condemned specifically without prejudice to the authority of Chalcedon. Hence the decision was rejected by the Mono-

---

[1] For Askidas' motives, see Liberatus, *Brev.* XXIV – though strongly prejudiced against Askidas to the extent of declaring that he was a Monophysite, 'dilectus et familiaris principum, secta Acephalus, Origenis autem defensor acerrimus et Pelagio aemulus'.

[2] Mansi, *Collectio* VIII, col. 829 = *ACO* 4. II, p. 181.

[3] Liberatus, *Brev.* XXIV; Facundus of Hermiana, *Pro defensione trium capitulorum* IV. 3 (*PL* 67, col. 624C). Leontius of Byzantium believed that Justinian hoped that the condemnation of the Three Chapters would rally the Monophysites to accept Chalcedon. See *De sectis* VI (*PG* 86. 1, col. 1238D).

physites. Even in this form, however, it was violently opposed in the west for the contrary reasons and nowhere more so than in the restored and re-invigorated Catholic church in North Africa. Whatever gratitude the African bishops may have felt to Justinian for the restoration of Catholicism in 535 had now worn off. Their spokesmen were motivated partly by a sense of their independence of Constantinople and the ties between church and state that Justinian's rule represented ('Only Christ is priest and king', urged Facundus),[1] and partly from the underlying kinship that existed between Antiochene and western Christology. No more than the Monophysites were the westerners prepared to abate one jot of their traditional theology. The story of the controversy that ensued in the next nine years emphasises the hopelessness not only of an attempt to conciliate the Monophysites without abrogating Chalcedon, but of establishing any overall comprehension between the eastern and western theologies even within the framework of Chalcedon.

The next move, involving the forceful removal of Pope Vigilius from Rome to Constantinople, was also attributed by the west to Monophysite intrigues.[2] At least Theodora and her circle were in the background ready to pick up any advantage to be gained from the situation. Vigilius arrived in the capital on 25 January 547. He failed to agree with the Patriarch Menas and soon they were excommunicating each other. According to Theophanes, one of Theodora's last official actions was to reconcile them on 29 June 547.[3] She died exactly a year later (28 June 548), but before this she had experienced a final triumph in Vigilius' signature to the condemnation of the Three Chapters by a verdict (*Judicatum*) which he sent to Menas on 11 April 548.

The ensuing controversies, leading to the summons of the Fifth General Council and Vigilius' *Constitutum* of 23 February 554 accepting its decision, belong more to the relations between the emperor and the western church

---

[1] *Pro defensione trium capitulorum* XII. 3 (*PL* 67, cols. 840–1), citing the fate of King Uzziah (2 Kings 6. 7–9). See Markus, 'Reflections on religious dissent in North Africa', pp. 146–50.

[2] Evagrius, *HE* IV. 38. Victor of Tunnuna, *Chron.* ad ann. 544: 'Justinianus imperator acephalorum subreptionibus instigatus, Vigilium Romanorum episcopum subtiliter compellit, ut ad urbem regiam properaret et sub specie congregationis eorum qui ab ecclesiae sunt societate divisi, tria capitula condemnaret.'

[3] Theophanes, *Chron.* A.M. 6039 (ed. Classen, I, 349–50). L. Duchesne, *L'Eglise au VIe siècle*, p. 186, comments that this entry is 'un passage qui ne paraît pas très rassurant'.

than to the story of the Monophysite movement. The events of these years demonstrated what had been evident since the accession of Justin and Justinian, that whatever the political aim of emperors the theology of Constantinople was now Byzantine, the product of the neo-Chalcedonian thought in the previous half-century, and it was opposed alike to the Diphysitism of the west and to the Severan Monophysites. Thus it was to remain so long as Constantinople stood. This time it was the west that tried unsuccessfully to wring concessions from the emperor. In 550 the Africans and Illyrians forced Vigilius to retract the *Judicatum*. The following year, however, Justinian renewed his condemnation of the Three Chapters, extending an olive branch only so far as to stress that the condemnation aimed at the heinous opinions of Ibas and Theodoret and their calumnies against Cyril, not against Chalcedon itself.[1] The opposition was mollified enough to attend the General Council summoned to meet in the capital in May 553. There, once more Justinian gained the day. The Chapters were condemned amid acclamations on the grounds that they were contradictory to the doctrines of Chalcedon! Of the Letter of Ibas, particularly, the bishops cried out, 'It had nothing to do with the Council of Chalcedon. Anyone who does not anathematise this letter places himself in opposition to the Council of Chalcedon. Long live the emperor! Long live the orthodox emperor!'[2] The wretched Vigilius was kept in captivity until he agreed, on 8 December 553 in a letter to the Patriarch Eutychius, and more formally in a solemn declaration condemning the Three Chapters on 23 February 554.[3]

There was no comfort for the Monophysites in all this. The eighth anathema in particular, while permitting the expression 'out of two natures' and confessing their 'hypostatic union', condemned the belief that this now resulted in 'one nature'.[4] In Anastasius' reign the involved phraseology might have been the subject for discussion between Severus and his fellow patriarchs, but now no confidence between the two sides existed and the apparent concession did nothing to bridge the cleavage between the two churches.

[1] See Hefele/Leclercq, *Histoire des conciles*, III. 1, 43ff. for the sequence of events, and L. Bréhier, 'La Lutte entre Vigile et Justinien', in Fliche and Martin, *Histoire de l'église*, IV, 467–82.
[2] Text in Hefele/Leclercq, *Histoire des conciles*, III. 1, 118–20.
[3] Duchesne, *L'Eglise au VIe siècle*, p. 217. Vigilius was not destined to see Rome again. He died at Syracuse on his return from Constantinople on 7 June 555.
[4] Text in Hefele/Lelercq, *Histoire des conciles*, III. 1, 118–20.

Justinian: the end of compromise

Meantime, the development of a separate Monophysite hierarchy had been proceeding slowly but irrevocably. As we have seen, continued persecution had forced Severus and his colleagues to commission the establishment of a priesthood through John of Tella. Severus himself felt there was little hope of a settlement so long as Justinian ruled,[1] and after his return from the capital near the end of 536[2] he took the further step of permitting John and other east Syrian bishops to consecrate bishops for his supporters across the Persian frontier. This was done because they were few and were threatened with extinction at the hands of 'Nestorians' (i.e. Persian Christians).[3]

No new bishops had been consecrated on the territory of the empire as yet, and the hesitation to challenge the hierarchy approved by the emperor is significant. There can be no greater contrast between the traditional proneness of the westerners to schism, demonstrated by the immediate setting up of 'altar against altar' by the opponents of Caecilian in Africa in 312, or the actions of the Novatianists in Rome in the mid third century, than the shuffling and reluctant steps taken on purely theological grounds for the salvation of 'rational souls' that established Severan Monophysitism as an independent church in the east after 536. The social and even regional background existed already – witness the popular response to John of Tella – but nothing was further from the thoughts of Severus and his colleagues than to establish their creed on the basis of provincial or national churches. The one-nature Christology presupposed religious unity in the empire, directed by the emperor. Nestorianism was the doctrine of schism.

To John of Tella must go the credit of consolidating Monophysitism on each side of the Romano-Persian frontier in north-east Syria, in Euphratesia, Osrhoëne, Mesopotamia and Adiabene. The violence of the reaction by the Patriarch Ephraim and his allies in these areas in 537–8 testifies to

---

[1] John of Ephesus records Severus as saying before he left for the capital, 'Don't be deceived. In the lifetime of these emperors no means of peace will be found, but so that I do not appear to hinder or oppose it, I will go, though with heartsearchings. I will return without anything accomplished.' *PO* 2, p. 303, and *Lives of Five Patriarchs*, (ed. Brooks), *PO* 18, p. 687.

[2] John of Ephesus, *Lives of Five Patriarchs*, gives Severus two years in Constantinople which would bring him to the winter of 536/7 (*PO* 18, p. 687). But see above, p. 273.

[3] Elias, *Vita Johannis episcopi Tellae*, p. 39: 'quae ibi propter errorem Nestorii miseri hominis cultoris quasi iam extincta erat [vera fides]'.

his success. On the capture and death of John (6 February 538) a new crisis arose. Severus survived him a bare two days. The renewal of the Persian war in 539 prevented ordination by bishops from that country. The Persian offensive leading to the fall of Antioch in 540 put a wide band of enemy-held territory between the Monophysites in the capital and Asia Minor and those within the Persian lines.

The years immediately succeeding the deaths of John of Tella and Severus were therefore crisis years for the Monophysites. As Michael the Syrian noted in retrospect, the sequence of deaths in the anti-Chalcedonian camp left the latter with an acute shortage of bishops.[1] There was Theodosius at Constantinople and Q'uiros in Persia, and the consecration of the latter had aroused the feeling that the faithful within the empire should have their bishops, but in such a way that the calumnies of enemies, perhaps to the effect that the Monophysites were pro-Persian, could be avoided.[2] The difficulties of these years are vividly illustrated in John of Ephesus' *Life* of James Bar'adai, when he states that 'the party of the believers had diminished, and deficiency too had arisen in the order of the priesthood over all the commonwealth of the party of the believers'.[3] There was absolutely no man to extend the hand of ordination to any believer in the whole Roman territory as far as the Persian frontier, except Theodosius and his entourage, and Theodosius was reluctant to act.[4]

The Monophysite dilemmas were solved in an unexpected way. The Arab tribes living along the length of the Romano-Persian frontier played a very considerable role in the struggle between the two empires. Persia had made much use of her Arab allies in the campaigns of 504–6 and 530–1, and she had exploited a tribal dispute as a pretext for the invasion of Syria in 540. The avoidance of a repetition of similar disasters on Rome's eastern frontier depended largely on the benevolent neutrality of at least a proportion of the more powerful tribes. By the early years of the sixth century two great confederations had come into being, the Lakhmids in the north and east with Hira as their centre, and the Ghassanids in the south and

[1] *Chron.* IX. 29 (ed. Chabot, II, 244).
[2] *Ibid.* p. 245.
[3] John of Ephesus, *Life of James Bar'adai* (ed. Brooks), PO 18, p. 692.
[4] *Life of John of Hephaestopolis* (ed. Brooks), PO 18, p. 529; cf. *Lives of James and Theodore*, PO 19, p. 153. Would-be priests were travelling yearlong between Constantinople and Alexandria in an effort to find someone orthodox to ordain them. (*Life of John of Tella*, PO 18, p. 522.)

Justinian: the end of compromise

west bordering the Roman province of Arabia. As one might imagine, they were hostile to each other and sought to derive every advantage from the permanent hostility between Romans and Persians. Both empires used the weapon of religion as a means of winning allies, and here the Romans had the advantage.[1] None of the Arab tribes seems to have been attracted either towards Nestorianism or Zoroastrianism, but between Manichaeism on the one hand and Chalcedon on the other, they wavered according to the impression missionaries and rival champions made on them. The Ghassanids had been in contact with Christianity since the mid fourth century. Later, Euthymius had been a prime mover of the conversion of some of their number, and in consequence their bishops had remained loyal to Chalcedon. Between 512 and 518, whatever the legendary details of the encounter between Severus' emissaries and the Arabs, it is evident that Severus' doctrines were unpopular.[2] Later, however, there was a change and in 541 the Ghassanid king, al Harith ibn Jabadah, with an eye no doubt to exploiting his political position, sent an embassy to Theodora with a request for the despatch of orthodox (i.e. Monophysite) bishops to his tribe.[3] This gave the empress, described in this context as 'desirous of furthering everything that would assist the opponents of the synod of Chalcedon',[4] another chance. At her suggestion, Theodosius consecrated two monks as metropolitans, James Bar'adai, an east Syrian, born at Tella, as metropolitan of Edessa, and Theodore as metropolitan of Bostra, the capital of the Roman province of Arabia. The latter departed to take up his duties among the Ghassanids, while James became one of the great religious and missionary leaders of all time.[5] Not for nothing did the Syrian Monophysites come to be called 'Jacobites' after him.

According to his biographer, James was invested with authority 'over all countries not only of Syria and the whole of Armenia and Cappadocia' but over Isauria, Lycia, Phrygia, Cyprus and the Islands; in fact the whole

---

[1] See D. Oates, *Studies in the Ancient History of Northern Iraq* (OUP for the British Academy, 1968), p. 113.

[2] See above, p. 229. For the fact of their rejection of Severus' doctrines, see Victor of Tunnuna, *Chron.* ad ann. 512.

[3] Michael the Syrian, *Chron.* IX. 29 (ed. Chabot, II, 245–6).

[4] John of Ephesus, *Lives of James and Theodore* (ed. Brooks), *PO* 19, p. 154.

[5] For a sketch of his life and work, see E. Honigmann, 'La Hiérarchie monophysite au temps de Jacques Baradée, 542–578', *CSCO*, Subsidia 2 (Louvain, 1951); also A. van Roey, 'Les débuts de l'église jacobite', in Grillmeier/Bacht, *Das Konzil von Chalkedon*, II, 339–60, especially pp. 356–9.

area between Jerusalem and Constantinople.[1] Nothing in John of Ephesus' account suggests that the Monophysite churches were designed to be organised on a regional basis. Indeed, at this stage the restoration of the church throughout Asia Minor seems to have had priority in the minds of the leaders rather than its consolidation in what had become its homeland, east Syria and Egypt. In the 580s Pamphylia was regarded as a Monophysite stronghold with its monasteries, churches and villages.[2] John himself, though he was a monk from Amida on the Tigris, is known to history from his titular archbishopric of Ephesus which he received from the Monophysites in 558, and he was commissioned by Justinian in 542 to convert the remaining islands of paganism in the diocese of Asia; this he did so successfully that 70,000 inhabitants were baptised, and ninety-eight new churches and twelve monasteries were built for them. Despite his known sympathies the emperor supported him in a conflict with the bishop of Tralles when the latter attempted to take over as a summer residence a monastery which John had built as a missionary centre.[3] John himself accepted an invitation from Justinian for religious discussion (in 558) and on the accession of Justin II he even hoped for the emperor's rejection of Chalcedon. Though originally a monk from Amida, he felt himself increasingly at home in Constantinople and its court. In his *History* he shows marked sympathy with Tiberius II as one 'who loved God'.[4] James Bar'adai's appointments to vacant metropolitanships, however, coupled with intense mutual distrust between the Monophysites and their opponents ended these hopes for practical purposes.[5] Moreover, the new opposition bishoprics seem to have been filled predominantly from among monks of great Syrian houses.[6] Inevitably, whatever the original intention of the leaders, the anti-

[1] John of Ephesus, *Life of James and Theodore* (ed. Brooks), *PO* 19, p. 154. Elsewhere, John says that James' 'diocese' extended from the imperial capital to Alexandria (*PO* 18, p. 693).

[2] John of Ephesus, *HE* (Part iii) v. 6: 'regio igitur Pamphyliae ex initio orthodoxorum erat'.

[3] *Ibid.* III. 37 (ed. Brooks, p. 127). For John's missionary activities, see also his *History of the refugees in Constantinople* (ed. Brooks), *PO* 18, p. 681.

[4] *HE* III. 5 and 6 (ed. Brooks, pp. 92 and 95).

[5] See *ibid.* II. 1 (ed. Brooks, p. 38) for this antipathy towards the 'Diphysites'.

[6] For instance, John, bishop of Chios, was a native of Aina dhe-Phraka near Amida on the Tigris; his friend John of Amida became bishop of Ephesus, and Sergius, patriarch of Antioch, was once a presbyter at Tella. For other Syrians among James' appointments, see John of Ephesus, *Lives of the Eastern Saints* (ed. Brooks), *PO* 19, pp. 156–8.

Justinian: the end of compromise

Chalcedonian church that emerged outside Egypt had a strong native Syrian imprint which was to survive permanently. This emphasised the increasing cultural differences between the Monophysites and their opponents.

Justinian and his advisers quickly recognised the danger represented by James and vain efforts were made to apprehend him and submit him to the fate of John of Tella. James, however, was never betrayed – another indication of underlying popular support for the Monophysite cause – and dressed as a beggar, 'sometimes travelling thirty or forty miles in a day, never staying long in any one district', he added to the numbers of believers in every place, 'both Greeks and Syrians' (the two groups were thus by now culturally distinct even though inhabiting the same province).[1] His opponents 'gnashed their molars at this mighty man in the Lord'.[2]

James' mission occupied more than thirty-five years from 542 to 578, and represents a slow but continuous development of the separate Monophysite church, especially after the Fifth General Council. 'Swift as Azaël' he covered great areas of Syria, Armenia, Cappadocia, Cilicia, Isauria, Pamphylia and Asia, and visited Rhodes, Cyprus, Chios and Mitylene. The first stage was the consecration of two suffragans, Conon of Tarsus and Eugenius of Seleucia in Isauria, both monks who accompanied him from Constantinople on his first mission through Asia Minor. John of Ephesus relates that leaving Lycaonia they sailed to Alexandria and were consecrated bishops there.[3] The date, unfortunately, is unknown, for it would have provided a hint of conditions in Egypt, but it was an important step. It enabled James to consecrate en route bishops as well as lesser clergy, 'causing the priesthood to flow like great rivers over the whole world of the Roman domains',[4] and the eventual tally of twenty-seven metropolitans and a claimed 100,000 clergy all over the Roman east was the result.

Another important series of missions *circa* 540–1 were those of John bishop of Hephaistos in Egypt, also a protégé of Theodora and originally a monk from Maiuma, who had been consecrated bishop by Theodosius in 536. He accompanied the latter to the capital in the next year but soon after he was hunted out of Constantinople and travelled through Asia Minor and the Aegean islands ordaining clergy as he went. A high point in his

---

[1] John of Ephesus, *Life of James Bar'adai* (ed. Brooks), *PO* 18, p. 693; compare ibid. p. 695.
[2] *Ibid.* p. 694.
[3] *Ibid.* p. 697, and *PO* 19, pp. 155–6.
[4] *Ibid.* p. 696.

adventurous career was on his third journey in 541 when, accompanied by John of Ephesus, he celebrated in the orthodox cathedral of Tralles and then proceeded to ordain fifty priests in a gallery while the Chalcedonians were holding their own service down below. At Ephesus he ordained another seventy clergy on one night. Arriving in Cilicia he was hunted by the agents of the Patriarch Ephraim, but made good his escape, first to Chios and thence to Alexandria.[1]

These great missions should not disguise the fact that the power-house of the Monophysite movement in these years remained Constantinople. Here the Patriarch Theodosius held sway, first under the protection of the empress and then under that of Justinian.[2] His authority was unchallenged. He was addressed, like his Chalcedonian rival, as 'Ecumenical Patriarch' by his suffragans, including James Bar'adai,[3] and the canons which he promulgated provided the basis for the law of the new church. His few surviving writings show him a moderate man who followed almost exactly in the footsteps of Severus. A sermon[4] preached after the death of Theodora in 548 stresses loyalty to the empire and its ruler. The Monophysite Christology is argued as a logical deduction from the doctrine of the Trinity following the canons of orthodoxy laid down by the Cappadocian Fathers. Christ was united with the Godhead as God. 'We believe that Christ, our Lord, was composed out of two natures, divine and human.' His flesh, derived from the *Theotokos*, the Virgin Mary, resulted in the formation of one being by nature and *hypostasis*, and as it was impossible to numerate the nature or essence of the Godhead, so it was absurd to numerate nature in Christ. The Trinity was distinguished in so far as its characteristics (*proprietatibus*) might be concerned but not in its natures (*naturis*).[5] Thus, as always, Chalcedon that spoke of Christ subsisting 'in two natures' was

---

[1] *Life of John of Hephaestopolis*, PO 18, pp. 536–9, and Honigmann's sketch in 'La Hiérarchie monophysite', pp. 165–7.

[2] Liberatus, *Brev.* xx, gives a house next to the Basilica of Arisphoca, six miles from the city, as Theodosius' forced residence. See E. Stein's note, *Bas-Empire*, II, 385. On the other hand, Conon and Eugenius are recorded as making a declaration of orthodoxy to Theodosius at the palace of Hormisdas (*Documenta*, ed. Chabot, p. 109).

[3] *Epistula scripta ad sanctum et beatum patriarcham Theodosium ab episcopis Iacobo, Eugenio et Eunomio* = *Documenta* (ed. Chabot), p. 63.

[4] *Documenta* (ed. Chabot), pp. 26–55.

[5] Compare the presbyter Longinus' summary of his doctrinal position: 'tres hypostases sunt quae distinguuntur non naturis sed proprietatibus' (*Documenta*, ed. Chabot, p. 59).

Justinian: the end of compromise

unacceptable. The *Henotikon*, on the other hand, could be received, but in the Severan sense of cancelling the synod.

Theodosius was reluctant to see the establishment of a rival hierarchy as a permanent expression of this difference of view.[1] As Severus before him, he refused to allow converts from the Diphysites to be re-ordained, being content with two years' penance before being re-admitted to their grade; i.e. Diphysite sacraments were not in all cases to be regarded as invalid[2] – once again one notes the contrast with the attitude of adherents to rival churches in the west. The tradition followed by the Monophysites was that of Dionysius and Peter of Alexandria rather than of Donatus of Carthage.

Theodosius also kept a firm hand on the theological debates within his church. The increasing degree of separation from the Chalcedonians during the 550s was accompanied by intellectual tension among the Monophysite leaders. The disputed issues arose out of the imprecisions of their creed. Debate was as fierce as in the Chalcedonian camp. To the existing Julianist schism and its various offshoots was added that of Tritheism which was to involve the patriarch's chosen suffragans, Conon and Eugenius. This dispute arose partly out of the return to fashion of Aristotelian philosophy applied to the mystery of the Trinity, and demonstrated incidentally how the Monophysites even under pressure continued to combine intellectual with popular monastic support as they had in the time of Severus. The Aristotelians distinguished two types of 'nature', the one abstract, representing the sum of common properties among all individual members of the same species, the other concrete and related to each individual, or in theological terms to each *hypostasis*. The Monophysites, following Severus, had been maintaining that while Christ existed in one indivisible *hypostasis*, this *hypostasis*, though united in essence to God, must be distinguished from the *hypostaseis* of God the Father and God the Holy Spirit. Now, through the assimilation of *hypostasis* and *physis* (nature), the distinction between the persons of the Trinity was elaborated to the extent that not only individualities (*hypostaseis*) but individual natures within each person had to be recognised and the sense of their

---

[1] John of Ephesus' views were similar. He regretted that by the death of Justinian 'nothing whatever had been done in the matter of the union of the church': *Lives of Five Patriarchs* (ed. Brooks), *PO* 18, p. 688.

[2] See F. Nau, 'Littérature canonique syriaque inédite', *Revue de l'Orient chrétien* 4, ser. II, 1909, pp. 113–16. Severus' canons were drawn up by his colleagues in Alexandria between February and August 535. See van Roey, 'Les débuts de l'église jacobite', p. 353 n48. Eating with Diphysites was, however, forbidden.

unity through common possession of the general essence or nature of Godhead became correspondingly attenuated.[1]

Such ideas deserved the term 'Tritheist'. They compromised the delicate balance of unity and distinction within the Trinity worked out by the Cappadocians, that God existed 'in one nature and three *hypostaseis*', which had been enshrined in the definition of faith in the Second Ecumenical Council of 381. During the 550s they began to gain ground in the Monophysite centres of Alexandria and Edessa, and they won the adherence of the Aristotelian philosopher, John Philoponos. John (d. *circa* 565) was one of the great intellects of the day whose active career spans the reign of Justinian. He was a man who combined zeal for ascetic Christianity, hence his title 'Philoponos', with eminence in the Alexandrian philosophic schools.[2] He represented the view that all existing nature was necessarily individual, and hence constituted an *hypostasis*. In Jesus Christ there was one nature and one *hypostasis*, and thus it followed that in the Trinity there were three natures and three *hypostaseis*. These ideas, logically presented by an Alexandrian scholar, were to have considerable effect on the Monophysite leaders, not least on Sergius, an east Syrian from Tella, whom Theodosius consecrated as patriarch of Antioch in 557.[3] With James Bar'adai's disciples Eugenius and Conon active as Tritheists in Isauria and Cilicia, the Monophysite cause was becoming threatened with Trinitarian as well as Christological dissensions.

In the capital, apart from Sergius who preferred life there to the rigours of the mission field, the Tritheists were represented by the picturesque figure of John Asconaghes (apparently he wore shoes of leather used for making water bottles), who arrived there about 557 and won the support of a powerful personage at court in the person of Athanasius, the grandson of the Empress Theodora. Athanasius was to be a stormy petrel for the next

[1] I have followed Duchesne, *L'Eglise au VIe siècle*, pp. 342–3. For other deviations in the Monophysite camp, see *ibid.* pp. 341ff.

[2] See H. D. Saffrey, 'Le Chrétien Jean Philopon et la survivance de l'Ecole d'Alexandrie', *Revue des études grecques* 67, 1954, pp. 396–410 (especially p. 408 where the author dates John's Tritheism to the early 550s), and T. Herrmann, 'Johannes Philoponos als Monophysit', *ZNTW* 29, 1930, pp. 209–64.

[3] Apparently not as Severus' successor. Since the latter's death in 538, Constantine of Laodicea had nominally been patriarch until his death in 553. See E. Honigmann, 'La Hiérarchie monophysite', p. 170. John dedicated his *De opificio mundi* to Sergius and Athanasius, and according to Nikephorus Kallistus, his work on the Hexaemeron also (*HE* XVIII. 47, *PG* 147, col. 424C).

Justinian: the end of compromise

two decades, aiming perhaps at the patriarchate of Alexandria.[1] In the crisis, Theodosius displayed unexpected powers of argument and diplomacy. In the debate with the Tritheists he was able to follow Severus' lead, and while accepting the difference in the 'properties' of the persons of the Trinity he rejected the idea of separate 'natures'. Having asserted this, he set about the dissidents. John Asconaghes was excommunicated and died shortly after, and the Patriarch Sergius followed circa 560/1. Conon and Eugenius wavered, continuing to be in and out of Tritheism for the remainder of their careers.[2]

The patriarchate of Antioch was left vacant for four years, before Theodosius determined to fill it with someone he could trust. In 563 he wrote to James Bar'adai asking his co-operation in consecrating his *syncellus* (secretary) Paul.[3] The latter was ostensibly a good choice, being an anti-Tritheist and Alexandrian-born, calculated therefore to harmonise the policies of the Syrians and Egyptians. As Theodosius declared, he had taken this step partly 'to maintain the unity of the holy Church', including Armenia, and partly because he was growing old.[4] His hopes were disappointed. Paul was consecrated in 564, and was destined to a stormy career. Though James Bar'adai was among his consecrators, he may have been passed over himself and resented this. The emphasis on unity in Theodosius' letter and the fact that he had opposed the Tritheists almost to the extent of slipping into the opposite extreme of Sabellianism may have influenced Theodosius' decision. Moreover, his enthusiasm for establishing a separate Monophysite hierarchy with great numbers of clergy aroused opposition. It is interesting that a letter ascribed to Anthimus, but almost certainly representing Theodosius' viewpoint, was sceptical about the

[1] See Michael the Syrian, *Chron.* x. 1 (ed. Chabot, II, 285).
[2] Theodosius, *Letter on the Canons* (published by Nau, 'Littérature canonique syriaque inédite', *Revue de l'Orient chrétien* 4, ser. II, 1909, pp. 120–3). For Conon's and Eugenius' recantation, see *Documenta* (ed. Chabot), pp. 109–10. Conon, however, lapsed into Tritheism: see Michael the Syrian, *Chron.* IX. 30 (ed. Chabot, II, 256) and x. 3; also John of Ephesus, *HE* v. 1–2. Following the pattern of other Monophysite leaders, Conon and Eugenius were missionaries in their cause. John of Ephesus complains that they established conventicles in Rome, Corinth, Athens and in Africa, and tried to win over the general Narses (*HE* v. 2).
[3] Theodosius, *Ep. ad episcopos orientales*, in *Documenta* (ed. Chabot), pp. 60–1. The dating of these events is worked out by E. W. Brooks, 'The Patriarch Paul of Antioch and the Alexandrine Schism of 575', *BZ* 30, 1929–30, pp. 468–76 at p. 469.
[4] Theodosius, *Ep. ad episcopos orientales*, p. 60; cf. pp. 66–7.

value of James' mass ordinations. 'As for us', James was told, 'one ought to meditate on the wise words written for our instruction, "Do not desire many useless children" (Eccles. 15. 22)' and, further on, 'One is greater worth than a thousand'.[1] Only ordinations that were strictly necessary were to be undertaken. Significantly for the spirit that animated the Monophysite leaders, the writer of the letter looked to 'the illumination of the heart of the peaceful and victorious emperor' and the reform and rapid reunification of members of the church 'separated for the moment'.

The momentum of the Monophysite church, however, could not be reversed. Indeed it would seem that most, if not all, of James' episcopal ordinations took place in the period between the Fifth General Council and Theodosius' death in 566; the years 557-8 were particularly busy, with the consecration of important figures such as John of Ephesus and Sergius of Antioch. The circumstances under which Theodosius' authority was wielded also presupposed his own 'Home Synod' rivalling that of the Chalcedonian patriarch. Already during their exile in Alexandria Severus and his colleagues had drafted disciplinary canons.[2] These were supplemented by Theodosius. Some of his canons for clergy ministering in the capital – a piece of evidence for the inconsistent practice of Justinian towards the Monophysites living under his nose – have survived.[3] Contact was also maintained with the churches within and beyond the boundaries of the empire, and prominent among these was the Armenian.[4] A further, almost inevitable step towards the establishment of a permanent independent hierarchy came in 564 or 565 when Theodosius commissioned Paul, the new patriarch of Antioch, to act as his representative in Egypt with the specific object of ordaining bishops in those Egyptian cities that lacked them.[5] That Justin II received Theodosius with the honour due to a patriarch early in 566 and accorded him a magnificent funeral when he died

---

[1] Nau, 'Littérature canonique syriaque inédite', p. 124. If written by Anthimus the letter must date to before 548 and reflect the restraint still felt by the Monophysite leaders at this stage regarding the establishment of a separate episcopal hierarchy.

[2] *Ibid.* pp. 113–16.

[3] *Documenta* (ed. Chabot), pp. 57–8.

[4] Theodosius, *Ep. ad episcopos orientales* (*Documenta*, ed. Chabot), p. 61, 'Scripta autem ad Armenos, cum istis scriptis brevibus nostris misimus'.

[5] *Ep. ad Iohannem et Leonidam et Iosephum venerabiles episcopos*, in *Documenta* (ed. Chabot), p. 95; also a letter to Theodore of Philae in the same sense (*ibid.* p. 97) and 'brethren in Thebaid and Arcadia' (*ibid.* pp. 98–9).

a few months later (22 June) made no difference to the situation. The Monophysite succession was not to die out with Theodosius.

By this time a new church had come into being. John of Ephesus writing in 566 gives the tally of twenty-seven bishops consecrated by James and his companions to this date.[1] They included the successive patriarchs of Antioch, Sergius and Paul, five metropolitans and three other bishops in Syria I. Cilicia, Isauria, Euphratesia, Mesopotamia, all had metropolitans, and in the other provinces of Asia Minor, large centres such as Smyrna and Ephesus had bishops. Bishops were also placed in some centres traditionally loyal to Severus, as Alabanda near Aphrodisias (as well as Aphrodisias itself) in Caria.[2] In 564 Theodosius regarded the situation as 'not unsatisfactory'.[3]

Less successful was Theodosius' attempt to refurbish the Egyptian episcopate confronted by the renewal of the Chalcedonian challenge which followed Justinian's appointment of Zoilus as patriarch. There the situation thanks to 'difficulties and persecutions' was less healthy.[4] Alexandria itself had been 'cast into the heresy of the Diphysites'.[5] Theodosius had 'sighed and wept' with good reason, for the Alexandrians had a reputation for acquiescing in orders from the emperor.[6] He had countered by agreeing to the appointment of no less than twelve new bishops for the towns of the Thebaid to consolidate the Monophysites' hold down the Nile valley on both sides of the Roman frontier.[7] The project however misfired, for the bishops do not seem to have reached their destinations and at the end of Justinian's reign there were only four Monophysite bishops in Egypt including the redoubtable Theodore of Philae. Jealousies, too, between the Egyptians and the leaders in the capital remained to plague the Monophysite cause for another generation.

[1] John of Ephesus, *Lives of James and Theodore* (ed. Brooks), *PO* 19, pp. 156–8. See Honigmann's list in 'La Hiérarchie monophysite', pp. 172–3.

[2] Both Bishop Zeuxis of Alabanda and Euphemius, metropolitan of Aphrodisias, were supporters of Severus and had been exiled by Justin. See *Chron. ad ann. 846* (ed. Brooks and Chabot), p. 173, and above, p. 249.

[3] *Ep. ad eos qui sunt Alexandriae*, *Documenta* (ed. Chabot), p. 97: 'Verum Oriens totus et loca alia per Christum plus minus sacerdotibus venerabilibus et archiepiscopis plena sunt.'

[4] *Ibid.* pp. 97–8.

[5] Michael the Syrian, *Chron.* IX. 29 (ed. Chabot, II, 243–4).

[6] *History of the Patriarchs* I, p. 467.

[7] John of Ephesus, *Lives of James and Theodore* (ed. Brooks), *PO* 19, p. 157.

The rise of the Monophysite movement

Though the organisation of the new bishoprics followed a traditional pattern, with the patriarchs of Alexandria and Antioch and other incumbents taking their titles from major cities,[1] the Monophysite church reflected the popular monasticism of Syria and Egypt. Its main centres lay beyond the city walls, in the great monasteries in north-east Syria, such as Mardin and Q'ennesrim, and in rural Egypt such as the great clusters of houses in the Wadi Habib and south-west of Alexandria. In the latter part of the sixth century the patriarchs both of Antioch and Alexandria lived in monasteries outside their primatial cities,[2] partly from necessity because they were banned entry to Alexandria and Antioch by the authorities, but partly perhaps from choice. Peter of Callinicum, patriarch of Antioch from 581, stated that he had never been to the city.[3]

There was another factor that was to make the separation of the churches difficult to heal. The sixth century had witnessed not only a revival of the military power and the prosperity of the cities of the east Roman Empire. Great changes had been taking place in the villages as well. In northern Syria the patient fieldwork of French archaeologists has established how in the mountains and plains east of Antioch what had once been an area dominated by landed proprietors on whom individual villages depended was now becoming an area where land was held by individual families engaged almost exclusively in olive culture in close association with the monasteries.[4] The fine construction of these and the churches and, above all, the olive presses witness their prosperity. Moreover, these north Syrian monasteries were becoming the intellectual and economic centres of Monophysitism. When within a year of Justinian's death the Tritheists threatened the tradition of the Patriarchs Severus and Theodosius, the north Syrians played a decisive part in upholding the doctrine of the latter. No less than fifty out of eighty whose names survive in the correspondence of the years 567–9 can be identified as north Syrian houses and thirty of

---

[1] This was not merely tradition. In the confusion following Phocas' disastrous war with the Persians, the Monophysite villages of north-east Syria refused bishops whom they believed had not been consecrated by a patriarch of Antioch. See Michael the Syrian, *Chron.* x. 26, and below, p. 333.

[2] *History of the Patriarchs*, part II (ed. Evetts), p. 472; cf. *ibid.* p. 471 regarding the Patriarch Peter. He resided at the Enaton monastery.

[3] Michael the Syrian, *Chron.* x. 22 (ed. Chabot, II, 370): Peter's explanation why he would not receive Damian of Alexandria in Antioch in 587.

[4] G. Tchalenko, *Villages antiques de la Syrie du Nord* (Paris, 1953–8), I, 376. Compare *ibid.* pp. 181–2.

Justinian: the end of compromise

these may be located from the restricted area of the plain of Dana.[1] Through them and other similar monastic agglomerations further east, the Monophysite church there had come into being. The combination of monastery and village as a single religious and economic unit became as significant for the survival of Monophysitism in Syria as a similar combination of martyr's shrine and village had been for Donatism in Numidia two centuries before.

The language of the Monophysite liturgies was following the trend of the times and becoming increasingly Syriac and Coptic, the language of the monks. The regional and autocephalous nature of its organisation was to be emphasised by the development of churches in Armenia and Persia and the great success of its missions beyond the boundaries of the empire, to Nubia and down the Red Sea to Arabia and thence to Ethiopia. It was an achievement, however, that had taken place less by the will of its leaders than by the logic of events that extended back over a century from the fateful decisions of Chalcedon.

[1] See A. Caquot, 'Couvents nommés dans les quatre lettres monophysites', in Tchalenko, *Villages antiques*, III, 63–83. For the correspondence, see *Documenta* (ed. Chabot), pp. 101–26.

Chapter 8

THE MONOPHYSITE KINGDOMS

During the first half of the sixth century Mediterranean Christianity reached the climax of its achievement. One aspect of this was the passionate and profound search for dogmatic truth that engrossed the Byzantines from the emperor downwards. The other was the propagation of that truth by every visible means. The age is symbolised by Sancta Sophia, completed in 537, and by its western counterparts in Ravenna, but wherever the emperor's writ ran churches, monasteries and other religious houses were being built, often on a sumptuous scale. At Gerasa (Jerash) eight entire new churches were built in the town in Justinian's reign.[1] In reconquered North Africa the surviving cities became resplendent with churches in this period. 'Eglise paléo-chrétienne', so beloved of archaeologists' reports of work done in the eastern Mediterranean, means in very many cases a church built or in use in the reigns of Justin and Justinian.

This explosion of church-building had propagandist and missionary aims.[2] It was a means by which Justinian gave tangible expression to the neo-Chalcedonian orthodoxy of his empire. Dedications were now to the Theotokos in preference even to Christ, and where the church confronted its enemies either on the frontiers or in hostile Samaria and the Judaean deserts, its role as an arm of the state was emphasised. Fortress and church were often associated, just as Benedictine monastery and Norman castle were associated in the Marcher earldoms of Norman England. Within the frontiers of the empire the remnants of paganism were being swept away by a mixture of repression and intensive missionary preaching.[3] Beyond them a motley crew of merchant adventurers and wandering monks and clergy were carrying the Gospel in one form or another to Arabs, Ethiopians, Nubians and Indians. In these enterprises the anti-Chalcedonians had already been active in Anastasius' reign. We read of a Bishop Simeon

---

[1] See C. H. Kraeling, *Gerasa, City of the Decapolis* (New Haven, 1938).

[2] See G. H. Armstrong, 'Fifth and sixth century church building in the Holy Land', *Greek Orthodox Theol. Review* 14, 1969, pp. 17–30.

[3] For the forceful suppression of paganism in Carrhae (Harran) by the Emperor Maurice, see *Chron. ad ann. 1234* (ed. Chabot), p. 165. For John of Ephesus' more peaceful and successful enterprise in western Asia Minor, see above, p. 286.

The Monophysite kingdoms

travelling far and wide 'from Jerusalem to Illyricum', before moving into Persia to combat the Nestorians there.[1] Christianity had made progress among the Himyarites in southern Arabia in the reign of Anastasius and a bishop had been sent thither on their request.[2] In Justin's reign Bishop James of Serug and monks who had been expelled from their Syrian monasteries as opponents of Chalcedon inspired missions thither, or went as missionaries themselves. Their success anticipated that of similar ventures sponsored by Theodora in the Monophysite cause.

The rise of the Monophysite kingdoms on the southern borders of the empire and beyond was the direct result of sixth-century missions in which the Monophysites were more successful than their Chalcedonian rivals. Thus the Nobatae (Nubians) south of the frontier of Egypt were convinced by Monophysite preaching that Christianity represented true monotheism, whereas Justinian's Chalcedonian emissaries were rejected, possibly because their Gospel might be held to represent duality, namely 'two Christs'.[3] Monophysitism was to survive for centuries as the national religion of the Nubian kingdoms and Ethiopia. In Armenia and among the Arab tribes living in the debatable land between Rome and Persia, the success of Monophysitism was also helped by antipathy felt for Persia and any form of Christianity connected with Persia, e.g. Nestorianism. The *Henotikon* of Zeno was accepted as the rock on which Armenian Christianity was built, while the Ghassanid Arab tribes, having at one time rejected Severus, accepted the theology of his successors. The combination of monastic-inspired devotion allied to political and cultural forces resulted in the emergence of the Monophysite kingdoms on Rome's eastern and southern borders. Their existence was to guarantee the survival of the work of Severus and Theodosius for many generations to come.

NUBIA

The most striking example of the missionary zeal of the Monophysites in the sixth century was the conversion of the three Nubian kingdoms south of the Egyptian border. This eventually brought a vast area, extending from Aswan to the foothills of Ethiopia, into the Monophysite fold. The Nubian kingdoms seem to have arisen out of the ruins of the Meroitic Empire

---

[1] John of Ephesus, *Life of Simeon the Bishop* (ed. Brooks), *PO* 17, p. 138.
[2] John Diakrinomenos, *HE* x (fragments, ed. Miller, p. 403).
[3] See John of Ephesus, *HE* IV. 7 (ed. Brooks, p. 138).

The rise of the Monophysite movement

from the middle of the third century onwards. Piecing together the results of excavations with the evidence provided by John of Ephesus, it would seem that towards the middle of the sixth century there was a northern kingdom (Nobatia) which extended down the west bank of the Nile from the Egyptian frontier at Aswan as far as the Third Cataract peopled by Nobatae. Its capital was at Faras (Pachoras). Further south lay the kingdom of Makurrah stretching as far as a site known to Arab writers as al-Abwab ('the doors'), perhaps near Kabushia, and whose capital was at Old Dongola. Beyond this was Alwah whose capital, Soba, was near Khartoum. In the vast, waterless tracts east of the Nile were the Blemmyes, one of whose principal strongholds was the cliff-fort of Q'asr Ibrim (Primis).

Between them, the Blemmyes and Nobatae had been the scourge of the Thebaid and in their raids had carried off enormous quantities of valuables looted from the Egyptians.[1] Not only do the contents of the royal tombs of Q'astel and Ballana bear witness to the barbaric splendour of their warrior kings in the fifth century, but even in the crudely built Blemmye houses which preceded the great church at Q'asr Ibrim Roman ivories and bronze figures were found.[2] The security of the frontier near Aswan was a major undertaking, but in 453 the Roman commander Maximinus defeated the Blemmyes and Nobatae and forced them to sue for peace. One concession was, however, granted to them, namely the right to an annual visit to Philae just below Aswan, there to bring offerings to the temple of Isis and to borrow the statue of the goddess for her oracular powers for use in their own territories. The treaty was for 100 years and lasted until sometime *circa* 540 when Justinian, angered at the continued existence of paganism anywhere in his dominions, alleged the expiry of the treaty and sent his general, Narses, to destroy the temple of Isis and end the cult.

This action may not have endeared the emperor to the tribesmen, but the mission to them began independently. According to John of Ephesus, the idea originated *circa* 541 with an elderly monk named Julian in the entourage of Theodosius at Constantinople.[3] He persuaded Theodora that

[1] See W. B. Emery, *The Royal Tombs of Ballana and Qustul* (Cairo, 1938) for an account of the Blemmyes and the excavation of their royal tombs.

[2] By the writer, to be published by Rev. Professor J. M. Plumley and himself on behalf of the Egypt Exploration Society.

[3] John of Ephesus, *HE* IV. 6. For a translation of John's account of the incident, see Bury, *History of the Later Roman Empire*, II, 328.

the Nubians' conversion was possible, but the empress in her enthusiasm informed Justinian of her aims. The emperor, while sympathising with these, resolved that any mission must be Chalcedonian in allegiance. There had probably been some Christian contact with Nubia through the bishops of the Thebaid, and Theodore of Philae seems to have been acceptable immediately the mission crossed into Nubian territory. One result of the Polish excavations at Faras (Pachoras) was the discovery of the remains of a church below the palace of the pagan ruler of Nobatia, itself destroyed *circa* 617, dating perhaps to the fifth century, and of simple Christian graves of similar date belonging to the poorer classes.[1] Egypt, however, was Monophysite in sentiment, though Justinian attempted to anticipate Theodora by enlisting the help of his Chalcedonian bishops in the Thebaid for the mission. In his zeal he fitted out a caravan with gifts, including gold and baptismal robes for the prospective converts. Theodora used the same cunning she had employed four years before with Pope Vigilius but with considerably more success. She wrote to the *dux* of the Thebaid, informing him that both she and the emperor intended to send a mission to the Nobatae, and that her emissary the blessed Julian would be in charge of the ambassadors. Her speed and boldness succeeded. The *dux* after some hesitation between the emperor's instructions and his queen's accepted hers, and a richly equipped expedition was soon on its way to the Nubian frontier. Julian succeeded in converting Silko, king of the Nobatae, and a number of the nobility and people, and even persuaded them of the grounds on which Chalcedon was to be rejected. When the emperor's mission eventually arrived the king rejected it, branding it as 'the wicked faith' of the emperor.[2] Meantime, Julian was supported by Theodosius' bishop, Theodore of Philae, who remained for a while at the court of Silko after Julian had returned to Constantinople.

The next step was a successful war waged by Silko against the Blemmyes. Despite his rejection of Chalcedonian Christianity the emperor's general, Narses, co-operated with him, and he advanced down the east bank of the Nile to take Talmis (Kalabscha) and Q'asr Ibrim (Primis). In the latter

[1] See K. Michalowski, *Kunst und Geschichte Nubiens in christlicher Zeit* (ed. E. Dinkler, Bongers, Recklinghausen, 1970), p. 12.

[2] John of Ephesus, *HE* IV. 7. Silko replied cunningly to the imperial envoys: 'We accept the gift of the king of the Romans and we will send him a gift, but his faith we will not accept. If we deserve to become Christians we will follow after the Pope Theodosius, whom because he would not accept the evil faith of the king he expelled and ejected.' Julian had done his work well.

The rise of the Monophysite movement

there is clear archaeological evidence that the 'X-Group people', almost certainly Blemmyes, had their houses in the fortress area or were squatting amid the litter of the disused forecourt of the great Meroitic temple.[1] An inscription from Kalabscha in rustic Greek commemorates Silko's campaign including the boastful expression, 'I did not allow my foes to rest in the shade, but compelled them to remain in the full sunlight [he would not have had much trouble at Q'asr Ibrim] with no one to bring them water to their houses; I am a lion for the lands below, a bear for the lands above'. And Silko claimed to be 'king of the Nobatae and all the Ethiopians'.[2] His defeat of the Blemmyes and their conversion had one important result. The peoples on the eastern bank of the Nile also accepted the Monophysite version of Christianity (*circa* 560), and probably within not much more than a generation the old Meroitic temple at Q'asr Ibrim was being ransacked for stone to build the most imposing stone church in all Nubia.

Further south in Makurrah, the emperor at first had more success. Julian's return to Constantinople, where he died, and Theodore's inability to make more than passing visits to Nobatia left the way open for Chalcedonian emissaries. These had a better reception in Makurrah, and by the time of his death in 565 Justinian had blocked temporarily the way for Monophysite expansion south. Once again, however, the superior attractive power of Monophysite teaching in tribal environments asserted itself. The presbyter Longinus had been appointed by the Patriarch Theodosius shortly before his death in 566 to succeed Julian, and had been consecrated bishop of the Nobatae, but for some time he was detained in Constantinople. Only in 568–9 did he manage to escape and make his way to Nubia, and then in disguise. 'Aware that he was watched and would not be permitted to leave, he disguised himself and put a wig on his head, for he was very bald',[3] wrote John of Ephesus, and so he arrived in Nubia. Except for three wretched years in Egypt (575–8) in which he was caught up in the whirlpool of ecclesiastical intrigue there,[4] he remained in Nobatia until in

---

[1] See the forthcoming report (ed. J. M. Plumley) on the excavations at Q'asr Ibrim. The writer found X-Group material (including a fine bronze skillet) lying just above the level of the temple forecourt, separated from the floor by a thin layer of wind-blown silt. X-Group houses underlay the great artificial mound on which the west end of the church and its approaches had been built.

[2] *CIG* III. 5072. See Bury, *History of the Later Roman Empire*, II, 330 n1.

[3] John of Ephesus, *HE* IV. 8 (ed. Brooks, p. 140).

[4] *Ibid.* IV. 9ff.

The Monophysite kingdoms

580 he was invited urgently by the king of Alwah, the southernmost of the three Nubian kingdoms, who was an ally of Nobatia, to preach the Gospel there.[1] Makurrah lay between and was pro-Chalcedonian and hostile. Longinus could not use the river route but was helped by the Blemmyes through the eastern desert, thus bypassing Makurrah. Again, John of Ephesus writes, 'But because of the wicked devices of him who dwells between us, I sent my saintly father to the king of the Blemmyes that he might conduct him thither [to Alwah] by routes further inland; but the Makaritae heard also of this, and set people on the look-out in all the passes of his kingdom, both in the mountains and in the plains'.[2] Even so, Longinus arrived in Soba in 580 and once again had brilliant success, despite intrigues by his enemies in Egypt. Even Julianist supporters carrying out a mission from Axum were refuted.[3] Not long after, Christianity had become the official religion of the whole of the northern Sudan as far as the foothills of Ethiopia. Between Alexandria and Axum the greater part of the population had been converted.

How long Makurrah remained Chalcedonian is not certain. Sometime between 560 and 710 the two kingdoms of Nobatia and Makurrah united to form one realm, perhaps through the great Nobatian ruler Mercurius (*circa* 700–60), and by then all Nubia was Monophysite. In Nobatia itself, however, Chalcedon may have been represented by the Byzantine agent established by Justinian at Talmis and by a bishopric at Taifa.[4]

It is not our purpose to pursue the story of Nubian Christianity beyond the period of the Arab invasions. Two points may, however, be made briefly. First, one would note the extraordinarily tenacious hold which the new faith had won in Nubia, which made it proof against constant Moslem pressure for nearly 800 years; and secondly, the predominantly Byzantine character of the church and administration of the Nubian kingdoms. Both these are remarkable, for one would have expected Nubia to have been an extension of the Coptic church and to have shared its vicissitudes. Whereas, however, the Christianity of Coptic Egypt after a period of great

---

[1] *Ibid.* IV. 49 (ed. Brooks, p. 175).
[2] *Ibid.* IV. 53 (ed. Brooks, p. 182).
[3] *Ibid.* IV. 53 (ed. Brooks, pp. 180–1). This sheds an interesting sidelight on the connections between Soba and Axum and the way in which the ground may have been prepared for Longinus' mission.
[4] *CIG* IV. 8647–9 (Talmis, later than Justinian's reign). See Bury, *History of the Later Roman Empire*, II, 330.

The rise of the Monophysite movement

prosperity between 650 and 700 gradually dissolved before Moslem pressures, the Nubians retained their independence and their Christianity until both were overthrown by military force after a resistance which prolonged the final issue until midway through the fifteenth century.[1] The Moslems had undoubtedly expected an easy conquest, for their raids started right after the surrender of Egypt to them in 641, but in subsequent encounters the discipline of generations of cavalry razzia into southern Egypt proved a match for the Arabs, and after a hard-won victory near Dongola in 652 they accepted a treaty which respected Nubian independence in exchange for an annual tribute. The unification of the Nubian kingdoms in the course of the next half-century enabled the Nubians to hold their own and at times even to come to the rescue of the Copts. At the end of the twelfth century archaeological discoveries have proved their recovery from the invasion of Saladin's brother, Shams-ed-Doula, in 1173 and the survival of an organised Christian kingdom round Q'asr Ibrim in the north and Soba in the south until the dawn of the modern epoch. In this kingdom administrative and episcopal offices were sometimes united; some of the medieval bishops whose memorial stones were found at Q'asr Ibrim also had civil titles.[2] One gains the impression of a strongly organised kingdom, administered on Byzantine lines, in which the church as guardian of national tradition and language played a major role, and that Nubian survival was due as much to its organisational strength as to the prowess of its archers.

The church and administration of the Nubian kingdoms, though Monophysite in allegiance and accepting its bishops from the patriarch of Alexandria, remained true to Byzantine forms. Considering that direct contact with Byzantium was broken after the conquest of Egypt by the Arabs, this is not what one would expect. Yet the discoveries of considerable quantities of Nubian manuscripts and inscriptions at Q'asr Ibrim and the analysis of the influences behind the magnificent frescoes discovered at

---

[1] The probable dating of the last phase at Q'asr Ibrim (one of the leather scrolls found by the writer appears to date 1137 of the Era of the Martyrs, i.e. 1421 A.D.). See my 'Christianity in the Middle East, survey down to 1800', ch. 5 of vol. 1 of *Religion in the Middle East*, ed. A. J. Arberry (Cambridge, 1969), pp. 270–5 for the period to 1400. Also P. L. Shinnie, *Medieval Nubia* (Khartoum, 1954).

[2] See my 'Nubia as a Byzantine cultural outpost', *Byzantino-Slavica* 18, 1968, pp. 319–26, and Kurt Weitzmann's article on Nubian art, 'Some remarks on the fresco paintings of the Cathedral of Faras' in *Kunst und Geschichte Nubiens*, ed. Dinkler, pp. 325–40.

The Monophysite kingdoms

Faras (Pachoras) leave very little doubt of the truth of this.[1] The high-sounding titles of 'new Constantine', 'king worthy of three hundred years' reign' or 'president of the Caesars' applied to the kinglets of Nubia in the eighth century could indeed be reminiscences of Byzantine titles from the period when direct contact with the court at Constantinople was possible. So too could the survival of titles such as 'eparchos' applied to the ruler of Q'asr Ibrim, who seems to have been a sort of viceroy of the northern kingdom in the Middle Ages; 'domesticus', 'primicerius' and others that suggested the Byzantine civil hierarchy. What is surprising, however, is the continued use of these titles, together with Greek and Nubian as the languages of liturgy and administration as long as the Nubian kingdoms lasted. Coptic indeed was read as the language of the Biblical text, but prayers were said in Greek when not in the native language.[2] One may detect the same dual influences in Nubian ecclesiastical art and architecture. Q'asr Ibrim was built on a basilican plan and could have been placed among Byzantine churches in Syria or North Africa of the sixth century. Regarding the frescoes on the walls of the church at Faras, it has been noted that apart from isolated scenes the general cast of features of the figures depicted and their arrangement and proportion is in keeping with the accompanying legends in Greek as well as Nubian. 'There is no doubt', their discoverer commented, 'that here we have an example of Greek-Byzantine art, without trace of the typical style that marks Coptic art.'[3] To an extent not previously appreciated, Christian Nubia was a cultural offshoot of Byzantium.[4] That it became so was primarily the work of Theodora and the Monophysite missionaries of the sixth century.

[1] K. Michalowski, 'The Polish Excavations at Faras, 1961', *Kush* 10, 1962, pp. 220–44 at p. 231. See for details, Michalowski's *Faras: die Kathedrale aus dem Wüstensand* (Benziger, Zurich, 1967), pp. 105–70.

[2] A fragment of Greek psalmody was found at Faras: see Michalowski, 'Polish excavations at Faras, 1962–63', *Kush* 12, 1964, pp. 195–207 at p. 196.

[3] K. Michalowski, quoted in the *Sunday Times* Colour Supplement of 14 July 1963, and compare U. Monneret de Villard's view that the Christian art and architecture of Nubia 'was entirely independent of Christian art in Egypt': *La Nubia medioevale* (Cairo, 1934–57), I, p. iv.

[4] See, for instance, K. Michalowski, 'Open problems of Nubian art and culture in the light of the discoveries at Faras', in *Kunst und Geschichte Nubiens*, ed. Dinkler, pp. 11–20, and other essays in this volume.

The rise of the Monophysite movement

ETHIOPIA AND THE RED SEA KINGDOMS

In Nubia the progress of the conversion of the three kingdoms to Monophysitism can be traced in outline with some accuracy. For the similar process that placed Ethiopia in the anti-Chalcedonian camp, the evidence is obscure.[1] Today, Ethiopian Christianity is monastic and Monophysite but is imbued throughout its ceremonial and expression with strong undercurrents of Jewish practice. This could only suggest that the way for Christianity had been prepared by long-standing contacts with Judaic influences, perhaps through the colonies of Jewish merchants to be found in south Arabia where Ethiopia itself had political and trading connections.[2] When Cosmas Indicopleustes visited the kingdom of Axum in *circa* 525 he found its port of Adulis a flourishing one with close relations with Arabia and beyond.[3]

The earliest evidence for Christianity in Ethiopia was also associated with traders along the Red Sea coast, this time from Alexandria. Frumentius and his brother Aedesius were the two young companions of a Tyrian merchant, Meropius, who traded with 'India' – probably in this case southern Arabia. They were captured *circa* 320 by the Ethiopians and taken to their capital at Axum. Meropius had either died or been executed; but somehow or other Frumentius and Aedesius became accepted at the Ethiopian court. On the death of the king, who left his wife and a young family behind him, they gradually assumed a considerable role in the administration of the country and in the education of the young princes, Frumentius even becoming regent. He and his brother were Christians, and they influenced some of the Roman merchants in the capital to take a positive interest in the spread of the faith. A small church was built and Christianity became influential.[4] It seems evident that in the latter part of his reign, which lasted *circa* 320–60, King Ezana was converted to Christianity. The researches of the Ethiopian scholar Bairu Tafla have shown that whereas on his earlier inscriptions the king shows strong adherence

[1] The most recent study is that of Edward Ullendorf, *Ethiopia and the Bible*, Schweich Lectures 1967 (London, 1968). The author provides an extensive bibliography. See also G. Bardy and L. Bréhier, 'L'Expansion chrétienne aux Ve et VIe siècles', in *Histoire de l'église*, ed. Fliche and Martin, vol. IV, pp. 513–29.

[2] Ullendorf, *Ethiopia and the Bible*, p. 23.

[3] Cosmas Indicopleustes, *The Christian Topography* II. 40 (ed. McCrindle, p. 54).

[4] See Socrates, *HE* I. 19, and Rufinus, *HE* I. 9 (*PL* 21, cols. 478–80).

to traditional pagan beliefs, attributing his successes to Ares[1] and other pagan gods, a later inscription attributes benefits to 'the Lord of Heaven', and abandons claim to descent from the gods.[2] This development would seem to coincide with Frumentius' return to Alexandria *circa* 348, and his consecration by Athanasius as bishop for the kingdom of Axum,[3] against which Constantius II protested so vigorously in his letter to the rulers.[4] We also hear of Constantius' missionary who established Christianity among Roman merchant communities in the Red Sea and Socotra, visiting Axum on behalf of the emperor to 'order all things correctly there'.[5] There is little doubt, however, as to the general truth of the story of Frumentius told by both Socrates and Rufinus, and the clear implication that in the first instance Ethiopian Christianity was controlled by Alexandria. Frumentius' consecration by Athanasius set a precedent for the subordination of the church of Ethiopia to that patriarchate.

The next phase, however, in the history of the Ethiopian church is extremely difficult to piece together. Tafla considers that part of the evangelisation of northern Ethiopia was undertaken by refugee Monophysites after Chalcedon, but there is no clear evidence to support this.[6] So far as we know, neither Proterius nor his Chalcedonian successors were in a position to exercise pressure on monks sufficient to drive them to seek refuge in Ethiopia. That there were, however, continuing links between the Monophysites in Egypt and Christians in Axum is clear from the explicit mention by John of Ephesus of followers of Julian of Halicarnassos from Axum attempting to spread their heretical views in the southernmost Nubian kingdom of Alwah.[7]

Tafla places the epochal event of the arrival of the Nine Saints at Axum in about A.D. 502. Their names traditionally preserved suggest diverse origins, perhaps united through a common training. The central figure of the group was Apa Michael Aragawi, who is credited with founding the great monastery of Debra Dame on a hill overlooking Axum, and giving

[1] Perhaps derived from Ptolemaic Egypt: see Cosmas Indicopleustes, *The Christian Topography* II. 143 (ed. McCrindle, p. 66).
[2] B. Tafla, 'The establishment of the Ethiopian church', *Tarikh* 2. 1 (Ibadan, 1967), pp. 28–42. A note in the *Numismatic Chronicle* of 1884, p. 205, shows coins of Ezana bearing a cross on the reverse.
[3] The episode must date after Athanasius' recall from exile in 346.
[4] See above, p. 56.　　[5] Philostorgius, cited by Photius, *Bibl.* II. 6.
[6] Tafla, 'The establishment of the Ethiopian church', p. 32.
[7] See above, p. 301.

it a Rule based on a Pachomian model. These missionaries and their immediate followers gave great impetus to the spread of Christianity and are also credited with the translation of the Scriptures into Gəʽəz, the language of northern Ethiopia.[1]

If the monastic rule established by them was Pachomian one would expect a strongly Coptic influence, but this does not seem to have been the case. There is a large measure of agreement that the translation of the Scriptures was from both Greek and Syriac originals and not Alexandrine or Coptic. Vööbus in particular invites attention to specifically Syriac translation techniques and modes of transliteration.[2] It has been usually assumed, moreover, that the Nine Saints were Syrian monks and that they arrived in Ethiopia by way of southern Arabia,[3] and their names, such as Liganio, Pantaleon, Guba and Yemata, recall those of Syrian monasteries.[4] It seems evident from this that the previously predominant Alexandrian type of monastic Christianity was modified and even displaced by a Syrian type. Both, however, were strongly anti-Chalcedonian in allegiance, but were anti-Eutychian also. The Monophysite mission thus seems to have been Severan in outlook, and despite every vagary of liturgical and ceremonial practice it has remained so. The strong infusion, however, of Syrian influence at this juncture might also have had an indirect effect of preserving underlying Jewish influences.

Only in the reign of Justin is the curtain lifted slightly on the relations between Ethiopia and the empire, and these show the usual complicated patterns in which the pro-western and Chalcedonian emperor was obliged to make use of the good offices of anti-Chalcedonians to develop relations with the peoples beyond his southern frontiers. Christian missions via the oases dominated by the Arab tribes and down the Red Sea coast as far as Yemen seem also to have been very largely Syrian and anti-Chalcedonian. The connection between the two areas was demonstrated when in *circa* 520 James of Serug wrote from his see of Batnai in north-east Syria to the Himyarite Christians, commending their faith and pointing to the quiet conditions existing in the Roman Empire under Justin.[5] The

[1] Ullendorf, *Ethiopia and the Bible*, pp. 39ff.
[2] A. Vööbus, *Early Versions of the New Testament* (Stockholm, 1954), p. 250.
[3] Ullendorf, *Ethiopia and the Bible*, p. 52.
[4] Bardy/Bréhier, 'L'Expansion chrétienne', p. 525.
[5] Cited from A. A. Vasiliev, *Justin the First*, Dumbarton Oaks Studies 1 (Cambridge, Mass., 1950), p. 290.

The Monophysite kingdoms

Chronicle of Séert also says that Monophysites expelled by Justin carried out successful missionary work in these parts.[1] Three years later occurred the disastrous war between the Jews and Christians in Yemen and the massacre of the latter at Najran. Significantly the Jews were supported by the Persians, while the Christians were regarded as protégés of Byzantium. Though they were anti-Chalcedonians this was clearly justified, for Justin at once intervened through the king of Ethiopia, and the latter used Timothy, patriarch of Alexandria, as his intermediary, promising to make war on the Yemenites if the Romans provided the ships. Justin, also using Timothy as go-between, accepted this condition. After one unsuccessful campaign the Ethiopians decisively defeated the Yemenites and Christianity was restored to its former tolerated position.[2] Indeed, after a period of anarchy in the Yemen, Christianity progressed there. We hear how in 567 Abraha, the Christian king of Yemen, built a new cathedral at Sana with the aim of making it a rival pilgrimage centre to Mecca. However, this was frustrated by hostile Arabs and Abraha's punitive expedition against Mecca was defeated, and in 571 the Jews supported by the Persians again asserted themselves.[3] These events, half-legendary though their transmission has been, show us how in the sixth century Yemen was a cockpit for the rival religions in the east, Jews, Zoroastrians, Nestorians and Monophysites. Out of this confusion Mahomet was to develop his synthesis in the next century and at the same time free Arabia from the rival armies of the Persians and Ethiopians.

The Monophysite success in Ethiopia was due to the country falling within an Alexandrian sphere of influence and, in addition, to evangelism in the sixth century being carried out largely by individual monks from Syria and Egypt pledged to the anti-Chalcedonian cause. There were also the Julianists as elsewhere in the Monophysite east, but they failed to make much headway. As in Nubia also, translation of the Scriptures into the predominant local language resulted in Monophysite Christianity becom-

---

[1] *Chronicle of Séert* XXII (ed. Scher, *PO* 7, pp. 143ff.), which claims that they were Julianists.

[2] The story is told by A. Moberg in his Introduction to *The Book of the Himyarites* (Lund, 1924). He regards this as an excellent source written up soon after the second Abyssinian expedition, i.e. circa 525, and relying partly on eyewitness accounts of events.

[3] See Moberg, *Himyarites*, p. cxxxiv, and J. Stewart, *Nestorian Missionary Enterprise* (Edinburgh, 1928), p. 68. Stewart, mistakenly in my view, considers the predominant Christian influence in Yemen Nestorian.

ing associated with the people at large. The Bible and liturgy in the native language provided a foundation for the growth of a national literature and system of education, and thus became the vehicle of what one may reasonably call national unity. One notices, as in Nubia, how Greek continued to be known and Bible translations were made direct from that language. One may suspect that in Ethiopia also Byzantium continued to exercise a distant influence, even though the emperor was associated with the hated Council of Chalcedon.

ARMENIA

The story of the Armenian church, like that of the Armenian people, is of a long struggle for survival against more powerful creeds and neighbours.[1] The rejection of Chalcedon and the acceptance by the middle of the sixth century of the works of Timothy the Cat and the *Henotikon* of Zeno as the touchstones of orthodoxy can best be understood within the context of the demands of national survival. The scanty available evidence suggests that from the outset there were two main influences on Armenian Christianity: the first derived from the neighbouring Greek-speaking province of Cappadocia which gave the Armenians their apostle, Gregory the Illuminator, *circa* 300; the second, more obscure but nonetheless almost equally important, from the south, principally through the Christianised client state of Osrhoëne where a Syriac and perhaps even Judaised interpretation of the faith seems to have penetrated into southern Armenia by the mid-third century.

Armenia became a Christian kingdom with the conversion of King Tiridates *circa* 301, and resisted the efforts of Maximin Daia to impose paganism by force in 311–12.[2] The fact that Christianity was accepted as the national religion before it became the religion of the Roman Empire gave the Armenians a sense of pride which made negotiations between the Byzantines and themselves rather more difficult than perhaps they need

[1] I have relied for this section mainly on K. Sarkissian, *The Council of Chalcedon and the Armenian Church* (London, 1965), V. Inglisian's essay, 'Chalkedon und die armenische Kirche', in Grillmeier/Bacht, *Das Konzil von Chalkedon*, II, 361–417, and Petermann and Gelzer, 'Armenien', in Herzog–Hauck, *Realencyclopädie für protestantische Theologie und Kirche*, vol. II (Leipzig, 1897), pp. 63–92.

[2] For the dating, see A. H. M. Jones, *The Prosopography of the Later Roman Empire* I, p. 916 and P. Ananian, 'La data e circostanze della consecrazione di S. Gregorio Illuminatore', *Le Muséon* 74, 1961, pp. 43–73.

The Monophysite kingdoms

have been. While there must have been a strong Christian element in Armenia by the end of the third century, the official conversion of the kingdom had taken place 'from above', that is through the conversion of the ruling dynasty and an influential part of the aristocracy. This gave Christianity from the outset the characteristics of a national movement, a symbol of identity in face of the rival empires of Rome and Persia. The old pagan priesthood tended to merge into the new ecclesiastical hierarchy.[1] The relationship between the head of the church, or Catholicus, and the king resembled that of ruler and chief minister, and for more than a century the Catholicate was occupied by a member of the house of Gregory the Illuminator.

Through most of the fourth century this situation worked in favour of Greek ecclesiastical influences dominating Armenia. Gregory himself had been educated in Cappadocia and had been consecrated bishop at its capital, Caesarea. Teachers and missionaries had accompanied him from Sebastea in eastern Cappadocia and continued to be supplied largely from that province. The liturgy was conducted in Greek, and the Council of Nicaea at which Armenia had a representative was accepted as the basis of orthodox faith. This attitude also coincided with the political bias of Armenia, for though both Romans and Persians sedulously courted Armenian support, this was usually lent to the Roman side. Faustus of Byzantium (*circa* 400), for instance, relates how in *circa* 356 King Arsak of Armenia was approached by the Persian monarch Sapor to conclude an alliance, but 'he refused either to give presents or draw near to him at all: he would not even hear the [Persian] ambassadors' names'.[2] Arsak was, generally speaking, loyal to Constantius II and Julian. The death of the latter and the disastrous treaty which Jovian was forced to sign in 363 had repercussions for the whole of Rome's eastern frontier and brought a profound and permanent change in Armenia's position. Rome had surrendered all Armenia as well as many other military advantages to the enemy.[3]

Jovian agreed not only to give up Nisibis, but to allow Sapor a free hand to conquer Armenia, promising not to go to the Armenians'

---

[1] Sarkissian, *Council of Chalcedon*, p. 82, but does not cite specific examples.

[2] Faustus of Byzantium IV. 21 (ed. M. Lauer, Cologne, 1879); compare Ammianus Marcellinus, *Res gestae* XX. 11. 1–3. For the twists of Armenian policy during the period, see N. H. Baynes, 'Rome and Armenia in the fourth century', in *Byzantine Studies, and Other Essays*, pp. 186–208.

[3] Libanius, *Orat.* XXIV. 9 (ed. Foerster, Leipzig, 1904, II, 518, line 12).

The rise of the Monophysite movement

help.¹ The result was a gradual wearing down of Armenian resistance by Persian forays, and the re-emergence of a pro-Persian and anti-Christian movement among the nobility. Fire-worshipping was better than sudden death. This development culminated in 373/4 in an acute crisis in which the Catholicus, Narses, was poisoned by King Pap, who then set about reducing the privileges of the church in favour of a restoration of paganism associated with an alliance with Persia. The fifth-century Armenian historian Mouses Xorenaci indicates that the Persian object in these negotiations was to root out the Greek element in Armenian Christianity.² At this juncture the bitter quarrel between the Emperor Valens and Basil of Caesarea inhibited effective counter-action, even though Pap was murdered on a visit to Roman territory.³ The Catholicate became henceforth entirely Armenian and the Catholicus was consecrated without reference to Caesarea. When eventually a *modus vivendi* between Rome and Persia was reached by the emperor Theodosius I in 387, the division of spheres of influence in Armenia between the two empires left more than three-quarters of the kingdom in Persian hands, including the ecclesiastical centres of Dvin, Etzimodzin and Archdidad.

This development coincided with the rise of the Antiochene school of theologians. Their influence on the Christians in Persia led to the revival of the Syriac Christian tradition in Armenia which had been partly overlaid by a century of Cappadocian-Greek influence.⁴ In Persian Armenia Christianity was only to be taught through Syriac. The Catholicus Ishak who governed the Armenian church for nearly half a century (390–439) was son of the murdered Narses, and at heart he was pro-Byzantine, but in his continuous efforts to hold a balance between the pro-Persian and pro-Byzantine elements in the country he was partly responsible for Christianity tending towards both a national and a Nestorian outlook, against which latter, however, there was to be a vigorous and lasting reaction.

The basic need of the time was to set down the Scripture and liturgy in

---

[1] See Baynes, 'Rome and Armenia', pp. 197–8.

[2] Cited from Sarkissian, *Council of Chalcedon*, p. 84.

[3] Faustus of Byzantium v. 31, and Ammianus Marcellinus, *Res gestae* XXX. 2. 1. 'Papam [=Pap] sociare sibi conabatur Sapor', but Pap was murdered by Roman military commanders in Armenia before anything could take place (Ammianus Marcellinus XXX. 1. 18–22).

[4] Though probably not intentionally, for Christian schools were established using both Greek and Syriac; see Sarkissian, *Council of Chalcedon*, p. 82.

The Monophysite kingdoms

the national language. Without this, native paganism could not be eradicated and the way would always be open to the intrusion of Persian Zoroastrianism. This was grasped by missioners who had worked in the largely pagan north-east of Armenia and one of their number, Mesrop Mastoc (d. 440), received permission from the Catholicus to visit east Syria where it was said an Armenian alphabet existed. Though this was legendary, Mastoc returned not only with the makings of an Armenian alphabet, which he proceeded to perfect, but with a profound respect for Antiochene theology confirmed by personal contact with Theodore of Mopsuestia.[1]

There was already opposition to this tendency from the pro-Byzantine element in the church before the Council of Ephesus met in 431. Against Ishak's advice, the Armenian princes had petitioned the Persian king to abolish their own monarchy and replace it with a viceroy. This was done in 428. Ishak was temporarily deposed and the Armenian church moved further in the direction of the Antiochene theology which was dominant among the Persian Christians.[2] The condemnation of Nestorius, however, and by implication the whole Antiochene theological system, once more strengthened the pro-Byzantine position. At the same time powerful pro-Cyrilline bishops in Syria itself attempted to persuade the Armenians to abandon Theodore. As early as 432, Cyril's supporter and correspondent, Acacius of Melitene, near the Armenian border, besought Ishak to beware of the 'stain of Jewish heresy that might have gained space in some of your churches', criticised Theodore's Christological teaching and informed him of Nestorius' condemnation at Ephesus. The doctrinal battle that was unleashed in Armenia by this – and probably other similar letters – resulted in the despatch of envoys to Constantinople in 434/5, bearing with them one of Theodore's works and asking for the opinion of the Patriarch Proclus upon it. The upshot was the *Tome* of Proclus, perhaps the most decisive document in Armenian church history.

Proclus had belonged to the pro-Cyrilline party in Constantinople and his letter was a straightforward statement of Cyril's Christology. He pointed out how Christ as Word of God became truly man without passing through human experience ($\dot{\alpha}\pi\alpha\theta\tilde{\omega}\varsigma$) and took upon himself the form of a servant, but remaining as he was without change or addition. The Word

[1] *Ibid.* pp. 88 and 102–3.
[2] For the political history of this period, see C. Tourmanoff, 'Armenia and Georgia', *CMH* IV. 1, pp. 595–9.

The rise of the Monophysite movement

was not united with a perfect man but 'became flesh by having descended into the nature itself' and voluntarily underwent human experiences. Any concept of a unity of opposites such as was implied by two distinct natures in Christ was absurd; the Word became man to repay the debt of man's sin and to save man from the power of death, and as Word incarnate suffered on the cross. Though Proclus did not denounce Theodore by name, his castigation of 'newly invented impieties of those who divide into two him who united the divided' left the recipients no doubt what doctrines were intended.[1] The importance of the letter was not in its immediate effect, for the Armenian leaders merely told Proclus in their reply that they would persecute anyone who held such views if any such appeared, but that in the long run it put Armenia decisively on the side of Cyrilline as opposed to Antiochene Christology. Ephesus and all it implied was accepted as orthodox.

The Armenians took no part at Chalcedon. Indeed, at that moment they were engaged in a life-and-death struggle to preserve Christianity as their national religion. The Persian King Yazdgard II (438–57) realised that the continuance of close relations between Constantinople and Armenia boded no good for Persian rule there, and *circa* 450 attempted to oust Christianity in favour of Zoroastrianism. Military success at the battle of Avarayr (2 June 451) at first went to the Persians. They found, however, that the enforcement of apostasy was impossible and after some years the new ruler Peroz (457–84) reverted to the previous policy of putting the Catholicate into the hands of a Syriac-speaking bishop and encouraging community of doctrine between the Armenian and Persian Christians. The latter were now unreservedly Antiochene in their Christology. Even this move failed, and in 485, after Peroz had fallen in battle against the Huns, the Persians were forced to concede freedom of religion to Armenia under its own governor who would remain responsible to the Persian king.

This period coincided exactly with the promulgation of Zeno's *Henotikon* and its formal rejection together with all ties with Antioch by the church in Persia at the Council of Beth-Lapat in 484. Once again the Armenians were obliged to choose, and they chose the *Henotikon*. In addition they may have been influenced by the works of Timothy the Cat, which were probably translated into Armenian about this time. These, as we have seen,

[1] For discussion of the important differences between the Greek and Armenian texts, see Sarkissian, *Council of Chalcedon*, pp. 119ff. In the Armenian text the Antiochene leaders are denounced by name.

The Monophysite kingdoms

denounced the *Tome* of Leo and Chalcedon as 'Nestorian',[1] and therefore associated Chalcedon in the minds of their readers with Nestorianism. The cumulative effect was decisive. Desire to be free from Persian influence so far as possible, together with religious sentiment accepting Cyrilline theology, led the Armenian church to reject the doctrines of the majority of the Persian Christians and the Council of Chalcedon. These attitudes prevailed at the important council held at Dvin in eastern Armenia in 506.

At this council pro-Monophysite delegates from the church in Persia had arrived with a tale of woe and a plea for support. They attempted to assure the Armenians that they accepted Nicaea and that their faith was the 'same as that held by the Greeks, Armenians, Georgians and Albanians' (i.e. the client kingdoms of Armenia), and they deplored the troubles that had befallen the church 'since the twenty-seventh year of the reign of Peroz' (i.e. 484) when 'the leaders of blasphemous heresy' held a series of councils that enforced the teaching not only of Nestorius, Diodore and Theodore, but of Mani (!) and Paul (of Samosata). The opposition minority had been accused (of disloyalty?) before the rulers of the kingdom and hence their request for assurance that theirs was the orthodox faith.[2]

The Catholicus and his bishops praised the endurance of the 'orthodox' in Persia, assured them of their own acceptance of Nicaea as the basis of the faith, and then in two letters condemned the Nestorianism of the church in Persia. In the first, the delegates were informed that 'Nestorian blasphemies' were anathema and that Nicaea and Constantinople formed the basis of the faith of the Armenians (Ephesus was not mentioned by name). In the second the Catholicus, bishops and nobles addressed the church in Persia as a whole. In this letter it was alleged that the Nestorians had renewed their attacks 'being strengthened by the Council of Chalcedon', mention as orthodox documents letters by 'the great Ampelis bishop of the city of Kerion' (surely Timothy the Cat (*Ailuros*) who spent a decade of his exile at Cherson), Anatolis of Constantinople (i.e. Anatolius) 'a devout priest', and Cyril's Twelve Chapters and the 'letter of the blessed Zeno' (the *Henotikon*). Significantly, among the 'orthodox Fathers' are those whose 'works' were included among the Apollinarian forgeries, such as Julius 'the guide of the way of life for the westerns', and Ignatius of

[1] See above, p. 207.
[2] I have followed Sarkissian's account, *Council of Chalcedon*, ch. 7.

Antioch, as well as the Cappadocian Fathers, the Alexandrians, Athanasius, Cyril and Theophilus, and the patriarchs of the capital, John Chrysostom, Atticus and Proclus. The Armenian church had made an official declaration of its view of orthodoxy in the name of both the religious and secular leaders of the people.

The object of the Council of Dvin had been to condemn Nestorianism. Chalcedon had only been involved as buttressing Nestorianism, and much of the history of the church in Armenia in the next centuries is centred round the efforts by the Byzantines to convince the Armenians that Chalcedon was not Nestorian. Despite temporary success in 571 and 632 these efforts failed, partly because the Armenians, though preferring Byzantine to Persian suzerainty, could not renounce the latter without danger, and secondly because the ideas of Monophysite leaders such as Philoxenus continued to exercise influence on the strongly monastic Christianity of the country. In the south of the country too, in Ingelene, John of Ephesus records continued Monophysite missionary activity in Justinian's reign.[1] Thus Chalcedon was again rejected at another council at Dvin between 524 and 527, and at a more important gathering there on 14 December 552 when the calendar was reformed and the date 11 July 552 fixed as the beginning of the common era. By then Armenian theology was moving further towards the extremes represented by Julian of Halicarnassos. For some time Syrian supporters of Julian had been in the habit of seeking consolation from the Armenians, and *circa* 555 they sought Armenian episcopal consecration for their priest Abdisho. This was forthcoming and in a letter written by the Catholicus Narses of Bagrevand (548–57) to Monophysites in Persia about the same time, Severus of Antioch 'and his corrupt writings' were condemned in company with those of Theodore, Eutyches, Apollinarius and Leo![2] Even so, connections were maintained with the Severan Monophysites in Constantinople. The momentary union between the Armenians and Byzantines in 571,[3]

[1] John of Ephesus, *Life of Leontius* (ed. Brooks), PO 18, p. 646.

[2] See R. W. Thomson, 'An Armenian list of heresies', *JTS*, n.s. 16, 1965, pp. 358–67 at p. 359, and Sarkissian, *Council of Chalcedon*, pp. 215ff. Julian's works were translated into Armenian. I have accepted G. Bardy's dating (in *Histoire de l'église*, ed. Fliche and Martin, IV, 511) for the Council of Dvin in 552.

[3] Michael the Syrian, *Chron.* x. 7, says that the Catholicus communicated with the patriarch out of ignorance ('for they knew nothing of the corruption of the synod that prevailed among the Romans'), but his action was repudiated by his countrymen on his return.

The Monophysite kingdoms

when the Persians set up a fire-temple in Dvin itself and forced the Catholicus to seek refuge in Constantinople, showed also that the Armenians would even be prepared to accept the emperor's creed temporarily in return for the emperor's protection. As in other parts of the Byzantine world where Monophysitism was strong, it was only in the reign of Maurice, 582–602, that disillusion with the empire set in, and even then, as the sequel to Maurice's treaty with the Persians of 591 and Armenian support for Heraclius showed,[1] there was still room for manoeuvre.

When one takes the Monophysite kingdoms together, it is difficult to point to common factors that brought them into the Monophysite rather than the orthodox fold. For Nubia and Ethiopia, the authority of the patriarch of Alexandria was decisive either as the original source of the Christian mission or as the natural authority to whom to turn for legitimate consecration of bishops. For Armenia, the decisions were largely political, based on the necessity for keeping a balance between the two great empires on her borders. It was to some extent accidental that Chalcedon was rejected in favour of the *Henotikon*. Yet beneath all these considerations was the idea that somehow the one incarnate nature of Christ represented true religion – 'the true monotheism', as the Nubian king expressed it – and fed by the assiduity of Syrian monastic missionaries this view prevailed over the compromise and ambiguities represented by Chalcedon even though this was the emperor's creed. Finally, the autocephalous nature of the organisation of the Byzantine church ensured that once accepted by the ruling families Monophysitism would remain the religion of the kingdom.

[1] See below, p. 345.

Chapter 9

'TO SYRIA, A LONG FAREWELL' (THE EMPEROR HERACLIUS)[1]

The year 553 was an *annus mirabilis* in Justinian's reign. In Italy during the summer the gallant and long-drawn-out resistance of the Goths was finally broken by Narses at Busta Gallorum. In December Pope Vigilius submitted to the decisions of the Fifth General Council while by a mixture of diplomatic skill and show of force Justinian had possessed himself of about one-third of the Visigothic kingdom in Spain.[2] Only the Franks and the far-away Saxons and Britons remained beyond the range of the emperor's ambitions. Then within a decade the tide turned and the series of events was set in motion which resulted in the loss not only of all the western conquests together with Illyricum but of the Monophysite areas of Egypt and Syria as well. The last half of the sixth century is in every way an anticlimax from the great days of Justinian. In turn Avars, Lombards and Slavs broke over the extended frontiers of the empire, the Avars to swarm round Constantinople itself, the Lombards to wrest more than half Italy from Byzantine rule, and the Slavs moving in like a creeping flood of humanity to erode and finally to destroy the Roman and Byzantine heritage in the Balkans, reducing Illyricum once more to the level of subsistence agricultural economy whence it had emerged six centuries before with the Roman conquest.[3]

[1] The occasion as recorded in Michael the Syrian, *Chron.* XI. 7 (ed. Chabot, II, 424), was the sight of the devastation caused by the Arabs in the neighbourhood of Antioch and Aleppo in 638. He left Antioch 'saying farewell and crying "May Syria rest in peace"'.

[2] See E. A. Thompson, *The Goths in Spain* (Oxford, 1969), Appendix, for the date of Justinian's help to Athanagild and the extent and history of the Byzantine province of Spania.

[3] For a brief but vivid description of the Slav occupation of devastated and empty Roman cities in Illyricum, see John of Biclar, *Chron.* ad ann. 576 (ed. Mommsen, pp. 211ff.), and *ibid.* ad ann. 581; also Michael the Syrian, *Chron.* x. 18. The archaeological remains of the sixth century housed in the National Museum at Belgrade show a staggering decline of material standards resulting from the Slav occupation of the Balkans. For the devastation of Greece by the Slavs in the first decade of the seventh century, see M. S. F. Hood, *Acta Musei Nationalis* 20, Prague, 1966, pp. 165–71.

'To Syria, a long farewell' – the Emperor Heraclius

The progressive disintegration of the Byzantine position in Italy, Africa and Illyricum is chronicled gloomily by the historians of the day. The problem for the historian of the Monophysite movement is how in the years following the death of Justinian the loyalism of the Monophysites gradually soured until when the supreme test of the Arab invasions came, the Monophysite populations stood aside from the conflict and even welcomed 'the sons of Ishmael' at the expense of the 'Chalcedonian persecutors'. Byzantine rule in Egypt and Syria disappeared with hardly a tear being shed.

On the accession of Justinian's nephew Justin II (565–78) few could have foreseen this development. The new reign opened with demonstrations of loyalty. The arrival of the imperial effigies in parts of rural Egypt was hailed by local Coptic worthies in ecstatic if execrable Greek verse.[1] Indeed for the whole of this reign and that of his successor, Tiberius II (578–82), relations between the Chalcedonians and Monophysites remained, as it were, negotiable. Justinian had died before his effort to impose Julianism plus Chalcedon as the religion of the empire could come to anything. His successor was personally more favourable to Severan Monophysitism and his wife Sophia, a woman of similar character but with less ability than her aunt Theodora,[2] was reputed to be an active adherent. In the first months of the new reign, as we have seen, the aged Theodosius was received by Justin with the honour due to a patriarch and the emperor promised peace would be made and that Theodosius would be restored to Alexandria. When he died on 22 June 566 the funeral oration pronounced by the monk Athanasius with all the pomp and circumstance of a great ecclesiastical occasion condemned Chalcedon.[3]

Until he became insane in 573, Justin's policies showed many features in common with those of Zeno and Anastasius. Without abandoning his uncle's conquests in the west he concentrated on the protection of Rome's central and eastern provinces threatened by the Avars and Slavs from the north and the Persians from the east. His attempts between 566 and 571 to find permanent common ground with the Monophysites fit into this

---

[1] See H. I. Bell, 'An Egyptian village in the age of Justinian', *JHS* 64, 1944, pp. 21–36 at p. 28.
[2] On her violent character, see Evagrius, *HE* v. 2, but more self-controlled than Theodora, see Michael the Syrian, *Chron.* x. 17. On her religion, see Michael, *Chron.* x. 7 (ed. Chabot, II, 306), and John of Ephesus, *HE* II. 10 (ed. Brooks, p. 50).
[3] Michael the Syrian, *Chron.* x. 1 (ed. Chabot, II, 283).

picture. His first step after the death of Theodosius was to convoke, largely on the inspiration of Sophia, a series of conferences with Monophysite leaders in the capital. Curiously enough, the original initiative came from the Tritheists who appealed to the emperor for fair play in their quarrel with the Severan Monophysites. The upshot was a three-way conference late in 566 between the two groups of Monophysites and the Chalcedonians under the chairmanship of the Patriarch John the Scholastic.[1] This was followed by meetings of monks and clergy which lasted about a year (566–7). James Bar'adai was among those who attended. The conference seems to have resulted in a temporary reconciliation between the Tritheists and orthodox Monophysites. These were supported strongly by the Syrian monasteries and even Eugenius and Conon asked for restoration to their former sees, which was granted to them.[2] With the Chalcedonians, however, no agreement was reached but the Monophysites themselves produced proposals for compromise.[3] If 'out of two natures, one' were accepted, and the words 'nor of two natures' were added to Justin's draft edict of reconciliation that outlawed 'two sons, two persons and two *hypostaseis*' and declared Cyril's Twelve Anathemas canonical, they would be satisfied. Alternatively, an explicit acceptance of the *Henotikon* in the (Severan) sense of its condemnation of Chalcedon, and the restoration of Severus to the diptychs, would be enough. For their part, they would be prepared to communicate with Anastasius, the Chalcedonian patriarch of Antioch (559–98), if he accepted the formula.[4] This was an astonishing concession, since it involved dropping their own Patriarch Paul whom James Bar'adai had consecrated only two years before. Anastasius I, however, was a remarkable man, who managed to remain on good personal terms with the Monophysites and, to judge from his few surviving works, was preparing the way for the attempted Monenergist compromise of the next century.[5] Paul, on the other hand, was *persona non grata* with Justin, whereas even James and Theodore, bishop

[1] *Ibid.* IX. 30 (II, 257).   [2] See *Documenta* (ed. Chabot), pp. 112 and 126.
[3] Michael the Syrian, *Chron.* X. 2 (II, 286).
[4] *Ibid.* X. 2 (II, 287). Anastasius was Chalcedonian patriarch of Antioch for two periods, 559–70 and 593–8.
[5] Thus he concedes in a work directed against John Philoponos 'that we also speak of one activity in Christ': cited by Maximus the Confessor, *PG* 91, col. 232B. See G. Weiss, 'Studien zum Leben, zu den Schriften und zur Theologie des Patriarchen Anastasius I von Antiochien, 559–598', *Miscellanea Byzantina monacensia*, vol. IV (Munich, 1965), pp. 204ff.

to the Arabs, despite all the damage they had caused were trusted by him.¹

The emperor delegated the negotiations to the Patrician John, who arranged to meet the Monophysites in the monastery at Mar Zakai at Callinicum on the Euphrates frontier and discuss the edict prior to embarking on an embassy to Persia. The meeting, probably in 568, was attended by a vast concourse of monks and clergy. John spoke warmly of the need for unity and urged his hearers to imitate apostolic times when disputes over even important details did not lead to schism. The edict he brought with him was short. The sole faith was that of Nicaea. It confessed Christ 'out of two natures, one *hypostasis* and *persona*', anathematised the Three Chapters, declared the edict against Severus abrogated, and abolished 'all anathemas from the time of Cyril to the present'.² The bishops and archimandrites were impressed. All seemed set for success when the monks created a tumult. 'Show us what you have written', they shouted to John; 'if it is orthodox we will accept it, if not, we will not accept it.' Riot immediately broke out, the *Libellus* was torn to shreds. James Bar'adai himself was threatened with anathema. John crossed the Euphrates to Persian territory without even staying for a meal.³

If any single incident can be considered as marking the completion of the break between Chalcedonian and Monophysite communities in the eastern provinces of the empire, it was the fiasco of the conference of Callinicum. In many respects the prospects for reconciliation before the organisation of the Monophysite church hardened irrevocably were favourable. With the death of Justinian some of the mistrust associated with the throne lapsed. The new emperor and his consort were well-disposed towards Monophysite theology, and the Monophysite leaders John of Ephesus and James Bar'adai were now old men who were fundamentally loyal to the emperor and wanted religious unity. In the west, Pope Pelagius was embarrassed by schisms in north Italy occasioned by his predecessor's acceptance of the condemnation of the Three Chapters and unable to intervene effectively, while the *force majeure* of the Lombard

---
¹ See Justin's revealing letter to the Dux Sergona of Dara in 569/70: Michael the Syrian, *Chron.* x. 2 (ed. Chabot, II, 289–90).
² For this edict, see Michael the Syrian, *loc. cit.* The text is not given in Evagrius as L. Bréhier supposes (*Histoire de l'église*, ed. Fliche and Martin, IV, 486). Bréhier seems to have confused the edict of 567/8 with that of 571.
³ Michael the Syrian, *Chron.* x. 2 (II, 287).

The rise of the Monophysite movement

invasions of Italy was rendering the links between Old and New Rome more tenuous. The empire was becoming 'Greek' rather than residually 'Roman',[1] and the concentration of Monophysitism in Egypt and astride the vital frontier area with Persia urged, as always, the need for compromise. Callinicum in the heart of Monophysite territory as the site of the conference had been a bold and imaginative choice.[2]

It would be facile, however, to see the absence of a specific condemnation of Chalcedon as the only cause of the breakdown. Neither the emperor nor his advisers, nor even the Monophysite leaders themselves seem to have realised the change that had come about since the condemnation of Severus and Anthimus a generation before. At that stage, apart from Egypt and, for very different reasons, Armenia, adherence to Severus' anti-Chalcedonianism was still largely a matter of individual choice based on the scrupulosity of families who insisted on a 'truly orthodox' Eucharist. A vigorous Chalcedonian patriarch of Antioch such as Ephraim could still enforce an appearance of conformity throughout his diocese, even in the rural monasteries of north and east Syria. The missions, however, of James Bar'adai had opened precisely the Pandora's box of organised dissidence that the bishops at the time of Chalcedon had feared so much, and in the thirty years of James' activity the 'Jacobite' element in what from now on was the Coptic-Jacobite church had come into being. It was largely a church of the monasteries and the Syrian countryside. The residence of the Monophysite patriarchs from 580 onwards was the monastery of Gubba Barraya between Aleppo and Maboug and not Antioch, and when Monophysite leaders wished to confer it was more often than not in some selected village in preference to a city where a Chalcedonian bishop governed.[3] The Church's organisation also took no account of the political frontier between the Roman and Persian empires, a factor which was to have considerable significance in the

---

[1] Michael the Syrian regards Justin II as the last 'emperor of the Romans', and Tiberius II his successor, though a Thracian, the first of the 'Greek emperors' (*Chron.* x. 11). With Maurice's assumption of the title of Basileus the last shreds of a Roman past may be said to have been cast off. See L. Bréhier, *La Civilisation byzantine* (Paris, 1950), p. 350.

[2] For the strength of the Severans in the area of the desert *Limes* on this frontier, see Evagrius, *HE* vi. 22, and below, p. 334.

[3] E.g. in 563 James' meeting with Bishop Eugenius to confute the latter's Tritheism took place at the village of Arbadis (Michael the Syrian, *Chron.* ix. 30, ed. Chabot, ii, 256).

'To Syria, a long farewell' – the Emperor Heraclius

relations between the Monophysites and the enemies of the Roman world, the Persians and later the Arabs.

One instance of this new development was in 559 when James had consecrated a converted Nestorian bishop named Ahoudemmeh as 'metropolitan of the east' and deputy to the patriarch of Antioch, with his see at Tagrit east of the Tigris on Persian territory.[1] Ahoudemmeh became a great missionary figure in the Monophysite cause. He converted a number of Arab tribes in Mesopotamia and ousted the Nestorians from the southern part of the plain of Nineveh.[2] By 570 his ambitions extended even to the conversion of Persia itself to Monophysitism. A successful debate with the Nestorians before King Chosroes in 573 marked the climax of his success, but his ambition overreached itself when he baptised a prince of the Persian royal house. He was arrested and died in prison in August 575. Such a man had no interest in coming to terms with a Constantinople-oriented faith and at the same time he inspired his followers with 'zeal and ardour for the faith and readiness for martyrdom'.[3] The monastic settlements, clustered astride the Roman–Persian frontier, represented this outlook, and at Callinicum they had shown their strength.

At the parley the monks had the last say and James himself was obliged to bow to their will. Nevertheless the emperor persevered, interpreting correctly the mood of the Monophysite leaders. He kept his temper and in a letter to the military commander of the fortress city of Dara he instructed him to send the Monophysite leaders (the *Diakrinomenoi*) James and Theodore once again to the capital, assuring them that he was no persecutor. He excused his retention of Bishop Longinus there on the grounds that he was a trouble-maker (a friend of Paul 'the Black' of Antioch), and Paul himself was singled out to be excluded from the diptychs.[4] Theodore obeyed, but James was kept behind by the monks. There followed in 569–70 further detailed conversations in the capital involving John of Ephesus, Longinus, and even Paul of Antioch and others. Again there were momentary hopes of reconciliation, and in 571

---

[1] See *History of Mar Ahoudemmeh* (ed. F. Nau, *PO* 3, pp. 15ff.).

[2] For a discussion of the religious situation in this area in the late sixth century, see J. Fiey, 'Mossoul chrétienne', *Recherches publ. par la direction de l'Institut oriental de Beyrouth* 12, 1961, and 'Assyrie chrétienne', *ibid.* 22, 1964 and 23, 1965, especially pp. 327–33. Fiey believes that despite Ahoudemmeh's efforts the Nestorians remained in the majority in the Mosul area.

[3] *History of Mar Ahoudemmeh* (ed. Nau), pp. 32, 37 and 43–4.

[4] Michael the Syrian, *Chron.* x. 2.

The rise of the Monophysite movement

the emperor published what he regarded as his final verdict. The second *Henotikon*[1] reiterated Cyrillian Christology in every sentence, refined as it had been in the previous half-century by Theopaschism, the condemnation of the Three Chapters, and neo-Chalcedonian orthodoxy. It also took account of the Tritheist controversies in the Monophysite camp by spelling out the differences in unity between the persons of the Trinity. Its Christology affirmed the hypostatic unity between the Godhead and manhood of Christ. It was 'not a human being that gave himself up on our behalf, but the Word-God himself' (the Christ therefore who died on the cross was 'one of the Trinity'). If in contemplation two natures were to be confessed, there was no division between them, for both natures were united in Christ as 'one Son, one person, one subsistence, both God and man together'.[2] Hence it was 'right to confess one incarnate nature of the God-Logos'. Finally, there must be no more unnecessary dispute about persons and words. The edict made no mention of Chalcedon or of any other decision. It reaffirmed Cyril's theology leaving, however, its strict interpretation open.[3] As with Zeno's *Henotikon* it was satisfactory to the Monophysites up to a point. John of Ephesus and Paul of Antioch actually received communion publicly on two occasions in Sancta Sophia from the Patriarch John in the belief that Chalcedon was about to be denounced explicitly, only to recant immediately on discovering their error.[4] Once more, however, an attempt by the emperor to restore peace by a general formula without meeting the specific Monophysite demands failed, especially on the status of Chalcedon. The clock could not be put back 140 years to the time of the Formula of Reunion. Justin became exasperated. The Monophysite leaders in the capital were imprisoned and their church seized, thus ending a peace that had lasted there for nearly forty years.[5] From now on, except for the short interlude of Tiberius II's reign (578–82), there were to be desultory but severe per-

[1] Evagrius' text is given in translation in the Appendix, p. 366 below.
[2] The Greek text shows the explicit use of Cyrillian terms. For instance, Ἡ δὲ καθ' ὑπόστασιν ἕνωσις...; ἐννοοῦντες δὲ αὐτοῦ τὴν ἄφραστον ἕνωσιν, ὀρθῶς ὁμολογοῦμεν μίαν φύσιν τοῦ Θεοῦ Λόγου σεσαρκωμένην σαρκὶ ἐψυχωμένῃ ψυχῇ λογικῇ τε καὶ νοερᾷ καὶ πάλιν ἐν θεωρίᾳ λαμβάνοντες τὴν τῶν φύσεων διαφοράν...
[3] Text in Evagrius, *HE* v. 4, Michael the Syrian, *Chron.* x. 4, and Nikephorus Kallistus, *HE* XVII. 35. Evagrius' text is given in translation in the Appendix, p. 366 below.
[4] Michael the Syrian, *Chron.* x. 3 (ed. Chabot, II, 294); compare *ibid.* 6 and 12.
[5] John of Ephesus, *HE* (Part iii) I. 4 (ed. Brooks, p. 3).

secutions in the capital and in the provinces which kept alive the latent anger against the very name of Chalcedon and its representatives.

The fact of the matter was that the empire had been forced into the position of permanent opposition towards the Monophysites. There was no place for two organised churches. Its political philosophy could never have envisaged the emperor being head of two separate and rival groups of Christians. Though every theological concession that man could devise could be made to the Monophysites, the empire was wedded to an acceptance of the canonical status of Chalcedon at least as a purely disciplinary synod dealing with the rival heresies of Nestorius and Eutyches. The ingenious phrasing of Zeno's *Henotikon* had postponed the day when schism became inevitable. Its abrogation by Justin I removed the common ground between the parties. After their experiences under Justinian, the Monophysites could not be satisfied with theological agreement only. Chalcedon had to go.[1] Against this stumbling-block the good will of Justin II and Tiberius II availed nought. The intermittent persecutions which developed after 571 foreshadowed what was to come as soon as an emperor convinced of the rightness and not merely the expediency of the creed of Chalcedon ascended the throne.

The crisis that developed in the reign of Maurice (582–602) in which the central figure was al-Moundhir, the phylarch of the great confederation of the Ghassanid Arabic tribes, had been long in preparation. The opening events indeed had nothing to do with Monophysite relations with the emperor, but concerned their own internal rivalries. The Patriarch Paul of Antioch had been a controversial figure from the outset.[2] He had been Theodosius' secretary and his choice as patriarch, perhaps passing over

[1] Thus the bishops informed the emperor, who had sent them a revised draft of his edict while they were in prison and asked their comments, 'If you put the Council of Chalcedon out of the church the union is already made. So long as its name is proclaimed we shall not consent to be united with you. We are deeply sorry to have stated that we would be united before it has been rejected.' Michael the Syrian, *Chron.* x. 6 (ed. Chabot, II, 300).

[2] For the unravelling of the complicated story of personal intrigue and doctrinal bickerings in the Monophysite camp in the years 571–7, see E. W. Brooks, 'The Patriarch Paul of Antioch and the Alexandrine schism of 575', *BZ* 30, 1929–30, pp. 468–76, supplemented by E. Honigmann, 'La Hiérarchie monophysite au temps de Jacques Baradée, 542–578', *CSCO*, Subsidia 2 (Louvain, 1951), pp. 195–205. Also, Th. Herrmann, 'Patriarch Paul von Antiochia und das alexandrinische Schisma', *ZNTW* 27, 1928, pp. 213–304 at pp. 263ff.

intentionally the far more impressive claims of James Bar'adai. James, however, was among the bishops who consecrated him in 564. Paul was also a friend of John of Ephesus and represented a moderate Severan position, but this made him suspect to extremer elements in Syria and Egypt. His anti-Tritheism, too, precipitated a quarrel with the monk Athanasius which undermined his standing in the capital. In 565 his mission to Alexandria undertaken at Theodosius' behest to refurbish the Egyptian episcopate failed. The Egyptians preferred to have no patriarch and no new bishops at all rather than accept intervention from Constantinople – even though Paul was Alexandrine-born. The consecration of Longinus in Constantinople immediately after Theodosius' death, with the object probably of his replacing Theodosius as patriarch of Alexandria, was equally unacceptable to the Egyptians, apostle to the Nubians though he was.[1] Their self-conscious parochialism and the ill-concealed hostility of James towards Paul himself placed the patriarch in a difficult position. There was only one ally he could trust, namely the Ghassanid Arabs in the Syrian desert.

There had been every justification for Theodosius' decision to send Paul to Egypt. The Severan Monophysites needed a leader.[2] Their Julianist rivals had plucked up courage to appoint a patriarch, but Justinian in the last year of his life had him deported and he died.[3] The incident was a salutary warning that something had to be done if the tradition of the two Timothies and Severus was to be upheld. There was also some threat from the Chalcedonians, especially in the towns and the Delta. The scanty evidence for the period following Justinian's reconstitution of the Melkite patriarchate suggests that this move had been well timed. Some of the Egyptian episcopate had conformed, and after a generation the Chalcedonians had built up a respectable following in Alexandria where they held all the famous churches, and some genuine support in larger centres such as Antinoë and Rhinoclura on the Palestinian frontier, as well as in Cyrenaica. Here it may be significant that the 'rich men of the province' as well as officials seem to have been the most ardent defenders of the

[1] In his old age Theodosius had granted to Longinus the position of deputy to him ('mandavit et permisit ut in loco eius staret'): John of Ephesus, *HE* IV. 5.

[2] At one time Justinian had been prepared to allow the monk Athanasius to become priest (but not bishop) in Alexandria, but the Monophysites demanded the recall of Apollinaris before they accepted Athanasius, and this was refused (Michael the Syrian, *Chron.* IX. 30, ed. Chabot, II, 253).

[3] Theophanes, *Chron.* A.M. 6057.

'*To Syria, a long farewell*' – *the Emperor Heraclius*

Byzantine regime in the seventh century.[1] There were also groups of Chalcedonians in the Choite and Agharwah nomes in the Delta who survived into the time of the Arab invasions,[2] and they also retained their traditional strongholds among the Pachomian monasteries. Moreover, they had also been served well by their patriarchs. Justinian's appointment of Apollinaris (551–70) had much to commend it. In the next century Apollinaris was credited by John of Nikiou as a supporter of Theodosius,[3] and he was open-handed in his charity.[4] Even so, he had been at one time in high state service and the story grew up of how he arrived in Alexandria, assembled his congregation in the church, and there threw off his military uniform to reveal himself in the robes of a priest (how he managed to wear both the story does not tell). Then he read the Chalcedonian Definition and ordered a massacre of those who protested.[5] Whatever the likelihood of this yarn (which hardly agrees with John of Nikiou's description of his 'gentle disposition'), it is nonetheless typical of the way in which Chalcedon had become linked in the popular mind with the emperor's religion and the use of military power to enforce it.

In contrast, despite their hold over the people, the Monophysite leadership on Justinian's death had been reduced to a dispirited group of four or five bishops of whom only the immensely long-lived Theodore of Philae was of any stature.[6] The church was riddled with sectarianism and

[1] For an estimate of the strength of the two churches in Egypt at this time, see Hardy, *Christian Egypt*, pp. 135ff. For Cyrenaica, see R. G. Goodchild, 'Byzantines, Berbers and Arabs in 7th-century Libya', *Antiquity* 41, 1967, p. 119–22. Without further evidence it is not possible however to state that the existence of two or more churches in a Cyrenaican settlement indicated division of religious loyalties. They could represent dedication to different saints.

[2] *History of the Patriarchs*, part I, ch. XV (ed. Evetts, *PO* 5, pp. 18–19).

[3] John of Nikiou, *Chron.* ch. 92. 9: 'He was gentle of disposition and a member of the Theodosian party.' In ch. 94.8 he says he was *comes* (count) of a monastery. For once John can hardly be correct. For a résumé of the contradictory estimates of the personality of Apollinaris, see Maspero, *Histoire des patriarches d'Alexandrie*, pp. 157–65.

[4] John Moschos, *Pratum spirituale*, ch. 193 (*PG* 87. 3, cols. 3072–6).

[5] Eutychius of Alexandria (Melkite, circa 950), *Annales*, *PG* 111, col. 1069, agrees that he had been sent to Alexandria as military commander (*dux*), and that at this period the Monophysites controlled both Alexandria and Egypt. See Stein, *Bas-Empire*, II, 629–30.

[6] He had been consecrated by the Patriarch Timothy *circa* 525 and was still bishop in 577 (see E. Honigmann, 'Evêques et Evêchés monophysites d'Asie antérieure au VIe siècle', *CSCO*, Subsidia 2, Louvain, 1951, p. 22﹒).

The rise of the Monophysite movement

strife. There were relics of long-past conflicts represented by the Meletians. Of those of more recent origin, the *Acephaloi* who had opposed the *Henotikon* in 482 were strong in eastern Egypt, and there were Julianists, Tritheists and many weird offshoots intriguing and quarrelling among themselves.[1] Yet all these, including the Meletians, seem to have regarded themselves in some way as anti-Chalcedonians.[2] In addition, the monasteries, and with them the countryside, had remained immovable. Descriptions of religious life in the latter part of the sixth century preserved in the *History of the Patriarchs* tell for instance of 'Monasteries in the Wadi Habib growing up like the plants of the field, in security and under the guidance of God', or of an area near Alexandria where 'there are 600 flourishing monasteries, all inhabited by the orthodox'. These houses were also landowners, and wealthy, and the patriarch himself administered the estates. The cultivators 'all held the true faith'.[3] The loss of Alexandria to the Chalcedonians had the effect of polarising differences between an 'imperial' or 'Melkite' church in Alexandria and the 'Coptic' and Monophysite church in the remainder of Egypt, whose centre was now the monastery of St Macarius in the south-west of the Delta. This division was to last until the Arab invasions and fatefully influenced the history of Christianity in Egypt.

In this edgy and quarrelsome society Paul was not welcome. In 566 he returned to Syria and took up his quarters with the formidable al-Hareth bar Gabala, ruling sheikh of the Ghassanid tribal confederation. This was the same al-Hareth who twenty-five years before had asked Theodora for a bishop for his people and thus set in train the great missions of James Bar'adai. He and his house began to assume an increasing importance in the affairs both of the Monophysites and the empire. The degree of the power he exercised over the vast no-man's-land that separated the Byzantine and Persian empires can be appreciated from the sumptuous hall of judgement at Resapha where audiences would be held and delegations of Arab sheiks received. Hard by was the church of St Sergius the martyr saint whose anniversary on 15 November made Resapha and al-Hareth's court

---

[1] See Maspero, *Histoire des patriarches d'Alexandrie*, pp. 191–4.

[2] *History of the Patriarchs*, part 1 (ed. Evetts), p. 473.

[3] *Loc. cit.* This information may be completely trustworthy, as an earlier chronicle from which the *History* was compiled was written by Abba George, archdeacon of the Patriarch Simon (689–701) 'on the mountain of St Macarius in the Wadi Habib', and he may have learnt it at first hand from the local population.

the scene of pilgrimages from far and wide.[1] Sergius had become the patron of Monophysitism along the *Limes*, to such an extent that Chosroes, not to be outdone, established a rival shrine to the saint on Persian territory 60 miles north-west of Mosul to retain the loyalty of Monophysites on Persian soil.[2] Al-Hareth's will was not to be thwarted either by Paul's enemies or by the emperor's generals.

Next year, however, Paul was back in the capital where he participated in the final negotiations with the emperor, and like John of Ephesus and the other bishops communicated with the Chalcedonians in 571 in the erroneous belief that Chalcedon would be denounced.[3] He recanted, was imprisoned, offered the prospect of a bishopric by the emperor and finally escaped only to find himself a discredited man. Most of the Arabs, however, remained loyal to him. Al-Hareth's son and successor, al-Moundhir, gave him hospitality and from the Arab camp he wrote to his Syrian colleagues asking forgiveness; then in 574 he moved to Egypt where he lived disguised as a soldier. The following year the Syrians agreed conditionally to receive Paul back, but sent two bishops to Alexandria to consult with the Egyptians. There they found continuing confusion. Theodosius had died in Constantinople nine years ago and the election of a new patriarch was urgent. Apart from the continuance of sectarian squabbles the Egyptian Monophysite episcopate was nearing extinction.[4] As a means of securing a rapid canonical election Paul persuaded Longinus to return from Nubia to assist at the consecration of the new patriarch. Unfortunately, the choice fell on a Syrian archimandrite named Theodore, and he was consecrated in the desert (between 25 June and 25 August 575). The reaction of the Alexandrines could have been anticipated. They had delayed making their own choice and now they would not accept Paul's. An aged deacon named Peter who had been an associate of Theodosius was persuaded to accept consecration, and his first act was to consecrate a veritable Sanhedrin of seventy bishops which put the Monophysite church in Egypt on a firm footing once more under an Egyptian patriarch (576).[5]

Paul retired once more to Syria and the welcoming tents of al-Moundhir.

---

[1] See Cl. Mondésart, 'Inscriptions et objets chrétiens de Syrie et de Palestine', *Syria* 37, 1960, p. 125, and J. Sauvaget, 'Les Ghassanides et Sergiopolis', *Byzantion* 14, 1939, pp. 115–30.

[2] See [E. E.] D. Oates, *Studies in the Ancient History of Northern Iraq* (OUP for the British Academy, 1968), pp. 115–18.   [3] Michael the Syrian, *Chron.* x. 6.

[4] That of the *Acephaloi* had practically reached this stage: *History of the Patriarchs*, part II (ed. Evetts), p. 474.   [5] John of Ephesus, *HE* IV. 12. He died in January 578.

Longinus was unable to help him and returned to more profitable tasks in Nubia in 577. James Bar'adai after hesitation again sided with the strongest party, in this case the Alexandrians. Paul was again excommunicated, on the grounds stated succinctly by Michael the Syrian. 'He had communicated at the hands of the Synodites and secondly, he had consecrated as patriarch for the Alexandrians a certain Theodore of Rhamnis without the Alexandrians being informed.'[1] James' death, however, on 30 July 578 only intensified the schism among the Syrian Monophysites, for the bishops and monks who had rejected Paul chose a certain Peter of Callinicum from the monastery of Mar-Hananiah as patriarch (578–91) in his stead.[2] Al-Moundhir, however, did not abandon his friend, even though Paul again left Syria for Constantinople and this time did not return.

After years of incapacity through insanity Justin II had died in October 578 and his successor was his Caesar, Tiberius II, a youngish, amiable but spendthrift ruler, who was popular and trusted by both Chalcedonians and Monophysites. Once more there was freedom of worship in the capital, and in February 580 al-Moundhir arrived thither with his sons on a state visit.[3] For the previous eight years the empire had been engaged in a severe and fluctuating conflict with the Persians and the active help of the Ghassanids could be the key to the victory. Al-Moundhir was received as 'the magnificent patrician' with every honour. The most significant of these was permission to wear a diadem of royalty. He was now king. On 2 March he convoked the supporters of Paul and James and patched up a truce. 'The council ended in peace and joy', we are told.[4] In fact the peace was purely temporary, and Paul died in obscurity in 581 without ever having been restored to Antioch.[5] Satisfied with his apparent success,

---

[1] Michael the Syrian, *Chron.* x. 21 (ed. Chabot, II, 360–1); John of Ephesus, *HE* IV. 11. See E. W. Brooks, 'The Alexandrine schism'.

[2] Peter was not actually consecrated until 580 after the Alexandrians had denounced the agreement made in the capital with al-Moundhir: see Michael the Syrian, *Chron.* x. 17.

[3] John of Ephesus, *HE* IV. 39. See also P. Goubert, *Byzance avant l'Islam sous les successeurs de Justinien*, vol. I (Paris, 1951), p. 81.

[4] John of Ephesus, *HE* IV. 40–1. The Egyptians under their patriarch Damian broke the agreement by rejecting Paul as soon as they returned to Alexandria. Michael the Syrian shows his bitterness towards the Egyptians in his description of this incident despite its having taken place 600 years before he was writing! (*Chron.* x. 17).

[5] Rumour had it that he withdrew to a cave in Isauria where he lived for four years (John of Ephesus, *HE* IV. 47, 54 and 57). For his death at Constantinople and burial there, see Michael the Syrian, *Chron.* x. 18 (ed. Chabot, II, 348).

however, al-Moundhir returned home. There he emphasised his primacy over all the frontier Arabs by winning a resounding victory over his Lakhmid enemies. Apart from the emperor himself he was now the most influential man in the empire, and he was ready to place his tribes at his master's disposal for a decisive blow against the Persians, or so it seemed.

The Roman armies in the east were commanded by Count Maurice, the Armenian whom Tiberius had appointed Caesar.[1] He came from the southern part of the Roman province and his family had a strongly orthodox ecclesiastical tradition which he maintained. In 580 he considered the moment had come for a powerful counter-attack on the Persians by crossing the Euphrates with a mixed Arab and Roman army and striking at the enemy capital, Ctesiphon. The key point was the bridge over the river at Circesium. However, when the Roman and Arab forces arrived in strength they found that it had been destroyed by the Persians and the campaign had to be abandoned.[2] Maurice at once suspected al-Moundhir of treachery, and personally accused him before Tiberius. As a result Tiberius agreed to al-Moundhir's arrest. In the summer of 581 this was effected treacherously and eventually al-Moundhir was condemned in Constantinople for treason and exiled to Sicily. In addition, however, his family was insulted and urged to turn Chalcedonian. In anger the Ghassanids rose against their former friends and devastated wide areas of Palestine and Phoenicia. Al-Moundhir's heir swore he would never willingly look on the face of a Roman again.[3]

What is one to make of this strange affair? Al-Moundhir undoubtedly had great ambitions. The constant use of his good offices to heal quarrels among the Monophysites may have given him the hope of restoring peace between them and the Chalcedonians, and in this he had been encouraged by Tiberius. He may also have been considering how to use his formidable power and strategic position to arbitrate between the two empires whose constant warfare damaged the free movement of his people from pasture to pasture. Given these ideas his course of action seems clear. He preferred Roman to Persian suzerainty, but he had good reason not to trust the Romans entirely. In 573 he had discovered a plot against his life involving

---

[1] On Maurice's birth and parentage, see Goubert, *Byzance avant l'Islam*, I, 36ff.
[2] John of Ephesus, *HE* III. 40.
[3] *Ibid.* III. 56, and Michael the Syrian, *Chron.* x. 19 (ed. Chabot, II, 350). See also Goubert, *Byzance avant l'Islam*, I, 81–3 and 252–6.

The rise of the Monophysite movement

Justin himself at the time of the Persian siege of Dara.[1] He was confronted also by hereditary enemies in the Lakhmid Arabs who were pro-Persian, and by the deadly jealousies of his own tributary rulers. At the same time, he was a convinced Monophysite, and pledged to the furtherance of Monophysite interests. He had been an unwavering supporter of the Patriarch Paul in his adversities. In the capital his influence had aroused suspicion and jealousy among the Chalcedonians.[2] All these circumstances would have counselled him not to leave himself at the mercy of a pro-Chalcedonian monarchy. Options, even Persian options, must remain open.

So far as the bridge at Circesium is concerned, the contemporary evidence is blighted by partisanship. To Evagrius, representing the Syrian Melkites, al-Moundhir was a rogue 'who had betrayed the commonwealth and Maurice himself' and 'filled the empire with endless mischiefs', and he was lucky to have the death sentence passed upon him commuted to exile.[3] To Theophylact Simocatta, a civil servant writing in Heraclius' reign who devoted a detailed history of eight books to the reign of Maurice, but was not a Chalcedonian fanatic, al-Moundhir was 'a traitor',[4] and his people 'devoid of good faith'. To John of Ephesus, however, the charge of treachery was 'false',[5] and though Michael the Syrian passes no judgement on the truth of the accusation, his description of the behaviour of the Roman officers detailed with the arrest of al-Moundhir indicates where he thought the rights and wrongs lay.[6]

The long-term effect of the quarrel was disastrous. In 584 Maurice, now emperor, abolished the phylarchy and al-Moundhir's kingdom fell apart into fifteen tribes, many of whom joined the Persians. The cause of Christianity itself was severely shaken by what the Arabs regarded as its association with fraud. Rome lost a powerful ally in her struggle with Persia and, even more important, the protection of her south-east frontier from raids by hostile Arabs from Arabia. From this time on the empire of the Christian Arabs ended on account of the treachery of the Romans, commented Michael.[7] The Arab raider had always been feared. In Ana-

---

[1] John of Ephesus, *HE* VI. 4. He received by mistake a letter written by the Emperor Justin to the general Marcianus ordering the latter to have him executed!
[2] *Ibid.* IV. 42 (ed. Brooks, p. 169).
[3] Evagrius, *HE* VI. 2, and compare V. 20.   [4] Theophylact, *Historiae* III. 17.
[5] John of Ephesus, *HE* VI. 16 (ed. Brooks, p. 237).
[6] Michael the Syrian, *Chron.* X. 19.
[7] *Ibid.*, ed. Chabot, II, 351. Compare John of Ephesus, *HE* III. 56.

'To Syria, a long farewell' – the Emperor Heraclius

stasius' reign the Ghassanids had supported Persia and their conversion to Christianity had been a diplomatic triumph. Even so, in Justinian's time Palestinian monks were demanding protection from the Saracen Arabs.[1] Now they would have had even more justification. The immediate upshot was the systematic pillage of the prosperous areas of Palestine and Phoenicia by the exasperated Ghassanids in 582, and this should have warned the emperor of what was in store when the Arabs turned their swift cavalry,[2] superior in range to anything the Byzantines could field against them, against an inadequately defended populace. The Byzantines realised too late how the expansion of their religious and commercial contacts with Arabia could also involve formidable new military commitments. They remained wedded to obsolete ideas of positional warfare against the Persians. The rise of Mahomet was to give the Arabs ample opportunities for paying off old scores, and at the battle of the Yarmuk their treachery to the Byzantine cause was decisive.

Ostensibly, however, the policies of Maurice were both justified and successful. To Chalcedonians he was a model ruler, 'a living image of virtue', as Evagrius described him.[3] In fact, he was an able general and diplomat, and a shrewd if mean financier with the heart of an accountant. In his twenty years' reign, from August 582 to November 602, he held the essential provinces of the east Roman Empire against all comers. Illyricum, the Danube and Persian frontiers, and in the west, Rome, Ravenna and Africa were defended with skill. Reinforcements even were spared to succour Justinian's outlying conquests in Spain against Visigothic counter-attack.[4] No serious effort, however, was made to oust the Lombards from Italy. In the east advantage was taken of the outbreak of civil war in Persia in 590 to restore the Roman frontier to its line before the outbreak of hostilities nearly twenty years before. In 591 Maurice's diplomacy gained a very favourable settlement of the Roman claims in Armenia which increased the Roman share of the country from rather over one-fifth to more than one-half.[5] The frontier was advanced to Lake Van. Had he been less avaricious and remembered the first rule of every successful

---

[1] Cyril of Scythopolis, *Vita Sabae*, ch. 72 (ed. Schwartz, p. 175).
[2] Already in 593 Evagrius was commenting on 'the fleetness of the Arabs' horses': *HE* V. 20.   [3] *Ibid.* VI. 1.
[4] For Byzantine policy towards the west in this period, see W. Goffart, 'Byzantine policy in the West under Tiberius II and Maurice; the pretenders Hermenegild and Gundwald', *Traditio* 13, 1957, pp. 73–118.
[5] For the detailed terms of the treaty, see Goubert, *Byzance avant l'Islam*, I, 167–70.

emperor since Septimius Severus, namely to keep the army well-paid, the revolution of 602 which overthrew him and his family and everything he had achieved for Byzantium in the previous twenty years might never have occurred.

Maurice was first and foremost a Chalcedonian. There was no attempt to come to terms with the Monophysites.[1] The 'faith of the Lord Jesus Christ' that he proclaimed had no place for those who refused to accept the emperor's creed. He is described from the outset of his reign as being a prey to those who wished to calumniate opponents of the synod, and among these was his cousin Domitian, tutor to his children, an able ecclesiastic of fanatical cast of mind.[2] On the other hand, he was respected by ascetics such as Theodore of Sykeon and received blessings and favours from them;[3] and even to John of Ephesus who remained in the capital as leader of the Monophysites until his death *circa* 585/6 he was the 'God-loving' emperor.[4] In the capital, however, the change of policy from that of Tiberius made itself felt immediately. Monophysites, including men as loyal to the emperor as John himself, were persecuted and even imprisoned. The Patriarch John the Faster (582–95) protested. 'What have the *Diakrinomenoi* done that we persecute them?' he asked. Even self-confessed pagans were treated more lightly.[5] To him indeed, the Monophysites were not heretics at all. 'Their beliefs are excellent', he said, 'with this exception, that they shun the church and are unwilling to communicate with us.' The state was better served in fighting the barbarians than its own citizens.[6] Even so, pressure continued on the Monophysites in the capital throughout the reign, and it was to spread to Egypt and Syria with fateful results.

In Armenia, meantime, the advance of the Roman frontier caused a crisis. It will be remembered how in 571–2 the Catholicus John, while a refugee in Constantinople, had accepted Justin's *Henotikon*. This had carried no weight at the time, but with the restoration of Byzantine influence in Armenia Maurice at once attempted to bring about the substitu-

---

[1] John of Nikiou, *Chron.* ch. 99. 1.   [2] John of Ephesus, *HE* v. 19 and 21.
[3] See *Life of St Theodore of Sykeon* (ed. Dawes and Baynes, *Three Byzantine Saints*), ch. 54.
[4] John of Ephesus, *HE* v. 14. For penalties against those who blasphemed the Theotokos at dinner parties, see Nikephorus Kallistus, *HE* XVIII. 33.
[5] John of Ephesus, *HE* v. 15.
[6] *Ibid.* III. 12 (ed. Brooks, p. 101) referring to John's attitude in the time of Tiberius. He refused to be an instrument of 'a Diocletian'.

tion of Chalcedon for Monophysitism in the kingdom as a whole. A council attended by twenty-one Armenian bishops from the Roman sphere met at Constantinople and accepted Chalcedon, and a Chalcedonian patriarch was established across the River Azat from Dvin, the capital of what had been Persearmenia. This formed the new frontier. The Armenian Catholicus Moses at Dvin, however, refused to be tempted. Why should he go to Constantinople in order to eat bread cooked in an oven and drink warm water – allusions to reported Byzantine liturgical practices.[1] Moses showed a traditional Armenian contempt for the 'Greeks' and Chalcedon, and for the heavy-handed ways in which they attempted to enforce acceptance of the council.[2] Maurice, however, gained one important success in that the Armenian client kingdom of Georgia was induced to move from Monophysitism to Chalcedon, and even in Phocas' reign the schism between the Armenian and Georgian Catholicates persisted. No doubt the powerful but distant suzerainty of Byzantium was more welcome than the unneighbourly interferences of the Armenian princes.

In Syria, despite internal dissensions and doctrinal disputes concerning Tritheism which resulted in their patriarchate being out of communion with the Egyptians for nearly thirty years, the Monophysites continued to gain ground. Writing of this period, Michael the Syrian speaks of the axis of the movement extending from Antioch to the Euphrates with its main support between Aleppo and Maboug.[3] In this great area the Chalcedonians were confined to the cities, while the villages were fanatically loyal to the Monophysite patriarch of Antioch and would accept no ministrations apart from his.[4] Here one would point to an economic factor which in the sixth and early seventh centuries consolidated rural Monophysitism around the monasteries of Syria I. These monasteries resembled their Egyptian counterparts. In an area given over to dry farming, dominated by olive culture, they were agricultural units as well as hospices, and formed natural economic as well as religious centres, playing a vital part in the lives of the people.[5] In addition to their hold on Syria I, Evagrius,

[1] Isaac of Armenia, *De rebus Armeniae* = *PG* 132, cols. 1248–9.

[2] See P. J. Alexander, 'An ascetic sect of Iconoclasts in 7th century Armenia', *Studies in Honor of A. M. Friend* (Princeton, 1955), pp. 151–60 for the cross-currents in the religious situation in Armenia at this time.

[3] Michael the Syrian, *Chron.* x. 22 (ed. Chabot, II, 366).

[4] *Ibid.* x. 21. 5 (Chabot, II, 380).

[5] On the other hand, the monasteries in Syria II (Apamea) tended to be more self-contained and inward-looking. See M. Rodinson's valuable commentary on the

writing of his own day, i.e. *circa* 590, speaks of the Severans predominating over the whole desert area of the (Persian) frontier, the *Limes*. Further north in eastern Cappadocia around Melitene, the Monophysites were also progressing, and here in 599 a persecution long remembered in Syria broke out.

The author was Maurice's cousin, Bishop Domitian of Melitene,[1] apart from the emperor the most powerful man of his time, who seems to have had the idea of welding Chalcedonianism both in Syria and Egypt into a viable force. The Coptic Bishop John of Nikiou (*circa* 670) describes him as 'a true Chalcedonian', one 'who forced heretics to be enrolled in the orders of the church'.[2] The Chalcedonian patriarch of Alexandria, Eulogius, however, sent him a work written in favour of the *Tome* of Leo. In his own diocese his measures were ruthless and thorough, and as 'archbishop' he extended his activities into the province of Mesopotamia where monasteries and churches of 'the Syrians' were seized and handed over to the Chalcedonians. Monophysite leaders were forced to leave the dioceses and flee to Egypt.[3] The terminology used by Michael the Syrian indicates how along the Armenian frontier 'Syrian' was being equated with Monophysite and 'Chalcedonian' with the Greeks, just as in Egypt 'Copt' was now Monophysite and 'Chalcedonian' was Greek. In east and west alike people were becoming known by their nationalities, Greeks, Romans, Syrians, Jews or Goths, each with their distinctive language, laws and religion.[4] Meantime, at Edessa the monks resisted orders to leave their monasteries and were massacred by soldiers.[5] This wave of persecution,

evidence brought together by G. Tchalenko on the economic situation of Syria in his article 'De l'archéologie à la sociologie historique. Notes méthodologiques sur le dernier ouvrage de G. Tchalenko', *Syria* 38, 1961, pp. 170–200, especially pp. 186–7. I agree with Rodinson's judgement, 'Il paraît certain que cette étroite liaison des moines avec la vie économique a conditionné leur influence et leur a permis de jouer un très grand rôle dans la propagation du monophysisme'.

[1] Evagrius, *HE* IV. 18, and Michael the Syrian, *Chron.* x. 23 (ed. Chabot, II, 372). He suggests that one of the reasons for the persecution was Monophysite progress in the region of Melitene. For Domitian's crusading zeal, see Theophylact, *Historiae* V. 4.

[2] *Chron.* ch. 99. 2. For a sketch of his life, see E. Honigmann, 'Patristic studies', *Studi e Testi* 173 (Vatican City, 1952), pp. 217–25.

[3] Michael the Syrian, *Chron.* x. 25 (ed. Chabot, II, 381). His persecution was directed against 'the Syrians': see *ibid.* p. 379, and *Chron. ad ann. 1234*, ch. LXXXII.

[4] For the Visigothic kingdom, see Thompson, *The Goths in Spain*, p. 24. For Syrians in Spain founding their own 'Acephalic' church in the early seventh century, see *ibid.* p. 164.   [5] Michael the Syrian, *Chron.* x. 23.

'To Syria, a long farewell' – the Emperor Heraclius

coming near the end of Maurice's reign, left the emperor with the worst of popular reputations throughout the east. Commenting on an earthquake in the Antioch area, John of Nikiou wrote, 'this chastisement has befallen the earth owing to the heresy of the Emperor Maurice'.[1] In so doing, he was giving an accurate reflection of the attitude of both the Copts and the Syrians towards the Persian and Arab conquests, regarding them as punishments for the wickedness of the Chalcedonian emperors. With Domitian's death in January 602, it was evident that the effort to force the peoples of Syria and Egypt into an acceptance of Leo and Chalcedon had failed. At a crucial moment in Byzantine history the cleavage between the government and the inhabitants of key provinces was complete.

Maurice and the dynasty he had attempted to found were cut down in the revolution that broke out at Constantinople in November 602. The Persian king, Chosroes II (590–628), who owed his throne to Maurice may have been deeply indignant at the treatment of his benefactor by Phocas and his partisans, but he was shrewd enough also to realise that Persia's hour had struck. The confused situation in the empire offered the finest opportunity ever presented to subjugate Rome's eastern provinces and restore Persia to the frontiers of Darius the Great. The campaigns, first against the Roman frontier fortresses, 604–7, then against Osrhoëne and Syria, 608–11, then Asia Minor and Palestine, 611–14, and finally Egypt, 616–20, do not concern us directly.[2] Important, however, is an estimate of Chosroes' religious policy towards the provincials who passed for nearly a generation under Persian rule, and their reaction towards their conquerors.

There is no reason to believe that the Persian armies were aided actively by the Monophysites, in the same way as they were by the Jews and Samaritans. These rose en masse and wherever they could vented their long-suppressed rage upon the Christians.[3] The uprising in Palestine where Jerusalem and Galilee were the centres[4] and which put Jerusalem itself in Jewish hands for three years (614–17) explains perhaps why the emperor's creed was always accepted there. The Christians knew where

[1] *Chron.* ch. 101. 5.
[2] For an account of Chosroes' campaigns, see A. N. Stratos, *Byzantium in the Seventh Century* (Amsterdam, 1968), chs. 3 and 7.
[3] Michael the Syrian, *Chron.* x. 25 (ed. Chabot, II, 379), XI. 1 (p. 400) and XI. 3 (p. 410).
[4] Eutychius of Alexandria, *Annales*, PG 111, cols. 1089–90.

The rise of the Monophysite movement

they must look for protection. Among the first targets for destruction by the Persian invaders was the *lavra* of St Sabas where forty-four monks were massacred.¹ Personally, however, Chosroes was not unfavourable to Christianity.² His wife Maria was a daughter of Maurice and built a church and monastery near the royal palace, and a favourite mistress whom he later married, Shirin, was a Jacobite convert. On two occasions, in 591 on his restoration to his throne and in 593 in thanks for Shirin's conception, he had made elaborate gifts at the shrine of St Sergius at Circesium.³ As his ancestor had done in his campaign against Anastasius in 502,⁴ Chosroes distinguished between the 'Romans', i.e. soldiers and officials, who were his enemies, and provincials, who were not,⁵ this time however with greater hope of effect. Nestorian and Monophysite bishops accompanied his armies, and on the capture of a city, the Chalcedonian bishop would be expelled and replaced by one or the other. Not even Chalcedonians of the standing of the Patriarch Zacharias of Jerusalem were spared, and he, together with 35,000 Chalcedonians and the fragments of the True Cross, was transported to Ctesiphon when Jerusalem fell on 5 May 614.

The Monophysites in contrast were left in peace. Bishops who had found refuge in Egypt returned and were welcomed in their former sees. In the conquered territories Chalcedon was practically eliminated as a political and religious force. Michael the Syrian writes of the period as one when 'the episcopal sees were everywhere directed by our bishops and the memory of the Chalcedonians disappeared from the Euphrates to the Orient [Syria]. The Lord made the iniquity of the Chalcedonians rebound on their own heads. What they had done by the intermediacy of the

---

¹ See Stratos, *Byzantium*, p. 108.

² Though note the view of the anonymous Nestorian chronicler (*Chron. anon.*, ed. I. Guidi, *CSCO*, Scriptores Syri III. 4, Paris, 1903, p. 19) that Chosroes only 'pretended to show favour to the Christians'. He seems to have distrusted the Nestorians.

³ *Chron. ad ann. 1234*, ch. LXXXI (marriage to Maria), Evagrius, *HE* VI. 21 and Theophylact, *Historiae* V. 14. 2 (offerings on behalf of Shirin). See M. J. Higgins, 'Chosroes II's votive offerings at Sergiopolis', *BZ* 48, 1955, pp.89–102. It is not easy to sort out Chosroes' matrimonial affairs. He was certainly married to Maria and since he built two churches for her, her early death cannot be presumed. Equally, the offerings at the shrine of St Sergius were on behalf of Shirin. If she had formally ousted Maria, Maurice would hardly have remained his friend. Possibly as Maria was a child this would not prevent the king marrying Shirin.

⁴ Joshua Stylites, *Chron.* (ed. Wright), p. 46.

⁵ Michael the Syrian, *Chron.* X. 25 (ed. Chabot, II, 378).

emperor of the Romans was repaid them by the intermediacy of the Persians, the kings of Assyria.'[1] The situation outlined in this important passage is corroborated by a statement in a letter *circa* 614 from the Monophysite Patriarch Athanasius of Antioch (the Camel-Driver, 595–631) to his colleague in Alexandria that 'the world rejoiced in peace and love' because the Chalcedonian night had been chased away.[2] At Antioch this had come to pass all too tragically, the Chalcedonian patriarch, Anastasius II, being killed in the triangular struggle that wracked the city between Jews, supporters and opponents of Phocas before its fall to the Persians in 611.[3] There was to be no successor for thirty-eight years, and even then the title was only nominal for the holder resided in Constantinople. It would seem that what had been largely true for a very long time had come to pass, that the monasteries and countryside of Syria I and Osrhoëne had now consolidated into a region as firmly Monophysite as Egypt and Armenia. It is, however, doubtful if in Syria II or Palestine the Monophysites were more popular than they had been. What the Persian era showed was that a foreign overlord was not necessarily a persecutor, but a Chalcedonian nearly always was.

Chosroes' policy seems to have been to give the Monophysites the status of majority religion in the conquered provinces of Syria, Palestine and parts of Asia Minor, while maintaining the Nestorians in this role among the Christians in Persia. So much emerges from the accounts of the strange pan-Christian assembly of 'all the bishops in the east' held under the presidency of the king's Armenian physician at Seleucia either in 612 or shortly after the fall of Jerusalem in May 614.[4] According to the Armenian historian Sébéos the king accepted the Armenian confession of faith as the faith of Christians throughout Persia,[5] but from the silence regarding the

[1] *Ibid.* x. 25 (pp. 380–1). Compare *Chron. ad ann. 1234* (ed. Chabot), ch. LXXXVIIII: 'Et omnino deleta est memoria synodi chalcedonensis ad orientem Euphratis.'

[2] *History of the Patriarchs*, part I (ed. Evetts), p. 481.

[3] *Chron. Paschale* ad ann. 610 (ed. Niebuhr, I, 699), says that Anastasius was killed by soldiers; Michael the Syrian, *Chron.* x. 25, by the Jews.

[4] J. B. Chabot dates the Nestorian confession presented at the conference to 612 (*Synodicon Orientale*, pp. 580–98). Sébéos, *Histoire d'Héraclius*, ed. F. Macler (Paris, 1904), p. 113, dates the assembly to 614 'après la captivité de Jérusalem'.

[5] *Ibid.* pp. 113–16, recording a letter which the Armenians sent to the Emperor Constans II (642–68). This is clearly, as Bréhier indicates (*Histoire de l'église*, v, 89 n4), a one-sided account of the proceedings, but suggests that in Armenia also Chosroes was prepared to accept the *status quo* among the Christians. It seems doubtful whether Chosroes 'expelled the Nestorians' as Sébéos claims.

whole affair from the Syrian Monophysites it hardly looks as though they came out satisfied. Perhaps they had pinned too many hopes on the influence of Queen Shirin. The only surviving confession presented to the conference for the king's approval is the Nestorian.[1] After a prayer that Chosroes would extend his dominions over the whole world, this affirmed that 'as created natures could not contemplate the glorious nature of Christ's divinity', Christ was 'marvellously fashioned of the Blessed Virgin Mary, a holy temple, a perfect man, formed outside all human participation according to the order of nature'. He was clothed in this manhood, united to it and thus appeared to the world. There was 'from the beginning' an indissoluble union between the human and divine natures in one *prosopon*. The Nestorians went on to contrast their doctrine with 'the heresies that abounded in the Roman empire' and in particular that of the 'Theopaschite Severans', and they hoped that the king would declare their teaching the religion of all his empire.

The Nestorians also were disappointed, for at the end of their statement a scribe has written a note that 'they received no reply from the king, first because he was a pagan and could not understand their arguments', and secondly 'because the king had consideration for Gabriel the chief of the faction of the Theopaschite heretics'.[2] That is to say, Chosroes, while ready to listen to everyone who opposed the creed of the emperor at Constantinople, intended to maintain a balance between the Nestorians and the Monophysites in his vast new domains, not fully trusting either.

This strange conference illustrates the situation of Christianity where it was not a state religion, but represented nonetheless the beliefs of an important minority of the inhabitants. Since 410 an elementary *millet* system had been in force in the Sassanian dominions and Chosroes was simply continuing the policy of his predecessors towards Christians. The Acts of the Synod of Seleucia of that date show how after he had failed to destroy the Christians in Persia, King Yazdgard I (399–420) had accepted the choice by the synod of a 'head of all the Christians in the East', a chief bishop (Catholicus) who was to act as intermediary between the

[1] Published by Chabot, *Synodicon Orientale*, pp. 580–98.
[2] *Synodicon Orientale* (ed. Chabot), p. 598. Regarding Gabriel, see *Chron. anon.* (ed. Guidi), *CSCO* III. 4, pp. 20–1. He was physician to Queen Shirin. In addition, the Nestorians had cause to complain that Chosroes had not appointed another Nestorian Catholicus to succeed Gregorius who had died in 608, largely on Gabriel's instigation. A confrontation between Nestorian and Monophysite bishops in 609 also proved indecisive.

'To Syria, a long farewell' – the Emperor Heraclius

Christians and the Persian authorities, and whose inviolability was guaranteed by the king.[1] The bishop of Seleucia-Ctesiphon was to be Catholicus. In return for legal toleration the Christians had accepted the status of a subject community within the Persian Empire (which, but for Constantine, might have been their situation at the end of the Great Persecution in the Roman Empire). Their influence at court was exercised through powerful individuals who as specialists, such as physicians, made themselves indispensable, foreshadowing the role of Nestorian physicians at the courts of the Moslem emirs. As a result of the pan-Christian conference, Chosroes evidently confirmed the position of the Nestorian Catholicus as leader of the Christians within the former Sassanid frontiers, but he had also extended this privilege to the Monophysites in the newly conquered Byzantine provinces. The Syrian Christians were thus given an idea of how they might fare if they were no longer ruled politically from Constantinople. At least the invaders had banished 'the Chalcedonian darkness' and given them control of the monasteries and bishoprics.

In Egypt the Persian occupation was much shorter, lasting a dozen years at the most, between 617 and 629. In the few years between the accession of Heraclius and the Persian invasions, the *Life* of John the Almsgiver, Chalcedonian patriarch between 611 and 619, throws interesting light on the religious situation there. From this also one can detect how in the previous half-century the two communities in Egypt, the Greeks and Copts, had become more polarised. Figures are hard to come by and unreliable, but most authorities suggest that in *circa* 600 there were about 200,000 Greeks and between five and six million Copts.[2] Among the latter Coptic was being used increasingly in legal and other documents as well as in the liturgy. In the sixth century a village notable might still express himself in Greek, and even know a smattering of Homer and Menander. In the seventh century, Greek papyri, especially ecclesiastical papyri, become very corrupt, and it is clear that the scribes had only a hazy idea what they were writing.[3] As we have seen, Justinian's restoration of the Chalcedonian patriarchate had divided the Egyptians into two camps along cultural and linguistic lines. The writer of the *Life* of John the Almsgiver indicates how this was the case. He describes, for instance, how in 611 the Monophysites 'swarmed in the countryside' and held all except seven churches

---

[1] See *Synodicon Orientale* (ed. Chabot), pp. 254 and 260–1.
[2] 'Monophysite (Eglise copte)', *DTC* 20, cols. 2251–306 at 2255–6.
[3] Cited from Bell, *Egypt from Alexander the Great to the Arab Conquests*, pp. 127–8.

in Alexandria.¹ On the other hand, the Chalcedonians were relatively wealthy. The patriarch controlled a fleet of merchantmen which traded in the Mediterranean and as far afield as western Britain.² On taking up his post John found 8,000 lb. of gold in his house.³ He rapidly acquired resources sufficient to sustain 7,500 poor of Alexandria who were on the lists of his church of Alexandria.⁴

John himself was not an Alexandrian, but the son of a former governor of Cyprus. He was a layman and a widower before his sudden translation to ecclesiastical office, a further example of the official character of the position of Chalcedonian patriarch in Egypt. Once installed he set about his task of restoring Chalcedon with zeal. The Monophysite *Trishagion*, which had evidently become accepted by now in Egypt as elsewhere in the Monophysite world, was abolished and John took back a large number of churches in Alexandria for Chalcedonian use, which he staffed with refugee clergy from Syria.⁵ Above all, he built up an enormous repute through shrewd but open-handed charity. Homes for the poor, hospitals and institutions of every sort were built from church funds. In particular, a vast sum of 100,000 solidi together with 100 craftsmen was sent to Jerusalem to aid the reconstruction of the city even before the expulsion of the Jewish administration in 617.⁶ All this became legendary, and as no other Chalcedonian before him he began to make an impression even in the monasteries when the Persian invasion cut his efforts short.⁷ After his death in November 619 he came to be accepted as a saint in the Coptic Monophysite church.⁸

Relations with the Monophysites had remained surprisingly good. All Egypt had suffered in the ferocious civil war that had raged before Heraclius' triumph in 610. His cousin Niketas whom he appointed governor

---

[1] *Life of John the Almsgiver* (ed. and tr. Dawes and Baynes, *Three Byzantine Saints*), ch. 5, and compare Leontius, Supplement, ch. 18 (Dawes and Baynes, p. 228).

[2] Leontius, Supplement, chs. 11 and 13.

[3] *Ibid.* ch. 45.   [4] *Ibid.* ch. 2.

[5] *Life of John the Almsgiver*, chs. 5 and 12. Converts to orthodoxy were obliged to accept 'the four holy ecumenical councils' and declare repentance, but no other penalty was imposed (*ibid.* ch. 5).

[6] *Ibid.* ch. 6.

[7] Leontius claims that he was 'regaining monasteries and villages for orthodoxy': Supplement, ch. 32. John left Egypt during 619 while Alexandria was besieged by the Persians. He died in Cyprus not long afterwards.

[8] His feast is kept on 11 November; cf. Bréhier, *Histoire de l'église*, ed. Fliche and Martin, v, 82 n2.

though a Chalcedonian seems to have been determined to unite the country, and ensure that the Monophysites had no cause to regret their support for his master. In Anastasius I (604–16) the Monophysites also possessed a leader characterised in the tradition of the great Athanasius as 'a monk, a priest and a scholar', and a man capable of statesmanship as well. He was ready to co-operate with Niketas when the latter took up the cause of healing the generation-old schism between the Monophysite churches of Egypt and Syria.[1]

Personalities as well as doctrinal questions had lain at the bottom of the dispute. Monophysitism had not meant the end of rivalry between Alexandria and Antioch. The Alexandrians had been determined to call the tune there regardless of Syrian susceptibilities.[2] Anastasius' predecessor, Damian (578–604), was a hothead who tried to suppress his own Syrian background by aggressive behaviour. Also, in attempting to find a compromise between Severan orthodoxy and the various Monophysite sects in Egypt he had gone perilously near to accepting the Tritheist position himself. He had proclaimed that the individual properties of the divine persons of the Trinity were identical in every way with the persons themselves, i.e. the 'non-generation' and 'eternity' of the Father, the 'sonship' of the Son and the 'procession' of the Holy Spirit each formed its own *hypostasis*. All, however, were merged without distinction into a single Godhead. God was thus the common divinity in which each person participated by nature and 'essence'.[3] One-nature Christology could therefore be interpreted to mean that the Father and Holy Spirit suffered as well as the Son. The reaction of the Syrian patriarch, Peter, and his bishops was to charge Damian with Sabellianism. This the Egyptians rejected with insult, called Peter 'a deaf asp' and a heretic,[4] who sought 'to divide the Trinity'. True to their parochialism they refused to meet the Syrians in the 'distant and barbarous country' between Hierapolis (Maboug) and Aleppo. Eventually a series of conferences was held in Arabia (*circa*

---

[1] See Michael the Syrian, *Chron.* x. 26 (ed. Chabot, p. 385), recording Athanasius of Antioch's letter to Cyriacus, bishop of Amida, outlining how the settlement came about.

[2] See the tone adopted by Damian in his relations with Patriarch Peter of Antioch. Though himself suspected of Tritheism he convoked his colleague to a discussion at a town in Egypt, and when they eventually met abused him without measure: Michael the Syrian, *Chron.* x. 22 (Letter of the Syrian Patriarch Peter).

[3] See J. Tixeront, *Histoire des dogmes*, III, 196–7.

[4] *History of the Patriarchs*, part I (ed. Evetts), p. 477.

The rise of the Monophysite movement

586–7), and after a public wrangle communion between Alexandria and Antioch was suspended.[1] The arrival, however, of the Syrian bishops as exiles at the end of Maurice's reign brought about a better understanding of respective positions, based on the assertion of the mutual co-inherence of the properties of the divine persons. Once peace was restored in Egypt with the fall of Phocas, the Patriarch Anastasius took up the negotiations again. Urged on by Niketas and his lieutenants, he held conversations with the Syrian bishops Mar Thomas of Hierapolis (Maboug) and Paul of Tella. The upshot was a meeting between the two patriarchs, probably in the autumn of 616. This was a long-drawn-out affair, and Niketas again intervened to bring about agreement. Finally the patriarchs held a joint service in the monastery of Caesaria Patricia, west of Alexandria, and signed a synodical letter which restored peace late in 616.[2] Niketas, relative of Heraclius and a Chalcedonian, had done signal service to the Monophysite cause.

Next year the Persians invaded Egypt in force. Byzantine resistance surprisingly collapsed. Alexandria fell by treachery and by 620 the Persians had occupied the Nile valley and Cyrenaica. Their forces advanced as far even as Faras where damage to the palace of the ruler of Nobatia may be attributed to them.[3] Their policy to the Copts stood in marked contrast to their attitude towards the Syrians. John of Nikiou is strangely silent regarding this period but the *History of the Patriarchs* tells of the deliberate massacre of monks near Alexandria and Nikiou; those in the patriarchal group of monasteries of the Enaton being singled out for destruction because they were wealthy, 'insolent [and] without fear' and independent.[4] Far from welcoming the invaders, the Copts, apart from a

[1] See Michael the Syrian, *Chron.* x. 22 and 26, particularly the joint synodical letter signed by Athanasius and Anastasius following the reconciliation.

[2] Michael the Syrian, *loc. cit.* The dating is not absolutely clear. Most of the Syrian exiles must have returned to their own country long before 615, and the *Synodicon Orientale* makes the reception of Athanasius of Antioch by Anastasius take place in the year of the Persian capture of Jerusalem, i.e. 614. On the other hand, one Syriac version of the Bible compiled by Paul of Tella and Thomas of Maboug records the presence of Athanasius in Alexandria in 616. Agreement must have been reached before 18 December when Anastasius died. September–October for the discussions therefore seems correct. See Bréhier, *Histoire de l'église*, ed. Fliche and Martin, v, 87 n4.

[3] K. Bittel (ed.), 'Das Wunder aus Faras' (Essen, 1969), p. 15. Alexandria itself fell to a 'fifth column' instigated by Peter, a merchant who had originally come from Q'atar in Chosroes' dominions. See *Chron. anon.* (ed. Guidi), CSCO III. 4, p. 22.

[4] *History of the Patriarchs*, part I (ed. Evetts), p. 485.

few time-servers,[1] regarded their arrival with dread. Far down the Nile valley at Coptos, Bishop Pisentios fled at news of their approach. 'Because of our sins, God has delivered us to the nations without mercy.'[2] In a *Life* of the great Shenute, the latter is made to prophesy that the Persians would invade Egypt 'causing great slaughter and would sacrilegiously seize the holy vessels in the churches and drink the communion wine, and cause every type of suffering and distress'.[3] Even so, there was no Coptic rising against the Persians, only a fatalistic acceptance of events, an attitude which the onset of the Arab invasion was to harden and perpetuate.

Despite their tolerance of the Syrian Monophysites, and after 617 their restraint of the Jews, the Persian occupation of the Byzantine provinces was unpopular. Monophysites could not trust a ruler who had imposed a Persian Nestorian as bishop of Edessa[4] – a new Ibas – and in Edessa the rapacity of the Persian authorities had allegedly cost the citizens 120,000 *litra* of silver.[5] Populations were never safe from personal injustices, crushing taxation and in the last resort the Persians' traditional weapon, deportation to Persia. Heraclius' final counter-offensive, dramatic in its suddenness and its overwhelming power, had all the appearance of a divine intervention. In a few months, 627–8, the Persian conquests in the east and Egypt had been swept away, Persia itself had been invaded,[6] Chosroes had been overthrown and his successor sued for peace. In April 630 the True Cross was solemnly brought back in triumph to Jerusalem by the emperor himself, and the Roman Empire was restored to the frontiers it had possessed on the death of Maurice.

At this moment Heraclius' prestige stood higher than even that of Justinian. The morrow of the great victory provided a final chance of healing the religious differences in the east. Hopes may have been pitched too high and the disappointment therefore was correspondingly greater, for the ensuing events showed that on the level of individuals the Chalce-

---

[1] There were a few prominent apostasies, significant perhaps of what was to happen in the Arab invasions. So I read John of Nikiou, *Chron*. ch. 109. 20.

[2] See E. Amélineau, *Vie d'un évêque de Keft au VIIe siècle* (Paris, 1887), p. 30.

[3] E. Amélineau, *Monuments pour servir à l'histoire de l'Egypte chrétienne, Mission archéologique française au Caire*, vol. IV (Paris, 1888), p. liii; the Coptic text was written circa 685–90.

[4] Michael the Syrian, *Chron*. x. 25 (ed. Chabot, II, 379).   [5] *Ibid*. XI. 1 (II, 403).

[6] For the sequence of events, see Stratos, *Byzantium*, chs. 16 and 17. Alexandria was probably evacuated by the Persians only in June 629.

The rise of the Monophysite movement

donians now hated the Monophysites as fiercely as the Monophysites hated them. Heraclius at once set about the perennial task of east Roman emperors, namely to work out a formula on which the union of the churches could be based without involving the total abandonment of Chalcedon. The Monophysites were in a commanding position in the reconquered territories. Armenia was theirs. The only patriarchs of Antioch and Alexandria were Monophysite,[1] and their bishops controlled the cities as their monks dominated the countryside. They had spread their mission and authority wider in Persia itself by the establishment of a grand metropolitan (*maphraim*) at Tagrit.[2] In Constantinople, however, the Patriarch Sergius (610–38) believed that progress could be made. He was a Syrian by birth, and indeed of Monophysite parentage,[3] and it may not be accidental that he came to the conclusion that by defining the place of the will in the incarnate Christ a compromise might be found. He suggested that the long-standing Monophysite teaching that Christ possessed one impulse of action (ἐνέργεια) corresponding to his one nature could be accepted if the will were attributed not to the nature of Christ but to his individuality (that is to the *hypostasis* rather than the *ousia* of the divine economy).[4]

This represented a real effort to think through the main problem raised by the Chalcedonian Definition. Two natures were still to be confessed, but they were not to be represented existentially, and the logical conclusion was to be drawn from their complete inseparability. The great merit of Sergius' ideas also was that it proposed unity on the basis of a positive notion that was emerging almost simultaneously on both sides, rather than on the condemnation of the work of long dead theologians, as at the Fifth General Council. Apollinarius had claimed that as Christ was one, 'we worship him in one nature, one will and one operation (ἐνέργεια)'.[5] Severus had said much the same, and had been opposed by Leontius of

---

[1] John the Almsgiver had died on his way to Cyprus in 619 and had not been replaced. See below, p. 349.

[2] See the Letter of the Patriarch Athanasius granting to Bishop Ahoudemmeh's monastery of Mar Matthai near Nineveh the 'honour and primacy over all the Orthodox convents that are in Persia': Michael the Syrian, *Chron.* XI. 4 (ed. Chabot, II, 416).

[3] Theophanes, *Chron.* A.M. 6121 (ed. Classen, I, 506). Eutychius labels him 'a Maronite': *Annales*, PG 111, col. 1083.

[4] See also L. Duchesne, *L'Eglise au VIe siècle*, pp. 391ff.

[5] H. Lietzmann, *Apollinaris von Laodicea und seine Schule* (Tübingen, 1964), p. 248, lines 5–7. See Wolfson, *Philosophy of the Church Fathers*, I, 468–9.

'To Syria, a long farewell' – the Emperor Heraclius

Byzantium who like other Chalcedonians maintained the existence of two operations.[1] Popular Egyptian thought had followed Severus as can be demonstrated by the curious sixth-century confession of faith attributed to Dioscorus I.[2] By the middle of the sixth century the Chalcedonian position also had begun to be less rigid. Even if the alleged letter from Menas to Vigilius asserting 'one source of activity of the God-man' (μία θεανδρικὴ ἐνέργεια) was a later forgery,[3] it seems evident that the Chalcedonian patriarch at Antioch, Anastasius, held similar views.[4]

If there was to be any settlement 'one operation' would contribute towards it. Sergius had pondered the question, and by 622 had won Heraclius for Monenergism. The emperor had discussed this solution with the Monophysite leader, Paul the One-eyed, while at Erzerum (Theodosopolis) in 623 at the outset of his counter-attack against the Persians.[5] He had not been rebuffed. Three years later while in the Black Sea state of Lazica preparing his final blow, he met the metropolitan Cyrus and convinced him of its orthodoxy. Cyrus from now on shared with Sergius the role of Heraclius' spiritual and political adviser. In 630, the Persian wars over and the True Cross restored, Heraclius began to put his plans into effect. At first all went well. Ezr, the new Catholicus of Armenia, was also induced to accept the 'one activity' formula late in 630, and his acceptance was confirmed by a national synod at Erzerum in 633, at which Heraclius

---

[1] Tixeront, *Histoire des dogmes*, III, 158. Leontius pointed to the inconsistency of Severus, for if in Christ, Word and flesh each retained their characteristics (ἰδιότητες) of incorruptibility and corruptibility they must also retain their ἐνέργειαι (*Libri tres contra Nestorianos et Eutychianos*, PG 86. 1, cols. 1320A–B).

[2] Preserved in a sixth-century (?) manuscript found in the monastery of Abu Makar. It reads: 'The Lord Jesus Emmanuel, our God, has never been divided in all his works, but [he is] one only Lord, one only nature, he has one only will and the deity has united with the humanity as the soul unites with the flesh.' The emperor's concession merely proved the truth of what the Copts had been asserting. See W. H. P. Hatch, 'A fragment of a lost work on Dioscorus', *HTR* 19, 1926, pp. 377–81.

[3] See Hefele/Leclercq, *Histoire des conciles*, III. 1, 329–31. But not much later as Sergius sent a copy to Paul the One-eyed (Mansi, *Collectio* XI, col. 529E).

[4] See above, p. 318. Monenergism may have prevailed in Syria since the end of the fifth century, as is asserted by Eutychius, *Annales*, PG 111, cols. 1077–8.

[5] Sergius in a letter to Pope Honorius in 634=Mansi, *Collectio* XI, cols. 529–37 (included among the *Acta* of the Sixth General Council at Constantinople in 680). The initiative in putting forward Monenergism as a formula for peace seems to have come from Heraclius. Paul himself was leader of the Monophysites in Cyprus and on a visit to Armenia in connection with Armenians in the island. Sergius is careful to call him an 'execrable heretic' and the 'Severans' similarly (col. 529).

may have been present in person.¹ The meeting between the emperor and Ezr had taken place at Edessa, and from there Heraclius addressed a general encyclical to the *Diakrinomenoi* stressing his adherence to Cyril's formula 'one incarnate nature of the God-Logos', understood as the two natures of Godhead and manhood inseparably and unconfusedly united, and condemning every other opinion 'even if found in the four synods'.²

In reply the Patriarch Athanasius wrote a long letter setting out in detail the Syrian Monophysite position, and making clearer than had often been the case exactly why Chalcedon was to be rejected. The council laid down a definition of faith other than that of Nicaea. It had asserted Christ in two separate natures, and condemned the term used by the Fathers, 'of two natures'. It had accepted Ibas' letter condemning Cyril's Twelve Anathemas as well as the work of Theodoret and the *Tome* of Leo. Such were the causes of the division between the churches. If they were removed then unity would be restored at once.³ The tone was not unconciliatory but reproduced traditional Monophysite arguments and showed that there had been little interest on the Monophysite side in the development of neo-Chalcedonian ideas. Much had been done to remove these particular stumbling blocks, particularly by the condemnation of the Three Chapters and by Justin's 'Second *Henotikon*'. At this stage there was a good deal in the Chalcedonian contention that the dispute with the followers of Severus had become nothing more than a matter of words. Unfortunately, neither Heraclius nor anyone else at the time was capable of dealing with the instinctive revulsion produced by the very names of Chalcedon and the *Tome* on the minds of the Monophysites.

In the spring of 631, however, conferences took place at Maboug between Heraclius and the Patriarch Athanasius accompanied by twelve bishops, at which the emperor proposed the formula, that in the two natures of Christ there was one will and one activity 'according to Cyril'. Michael states that the bishops simply repeated their patriarch's objections to Chalcedon,⁴ but it would seem that the meetings were not altogether

¹ Bréhier, *Histoire de l'église*, ed. Fliche and Martin, v, 116–17. Opposition to Chalcedon, however, continued in Armenia.
² Text in Michael the Syrian, *Chron.* xi. 2, whose sequence of events is followed here.
³ *Ibid.* xi. 2.
⁴ *Ibid.* xi. 3. The reference to 'one will' has led some critics to doubt the accuracy of Michael's account (Stratos, *Byzantium*, p. 296). 'One will' did not become an issue until 634, but it is implicit in 'activity' and may have been used even as an additional concession by the emperor at these conferences.

fruitless. There were strong rumours in Palestine that Heraclius and Athanasius had reached agreement, and that Athanasius would occupy, like Severus before him, the patriarchal throne of Antioch.[1] The fact that no Chalcedonian was appointed by Heraclius to the see at this time lent colour to this. A number of the major monasteries in Syria such as Beth-Maron, Emesa, Maboug itself and many monasteries in southern Syria rallied to Monenergism, and these represented both Monophysite and Chalcedonian traditions. Confidence, however, was not restored in areas decisive for the success of reunion, namely east Syria and Palestine. Heraclius found himself humiliated at Edessa before a number of Syrian notables – one accepts Michael's account – when he was refused communion by the bishop unless he condemned Chalcedon. Like Justin II he allowed himself to be provoked. The Great Church at Edessa was handed over to the Chalcedonians and Heraclius reaffirmed acceptance of Chalcedon as orthodoxy threatening dire punishment against those who refused.[2] Meantime, the Patriarch Athanasius had died (July 631) and the Monophysites became angry and suspicious at the success of the emperor's formula among some of the most influential monasteries in Syria, and they feared the consequences of the restoration of a Chalcedonian hierarchy. Both sides evidently became exasperated. This was the situation that the Arab raiders encountered when they started their conquest of Palestine and Syria in 634. Michael's angry comment was that even though the Great Churches of Edessa and Carrhae remained in Chalcedonian hands, 'it was no light benefit to be delivered from the cruelty of the Romans, from their bad faith, their anger and cruel zeal towards us, and to find rest'.[3] In this he summed up much of the psychology that led to the fateful decision of the Monophysites to prefer a permanent second-class status under the Arab Moslems to continued allegiance to the emperors.

Meantime, the situation in the years 631–4 had been building up into the same pattern that had wrecked the efforts of all previous emperors to find a solution to the empire's religious problems. The further Heraclius went in his attempt to meet the Monophysites, the more certain he was to encounter opposition from the Chalcedonians, and in particular from the west. In 632/3 the Monenergist compromise had won a further success through the adherence of influential Persian Christians, a success which

---

[1] Antiochus the Monk, *Homil.* cxxx (*PG* 89, col. 1844). Athanasius himself was regarded as the 'precursor of Antichrist' by this monk.
[2] Michael the Syrian, *Chron.* xi. 3.   [3] *Ibid.*, ed. Chabot, II, 413.

could have been of great historical importance if the settlement between Rome and Persia had survived.[1] In Palestine, however, the rumours of Heraclius' diplomatic successes, particularly in Syria, had aroused profound misgivings.[2] For reasons which may have been connected with events of the Persian war the Palestinian monks were as much opposed to the Monophysites as they were to the Jews. They regarded them as sectaries, 'followers of the devil', just as fervently as the Monophysites regarded the Chalcedonians. In the monk Sophronius, experienced dialectician and western-oriented, they found a leader. In the summer of 633, this venerable figure aged over eighty travelled to the capital to protest to Sergius. In vain the latter tried to explain the great benefits of what had been achieved, its political necessity and the dangers of going back. Sophronius urged with the persistence of senility the need for keeping the faith intact. Sergius was not to be beaten easily, challenged his opponent to produce texts of the Fathers that justified the attribution of 'two activities' in the incarnate Christ, and when he could not, put the matter to the Home Synod which decided that this 'dispute over words should be put aside'.[3]

Sophronius was momentarily outwitted and obliged to accept the synod's ruling, but with one of those turns of the wheel of fate that dogged Heraclius from then onwards, no sooner had he returned to Jerusalem than he was elected patriarch at the beginning of 634. Now his views could not be ignored, and Sergius, perhaps on Heraclius' orders, wrote to inform Pope Honorius of the situation and explain the doctrine of the 'one activity'. It was a long letter,[4] outlining all that the compromise formula had achieved in Armenia, Syria and even as he wrote, in Egypt; and he proposed a possible further refinement if 'one activity' was not acceptable, that the one and same Christ activated Godhead and humanity and that all his activity whether human or divine was 'without division' (ἀδιαιρέτως), thus using the term taken from the Chalcedonian definition and attempting even to justify the formula by reference to the *Tome* of Leo. But, however one looked at it, Monenergism involved the passivity of Christ's human ἐνέργεια and hence the unreality of his human nature as understood in the west. It had no more chance of acceptance than the *Henotikon* or the Theopaschite formula. As it was, Honorius did his best

---

[1] See Bréhier, *Histoire de l'église*, ed. Fliche and Martin, v, 116.
[2] Antiochus the Monk, *Homil.* cxxx (*PG* 89, col. 1844).
[3] Mansi, *Collectio* xi, cols. 533–6.   [4] *Ibid.* cols. 529–37, cited above.

to avoid a break with Sergius. In his reply he praised his work, but pointed out that no subjects should be added to dogmatic teaching that had not been discussed at ecumenical councils. He urged that the 'activities' of Christ should cease to be a matter for debate and that Christ should be worshipped as operating in two natures, human and divine.[1] Though he must have thought Monenergism heretical, he had the tact not to say so. He hardly deserved excommunication by the Sixth General Council for offering his advice.

Egypt, however, was to be the scene of Heraclius' decisive failure. Here also, the end of the Persian occupation had left the Monophysites all-powerful. No Chalcedonian was enthroned following the departure of John the Almsgiver from Alexandria in 619. The Monophysites, however, had elected first Andronicus, and on his death in 623 Benjamin, known in the *History of the Patriarchs* as the 'Coptic Patriarch'. He took up his quarters in Alexandria, where he stayed throughout the Persian occupation. As with Athanasius of Antioch, Heraclius was ready to negotiate with him, and discussions took place during 630 with the Byzantine representatives. Though for the moment all rejoiced in the departure of the Persians, there was not the same *rapport* between Benjamin and the Byzantines as had existed between them and the Syrians. Sometime towards the end of 630 he left Alexandria for the monasteries, the classic act of an Egyptian patriarch declaring his non-cooperation with the authorities. He was to go from place to place for the next decade until the arrival of the Arabs restored him to Alexandria. Heraclius then made a far-reaching and ultimately disastrous decision. In 631 he appointed his friend Cyrus, metropolitan of Phasis, to combine the offices of patriarch and governor of Egypt. Rightly, Heraclius had appreciated the importance of winning Egypt for the Monenergist compromise, but wrongly he appointed Cyrus to carry out the task. For the people, not only had their own patriarch been shunned, but he had been replaced by a foreigner. Moreover his appointment symbolised once more the identification of Chalcedon with the imperial administration of Egypt.[2] In the next few years 'Cyrus the Caucasian' became a hated name.

Cyrus reached Alexandria in the autumn of 631. Benjamin immediately

---

[1] *Ibid.* cols. 537–44. Honorius' conclusion, however, 'Unde et unam voluntatem fatemur' had become objectionable in 680.

[2] *History of the Patriarchs*, part II (ed. Evetts), p. 495, describes Cyrus as 'that infidel' who was 'both prefect and patriarch of the city under the Romans'.

went into hiding and instructed his bishops to do likewise. The new patriarch lost no time in setting about his task. Once again in Alexandria the major churches were taken back into Chalcedonian use. Negotiations were opened with leaders other than Benjamin to accept the Monenergist formula. At first these were fruitful, for to many educated Copts Monenergism seemed to provide a possible compromise. In the summer of 633 Cyrus summoned a synod at Alexandria at which not only the followers of Benjamin but representatives of the splinter sections of the Monophysite movement were represented, the Julianists, Tritheists and others more obscure. A Tome of Union in nine headings was drawn up, of which Chapter 7 acknowledging the 'single activity' in Christ (καὶ ἀνθρώπινα μιᾷ θεανδρικῇ ἐνεργείᾳ) 'according to the holy Dionysius' (the Areopagite) was the most important. Two bishops defied Benjamin and signed, and so did 'all the clergy of the party of the Theodosians'[1] in Alexandria, accepting communion from Cyrus at a solemn Te Deum celebrated in the Chalcedonian cathedral on 3 June 633.[2] Cyrus reported in triumph to Sergius, 'Even the heavenly beings rejoiced.'[3] Among the populace the turn of events was not displeasing, for with native shrewdness they realised that 'one activity' involved 'one nature', and hence the tacit abrogation of Chalcedon.[4] As with the *Henotikon* this was the only consideration that mattered.

Heraclius sent a letter of congratulation to Cyrus, as well he might. The year 633 marked the climax of his endeavours. For a few months it looked as though he might succeed in accomplishing the aims of Zeno, Anastasius and Justin II of uniting the east round unequivocal Cyrillian theology without explicitly denouncing Chalcedon. All imperial thinking for the previous century had been moving towards that goal, but none of Heraclius' predecessors had come so near to its fulfilment. The circle appeared to be squared. All the phraseology dear to the Monophysites had been conceded together with the condemnation of the Three Chapters, but with explanations that could just be compatible with Chalcedon. Three factors brought all this to nought even before the Arabs destroyed hopes

---

[1] Cyrus' report to Sergius in Mansi, *Collectio* XI, col. 562 (thirteenth session of the Sixth General Council). The 'Theodosians' must mean the majority Severan party as opposed to the Julianists.

[2] See Hefele/Leclercq, *Histoire des conciles*, III. 1, 339–41, for the text of the Tome of Union.

[3] Mansi, *Collectio* XI, col. 564A.

[4] Theophanes, *Chron.* A.M. 6121 (ed. Classen, I, 507).

of settlement for ever. First, the activities of Sophronius, supported by the arguments of the more cultivated and even more illustrious Maximus the Confessor, sufficed to prevent a theology based on the affirmation of one activity and one will in Christ from becoming accepted as orthodox. In particular, failure to win Honorius' support was fatal. Secondly, the reunion of the rival hierarchies was beyond the statesmanship of the time. Heraclius had done his best by not appointing a Chalcedonian to Antioch while hope remained of the Syrians accepting Monenergism. Egypt, however, would have remained loyal to Benjamin whether the Arabs had appeared or not. When in 634/5 Heraclius was forced to withdraw his project and forbid discussion of the divine activities, the decision was greeted with popular derision in Egypt. He had shown that he was no more to be trusted than previous Chalcedonian rulers.

Thirdly and even more important in a finely balanced situation was the character of the patriarch. All sources testify to Cyrus' ability, courage and singleness of purpose, but he was harsh in his administration and merciless towards his opponents. The Copts were right not to trust him. If one looks carefully at his correspondence one can detect a readiness to proclaim the orthodoxy of Leo's *Tome* as well as Monenergism.[1] He re-established a Chalcedonian episcopate even in the Thebaid, and personally visited monasteries. The torture and death of his rival's brother Menas on the latter's refusal to acknowledge Chalcedon was only one of the horrors of which he was accused.[2] 'The Caucasian', as he was called, opened a reign of terror the like of which the Egyptians had not experienced since the Great Persecution. In the six years 635–41 whatever loyalty had been felt towards Heraclius and the Roman Empire[3] ebbed away. None was left unmolested, even Gaianites, suspected of plotting Cyrus' murder, were seized and mutilated without trial.[4] As Butler has described it, a 'sullen gloom' descended on the land.[5]

Meantime, Heraclius' hopes had fallen before the Moslem onslaught. In April 634 the Arab invasion of Palestine and Syria had begun in earnest.

---

[1] See his first letter to Sergius = Mansi, *Collectio* XI, col. 561.
[2] *History of the Patriarchs*, part I (ed. Evetts), p. 491. See A. J. Butler, *The Arab Conquest of Egypt* (Oxford, 1902), pp. 184ff., who lists this and other incidents.
[3] The reality of the sentiment towards the empire as such is shown by John's story of the popular rumour that Heraclius' death was due 'to stamping his gold coinage with the heads of the three emperors, himself and his two sons – and so no room was left for inscribing the name of the Roman Empire'.
[4] John of Nikiou, *Chron.* ch. 116. 10–11.   [5] Butler, *Arab Conquest*, p. 191.

It was a cruel business. No quarter was given. The Monophysite writer of the *Chron. ad ann. 724* records the slaughter of 40,000 of the peasantry in Palestine and of Jews, Samaritans and Christians indiscriminately.[1] The onset was worse than that of the Persians twenty years before. The Arabs at this stage had no intention of liberating anyone. Monophysite monasteries such as Mardin and Q'atar in north-east Syria[2] suffered as much as the Byzantine-held towns and fortresses. Soon Heraclius' forces had been defeated in the battle of Ajnadain, and Damascus fell to the invader (20 August 635). The Arabs still lacked the discipline to occupy the province permanently. They scattered and Heraclius succeeded in rallying his forces and raising a new army mainly from Armenia. Central Syria was cleared, Damascus was retaken in the spring of 636, but in July the emperor's forces were completely defeated on the Yarmuk river. This time there was no recovery, Syria and Palestine were lost, though Jerusalem held out until 638 and Caesarea reinforced by the Byzantine fleet until the following year. In such conditions, Heraclius' last effort at religious compromise contained in the *Ecthesis* of 638, which, while condemning the usage of the terms 'one' or 'two activities', declared that in Christ there was one will (Monothelitism), was doomed to failure. If the capital accepted it, neither of those whom it was hoped to unite, namely the Monophysites and the west, would do so. In the same year the emperor ordered resistance to the Arabs to cease in Syria, and bade the province farewell.

In this period of disaster Cyrus had held Egypt. For two years the Arabs were bought off with tribute, but the lure of conquest proved too strong. Perhaps contrary to a strict interpretation of their orders the Arab armies arrived in Egypt in mid-December 639 to find the country ripe for revolt. The *Ecthesis* had been promulgated and it roused a storm of indignation. There was 'hostility of the people to the Emperor Heraclius, because of the persecution wherewith he had visited all the land of Egypt in regard to the orthodox faith, at the instigation of Cyrus the Chalcedonian patriarch'.[3] Though in the ensuing campaigns many of the Copts, particularly the townsmen, fought hard in defence of their lives and possessions, once they saw that the Moslems were winning they changed sides.[4] Some openly aided the invader and harassed the retreating Roman troops. Some actually apostasised from Christianity. John of Nikiou gives

---

[1] *Chron. ad ann. 724* (ed. Brooks and Chabot), p. 114.   [2] *Loc. cit.*
[3] John of Nikiou, *Chron.* ch. 115. 9.   [4] *Ibid.* chs. 113. 2 and 115. 11.

'To Syria, a long farewell' – the Emperor Heraclius

the impression of utter confusion and division reigning throughout the country. Chalcedonians fought Monophysites, men of Lower Egypt fought inhabitants of towns in the Delta, Blues attacked Greens.[1] Even at the moment of the surrender of the fortress of Babylon to the Moslems, the Chalcedonian garrison scourged and mutilated Monophysites they were holding prisoner.[2] Often personal experience of injustice at the hands of the authorities persuaded otherwise loyal citizens to throw in their lot with the Moslems.[3] Over all, blame for the situation was laid on Cyrus and his master. 'These were the years', said Severus of Asmounein, the Coptic editor of the *History of the Patriarchs*, 'during which Heraclius and al Mucaukas (the Caucasian) were ruling over Egypt: and through the severity of the persecution and the oppression and the chastisements which Heraclius inflicted on the orthodox in order to force them to adopt the faith of Chalcedon, innumerable multitudes were led astray, some by tortures, others by promise of honours, some by persuasion and guile.'[4] In the folk-memory there had been a total breakdown of confidence between government and governed. 'The Lord abandoned the army of the Romans as a punishment for their corrupt faith, and because of the anathemas uttered against them by the ancient fathers, on account of the council of Chalcedon.'[5] Thus, the popular verdict a generation after the event.

---

[1] John tells also of Blues and Greens uniting to attack the Romans in the town of Misr: *ibid.* ch. 118. 3. For the mutual hostility of the factions persisting to the end, *ibid.* ch. 119. 9.

[2] *Ibid.* ch. 117. 45.   [3] *Ibid.* ch. 114. 9–10.

[4] *History of the Patriarchs*, part I (ed. Evetts), p. 491.   [5] *Ibid.* pp. 492–3.

EPILOGUE

Heraclius was defeated because the Arabs were stronger militarily. Their cavalry was superb. They were better led and equipped than their opponents, and they fought with greater skill and conviction. Their succession of victories culminating in the battle of the Yarmuk, followed by the disintegration of the Persian Empire and Amr's reduction of Egypt, tell their story of the conquerors' genius and dash.[1] Not since the campaigns of Alexander had so great a change been brought about in the political control of the lands of the Fertile Crescent. Even so, the Arabs were first and foremost marauders covering vast tracts of country spreading death and destruction indiscriminately among the cultivators and townsfolk whom they hated and despised. The cities, indeed, they feared, and for a generation they showed no great gifts of administration over the immense empire they had conquered. Without the passive consent of the governed and the willingness of some of the ex-provincial leaders to serve them as administrators they would never have consolidated their power. Their occupation of Syria, Palestine and Egypt would have been an episode, like that of the Persian occupation or their own previous raids at the turn of the sixth century, to be ended as soon as a new, vigorous ruler occupied the throne at Constantinople.

The chroniclers, however, whether Egyptian, Syrian or Armenian, record the complete alienation of the local populations. 'Chalcedon' had become part of a folk-memory, symbolising oppression and nagging religious persecution by the Byzantines which rendered Moslem rule preferable to Byzantine. Typical is the complaint of the Armenian historian Matháos (Matthew of Edessa) who described how the Byzantines even before the Arab invasions, 'investigated all people to see whether their beliefs were false, and instead of fighting the enemy with the sword, they introduced troubles and disputes into the Church (of Armenia)'.[2]

Harsh words, but they are echoed by writers as diverse as Theophilus of

---

[1] See Michael the Syrian, *Chron.* XI. 4–7, for this explanation of the Arab victories over the Byzantines and Persians.

[2] Matthew of Edessa, *Chronique arménienne* ii. 84 (ed. and tr. E. Dulaurier, Paris, 1858), p. 114. See J. B. Aufhauser, 'Die orientalischen christlichen Zweigkirchen und der Missionsgedanke', *BZ* 30, 1929–30, pp. 502–10 at p. 505.

Epilogue

Alexandria (late seventh century) who welcomed the Arabs as a 'powerful nation who would have care for the welfare of the churches of Christ',[1] and Michael the Syrian himself.[2]

These expressions of exasperation concealed long-term factors that had gradually been making Byzantine rule less tolerable as the sixth century wore on. Beneath the imposing façade of the Byzantine cities defended by great stone fortresses and crowded with resplendent churches the old, long-submerged native, pre-Hellenic cultures were re-emerging. Reconquered North Africa even was Latin only in appearance. Many of the one-time prosperous cities had become ruined and abandoned, others resembled native villages, and the baths, fora and public buildings were filled with rubble or used as the shelter of crude olive presses. Berber Africa was replacing Latin Africa a generation before the Arabs arrived.[3] In the eastern provinces, meantime, similar changes were taking place. Syriac and Coptic were becoming increasingly the *lingua franca* of Syria and Egypt, and in ordinary speech Greek place-names after centuries of use gave way to their more ancient native counterparts. Alexandria becomes Rakote, with Coptic as the language of the people,[4] and Hierapolis in Syria, Maboug. Village life with its multiplicity of monasteries and small-holdings was replacing city life.[5] Amid these changes, provincial boundaries resulting from imperial administrative reforms and the frontier between Rome and Persia brought about by military stalemate were losing their relevance in cultural and religious terms. Instead the age-old oasis routes linking one part of the Fertile Crescent to another were coming into their own once more. Down these, Nestorian and Monophysite missionaries moved from Syria or Persia

---

[1] H. Fleisch (ed.), 'Une homélie de Théophile d'Alexandrie', *Revue de l'Orient chrétien* 30, 1935–6, pp. 374–5.

[2] *Chron.* XI. 4 (ed. Chabot, II, 412–13).

[3] See my 'The end of Roman North Africa', *Trans. Royal Hist. Soc.*, no. 5, 1955, p. 73, and for the detailed discussion of one of the latest Latino-Christian inscriptions of the Byzantine period from Numidia, see J. Duval and P.-A. Février, 'Procès-verbal de déposition de reliques de la région de Telergma (VIIe s.)', *Mélanges* 81, 1969, pp. 257–320.

[4] See Anastasius of Sinai, *Hodegos*, PG 89, col. 161. Characteristically, the people of Alexandria are recorded as shouting theological slogans 'in their own language' – 'if "nature" signifies "person", destroy and burn everything especially saint Cyril who says that the natures in Christ remain unconfused!'

[5] For instance, see G. Tchalenko, 'La Syrie du Nord: étude économique', in *Actes du VIe Congrès international des études byzantines* (Paris, 1950), II, 389–97.

Epilogue

via Hira to the Yemen and back again.[1] The Persian conquests by uniting Iran, Syria, Palestine and for a short time Egypt under a single government aided this development, and in particular the spread of Monophysitism eastwards into Persian territory. The still more dramatic sweep of the Arab armies through the desert routes broke for ever the moulds in which the religious life of Byzantine and Persian worlds had been setting.

Against such powerful tides favouring the disruption of the cultural patterns that had existed in the Mediterranean world in their essentials since the conquests of Alexander, Byzantium could offer little. At Chalcedon the die had been cast. The first priority in Byzantine ecclesiastical statesmanship became the unity of the two Romes. It never seems to have been realised how impossible was this ideal. So, when after nearly half a century of bickering the final effort at compromise with the Monophysites through Monergism and Monotheletism ended with the Sixth General Council in 680/1, the wheel had turned its full cycle once more. Chalcedon had won, but at a price. Two more heresies had been added to the already overburdened catalogue, and this time the separation between the two branches of Greek Christianity was final.

At first it seemed as though Alexandria was finally to reap the reward of Dioscorus' and Timothy's obstinacy. The first generation of the Moslem occupation witnessed the Coptic-Monophysite church prosper as never before. The Chalcedonian opposition collapsed. Some of its members were indeed among the first converts to Islam in Egypt. The Patriarch Benjamin took over its property,[2] and built churches and monasteries, including a great new house dedicated to St Macarius in Alexandria, while his successors reabsorbed isolated pockets of Chalcedonianism in the Delta.[3] More important even than this was the extension of the authority of the see of Alexandria among Christians left behind in the whirlwind advance of the Arab armies.[4] By the last quarter of the seventh century its supremacy seems to have been acknowledged by the Christians in North Africa as well as by the churches in India, Nubia and

---

[1] *Chronicle of Séert* LXXIII (ed. Scher, *PO* 5, p. 331).
[2] *History of the Patriarchs*, part I, ch. XVIII (ed. Evetts, *PO* 5, p. 123).
[3] *Ibid.* ch. XV, pp. 18–19.
[4] See H. Gelzer's article, 'Ungedrückte und wenig bekannte Bistümerverzeichnisse der orientalischen Kirche', *BZ* 2, 1893, pp. 22ff. For a critical assessment of the Alexandrian *Thronos*, see E. Honigmann, *Histoire et Géographie de l'Orient chrétien* (Brussels, 1961), pp. 127–207.

Epilogue

Ethiopia.[1] When Benjamin ended a triumphant rule of nearly forty years in 661 it might appear that the dreams of his great predecessors of making Alexandria the centre of Christianity throughout the Mediterranean, and a great missionary patriarchate as well, had been fulfilled under the protection of the Arabs. Chalcedon had been banished for ever.

If such hopes were ever entertained they were doomed to be disappointed. Down to A.D. 700 the Monophysites in Egypt and Syria could congratulate themselves on having made terms with the Arabs. Subsequent events were to show just how disastrous the change of rulers had been. Monophysitism could only flourish in the setting of the Byzantine church-state. For all their theological and ecclesiastical differences, Constantinople, Antioch and Alexandria spoke the same religious language, a language different from that of the west and totally different from Islam. Much as the Monophysites may have come to hate Constantinople they needed the constant debate with the Chalcedonians and the constant refinements of doctrine that subtle minds could devise in order to flourish. For centuries after the Arab conquest became a fact their chroniclers continued to live in a Byzantine world, as though their religious and political centre was still on the Bosporus and the Arab conquest was an interlude. What else made them catalogue so minutely every bishopric and monastery whose orthodox incumbent had been exiled at the end of the Acacian schism, or record obscure acts of persecution and heroism in the reign of Justinian, or remember the detail of equally obscure quarrels between the Monophysite patriarchs of Alexandria and Antioch 600 years previously?[2] They remained at heart Byzantines. The 'one nature' doctrine implied the rule over mankind of the imperial monarch freed, however, from all traces of Chalcedonian dualism. A Monophysite, even a Coptic Monophysite, was a reluctant separatist.

How strongly the relationship with Byzantium was felt even in the remote outposts of Monophysite influence can be seen from the Christianity that flourished in medieval Nubia. Faras and Q'asr Ibrim remained Byzantine cultural outposts for eight centuries after direct contact

---

[1] *History of the Patriarchs*, part I, ch. XVI (ed. Evetts, *PO* 5, pp. 36–7). Compare my survey of Christianity in the Middle East, 600–1800, published as ch. 5 of *Religion in the Middle East*, ed. A. J. Arberry (Cambridge, 1969), at pp. 262ff.

[2] For instance in *Chron. ad ann. 846* (ed. Brooks and Chabot), pp. 169–73. For long and bitter memories of attempted Egyptian domination over Syrian Monophysitism, see Michael the Syrian, *Chron.* X. 17 (ed. Chabot, II, 345).

Epilogue

with the Byzantine empire via Egypt had been lost. The writer remembers his amazement at finding beneath a fallen column in the cathedral of Q'asr Ibrim a manuscript written in Greek but in the typical thick angular writing of the medieval Nubian scribes recording the story of a combat between St Mercurius and a priest of Apollo during the reign of Julian the Apostate a thousand years before.[1] It was as though twentieth-century Britain was living on the memory of Hereward the Wake. Q'asr Ibrim even at the moment of its downfall probably sometime in the first half of the fifteenth century remained true to its Byzantine heritage.[2]

One sees how, bereft of Byzantine inspiration and opposition, Monophysitism gradually became a religion of survival only. Copts and Syrians soon found it difficult to establish a satisfactory terminology even for the various key Christological terms that existed only in Greek.[3] Without a developing theology they found themselves being worsted in religious debate with the Moslem leaders.[4] They were embarrassed also by the remnants of schisms whose origins were becoming lost in the mists of time. Gradually the attraction of the religion of the conqueror began to make itself felt among the Coptic and Syrian populations as a whole. One small example of the silent pressure of Islam comes from the village of Aphrodite in Upper Egypt, whose records throw so much light on what the transition from Byzantine to Arab rule meant to the rural population of Egypt. There, papyri of the early part of the eighth century show how the Christian cross was already being placed in an inferior status to the invocation of Allah and his Prophet. There also, a Moslem administration felt few of the inhibitions of its Byzantine predecessor in imposing the death penalty on those responsible for collecting the village taxes if the slightest discrepancy emerged.[5]

The Arabs like the Persians brought relief from the harassments of the Chalcedonians. In Persia under the Arabs the Nestorians also, saw the

---

[1] To be published by J. M. Plumley and the writer on behalf of the Egypt Exploration Society.

[2] The latest documents found on the site date to the Era of the Martyrs 1137 (i.e. A.D. 1421).

[3] For instance, it was apparently impossible to find a synonym for *hypostasis* in Syriac.

[4] See for instance *History of the Patriarchs*, part I, ch. XVI (ed. Evetts, *PO* 5, p. 25).

[5] H. I. Bell, 'An Egyptian village in the age of Justinian', *JHS*, 64, 1944, pp. 21–36 at p. 35.

Epilogue

advantage in being ruled over by a non-Christian king.[1] The price, however, proved to be disproportionately heavy. We can trace the gradual reduction of the Monophysites from their proud standing as something akin to national representatives for the Coptic and Syrian peoples, to one of dependence on the Arab rulers, and then step by step to fatalistic submissiveness and peonage. No communities of converted Moslems developed within the Islamic dominions, while throughout the centuries losses to Islam have continued. No people or religion can accept the domination of another without risk of absorption and decline. By accepting the 'Ishmaelites' as instruments of God wherewith to punish the Chalcedonians, the Monophysites purchased not their liberty but their grave.

[1] Patriarch Timotheus writing to the monks of Mar Maron (Monotheletes) about 793 says: 'In our case at least, orthodox doctrine has been strictly adhered to without change. Our faith has never been opposed ... In your case on the other hand, Christian kings have held absolute sway and whenever they incline towards heretics or orthodox the priests and faithful follow their lead.' His church, however, had never been compelled to revise its doctrine by a Magian or Moslem ruler (letter 30, ed. Bidawid, *Les lettres du Patriarche Timothéus* (Vatican, 1954), pp. 120–1).

APPENDIX

The text is given of three important doctrinal statements reflecting the views of the emperors and the Severan Monophysites. Evagrius' text of the *Henotikon* and the Edict of Justin II is given without emendation from other sources,[1] thus preserving the outlook of the court at the end of the sixth century.

The translations are those of the Bohn edition for Evagrius and Hamilton and Brooks for Zacharias.

THE 'HENOTIKON'
Letter of Zeno to the bishops, monks and laity of Egypt, A.D. 482
Evagrius, text in *Ecclesiastical History* III. 14

The emperor Caesar Zeno, pious, victorious, triumphant, supreme, ever worshipful Augustus, to the most reverend bishops and clergy, and to the monks and laity throughout Alexandria, Egypt, Libya, and Pentapolis. Being assured that the origin and constitution, the might and invincible defence, of our sovereignty is the only right and true faith, which, through Divine inspiration, the three hundred holy fathers assembled at Nicaea set forth, and the hundred and fifty holy fathers, who in like manner met at Constantinople, confirmed; we night and day employ every means of prayer, of zealous pains and of laws, that the holy catholic and apostolic church in every place may be multiplied, the uncorruptible and immortal mother of our sceptre; and that the pious laity, continuing in peace and unanimity with respect to God, may, together with the bishops, highly beloved of God, the most pious clergy, the archimandrites and monks, offer up acceptably their supplications in behalf of our sovereignty. So long as our great God and Saviour Jesus Christ, who was incarnate and born of Mary, the holy Virgin, and *Theotokos*, approves and readily accepts our concordant glorification and service, the power of our enemies will be crushed and swept away, and peace with its blessings, kindly temperature, abundant produce, and whatever is beneficial to man, will be liberally bestowed. Since, then, the irreprehensible faith is the preserver both of ourselves and the Roman weal, petitions have been offered to us from pious archimandrites and hermits, and other venerable persons, imploring us with tears that unity should be procured for the churches, and the limbs should be knit together, which the enemy of all good has of old time been eagerly bent upon severing, under a consciousness that defeat will befall him whenever he assails the body while in an entire condition. For since it happens, that of the unnumbered generations

---

[1] For these, see above, p. 177 n4.

Appendix

which during the lapse of so many years time has withdrawn from life, some have departed deprived of the laver of regeneration, and others have been borne away on the inevitable journey of man, without having partaken in the Divine communion; and innumerable murders have also been perpetrated; and not only the earth, but the very air, has been defiled by a multitude of blood-sheddings; that this state of things might be transformed into good, who would not pray? For this reason, we were anxious that you should be informed, that we and the churches in every quarter neither have held, nor do we or shall we hold, nor are we aware of persons who hold, any other symbol, or lesson, or definition of faith or creed, than the before-mentioned holy symbol of the three hundred and eighteen holy fathers, which the aforesaid hundred and fifty holy fathers confirmed; and if any person does hold such, we deem him an alien: for we are confident that this symbol alone is, as we said, the preserver of our sovereignty, and on their reception of this alone are all the people baptized when desirous of the saving illumination: which symbol all the holy fathers assembled at Ephesus also followed; who further passed sentence of deposition on the impious Nestorius and those who subsequently held his sentiments: which Nestorius we also anathematize, together with Eutyches and all who entertain opinions contrary to those above mentioned, receiving at the same time the twelve chapters of Cyril, of holy memory, formerly archbishop of the holy Catholic church of the Alexandrians. We moreover confess, that the only begotten Son of God, himself God who truly assumed manhood, namely, our Lord Jesus Christ, who is con-substantial with the Father in respect of the Godhead, and con-substantial with ourselves as respects the manhood; that He, having descended, and become incarnate of the holy Spirit and Mary, the Virgin and *Theotokos*, is one and not two; for we affirm that both his miracles, and the sufferings which he voluntarily endured in the flesh, are those of a single person: for we do in no degree admit those who either make a division or a confusion, or introduce a phantom; inasmuch as his truly sinless incarnation from the *Theotokos* did not produce an addition of a son, because the Trinity continued a Trinity even when one member of the Trinity, the God-Word, became incarnate. Knowing, then, that neither the holy orthodox churches of God in all parts, nor the priests, highly beloved of God, who are at their head, nor our own sovereignty, have allowed or do allow any other symbol or definition of faith than the before-mentioned holy lesson, we have united ourselves thereto without hesitation. And these things we write not as setting forth a new form of faith, but for your assurance: and every one who has held or holds any other opinion, either at the present or another time, whether at Chalcedon or in any synod whatever, we anathematize; and specially the before-mentioned Nestorius and Eutyches, and those who maintain their doctrines. Link yourselves, therefore, to the spiritual mother, the church, and

Appendix

in her enjoy the same communion with us, according to the aforesaid one and only definition of the faith, namely, that of the three hundred and eighteen holy fathers. For your all-holy mother, the church, waits to embrace you as true children, and longs to hear your loved voice, so long withheld. Speed yourselves, therefore, for by so doing you will both draw towards yourselves the favour of our Master and Saviour and God, Jesus Christ, and be commended by our sovereignty.

PETITION OF THE MONOPHYSITES TO JUSTINIAN, A.D. 532
Text in Zacharias Rhetor, *Ecclesiastical History* IX. 15[1]

Various other men crown your believing head, O victorious king, with a crown of praises – men who take occasion from the case of other persons to write words about your favours towards them; but we, who have been ourselves judged worthy to experience your virtues, render thanks to you with a crown of laudation, which we weave with splendour. And, while in the desert, and, so to speak, at the end of the world, we have been this long time dwelling in quietness, praying to the good and merciful God during such days as those on behalf of your Majesty and on behalf of our sins: and your tranquillity has inclined towards our vileness and in your believing letters summoned us to come to you. And the thing is a wonder to us that you did not receive this our request with scorn, but, with the kindness innate in you, sympathised with us, so as to bring us out of affliction, making the pretext that this or that man had interceded for us.

Now we, since it is our duty to obey when commanded, immediately left the desert, and, journeying quietly along the road in peace without our voice being heard, have come before your feet; and we pray God, the bountiful giver, on our behalf to reward your serenity and the God-loving queen with good gifts from on high, and to bestow peace and tranquillity upon you, and to set every rebellious people as a stool beneath your feet.

However, now that we have come, we present a supplication to your peacefulnesses containing our true faith, not wishing to hold an argument with any man on any matter that is not profitable, as it is written, lest we annoy your ears; for it is very hard for a man to convince persons of a contentious disposition, although he make the truth manifest. And so, as we have said, we refuse to engage in a dispute with the contentious, who will not receive instructors; for our master the apostle said, 'We have no such custom, neither the Churches of God'.

Accordingly, victorious king, we do now also declare the freedom of our faith; although in the desert, when we received your edict at the hands of Theo-

[1] For a second text, see Michael the Syrian, *Chron.* IX. 22 (ed. Chabot, II, 196–203).

Appendix

dotus the duke, we also wrote and declared what we thought, and your Majesties gave us a message of truth free from affliction in that you were graciously moved and summoned us to your presence. And, since we have been judged worthy of the mercies of God, we do in this supplication inform your orthodoxies that by the grace of God we have from our earliest infancy received the faith of the apostles, and have been brought up in it and with it, and we think and believe even as our three hundred and eighteen God-inspired holy fathers, who drew up the faith of life and salvation, which was confirmed by our one hundred and fifty holy fathers who once met here, and ratified by the pious bishops who assembled at Ephesus and rejected the impious Nestorius. And so in this faith of the apostles we have been baptised and do baptise, and this saving knowledge is grounded in our hearts, and this same doctrine alone we recognise as a rule in the faith, and beyond it we receive no other; because it is perfect in all points, and it does not grow old nor need renovation.

Now we acknowledge a worshipful and holy Trinity of one nature, power, and honour, which is made known in three persons; for we worship the Father and His only Son, God the Word, Who was begotten of Him eternally beyond all times, and is with Him always without variation, and the Holy Spirit, which proceeds from the Father, and is of the nature of the Father and of the Son. One of the persons of this holy Trinity, that is, God the Word, we say by the will of the Father in the last days for the salvation of men took flesh of the Holy Spirit and of the holy Virgin the *Theotokos* Mary in a body endowed with a rational and intellectual soul, passible after our nature, and became man, and was not changed from that which He was. And so we confess that, while in the Godhead He was of the nature of the Father, He was also of our nature in the manhood. Accordingly He Who is the perfect Word, the invariable Son of God, became perfect man, and left nothing wanting for us in respect of our salvation, as the foolish Apollinaris said, saying that the Humanisation of God the Word was not perfect, and deprives us, according to his opinion, of things that are of prime importance in our salvation. For, if our intellect was not united with Him, as he absurdly says, then we are not saved, and in the matter of salvation have fallen short of that which is of the highest consequence for us. But these things are not as he said; for the perfect God for our sake became perfect man without variation, and God the Word did not leave anything wanting in the Humanisation, as we have said, nor yet was it a phantom of Him, as the impious Mani supposes, and the erring Eutyches.

And, since Christ is truth and does not know how to lie and does not deceive, because He is God, therefore God the Word truly became incarnate, in truth again, and not in semblance, with natural and innocent passions, because of His own will He for our sake among the things which He took upon Himself in the passible flesh of our nature of His own will endured also our death, which He

Appendix

made life for us by a Resurrection befitting God, for He first restored incorruption and immortality to human nature.

And, indeed, as God the Word left nothing wanting and was not phantasmal in the Incarnation and Humanisation, so He did not divide it into two persons and two natures according to the doctrine introduced by Nestorius the man-worshipper and those who formerly thought like him, and those who in our day so think.

And the faith contained in your confession refutes the doctrine of these men and contends with it, because in your earnestness you said thus: 'God appeared, Who became incarnate. He is in all points like the Father except the individuality of His Father. He became a sharer of our nature, and was called Son of Man. Being one and the same, God and man, He showed Himself to us, and was born as a babe for our sake; and, being God, He for men and for the sake of their salvation became man.'

If those who dispute with us adhered to these things in truth and were not content to hold them in appearance only, but rather consented to believe as we do and you do and as our holy God-inspired fathers did, they would have abstained from this stirring of strife. For that Christ was joined by composition and that God the Word is joined by composition with a body endowed with a rational and intellectual soul the all-wise doctors of the Church have plainly stated. Dionysius, who from the Areopagus and from the darkness and error of heathendom attained to the supreme light of the knowledge of God through our master Paul, in the treatise which he composed about the divine names of the Holy Trinity says, 'Praising it as kindly, we say, as is right, that it is kindly, because it in truth partook perfectly of our attributes in one of its persons, drawing to itself and raising the lowliness of our manhood, out of which the simple Jesus became joined by composition in a manner that cannot be described; and He who was from eternity and beyond all times took upon Him a temporal existence, and He who was raised and exalted above all orders and natures became in the likeness of our nature without variation and confusion'.[1] And Athanasius again in the treatise upon the faith named the unity of God the Word with soul-possessing flesh 'a composition' (*synthetos*), speaking thus: 'What sort of resultant unbelief befalls those who call it an indwelling instead of an Incarnation, and instead of a union and composition a human energy?'[2]

If, therefore, according to our holy fathers, whom your peacefulnesses have followed, God the Word, who was before simple and not composite, became incarnate of the Virgin, the *Theotokos* Mary, and [hypostatically][3] united soul-possessing and intellectual flesh to Himself personally and made it His own and was joined with it by composition in the dispensation [of the incarnation][3], it

---

[1] Published in *PG* 3, col. 592.
[2] *PG* 28, col. 124, from *Quod unus sit Christus*, a pseudo-Athanasian work.
[3] This term occurs in Michael the Syrian's text, p. 202.

Appendix

is manifest that according to our fathers we ought to confess one nature of God the Word, who took flesh and became perfectly man. Accordingly God the Word, who was before simple, is not recognised to have become composite in a body, if He is again divided after the union by being called two natures. But, just as an ordinary man, who is made up of various natures, soul and body and so forth, is not divided into two natures because a soul has been joined by composition with a body to make up the one nature and person of a man, so also God the Word, who was personally united and joined by composition with soul-possessing flesh, cannot be 'two natures' or 'in two natures'[1] because of His union and composition with a body. For according to the words of our fathers, whom the fear of God that is in you has followed, God the Word, Who was formerly simple, consented for our sake to be united by composition with soul-possessing and intellectual flesh and without change to become man. Accordingly one unique nature and person (*hypostasis*) of God the Word, Who took flesh, is to be proclaimed, and there is one energy of the Word of God which is made known, which is exalted and glorious and fitting for God, and is also lowly and human. [How is it that our brethren cannot apply themselves to annul the things which Leo has written in his *Tome*?][2]

[There follow passages of Leo, Nestorius, Theodore, Diodore, Theodoret and the Council of Chalcedon which proclaimed two natures after the union and incarnation of God the Word, and two *hypostaseis*. These are refuted by other statements from the Fathers, asserting one nature and one person of the incarnate Word. Neither Zacharias nor Michael reproduce these, the latter commenting that these texts are to be found in 'the work against the Diophysites'.

The petition ended as follows:]

And for this reason we do not accept either the Tome or the definition of Chalcedon, O victorious king, because we keep the canon and law of our fathers who assembled at Ephesus and anathematised and deprived Nestorius and excommunicated any who should presume to compose any other definition of faith besides that of Nicaea, which was correctly and believingly laid down by the Holy Spirit. These we reject and anathematise. And this definition and canon those who assembled at Chalcedon deliberately set at naught and transgressed, as they state in the Acts of that Synod; and they are subject to punishment and blame from our holy fathers in that they have introduced a new definition of faith, which is contrary to the truth of the doctrine of those who from time to time have been after a pure manner doctors of the Church, who, we believe, are now also entreating Christ with us, that you may aid the truth of their faith, honouring the contests undergone by their priesthoods, by which the Church has been exalted and glorified. For thus shall peace prevail in

---

[1] Chabot's translation is accepted here as more precise.
[2] The reference to Leo is given by Michael the Syrian (Chabot, II, 203).

Appendix

your reign by the power of the right hand of God Almighty, to whom we pray on your behalf that without toil or struggle in arms He will set your enemies as a stool beneath your feet.

'SECOND HENOTIKON'
Edict of Justin II, A.D. 571
Evagrius, text in *Ecclesiastical History* v. 4

In the name of the Lord Jesus Christ, our God, the Emperor Caesar Flavian Justin, faithful in Christ, clement, supreme, beneficent, Alemannicus, Gothicus, Germanicus, Anticus, Francicus, Herulicus, Gepidicus, pious, fortunate, glorious, victorious, triumphant, ever-worshipful Augustus.

'My peace I give to you', says the Lord Christ, our very God. 'My peace I leave to you', he also proclaims to all mankind. Now this is nothing else than that those who believe on him should gather into one and the same church, being unanimous concerning the true belief of Christians, and withdrawing from such as affirm or entertain contrary opinions: for the prime means of salvation for all men is the confession of the right faith. Wherefore we also, following the evangelical precepts and the holy symbol or doctrine of the holy fathers, exhort all persons to unite in one and the same church and sentiment; and this we do, believing in the Father, Son, and Holy Spirit, holding the doctrine of a consubstantial Trinity, one Godhead or nature and substance, both in terms and reality; one power, influence, and operation in three subsistences or persons; into which doctrine we were baptised, in which we believe, and to which we have united ourselves. For we worship a Unity in trinity and a Trinity in unity, peculiar both in its division and in its union, being Unity in respect of substance or Godhead, and Trinity with regard to its proprieties or subsistences or persons; for it is divided indivisibly, so to speak, and is united divisibly: for there is one thing in three, namely, the Godhead; and the three things are one, namely, those in which is the Godhead, or, to speak more accurately, which are the Godhead: and we acknowledge the Father to be God, the Son God, and the Holy Spirit God, whenever each person is regarded by itself – the thought in that case separating the things that are inseparable – and the three when viewed in conjunction to be God by sameness of motion and of nature; inasmuch as it is proper both to confess the one God, and at the same time to proclaim the three subsistences or proprieties. We also confess the only begotten Son of God, the God-Word, who, before the ages and without time, was begotten of the Father, not made, and who, in the last of the days, for our sakes and for our salvation, descended from heaven and was incarnate of the Holy Spirit and of our Lady, the holy glorious Mother of God and ever virgin Mary, and was born of her; who is our Lord Jesus Christ, one of the Holy Trinity, united

Appendix

in glorification with the Father and the Holy Spirit: for the Holy Trinity did not admit the addition of a fourth person, even when one of the Trinity, the God-Word, had become incarnate; but our Lord Jesus Christ is one and the same, being consubstantial with God the Father as respects the Godhead, and at the same time consubstantial with ourselves as respects the manhood; passible in the flesh, and at the same time impassible in the Godhead: for we do not admit that the Divine Word who wrought the miracles was one, and he who underwent the sufferings was another; but we confess our Lord Jesus Christ to be one and the same, namely, the Word of God become incarnate and made perfectly man, and that both the miracles and the sufferings which he voluntarily underwent for our salvation belong to one and the same; inasmuch as it was not a human being that gave himself on our behalf; but the God-Word himself, becoming man without undergoing change, submitted in the flesh to the voluntary passion and death on our behalf. Accordingly, while confessing him to be God, we do not contravene the circumstance of his being man; and while confessing him to be man, we do not deny the fact of his being God: whence, while confessing our Lord Jesus Christ to be one and the same, composed of both natures, namely, the Godhead and the manhood, we do not superinduce confusion upon the union; for he will not lose the circumstance of being God on becoming man like ourselves; nor yet, in being by nature God, and in that respect incapable of likeness to us, will he also decline the circumstance of being man. But as he continued God in manhood; in like manner, though possessed of Divine supremacy, he is no less man; being both in one, God and man at the same time, our Emmanuel. Further, while confessing him to be at the same time perfect in Godhead and perfect in manhood, of which two he was also composed, we do not attach to his one complex subsistence a division by parts or severance; but we signify that the difference of the natures is not annulled by the union: for neither was the Divine nature changed into the human, nor the human nature converted into the Divine; but, each being the more distinctly understood and existent in the limit and relation of its own nature, we say that the union took place according to subsistence. The union according to subsistence signifies, that the God-Word, that is to say one subsistence of the three subsistences of the Godhead, was not united with a previously existing human being, but in the womb of our Lady, the holy glorious *Theotokos* and ever virgin Mary, formed for himself of her, in his own subsistence, flesh consubstantial with ourselves, having the same passions in all respects except sin, and animated with a reasonable and intelligent soul; for he retained his subsistence in himself, and became man, and is one and the same, our Lord Jesus Christ, united in glorification with the Father and the Holy Spirit. Further, while considering his ineffable union, we rightly confess one nature, that of the Divine Word, to have become incarnate, by flesh animated with a reasonable and intelligent soul; and, on the other hand, while contemplating the difference of the natures, we affirm that they are two, without, however, introducing any division, for either nature is in him; whence we confess one and the same Christ, one Son, one person, one subsistence, both God and man together: and all who have held or do hold opinions at variance with these, we anathematise, judging them to be alien from the Holy and Apostolic Church of God. Accordingly, while the right doctrines which have been delivered to us by the holy fathers are being thus proclaimed, we exhort you all to gather into one and the same Catholic and Apostolic Church, or rather we even entreat you; for though possessed of imperial supremacy, we do not decline the use of such a term, in behalf of the unanimity and union of all Christians, in the universal offering of one doxology to our great God and Saviour Jesus Christ, and in abstinence for the future on the part of all from unnecessary disputes about persons and words – since the words lead to one true belief and understanding – while the usage and form which have hitherto prevailed in the holy Catholic and Apostolic Church of God, remain for ever unshaken and unchanged.

BIBLIOGRAPHY

The Monophysite movement has produced an enormous bibliography. An attempt is made here to provide a list of representative works for its origins and development between the First Council of Ephesus and the Arab invasions. Works covering general themes have been grouped together, followed by studies relevant to particular chapters. Heed has also been paid to the comparative availability of works. For instance, while Schwartz's *Acta Conciliorum Oecumenicorum* is indispensable, it was never completed, is not always easy to use and copies are relatively scarce. The more commonly available Mansi, *Sacrorum Conciliorum nova et amplissima Collectio* is therefore usually quoted alongside, and the same principle has been applied to the use of Migne's *Patrologia Latina* and *Graeco-Latina* in conjunction with more modern editions of the Fathers. For the Byzantine historians, the Bonn edition has generally been used throughout, and the Latin translation of Syriac writings published in the *Corpus Scriptorum Christianorum Orientalium* has been cited where possible. Reference has also been made to well-known collections and translations of use to English-speaking students, such as Bindley/Green, *Oecumenical Documents of the Faith* (London, 1950) or J. Stevenson's *Creeds, Councils and Controversies* (London, 1966).

The various works attributed to Severus of Antioch's friend Zacharias Scholasticus have been divided out as between Zacharias Scholasticus, Severus' biographer, Zacharias Rhetor, the Constantinopolitan historian and main source for the ecclesiastical history of the period 451–91, and 'pseudo-Zacharias', the Syrian writer who continued the history of Zacharias Rhetor to A.D. 569. It is difficult to see Zacharias, bishop of Mitylene, who was present at the great Home Synod that condemned Severus and his friends in June 536 as coinciding with any of these though, as Brooks' edition of Zacharias' *Ecclesiastical History* has been used throughout, the equation Zacharias Rhetor = Zacharias of Mitylene has been retained without prejudice. In the Vatican Syriac MS translated by Mai (*Scriptorum Veterum Nova Collectio*, vol. x, p. 361, Rome, 1839), Zacharias is styled 'Episcopus Melitensis', and this location seems possible for the continuator of the work.

PRIMARY SOURCES AND COLLECTIONS

Acta Archelai, ed. C. H. Beeson, *GCS* 16, Leipzig, 1906.

Acta Conciliorum Oecumenicorum, 4 tomes in 13 volumes, ed. E. Schwartz, Strasbourg, Berlin and Leipzig, 1914–40, and vol. 14, ed. J. Straub, Bonn, 1970.

Bibliography

Akten der ephesinischen Synode vom Jahre 449, ed. J. Flemming, *Abh. der Kgl. Ges. der Wiss. zu Göttingen*, Phil.-hist. Kl., n.s. 15, 1917, pp. 1–159.

Ambrose of Milan, *De fide, PL* 16.
    De incarnatione, PL 16.
    Epistulae, PL 16.
    Sermo contra Auxentium, PL 16 (cols. 1049–62).

Ammianus Marcellinus, *Res gestae*, Loeb Classical Library, London, Cambridge, Mass., 1935–9.

Anastasius, monk of Sinai, *Hodegos, PG* 89.

Antiochus the Monk, *Homiliae, PG* 89.

Apocryphal New Testament, ed. M. R. James, Oxford, 1924.

Apollinarius of Laodicea, *Fragmenta*, ed. H. Lietzmann (*Apollinaris von Laodicea und seine Schule*), Tübingen, 1904.

Apophthegmata Patrum, PG 65.

Athanasius of Alexandria, *Apol. ad Constantium, PG* 25.
    Apol. contra Arianos, PG 25.
    De incarnatione verbi, PG 25.
    Ep. ad Epictetum, PG 26.
    Ep. ad Jovianum de fide, PG 26.
    Historia Arianorum ad monachos, PG 25.
    Oratio contra gentes, PG 25.
    Orationes contra Arianos, PG 26.
    Tomus ad Antiochenos, PG 26.
    Vita Sancti Antonii, PG 26.

*Athanasius Scriptor, *The Conflict of Severus, patriarch of Antioch*, ed. E. J. Goodspeed and W. E. Crum, *PO* 4. 6, Paris, 1908.

Augustine, *De civitate Dei*, ed. E. Hoffmann, *CSEL* 40. 1 and 2, Vienna, 1899–1900.

Basil of Caesarea, *Epistulae, PG* 32 (Fr. ed. and tr. Y. Courtonne, Collection Budé, 3 vols., Paris, 1957–66).
    Homiliae, PG 31.

*Besa, *Life of Shenute*: Coptic text ed. J. Leipoldt and W. E. Crum, *CSCO*, Scriptores Coptici II. 2, Paris, 1906; translation by H. Wiesman, *ibid.* II. 4, Paris, 1931.

Bibliotheca orientalis, ed. J. S. Assemani, 4 vols., Rome, 1719–28.

Bibliothek der Symbole, ed. A. Hahn, Breslau, 1897.

Bindley/Green, *Documents*: see under *Oecumenical Documents*, below.

Chronica minora, ed. Th. Mommsen, *MGH*, AA 9 (vol. I) and 11 (vol. II), Berlin, 1892–4.

* Monophysite source.

Bibliography

Chronicle of Séert, ed. and tr. A. Scher, *PO* 4, 5, 7 and 13, Paris, 1907–18 (Nestorian, eleventh century).
**Chronicon ad annum Domini 724 pertinens*, anon., ed. and tr. E. W. Brooks and J. B. Chabot, *CSCO*, Scriptores Syri III. 4, Paris, 1903, pp. 61–119.
**Chronicon ad annum Domini 819 pertinens*, anon., ed. and tr. J. B. Chabot, *CSCO*, Scriptores Syri III. 14, Louvain, 1937, pp. 1–16.
**Chronicon ad annum Domini 846 pertinens*, anon., ed. and tr. E. W. Brooks and J. B. Chabot, *CSCO*, Scriptores Syri III. 4, Paris, 1903, pp. 121–80.
**Chronicon ad annum Domini 1234 pertinens*, anon., ed. and tr. J. B. Chabot, *CSCO*, Scriptores Syri III. 14, Paris, 1920, Louvain, 1937, pp. 17–266.
**Chronicon Edessenum*, ed. I. Guidi, *CSCO*, Scriptores Syri III. 4, Paris, 1903, pp. 1–11.
Chronicon Paschale, ed. B. G. Niebuhr, 2 vols., Bonn, 1832 (also, L. Dindorf, Leipzig, 1870).
Codex Justinianus, ed. P. Krueger, Berlin, 1877.
Codex Theodosianus, ed. Th. Mommsen and P. M. Meyer, Berlin, 1905.
Collectio, ed. Mansi: see under *Sacrorum . . . Collectio*, below.
Collectio Avellana, Epistulae imperatorum, pontificum, aliorum, A.D. 367–553, ed. O. Guenther, *CSEL* 35. 1 and 2, Vienna, 1895.
Constantine Porphyrogenitus, *De cerimoniis aulae byzantinae libri II*, ed. J. J. Reiscke, Bonn, 1829–30.
Cosmas Indicopleustes, *The Christian Topography*, ed. E. O. Winstedt, Cambridge, 1909 (also, Eng. tr. by J. W. McCrindle, Hakluyt Society Publications 98, London, 1897).
Creeds, Councils and Controversies, ed. J. Stevenson, London, 1966.
Cyril of Alexandria, *Opera*, *PG* 72–7.
Cyril of Scythopolis, *Vita Euthymii*, *Vita Hesychasti* and *Vita Sabae*, ed. E. Schwartz, *TU* 49 (ser. IV. 4), Leipzig, 1939, no. 2.
**pseudo-Dionysius, *Chronicon pseudo-Dionysianum vulgo dictum*, ed. and tr. J. B. Chabot, *CSCO*, Scriptores Syri III. 1, Louvain, 1927–49.
**Documenta ad origines monophysitarum illustrandas*, ed. and tr. J. B. Chabot, *CSCO*, Scriptores Syri II. 37, Paris, Louvain, 1907–33.
**Elias, *Vita Johannis episcopi Tellae*, ed. and tr. E. W. Brooks, *CSCO*, Scriptores Syri III. 25, Paris, 1907, pp. 21–60.
Epiphanius, *Panarion*, vol. III, ed. K. Holl, *GCS* 37, Leipzig, 1933.
Epistulae romanorum pontificum genuinae, ed. A. Thiel, Braunsberg, 1867–8.
Eusebius of Caesarea, *Historia ecclesiastica*, ed. and Eng. tr. K. Lake and J. E. L. Oulton, London, 1926–32.
  Tricennial Oration, ed. I. A. Heikel, *GCS* 7, Eusebius Werke I, Leipzig, 1902.
  Vita Constantini, ed. I. A. Heikel, *GCS* 7, Eusebius Werke I, Leipzig, 1902.

* Monophysite source.

Bibliography

Eustathius of Antioch, *Fragmenta*, ed. M. Spanneut, Lille, 1948 (*Recherches sur les écrits d'Eustathe d'Antioche*); also *PG* 18.

Eutychius of Alexandria, *Annales ecclesiasticae*, *PG* 111, cols. 907–1156 (tenth-century Melkite).

Evagrius Scholasticus, *Historia ecclesiastica*, ed. J. Bidez and L. Parmentier, London, 1898 (Syrian Melkite, reflects the views of the period of the Emperor Maurice).

Facundus of Hermiana, *Pro defensione trium capitulorum Concilii Chalcedonensis*, *PL* 67.

Gelasius, *Epistulae*, ed. A. Thiel, *Epist. rom. pontif.* pp. 287–483.

Gennadius of Marseille, *Liber de scriptoribus ecclesiasticis*, *PL* 58, cols. 1059–1120.

George Cedrenus, *Historiarum compendium*, ed. I. Bekker, 2 vols., Bonn, 1839.

Georgius Pisida, *De expeditione persica*, ed. A. Pertusi, 1959.

Gregory of Nazianzus, *Epistulae*, *PG* 35.
   Orationes, *PG* 35–6.
   Poemata de seipso, *PG* 37.

Gregory of Nyssa, *Contra Eunomium*, *PG* 45.

Histoire d'Ahoudemmeh, métropolitain jacobite de Tagrit, anon., *PO* 3. 1., ed. F. Nau, Paris, 1909.

History of the Patriarchs: see under Severus of Asmounein, below.

Innocent of Maronia, *Epistula de collatione cum Severianis habita*, ed. Mansi, *Collectio* VIII, cols. 818–33, and Schwartz, *ACO* 4. II, pp. 169–84.

Inscriptiones Latinae Christianae Veteres, ed. E. Diehl, Berlin, 1961.

Inscriptions grecques et latines de la Syrie, ed. L. Jalabert and R. Mouterde, Paris, 1929– .

*James of Edessa, *Chronicon*, ed. and tr. E. W. Brooks, *CSCO*, Scriptores Syri III. 4, Paris, 1903, pp. 197–258.

*James of Saroug (Serug), *Epistulae quotquot supersunt*, *CSCO*, Scriptores Syri II. 45 ed. G. Olinder, Paris, 1937.

*John of Beith-Aphthonia, *Vita Severi*, ed. and tr. M. A. Kugener, *PO* 2. 3, Paris, 1907.

John of Biclar, *Chronicon*, ed. Th. Mommsen, *MGH*, AA 9=*Chron. min.*, I, 211–20.

John Chrysostom, *Adversus Iudaeos orationes*, *PG* 48.
   Homiliae, *PG* 49.

John Diakrinomenos, *Fragmenta*, ed. E. Miller (as 'John of Egea'), *Revue archéologique*, n.s. 26, 1873, pp. 400–2, and *PG* 86. 1 (fragmenta II. 38–59 attributed to Theodore Lector) (Henoticist but anti-Severan).

John of Egea: see under John Diakrinomenos, above.

* Monophysite source.

Bibliography

*John of Ephesus, *Historiae ecclesiasticae pars tertia*, ed. and tr. E. W. Brooks, *CSCO*, Scriptores Syri III. 3, Paris, Louvain, 1935–6. Syriac fragments of part two were published by Brooks in *ibid*. III. 2, Paris, 1933, pp. 401–20.

Lives of the Eastern Saints, ed. and tr. E. W. Brooks, *PO* 17–19, Paris, 1923–6.

John Lydus, *De magistratibus populi Romani libri tres*, ed. R. Wuensch, Bibl. Teubner, Leipzig, 1903.

*John Malalas, *Chronographia*, ed. L. Dindorf, Bonn, 1831 (Crypto-Monophysite).

John Moschos, *Pratum spirituale*, *PG* 87. 3, cols. 2855–3112 (Palestinian and Chalcedonian).

*John of Nikiou, *Chronicle*, ed. R. H. Charles, London, 1916.

*John Philoponos, *De opificio mundi*, ed. W. Reichardt, Leipzig, 1897.

Opuscula monophysitica, ed. A. Šanda, Beirut, 1930.

*John Rufus (Beit Rufin), *Plerophoria*, ed. F. Nau, *PO* 8. 1, Paris, 1912.

Vita Petri Iberi, ed. R. Raabe, Leipzig, 1895.

Jordanes, *Getica* and *Romana* (*Regni romanorum successio*), ed. Th. Mommsen, *MGH*, AA 5. 1, Berlin, 1882.

*Joshua Stylites, *Chronicle*, ed. and tr. W. Wright, Cambridge, 1882 (sixth century).

*Julian of Halicarnassos, *Fragmenta*, ed. R. Draguet, Louvain, 1924.

Justinian, *Novellae*, ed. C. E. Zachariae von Lingenthal, Bibl. Teubner, Leipzig, 1881–4. Also R. Schoell and W. Kroll (*Corpus Iuris Civilis* III), Berlin, 1928.

Theological Works, ed. E. Schwartz, *Abh. der bayer. Akad. der Wiss.*, Phil.-hist. Abt., n.s. 18. 1, 1939 ('Drei dogmatische Schriften Justinians'); also *PG* 86.

Landolphus, *Additamenta ad Pauli historiam romanam*, ed. H. Droysen, *MGH*, AA 2, Berlin, 1879, pp. 225–376.

Leo, *Epistulae*, *PL* 54, cols. 593–1218. Also ed. E. Schwartz, *ACO* II, 4, Berlin, 1932.

Sermones, *PL* 54, cols. 141–468.

Leontius of Byzantium, *Adversus fraudes Apollinaristarum*, *PG* 86. 2, cols. 1947–76.

De sectis, *PG* 86. 1, cols. 1193–1268.

Libri tres contra Nestorianos et Eutychianos, *PG* 86. 1, cols. 1268–1357.

Leontius of Neapolis, *Vita Sancti Ioannis Eleemosynarii*, ed. H. Gelzer, Freiburg and Leipzig, 1893; Eng. tr. E. Dawes and N. H. Baynes, *Three Byzantine Saints*, Oxford, 1948.

Liber pontificalis, ed. L. Duchesne, Paris, 1886.

* Monophysite source.

Bibliography

Liberatus (archdeacon of Carthage), *Breviarium causae Nestorianorum et Eutychianorum*, ed. Schwartz, *ACO* 2. v, pp. 98–141; also *PL* 68, cols. 969–1050.
Mansi, *Collectio*: see under *Sacrorum . . . Collectio*, below.
Marcellinus Comes, *Chronicon*, ed. Th. Mommsen, *MGH*, AA 11 = *Chron. min.*, II, 37–108.
Maximus of Turin, *Sermones*, ed. A. Mutzenbacher, *Corpus Christianorum*, ser. Latina, vol. XXIII, Turnhout, 1962.
Michael the Syrian, *Chronicle*, ed. J. B. Chabot, vols. I–III, Paris, 1899–1905.
Nestorius, *The Bazaar of Heraclides*, ed. G. R. Driver and L. Hodgson, Oxford, 1925 (Fr. ed. and tr. F. Nau, *Le Livre d'Héraclide*, Paris, 1910).
Nikephorus Kallistus Xanthopulus, *Historiae ecclesiasticae libri XIV–XVIII*, *PG* 146, col. 1055 – 147, col. 448.
Oecumenical Documents of the Faith, ed. T. H. Bindley and F. W. Green, 4th ed., London, 1950.
Optatus of Milevis, *De schismate Donatistarum*, ed. C. Ziwsa, *CSEL* 26, Vienna, 1893.
Origen, *Contra Celsum*, ed. P. Koetschau, *GCS* 2 and 3, Origenes Werke 1 and 2, Leipzig, 1897–9.
    Entretien avec Héraclide, ed. J. Scherer, *Sources chrétiennes* 67, Paris, 1960 (Eng. tr. J. E. L. Oulton and H. Chadwick, *Alexandrian Christianity*, London, 1954, pp. 430–55).
Palladius, *Historia Lausiaca*, ed. C. Butler, *Cambridge Texts and Studies* VI. 1 and 2, Cambridge, 1898–1904 (also, W. K. Lowther Clarke, *Translations of Christian Literature*, series 1, Greek Texts, London, S.P.C.K., 1918).
A Patristic Greek Lexicon, ed. G. W. H. Lampe, Oxford, 1961–9.
Paul the Deacon, *Historiae romanae libri XI–XVI*, ed. H. Droysen, *MGH*, AA 2, Berlin, 1879, pp. 185–224.
Paulinus of Nola, *Carmina*, ed. W. Hartel, *CSEL* 30, Vienna, 1894.
    Epistulae, ed. W. Hartel, *CSEL* 29, Vienna, 1894.
Philostorgius, *Historia ecclesiastica*, ed. J. Bidez, *GCS* 21, Leipzig, 1913.
*Philoxenus of Maboug, *Discourses*, ed. and Eng. tr. W. Budge, 2 vols., London, 1893–4.
    Letter to the monks of Senoun, ed. A. de Halleux, *CSCO*, Scriptores Syri 98–9, Louvain, 1963.
    Textes inédits, ed. J. Lebon, *Le Muséon* 43, Louvain, 1930, pp. 17–84 and 149–220.
    Three Letters of Philoxenus, ed. A. Vaschalde, Rome, 1902.
    Tractatus de Trinitate et de incarnatione, ed. A. Vaschalde, *CSCO*, Scriptores Syri II. 27, Rome, Paris, 1907.
Photius of Constantinople, *Bibliotheca*, *PG* 103 and 104.

* Monophysite source.

Bibliography

Priscus of Paniou, *Fragmenta*, ed. L. Dindorf, *Hist. graec. minores* 1, Bibl. Teubner, Leipzig, 1870, pp. 275-352.
Proclus of Constantinople, *Tomus ad Armenios*, *ACO* 4. II, pp. 187ff.
Procopius of Caesarea, *Wars* and *Anecdota*, ed. and tr. H. B. Dewing, Loeb Classical Library, 7 vols., London, 1914-40.
Prosper Tiro, *Chronicon*, *PL* 51, cols. 555-606; ed. Th. Mommsen, *MGH*, AA 9 = *Chron. min.*, I, 341-499.
Regesten der Kaiser und Päpste für die Jahre 311 bis 476 nach Chr., ed. O. Seeck, Stuttgart, 1919.
Rufinus, *Historiae ecclesiasticae libri duo*, *PL* 21, cols. 461-541, and ed. Th. Mommsen, *GCS* 9. 2, Leipzig, 1908.
Historia monachorum, *PL* 21, cols. 387-461.
Sacrorum Conciliorum nova et amplissima Collectio, ed. J. D. Mansi, Florence and Venice, 1759-98 (reprinted Paris, 1901-27).
Salvian of Marseille, *De gubernatione Dei*, ed. F. Pauly, *CSEL* 8, Vienna, 1883 (Eng. ed. and tr. E. M. Sanford, New York, 1930).
Sergius of Constantinople, *Epistulae*, ed. Mansi, *Collectio* XI, cols. 529-61.
*Severus of Antioch, *Anti-julianist Writings*, vol. I, ed. R. Hespel, *CSCO*, Scriptores Syri 104-5, Louvain, 1964, and vol. II, ed. R. Hespel, *ibid.* 124-7, Louvain, 1968.
Cathedral Homilies, ed. M. Brière, R. Duval, I. Guidi and M. A. Kugener, PO 4. 1, 8. 2, 12. 1, 16. 5, 20. 2, 22. 2, 23. 1, 25. 1 and 4, 26. 3, 29. 1 and 35. 1.
A Collection of Letters of Severus of Antioch from numerous Syriac Manuscripts, ed. and tr. E. W. Brooks, *PO* 12. 2 and 14, Paris, 1916 and 1920.
Liber contra impium grammaticum, ed. J. Lebon, Paris, Louvain, vol. I (1938), vol. III, part 1 (1929), vol. III, part 2 (1933), *CSCO*, Scriptores Syri IV. 4, 5 and 6.
Orationes ad Nephalium: Severi ac Sergii Grammatici epistulae mutuae, ed. J. Lebon, *CSCO*, Scriptores Syri IV. 7, Louvain, 1949.
Philalethes, ed. R. Hespel, *CSCO*, Scriptores Syri 69, Louvain, 1952.
The Sixth Book of the Select Letters of Severus, Patriarch of Antioch in the Syriac version of Athanasius of Nisibis, ed. and tr. E. W. Brooks, 4 vols. in continuous pagination, London, 1902-4.
*Severus of Asmounein, *History of the Patriarchs*, ed. and tr. B. T. A. Evetts, *PO* 1, Paris, 1907, and *PO* 5, Paris, 1910.
Socrates Scholasticus, *Historia ecclesiastica*, *PG* 67.
Sophronius of Jerusalem, *Epistula synodica ad Sergium patriarcham Constantinopolitanum*, *PG* 87. 3, cols. 3147-200.
Sozomen, *Historia ecclesiastica*, ed. J. Bidez and G. C. Hansen, *GCS* 50, Berlin, 1960.

* Monophysite source.

Bibliography

Synesius, *De regno* and *Epistulae*, *PG* 66 (ed. and Eng. tr. A. FitzGerald, 1926 and 1930).
Synodicon orientale, ed. J. B. Chabot, *Notices et extraits des manuscrits de la Bibliothèque Nationale* 37, Paris, 1902.
Tertullian, *Adversus Praxean*, ed. E. Kroymann, *CSEL* 47, Vienna, 1908.
Theodore Lector, *Historia ecclesiastica* (Chalcedonian, *circa* 520):
  (*a*) in *PG* 86. 1, cols. 165–204 (fragmenta I. 1 – II. 37) (fragmenta II. 38–59 are attributed to John Diakrinomenos);
  (*b*) ed. E. Miller, *Revue archéologique*, n.s. 26, 1873, pp. 273–88 and 396–9 (fragments attributed to John of Egea belong to John Diakrinomenos);
  (*c*) ed. F. Diekamp, *Historisches Jahrbuch der Görresgesellschaft* 24, 1903, pp. 553–8. (*d*) ed. G. C. Hansen, *GCS*, Berlin, 1971.
Theodore of Mopsuestia, *In epistulas Beati Pauli commentarii*, ed. H. B. Swete, 2 vols., Cambridge, 1880–2.
Theodoret of Cyrrhus, *Correspondance*, ed. Y. Azéma, *Sources chrétiennes* 40, 98 and 111, Paris, 1955–65.
  Eranistes, *PG* 83.
  Historia ecclesiastica, ed. L. Parmentier, *GCS* 19, Leipzig, 1911; 2nd ed. F. Scheidweiler, *GCS* 44, Berlin, 1954.
  Historia religiosa, *PG* 82.
Theophanes, *Chronographia*, ed. J. Classen, 2 vols., Bonn, 1839–41.
Theophylact Simocatta, *Historiarum libri octo*, ed. B. G. Niebuhr, Bonn, 1834.
Timothy the Cat, *Fragments*:
  (*a*) in *Textes Monophysites*, ed. F. Nau, *PO* 13, Paris, 1919, pp. 201–47;
  (*b*) ed. R. Y. Ebied and L. R. Wickham, 'A collection of unpublished Syriac letters of Timotheus Aelurus', *JTS*, n.s. 21. 2, 1970, pp. 321–69.
Victor of Tunnuna, *Chronicon*, ed. Th. Mommsen, *MGH*, AA 11 = *Chron. min.*, II, 184–206.
Victor of Vita, *Historia persecutionis africanae provinciae*, ed. M. Petschenig, *CSEL* 7, Vienna, 1881.
Vita Isaiae monachi, ed. and tr. E. W. Brooks, *CSCO*, Scriptores Syri III. 25, Paris, 1907, pp. 1–10.
Vita Sancti Danielis Stylitae, ed. P. Peeters, *AB* 32, 1913, pp. 121–214 (ed. and Eng. tr. E. Dawes and N. H. Baynes, *Three Byzantine Saints*, Oxford, 1948).
Vitae virorum apud Monophysitas celeberrimorum, ed. and tr. E. W. Brooks, *CSCO*, Scriptores Syri III. 25, Paris, 1907.
*Zacharias Rhetor, *Historia ecclesiastica*, ed. and tr. E. W. Brooks, *CSCO*, Scriptores Syri III. 5 and 6, Paris, Louvain, 1919–24 (Eng. tr. F. J. Hamilton and E. W. Brooks, London, 1899).

* Monophysite source.

Bibliography

*Zacharias Scholasticus, *Vita Severi*, ed. and tr. M. A. Kugener, *PO* 2. 1, Paris, 1907.
*pseudo-Zacharias, *Historia ecclesiastica* (continuator), ed. and tr. E. W. Brooks, *CSCO*, Scriptores Syri III. 6, Paris, Louvain, 1921-4.
Zonaras, *Epitomae historiarum*, ed. T. Büttner-Wobst, Bonn, 1897.
Zosimus, *Historia nova*, ed. I. Bekker, Bonn, 1839 (also, ed. L. Mendelssohn, Leipzig, 1887).

GENERAL WORKS

Altaner, B. and Stuiber, A. *Patrologie*. 7th ed., Freiburg, 1966.
Armstrong, A. H. (ed.). *The Cambridge History of Later Greek and Early Medieval Philosophy*. Cambridge, 1967.
Atiya, A. S. *A History of Eastern Christianity*. London, 1968.
Bacht, H. 'Die Rolle des orientalischen Mönchtums in den Kirchenpolitischen Auseinandersetzungen um Chalkedon (432-519)'. Grillmeier/Bacht, *Das Konzil von Chalkedon*, vol. II, pp. 193-314.
Bardenhewer, O. *Geschichte der altchristlichen Literatur*, vol. IV and V. Freiburg, 1924, 1932.
Baynes, N. H. *Byzantine Studies, and Other Essays*. London, 1955.
Baynes, N. H. and Moss, H. St L. B. (ed.). *Byzantium: an introduction to East Roman civilisation*. Oxford, 1955.
Beck, H. G. *Kirche und theologische Literatur im byzantinischen Reich*. Handbuch der Altertumswissenschaft 12. II. 1, Munich, 1959.
Bell, H. I. *Egypt from Alexander the Great to the Arab Conquests*. Oxford, 1948.
Beskow, P. *Rex gloriae, the Kingship of Christ in the Early Church*. Uppsala, 1962.
Bréhier, L. *Le Monde byzantin*. 3 vols., Paris, 1947-50.
Brown, P. [R. L.] *The World of Late Antiquity from Marcus Aurelius to Muhammed*. London, 1971.
Bury, J. B. *History of the Later Roman Empire*. 2 vols., London, 1923.
von Campenhausen, H. *The Fathers of the Greek Church*. Eng. tr., London, 1963.
Caspar, E. *Geschichte des Papsttums, von den Anfängen bis zur Höhe der Weltherrschaft*. 2 vols., Tübingen, 1930-3.
Chapot, V. 'La frontière de l'Euphrate de Pompée à la conquête arabe'. *Bibl. des écoles françaises d'Athènes et de Rome* 19, 1907.
Chitty, D. J. *The Desert a City*. Oxford, 1966.
Coleman-Norton, P. R. *Roman State and Christian Church*, vol. III. London, 1966.
Cramer, M. 'Der anti-chalkedonische Aspekt im historisch-biographischen Schrifttum der koptischen Monophysiten'. Grillmeier/Bacht, *Das Konzil von Chalkedon*, vol. II, pp. 315-38.

* Monophysite source.

Bibliography

Dawes, E. and Baynes, N. H. *Three Byzantine Saints*. Oxford, 1948.
Delehaye, H. 'Les Saints stylites'. *Subsidia Hagiographica* 14, Brussels, 1923.
Devreese, R. *Le Patriarcat d'Antioche depuis la paix de l'église jusqu'à la conquête arabe*. Paris, 1945.
Diehl, C. and Marçais, H. *Le Monde oriental de 395–1081*. 2nd ed. Paris, 1944.
Duchesne, L. *L'Eglise au VIe siècle*. Paris, 1924.
    Early History of the Christian Church, vol. III. Eng. tr. C. Jenkins, London, 1924.
Dvornik, F. 'Emperors, Popes and General Councils'. *Dumbarton Oaks Papers* 6, 1951, pp. 1–23.
    The Idea of Apostolicity in Byzantium and the Legend of the Apostle Andrew. Dumbarton Oaks Studies 4, Cambridge, Mass., 1958.
    Byzance et la primauté romaine. Paris, 1964.
    Early Christian and Byzantine Political Philosophy. 2 vols., Dumbarton Oaks Studies 9, Washington, 1966.
Ehrhardt, A. A. T. *Politische Metaphysik von Solon bis Augustin*. 3 vols., Tübingen, 1959–69.
Every, G. *The Byzantine Patriarchate (451–1204)*. London, 1948 (2nd ed. 1962).
Festugière, A. J. *Antioche païen et chrétien*. Paris, 1959.
    Les Moines d'Orient. 4 vols., Paris, 1961–4.
Fliche, A. and Martin, V. *Histoire de l'église*, vols. III and IV. Paris, 1936 and 1937.
Gaudemet, J. *L'Eglise dans l'empire romain (IVe et Ve siècles)*. Paris, 1958.
Greenslade, S. L. *Schism in the Early Church*. London, 1953.
Grillmeier, A. *Christ in Christian Tradition*. Eng. tr. J. S. Bowden, London, 1965. (Indispensable.)
Grillmeier, A. and Bacht, H. *Das Konzil von Chalkedon; Geschichte und Gegenwart*. 3 vols., Würzburg, 1953–62. (Indispensable.)
Haacke, R. 'Die Kaiserliche Politik in den Auseinandersetzungen um Chalkedon, 451–533'. Grillmeier/Bacht, *Das Konzil von Chalkedon*, vol. II, pp. 95–177.
Hardy, E. R. *Christian Egypt, Church and People*. New York, 1952.
Harnack, A. von. *History of Dogma*, vols. IV and V. Eng. tr., London, 1898.
Hefele, C. J. and Leclercq, H. *Histoire des conciles*, vols. I–III, Paris, 1907.
Honigmann, E. 'Patristic studies'. *Studi e Testi* 173, Vatican City, 1952.
Hussey, J. M. (ed.). *Cambridge Medieval History*, vol. IV, parts 1 and 2. Cambridge, 1966–7.
Jalland, T. G. *The Life and Times of St Leo the Great*. London, 1941.
    The Church and the Papacy. London, 1944.
Jones, A. H. M. *The Later Roman Empire*. 3 vols., Oxford, 1964.
Jugie, M. *Le Schisme byzantin, aperçue historique et doctrinale*. Paris, 1941.
    'Monophysisme'. *DTC* 20, cols. 2216–51.
Kelly, J. N. D. *Early Christian Doctrines*. London, 1958.

Bibliography

Kidd, B. J. *A History of the Church to A.D. 461*, vol. III. Oxford, 1922.
 The Roman Primacy to A.D. 461. London, 1936.
Krüger, G. 'Monophysiten'. Herzog–Hauck, *Realencyclopädie für protestantische Theologie und Kirche*, vol. XIII, Leipzig, 1905, pp. 372–401.
Labourt, J. *Le Christianisme dans l'empire perse sous la dynastie sassanide*. Paris, 1904.
Lebon, J. 'La Christologie du monophysisme syrien'. Grillmeier/Bacht, *Das Konzil von Chalkedon*, vol. I, pp. 425–580, and *Le Monophysisme sévérien*, Louvain, 1909. (Important.)
Maspero, J. *Histoire des patriarches d'Alexandrie depuis la mort de l'empereur Anastase jusqu'à la réconciliation des églises jacobites*. Paris, 1923. (Review and discussion by A. Jülicher in *ZNTW* 24, 1925, pp. 17–43.)
Momigliano, A. (ed.). *The Conflict between Paganism and Christianity in the Fourth Century*. Oxford, 1963.
Morrison, K. F. *Tradition and Authority in the Western Church*. Princeton, 1970.
Moss, H. St L. B. *The Birth of the Middle Ages, 395–814*. London, 1935.
Ostrogorsky, G. *History of the Byzantine State*. Eng. tr. J. M. Hussey, Oxford, 1956.
Prestige, G. L. *God in Patristic Thought*. London, 1956.
Rubin, B. *Das Zeitalter Justinians*. Berlin, 1960.
Schmemann, A. *The Historical Road of Eastern Orthodoxy*. London, 1963.
Schwartz, E., 'Aus den Akten des Konzils von Chalkedon'. *Abh. der bayer. Akad. der Wiss.*, Phil.-hist. Abt. 32. 2, 1925.
Seeck, O. *Geschichte des Untergangs der antiken Welt*, vol. VI. Stuttgart, 1920.
Sellers, R. V. *The Council of Chalcedon: a historical and doctrinal survey*. London, 1961. (Indispensable.)
Stein, E. *Histoire du Bas-empire*, vol. II, 476–565. Publ. by J.-R. Palanque, Paris, Bruxelles, Amsterdam, 1949.
 Geschichte des spätrömischen Reiches, vol. I, Vienna, 1928; Fr. ed. J.-R. Palanque, Bruges, 1959.
Tchalenko, G. *Villages antiques de la Syrie du Nord*. 3 vols., with contributions by H. Seyrig and A. Caquot, Institut français d'archéologie de Beyrouth, *Bibl. archéologique et historique* 50, Paris, 1953–8. (Important for the economic background of Syrian Monophysitism.)
Tixeront, J. *Histoire des dogmes*, vol. III: *La Fin de l'âge patristique, 430–800*. Paris, 1928.
Ullmann, W. *The Growth of Papal Government in the Middle Ages*. London, 1955.
Vasiliev, A. A. *The Byzantine Empire*. 2 vols., Madison, 1952.
Vööbus, A. *A History of Asceticism in the Syrian Orient*. *CSCO*, Subsidia 14 (vol. I) and 17 (vol. II), Louvain, 1958 and 1960. (Important.)

Bibliography

Wigram, W. A. *The Separation of the Monophysites*. London, 1923.
Wiles, M. F. *The Making of Christian Doctrine*. Cambridge, 1967.
Wolfson, H. A. *The Philosophy of the Church Fathers*, vol. 1. Cambridge, Mass., 1956.
Zernov, N. *Eastern Christendom*. London, 1961.

CHAPTER ONE

Amann, E. 'L'Affaire Nestorius vue de Rome'. *Revue des sciences religieuses* 23, 1949, pp. 5–37 and 207–44; and 24, 1950, pp. 28–52 and 235–65.
Baynes, N. H. 'Alexandria and Constantinople, a study in ecclesiastical diplomacy'. *Byzantine Studies, and Other Essays*, London, 1955, pp. 97–116.
Bethune Baker, J. F. *Nestorius and his Teaching*, Cambridge, 1908.
Bright, W. *Notes on the Canons of the First Four General Councils*. Oxford, 1882.
Camelot, T. 'De Nestorius à Eutychès'. Grillmeier/Bacht, *Das Konzil von Chalkedon*, vol. 1, pp. 213–42.
Chadwick, H. 'The exile and death of Flavian of Constantinople: a prologue to the Council of Chalcedon'. *JTS*, n.s. 6. 1, 1955, pp. 17–34.
  'Faith and order at the Council of Nicaea: a note on the background of the sixth canon'. *HTR* 53, 1960, pp. 171–95.
Draguet, R. 'La Christologie d'Eutychès d'après les Actes du Synode de Flavien, 448'. *Byzantion* 6, 1931, pp. 441–57.
Drijvers, H. J. W. 'Edessa und das Jüdische-Christentum'. *Vig. Christ.* 24, 1970, pp. 4–33.
Durand, G. M. de. Introduction to *Cyrille d'Alexandrie; deux dialogues christologiques*. Sources chrétiennes 97, Paris, 1964.
Ensslin, W. 'Zur Frage nach der ersten Kaiserkrönung durch die Patriarchen'. *BZ* 42, 1943–50, pp. 101–15 and 369–72.
Galtier, P. 'Saint Cyrille et Saint Léon à Chalcédoine'. Grillmeier/Bacht, *Das Konzil von Chalkedon*, vol. 1, pp. 345–87.
Goubert, P. 'Le Rôle de Sainte Pulchérie et de l'eunuche Chrysaphios'. Grillmeier/Bacht, *Das Konzil von Chalkedon*, vol. 1, pp. 303–21.
Greenslade, S. L. 'The Illyrian churches and the vicariate of Thessalonica, 378–395'. *JTS* 46, 1945, pp. 17–36.
Haase, F. 'Patriarch Dioskur I nach monophysitischen Quellen'. *Kirchengeschichtliche Abhandlungen* 6, 1908.
Hodgson, L. 'The metaphysic of Nestorius'. *JTS* 19, 1917, pp. 49–53.
Honigmann, E. 'The original list of members of the Council of Nicaea, the Robber Synod and the Council of Chalcedon'. *Byzantion* 16, 1942–3, pp. 20–80.
  'Juvenal of Jerusalem'. *Dumbarton Oaks Papers* 5, 1950, pp. 211–79.

Kraatz, W. *Koptische Akten zum ephesinischen Konzil vom Jahre 431.* TU 26 (n.s. 11), Leipzig, 1904, no. 2.
Loofs, F. 'Eutyches'. Herzog–Hauck, *Realencyclopädie für protestantische Theologie und Kirche*, vol. v, Leipzig, 1898, pp. 641–4.
Mohrmann, C. 'Linguistic problems in the early Christian Church'. *Vig. Christ.* 11, 1957, pp. 11–36.
Oost, S. I. *Galla Placidia Augusta.* Chicago, 1968.
Rahner, H. 'Leo der Grosse, der Papst des Konzils'. Grillmeier/Bacht, *Das Konzil von Chalkedon*, vol. I, pp. 323–39.
Schwartz, E. 'Die Kaiserin Pulcheria auf die Synode von Chalkedon'. *Festgabe für A. Jülicher*, Tübingen, 1927, pp. 203–12.
'Der Prozess des Eutyches'. *Sitz. der bayer. Akad. der Wiss. zu München*, Phil.-hist. Abt. 1929, no. 5, pp. 64–93.
'Der sechste nicaënische Kanon auf der Synode von Chalkedon'. *Sitz. der preussischen Akad. der Wiss.*, Phil.-hist. Kl. 1930, pp. 611–40.
'Zweisprachigkeit in der Konzilienakten'. *Philologus* 88, 1933, pp. 245–53.
Thompson, E. A. *Attila and the Huns.* Oxford, 1948.
'The foreign policies of Theodosius II and Marcian'. *Hermathena* 76, 1956, pp. 58–75.
Urbina, I. Ortiz de. 'Das Glaubenssymbol von Chalkedon, sein Text, sein Werden, seine dogmatische Bedeutung'. Grillmeier/Bacht, *Das Konzil von Chalkedon*, vol. I, pp. 389–418.

CHAPTER TWO

Alexander, P. J. 'The strength of empire and capital as seen through Byzantine eyes'. *Speculum* 37, 1962, pp. 339–57.
Amélineau, E. 'Le Christianisme chez les anciens Coptes'. *RHR* 14, 1886, pp. 308–45, and *RHR* 15, 1887, pp. 52–87.
Antonini, L. 'Le chiese cristiane nell'Egitto dal iv al ix secolo'. *Aegyptus* 20, 1940, pp. 130–208.
Bardy, G. 'Le Patriotisme égyptien dans la tradition patristique'. *RHE* 45, 1950, pp. 1–24.
Bauer, W. 'Jedermann sei untertan der Obrigkeit'. *Aufsätze und Kleine Schriften*, Tübingen, 1967, pp. 263–84.
Baynes, N. H. 'Eusebius and the Christian empire'. *Byzantine Studies, and Other Essays*, London, 1955, pp. 168–72.
Bousset, W. *Apophthegmata Patrum.* Tübingen, 1923.
Brown, P. R. L. 'Christianity and local culture in Late Roman Africa'. *JRS* 58, 1968, pp. 85–95.

Bibliography

Brown, P. R. L. 'The diffusion of Manichaeism in the Roman Empire'. *JRS* 59, 1969, pp. 92–103.
Browning, R. 'The riot of A.D. 387 in Antioch'. *JRS* 42, 1952, pp. 13–20.
Coster, C. H. 'Synesius, a *curialis* of the time of the Emperor Arcadius'. *Byzantion* 15, 1940–1, pp. 17–37.
Cranz, F. E. 'Kingdom and polity in Eusebius of Caesarea'. *HTR* 45, 1952, pp. 47–66.
Diesner, H. J. 'Die Lage der nordafrikanischen Bevölkerung im Zeitpunkt der Vandaleninvasion'. *Historia* 11, 1962, pp. 97–111.
Kirche und Staat im spätrömischen Reich. Berlin, 1963.
Dölger, F. J. 'Rom in der Gedankenwelt der Byzantiner'. *Zeitschr. f. Kirchengeschichte* 56, 1937, pp. 1–42.
Downey, G. 'Coptic culture in the Byzantine world, nationalism and religious independence'. *Greek, Roman and Byzantine Studies* 1, 1958, pp. 119–35.
Eger, H. 'Kaiser und Kirche in der Geschichtestheologie Eusebs von Käsarea'. *ZNTW* 38, 1939, pp. 97–115.
Ensslin, W. 'Das Gottesgnadentum des autokratischen Kaisertums der frühbyzantinischen Zeit'. *Studi bizantini neoellenici* 5, 1939, pp. 154–66.
'Gottkaiser und Kaiser von Gottes Gnaden'. *Sitz. der bayer. Akad. der Wiss. zu München*, Phil.-hist. Abt., 1943.
Fennelly, J. M. 'Roman involvement in the affairs of an Egyptian shrine'. *Bull. of John Rylands Library* 50, 1968, pp. 317–35.
Frend, W. H. C. 'The Roman Empire in the eyes of the western schismatics'. *Miscellanea historiae ecclesiasticae*, vol. I, Louvain, 1961, pp. 9–22.
Martyrdom and Persecution in the Early Church. Oxford, 1965.
'Paulinus of Nola and the last century of the western empire'. *JRS* 59, 1969, pp. 1–11.
Geankopolos, D. J. 'Church and state in the Byzantine Empire. A reconsideration of the problem of Caesaropapism'. *Church History* 34, 1965, pp. 381–403.
Gmelin, U. 'Auctoritas. Römischer Princeps und päpstlicher Primat'. *Forschungen zur Kirchen- und Geistesgeschichte* 11, 1937, pp. 1–154.
Grabar, A. 'L'Empereur dans l'art byzantin'. *Publications de la Faculté des Lettres à l'Université de Strasbourg*, fasc. 75, Paris, 1936, pp. 95–122.
Greenslade, S. L. *Church and State from Constantine to Theodosius.* London, 1954.
Hardy, E. R. 'The patriarchate of Alexandria. A study in national Christianity'. *Church History* 15, 1946, pp. 81–100.
Heussi, K. *Der Ursprung des Mönchtums.* Tübingen, 1934.
Honigmann, E. 'Le Couvent de Barṣaumā et le patriarcat jacobite d'Antioche et de Syrie'. *CSCO*, Subsidia 7, Louvain, 1954.

Bibliography

Jones, A. H. M. 'Were ancient heresies national or social movements in disguise?' *JTS*, n.s. 11, 1959, pp. 280–98. (Important study.)

Kaegi, W. E. *Byzantium and the Decline of Rome*. Princeton, 1968.

Karayanopulos, J. 'Der frühbyzantinische Kaiser'. *BZ* 49, 1956, pp. 368–84.

Labriolle, P. de. 'Les Débuts du Monachisme'. *Histoire de l'église*, ed. Fliche and Martin, vol. III, part 3, ch. 1.

Leipoldt, J. *Schenute von Atripe*. *TU* 25 (n.s. 10), Leipzig, 1904, no. 1.

Lietzmann, H. 'Das Mönchtum'. *Geschichte der alten Kirche*, vol. IV, Berlin, 1944, ch. 6. (Important study.)

Macmullen, R. 'Nationalism in Roman Egypt'. *Aegyptus* 44, 1964–5, pp. 179–99.

'Provincial languages in the Roman Empire'. *AJP* 87, 1966, pp. 1–17. (Important article.)

Pargoire, J. 'Les Débuts du Monachisme à Constantinople'. *Revue des questions historiques*, n.s. 21, 1899, pp. 67–143.

Parker, T. M. *Christianity and the State in the Light of History*. Bampton Lectures for 1954, London, 1955.

Peterson, E. *Der Monotheismus als politisches Problem*. Leipzig, 1935.

Schneemelcher, W. 'Athanasius von Alexandrien als Theologe und als Kirchenpolitiker'. *ZNTW* 43, 1950–1, pp. 242–56.

Seston, W. 'Constantine as a "bishop"'. *JRS* 37, 1947, pp. 127–31.

Setton, K. M. *The Christian Attitude towards the Emperor in the Fourth Century*. Columbia, 1941.

Simon, M. 'La polémique anti-juive de S. Jean Chrysostome et le mouvement judaïsant d'Antioche'. *Mélanges Cumont = Annuaire de l'Institut de Philologie et d'Histoire orientales* 4, 1936, pp. 403–21.

'Les Saints d'Israël dans la dévotion de l'église ancienne'. *Revue d'histoire et de philosophie religieuses* 34, 1954, pp. 98–127.

Stockmeier, P. '"Imperium" bei Leo dem Grossen'. *Studia Patristica* 3 (= *TU* 78), Berlin, 1961, pp. 413–20.

Tchalenko, G. 'La Syrie du Nord: étude économique'. *Actes du VIe Congrès International des Etudes byzantines*, Paris, 1950, pp. 389–97.

Turcan, R. 'L'Abandon de Nisibe et l'opinion publique'. *Mélanges André Piganiol* II, Paris, 1966, pp. 875–90.

Ullmann, W. 'Leo I and the theme of papal primacy'. *JTS*, n.s. 11, 1960, pp. 25–51.

Voigt, K. P. 'Papst Leo der Grosse und die "Unfehlbarkeit" des oströmischen Kaisers'. *Zeitschr. f. Kirchengeschichte* 47, 1928, pp. 11–17.

Williams, C. H. 'Christology and church–state relations'. *Church History* 20, 1951, pp. 17–23.

Woodward, E. L. *Christianity and Nationalism in the Later Roman Empire*. London, 1916.

Bibliography

CHAPTER THREE

Abramowski, L. 'Die Streit um Diodor und Theodor zwischen den beiden ephesinischen Konzilien'. *Zeitschr. f. Kirchengeschichte* 57, 1955-6, pp. 252-87.

'Untersuchungen zum Liber Heraclidis des Nestorius'. *CSCO*, Subsidia 22, Louvain, 1963.

Alexander, P. J. *The Oracle of Baalbek*. Dumbarton Oaks Studies 10, Washington, 1967.

'Mediaeval Apocalypses as historical sources'. *AHR* 73. 4, 1968, pp. 997-1018.

Amann, E. 'Nestorius'. *DTC* 21, cols. 76-157.

Bardy, G. 'Sur une citation de saint Ambroise dans les controverses christologiques'. *RHE* 40, 1944-5, pp. 171-6.

Burghardt, W. J. *The Image of God in Man according to Cyril of Alexandria.* Washington, 1957.

Chadwick, H. 'Eucharist and Christology in the Nestorian controversy'. *JTS*, n.s. 2. 2, 1951, pp. 145-64. (Important article.)

Devreese, R. 'Essai sur Théodore de Mopsuestie'. *Studi e Testi* 141, Vatican City, 1948.

Dupré la Tour, A. 'La *Doxa* du Christ dans Saint Cyrille'. *Revue des sciences religieuses* 49. 1, 1961, pp. 68-94.

Galtier, P. 'Saint Athanase et l'âme humaine du Christ'. *Gregorianum* 36, 1955, pp. 553-89.

Gesché, A. 'L'Ame humaine de Jésus dans la christologie du IVe siècle'. *RHE* 54, 1959, pp. 385-425.

'La Christologie du commentaire sur les Psaumes découvert à Toura'. *Univ. Cath. Lovaniensis Dissertationes*, ser. III. 7, Gembloux, 1962. (Summarised in *Studia Patristica* 3 = *TU* 78, Berlin, 1961, pp. 205-13.)

Greer, R. A. *Theodore of Mopsuestia, Exegete and Theologian.* London, 1961.

'The Antiochene Christology of Diodore of Tarsus'. *JTS*, n.s. 17, 1966, pp. 327-41.

Griffith, F. Ll. 'Oxford excavations in Nubia VII'. *Annals of Archaeology and Anthropology* 15, Liverpool, 1927.

Kuhn, E. H. 'A fifth century Egyptian Abbot'. *JTS*, n.s. 5, 1954, pp. 36-48 and 174-87.

Lebon, J. 'Altération doctrinale de la lettre à Epictète de Saint Athanase'. *RHE* 31, 1935, pp. 713-61.

Lietzmann, H. *Apollinaris von Laodicea und seine Schule.* Tübingen, 1904.

Loofs, F. *Nestorius and his Place in the History of Christian Doctrine.* Cambridge, 1914.

Bibliography

Mahé, J. 'L'Eucharistie après Saint Cyrille d'Alexandrie'. *RHE* 8, 1907, pp. 677–96.
Mingana, A. *The Commentary of Theodore of Mopsuestia on the Nicene Creed.* Woodbrooke Studies 5, Cambridge, 1932. (First published in part as 'The Christian faith and the interpretation of the Nicene Creed, by Theodore of Mopsuestia (c. 350–428)', Woodbrooke Studies, fasc. 10, *Bull. of John Rylands Library* 16, 1932, pp. 200–318.)
The Commentary of Theodore of Mopsuestia on the Lord's Prayer and on the Sacraments of Baptism and the Eucharist. Woodbrooke Studies 6, Cambridge, 1933.
Nau, F. 'Histoire des solitaires égyptiens'. *Revue de l'Orient chrétien* 12, 1907, pp. 43–69, 171–89 and 393–413.
Norris, R. A. *Manhood and Christ: a study in the Christology of Theodore of Mopsuestia.* Oxford, 1963.
Opitz, H. G. 'Euseb von Caesarea als Theologe'. *ZNTW* 34, 1935, pp. 1–19.
Otis, B. 'Cappadocian thought as a coherent system'. *Dumbarton Oaks Papers* 12, 1958, pp. 95–124.
Prestige, G. L. *Fathers and Heretics.* London, 1954.
St Basil the Great and Apollinaris of Laodicea. Ed. H. Chadwick, London, 1956.
Raven, C. E. *Apollinarianism.* Cambridge, 1923.
Richard, M. L'Introduction du mot *hypostase* dans la théologie de l'Incarnation'. *Mélanges de science religieuse* 2, 1945, pp. 5–32 and 243–70.
'Saint Athanase et la psychologie du Christ selon les Ariens'. *Mélanges de science religieuse* 4, 1947, pp. 5–54.
Riedmatten, H. de. *Les Actes du procès de Paul de Samosate.* Fribourg, Switzerland, 1952. (Reviewed by H. Chadwick, *JTS*, n.s. 4, 1953, pp. 91–4.)
'La Christologie d'Apollinaire de Laodicée'. *Studia Patristica* 2 (=*TU* 64, ser. v. 9), Berlin, 1957, pp. 208–34.
Roldanus, A. *Le Christ et l'homme dans la théologie d'Alexandrie.* Leiden, 1968.
Schneemelcher, W. 'Athanasius von Alexandrien als Theologe und als Kirchenpolitiker'. *ZNTW* 43, 1950–1, pp. 242–56.
Sellers, R. V. *Eustathius of Antioch.* Cambridge, 1928.
Two Ancient Christologies. London, 1954.
Spanneut, M. *Recherches sur les écrits d'Eustathe d'Antioche.* Lille, 1948.
Sullivan, F. A. 'The Christology of Theodore of Mopsuestia'. *Analecta Gregoriana* 82, Rome, 1956.
Turner, H. E. W. *The Patristic Doctrine of Redemption.* London, 1952.
Weijenborg, R. 'Apollinaristic interpolations in the Tomos ad Antiochenos of A.D. 362'. *Studia Patristica* 3 (=*TU* 78), Berlin, 1961, pp. 324–30.
Wiles, M. F. *The Spiritual Gospel.* Cambridge, 1960.

Wiles, M. F. 'The nature of the early debate about Christ's human soul'. *JEH* 16. 2, 1965, pp. 139–51.
Wolfson, H. A. 'Philosophical implications of Arianism and Apollinarianism'. *Dumbarton Oaks Papers* 12, 1958, pp. 3–28.
Young, F. M. 'Christological ideas in the Greek Commentaries on Hebrews'. *JTS*, n.s. 20. 1, 1969, pp. 150–63.

CHAPTER FOUR

Bareille, G. 'Diacrinomènes'. *DTC* 7, cols. 732–3.
Baynes, N. H. 'The Vita S. Danielis Stylitae'. *EHR* 40, 1925, pp. 397–402.
Beck, G. H. 'Eudocia'. *Reallexikon für Antike und Christentum* 6, cols. 843–7.
Brooks, E. W. 'The Emperor Zeno and the Isaurians'. *EHR* 8, 1893, pp. 209–38.
Ebied, R. Y. and Wickham, L. R. 'A collection of unpublished Syriac letters of Timotheus Aelurus'. *JTS*, n.s. 21. 2, 1970, pp. 321–69.
Ensslin, W. 'Leo'. *PW* 12. 2, cols. 1947–62.
Gautier, E. F. *Genséric, Roi des Vandales*. Paris, 1932.
Grégoire, H. 'Le Peuple de Constantinople'. *Comptes rendus à l'Académie des inscriptions et belles lettres*, 1946, pp. 568–78.
Grégoire, H. and Manojlovic, G. 'Le Peuple de Constantinople'. *Byzantion* 11, 1936, pp. 616–716.
Herrmann, E. 'Chalkedon und die Ausgestaltung des konstantinopolitanischen Primats'. Grillmeier/Bacht, *Das Konzil von Chalkedon*, vol. II, pp. 459–90.
Hofmann, F. 'Der Kampf der Päpste um Konzil und Dogma von Chalkedon von Leo bis Hormisdas'. Grillmeier/Bacht, *Das Konzil von Chalkedon*, vol. II, pp. 13–94.
Honigmann, E. 'Patristic studies'. *Studi e Testi* 173, Vatican City, 1952.
Jarry, J. 'Hérésies et factions à Constantinople du Ve au VIIe siècle'. *Syria* 37, 1960, pp. 348–71.
Kugener, M. A. 'La compilation historique de Pseudo-Zacharie le Rhéteur'. *Revue de l'Orient chrétien* 5, 1900, pp. 201–14 and 416–80.
Lang, D. M. 'Peter the Iberian and his biographers'. *JEH* 2, 1951, pp. 158–68.
Lebon, J. 'La Christologie de Timothée Aelure'. *RHE* 9, 1908, pp. 677–702.
Meyer, H. 'Der Regierungsantritt Kaiser Majorians'. *BZ* 62, 1969, pp. 5–13.
Michel, A. 'Der Kampf um das politische oder petrinische Prinzip der Kirchenführung'. Grillmeier/Bacht, *Das Konzil von Chalkedon*, vol. II, pp. 491–562.
Peeters, P. 'Sur une contribution récente à l'histoire du Monophysisme'. *AB* 54, 1936, pp. 143–59. (Review of Schwartz, 'Publizistische Sammlungen'.)
Raabe, R. *Petrus der Iberer, ein Charakterbild zur Kirchen- und Sittengeschichte des fünften Jahrhunderts*. Leipzig, 1895.

Bibliography

Schwartz, E. 'Das Nicaenum und das Constantinopolitanum auf der Synode von Chalkedon'. *ZNTW* 25, 1926, pp. 38-88.
    'Codex Vaticanus graecus 1431, eine anti-chalkedonische Sammlung aus der Zeit Kaiser Zenos'. *Abh. der bayer. Akad. der Wiss.*, Phil.-hist. Abt. 32. 6, 1927.
    'Publizistische Sammlungen zum acacianischen Schisma'. *Abh. der bayer. Akad. der Wiss.*, Phil.-hist. Abt., n.s. 10. 4, 1934. (Documents and commentary – indispensable.)
Topping, E. C. 'The poet priest in Byzantium'. *Greek Orthodox Theological Review* 14. 1, 1969, pp. 31-41.
Vailhé, S. 'Le Titre de patriarche œcuménique avant S. Grégoire le Grand'. *Echos de l'Orient* 2, 1908, pp. 65-9.

CHAPTERS FIVE AND SIX

Amann, E. 'Scythes (moines)'. *DTC* 14, cols. 1746-53.
    'Théopaschite (controverse)'. *DTC* 15, cols. 507-12.
Bardy, G. 'Sous le régime de l'Hénotique: la politique religieuse d'Anastase'. *Histoire de l'église*, ed. Fliche and Martin, vol. IV, part 2, ch. 2.
    'Sévère d'Antioche'. *DTC* 14, cols. 1988-2000.
    'Zachare le Rhéteur'. *DTC* 30, cols. 3676-80.
Bauer, W. 'Die Severus-Vita des Zacharias Rhetor'. *Aufsätze und kleine Schriften*, ed. G. Strecker, Tübingen, 1967, pp. 210-28.
Casey, R. P. 'Julian of Halicarnassus'. *HTR* 19, 1926, pp. 206-13.
Charanis, P. *Church and State in the Later Roman Empire: the Religious Policy of Anastasius I, 491-518*. Madison, Wisconsin, 1939.
Crum, W. E. 'Sévère d'Antioche en Egypte'. *Revue de l'Orient chrétien* 3, ser. III, 1922-3, pp. 92-104.
Diesner, H. J. 'Die Auswirkungen der Religionspolitik Thrasamunds'. *Sitz. der sächsischen Akad. der Wiss. zu Leipzig*, Phil.-hist. Kl. 113. 3, 1965.
Draguet, R. 'Julien d'Halicarnasse et sa controverse avec Sévère d'Antioche sur l'incorruptibilité du corps du Christ'. Diss., Louvain, 1924.
Dvornik, F. 'Pope Gelasius and the emperor Anastasius I'. *BZ* 44, 1951, pp. 111-16.
Ensslin, W. *Theodorich der Grosse*. Munich, 1947.
    'Papst Johannes I als Gesandter Theodorichs des Grossen bei Kaiser Justinus I'. *BZ* 44, 1951, pp. 127-34.
Haacke, W. 'Die Glaubensformel des Papstes Hormisdas im Acacianischen Schisma'. *Analecta Gregoriana*, Rome, 1939, pp. 22-6.
Halleux, A. de. *Philoxène de Mabbog, sa vie, ses écrits et sa théologie*. Louvain, 1963. (Reviewed by L. Abramowski, *RHE* 60, 1965, pp. 859-66.)

Bibliography

Honigmann, E. 'Evêques et Evêchés monophysites d'Asie antérieure au VIe siècle'. *CSCO*, Subsidia 2, Louvain, 1951. (Important contribution.)

Jugie, M. 'Julien d'Halicarnasse et Sévère d'Antioche'. *Etudes orientales* 24, 1925, pp. 129–62 and 257–85.

Krüger, G. 'Theopaschiten'. Herzog–Hauck, *Realencyclopädie für protestantische Theologie und Kirche*, vol. XIX, Leipzig, 1907, pp. 658–62.

Kugener, M. A. 'Allocution prononcée par Sévère après son élévation sur le trône patriarcal d'Antioche'. *Oriens Christianus* 2, Rome, 1902, pp. 265–82.

Lebon, J. 'La Christologie de Timothée Aelure'. *RHE* 9, 1908, pp. 677–702.

'Textes inédits de Philoxène de Maboug'. *Le Muséon* 43, 1930, pp. 39–56.

Moeller, Ch. 'Le chalcédonisme et le néo-chalcédonisme'. Grillmeier/Bacht, *Das Konzil von Chalkedon*, vol. I, pp. 637–720.

'Nephalius d'Alexandrie; un représentant de la Christologie néochalcédonienne au début du VIe siècle'. *RHE* 40, 1944–5, pp. 73–140.

'Le *Type* de l'empereur Anastase I'. *Studia Patristica* 3 (= *TU* 78), Berlin, 1961, pp. 240–7.

Nau, F. 'La patrice Césaria, correspondante de Sévère d'Antioche'. *Revue de l'Orient chrétien*, 6, 1901, pp. 470–3.

Nicol, D. M. 'The Byzantine view of western Europe'. *Greek, Roman and Byzantine Studies* 8, no. 4, 1967, pp. 315–39.

Parker, T. M. 'The Mediaeval origins of the church as a "Societas perfecta"'. *Miscellanea historiae ecclesiasticae*, vol. I, Louvain, 1961, pp. 23–31.

Peeters, P. 'Jacques de Saro, appartient-il à la secte monophysite?' *AB* 66, 1948, pp. 134–98.

Schnürer, G. 'Die erste päpstliche Kaiserkrönung'. *Festschr. f. Felix Porsch zum siebzigsten Geburtstag dargebracht von der Görres-Gesellschaft*, Paderborn, 1923, pp. 211ff.

Schwartz, E. 'Johannes Rufus, ein monophysitischer Schriftsteller'. *Sitz. der heidelberger Akad. der Wiss.*, Phil.-hist. Kl. 3. 16, 1912.

Tisserant, E. 'Jacques de Saro'. *DTC* 15, cols. 300–3.

'Philoxène de Mabboug'. *DTC* 24, cols. 1509–32.

Vasiliev, A. A. *Justin the First*. Dumbarton Oaks Studies 1, Cambridge, Mass., 1950. (Indispensable.)

CHAPTER SEVEN

Amman, E. 'Les trois chapitres'. *DTC* 15, cols. 1868–924.

Armstrong, G. T. 'Imperial church building and church–state relations'. *Church History* 36, 1967, pp. 3–17.

Bréhier, L. 'La politique religieuse de Justinien'. *Histoire de l'église*, ed. Fliche and Martin, vol. IV, pp. 437–82.

Bibliography

Cameron, A. 'The last days of the Academy at Athens'. *Proc. of the Cambridge Philol. Soc.* 195, 1969, pp. 7–30.
Devreese, R. 'Le Début de la querelle des trois chapitres'. *Revue des sciences religieuses* 11, 1931, pp. 543–65.
  'Le cinquième concile et l'œcuménicité byzantine'. *Miscellanea Giovanni Mercati*, vol. III, Vatican City, 1946 (=*Studi e Testi* 123), pp. 1–15.
Diehl, Ch. *Justinien et la civilisation byzantine du VIe siècle*. Paris, 1901.
Diekamp, F. *Die origenistischen Streitigkeiten im sechsten Jahrhundert und das fünfte allgemeine Concil*. Münster, 1899.
Dölger, F. J. 'Rom in der Gedankenwelt der Byzantiner'. *Zeitschr. f. Kirchengeschichte* 56, 1937, pp. 1–42.
Downey, G. 'Ephraemius, patriarch of Antioch'. *Church History* 7, 1938, pp. 364–70.
Duchesne, L. 'Les Protégés de Théodora'. *Mélanges d'archéologie et d'histoire de l'école française de Rome* 35, 1915, pp. 57–9.
Ensslin, W. 'Papst Agapet und Kaiser Justinian I'. *Historisches Jahrbuch* 77, 1958, pp. 459–66.
Evans, D. B. '*Leontius of Byzantium; an Origenist Christology*. Dumbarton Oaks Studies 13, Washington, 1970.
Herrmann, Th. 'Johannes Philoponos als Monophysit'. *ZNTW* 29, 1930, pp. 209–64.
Honigmann, E. 'La Hiérarchie monophysite au temps de Jacques Baradée, 542–578'. *CSCO*, Subsidia 2, Louvain, 1951. (Important, with excellent bibliography.)
Kraeling, C. H. *Gerasa, City of the Decapolis*. New Haven, 1938.
Lebon, J. 'Ephrem d'Amid, patriarche d'Antioche (526–544)'. *Mélanges d'histoire offerts à Ch. Moeller*, vol. I, Louvain, Paris, 1914, pp. 197–214.
  'Encore le Pseudo-Dionysius'. *RHE* 28, 1932, pp. 296–313.
Loofs, F. *Leontius von Byzanz und die gleichnamigen Schriftsteller der griechischen Kirche*. *TU* 3, Leipzig, 1887.
Markus, R. A. 'Reflections on religious dissent in North Africa in the Byzantine period'. *Studies in Church History*, vol. III, Leiden, 1966, pp. 140–50.
Martin, H. 'Jean Philopon et la controverse trithéiste'. *Studia Patristica* 5 (=*TU* 80), Berlin, 1962, pp. 519–25.
Richard, M. 'Le Traité "De Sectis" et Léonce de Byzance'. *RHE* 35, 1939, pp. 695–723.
  'Léonce de Jérusalem et Léonce de Byzance'. *Mélanges de science religieuse* 1, 1944, pp. 35–88.
  'Le Néochalcédonisme'. *Mélanges de science religieuse* 3, 1946, pp. 156–61.
  'Léonce de Byzance était-il origéniste?' *Revue des études byzantines* 5, 1947, pp. 31–66.

Rubin, B. 'Prokopios von Kaisareia'. *PW* 23. 1, cols. 273–599.
Saffrey, H. D. 'Le Chrétien Jean Philopon et la survivance de l'Ecole d'Alexandrie'. *Revue des études grecques* 67, 1954, pp. 396–410.
Schwartz, E. 'Drei dogmatische Schriften Justinians'. *Abh. der bayer. Akad. der Wiss.*, Phil.-hist. Abt., n.s. 18. 1, 1939.
Kyrillos von Skythopolis. *TU* 49 (ser. IV. 4), Leipzig, 1939, no. 2. (Reviewed by E. Stein in *AB* 62, 1944, pp. 169–86.)
'Zur Kirchenpolitik Justinians'. *Sitz. der bayer. Akad. der Wiss. zu München*, Phil.-hist. Abt. 1940, no. 2. (Reprinted in *Gesammelte Schriften*, Berlin, 1938–63, vol. IV, pp. 276–328.) (Indispensable.)
van Roey, A. 'Les Débuts de l'église jacobite'. Grillmeier/Bacht, *Das Konzil von Chalkedon*, vol. II, pp. 339–60.
Wloska, W. *La Topographie chrétienne de Cosmas Indicopleustes*. Paris, 1962.

CHAPTER EIGHT

Armstrong, G. H. 'Fifth and sixth century church building in the Holy Land'. *Greek Orthodox Theol. Review* 14, 1969, pp. 17–30.
Bardy, G. 'Eglises de Perse et de l'Arménie au Ve et au VIe siècle'. *Histoire de l'église*, ed. Fliche and Martin, vol. IV, pp. 321–36 and 497–512.
Bardy, G. and Bréhier, L. 'L'expansion chrétienne aux Ve et VIe siècles'. *Histoire de l'église*, ed. Fliche and Martin, vol. IV, pp. 513–29.
Baynes, N. H. 'Rome and Armenia in the fourth century'. *EHR* 25, 1910, pp. 625–42 (reprinted in his *Byzantine Studies, and Other Essays*, pp. 186–208).
Bittel, K. (ed.). 'Das Wunder aus Faras'. Essen, 1969.
Burkitt, F. C. *Early Eastern Christianity*. London, 1904.
Der-Nersessian, S. *Armenia and the Byzantine Empire*. Cambridge, Mass., 1947.
Dinkler, E. (ed.). *Kunst und Geschichte Nubiens in christlicher Zeit*. Bongers, Recklinghausen, 1970. (Indispensable.)
Duchesne, L. 'Les missions chrétiens au sud de l'empire romain'. *Mélanges d'archéologie et d'histoire de l'école française de Rome* 16, 1896, pp. 82–90.
Frend, W. H. C. 'Christianity in the Middle East, survey down to 1800' (sections on Nubia and Ethiopia). A. J. Arberry (ed.), *Religion in the Middle East*, Cambridge, 1969, vol. I, ch. 5.
Hable-Selassie, S. *Die Beziehungen Äthiopiens zur griechisch-römischen Welt*. Bonn, 1964.
Inglisian, V. 'Chalkedon und die armenische Kirche'. Grillmeier/Bacht, *Das Konzil von Chalkedon*, vol. II, pp. 361–417.
Maspero, J. 'Théodore de Philae'. *Revue d'histoire des religions* 59, 1909, pp. 299–317.

Bibliography

Michalowski, K. 'Polish excavations at Faras, Second Season, 1961-2'. *Kush* 11, 1963, pp. 235-56, and *ibid.* 12, pp. 195-207.
Faras: die Kathedrale ans dem Wüstensand. Benziger, Zurich, 1967.
Moberg, A. *The Book of the Himyarites: fragments of a hitherto unknown Syriac work.* Lund, 1924.
Monneret de Villard, U. 'Storia della Nubia cristiana'. *Orientalia Christiana Analecta* 118, Rome, 1938.
Petermann and Gelzer. 'Armenien'. Herzog-Hauck, *Realencyclopädie für protestantische Theologie und Kirche*, vol. II, Leipzig, 1897, pp. 63-92.
Ryckmans, J. *La Persécution des chrétiens himyarites au sixième siècle.* Istanbul, 1956.
Sarkissian, K. v. *The Council of Chalcedon and the Armenian Church.* London, 1965. (Indispensable.)
Shinnie, P. L. *Mediaeval Nubia.* Sudan Antiquities Service, Khartoum, 1954.
Tafla, B. 'The establishment of the Ethiopian church'. *Tarikh* 2. 1, Ibadan, 1967, pp. 28-42.
Ter-Minassiantz, E. *Die armenische Kirche in ihren Beziehungen zu den syrischen Kirchen bis zum Ende des 13. Jahrhunderts. TU* 26 (n.s. 11), Leipzig, 1904, no. 4.
Thomson, R. W. 'An Armenian list of heresies'. *JTS*, n.s. 16, 1965, pp. 358-67.
Ullendorf, E. *Ethiopia and the Bible.* Schweich Lectures 1967, London, 1968.

CHAPTER NINE

Amélineau, E. *Etude sur le christianisme en Egypte au VIIe siècle.* Paris, 1887.
Monuments pour servir l'histoire de l'Egypte chrétienne, Paris, 1895.
Baynes, N. H. 'The first campaign of Heraclius against Persia'. *EHR* 19, 1904, pp. 694-702.
Bell, H. I. 'An Egyptian village in the age of Justinian'. *JHS* 64, 1944, pp. 21-36. (Valuable information.)
Bréhier, L. 'La Crise de l'empire et le redressement d'Héraclius'. *Histoire de l'église*, ed. Fliche and Martin, vol. V, ch. 3; and *ibid.* chs. 4, 5 and 6.
Brooks, E. W. 'The Patriarch Paul of Antioch and the Alexandrine schism of 575'. *BZ* 30, 1929-30, pp. 468-76.
Butler, A. J. *The Arab Conquest of Egypt.* Oxford, 1902.
Ensslin, W. 'Mauricius'. *PW* I. 14, cols. 2387-93.
Fiey, J. 'Mossoul chrétienne'. *Recherches publ. par la direction de l'Institut oriental de Beyrouth* 12, 1961; and 'Assyrie chrétienne', *ibid.* 22 and 23, 1964 and 1965.

Bibliography

Goodchild, R. G. 'Byzantines, Berbers and Arabs in 7th-century Libya'. *Antiquity* 41, 1967, pp. 119–22.

Goubert, R. *Byzance avant l'Islam sous les successeurs de Justinien*, vol. 1: *Byzance et l'Orient*. Paris, 1951.

Grégoire, H. 'Mahomet et le Monophysisme'. *Mélanges Charles Diehl*, vol. 1, Paris, 1930.

Grousset, R. *Histoire de l'Arménie des origines à 1071*. Paris, 1951.

Guillaumont, A. 'Un colloque entre orthodoxes et théologiens nestoriens de Perse sous Justinien'. *Comptes rendus de l'Académie des inscriptions et belles-lettres*, 1970, pp. 201–7.

Hatch, W. H. P. 'A fragment of a lost work on Dioscorus'. *HTR* 19, 1926, pp. 377–81.

Herrmann, Th. 'Patriarch Paul von Antiochia und das alexandrinische Schisma von 575'. *ZNTW* 27, 1928, pp. 213–304.

Higgins, M. J. 'Chosroes II's, votive offerings at Sergiopolis'. *BZ* 48, 1955, 89–102.

Honigmann, E. 'L'histoire ecclésiastique de Jean d'Ephèse'. *Byzantion* 14, 1939, pp. 615–25.

Janssens, Y. 'Les Bleus et les Verts sous Maurice, Phocas et Héraclius'. *Byzantion* 11, 1936, pp. 499–536.

Jülicher, A. 'Die Liste der alexandrinischen Patriarchen im 6. und 7. Jhd.' *Festgabe K. Mueller zum 70. Geburtstage*, Tübingen, 1922, pp. 7–23.

'Zur Geschichte der Monophysitenkirche'. *ZNTW* 24, 1925, pp. 17–43.

Monks, G. R. 'The church of Alexandria and the city's economic life in the sixth century'. *Speculum* 28, 1953, pp. 349–62.

Müller, L. D. G. 'Stellung und Bedeutung des Katholikos-Patriarchen von Seleukeia-Ktesiphon'. *Oriens Christianus* 53, 1969, pp. 227–45.

Oates, E. E. D. *Studies in the Ancient History of Northern Iraq*. OUP for the British Academy, 1968.

Sauvaget, J. 'Les Ghassanides et Sergiopolis'. *Byzantion* 14, 1939, pp. 115–30.

Sharf, A. 'Byzantine Jewry in the seventh century'. *BZ* 48, 1955, pp. 103–15.

Stratos, A. N. *Byzantium in the Seventh Century*. Amsterdam, 1968.

Thompson, E. A. *The Goths in Spain*. Oxford, 1969.

Weiss, G. 'Studien zum Leben, zu den Schriften und zur Theologie des Patriarchen Anastasius I von Antiochien, 559–98'. *Miscellanea Byzantina monaciensia*, vol. IV, Munich, 1965.

INDEX

Note. The title patriarch is used for the bishops of Constantinople, Antioch, Alexandria and Jerusalem appointed after the Council of Ephesus in 431.

Acacian schism, 182–3, 193–4, 199, 235–9
Acacius, bishop of Melitene, 22, 23, 124, 311
Acacius, patriarch of Constantinople, 93, 169–74, 175, 187, 190, 194, 198, 229, 232, 235, 236, 237, 239, 243, 246
   relations with the papacy, 175–6, 181–3
   relations with Timothy the Cat, 170–3
Acephaloi, xiii, 180, 187, 193, 234, 243n., 326
Acts of Archelaus, 108, 128, 138, 140
Adelphians, 216, 226
Aetius, archdeacon of Constantinople, 6n., 48, 49, 156
Aetius, general, 1
Agapetus, bishop of Rhodes, 58
Agapetus, pope, 272
Ahoudemmeh, Monophysite metropolitan of Tagrit, 321
Alabanda, 249, 293
Alcison, bishop of Nicopolis, 228, 230, 231
Alexander, archimandrite, 229
Alexander, bishop of Hierapolis, 23
Alexander, monk, 90
Alexander, P. J., 140
Alexandria, patriarchate of, 5, 40–3, 47–8, 81–3, 144, 173, 175, 180, 229, 302, 307
   Chalcedonians in, 154, 163, 274–5, 293, 324–5, 339–40, 349–50
   Council of, 114, 116
   Eutychists in, 154–5, 206, 263
   'guardian of orthodoxy', 15, 43, 83
   missions, 15, 83, 304–5, 307
   mobs in, 73, 142, 151, 154–5, 159
   monks in, 73, 155, 263, 270, 326
   Monophysitism in, 253, 262, 270, 290, 294, 324, 326, 344, 349–51, 356–7
   paganism in, 202–3
   relations with: Antioch, 21–2, 28, 34, 88, 216, 341–2; Constantinople, 15, 17–18, 25, 63, 170, 176, 177, 186–7, 193; Rome, 15, 27, 131, 155, 198–9

theology of, 13, 14, 105–7, 109, 112–13, 119–20, 128, 138, 210–11, 213
other references, 50, 54, 56, 59, 73, 80, 87, 93, 94, 160–1, 167, 175, 177, 213, 241, 242, 252, 265, 269, 288, 317
see also Cyril
al-Hareth, *see* Hareth
al-Moundhir, *see* Moundhir
Alwah, kingdom of, 301, 305
Ambrose, bishop of Milan, 16, 17, 57, 98–9, 111, 132, 133, 134
Amida, 185, 275, 286
Amphilochius, bishop of Side, xvi, 162
Anastasius I, Chalcedonian patriarch of Antioch, 318, 345
Anastasius II, Chalcedonian patriarch of Antioch, 337
Anastasius, emperor, xi, 54, 61, 73, 83, 96, 140, 195, 200, 214, 216, 220, 221, 222, 228, 231–3, 236, 237, 317
   economic policy, 191–2
   religious policy, 192, 214, 217–19
Anastasius, law student, 150
Anastasius I, Monophysite patriarch of Alexandria, 341–2
Anastasius, patriarch of Jerusalem, 174
Anastasius II, pope, 197, 199, 200, 244
Anatolius, patriarch of Constantinople, 3, 5, 10, 11n., 31n., 43, 45, 46, 58, 145–7, 156, 157, 160–2, 164, 170, 172, 313
Anatolius, patrician, 67
Ancyra, 11, 83
Andrew, archdeacon of Constantinople, 156
Andrew, bishop of Samosata, 189
Anthimus, patriarch of Constantinople, 271–3, 291, 320
Antioch, city of, 61, 66, 181, 215, 220, 222, 284, 337
   Circus factions, 157–8, 175, 242n.
   councils at, 107, 110
   monks in, 85, 136, 140–1, 219, 248

393

Index

Antioch (cont.)
  Monophysitism in, 140, 166–8, 175, 290–1, 294, 320, 321, 323, 333, 341–2, 344
  patriarchate of, 3, 5, 10, 21, 24, 25, 26, 35, 39, 83–91, 131, 144, 156, 175, 180–1, 187–8, 217, 223–4, 271, 294, 345, 347
  Severus at, 214, 221–8
  theology of, 13–14, 19, 21–3, 27, 43, 108, 111–12, 114, 123–4, 126–30, 133–4, 234–5, 256, 271, 277, 279, 310–12
  other references, 34, 39, 105, 117, 152, 176, 184, 213, 215, 249, 280, 294, 320, 328
Antonia, wife of Belisarius, 276
Antony, monk, 72, 95, 137
Apamea, 181, 191, 215, 221, 228
Aphraates, 140
Aphrodisias, 140, 181, 193
Aphrodite, village, 358
Aphthartodocetism, 255
Apion, pretorian prefect, 193, 265
Apocalyptic, 68, 77, 79, 99, 140–1
Apollinarian forgeries, 33, 41, 120, 121, 140, 206, 207, 230, 263, 266
Apollinarianism, 26, 79, 118, 120, 136, 263
Apollinaris, Chalcedonian patriarch of Alexandria, 325
Apollinarius(is), bishop of Laodicea, 13, 19, 41, 109, 113–121, 130, 206, 230, 253, 257, 264, 267, 344
  his teaching, 13, 113–18, 119
Aposchists (Separatists), xii, 176, 187, 216, 220, 270
Aquilinus, bishop of Byblos, 42
Arabs, 74, 229, 284, 302, 306–7, 317, 321, 330–1, 347, 351–2, 354
Arcadius, emperor, 16, 64, 94, 95
Ardaburius, 165, 166
Area, 224–5
Ariadne, empress, 168, 190–1, 233
Aristotle (Aristotelian), 105, 112, 116, 289
Arius, 109
  Arian controversy, 141
  Arianism, xii, 26, 57n., 93, 99, 109, 111–12, 116–17, 120, 132, 139, 159, 172, 191, 254, 256, 266
Armenia, Christianity in, 22, 92, 253, 261, 268, 291, 295, 297, 308–15, 337

  relations with Byzantines, 331–3, 344–5, 348, 352
Arsak, king of Armenia, 309
Aspar, *magister militum*, 159, 165, 166, 168–9
Athanasius, bishop of Alexandria, 13, 15, 20n., 52n., 54, 56, 57n., 59, 74, 82, 88, 109, 121, 131, 139, 304–5, 314, 341
  christology, 112–13, 114, 118, 128, 211
  forged writings, 120, 230
Athanasius, monk of Constantinople, 290–1, 317, 324
Athanasius, Monophysite patriarch of Antioch, 337, 346, 347, 349
Athanasius II, Monophysite patriarch of Alexandria, 193, 198
Athanasius, presbyter of Alexandria, 28
Athanasius of Nisibis, xvi
Atonement, 132, 134, 140, 162–3
Attila, 45
Audians, 89
Augustine, bishop of Hippo, xii, 64, 102, 196
  christology, 133
Augustus, 54, 76
Axum, 15, 56, 301, 304–5

Bagaudae, 65
Ballana, 298
Baptism, 49, 97, 105, 108, 150, 197, 221, 226–7, 234
Baradotus, monk, 95, 161
Barbarians, 63, 158–9, 166
Barsaumas, bishop of Nisibis, 223
Barsaumas, monk, 35, 39, 42, 91, 95, 140
Barsaumas, Persian agent, 67
Basil, bishop of Caesarea, 77, 114, 118, 186, 202, 213, 215, 310
Basil, bishop of Seleucia, 33n., 150
Basiliscus, usurping emperor, 59, 141, 166, 169–74, 189
Belisarius, 275, 276
Benjamin, Monophysite patriarch of Alexandria, 74, 349, 350–1, 356–7
Berytus, 34, 37, 53, 143, 150, 202, 203
Beth-Lapat (Baylhapat), synod of, 188, 312
Bible, 71, 97–8, 138–9, 201, 215, 225, 303, 307–8, 310
Bishops, secular duties, 62, 76, 225

394

Index

Blemmyes, 298, 299, 300–2
Blue Faction, 87, 158, 175, 242, 353
Boniface I, pope, 10n.
Boscoi, 89
Butler, A. J., 351

Caecilian, bishop of Carthage, 55, 283
Caesaria, niece of the emperor Anastasius, 260, 342
Caesarius, bishop of Arles, 78
Caesaro-Papism, 180; *see also* Emperors
Calendio, patriarch of Antioch, 175, 180, 181, 184, 187n., 188
Callinicum, 319, 320, 321
Canopus, monastery, 82, 163
Cappadocia, 15, 226, 240, 252, 261, 279
Cappadocians, theology of, 106, 109, 118–19, 207–8, 269, 288, 314
Caria, 181, 249, 293
Carrhae, 86, 91, 108, 347
Carthage, 68
Castor, bishop of Perga, 226
Castra Martis, 65
Celestine, pope, 17, 23–4, 31, 100, 131, 135, 171
Chalcedon, Council of, x, 1–12, 20, 23, 28, 46–9, 50, 91, 178–9, 192, 206, 207, 222, 226–7, 232, 241, 247, 255, 257, 264, 268, 275, 277, 278, 281–2, 285, 308, 317, 323, 340, 344, 350, 353, 354
  Canons of, 11, 143–4
  Canon 28, 11, 144–7, 162, 164, 195, 239
  Definition of, 1–2, 49, 325
  favoured in: Constantinople, 164, 244; Illyricum, 231; Makurrah, 301; Palestine, 189, 230–1
  opposed in: Alexandria, 163, 187, 192–3; Armenia, 308, 312, 314; Ethiopia, 305–8; Nubia, 299
  'plebiscite' over, 161–2
  policy of rulers towards: Anastasius, 192, 217–18; Basiliscus, 171–2; Justin I, 235; Justinian, 255
  reception of, 144–51
Chareas, *comes*, 37, 39, 42, 67, 94
Chosroes I, king of Persia, 321, 327
Chosroes II, king of Persia, 335–8, 343
Christianity, spread of, 67–8, 74–5
Christology, Ch. 3 *passim*

Alexandrian, 13, 112, 114
Antiochene, 13–14, 110–11, 126–30, 281, 312
Apollinarian, 13, 19, 115–18
Arian, 109–10
Athanasius', 112–13, 211
Constantinopolitan, 23, 311–12
defined 'in two natures', 2, 5, 6, 37, 129, 276
Docetic, 86, 109, 118, 140, 141
Eutychian, 29–32, 41, 142
expressed 'out of two natures', 5, 21, 215, 217, 276–7, 282, 318, 319
Monergist, 344, 348
neo-Chalcedonian, 186, 277–9
Neo-Platonist influence on, 107
Nestorius', 129–30, 131n.
One-nature, 5, 13, 19, 43, 109, 132, 211–13, 282–3, 322, 341–2, 346
Paul of Samosata's, 41, 108
Stoic influence on, 5, 112
two Christs, 2, 28, 131n., 297
Two-nature, 22, 108, 118–20, 148, 186, 188, 206, 240–1, 365
Western, 130–4, 281
word-flesh, 5, 107, 109, 115, 120, 210–12
word-man, 5, 13–14, 109, 138
see also Cyril and Severus of Antioch
Chrysaphius, grand chamberlain, 25–6, 28, 29, 45, 158
Cilicia I, 166, 240, 249
Cilicia II, 166, 248
Circesium, 329, 330
Circumcellions, 78, 90
Circus factions
  in Antioch, 157–8, 175
  in Constantinople, 93, 157–8, 220
  in Cyzicus, 158
  in Egypt, 353
Cledonius, presbyter, 118
Clement of Alexandria, 77
Codex Encyclius, 162
Communicatio Idiomatum, 1, 11, 38, 103
Conon, Monophysite bishop of Tarsus, 287, 289, 291, 318
Constans, emperor, 70, 96, 98
Constantine, emperor, 50, 55–6, 75–7, 95, 180
Constantine of Laodicea, xii, 275

395

Index

Constantinople (New Rome), city of, 51, 63, 66, 190, 236, 246
  Council of, 8, 11, 15, 27, 46, 49, 94, 118, 146–7, 171, 223, 290, 313
  Eutychian influence, 93, 166, 168–9, 172
  factions, 93, 156–7
  Germanic influence, 93, 166, 168–9, 172
  Isaurian influence, 165–6, 168–9
  monks, 29, 91–2, 171, 218, 220
  Monophysite influence, 260, 262, 270, 288, 317, 332
  patriarchate, 1, 5–7, 10, 15, 25, 46, 92–4, 103, 171–4, 229
  relations with: Alexandria, 15, 131, 160, 186–7, 192–3; Ephesus, 7–8, 93, 173–4; Rome, 9–12, 24, 100–1, 146–7, 156, 181–3, 194–5, 200, 232, 234–5, 238–9, 243, 348–9
  religious outlook, 93, 163–4, 171–2, 205, 233–5, 244, 282
  see also Home Synod
Constantius II, emperor, 15n., 50, 54, 56, 57, 60, 95–6, 98, 112, 179, 196, 305, 309
Copts, 50, 71, 193, 302, 317, 320, 335, 339, 342, 350–1, 352, 356–7, 359–60
Coptic language, 71, 295, 303, 355
Cosmas, bishop of Apamea, 227
Crispus, son of Constantine, 75
Cubicularii, 29
Cyprian, bishop of Carthage, 69, 194, 226
Cyrenaica, 64, 177, 324, 325n., 342
Cyriac, sub-deacon, 252
Cyril, bishop of Alexandria (412–444)
  succeeds Theophilus, 16
  triumphs over Nestorius, 17–18
  accepts Formula of Reunion, 21–2
  relations with: Antioch, 20, 22, 23, 123–4, 135–6; the Imperial Court, 18, 20, 83; monks, 82, 136, 139
  Christology, 18–19, 22, 47, 121–6, 211, 262–3, 277–8
  Eucharistic teaching, 124–5
  Twelve Anathemas, 19–20, 26, 124, 136, 178, 198, 266, 313
  influence, 20, 34, 48–9, 59, 142, 162, 170, 206, 208–9, 241, 281–2, 322
  other references, 25, 27, 31, 33, 45, 48, 73, 84, 88, 92, 113, 130, 140, 153, 170–1, 175, 186, 187, 235, 241, 244, 266, 269, 311, 314, 346
Cyril of Scythopolis, 256, 277
Cyrrhus, 226
Cyrus, 'the Caucasian', Chalcedonian patriarch of Alexandria, 345, 349–51, 353
Cyrus, pretorian prefect, xi, 94

Dalmatius, monk, 92
Damasus, pope, 102, 132
Damian, Monophysite patriarch of Alexandria, 341
Daniel, bishop of Harran (Carrhae), 42
Daniel stylites, 165, 172–4
Dara, 185, 191, 248, 321, 330
Decius, emperor, 61
Demons, 37, 72, 78, 81, 97, 222
Demophilus, bishop of Constantinople, 119
Diakrinomenoi, xii, 144, 248, 321, 332, 346
Didymus, bishop, 252
Didymus the Blind, 119–20
Diocletian, emperor, 61, 75
Diodore, bishop of Tarsus, 13, 22, 23, 88, 109, 128n., 135, 216, 217, 264, 277, 313
Diogenes, bishop of Cyzicus, 9
Dionysius 'the Areopagite', 265, 350, 364
Dionysius, bishop of Alexandria, 75, 226, 289
Dioscorus, deacon, 235, 237, 241, 245
Dioscorus I, patriarch of Alexandria
  succeeds Cyril, 25
  character, 26–7
  campaign against Constantinople and Antioch, 27–9, 33–5
  accusations against, 6n., 28
  at: Chalcedon, 47–8; Ephesus II, 36, 39–43
  exiled, 54, 163
  criticised by Severus of Antioch, 206, 226
  theology, 27, 28n., 41, 47–8, 141
  other references, 44, 45, 52, 70, 82, 84, 91, 92, 134, 139, 143, 134, 169–70, 198, 228, 232, 243, 270, 274, 345
Dioscorus II, patriarch of Alexandria, 73n., 229
Diphysites, 221, 227, 282, 289, 293, 365
Dometianus (Domitian), bishop of Melitene, xii, 322, 334, 335

396

Index

Domnus, patriarch of Antioch, 25, 26, 28–30, 34, 39, 41, 42, 43, 88, 91, 95, 136, 149, 152
Donatists, xiv, 69, 70, 96, 265
Donatus, bishop of Carthage, 55, 98, 194, 289, 295
Dorotheus, bishop of Thessalonica, 231, 246
Doxologies, 167–8, 181, 220, 269
Dvin, 310, 313, 314, 315, 333

Ebionites, 105, 110
Ecthesis, 179, 352
Edessa, 67, 83, 84, 91, 215, 241, 242, 290, 334, 343, 346, 347
Egypt
  anti-Chalcedonian, 50, 142, 241
  Chalcedonian restoration in, 273–4, 324–5
  Heraclius and, 349–53
  monasticism in, 70–1, 137–9, 326
  Monophysitism in, 293, 324–5
  Moslems and, 357–8
  national feeling, 71–4
  Persian occupation, 339–40
  other references, 70, 109, 137, 142, 144–5, 302
Elias, Monophysite writer, 261
Elias, patriarch of Jerusalem, 54, 201, 205, 218, 219, 228, 230
Emperors, office of, 51ff., 58
  Western attitude towards, 98–9
Enaton, monastery of, 155, 342
Encratites, 150
Energeia, 115, 212, 344, 345, 350
Ennodius, bishop of Ticinum, 232
Ephesus
  first Council of, 18–21, 26, 27, 41, 83, 88, 135, 136, 139, 175, 179, 202, 223, 270, 311–12
  second Council of ('Robber Council'), 3, 27, 39–43, 52, 91, 101, 134–6, 149, 170, 171n., 179, 238, 270
  third Council of, 171
  relations with Constantinople, 7–8, 171
Ephraim, Chalcedonian patriarch of Antioch, xi, 249, 252, 254, 271, 273, 275, 277n., 279, 283–4, 288, 320
Ephraim Syrus, 66, 139
Epictetus, bishop of Corinth, 13, 114–15, 207

Epiphanius, bishop of Tyre, 229, 234
Epiphanius, patriarch of Constantinople, 243, 267, 268, 270
Eranistes, 30
Etheria (Egeria), 67, 85, 91
Ethiopia, 15, 83, 295, 304–8
Eucharist, 62, 124–5, 141, 320
Euchites, monastery of, 200, 218
Eudocia, empress, 29, 153–4
Eudoxia, empress, 16
Eudoxius, bishop of Antioch and Constantinople, 88, 110
Eugenius, Monophysite bishop of Seleucia, 287, 289, 291, 318
Eulogius, Chalcedonian patriarch of Alexandria, 334
Eulogius, *comes*, 39
Eulogius, presbyter, 123
Eunomians, 26, 79
Eunomius, bishop of Nicomedia, 58
Euphemia, church of St, 1
Euphemia, wife of Justin I, 238
Euphemius, patriarch of Constantinople, 191, 194, 200
Euphratesia, 23, 188–9, 201, 215, 247, 248, 293
Eusebius, bishop of Caesarea, 16, 57, 76, 77, 110, 111
Eusebius, bishop of Dorylaeum, 25, 32, 41, 44
Eustathius, bishop of Antioch, 88, 109, 110–12, 180
Eustathius, bishop of Berytus, 53, 143
Euthymius, monk, 25, 152, 285
Eutyches, archimandrite, 5n., 22, 25, 30, 31, 34, 35, 38, 44, 52, 92, 101, 102, 114, 131, 136, 144, 148, 163, 173, 206, 229, 232, 241, 264, 268
  trial of, 31–3
  rehabilitation at Ephesus II, 41–2
  pronounced heretical, 47, 49, 178
Eutychism, 142, 145, 154, 171, 194, 205, 226
Eutychius, patriarch of Constantinople, 282
Evagrius, bishop of Antioch, 88
Evagrius, bishop of Samosata, 203
Evagrius, historian, 4n., 59, 156, 187, 192, 279, 330, 333
Ezana, king of Ethiopia, 304
Ezr, Armenian Catholicus, 345, 346

397

Index

Facundus, bishop of Hermiana, 257, 281
Faras (Pachoras), 138, 299, 303, 342
Faustus of Byzantium, 309
Felix III, pope, 102, 182, 186, 190, 193
Festus, senator, 198
Fifth General Council, 23, 281–2, 287, 292, 316, 344
Flacillus, bishop of Antioch, 88, 112
Flavian I, bishop of Antioch, 61n., 88
Flavian II, patriarch of Antioch, 87, 192, 201, 214–15, 220, 221, 230, 234, 240
   accepts *Henotikon*, 215
   deposed, 218–19
Flavian, patriarch of Constantinople, 3, 25, 28–9, 31–3, 35–7, 42, 43, 45, 46, 52, 54, 91, 93, 95, 101, 135, 136, 146, 206
   confession of faith, 5n., 14n., 38
   deposed at Ephesus II, 41
   exile and death, 42–4
   rehabilitation at Chalcedon, 48
Florentius, patrician, 29, 32n., 33, 37
Formula of Reunion, 21–2, 31, 44, 47, 88, 95, 116, 117, 121, 123–4, 167, 241
Fortunatus, African Manichee, xii
Fravitta, patriarch of Constantinople, 190, 193
Frumentius, bishop of Axum, 15, 56, 304–5

Gaianus, Julianist patriarch of Alexandria, 263n., 270
Gainites, 351
Gainas, barbarian general, 66, 93, 94, 159
Gaiseric, king of the Vandals, 63, 153, 159, 166
Gangra, 54
Gaza, 86
Gelasius, Pope, 52, 93, 100, 102, 175, 179, 193–7, 235, 237
Gennadius, patriarch of Constantinople, 164, 169, 172, 200
George of Pisidia, deacon and poet, 58
Georgia, kingdom, 333
Ghassanids, 284–5, 297, 323–4, 326–31
Gnostics, Gnosticism, 86
Gospel of Thomas, 80, 89
Gothia, 56
Goths, 93, 159, 172, 254, 256, 257, 272
Great persecution, 68, 69, 161, 351
'Greens', faction, 157–8, 175, 256, 263, 353
Gregory the Illuminator, 308–9

Gregory of Nazianzus, 94, 118–19, 227
Gregory of Nyssa, xii, 119
Gregory, pope, 78
Gregory the Wonderworker, 186, 202
   forged works of, 41, 230
Grillmeier, A., 120
Gurba Barraya, monastery, 320

Habsa, 137
al Hareth ibn Jabadah, Ghassanid chief, 285, 326–7
Harnack, Adolf von, 2, 115
Heliopolis (Baalbek), 86
Helpidius, *comes*, 39
Henotikon of Zeno, 54, 144–5, 174, 177–81, 182, 184, 187, 189, 192, 193, 198, 200, 215–16, 217, 223, 237, 240, 244, 269, 271, 289, 297, 308, 312, 318, 323, 360–2
Henotikon of Justin II, 322, 332, 346, 366–8
Heraclea, 8, 10, 232, 241
Heracleon, bishop of Chalcedon, 186
Heraclides, bishop, 105–6
Heraclius, emperor, 58, 74, 315, 340, 343, 345–8, 349–52, 354
Hierapolis (Maboug), 185, 188, 189, 333, 342, 355
Hilarus (Hilary), bishop of Arles, 102
Hilarus (Hilary), papal legate and later pope, 40, 41, 42n., 165
Himyarites, 137, 297, 306–7
Home synod, 31–2, 36, 37, 234, 272–3, 348
Homoiousion, 88
Homoousion, 12, 13, 120, 172, 241
Honorius, emperor, 66, 96
Honorius, pope, 348–9, 351
Hormisdas, palace, 274, 276
Hormisdas, praetorian prefect, 31
Hormisdas, pope, 199, 229, 231–3, 235–8, 242–3, 245–7
   libellus of, 236–8, 243
Horrea Margus, 65, 66
Hosius, bishop of Cordoba, 98, 110
Huns, 1, 3, 36, 63, 65
Hypatia, philosopher, 16
Hypostasis, 1, 2, 13, 13n., 19, 47, 115, 116, 122, 127, 209, 215, 252, 278, 288, 290, 318, 341, 344, 365
Hypostatic union, 22, 47, 124, 129, 209, 268, 282

Index

Ibas, bishop of Edessa, 9, 19, 21n., 25, 32, 34, 35, 42, 67, 84, 85, 136, 145, 150, 213, 217, 280, 282, 343, 346
Illus, Isaurian general, 177, 181, 188
Illyricum (Illyrian provinces), 9, 9n., 24, 66, 99, 145, 197, 236, 297, 316, 331
  bishops of, 43, 92, 100–1, 132, 156, 196, 220n, 231
Incarnation, *see* Christology
Innocentius, presbyter of Maronia, 265
Irenaeus, *comes* and later bishop of Tyre, 25, 28, 30
Isaac, monk, 91
Isaiah, bishop of Hermopolis, 206
Isauria, 123, 150, 219, 224, 248–9, 287, 293
Isaurians, 176, 181, 191, 200
Ishak, Catholicus of Armenia, 310–11
Isis, 203, 298

Jacobites, 285, 320, 336
James Bar'Adai
  consecrated bishop, 285
  missions, 285–7, 292, 326
  other references, xiv, 284, 290, 291, 318–20, 321, 324, 328
James, bishop of Nisibis, 66
James, monk, 95, 161
James of Serug, 60n., 242, 243, 297, 306
Jerome, 78, 80, 89, 110n.
Jerusalem, patriarchate, 144, 173, 200, 245, 248
  disorders, 149
  falls to Persians, 335–6, 337, 340
  synod of, 234
  other references, 74, 85, 97, 173, 230–1, 271, 297, 335, 343, 352
Jesus Christ, *see* Christology
Jews, Judaism
  influence: on Antiochene theology, 87–8, 105, 175; in Armenia, 308; in Ethiopia, 304; in the Yemen, 306–7
  reaction to Chalcedon, 148
  other references, 2, 35, 80, 87, 97–8, 109, 149, 152, 334, 343, 352
John the Almsgiver, Chalcedonian patriarch of Alexandria, 339–40, 349
John, Armenian Catholicus, 333
John Asconaghes, 290, 291
John, bishop of Antioch, 19, 24, 25, 88

John, bishop of Tella, 59, 242, 247, 248, 260–1, 274, 283, 284, 287
John Chrysostom, 7n., 15, 16, 54, 63, 82, 84–5, 87, 90, 91, 93, 159, 314
John of Claudiopolis, 222
John Codonatus, 181
John Diakrinomenos, historian, 167
John of Ephesus, historian, xv, 260, 274, 275, 284, 286–8, 292, 298, 300, 314, 318, 321–2, 324, 327, 332
John the Faster, patriarch of Constantinople, xiii, 332
John the Grammarian, 229
John, *hegemon* of Beith-Aphthonia, 203, 221
John Hemula, patriarch of Alexandria, 193
John of Hephaistos, missionary, 287–8
John I, pope, 254
John II, pope, 268, 269
John of Nikiou, historian, 325, 334, 335, 342, 352
John of Nikiou, patriarch of Alexandria, 83, 193, 216, 217n., 218, 219
John, patriarch of Constantinople, 233, 234, 236–8
John, patriarch of Jerusalem, 230, 248
John, patrician, 319
John Philoponos, 59, 290
John Rufus (Beit Rufin), 150, 184
John the Scholastic ('of Sirimis'), patriarch of Constantinople, 318, 322
John Talaia, 177, 181, 186, 199, 274
Jones, A. H. M., x
Joshua Stylites, 233
Jovian, emperor, 54, 66, 309
Judaism, *see* Jews
Julian, archimandrite, 261
Julian, bishop of Cóos, 25, 147, 160
Julian, bishop of Halicarnassos, 206, 253–4, 255, 257, 262–3, 305, 314
Julian, emperor, 12, 69, 113, 309, 358
Julian, monk and missionary, 298, 299, 300
Julian, presbyter of Tarsus, 225
Julianism, 270, 301, 317, 324, 350
Julius, bishop of Puteoli, 40
Julius, pope, 213, 230
  forged letters, 33, 41, 207, 313
Justin I, emperor, 56, 59, 147, 234, 238, 249, 252, 254, 297, 307, 323
  persecutes anti-Chalcedonians, 247

399

Index

Justin (cont.)
    relations with papacy, 243, 247
    religious policy, 238–9, 247
Justin II, emperor, 286, 292, 317–19, 323, 328, 332, 346
    Second Henotikon, 322, 366–8
Justinian, emperor, ix, xi, 5 1n., 96, 147, 152, 158, 235, 236, 240, 245, 246, 254, 261, 297, 299, 316, 317
    personal religion, 245, 255, 266, 271, 278n.
    relations with Monophysites, 261–4, 266, 275, 286–7, 292
    religious policy, 243, 255, 257, 267–8, 272–3, 275, 277, 279–80, 282, 296, 298
Juvenal, bishop of Jerusalem, 26, 39, 40–2, 47, 88, 149, 152–3, 231

Kelly, J. N. D., 115
Kenosis, 116, 122, 125, 210

Lactantius, 75
Lakhmids, 284–5, 329, 330
Lampsacus, Council of, 96
Laodicea, Council of, 219
Leo, pope, 24–5, 31–2, 35–6, 38–9, 44–9, 51, 53, 58, 102, 109, 134–5, 142, 153, 155–6, 160, 197, 198, 207, 238
    achievement, 164
    attitude to: Chalcedon, 49, 145–7; the emperor, 100–2
    reaction to Ephesus II, 44–5
    theology, 130, 134–5, 162–3
Leo, *Tome* of, 3, 38, 39, 40, 44, 48, 74, 132, 134, 143, 184, 221, 222, 232, 275, 277, 334, 346, 348, 351
    accepted by Justin I, 235
    criticised, 149, 170, 276–7
    rejected by: Armenians, 313; Christians in Persia, 188; Severus of Antioch, 212–13, 217; Timothy the Cat, 163
Leo I, emperor, 59, 155, 157–9, 163, 165, 168, 172, 256
Leo II, emperor, 169
Leontius, bishop of Antioch, 167
Leontius of Byzantium, 152, 207, 265, 277–8
Leontius, consular, 181, 188
Leontius, lawyer, 202, 203
Libanius, 77, 202
Liberatus, archdeacon of Carthage, 45, 276

Liberius, pope, 21n., 54, 57
Licinia Eudoxia, daughter of Theodosius II 24, 44, 153
Livy, 54
Logos-Theology, 105–7
Longinus, abbot, 155
Longinus, bishop of the Nobatae, 300–1, 321, 324, 327, 328
Lucian of Samosata, 75

Macedonius, patriarch of Constantinople, 186, 192, 200, 207, 216, 218, 220, 230, 234, 236, 237
Macedonius, monk, 95
Mahomet, 307, 331
Maiuma, 153, 201, 202, 205, 219, 221, 287
Makurrah, 300–1
Malchion, presbyter, 85, 107, 108, 113
Mani (Manichaeus), 41, 108, 139, 142, 257, 263, 264, 313
Manichaeism, 43, 45, 61, 71, 86, 100, 108–9, 132, 139, 152, 155, 191, 234
Mar Bassus, monastery, 261
Mar Zakai, monastery, 319
Marcellinus, *comes*, historian, 185
Marcian, emperor, 4, 45, 50, 61, 100, 143, 146–8, 151, 154–7, 158n., 159, 161, 170, 195, 238
Marcion, 139
Marcionites, 86, 89, 104, 139–40
Mardin, 185, 253, 294, 352
Maria, wife of Chosroes II, 336
Marius Mercator, 17, 129n.
Marinus of Apamea, 220
Maro, lector of Anazarba, 240
Maro (Beth Maron), monastery, 140, 229, 249, 347
Martyrdom, 68, 69, 138, 249, 295
Martyrius, patriarch of Antioch, 167, 175
Martyrius, patriarch of Jerusalem, 174–5, 189
Maurice, emperor, 158n., 315, 329–35, 336, 343
Maxentius, Scythian monk, 245, 246
Maxentius, usurping emperor, 75
Maximin, emperor, 52n., 161, 308
Maximin, general, 298
Maximus, bishop of Turin, 65
Maximus the Confessor, 351

Index

Maximus, patriarch of Antioch, 146, 156, 280
Meletians, 81–2, 139, 326
Meletius, bishop of Antioch, 88
Melkites, 180, 274, 275, 324, 326
Memnon, bishop of Ephesus, 18n., 19
Menas, brother of patriarch Benjamin, 351
Menas, patriarch of Constantinople, 272–3, 281, 345
Mesopotamia, province, 66, 247, 293, 321
Mesrop Mastoc, Armenian scholar, 311
Messalians, 89
Metras, monastery, 74
Michael the Syrian, 284, 330, 334, 347
Millet system, 338–9
Misenus, bishop of Cuma, 182
Monarchians, 104–6
Monenergism, 318, 344–5, 347, 349–51
Monks, monasticism
   Alexandrian, 31, 169–70, 187, 270
   anger at Chalcedon, 150, 319
   Armenian, 314
   in Constantinople, 29, 91–2, 218, 220
   Coptic, 31, 71–4, 80–2, 137–9, 176, 326, 342
   general, 5n., 6, 16, 31, 38, 42, 79–92, 136–41, 150–1, 264
   one-nature sympathies, 136–9, 176
   opposed to bishops, 85–6, 136, 143–4
   Palestinian, 189, 218, 271, 348
   regarded as 'philosophers', 77, 319
   successors of martyrs, 81
   Syrian, 61, 88–91, 95, 139–40, 216, 219, 239, 248, 333
Monophysites (Monophysitism), x, xii, xiii–xiv, 20, 59, 60, 62, 67, 72, 105, 139, 140, 141, 144, 145, 153, 184, 228, 229, 232, 241–2, 256, 257, 273, 275, 278, 280, 315, 317, 319, 326, 335, 347, 348, 352–3
   confession of faith, 264–5, 362–6
   debt to Severus, 213–14
   Egyptian, 73–4, 139, 193–293, 339–41, 356–7
   hierarchy, 260–1, 283–4, 291–3
   historians, 169, 352, 369ff.
   kingdoms, 62, 297ff.
   loyalty to empire, 60n., 264, 292
   missions, 296–7, 306–7, 314
   monasteries, 74, 249, 264, 326
   regions, 249, 253, 294–5, 320, 333, 334, 337
   schisms, 326, 341–2
   Syrian, 185, 333–4, 341, 346
   see also Severus, Tritheists and Julian of Halicarnassos
Monothelitism, 352, 356
Moslems, 352–3, 358–9
al-Moundhir, Ghassanid ruler, 323, 327–30
Musonius, bishop of Meloë, 224

Najran, 137n., 307
Narses, general, 298, 299, 316
Nature, *see physis*
Nationalism, x–xi, 51, 62, 69–71, 73–4
Nephalius, Alexandrian monk, 186, 201, 202, 207, 216
Neo-Chalcedonians, 186, 229, 241, 273, 278n., 346
Neo-Platonism, 107, 181
Nestor, bishop of Tarsus, 188
Nestorius, bishop of Constantinople, 7n., 14, 16–19, 20, 24, 25, 27, 31, 35, 37, 45, 54, 82, 93, 121, 129, 131, 135, 142, 173, 178, 213, 216, 222, 223, 226, 229, 232, 234, 257, 264, 268, 273, 311
   relations with Cyril, 18, 122–5
   theology, 129–30, 131n., 134
Nestorians, 137, 167, 188, 201, 226, 240, 297, 310, 313, 321, 337–9, 343
Nestorianism, 171, 252, 268, 283, 297, 313, 314
Nestorius, bishop of Phragon, 28
New Rome, *see* Constantinople
Nicaea, Council of, 7, 13, 20n., 21, 27, 41, 43, 49, 56, 82, 87, 111, 114, 138, 141, 174, 198, 223, 232, 257, 264, 270, 309, 346
   symbol of, 20, 49, 96, 110, 170, 178, 207
Nika Riot, 60, 96, 158, 263
Nikephorus Kallistus, historian, 29, 145
Niketas, 340–2
'Nine Saints', 305–6
Nisibis, 66, 167, 188, 191, 309
Nobatia, 298
North Africa
   Christianity in, 14, 55, 68, 71, 102, 256–7, 265, 281, 282

401

Index

North Africa (*cont.*)
  paganism in, 68
  see also Donatists
Nubia, 295, 297–303, 315
Numidia, 69, 70

Odoacer, 181, 186
Optatus, bishop of Milevis, 70, 90
Oracle of Baalbek, 140–1
Origen, 16, 75–7, 105–7, 109, 113, 118, 128, 213, 214, 278–9
Origenism, 88, 112, 216, 279
Osrhoene, 37, 83, 247, 249, 308, 335, 337
Ousia, 129, 210–11, 223, 252, 344
Oxyrhynchus, 80, 154

Pachomius, 82
Pachomian Monasteries, 72, 80, 137, 139, 163, 177, 274, 306
Paganism, 71, 72, 75–6, 81, 203–4, 296, 311
  repressed by Justinian, 257, 286, 298
Palestine
  devastated by the Arabs, 331
  favours Chalcedon, 189, 223, 230
  invaded by the Persians, 335–6
  lost to Byzantium, 351–2
  monks in, 152, 174, 189, 217, 223, 228, 230, 279, 348
  opposes Monergism, 348–9
  religious situation, 151–3, 189
Palladius, pretorian prefect, 154
Pamphylia, 226, 286
Pamprepius, philosopher, 181
Panopolis, 80
Pap, king of Armenia, 310
Papacy, *see* Rome
Paphnutius, confessor, 95
Paschasinus, bishop of Libybaeum, 10n., 53
Paul, bishop of Edessa, 242, 243
Paul, bishop of Ephesus, 174
Paul 'The Black', Monophysite patriarch of Antioch, 291, 293, 318, 321, 322–4, 326–7, 328
Paul, bishop of Olba, 224
Paul, bishop of Tella, 342
Paul 'The Jew', patriarch of Antioch, 241, 242, 249
Paul 'The One-Eyed', 345

Paul, St, 5, 115, 143
Paul of Samosata, 12, 41, 75, 85, 86, 105, 108, 110, 117, 277, 313
Paul the Tabennesiot, 274
Pax Deorum, 52
Pelagius, monk, 136
Pelagius, Pelagianism, 17, 23, 129, 134
Pelagius, deacon and later pope, 273, 274, 275, 279, 319
Peroz, king of Persia, 312, 313
Persia
  Christianity in, 56, 181, 188, 223, 297, 338–9, 347
  Monophysitism in, 283, 295, 313, 321
  Nestorianism in, 167, 201, 313, 337–9, 343
  relations with empire, 67, 185, 191, 201, 284–5, 309, 315, 321, 328–30, 335–6, 339–40, 432–3
Peter, bishop of Apamea, 228, 270
Peter, bishop of Ravenna, 36
Peter of Callinicum, Monophysite patriarch of Antioch, 294, 328, 333
Peter the Fuller, patriarch of Antioch, 167–8, 170, 174, 175, 181, 188–90, 229, 243
Peter I, bishop of Alexandria, 289
Peter II, bishop of Alexandria, 120
Peter the Iberian, 149, 153, 155, 173, 180, 184, 189, 202, 206
Peter Mongus, patriarch of Alexandria, 154, 174–6, 177, 179, 181, 184, 187, 190, 193, 194, 199, 229, 243
Peter, Monophysite patriarch of Alexandria, 327
Peter, patriarch of Jerusalem, 151n., 279
Philoponoi, 203
Philoxenus (Xenaias), bishop of Hierapolis, 186, 188–9, 201, 206, 214–17, 228, 230, 240, 248, 314
  theology, 215
Philoxenus, bishop of Doliche, 267
Phoenicia Libanesia, 249, 331
Phoenicia Maritima, 205, 244
Phocas, emperor, 333, 335, 337, 342
Photinus, bishop of Sirmium, 17
Photion, monk, xi
Physis, 2, 13n., 115, 121, 209–11, 288, 291
Pisentios, bishop of Coptos, 343
Plato, 72, 77, 113
Platonism, 115, 126

Plerophoria, 150–1
Porphyry, 31, 33, 273, 275
Possidius, bishop of Calama, 65
Praxeas, 104, 131
Priscus, historian, 65
Proclus, patriarch of Constantinople, 22, 25, 92, 212, 268, 314
    Tome of Proclus, 23, 92, 244, 245, 268, 311–12
Prosopon, 1, 2, 13, 13n., 18, 111, 115, 120, 128–30, 209–11, 319, 338
Prosper Tiro, 31
Proterius, patriarch of Alexandria, 142, 149, 154–5, 160–2, 184, 270
Proterians, 177–8, 180, 226, 252
Psathyrians, xii
Pulcheria, empress, 25, 29, 43, 45, 50, 53, 61, 94, 146, 147, 156, 238

Q'asr Ibrim, 298, 299, 302, 303, 358
Q'astel, 298
Q'ennesrim (Chalcis), 225–6, 248, 294
Q'iros, bishop, 284

Rabbula, bishop of Edessa, 22, 25, 34, 88, 135, 280
Ravenna, 36, 45, 102, 296
Redemption, 111, 113, 118, 127, 133, 134
Ricimer, 158, 159
Romanus, monk, 153, 154, 202
Romanus, patrician, 37
Rome, city of, 54, 153, 246, 269, 275, 281, 320
Rome, see of, 3, 5, 7, 11, 24, 36, 50, 100–3, 135, 173, 220, 234, 252
    claims to primacy, 11, 21, 53, 144, 164, 193–7, 232–3, 235–6
    Councils at, 44, 120, 132, 161, 182, 186
    relations with: Alexandria, 27, 131, 155, 197–8; Constantinople, 38, 44, 101–2, 145–7, 181–4, 194–9, 231–3, 235–8, 268, 272–3, 275–7, 281–2

Sabas, Palestinian monk, 54, 189, 205, 219, 230, 262n., 271, 279, 336
Sabellius, 12, 222, 341
Sallustius, patriarch of Jerusalem, 189
Salvian, presbyter of Marseille, 65
Samaritans, 152, 257, 296, 335, 352

Saracens, 205, 331
Scythian Monks, 244, 245
Seleucia, synod of, 338–9
Seleucus, bishop of Amasea, 161
Senoun, monastery of, 247
Serenus, monk, 81
Serdica, Council of, 96
Sergius, bishop of Cyrrhus, 252
Sergius, grammarian, 206, 209
Sergius, patriarch of Constantinople, 344–5, 348–9
Sergius, St, shrine of, 326, 327, 336
Sergius of Tella, Monophysite patriarch of Antioch, 290, 291, 292, 293
Severus, patriarch of Antioch
    early career, 202–5
    accused of pagan sympathies, 203–4
    in Constantinople, 205ff.
    opposes Apollinarians, 205–6, 214
    criticises Dioscorus, 206
    condemns Eutyches, 216
    opposes Origenism, 216
    struggle with Macedonius, 216–18
    elected patriarch, 219–20
    condemns Chalcedon, 228–9, 234, 240
    preaching, 214
    diocesan administration, 223–7
    theology, 207–13, 226
    sacramental teaching, 226–7, 252, 260
    opposition to, 221, 228–9, 234, 240
    exiled, 235
    quarrel with Julian of Halicarnassos, 253–4, 262–3, 265
    activities in exile, 252–3, 260, 283, 292
    final condemnation, 273, 276
    other references, 14n., 59, 77, 87, 153, 168, 186, 201, 230, 233, 235, 243, 254, 257, 265, 269, 271, 279, 289, 344
Severans, 265–6, 275, 282, 283, 306, 317, 324, 334, 338, 341, 345n.
Shapur I (Sapor), 85
Shapur II (Sapor), 309, 310n.
Shenute, 72, 73, 80–1, 91, 137–8, 343
Shirin, mistress and later wife of Chosroes II, 336, 338
Sibyllines, 140–1
Sicily, 102, 256, 272, 329
Sidon, Council of, 219, 228, 240
Silko, king of Nobatia, 299, 300

Index

Silverius, pope, 276
Simeon, bishop, 296
Simeon, presbyter monk, 136
Simeon stylites, 26, 90, 95, 148, 153, 161, 165, 166
Simplicius, pope, 173, 175, 176, 181, 182, 184, 187
Sixth General Council, 349, 356
Sleepless monks, 165, 167, 168, 182, 220, 235, 244, 269
Socrates, historian, 16, 24, 305
Sophia, empress, 317-18
Soterichus, bishop of Caesarea (Cappadocia), 240, 252
Sophronius, bishop of Tella, 42
Sophronius, monk and patriarch of Jerusalem, 348, 351
Sozomen, historian, 58, 79, 86, 99
Stephen, patriarch of Antioch, 175
Strategius, *comes largitionen*, 60, 265
Studius, Studite monks, 165
Symbol of faith, *see* Nicaea
Successus, 23, 123, 262
Symmachus, pope, 102, 200, 231
Synesius, philosopher and bishop of Ptolemais, 57, 64, 78n., 95
Syria, economic situation, 90, 294-5, 333-4
monks in, 88-91, 139-40, 215, 229, 294-5
Syria I, anti-Chalcedonian, 167, 249, 293, 333, 337
Syria II, pro-Chalcedonian, 140, 166, 186, 219, 228, 249, 337
monasteries, 219, 228, 333n.
relations with Rome, 229, 235, 239
Syriac, 84-6, 185, 215, 247, 310, 355

Tafla, Bairu, 304-5
Tagrit, 321, 344
Tarsus, 188, 226
Taurus, patrician, 29
Tertullian, 131, 194
Thalassius, bishop of Caesarea (Cappadocia), 39, 148
Theodahad, king of the Ostrogoths, 272
Theodora, empress, 260, 262, 263, 270-1, 276, 280, 281, 285, 288, 290, 297, 298-9, 303
Theodore, archimandrite, 327, 328
Theodore Askidas, 279-80

Theodore, bishop of Bostra, 285, 318, 322
Theodore, bishop of Mopsuestia, 13, 22, 88, 109, 126-9, 135, 136, 188, 216, 217, 245, 264, 277, 280, 311, 313
Theodore, bishop of Philae, 293, 298-9, 325
Theodore, law-student, 150
Theodore Lector, historian, 191
Theodore of Sykeon, ascetic, 332
Theodoret, bishop of Cyrrhus, 14n., 26, 27-30, 39, 40, 42, 44, 84, 86, 90, 95, 111, 129, 136, 145, 150, 189, 198, 217, 264, 267, 277, 280, 346
Theodoric, king of the Ostrogoths, 191, 198, 200, 254
Theodoric Strabo, *magister militum*, 166, 169
Theodosius, Augustal prefect, 73
Theodosius I, emperor, 15, 57, 61, 96, 164, 179, 196, 310
Theodosius II, emperor, 9, 21n., 24, 25, 30, 34-6, 38, 43-5, 50, 52, 91, 94-5, 97, 101, 156, 158, 161, 170
Theodosius, monastic leader in Palestine, 31, 149, 151, 176
Theodosius, patriarch of Alexandria, 270, 274, 276, 283-4, 285, 290, 291-3, 298, 300, 317, 323, 327
theology, 288, 289
Theodosius, pro-Chalcedonian monk, 230-1
Theopaschism (Theopaschites), 205, 245, 246, 252, 266, 271, 322, 338
Theophanes, historian, 159, 242, 281
Theophilus, bishop of Alexandria, 16, 82
Theophylact Simocatta, historian, 330
Theoria, 123, 136, 212, 322
Thessalonica, 36, 57, 95, 231, 265, vicariate of, 24
Thomas, bishop of Dara, 248
Three chapters, 217, 280, 281-2, 319, 246, 350
Tiberius II, emperor, 286, 317, 322, 328-9
Tilmognon, monastery, 215
Timothy 'The Cat', patriarch of Alexandria, 154-5, 159, 160, 161, 165, 170-2, 173-6, 198, 226, 228, 243, 308, 312, 313
theology, 155, 163, 206-7
Timothy IV, patriarch of Alexandria, 257, 269, 270, 307
Timothy, patriarch of Constantinople, 218, 233

Index

Timothy Salafaciolus, Chalcedonian patriarch of Alexandria, 163, 173, 175, 177
Tiridates, king of Armenia, 308
Trinitarian doctrine, 106, 133, 179, 208, 213, 252-3, 288, 289-90, 341
Trishagion, 96, 168, 212, 218, 220, 230, 231, 340
Tritheism, xvi, 289-91, 294, 318, 322, 350
True Cross, 336, 343, 345
Twelve Anathemas, 19-20, 26, 31, 34, 43, 44, 121, 134, 136, 178, 198, 266, 269, 270, 271, 313, 318, 346
Two Swords theory, 60, 196
Typos of Anastasius, 217, 219
Tyre, 34, 53n., 226
  Synod of, 227

Ullmann, W., 196

Valens, emperor, 95, 310
Valentinian I, emperor, 96
Valentinian II, emperor, 16, 196
Valentinian III, emperor, 24, 97, 158
Valentinus, 41
Valentinian heresy, 33, 104
Vandals, 65, 166, 192, 199, 256
Vasiliev, A. A., 233, 254
Verina, empress, 166, 169, 181
Victor, monk, 25
Vigilius, pope, 54, 239, 276, 277, 281, 282, 299, 316, 345
Viminacium, 65
Virgin Mary
  anthropotokos, 14n., 111, 130
  Christotokos, 14
  Theotokos, 1, 3, 4, 14, 18, 20, 28, 115, 125, 130, 134, 139, 178, 209, 234, 245, 247, 267, 288, 332n., 360-1, 363, 367
  other references, 41, 108, 114, 116, 118, 138, 338
Vitalian, general, 191, 220-1, 231-3, 235-6, 240, 244, 245
Vitalis, bishop of Antioch, 83
Vitalis, papal legate, 182
Vööbus, A., 306

White Monastery, 72, 80
Word-flesh, *see* Christology
Word-man, *see* Christology

Xystus II, pope, 227
Xystus III, pope, 23, 24, 100

Yaranshahr, 85
Yarmuk, battle of, 331, 352, 354
Yazdgard I, king of Persia, 338
Yazdgard II, king of Persia, 312
Yemen, 83, 87, 306-7, 356

Zacharias, patriarch of Jerusalem, 336
Zacharias Rhetor, bishop of Mitylene (?), 148, 161, 170, 176, 202n., 248, 265, 271, 369
Zacharias Scholasticus, 77, 202, 204
Zeno, emperor, 53, 59, 165-6, 168-9, 174, 176-7, 180-1, 184, 190, 236, 237, 313, 317
Zenonis, wife of Basiliscus, 169, 171
Zoilus, Chalcedonian patriarch of Alexandria, 275, 293
Zooras, monk, 270, 272
Zoroastrianism, 285, 311-12, 315
Zosimus, historian, 159
Zosimus, pope, 11n., 64